THE BEST OF
AMERICA'S TEST KITCHEN

THE YEAR'S BEST RECIPES,
EQUIPMENT REVIEWS, AND TASTINGS

2017

BY THE EDITORS AT
AMERICA'S TEST KITCHEN

Copyright © 2016 by the Editors at America's Test Kitchen

AMERICA'S TEST KITCHEN
17 Station Street, Brookline, MA 02445

THE BEST OF AMERICA'S TEST KITCHEN 2017
The Year's Best Recipes, Equipment Reviews, and Tastings

1st Edition

ISBN: 978-1-940352-68-8
ISSN: 1940-3925

Manufactured in the United States of America

10 9 8 7 6 5 4 3 2 1

Distributed by Penguin Random House Publisher Services
Tel: 800-733-3000

CHIEF CREATIVE OFFICER: Jack Bishop

EDITORIAL DIRECTOR, BOOKS: Elizabeth Carduff

EXECUTIVE EDITOR: Adam Kowit

SENIOR EDITOR: Debra Hudak

ASSOCIATE EDITOR: Melissa Herrick

ASSISTANT EDITOR: Samantha Ronan

ART DIRECTOR: Carole Goodman

ASSOCIATE ART DIRECTORS: Allison Boales and Jen Kanavos Hoffman

DESIGNER: Aleko Giatrakis

PRODUCTION DESIGNER: Reinaldo Cruz

PHOTOGRAPHY DIRECTOR: Julie Cote

ASSISTANT PHOTOGRAPHY PRODUCER: Mary Ball

FRONT COVER PHOTOGRAPH: Keller + Keller

ASSOCIATE ART DIRECTOR, PHOTOGRAPHY: Steve Klise

STAFF PHOTOGRAPHER: Daniel J. van Ackere

ADDITIONAL PHOTOGRAPHY: Carl Tremblay

FOOD STYLING: Catrine Kelty and Marie Piraino

PHOTOSHOOT KITCHEN TEAM:

    ASSOCIATE EDITOR: Chris O'Connor

    TEST COOK: Daniel Cellucci

    ASSISTANT TEST COOK: Allison Berkey and Matthew Fairman

ILLUSTRATIONS: John Burgoyne

PRODUCTION DIRECTOR: Guy Rochford

SENIOR PRODUCTION MANAGER: Jessica Quirk

PRODUCTION MANAGER: Christine Walsh

IMAGING MANAGER: Lauren Robbins

PRODUCTION AND IMAGING SPECIALISTS: Heather Dube, Sean MacDonald, Dennis Noble, and Jessica Voas

COPYEDITOR: Cheryl Redmond

PROOFREADER: Amanda Poulsen Dix

INDEXER: Elizabeth Parson

PICTURED ON FRONT COVER: Chocolate-Caramel Layer Cake (page 235)

CONTENTS

SALADS AND STARTERS

ISRAELI COUSCOUS WITH RADISHES AND WATERCRESS

ISRAELI COUSCOUS SALAD

✔ **WHY THIS RECIPE WORKS:** To make pasta salad using Israeli couscous, we first toasted the spheres in oil to bring out their nuttiness. We then cooked the couscous in a measured amount of water that was slowly soaked up during cooking. This absorption method produced more evenly cooked results than boiling. To turn the couscous into a salad, we let the spheres cool on a rimmed baking sheet, preventing built-up steam from cooking the couscous further. A bold vinaigrette of equal parts acid and oil worked well as our dressing. Finally, we mixed in plenty of fresh vegetables, cheese, nuts, and herbs for a vibrant finish.

When a recession hit Israel in the 1950s, rice—a kitchen staple—became scarce. In response, prime minister David Ben-Gurion called on food manufacturers to develop a wheat-based alternative. The result was the dense, pasta-like spheres called *ptitim* or, outside Israel, Israeli couscous. Like tiny, granular North African couscous, the Israeli kind is made from semolina flour, but it boasts smooth, small spheres and a pleasant chew. Like pasta, the little balls are made by forcing dough through an extruding machine. But unlike most pasta, which is air-dried, Israeli couscous is dried over a flame, giving it toasty, rich flavor.

That flavor, plus its springy texture, makes Israeli couscous a fresh choice for pasta salad, offering an alternative to customary shapes like fusilli or penne. The only real barrier is that the compact spheres are tricky to cook just right.

Whereas North African couscous is so tiny that it can be hydrated with boiling water off the heat, the Israeli kind needs to spend time on the stove. After paging through cookbooks, I noted two possible techniques. For the less common pasta method, the couscous is boiled and then drained. But when I tried this, it yielded spheres that overcooked and turned gummy on the exterior before the interior had a chance to become tender. The other option, the absorption method, seemed more promising, since it calls for slowly simmering the couscous in a measured amount of water that is entirely soaked up during cooking. Sure enough, this gentler approach produced more consistent results. After some tinkering, I determined that a couscous-to-water ratio of 1 to 1¼ was ideal. To ensure perfectly even cooking, I stirred the pot occasionally during simmering and then let the couscous stand covered off the heat for 3 minutes.

Before moving on, I tried toasting the couscous in fat before adding the water—a technique known as the pilaf method. This was well worth the effort, as the fat accentuated the unique nuttiness of the pearls. Oil was best since butter tended to solidify once the orbs cooled enough to be incorporated into a salad.

Although my tender-chewy Israeli couscous was good enough to eat warm as a simple side dish, I needed to quickly cool it down to use in salad. To do so, I spread it into a single layer on a baking sheet. (When left to cool in a bowl, it continued to steam and became mushy in spots.)

I mixed the cooled couscous with a basic vinaigrette, but it was far too mild. I bumped up the acid, eventually using equal parts acid and oil to dress the starchy orbs. Next came plenty of fragrant herbs, along with fresh vegetables and salty cheese. Whereas many pasta salads include large, chunky mix-ins, I chopped the ingredients small to ensure that each bite contained a balance of flavors and textures. With a sprinkling of crunchy, toasted nuts on top, this salad was ready for backyard parties, potlucks, or as a standalone for a simple meal.

—ERIN MCMURRER, *Cook's Illustrated*

Simple Israeli Couscous
MAKES ABOUT 4 CUPS

The warm couscous can be tossed with butter or extra-virgin olive oil and salt and pepper for a side dish or cooled and used in a salad. If you're making a salad, transfer the couscous to a rimmed baking sheet and let it cool completely, about 15 minutes. Our favorite brand of Israeli couscous is Roland.

1	tablespoon extra-virgin olive oil
2	cups Israeli couscous
2½	cups water
½	teaspoon salt

Heat oil and couscous in medium saucepan over medium heat, stirring frequently, until about half of grains are golden brown, 5 to 6 minutes. Add water and salt; stir to combine. Increase heat to high and bring to boil. Reduce heat to medium-low, cover, and simmer, stirring occasionally, until water is absorbed, 9 to 12 minutes. Remove saucepan from heat and let stand, covered, for 3 minutes. Serve.

Israeli Couscous with Lemon, Mint, Peas, Feta, and Pickled Shallots

SERVES 6

For efficiency, let the shallots pickle while you prepare the remaining ingredients.

⅓ cup red wine vinegar
2 tablespoons sugar
  Salt and pepper
2 shallots, sliced thin
3 tablespoons extra-virgin olive oil
3 tablespoons lemon juice
1 teaspoon Dijon mustard
⅛ teaspoon red pepper flakes
1 recipe Simple Israeli Couscous (page 3), cooled
4 ounces (4 cups) baby arugula, chopped coarse
1 cup fresh mint leaves, torn
½ cup frozen peas, thawed
½ cup shelled pistachios, toasted and chopped
3 ounces feta cheese, crumbled (¾ cup)

1. Bring vinegar, sugar, and pinch salt to simmer in small saucepan over medium-high heat, stirring occasionally, until sugar dissolves. Add shallots and stir to combine. Cover and let cool completely, about 30 minutes. Drain and discard liquid.

2. Whisk oil, lemon juice, mustard, pepper flakes, and ⅛ teaspoon salt together in large bowl. Add couscous, arugula, mint, peas, 6 tablespoons pistachios, ½ cup feta, and shallots and toss to combine. Season with salt and pepper to taste, and transfer to serving bowl. Let stand for 5 minutes. Sprinkle with remaining ¼ cup feta and remaining 2 tablespoons pistachios and serve.

Israeli Couscous with Tomatoes, Olives, and Ricotta Salata

SERVES 6

Crumbled feta cheese can be substituted for the ricotta salata.

3 tablespoons extra-virgin olive oil
3 tablespoons red wine vinegar
1 teaspoon Dijon mustard
  Salt and pepper
1 recipe Simple Israeli Couscous (page 3), cooled
12 ounces grape tomatoes, quartered
2 ounces (2 cups) baby spinach, sliced ¼ inch wide
1½ cups basil leaves, chopped coarse
3 ounces ricotta salata cheese, crumbled (¾ cup)
⅔ cup pitted kalamata olives, sliced
½ cup pine nuts, toasted
1 bunch chives, cut into ¼-inch pieces (¼ cup)

Whisk oil, vinegar, mustard, and ⅛ teaspoon salt together in large bowl. Add couscous, tomatoes, spinach, basil, ½ cup ricotta salata, olives, 6 tablespoons pine nuts, and chives and toss to combine. Season with salt and pepper to taste and transfer to serving bowl. Let stand for 5 minutes. Sprinkle with remaining ¼ cup ricotta salata and remaining 2 tablespoons pine nuts and serve.

Israeli Couscous with Radishes and Watercress

SERVES 6

Our favorite goat cheese is Laura Chenel's Chèvre Fresh Chèvre Log.

3 tablespoons extra-virgin olive oil
3 tablespoons sherry vinegar
1 teaspoon Dijon mustard
1 teaspoon smoked paprika
¼ teaspoon sugar
  Salt and pepper
1 recipe Simple Israeli Couscous (page 3), cooled
2 ounces (2 cups) watercress, torn into bite-size pieces
6 scallions, sliced thin
6 radishes, trimmed and sliced thin, then sliced into matchsticks
1½ cups parsley, chopped coarse
½ cup walnuts, toasted and chopped coarse
4 ounces goat cheese, crumbled (1 cup)

Whisk oil, vinegar, mustard, paprika, sugar, and ⅛ teaspoon salt together in large bowl. Add couscous, watercress, scallions, radishes, parsley, and 6 tablespoons walnuts and toss to combine. Season with salt and pepper to taste, and transfer to serving bowl. Let stand for 5 minutes. Sprinkle with goat cheese and remaining 2 tablespoons walnuts and serve.

PITA BREAD SALAD WITH TOMATOES AND CUCUMBER

✔ **WHY THIS RECIPE WORKS:** This Middle Eastern bread salad known as *fattoush* is at its best when it combines fresh produce with crisp pita and bright herbs. Many recipes eliminate excess moisture from the salad by seeding and salting the cucumbers and tomatoes. We skipped these steps in order to preserve the crisp texture of the cucumber and the flavorful seeds and jelly of the tomatoes. Instead, we made the pita moisture-repellent by brushing its craggy sides with olive oil before baking. The oil prevented the pita chips from absorbing too much moisture from the salad and becoming soggy while still allowing the chips to pick up flavor from the dressing.

Middle Eastern cooks have a knack for making the most of leftovers. Take flatbreads: These thin breads stale quickly, so leftovers—and dishes designed to use them up—abound. Pita bread salad, or *fattoush*, is a prime example. The vibrant mix combines day-old bread with ripe tomatoes, cucumber, romaine lettuce, parsley, mint, scallions, and a potent green like watercress, all simply dressed with fresh lemon juice and olive oil.

Some cooks don't mind (or even prefer) if the pita softens in the vegetable juices and vinaigrette, but I like the bread to have some crunch. My goal: a refreshing, easy-to-make salad boasting plenty of textural contrast.

I began by selecting the vegetables and herbs. Fresh tomatoes and a crisp English cucumber, which we have found to have fewer seeds than the American kind, were mandatory. A handful of chopped scallions was also a given. After sampling various combinations of lettuce, greens, and herbs, I eliminated the traditional parsley and romaine; mint, cilantro, and peppery arugula offered a brighter take on fresh, summery flavor.

For the vinaigrette, I looked to the test kitchen's favorite panzanella recipe, which also stars bread, tomatoes, and cucumbers. Figuring that a similar dressing would be appropriate here, I whisked together 3 tablespoons of fresh lemon juice, ½ cup of extra-virgin olive oil, 1 small clove of minced garlic, and salt and pepper.

On to the pita. Plain stale bread wasn't crisp enough from the get-go. Could it be as convenient as tearing open a bag of pita chips? No. Though they were super-crunchy straight from the bag, commercially made chips are low in fat and so became mushy within minutes of mixing the salad. I would have to make my own.

Following the test kitchen's recipe for pita chips, I divided two rounds into wedges, lightly spritzed them with vegetable oil spray, and toasted them in the oven. Once the brittle triangles cooled, I broke them into bite-size pieces and tossed them with my vegetables and vinaigrette. These chips had the right combination and ratio of ingredients; however, the garlic flavor in the dressing was overwhelming even though I had used only a small clove. What's more, the pita failed to stay crunchy.

To tame the garlic, I used a tried-and-true test kitchen trick and soaked it in lemon juice. The citric acid chemically changed the harsh-tasting allicin in the raw garlic into mellower flavor compounds.

As for the pita, one way to keep it crunchy would be to remove moisture from the vegetables. This meant seeding the tomatoes and cucumbers, salting them, and then letting their liquid drain away. But aside from being time-consuming, the trouble with this approach was that as the salt pulled moisture out, it also caused the vegetables' cell walls to collapse slightly, softening their textures. What's more, the jelly that surrounds a tomato's seeds is its tastiest part, so I was loath to toss it in the garbage.

Perhaps I needed an altogether different approach. Instead of removing moisture from the salad, what if I waterproofed the pita? Since oil repels water, my immediate thought was to deep-fry the pita, coating it in more oil than simply spritzing it. Sure enough, a batch of deep-fried pita chips retained its crunch even after being tossed with the vegetables and vinaigrette. The drawbacks: The chips had to be fried in batches and in lots of oil—about 2 cups.

I was fairly certain that I could achieve this same effect in the oven if I could determine how much oil the pita absorbed during frying. To find out, I made a couple more batches, carefully measuring the amount of oil I began with and the amount that remained after frying. I determined that two pita breads were soaking up about ¼ cup of oil. I set a rack in a rimmed baking sheet and arranged my pitas (first splitting them into two thin rounds and halving them) on the rack, brushing them with half the oil destined for the dressing. Then I baked the pitas in a 375-degree oven until crisp. Once they were cool, I broke the pitas into rough pieces and added the herbs, vegetables, garlic–lemon juice mixture, and remaining oil. It was a good start: The oil prevented most of the chips from absorbing so much moisture that they turned to mush while

PERFECTING PITA FOR SALAD

It took a few tries to figure out an easy way to produce pita chips that would maintain most of their crunch even when mixed with vinaigrette and juicy vegetables.

DAY-OLD PITA: We dismissed day-old bread from the get-go for its lack of crunch.

STORE-BOUGHT CHIPS: These chips are convenient but their low fat content meant they took on too much moisture and turned mushy.

SPRITZED AND BAKED: A light misting of oil didn't adequately waterproof the pita, resulting in soggy bread.

DEEP-FRIED: This option required 2 cups of oil and frying in multiple batches.

OVEN-FRIED: Our method produces chips that are truly water-repellent, for optimum crunch.

NEATER, TASTIER TOMATOES

Hold tomato on counter with cored stem end facing down and cut into ¾-inch-thick slices. Stack slices in pairs and cut into ¾-inch strips, then cut strips crosswise into ¾-inch pieces.

still allowing them to pick up flavor from the lemony dressing. Frustratingly, some of the chips were still soggy or oily.

I realized that I'd arranged the pitas on the rack with some smooth side up and others rough side up. The oil was sliding off the smooth sides of the bread while the craggy rough-side-up chips had gripped the oil and remained crisp. I prepared another batch, this time arranging all my pita chips rough side up. I also reduced the oil to 3 tablespoons to eliminate any greasiness. These chips hit the mark: During baking, the oil spread and soaked all the way through the bread, giving the same effect as deep frying. When a colleague raved about the bright flavors and quipped that every last pita piece was "crunchewy," I knew I had a winner.

—LAN LAM, *Cook's Illustrated*

Pita Bread Salad with Tomatoes and Cucumber (Fattoush)

SERVES 4

The success of this recipe depends on ripe, in-season tomatoes. A rasp-style grater makes quick work of turning the garlic into a paste.

  2 (8-inch) pita breads
  7 tablespoons extra-virgin olive oil
      Salt and pepper
  3 tablespoons lemon juice
  ¼ teaspoon garlic, minced to paste
  1 pound tomatoes, cored and cut into ¾-inch pieces
  1 English cucumber, peeled and sliced ⅛ inch thick
  1 cup arugula, chopped coarse
  ½ cup chopped fresh cilantro
  ½ cup chopped fresh mint
  4 scallions, sliced thin

1. Adjust oven rack to middle position and heat oven to 375 degrees. Using kitchen shears, cut around perimeter of each pita and separate into 2 thin rounds. Cut each round in half. Place pitas, smooth side down, on wire rack set in rimmed baking sheet. Brush 3 tablespoons oil over surface of pitas. (Pitas do not need to be uniformly coated. Oil will spread during baking.) Season with salt and pepper to taste. Bake until pitas are crisp and pale golden brown, 10 to 14 minutes. Set aside to cool. (Cooled pitas can be stored in zipper-lock bag for 24 hours.)

2. While pitas toast, whisk lemon juice, garlic, and ¼ teaspoon salt together in small bowl. Let stand for 10 minutes.

3. Place tomatoes, cucumber, arugula, cilantro, mint, and scallions in large bowl. Break pitas into ½-inch pieces and place in bowl with vegetables. Add lemon-garlic mixture and remaining ¼ cup oil and toss to coat. Season with salt and pepper to taste. Serve immediately.

ASPARAGUS SALAD

✔ **WHY THIS RECIPE WORKS:** Instead of roasting our asparagus, we took a drastically different approach and made a fresh, vibrant salad with raw spears. Slicing the spears thin was the key to keeping them crunchy, not woody. An herb-based dressing complemented the freshness of the asparagus. Spicy radishes, salty Pecorino Romano, and crunchy croutons were the perfect finishing touches.

Grilled or roasted asparagus, perfectly tender and browned, is hard to beat and pairs beautifully with fish, meat, chicken . . . you name it. Raw asparagus can be just as appealing, boasting a delicious, mildly sweet and nutty flavor with a delicate crunch. An added benefit: Raw asparagus is void of the sulfurous flavors that cooked asparagus sometimes has. Still, I knew that serving up uncooked spears would take a little bit of extra creativity, so I set my sights on a salad with bold flavor and off-the-charts crunch in every forkful.

During my research, I found that many recipes turn to simple cut-up lengths of asparagus as their base, but even when I painstakingly peeled the spears, I found them far too fibrous. After experimenting with a few different techniques, I found that this salad's success started in the produce aisle. The best flavor and texture came from spears that were bright green, firm, and crisp, with tightly closed tips. Slicing the asparagus very thin on the bias staved off any unpleasant woodiness without sacrificing the signature crunch I wanted. This technique worked best with thicker spears, a welcome discovery because they're available year-round.

To complement the fresh asparagus, I wanted an impactful, herby dressing. A basil-based vinaigrette proved too one-dimensional and seemed more suited to pasta, so I instead turned to zesty fresh mint, keeping basil as its supporting player. I used a high ratio of herbs to oil, to create a pesto-style dressing potent enough to enhance but not overshadow the distinct fresh flavor of the asparagus. A food processor made quick work of chopping the fresh herbs. Pecorino Romano cheese was the perfect salty complement to the herbs, and minced garlic solidified the pesto's flavor. I looked to lemon juice for some bright, citrusy bite, and extra-virgin olive oil contributed extra body and richness.

With my salad's base firmly in place, I sought out some crunchy, flavor-packed mix-ins to round it out. Radishes promised great texture and striking contrasting color. Shaved Pecorino Romano reinforced the pesto and homemade croutons delivered rich, buttery flavor in every bite. I served up this stunning but simple salad and my tasters agreed: Our favorite vegetable had earned its place on our salad plates.

—MORGAN BOLLING, *Cook's Country*

Asparagus Salad with Radishes, Pecorino Romano, and Croutons
SERVES 4 TO 6

Parmesan can be substituted for the Pecorino Romano. Grate the cheese for the pesto with a rasp grater or use the small holes of a box grater; shave the cheese for the salad with a vegetable peeler. For easier slicing, select large asparagus spears, about ½ inch thick.

CROUTONS
- 2 tablespoons unsalted butter
- 1 tablespoon extra-virgin olive oil
- 2 slices hearty white sandwich bread, crusts discarded, cut into ½-inch cubes (1⅓ cups)
- Salt and pepper

PESTO
- 2 cups fresh mint leaves
- ¼ cup fresh basil leaves
- ¼ cup grated Pecorino Romano cheese
- 1 teaspoon grated lemon zest plus 2 teaspoons juice
- 1 garlic clove, minced
- Salt and pepper
- ½ cup extra-virgin olive oil

SALAD

2 pounds asparagus, trimmed

5 radishes, trimmed and sliced thin

2 ounces Pecorino Romano cheese, shaved (¾ cup)

Salt and pepper

1. FOR THE CROUTONS: Heat butter and oil in 12-inch nonstick skillet over medium heat until butter is melted. Add bread cubes and ⅛ teaspoon salt and cook, stirring frequently, until golden brown, 7 to 10 minutes. Transfer croutons to paper towel–lined plate. Season with salt and pepper to taste.

2. FOR THE PESTO: Process mint, basil, Pecorino, lemon zest and juice, garlic, and ¾ teaspoon salt in food processor until finely chopped, about 20 seconds, scraping down bowl as needed. Transfer to large bowl. Stir in oil until combined and season with salt and pepper to taste.

3. FOR THE SALAD: Cut asparagus tips from stalks into ¾-inch-long pieces. Slice asparagus stalks ⅛ inch thick on bias into approximate 2-inch lengths. Add asparagus tips and stalks, radishes, and Pecorino to pesto and toss to combine. Season with salt and pepper to taste. Transfer salad to platter and top with croutons. Serve.

NOTES FROM THE TEST KITCHEN

TRIMMING ASPARAGUS

1. Remove 1 stalk of asparagus from bunch and bend at thicker end until it snaps.

2. With broken asparagus as guide, trim tough ends from remaining asparagus bunch using chef's knife.

VARIATIONS

Asparagus Salad with Oranges, Feta, and Hazelnuts

Omit radishes and Pecorino Romano. Cut away peel and pith from 2 oranges and, holding fruit over bowl, use paring knife to slice between membranes to release segments. Add segments with asparagus tip and stalks in step 3. Add 1 cup crumbled feta cheese and ¾ cup hazelnuts, toasted, skinned, and chopped, in step 3.

Asparagus Salad with Grapes, Goat Cheese, and Almonds

Omit radishes and Pecorino Romano. Add 6 ounces thinly sliced grapes (1 cup), 1 cup crumbled goat cheese, and ¾ cup whole blanched almonds, toasted and chopped, in step 3.

BRUSSELS SPROUT SALAD

WHY THIS RECIPE WORKS: To turn out a Brussels sprout salad with big flavor and a tender texture, we started with our slicing technique. Turning to a food processor seemed efficient, but hand-slicing the sprouts—trimming off the tough stems, halving, and slicing them thin—promised evenly shredded leaves. A little heat was necessary to tenderize the sprouts, so we turned to a warm vinaigrette, first microwaving red wine vinegar, whole-grain mustard, sugar, salt, and a thinly sliced shallot to meld their flavors and quickly pickle the shallots for a bright, acidic pop. We rendered the fat from chopped-up slices of bacon and stirred in the vinaigrette and shallots off the heat before adding the shredded sprouts to the warm skillet. The heat gently wilted the leaves, turning our boldly dressed salad appealingly tender. Adding shredded radicchio with the sprouts brought in some color and contrasting texture, and serving the salad with shaved Parmesan and toasted almonds made for a flavorful finish.

Though most often sautéed or roasted, raw Brussels sprouts make a great salad green. My method has always been to slice the raw sprouts thin, dress them, and let them sit—steps that help tenderize the tough leaves and brighten their pungent flavor. Sprouts also take well to punchy dressings and bold additions like rich nuts and cheeses, tangy dried fruit, and even smoky, salty bacon.

BRUSSELS SPROUT SALAD WITH WARM BACON VINAIGRETTE

A drawback to these slaw-like salads is that thin-slicing the sprouts is tedious—and they can literally be a lot to chew on. I had one idea that sounded faster: pulling the leaves from the stem whole instead of slicing them. But it only took a few minutes of plucking for me to realize that pulling apart the tightly packed leaves was actually more time-consuming than slicing. Scratch that.

In the end, I was able to streamline the shredding process with an assembly line approach: Rather than trimming, halving, and slicing the sprouts one by one,

NOTES FROM THE TEST KITCHEN

SPEEDIER BRUSSELS SPROUTS PREP
We prefer to thinly slice 1½ pounds of sprouts for Brussels Sprout Salad by hand rather than use a food processor, since its blades tend to cut the leaves unevenly. We've found it most efficient to complete one task at a time on all the sprouts and use an assembly line setup on the cutting board. In fact, employing this approach made some cooks more than 30 percent faster at the task.

1. TRIM GENEROUSLY: Trim base from sprouts, cutting high enough so that each sprout is roughly as tall as it is wide. This will allow tough outer leaves to fall away; pull off and discard any that remain.

2. HALVE SPROUTS: Pile trimmed sprouts at one end of board. Cut each in half, pushing halved sprouts to opposite end of board.

3. SLICE SPROUTS: Keep halved sprouts at 1 end near your non-dominant hand, reserve center for slicing, and pile shredded sprouts on remaining third of board.

I worked through all the trimming before moving onto the halving, and so forth.

Even shredded, the sprouts were very dense to eat; I decided to incorporate a second leafy vegetable. A handful of bitter but more tender radicchio, shredded into fine strips, was just the thing to break up the salad's slaw-like density and add complexity.

Softening raw Brussels sprouts with a regular dressing takes about 30 minutes, but what if I dressed them with a warm vinaigrette? Surely the heat would wilt them faster, and a warm dressing would be a nice change.

Like regular vinaigrettes, warm ones are mixtures of fat and acid (usually in a 3:1 ratio). The difference is that the fat in warm vinaigrettes is heated, which meant that I had options other than oil. This seemed like a perfect opportunity to use my favorite Brussels sprouts pairing: bacon.

While I crisped a few chopped slices in a skillet, I used the microwave to lightly pickle some thinly sliced shallots in a mixture of red wine vinegar, whole-grain mustard, sugar, and salt. Then I whisked the shallot mixture into the bacon. Instead of dressing the greens in a bowl, I added them to the skillet, where they were warmed not just by the dressing but also by the pan's residual heat.

Now for those aforementioned bold additions—toasted almonds and shaved Parmesan for the bacon version; dried cranberries, toasted hazelnuts, and Manchego for a variation with browned butter; and dried apricots and pistachios for yet another variation. These salads were as complex as they were elegant and have secured a starring role on my holiday table.

—LAN LAM, *Cook's Illustrated*

Brussels Sprout Salad with Warm Bacon Vinaigrette
SERVES 6

A food processor's slicing blade can be used to slice the Brussels sprouts, but the salad will be less tender. Toast the almonds in a skillet (without any oil) set over medium heat, shaking the pan occasionally to prevent scorching.

¼ cup red wine vinegar

1 tablespoon whole-grain mustard

1 teaspoon sugar

Salt and pepper

1 shallot, halved through root end and
sliced thin crosswise

4 slices bacon, cut into ½-inch pieces

1½ pounds Brussels sprouts, trimmed, halved,
and sliced thin

1½ cups finely shredded radicchio, long strands cut into
bite-size lengths

2 ounces Parmesan, shaved into thin strips using
vegetable peeler

¼ cup sliced almonds, toasted

1. Whisk vinegar, mustard, sugar, and ¼ teaspoon salt together in bowl. Add shallot, cover tightly with plastic wrap, and microwave until steaming, 30 to 60 seconds. Stir briefly to submerge shallot. Cover and let cool to room temperature, about 15 minutes.

2. Cook bacon in 12-inch skillet over medium heat, stirring frequently, until crisp and fat is rendered, 6 to 8 minutes. Off heat, whisk in shallot mixture. Add Brussels sprouts and radicchio and toss with tongs until dressing is evenly distributed and sprouts darken slightly, 1 to 2 minutes. Transfer to serving bowl. Add Parmesan and almonds and toss to combine. Season with salt and pepper to taste, and serve immediately.

Brussels Sprout Salad with Warm Browned Butter Vinaigrette

SERVES 6

Toast the hazelnuts in a skillet (without any oil) set over medium heat, shaking the pan occasionally to prevent scorching.

¼ cup lemon juice (2 lemons)

1 tablespoon whole-grain mustard

1 teaspoon sugar

Salt and pepper

1 shallot, halved through root end and
sliced thin crosswise

¼ cup dried cranberries

5 tablespoons unsalted butter

⅓ cup hazelnuts, toasted, skinned, and chopped

1½ pounds Brussels sprouts, trimmed, halved,
and sliced thin

1½ ounces (1½ cups) baby arugula, chopped

4 ounces Manchego cheese, shaved into thin strips using
vegetable peeler

1. Whisk lemon juice, mustard, sugar, and ¼ teaspoon salt together in bowl. Add shallot and cranberries, cover tightly with plastic wrap, and microwave until steaming, 30 to 60 seconds. Stir briefly to submerge shallot and cranberries. Let cool to room temperature, about 15 minutes.

2. Melt butter in 12-inch skillet over medium heat. Add hazelnuts and cook, stirring frequently, until butter is dark golden brown, 3 to 5 minutes. Off heat, whisk in shallot mixture. Add Brussels sprouts and arugula and toss with tongs until dressing is evenly distributed and sprouts darken slightly, 1 to 2 minutes. Transfer to serving bowl. Add Manchego and toss to combine. Season with salt and pepper to taste, and serve immediately.

Brussels Sprout Salad with Warm Mustard Vinaigrette

SERVES 6

Crumbled feta cheese can be substituted for the ricotta salata.

5 tablespoons white wine vinegar

1 tablespoon whole-grain mustard

1 teaspoon sugar

Salt and pepper

1 shallot, halved through root end and
sliced thin crosswise

¼ cup dried apricots, chopped

5 tablespoons vegetable oil

⅓ cup shelled pistachios, chopped

1½ pounds Brussels sprouts, trimmed, halved,
and sliced thin

1½ ounces (1½ cups) watercress, chopped

4 ounces ricotta salata, shaved into thin
strips using vegetable peeler

1. Whisk vinegar, mustard, sugar, and ¼ teaspoon salt together in bowl. Add shallot and apricots, cover tightly with plastic wrap, and microwave until steaming,

30 to 60 seconds. Stir briefly to submerge shallot and apricots. Let cool to room temperature, about 15 minutes.

2. Heat oil in 12-inch skillet over medium heat until shimmering. Add pistachios and cook, stirring frequently, until pistachios are golden brown, 1 to 2 minutes. Off heat, whisk in shallot mixture. Add Brussels sprouts and toss with tongs until dressing is evenly distributed and sprouts darken slightly, 1 to 2 minutes. Transfer to serving bowl. Add watercress and ricotta salata and toss to combine. Season with salt and pepper to taste, and serve immediately.

WHIPPED CASHEW NUT DIPS

✓ **WHY THIS RECIPE WORKS:** Creating a paleo and vegan-friendly nut-based dip with all the creamy, rich qualities of ricotta cheese starts with selecting the right nut. After soaking and pureeing macadamias, almonds, and cashews, it was clear that the mellow flavor and supremely creamy texture of pureed cashews created the perfect neutral base. Soaking the cashews for at least 12 hours proved critical; any less, and the dip turned out grainy. With our homemade nut "cheese" in place, we turned to a variety of simple ingredients to give our dip some flavor. For our first combination, we tried mildly smoky roasted red peppers paired with the briny saltiness of chopped kalamata olives. A bit of olive oil and lemon juice boosted the flavor further and thinned the dip to a perfect spreadable consistency. Some parsley, stirred in with the olives after processing, provided welcome freshness. Since our dip had come together so quickly and easily, we decided to create two more variations, one using smoky chipotle, tangy lime juice, and fresh cilantro; and another with sweet sun-dried tomatoes and earthy rosemary.

For anyone following a paleo diet, turning out a smooth, creamy dip is the ultimate challenge. Here in the test kitchen, we rely on the lush texture and creamy flavor of cheese, milk, and butter to boost richness in our recipes. In order to make a full-flavored dip that would impress even my non-paleo friends, I needed to get creative. During my research, I learned that simply soaking and pureeing macadamia nuts promised the buttery flavor and velvety, spreadable body of ricotta cheese. This technique piqued my curiosity. Was it possible that nuts alone could mimic dairy's best qualities?

I started by aiming for a basic nut "cheese." Many recipes rely on macadamias for their base, but I didn't want to limit myself to a single nut quite yet. Along with the macadamias, I also wondered how almonds and cashews would fare. Whirring the nuts alone in the food processor only chopped them up, so soaking the nuts would be key to achieving the right texture. I submerged the three different nuts in water overnight, drained them, and then gave them a spin in the food processor. All three emerged smooth and spreadable, but the cashew puree had the finest texture and most neutral flavor—perfect as a base for a range of flavors but also enjoyable on its own. Much to my surprise, the macadamias were the least favorite among our tasters, who found their flavor distracting, and though some liked the almond puree, it turned out coarser than I liked. Focusing on the cashew puree, I refined its creamy texture and boosted its richness by adding some extra-virgin olive oil. I was impressed—this very basic cheese alternative was well on its way to having the buttery, creamy characteristics I was seeking.

Nut cheeses are popular in a whole range of recipes—from hearty vegan lasagnas to bite-size stuffed dates—but I wanted to focus my efforts on turning out an appealing dairy-free dip without too much fuss. I first investigated the soaking time. After a few tests, I determined that 12 hours was the sweet spot—just enough time to properly soften the cashews—and anything over 24 hours was unnecessary, if not detrimental to the recipe. Next, I experimented with the puree's texture, aiming for an airy, whipped consistency. The liquid components—olive oil and water—were important to keeping the dip smooth and spreadable, so I played with different ratios until I settled on 3 tablespoons of each. Lemon juice promised to give the mixture ricotta's signature tang, so I also added 3 tablespoons of fresh juice. This base had all the qualities I loved in ricotta cheese, and I suddenly understood all the hype.

To turn my ricotta-esque base into a crowd-pleasing dip, I sought out some bold complementary flavors. I started with roasted red peppers, thinking their smoky-sweet flavor would pair well with the lush cashew puree. I patted the peppers dry (so as to not add any thinning

WHIPPED CASHEW NUT DIPS

liquid to my base), chopped them, and tossed them into the food processor. I added in some chopped kalamata olives and, minutes later, I had my first dip ready to go. With plenty of soaked cashews on hand, I kept going, adding in chipotle chile powder and cumin and replacing the lemon juice with lime for a smoky, Southwestern variation. I also tried swapping in sun-dried tomatoes and rosemary for a sweet and savory take. Aside from waiting for the nuts to soak, these dips could not have come together more quickly, and they tasted so rich and creamy that I had to remind my tasters that there wasn't even a whisper of dairy in them.

—LAWMAN JOHNSON, *America's Test Kitchen Books*

Whipped Cashew Nut Dip with Roasted Red Peppers and Olives
SERVES 6 TO 8

You can substitute an equal amount of slivered almonds for the cashews, but the dip will have a slightly coarser consistency. Serve with crackers, chips, or crudités.

1½	cups raw cashews
½	cup jarred roasted red peppers, rinsed, patted dry, and chopped
3	tablespoons extra-virgin olive oil
3	tablespoons lemon juice
	Kosher salt and pepper
1	garlic clove, minced
½	cup minced fresh parsley
½	cup pitted kalamata olives, chopped

1. Place cashews in bowl and add cold water to cover by 1 inch. Soak cashews at room temperature for at least 12 hours or up to 24 hours. Drain and rinse well.

2. Process soaked cashews, red peppers, 3 tablespoons water, oil, lemon juice, 1½ teaspoons salt, ½ teaspoon pepper, and garlic in food processor until smooth, about 2 minutes, scraping down sides of bowl as needed.

3. Transfer cashew mixture to serving bowl and stir in parsley and olives. Season with salt and pepper to taste. Cover with plastic wrap and let sit at room temperature until flavors meld, about 30 minutes. Serve. (Dip can be refrigerated for up to 5 days; if necessary, stir in 1 tablespoon warm water to loosen dip consistency before serving.)

VARIATIONS

Whipped Cashew Nut Dip with Chipotle and Lime

Omit red peppers and olives. Add ½ teaspoon chipotle chile powder and ½ teaspoon ground cumin to processor with soaked cashews and increase water to 6 tablespoons in step 2. Substitute ¼ cup lime juice (2 limes) for lemon juice and ⅓ cup minced fresh cilantro for parsley.

Whipped Cashew Nut Dip with Sun-Dried Tomatoes and Rosemary

Omit red peppers and parsley. Add 2 teaspoons minced fresh rosemary to processor with soaked cashews and increase water to 6 tablespoons in step 2. Substitute ½ cup finely chopped oil-packed sun-dried tomatoes for olives.

BAKED PEPPERONI PIZZA DIP

✓ **WHY THIS RECIPE WORKS:** To turn classic pepperoni pizza into an easy appetizer, we set our sights on a cheesy, rich dip. We started with the dip's base, combining mozzarella with cream cheese for a smooth texture. Adding pizza sauce boosted the base's pizza flavor and thinned it to a perfectly dippable consistency. Crisped pepperoni finalized the familiar flavor profile. We wanted this dip to stay warm from oven to table, so we harnessed the heat-retaining power of our trusty cast-iron skillet. Preparing and serving the dip in this vessel kept the cheese warm and gooey without the help of a Sterno or hot plate. Naturally, the perfect partner for our creamy, saucy dip was pizza dough. We rolled out dough balls, tossed them with garlic oil, and baked them right in the skillet, which created a crisp, golden bottom on the garlic rolls. We spooned the dip mixture into the center of the skillet, inside the ring of parbaked mini rolls, and baked the whole thing in the oven. A sprinkling of fresh basil and pepperoni crisps gave our all-in-one dip an authentic finish.

Nothing says casual party quite like cheesy pepperoni pizza and bowls of chips paired with creamy, gooey dips. These old standbys are mainstays at every Super Bowl party I've ever attended and are gobbled up as quickly as they hit the table. For this year's big game, I wanted to serve something with a bit more panache, so I started toying with the idea of combining my favorite gameday snacks into a single indulgent, flavor-packed app. My cast-iron skillet seemed like the perfect vessel for the job—its heat-retaining power would keep my all-in-one dip warm from oven to table. If I could find a way to turn out a rich, cheesy dip with bits of spicy pepperoni, crispy browned edges, and a chewy pizza crust for dipping, I knew I'd have a winner on my hands.

First, I focused on the dip itself. Mozzarella is our go-to pizza cheese, but when melted its heavy, stringy consistency made dipping impossible. To make the mozzarella creamier, I looked to the dairy aisle. Adding an additional shredded cheese would take away from the straightforward pizza flavor I wanted and sour cream was too watery, but cream cheese seemed promising. I mixed shredded mozzarella and cream cheese together and was pleased to discover that these two components melted down to a thick, indulgent consistency. To bring in more familiar pizza flavor, I decided to add a simple pizza sauce into the mix. Favoring the fresh flavor of homemade sauce over store-bought, I processed canned diced tomatoes, olive oil, minced garlic, and oregano in my food processor and thinned out this mixture with the juice drained from the canned tomatoes. I added my sauce to the mozzarella–cream cheese mixture and my dip finally hit its mark, boasting creamy, cheesy body and bright tomato taste. For a final boost, I crisped up some thinly sliced pepperoni and stirred it into to the dip. Now all that was missing was a chewy, crusty accompaniment to complement the dip.

I knew that serving (and keeping) this pizza dip warm at the table would make the biggest impact. Enter my trusty cast-iron skillet. Not only would heating the dip in it keep the cheesy nice and gooey, but its sloping sides also gave me a great idea: I could bake bite-size pizza crust rolls along the edges of my skillet and use them to scoop up the dip. I started with the test kitchen's favorite pizza dough recipe and rolled it out into small balls. I arranged the balls around the perimeter of the skillet and scooped the dip into the center. Though the cream cheese gave me some insurance against a grease slick, I knew that overheating would compromise the dip's lush texture, so I kept the baking time as brief as possible. After 10 minutes in the oven, my dip was perfectly melty but the dough had barely baked. Clearly parbaking the balls would be necessary.

I began again, crisping the pepperoni before arranging the dough. I was about to wipe out the pepperoni's rendered fat when another take-out favorite came to mind—garlic knots. These chewy rolls are made of knotted pizza dough and are loaded with major garlic flavor in every bite. What if I used the pepperoni's oil, boosted with some garlic, to infuse the dough with flavor? With the skillet still warm from cooking the pepperoni, I added olive oil and a few minced garlic cloves and let the flavors meld. I brushed the dough balls with this spicy garlic oil before arranging them in the now-empty skillet and left them to puff up before baking. This time around, I parbaked the garlic rolls on their own, allowing the rolls to begin to brown and bake without compromising the dip. After 20 minutes, I scooped in the dip and returned the skillet to the oven. After 10 minutes, the dip emerged creamy, bubbly, loaded with pizza flavor, and encircled by soft, chewy rolls which were easy to pull apart and use to scoop up the cheesy dip. A sprinkling of chopped fresh basil and some of the crisp pepperoni bits made for a fresh and appealingly crunchy finish. Win or lose, I think I just drafted this year's most valuable player.

—LEAH COLINS, *America's Test Kitchen Books*

Baked Pepperoni Pizza Dip
SERVES 8 TO 10

We like the convenience of using ready-made pizza dough from the local pizzeria or supermarket; however, you can use our Classic Pizza Dough (recipe follows). For the pizza sauce, consider using our No-Cook Pizza Sauce (recipe follows). To soften the cream cheese quickly, microwave it for 20 to 30 seconds.

- 3 **ounces thinly sliced pepperoni, quartered**
- 1 **tablespoon extra-virgin olive oil**
- 3 **garlic cloves, minced**
- 1 **pound pizza dough**
- 8 **ounces cream cheese, cut into 8 pieces and softened**
- ¾ **cup pizza sauce**
- 4 **ounces mozzarella cheese, shredded (1 cup)**
- 2 **tablespoons chopped fresh basil**

1. Adjust oven rack to middle position and heat oven to 400 degrees. Cook pepperoni in 10-inch cast-iron skillet over medium heat until crisp, 5 to 7 minutes. Using slotted spoon, transfer pepperoni to paper towel–lined plate; set aside. Off heat, add oil and garlic to fat left in skillet and let sit until fragrant, about 1 minute; transfer to medium bowl.

2. Place dough on lightly floured counter, pat into rough 8-inch square, and cut into 32 pieces (½ ounce each). Working with 1 piece of dough at a time, roll into tight ball, then coat with garlic oil. Evenly space 18 balls around edge of skillet, keeping center of skillet clear. Place remaining 14 balls on top, staggering them between seams of balls underneath. Cover loosely with greased plastic wrap and let sit until slightly puffed, about 20 minutes.

3. Remove plastic. Transfer skillet to oven and bake until balls are just beginning to brown, about 20 minutes, rotating skillet halfway through baking. Meanwhile, whisk cream cheese and pizza sauce in large bowl until thoroughly combined and smooth. Stir in mozzarella and three-quarters of crisped pepperoni.

4. Spoon cheese mixture into center of skillet, return to oven, and bake until dip is heated through and rolls are golden brown, about 10 minutes. Sprinkle with basil and remaining crisped pepperoni. Serve.

NOTES FROM THE TEST KITCHEN

MAKING PEPPERONI PIZZA DIP

Evenly space 18 balls around edge of skillet. Place remaining 14 balls on top, staggering between seams of lower row. There will be some gaps in top row.

A SUPERIOR SKILLET

The Lodge Classic Cast Iron Skillet is our favorite model. It browns foods deeply, and its thorough seasoning ensured that our Baked Pepperoni Pizza Dip's spicy garlic oil did not pick up any off-flavors.

Classic Pizza Dough
MAKES 1 POUND

    2   cups plus 2 tablespoons (11¾ ounces) bread flour
    1⅛ teaspoons instant or rapid-rise yeast
    ¾   teaspoon salt
    1   tablespoon olive oil
    ¾   cup warm water (110 degrees)

1. Pulse flour, yeast, and salt in food processor until combined, about 5 pulses. With processor running, add oil, then water, and process until rough ball forms, 30 to 40 seconds. Let dough rest for 2 minutes, then process for 30 seconds longer. (If after 30 seconds dough is very sticky and clings to blade, add extra flour as needed.)

2. Transfer dough to lightly floured counter and knead by hand to form smooth, round ball, about 1 minute. Place dough in large, lightly greased bowl, cover tightly with greased plastic wrap, and let rise until doubled in size, 1 to 1½ hours. (Alternatively, dough can be refrigerated for at least 8 hours or up to 16 hours.)

No-Cook Pizza Sauce
MAKES ¾ CUP

While it is convenient to use ready-made pizza sauce, we think it is almost as easy, and a lot tastier, to make your own.

    ¾   cup canned diced tomatoes, drained,
        juice reserved
    1   teaspoon extra-virgin olive oil
    1   small garlic clove, minced
    ½   teaspoon dried oregano
        Salt and pepper

Process tomatoes with oil, garlic, and oregano in food processor until smooth, about 30 seconds. Transfer mixture to 2-cup liquid measuring cup and add tomato juice until sauce measures ¾ cup. Season with salt and pepper to taste.

BAKED PEPPERONI PIZZA DIP

CRISPY PARMESAN POTATOES

✓ **WHY THIS RECIPE WORKS:** To turn out perfectly snackable Parmesan potatoes, we had to figure out how to cook the potatoes just right and how to get the cheese to stick. We opted for Yukon Gold potatoes because their high moisture content meant the spuds wouldn't dry out during roasting. We tossed the potato slices in cornstarch seasoned with salt and pepper to dry their surfaces and enhance crisping. Roasting the slices on a greased baking sheet in a hot oven created a creamy interior. We processed Parmesan cheese with rosemary, salt, pepper, and cornstarch in the food processor for a savory, easy-to-sprinkle cheese topping and spread the seasoned cheese over and in between the slices, pressing it onto the potatoes' exposed surfaces to be sure it stayed put. To ensure an even layer of cheese, we flipped the slices over (in the same footprint) and continued to bake until the cheese turned a light golden brown. The cooled potatoes came off the baking sheet with ease, covered in appealing crispy cheese.

Crispy. Cheesy. Potatoes. Three words that, put together, have to mean good, right? While none of the existing recipes we tried were inedible, some produced over-cooked potatoes, while others offered cheese that refused to cling to the oily potatoes. I wanted creamy potato slices (rather than thick wedges) with crispy, flavorful Parmesan adhering to each slice.

After my initial tests, I settled on 2 pounds of creamy Yukon Gold potatoes, sliced ½ inch thick and tossed with olive oil, salt, and pepper for maximum flavor. I knew that roasting the potatoes at a high temperature would achieve the best color and flavor: 500 degrees on the lower-middle rack was just right. Two teaspoons of cornstarch added to the pre-oven toss helped them get crunchy. Now I could turn my attention to the real sticking point with this recipe: the cheese.

I roasted a pan of potatoes for 20 minutes to a golden brown and then took them out of the oven and sprinkled a bit of grated Parmesan cheese onto each slice. I put them back in the oven to melt and crisp the cheese. But I'd been a bit careless in my cheese distribution, covering the pan as well as the potatoes. As I scraped the mess off the baking sheet, I realized I'd created a giant salty, savory, cheesy Parmesan chip, or *frico*. Not great looking but undeniably delicious.

If only I could get that frico to stick to the potato and not just the pan.

For my next test, I processed the cheese in the food processor for a finer texture. I also added some rosemary and pepper for flavor and a bit more cornstarch, which we've found helps the finely shredded Parmesan distribute evenly. I sprayed the baking sheet with vegetable oil spray to help prevent sticking; then, when the potatoes came out of the oven 20 minutes later, I sprinkled the cheese liberally over the potatoes and baking sheet. I turned each slice over and returned the sheet to the oven until the cheese turned golden, about 5 minutes. I let the potatoes cool for 15 minutes on a wire rack before removing them from the sheet. The interiors were creamy, the upper sides of the slices were golden brown, and the underside of each had a delicious Parmesan crisp firmly stuck to it.

The only improvement? A dipping sauce. I combined sour cream (a natural with potatoes), chives, rosemary, garlic and onion powders, and salt and pepper. Just right.

—DIANE UNGER, *Cook's Country*

Crispy Parmesan Potatoes
SERVES 6 TO 8

Try to find potatoes that are 2½ to 3 inches long. Spray the baking sheet with an aerosol (not pump) vegetable oil spray. Use a good-quality Parmesan cheese here. Serve with Chive Sour Cream (recipe follows), if desired.

- 2 **pounds medium Yukon Gold potatoes, unpeeled**
- 4 **teaspoons cornstarch**
  Salt and pepper
- 1 **tablespoon extra-virgin olive oil**
- 6 **ounces Parmesan cheese, cut into 1-inch chunks**
- 2 **teaspoons minced fresh rosemary**

1. Adjust oven rack to lower-middle position and heat oven to 500 degrees. Spray rimmed baking sheet liberally with vegetable oil spray. Cut thin slice from 2 opposing long sides of each potato; discard slices. Cut potatoes lengthwise into ½-inch-thick slices and transfer to large bowl.

2. Combine 2 teaspoons cornstarch, 1 teaspoon salt, and 1 teaspoon pepper in small bowl. Sprinkle cornstarch mixture over potatoes and toss until potatoes are thoroughly coated and cornstarch is no longer visible. Add oil and toss to coat.

3. Arrange potatoes in single layer on prepared sheet and bake until golden brown on top, about 20 minutes.

4. Meanwhile, process Parmesan, rosemary, ½ teaspoon pepper, and remaining 2 teaspoons cornstarch in food processor until cheese is finely ground, about 1 minute.

5. Remove potatoes from oven. Sprinkle Parmesan mixture evenly over and between potatoes (cheese should cover surface of baking sheet), pressing on potatoes with back of spoon to adhere. Using 2 forks, flip slices over into same spot on sheet.

6. Bake until cheese between potatoes turns light golden brown, 5 to 7 minutes. Transfer sheet to wire rack and let potatoes cool for 15 minutes. Using large metal spatula, transfer potatoes, cheese side up, and accompanying cheese to platter and serve.

Chive Sour Cream
MAKES ABOUT 1 CUP

This enhanced condiment makes an excellent topping for potatoes of all kinds.

  1 **cup sour cream**
  ¼ **cup minced fresh chives**
  ½ **teaspoon minced fresh rosemary**
  ½ **teaspoon salt**
  ½ **teaspoon pepper**
  ½ **teaspoon garlic powder**
  ¼ **teaspoon onion powder**

Combine all ingredients in bowl. Cover and refrigerate at least 30 minutes to allow flavors to blend.

NOTES FROM THE TEST KITCHEN

FLIPPING FOR FRICO

Using 2 forks, turn each potato slice over and return it to the same spot on the sheet. As the excess Parmesan bakes, it will transform into crispy cheesy bits called frico.

TERIYAKI MEATBALLS

✔ WHY THIS RECIPE WORKS: These bite-size meatballs get salty-sweet flavor from our homemade teriyaki sauce. Unlike thick, too-sweet bottled versions, we kept our sauce simple, combining soy sauce, sugar, mirin, and a little cornstarch for just the right thickness. For the meatballs, we opted for ground chicken; the mild meat paired well with the teriyaki sauce and other aromatic ingredients like ginger, garlic, and scallions. Sautéed shiitakes and cabbage added moisture and depth, while an egg added richness. Panko bread crumbs gave the meatballs structure, and mixing in a few tablespoons of the sauce reinforced the teriyaki flavor. Chilling the meatballs before baking helped them maintain their shape and allowed us to prep them in advance.

The perfect happy-hour meatball is bite-size, packed with flavor, and cloaked in a glossy sauce that clings to the meatball rather than dripping onto your little black dress. It's sweet and salty, complementing any cocktail in the bartender's canon. And it's good enough to make you spoil your dinner. I set out to create a meatball that was worthy of any fancy toothpick I stuck into it.

I targeted the teriyaki. Traditionally a glazy mixture of soy sauce, mirin (cooking wine), and sugar, teriyaki comfortably straddles sweet and savory. At least, it should. But ever since its first widespread flirtation with midcentury American palates, the sauce has taken many wrong turns, evolving into a sugary one-note wonder.

It didn't take much to bring the sauce back into balance. I played with a handful of existing recipes and tinkered with different ratios of the core ingredients (I chose supermarket mirin over more expensive sake and added cornstarch for thickening) until I found the right consistency to properly cling to a simple beef meatball. My colleagues loved the sauce, especially when I added complementary flavors like ginger, garlic, and scallions to the meatball mix. But the beefiness stubbornly overshadowed these additions.

I scoured the meat case for a replacement. Ground pork was sweet and promising, but ground chicken was even better—its neutral flavor and pleasant chew gave the teriyaki space to shine.

A couple of experiments showed me that an all-white-meat grind of chicken was too dry, so I used regular ground chicken (a mix of white and dark meats)

TERIYAKI MEATBALLS

fortified with sautéed shiitake mushrooms and green cabbage for added moisture and deep savory flavor. An egg added richness and structure while some panko bread crumbs helped the meatballs keep their shape. And, to amp up the teriyaki presence, I mashed in a bit of my sauce.

Since these meatballs were meant to be bite-size, I kept them small—just 1 tablespoon each—and baked them in a hot oven for about 20 minutes. Chilling them for about an hour before baking ensured they'd bake into balls, not disks, and also meant I could form them the day before serving. The golden meatballs that emerged from the oven were flavorful in their own right but even better after a roll around the skillet in the glazy teriyaki sauce. These meatballs were ready to party.

—CHRISTIE MORRISON, *Cook's Country*

Teriyaki Meatballs

MAKES 40 MEATBALLS

If you don't have mirin, use an equal amount of dry white wine and increase the sugar to ¼ cup. Toast the sesame seeds in a dry skillet over medium heat until fragrant (about 1 minute), and then remove the pan from the heat so the seeds won't scorch. Plan ahead: The meatballs need to chill for at least 1 hour before baking.

MEATBALLS

- 6 ounces shiitake mushrooms, stemmed and chopped coarse
- 1½ cups chopped green cabbage
- 2 tablespoons vegetable oil
  Salt and pepper
- 3 garlic cloves, minced
- 1 tablespoon grated fresh ginger
- 1 pound ground chicken
- ½ cup panko bread crumbs
- 4 scallions, minced
- 3 tablespoons minced fresh cilantro
- 1 large egg, lightly beaten
- 1 tablespoon toasted sesame oil

SAUCE

- 1 tablespoon cornstarch
- 1 tablespoon unseasoned rice vinegar
- ½ cup mirin

- ⅓ cup water
- ¼ cup soy sauce
- 3 tablespoons sugar
- 2 scallions, green parts only, sliced thin on bias
- 1 tablespoon sesame seeds, toasted

1. FOR THE MEATBALLS: Adjust oven rack to upper-middle position and heat oven to 400 degrees. Line rimmed baking sheet with aluminum foil and spray evenly with vegetable oil spray. Combine mushrooms and cabbage in food processor and pulse until chopped into ¼-inch pieces, about 5 pulses.

2. Heat vegetable oil in 12-inch nonstick skillet over medium-high heat until shimmering. Add mushroom mixture and ½ teaspoon salt and cook, stirring occasionally, until vegetables are lightly browned, 6 to 8 minutes. Add garlic and ginger and cook until fragrant, about 30 seconds. Transfer to large bowl.

3. FOR THE SAUCE: Wipe now-empty skillet clean with paper towels. Whisk cornstarch and vinegar in small bowl until combined; set aside. Bring mirin, water, soy sauce, and sugar to boil over high heat. Whisk in cornstarch slurry, reduce heat to medium-low, and simmer until thickened, about 1 minute. Remove pan from heat; transfer 3 tablespoons teriyaki sauce to mushroom mixture. Let mushroom mixture cool completely, about 15 minutes. Cover skillet and set remaining sauce aside.

4. Add chicken, panko, scallions, cilantro, egg, sesame oil, and ½ teaspoon pepper to cooled mushroom mixture and mix with your hands until thoroughly combined. Divide chicken mixture into 40 portions, about 1 tablespoon each. Roll between your wet hands to form 1¼-inch balls and space evenly on prepared sheet in 8 rows of 5. Cover lightly with plastic wrap and refrigerate until firm, about 1 hour.

5. Uncover sheet and cook until meatballs are firm and bottoms are lightly browned, 15 to 20 minutes, rotating sheet halfway through cooking. Rewarm sauce over medium-low heat. Add meatballs to skillet and toss to coat with sauce. Transfer meatballs and sauce to serving dish and sprinkle with scallions and sesame seeds. Serve.

TO MAKE AHEAD: Meatballs and sauce can be prepared through step 4, covered, and refrigerated for up to 24 hours. Add 2 tablespoons water to sauce when reheating.

CHAPTER 2

SOUPS, STEWS, AND CHILIS

PASTA E CECI (PASTA WITH CHICKPEAS)

PASTA E CECI

✔ **WHY THIS RECIPE WORKS:** The hearty Italian dish known as *pasta e ceci* combines chickpeas and pasta into a rich, satisfying stew. We began by pulsing carrots, celery, and garlic into a *soffritto* using a food processor; salty pancetta gave the aromatic base a meaty richness. We cooked the soffrito in a Dutch oven to build a flavorful fond and then added in minced anchovy for an umami boost. Red pepper flakes introduced some heat and minced fresh rosemary added a woodsy, herbal quality. Chopped tomatoes are essential, but to keep our pasta e ceci convenient we turned to canned peeled tomatoes and chopped them quickly using the food processor. We poured the tomatoes into the pot with canned chickpeas (including their starchy canning liquid for added body) and brought the mixture to a simmer. The chickpeas began to soften after 10 minutes, so we added in ditalini pasta and cooked the stew a little longer. The chickpeas took on a creamy softness that complemented the tender pasta and thick, silky broth. Lemon juice and minced parsley offered some brightness and grated Parmesan gave it an authentic finish.

Pasta e ceci—pasta and chickpeas—have been paired up in Italian cuisine for centuries. The combination is cheap, simple, and pantry-ready, and the dish itself—a sibling of *pasta e fagioli*—is hearty, flavorful, and fast to make. It's one of those one-pot meals that home cooks turn to over and over again. Just about every Italian household has a version, which explains why published recipes range dramatically—from brothy soups to hearty stews and even lightly sauced pastas. Simple aromatics like onion, celery, carrot, and garlic are common but not compulsory, as are additions like pancetta, tomato, rosemary, and parsley. In fact, the only constants are the namesake ingredients—and even those can vary. It's common to see both dried and canned chickpeas, as well as fresh and dried pasta of various shapes. Using up broken strands of spaghetti or linguine befits the dish's frugal nature, but short pastas pair particularly well with the chickpeas.

Preparing a handful of recipes helped me develop my own ideal: a loose stew that would be thick with creamy beans and stubby pasta but also savory enough to balance the starchy components. And it had to be on the table in well under an hour.

A quick version meant I'd be using canned chickpeas, but it wasn't a sacrifice. We've found that many canned chickpeas are uniform and well seasoned. I started by sautéing a *soffritto*—minced onion, carrot, celery, and garlic—in olive oil. I then stirred in a couple of cups of water (cleaner tasting than either chicken or vegetable broth) and two 15-ounce cans of chickpeas along with their liquid (the starchy, seasoned liquid adds body and flavor). I also added 8 ounces of ditalini, a popular choice for their chickpea-like size. The mixture simmered for about 10 minutes, by which point the pasta was tender and had released some starch that thickened the stew.

I liked that the pasta and chickpeas were chunky and distinct (some recipes puree some or all of the chickpeas), but I did want to soften up the beans a bit more. So rather than adding them along with the pasta, I gave them a 10-minute head start. The extra simmering time changed their texture from snappy to creamy, and because they broke down a bit, they added even more body to the cooking liquid.

With the consistency of the stew just right, I circled back to its flavor—which, despite the soffritto, was lackluster. My instinct was to add some diced pancetta, which I'd seen in a few recipes. It lent the stew meaty depth, but it also added chewy bits that marred the overall creamy texture. The solution was to grind the pork to a paste in the food processor and then incorporate it into the soffritto. While I had the appliance out, I saved myself some knife work and blitzed the vegetables, too.

Tomatoes and a minced anchovy, both packed with umami-enhancing glutamates, were good additions as well. I opted for a small can of whole tomatoes, chopped coarse. The final tweaks—minced rosemary and a dash of red pepper flakes added to the soffritto, plus last minute additions of parsley and lemon juice—provided bite and brightness.

I topped my bowl with grated Parmesan and a drizzle of oil and tucked into a savory, rib-sticking stew that I'd thrown together in about 30 minutes.

—ANDREW JANJIGIAN, *Cook's Illustrated*

Pasta e Ceci (Pasta with Chickpeas)

SERVES 4 TO 6

Another short pasta, such as orzo, can be substituted for the ditalini, but make sure to substitute by weight and not by volume.

 2 ounces pancetta, cut into ½-inch pieces
 1 small carrot, peeled and cut into ½-inch pieces
 1 small celery rib, cut into ½-inch pieces
 4 garlic cloves, peeled
 1 onion, halved and cut into 1-inch pieces
 1 (14-ounce) can whole peeled tomatoes, drained
 ¼ cup extra-virgin olive oil, plus extra for serving
 1 anchovy fillet, rinsed, patted dry, and minced
 ¼ teaspoon red pepper flakes
 2 teaspoons minced fresh rosemary
 2 (15-ounce) cans chickpeas (do not drain)
 2 cups water
     Salt and pepper
 8 ounces (1½ cups) ditalini
 1 tablespoon lemon juice
 1 tablespoon minced fresh parsley
 1 ounce Parmesan cheese, grated (½ cup)

1. Process pancetta in food processor until ground to paste, about 30 seconds, scraping down sides of bowl as needed. Add carrot, celery, and garlic and pulse until finely chopped, 8 to 10 pulses. Add onion and pulse until onion is cut into ⅛- to ¼-inch pieces, 8 to 10 pulses. Transfer pancetta mixture to large Dutch oven. Pulse tomatoes in now-empty food processor until coarsely chopped, 8 to 10 pulses. Set aside.

2. Add oil to pancetta mixture in Dutch oven and cook over medium heat, stirring frequently, until fond begins to form on bottom of pot, about 5 minutes. Add anchovy, pepper flakes, and rosemary and cook until fragrant, about 1 minute. Stir in tomatoes, chickpeas and their liquid, water, and 1 teaspoon salt and bring to boil, scraping up any browned bits. Reduce heat to medium-low and simmer for 10 minutes. Add pasta and cook, stirring frequently, until tender, 10 to 12 minutes. Stir in lemon juice and parsley and season with salt and pepper to taste. Serve, passing Parmesan and extra oil separately.

RED LENTIL SOUP WITH NORTH AFRICAN SPICES

✔ **WHY THIS RECIPE WORKS:** Red lentils cook quickly into a thick puree, but their mild flavor requires a bit of embellishment. To turn out a rich soup, we started by sautéing onions in butter and used the warm mixture to bloom some fragrant North African spices. Tomato paste and garlic boosted the savory base before the addition of the lentils, and a mix of chicken broth and water gave the soup a full, rounded character. After only 15 minutes of cooking, the lentils were soft enough to be coarsely pureed with just a whisk. A generous dose of lemon juice brought the flavors into focus; a drizzle of spice-infused butter and a sprinkle of fresh cilantro completed the transformation of commonplace ingredients into an exotic yet comforting soup.

If you'd like to cook more beans but are unsure of where to begin, red lentils are the ideal gateway legume. For one thing, they're quick to prepare. Unlike green and brown lentils, the red ones have had their skins removed; as a result, they split in two during processing, which leaves them so tiny that they cook in less than 20 minutes, with no presoaking or brining required. But the best thing about cooking red lentils is that you get to sidestep the biggest challenge of bean cookery: getting the interiors of the beans to soften before the skins rupture. With no skins to contain them, red lentils disintegrate when you cook them. No amount of vigilance or technique can prevent it. In countries like Egypt and Morocco, cooks embrace this inevitability by turning their red lentils into soup. They add them to sautéed aromatics, stir in some warm spices, and then simmer it all in broth or water. Less than half an hour later, they have a satisfying soup.

To develop my own recipe, I started simply. I sautéed onions in a bit of butter until they were soft, and then I stirred in some minced garlic, cumin, coriander, and black pepper and cooked them briefly in the warm mixture. When the spices were fragrant, I added a cup of lentils, and because many recipes called for some form of tomato, I added one can of diced. For my cooking liquid, I began with the easiest option: water.

After 15 minutes of simmering, the lentils were fully softened and about half had disintegrated, but the consistency of the soup was thinner than I had anticipated. The tomato added a nice acidity, but it made the soup seem even more watery. To thicken the soup, I added 50 percent more lentils in the next round. I ditched the diced tomatoes for a tablespoon of tomato paste, and to give the soup a bit more backbone, I replaced some of the water with chicken broth. I also added more of the warm spices found in North African versions of the soup: cinnamon, ginger, and just a pinch of cayenne.

This batch was more substantial, but the lentils had settled to the bottom; the top was somewhat watery. And the overall flavor was still a bit flat. Before I perfected the flavor, I evened out the consistency. A quick whir in the blender or food processor would do the trick, but it seemed like overkill for such a simple soup. Instead I tried boiling it vigorously after the lentils had softened, thinking that the turbulence would break up the lentils and help thicken things up. It did, but it also scorched on the bottom of the saucepan, so the soup tasted burnt.

I knew that constant stirring while boiling would prevent scorching, but then it occurred to me: Maybe I could skip the boiling if I just changed stirring implements. When the next batch of lentils had softened, I swapped my wooden spoon for a whisk. Thirty seconds of whisking did the trick: Now I had a coarse puree that was homogeneous from top to bottom.

Following the lead of North African cooks, I added 2 tablespoons of lemon juice to the pureed soup. The effect was like adjusting the focus on a manual camera: All the flavors were instantly more vibrant and defined. Now the soup needed just a touch of richness. I melted 2 tablespoons of butter and then stirred in some dried mint and paprika for even more authentic flavor. I ladled out my fragrant soup, drizzled some spiced butter on top, and sprinkled it with fresh cilantro for a rich, bright finish.

—ANDREA GEARY, *Cook's Illustrated*

NOTES FROM THE TEST KITCHEN

PUREEING BY HAND

When lentils have softened, vigorously whisk for 30 seconds to coarsely puree lentils into homogeneous mixture.

Red Lentil Soup with North African Spices

SERVES 4 TO 6

Do not substitute brown, green, or French lentils for the red lentils here; the texture of the red lentils is essential to the soup.

    4 tablespoons unsalted butter
    1 large onion, chopped fine
       Salt and pepper
    ¾ teaspoon ground coriander
    ½ teaspoon ground cumin
    ¼ teaspoon ground ginger
    ⅛ teaspoon ground cinnamon
       Pinch cayenne
    1 tablespoon tomato paste
    1 garlic clove, minced
    4 cups chicken broth
    2 cups water
 10½ ounces (1½ cups) red lentils, picked over and rinsed
    2 tablespoons lemon juice, plus extra for seasoning
 1½   teaspoons dried mint, crumbled
    1 teaspoon paprika
    ¼ cup chopped fresh cilantro

1. Melt 2 tablespoons butter in large saucepan over medium heat. Add onion and 1 teaspoon salt and cook, stirring occasionally, until softened but not browned, about 5 minutes. Add coriander, cumin, ginger, cinnamon, cayenne, and ¼ teaspoon pepper and cook until fragrant, about 2 minutes. Stir in tomato paste and garlic and cook for 1 minute. Stir in broth, water, and lentils and bring to simmer. Simmer vigorously, stirring occasionally, until lentils are soft and about half are broken down, about 15 minutes.

2. Whisk soup vigorously until it is coarsely pureed, about 30 seconds. Stir in lemon juice and season with salt and extra lemon juice to taste. Cover and keep warm. (Soup can be refrigerated for up to 3 days. Thin soup with water, if desired, when reheating.)

3. Melt remaining 2 tablespoons butter in small skillet. Remove from heat and stir in mint and paprika. Ladle soup into individual bowls, drizzle each portion with 1 teaspoon spiced butter, sprinkle with cilantro, and serve.

CHICKEN AND ZUCCHINI-NOODLE SOUP

✔ **WHY THIS RECIPE WORKS:** For a full-flavored paleo-friendly chicken soup recipe, we began by making our own broth using a whole chicken. We built a flavorful base by cooking aromatics in ghee and then placed an entire chicken in the pot with plenty of water, eliminating the need to hack up the chicken into parts. To keep the recipe cost-effective and streamlined, we also wanted to use the meat in our soup. To make this work, we removed the chicken from the broth as soon as it cooked through. We shredded the meat from the bones and set it aside for later; the carcass went back into the pot to fortify the broth with more rich chicken flavor. For paleo "noodles," we turned to mild, quick-cooking zucchini and used a spiralizer to speedily turn the squash into thin strands.

Nothing is more homey than a warm bowl of chicken noodle soup, but when I set out to make my favorite comfort food paleo-friendly, it seemed like the odds were stacked against me. One of the biggest challenges would be making the stock: My research revealed that store-bought chicken stocks that meet the paleo diet's requirements are hard to find, and those available are somewhat bland—unacceptable in a soup where a flavorful broth is critical. Making my own stock was clearly the way to go, but I wanted to keep the process simple enough that even non-paleo home cooks would be willing to give it a try. Egg noodles, the other major element of this classic soup, were also out of the question, as were butter, vegetable oil, and even table salt. Despite all of this, I was sure I could come up with a tasty alternative. I headed into the kitchen.

I started with the stock. To suit a humble soup like chicken noodle, I wanted a streamlined, cost-effective approach to making a stock that would also yield tender chicken to stir into my soup. For my first attempt, I cut a whole chicken into parts, browned them for flavor, added in chopped onions and water, and simmered. The resulting stock had rich flavor, but cutting up the chicken was time-consuming. For my second batch, I decided to try poaching a whole bird instead. Since the meat would be blander without the initial browning, this time I browned the aromatics first. Paleo cooks often use ghee (butter with all milk solids removed), coconut oil, and olive oil instead of vegetable oil for cooking. Ghee had a pleasant, mellow flavor and was the most affordable of the three, so I melted a tablespoon of it in my Dutch oven and softened the chopped onions before adding the chicken, bay leaves, and water to the pot. The chicken poached nicely and the aromatics imparted plenty of flavor to the stock. Once the chicken was cooked through, I removed it and shredded the meat into bite-size pieces. Keeping with my recipe's thrifty approach, I wondered if I could coax any more flavor out of the bones before discarding them. I returned the carcass to the pot and let the stock continue to simmer. Sure enough, this step proved integral: The simmering liquid transformed into a concentrated, full-bodied stock.

Next, I tackled the noodles. With all forms of pasta off the table, I wanted to use a spiralized vegetable to mimic the slurpable, tender texture of noodles. I spun out a few different vegetables, including butternut squash, carrots, and zucchini; tasters preferred the neutral flavor and pasta-like texture of the zucchini. With the vegetable settled, I tested zucchini "noodles" of different lengths and thicknesses. Mountains of spiralized squash later, I determined that noodles longer than 2 inches were too hard to spoon up and eat, and any thicker than ⅛ inch was a mouthful. Because zucchini is quick to overcook, they would have to be the last ingredient added to the pot. I set them aside for later.

Because the poached chicken was somewhat bland, I doubled down on flavor builders to finish off the soup. I heated some of the fat skimmed from the stock and used it to brown and cook sliced carrots, sliced celery, and chopped onion. I scooped in some umami-boosting tomato paste and minced plenty of thyme for a savory, herbal hit. I poured in my strained stock and brought the pot to a simmer, allowing all of the flavors to meld before stirring in the chicken and noodles. I served myself a bowl and savored my first spoonful of this new take on an old favorite. My soup's rich flavor, tender noodles, and hearty chunks of chicken and vegetables were as comforting as ever—and you don't have to be on a paleo diet to appreciate that.

—RUSSELL SELANDER, *America's Test Kitchen Books*

CHICKEN AND ZUCCHINI-NOODLE SOUP

Chicken and Zucchini-Noodle Soup

SERVES 6 TO 8

You can substitute 2 tablespoons ghee for the reserved chicken fat in step 5. Use a Dutch oven that holds 7 quarts or more for this recipe. If possible, use smaller, in-season zucchini, which have thinner skins and fewer seeds.

STOCK

- 1 tablespoon ghee
- 2 onions, chopped
- 1 tablespoon kosher salt
- 1 (3½- to 4-pound) whole chicken, giblets discarded
- 3½ quarts water
- 2 bay leaves

SOUP

- 1 pound zucchini, trimmed
- 4 carrots, peeled and sliced ¼ inch thick
- 3 celery ribs, sliced ¼ inch thick
- 1 onion, chopped
   Kosher salt and pepper
- 1 tablespoon tomato paste
- 1 tablespoon minced fresh thyme or 1 teaspoon dried
- ¼ cup minced fresh parsley

1. FOR THE STOCK: Heat ghee in Dutch oven over medium heat until shimmering. Add onions and salt and cook until softened and lightly browned, about 8 minutes. Place chicken breast side up in pot, then add water and bay leaves and bring to boil. Reduce heat to medium-low, partially cover, and simmer until breast registers 160 degrees and thighs register 175 degrees, 30 to 40 minutes.

2. Transfer chicken to carving board, let cool slightly, then shred meat into bite-size pieces using 2 forks; reserve bones and discard skin.

3. Add reserved bones to broth and return to simmer over medium heat. Cook, uncovered, until broth is deeply flavored, about 30 minutes.

4. Remove large bones from pot, then strain broth through fine-mesh strainer. Let broth settle for 5 to 10 minutes, then defat using wide, shallow spoon or fat separator, reserving 2 tablespoons fat. (Shredded chicken, strained broth, and reserved fat can be refrigerated in separate containers for up to 2 days; return broth to simmer before proceeding.)

5. FOR THE SOUP: Using spiralizer, cut zucchini into ⅛-inch-thick noodles, then cut noodles into 2-inch lengths. Heat reserved fat in now-empty pot over medium heat until shimmering. Add carrots, celery, onion, and 1 teaspoon salt and cook until softened and lightly browned, 8 to 10 minutes. Stir in tomato paste and thyme and cook until fragrant, about 1 minute. Stir in strained broth, scraping up any browned bits. Bring to simmer and cook until vegetables are tender, about 5 minutes.

6. Stir in zucchini noodles and shredded chicken and cook until zucchini is just tender, 6 to 8 minutes. Stir in parsley and season with salt and pepper to taste. Serve.

NOTES FROM THE TEST KITCHEN

MAKING ZUCCHINI NOODLES

Depending on your spiralizer, the amount of trimming required will vary. You can also make noodles using a mandoline or V-slicer fitted with an ⅛-inch julienne attachment. Make sure to position the zucchini vertically so the noodles are as long as possible.

1. Trim zucchini so it will fit on prongs and blade.

2. Set to ⅛-inch thickness and spiralize by turning crank.

3. Pull noodles straight and cut into 2-inch lengths.

CAROLINA CHICKEN MULL

✔ **WHY THIS RECIPE WORKS:** A dish not often seen outside of the Carolinas, chicken mull combines a few inexpensive ingredients—milk, water, chicken, and saltines—into a simple yet unbelievably comforting stew. For our version, we started with a base of chicken broth and added milk and heavy cream to create a lush, creamy texture. To give the stew more heft, we pulsed saltines in the food processor until they were finely ground and stirred them in. In keeping with the simple nature of this stew, we also used the food processor to chop the onion and then, after cooking bone-in chicken thighs in broth, we used it once again to shred the cooked meat into bite-size pieces. Plenty of butter stirred into the finished stew contributed even more richness and a little cayenne gave it a touch of heat.

I'm from North Carolina, but when I first saw a photo of chicken mull, I was skeptical. Was this pale yellow concoction of pulverized bits of chicken floating in a milky, butter-slicked liquid really something we wanted to bring into the test kitchen?

While mull (the word, food historian Robert Moss tells me, is derived from "muddle," a common Southern term for a range of soups and stews) is little known outside small pockets of North and South Carolina, devotees of this dish are dedicated. And competitive: Bear Grass, North Carolina, hosts a chicken mull festival every year that swells the town with throngs of mull fans.

Before I hit the kitchen with the handful of recipes I'd uncovered, I hit the road to get a taste of the real thing. I found myself in a lengthening procession of cars as I traveled down two-lane back roads shaded by Carolina pines. This was the Piedmont, a mountainous area of South Carolina, and it was uncharacteristically cold, even for February. I crossed into Buffalo and followed the snaking line of cars into the parking lot of Midway BBQ, already nearly full for the lunchtime rush.

I polished off my first bowl of mull in no time. Midway's mull was just as rich and warming as I'd heard, and when owner Jay Allen invited me into the back kitchen to see mull-making in action, I couldn't say no. Allen and his wife, Amy, took over the business from his father-in-law in 1994, but many of their recipes remain unaltered since Midway opened in 1941, and Allen won't share details. Still, I had to ask for the secret to the mull I'd enjoyed for lunch. He grinned. "Butter. A lot of butter."

Back in the test kitchen, I relied on a few existing mull recipes and my clear memory of Midway's comforting stew to cobble together a working recipe. I placed a chicken in a Dutch oven; covered it with water, milk, and chopped onions; and then let it simmer. Once it was cooked, I shredded the meat and added cayenne, salt, and pepper. My stew tasted cozy, but it looked curdled and the shredding took a long time.

I switched to chicken thighs, which were much easier to wrangle than a whole bird. Cooking them with onions, salt, and chicken broth created a much more robust base. Instead of adding the milk at the beginning, I held it until the end, just warming it through before serving.

This version tasted much better, but it still lacked richness. Replacing some of the milk with heavy cream and whisking in 4 tablespoons of butter helped, but the stew needed thickening. In my research I'd learned that some Carolina cooks use crushed saltines to do this. It worked brilliantly: Just 15 crushed saltines gave the stew the right heft.

One sticking point remained: the chunks of chicken were much too big. I changed up my shredding protocol: Instead of using two forks, I turned to the food processor. In seven pulses I had the perfect bite-size pieces.

I whipped up a final batch on a rainy Boston day. Slurping spoonful after spoonful, my misgivings faded into the past: I, too, was captivated by homey, faintly spicy chicken mull.

—MORGAN BOLLING, *Cook's Country*

Carolina Chicken Mull
SERVES 4 TO 6

An equal weight of bone-in split chicken breasts or a combination of breasts and thighs may be substituted. We prefer heavy cream, but half-and-half can also be used. When heating the finished stew in step 4, do not let it come to a boil, or it may break.

15 square or 17 round saltines, plus extra for serving
1 large onion, chopped coarse
2 pounds bone-in chicken thighs, trimmed
4 cups chicken broth
   Salt and pepper
2 cups whole milk
¼ cup heavy cream
4 tablespoons unsalted butter
¼ teaspoon cayenne pepper

1. Process saltines in food processor until finely ground, about 30 seconds; transfer to bowl and set aside. Pulse onion in now-empty food processor until finely chopped, 5 to 7 pulses.

2. Arrange chicken, skin side down, in single layer in bottom of Dutch oven. Add broth, 1 teaspoon salt, and onions and bring to boil over medium-high heat. Reduce heat to low, cover, and simmer for 30 minutes.

3. Remove pot from heat and transfer chicken to plate to let cool slightly, about 15 minutes; cover pot to keep stew warm. Discard chicken skin and bones. Tear chicken into large pieces. Transfer chicken to clean food processor and pulse until finely chopped, about 7 pulses.

4. Whisk chopped chicken, saltine crumbs, milk, cream, butter, cayenne, 1 teaspoon pepper, and ½ teaspoon salt into stew. Heat over medium heat until warmed through but not boiling, 3 to 5 minutes. Season with salt and pepper to taste. Serve with extra saltines.

PENNSYLVANIA DUTCH CHICKEN AND CORN SOUP

✔ WHY THIS RECIPE WORKS: This soup is at its best when it boasts sweet corn and tender, chewy dumplings, called *rivels*, in every spoonful. For the rivels, we created a simple dough by working eggs into flour and minced chives. While the dough rested, we readied the corn, cutting the kernels from two ears and, for extra starch and flavor, grating the kernels from two more. We then prepared the broth, starting with an aromatic base of onion and celery. We browned them in oil before pouring in chicken broth and water and poaching meaty bone-in chicken thighs in the broth. Adding the stripped cobs infused the broth with subtle corn flavor. We added bone-in chicken breasts second, as their lighter meat would cook more quickly. Once the chicken was cooked through, we removed it and shredded it into bite-size pieces. Adding the rivels was as easy as pinching off pieces of dough. An added bonus: The little dumplings held their shape in the warm broth while also releasing some body-building starch. We stirred in our kernel mixture and simmered the soup until the kernels were just tender. The shredded chicken came last, stirred in to heat through before serving. Chopped hard-cooked eggs are a traditional topping, so we sprinkled some on for good measure.

With its satisfying flavors and hearty, stick-to-your-ribs feel, chicken-corn soup is typical of Pennsylvania Dutch recipes. The soup is traditionally made by simmering a whole chicken for hours to create a rich broth in which to showcase the sweet, tender bite of local corn. But what really makes it special are its tiny rivels, a cross between dumplings and German spaetzle, which add an unexpected chewy component. As a girl, I spent many a Saturday afternoon watching my grandmother make this soup in her central Pennsylvania home. I wanted to capture all the slow-cooked flavor and texture I remembered without devoting an entire day to the process.

Re-creating the soup with an eye toward efficiency meant starting with chicken parts instead of a whole bird. I decided to go with bone-in, skin-on breasts and thighs, which provided a nice mix of light and dark meat. Since I didn't need to brown the chicken, I discarded the skin before cooking to prevent the broth from becoming greasy. To build long-cooked flavor without overcooking the lean white meat, I started by sautéing onion and celery, pouring in chicken broth, and then poaching the thighs—only adding the chicken breasts after the thighs were partially cooked (since thighs take longer). This technique yielded meat that was perfectly moist and a reinforced broth that tasted as if it had been simmering for hours.

Because corn is so important to this soup, I wanted to find a way to maximize its sweet flavor. I departed from tradition and added the stripped cobs to the broth while the chicken poached; I then added the kernels for the last 15 minutes to keep their flavor fresh. But this short cooking time left the kernels too starchy and firm. Extending the cooking time to 25 minutes yielded more tender corn. To get at even more of the flavor inside the corn kernels, I grated two of the four ears I was using on the large holes of a box grater; this had the added advantage of releasing extra starch and thickening this hearty soup.

The chicken and corn may pack all the flavor in this soup, but the dense, chewy rivels supply the texture that made my tasters go back for a second bowl. Traditional recipes call for a ratio of 2 cups of flour to two eggs and no additional milk or water to loosen the dough, making it quite dry and very hard to work together. The drier the rivels, the more they disintegrated into the soup, leaving me with floury sludge. I eased back on the flour to 1¼ cups, at which point I could easily work together the flour and egg (and some minced chives for added flavor). But the rivels were still a little tough. Letting the dough rest while I prepared the soup was the answer; this extra time gave the dough a chance to relax. When my soup was done, I stirred in some fresh parsley and topped each bowl with chopped hard-cooked egg, a traditional garnish that adds richness and texture.

I served my tasters each a bowl and watched with pride as my corn-packed Pennsylvania classic won over a new batch of devotees.

—CHRISTIE MORRISON, *Cook's Country*

Pennsylvania Dutch Chicken and Corn Soup

SERVES 6

Fresh corn kernels (plus the stripped cobs) give this soup its flavor; do not substitute frozen corn. Our favorite store-bought broth is Swanson Chicken Stock. Note that the chicken thighs and breast are added to the soup at different points. This soup cooks for about 90 minutes.

- 1¼ cups (6¼ ounces) all-purpose flour
- 2 tablespoons minced fresh chives
  Salt and pepper
- 2 large eggs, lightly beaten, plus 2 hard-cooked large eggs, chopped
- 4 ears corn, husks and silk removed
- 2 tablespoons unsalted butter
- 1 onion, chopped fine
- 2 celery ribs, chopped fine
- 8 cups chicken broth
- 2 (5- to 7-ounce) bone-in chicken thighs, skin removed, trimmed
- 1 (10- to 12-ounce) bone-in split chicken breast, skin removed, trimmed
- 2 tablespoons minced fresh parsley

1. Combine flour, chives, and ¾ teaspoon salt in bowl. Form well in center and add beaten eggs. Using fork, slowly work flour into eggs, using your hands when stirring becomes difficult. (Dough will be very firm.) Knead dough on lightly floured counter until smooth, about 1 minute. Return dough to bowl, cover with plastic wrap, and let sit at room temperature while assembling soup.

2. Cut kernels from 2 ears corn, transfer to bowl, and reserve cobs. Grate remaining 2 ears corn on large holes of box grater over same bowl; reserve cobs.

3. Melt butter in Dutch oven over medium-high heat. Add onion, celery, 1 teaspoon salt, and ½ teaspoon pepper and cook until lightly browned, 5 to 7 minutes. Add broth, chicken thighs, and reserved cobs and bring to boil. Reduce heat to low and simmer, partially covered, for 25 minutes. Add chicken breast and continue to simmer until breast registers 160 degrees, about 20 minutes longer.

4. Remove pot from heat; discard cobs. Transfer chicken to plate and let cool slightly. Pinch off pea-size pieces of dough and drop into soup. Stir in corn kernel mixture and bring soup to boil over high heat. Reduce heat to low and simmer, partially covered, until corn is just tender, about 25 minutes, stirring occasionally to keep rivels from sticking to bottom of pot.

5. Using 2 forks, shred chicken into bite-size pieces; discard bones. Stir shredded chicken into soup and cook until warmed through, 3 to 5 minutes. Stir in parsley and season with salt and pepper to taste. Serve, topped with hard-cooked eggs.

NOTES FROM THE TEST KITCHEN

LEAVE NO CORN FLAVOR BEHIND
To maximize sweet corn flavor in our Pennsylvania Dutch Chicken and Corn Soup, we stripped corn cobs in two ways:

1. To strip whole kernels from cob, cut cob in half and stabilize by standing it on cut end. Slice kernels from cob with chef's knife.

2. To grate kernels, set box grater in bowl and rub cob against coarse side of grater.

DUBLIN CODDLE

DUBLIN CODDLE

✓ **WHY THIS RECIPE WORKS:** This derivative of Irish stew layers pork sausage, bacon, onions, and potatoes and allows it to slowly simmer (or "coddle") in stock for hours. For a full-flavored version of this comforting stew, we bypassed the long simmer and focused on one ingredient at a time. Starting with the sausages, we crisped some bacon and used its rendered fat to partially brown bratwurst (a perfect stand-in for traditional but hard-to-find bangers), leaving behind a flavorful fond. Softening sliced onions and adding broth to the pan released the fond into the coddling liquid. A splash of cider vinegar helped rein in the liquid's richness. We arranged thinly sliced potatoes in a baking dish, carefully poured the liquid over them, and layered the sausages on top. We placed the coddle in the oven where the potatoes gently cooked to a soft, creamy texture and the sausages finished browning. Our coddle emerged with each element cooked to perfection, unified by a bold broth.

It's late, it's cold out, and you've just returned from a long day of work followed by a headache-inducing commute home. All you want is a big bowl of something warm and comforting. Enter simple, savory Dublin coddle, proof positive that the Irish know their way around rich, restorative meals.

Similar to Irish stew, that famous dish based on lamb and cabbage, coddle instead combines pork sausage, bacon, onions, potatoes, and stock—and rather than stew it all together, it's layered and cooked (or coddled) into a finished dish that is so much more than the sum of its parts. Or at least it should be—in my initial research into this dish, I found recipes that boiled the ingredients for hours on end, resulting in a mushy mess of barely identifiable starch-saddled meats. I wanted a flavorful version of this rustic dish that kept its elements intact.

Back in the old country, coddle is built on Irish bangers, a sausage of pork, bread crumbs, and various seasonings. I loved traditional bangers in this dish—but, recognizing that they aren't available in most grocery stores, I chose to develop my version with bratwurst, a sausage more widely available stateside.

Most recipes I found didn't brown any of the meats before simmering them, but I knew I could make major inroads into flavor depth by adding a browning step up front. Tests proved this to be true, and further tests helped me nail down the exact process: I cooked 2-inch pieces of thick-cut bacon to render its fat. I set aside these crispy pieces while I browned the sausages and onions in some reserved bacon fat, which left behind the flavorful browned bits, or fond, in the pan. Scraping this fond into chicken stock meant none of it went to waste.

Potatoes are generally a tricky component of braises like this one, as they always seem to take longer to cook than the other components. I twisted myself into pretzels coming up with easy ways to precook the potatoes—microwaving them, boiling them, roasting them—but ultimately found that I didn't need to. Instead, I sliced the potatoes thin (I chose Yukon Golds for their superior flavor), arranged them in the bottom of a baking dish, and covered them with the cooked onions and fond-bolstered cooking liquid. I then piled the sausages on top and slid the dish into a 350-degree oven. After 45 minutes, the sausages were on the verge of overdone, but the potatoes were still underdone. The fix was simple: I lowered the oven temperature to 325 degrees and cooked the dish for an hour and a quarter, gently coddling the potatoes to a soft, creamy texture.

My Dublin coddle was rich and full of flavor, but some testers wanted just a little bit of brightness. Cider vinegar was the answer: Just 2 tablespoons added to the broth gave the dish a subtle but invigorating punch, and a final sprinkle of chopped parsley and the reserved bacon finished it off to soul-warming perfection.

—CECELIA JENKINS, *Cook's Country*

NOTES FROM THE TEST KITCHEN

A BANG-ON SUBSTITUTION
"Banger" is British slang for a sausage made with ground pork, bread crumbs, and seasonings; it's so due to the tendency of the links to split open, or "bang" when cooked. Since bangers can be hard to find stateside, we instead call for bratwurst, a German sausage of pork, veal, and spices.

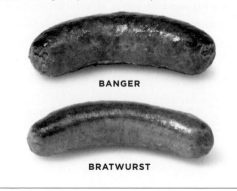

BANGER

BRATWURST

Dublin Coddle

SERVES 4 TO 6

An equal weight of traditional Irish bangers can be substituted for the bratwurst. We prefer to use Farmland Thick Sliced Bacon. Serve with crusty bread to soak up the sauce.

1¾ pounds Yukon Gold potatoes, peeled and
    sliced ¼ inch thick
    Salt and pepper
4 slices thick-cut bacon, cut into 1-inch pieces
1¼ pounds bratwurst
2 onions, sliced into ½-inch-thick rounds
1 tablespoon minced fresh thyme
1¾ cups chicken broth
2 tablespoons cider vinegar
2 tablespoons minced fresh parsley

1. Adjust oven rack to lower-middle position and heat oven to 325 degrees. Shingle potato slices in bottom of 13 by 9-inch baking dish. Sprinkle with ½ teaspoon salt and ¼ teaspoon pepper; set aside.

2. Cook bacon in 12-inch skillet over medium heat until crispy, 12 to 14 minutes. Using slotted spoon, transfer bacon to paper towel–lined plate.

3. Carefully add sausages to now-empty skillet and cook until lightly browned on tops and bottoms, about 5 minutes. Transfer to paper towel–lined plate.

4. Pour off all but 2 tablespoons fat from skillet and return to medium heat. Add onions, thyme, ½ teaspoon salt, and ½ teaspoon pepper. Cover and cook until onions are softened, 7 to 9 minutes, stirring occasionally and scraping up browned bits on pan bottom.

5. Add broth and vinegar, scraping up remaining browned bits, and bring to simmer. Carefully pour onion mixture over potatoes, spreading onions into even layer.

6. Place sausages on top of onions, browned side up. Transfer to oven and bake until paring knife inserted into potatoes meets little resistance, about 1¼ hours.

7. Remove from oven and let cool for 10 minutes. Sprinkle with parsley and reserved bacon. Serve.

PORTUGUESE-STYLE BEEF STEW

WHY THIS RECIPE WORKS: *Alcatra*, a classic Portuguese beef stew, features tender chunks of beef braised with onions, garlic, warm spices, and wine. Unlike beef stews that require searing the beef to build savory flavor or adding flavor boosters like tomato paste and anchovies, this dish skips those steps and ingredients, highlighting the warm and bright flavors of the spices and wine as much as the meatiness of the beef. We used beef shank because it is lean (which means the cooking liquid doesn't need to be skimmed) and full of collagen (which breaks down into gelatin and gives the sauce body). Submerging the sliced onions in the liquid helped them take on a great meaty dimension, enhancing the savory flavor of the broth.

A few times a year, I labor over a great beef stew. Based on a classic French approach to braising, the recipe I follow calls for batch-searing pieces of beef chuck—a step that splatters grease on my stovetop but generates valuable savory browning. From there, I sauté vegetables, aromatics, and flavor boosters like minced anchovies and tomato paste in the rendered fat, followed by a little flour to thicken the cooking liquid. Next I deglaze the pot with wine and scrape up the flavorful browned bits of fond on the bottom of the pot; add broth, water, and a chunk of salt pork for even more meaty flavor; and then braise the stew in the oven for a few hours, just enough time to turn the tough pieces of chuck roast fork-tender.

All those steps and ingredients yield a meaty, complex, and satisfying stew but one that I make infrequently. However, my assumption about making beef stew changed when a colleague brought in a Portuguese version, which called for just a handful of ingredients and was supposedly simple to make. Best of all, the dish, called alcatra, from the Azorean island of Terceira, tasted fabulous without requiring any browning of the meat or aromatics. All you do is pack chunks of beef into a pot (traditionally a clay pot called an alguidar) with onions, wine, bacon or chorizo, garlic, and spices; cover it and put it in the oven; and forget about it until it's done.

You wouldn't think that the result would taste nearly as good as a stew made the French way, but it does. The pork, onions, and spices (often peppercorns, allspice, and bay leaves) add surprising depth to what is, essentially, boiled beef and yield a brothy cooking liquid that's flavorful but clean-tasting. Crusty bread or boiled potatoes are often served alongside to sop up the flavorful juices. Needless to say, I could see myself making a dish this easy all winter long.

My recipe research revealed that, despite its narrow regional provenance, alcatra can vary quite a bit—from the cut of beef to the type of wine and particular seasonings. Tackling the beef first, I prepared batches of a basic recipe with three different cuts of meat: rump (the name "alcatra" comes from *alcatre*, the Portuguese word for rump), shank, and chuck, which is our usual choice for braising. After cutting the meat into roughly 2½-inch pieces and seasoning them with salt, I packed the pieces of each cut into three Dutch ovens (my alguidar substitute). I then added a couple of sliced onions; a cheesecloth bundle of peeled and smashed garlic cloves, black peppercorns, allspice berries, and bay leaves; 8 ounces of chopped bacon; and just a few cups of white wine (chosen over red for its cleaner taste), so as not to dilute the flavor of the meat, to each pot.

Next, I covered the pots, slid them into 325-degree ovens, and cooked each batch until the meat was very tender. Tasters agreed that the seasonings in each batch were more or less on target: savory and faintly sweet from the onions, garlic, and warm spices, with bright, clean acidity from the wine. They weren't wild about the bacon's heavy smoke flavor, but I'd revisit that after I settled on the beef.

As for the meat, the rump tasted comparatively dull and even a bit livery, which we've found can happen when this cut cooks for a prolonged period of time. It was the first to go. Meanwhile, the shank and chuck were super beefy and cooked up beautifully tender, but the shank offered two distinct advantages that made it particularly good for braising. First, whereas chuck is a relatively fatty cut that made the cooking liquid a bit greasy (it required skimming before serving), shank is quite lean, so its broth wasn't the least bit fatty. Second, shank is loaded with collagen, the major protein in connective tissue that breaks down during cooking into gelatin; the gelatin coats the muscle fibers, rendering the lean meat supple and silky and the cooking liquid full bodied and glossy.

Back to the pork: While bacon's assertive smokiness can be a great addition to stews, I liked the idea of a cleaner-tasting stew and hoped that chorizo would offer savory support with subtler smoke.

Markets in the United States usually carry two main varieties of chorizo, Mexican and Spanish. I picked Spanish because it's seasoned with smoked paprika and tastes faintly sweet and fruity (not unlike some varieties of dried chiles). When I sliced ½ pound into 1-inch chunks and added it to a fresh batch of my stew along with the onions, its sweet-smoky flavor matched up perfectly with the other warm spices. The downside was that it dried out considerably during the lengthy braise, so I tried delaying its addition until the last 20 minutes of cooking. The results were better but inconsistent; some pieces were fully submerged and overcooked quickly, while others sat on the surface and stayed nicely moist.

I finally got the texture right when I took advantage of Spanish chorizo's other notable trait: Unlike the Mexican variety, it's sold cured and/or fully cooked and thus doesn't need prolonged cooking. Going forward, I simply sliced it into ¼-inch-thick coins (they would warm through quickly); added them to the pot after braising the beef, making sure they were fully submerged by flipping the pieces of beef on top of the sausage; and let the stew sit covered off the heat for about 20 minutes.

My version of alcatra was solid and dead simple, but I had an idea for amping up its savory flavor just a bit more: packing the sliced onions at the bottom of the pot where they would be completely submerged in the liquid. The reason—though it sounds counterintuitive—is that cooking cut onions causes them to form a meaty-tasting compound called 3-mercapto-2-methylpentan-1-ol, or MMP for short. The payoff was evident in this latest batch of stew, which tasted even more flavorful. I also made a point of submerging the spice packet in the liquid to ensure that those flavors were thoroughly infused.

For due diligence, I ran a final series of tests in which I added supporting flavors I'd seen in published recipes: tomato paste (too sweet), butter (unnecessarily rich), and carrots (too vegetal). The only change I made was to add a little ground cinnamon, which underscored the warmth of the black pepper and allspice.

This stew was complex and bright-tasting—as satisfying as any beef stew I'd ever had. Even better, it was truly one of the easiest meals I'd ever made.

—LAN LAM, *Cook's Illustrated*

THE ULTIMATE CUT FOR BRAISING

Shank (also called shin), a cut from the upper portion of a steer's legs, is an excellent cut for braising for a number of reasons. First, it's at least as beefy-tasting as more popular stew cuts like chuck or short ribs—but unlike those cuts, shank is quite lean, so the cooking liquid requires little, if any, skimming. Second, it's loaded with collagen, the major protein in connective tissue that liquefies into gelatin during cooking, giving the meat and the cooking liquid a silky richness. Third, it's a bargain cut, cheaper than both chuck and short ribs.

Shank is typically sold in two forms: boneless long-cut and crosscut, which can be sold with or without the bone. We prefer long-cut because it contains more collagen, but crosscut can be used; remove the bones before cooking and reduce the cooking time by about half an hour.

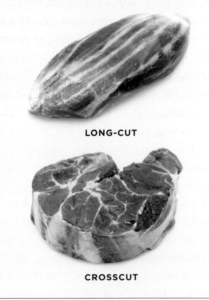

LONG-CUT

CROSSCUT

Portuguese-Style Beef Stew (Alcatra)
SERVES 6

Beef shank is sold both long-cut and crosscut (with and without bones). We prefer long-cut since it has more collagen. You can substitute 4 pounds of bone-in crosscut shank if that's all you can find. Remove the bones before cooking and save them for another use. Crosscut shank cooks more quickly, so check the stew for doneness in step 2 after 3 hours. A 3½- to 4-pound chuck roast, trimmed of fat and cut into 2½-inch pieces, can be substituted for the shank. Serve this dish with crusty bread or boiled potatoes.

- 3 pounds boneless long-cut beef shanks
  Salt and pepper
- 5 garlic cloves, peeled and smashed
- 5 allspice berries
- 4 bay leaves
- 1½ teaspoons peppercorns
- 2 large onions, halved and sliced
- 2¼ cups dry white wine
- ¼ teaspoon ground cinnamon
- 8 ounces Spanish-style chorizo sausage, cut into ¼-inch-thick rounds

1. Adjust oven rack to middle position and heat oven to 325 degrees. Trim away any fat or large pieces of connective tissue from exterior of shanks (silverskin can be left on meat). Cut each shank crosswise into 2½-inch pieces. Sprinkle meat with 1 teaspoon salt.

2. Cut 8-inch square of triple-thickness cheesecloth. Place garlic, allspice berries, bay leaves, and peppercorns in center of cheesecloth and tie into bundle with kitchen twine. Arrange onions in Dutch oven in even layer and place spice bundle on top. Add wine and cinnamon. Arrange shank pieces in single layer on top of onions. Cover and cook until beef is tender, about 3½ hours.

3. Remove pot from oven and add chorizo. Using tongs, flip each piece of beef over, making sure that chorizo is submerged. Cover and let stand until chorizo is warmed through, about 20 minutes. Discard spice bundle. Season with salt and pepper to taste. Serve.

BEST GROUND BEEF CHILI

✓ **WHY THIS RECIPE WORKS:** For a rich, distinct ground beef chili, we started with the meat. Seasoning the beef with salt and adding baking soda helped keep it moist and tender. To ensure that our chili had complex flavor, we made our own chili powder, combining toasted dried ancho chiles with a blend of herbs and spices in the food processor. Tortilla chips helped bulk up the mix, ensuring the potent ingredients blended evenly. Starting with an aromatic base of chopped onion and garlic, we browned the beef and stirred in our chili powder and smoky minced chipotle chiles in adobo sauce. We poured in some water, canned tomatoes, and a can of pinto beans, including their liquid for a thick, rich consistency. A little sugar promised to balance out the richness. The chili cooked and thickened in the oven, emerging tender and loaded with deep, smoky flavor. Many of the spices in the chili powder are fat-soluble, so we stirred any accumulated fat back into the pot before serving. A final hit of cider vinegar brought in some welcome brightness.

I'm not from Texas, so I've never thought that chili by definition could only mean a bowl made with hand-cut chunks of beef. If anything, I'm always more drawn to ground beef versions, since they skip the tedious step of breaking down a whole roast. That said, I've rarely encountered a ground beef chili that can hold its own against the chunky kind. It often suffers from dry, grainy, somewhat tough meat. I challenged myself to change that.

I wanted a big batch of thick, spicy, ultrabeefy chili—the kind I'd pile into a bowl with tortilla chips or rice and enjoy with a beer. In order to create that, I would first have to sort out how to give the ground meat the same juicy, tender texture found in chili made with chunks of beef.

As a first step toward improving dry meat, I opted to use 2 pounds of 85 percent lean (15 percent fat) ground beef. The fat in the mix would lubricate the meat fibers, creating a sense of moistness. As for how to cook it, most chili recipes—whether using ground beef or chunks—call for browning the meat in oil to build a flavor base. Since ground beef sheds a fair amount of liquid as it cooks, and liquid precludes browning, I cooked it in three batches so that any moisture could evaporate quickly.

The next big question was how long to simmer the meat in the liquid ingredients for the most tender results. Recipes vary widely: Some suggest an hour, others call for 2 hours, and more than a few say "the longer the better." But would the fact that the meat was ground make its proteins and collagen break down more quickly than stew meat, which requires roughly 2½ hours of simmering? All this confusion could, I figured, be cleared up by one simple test.

But first I needed a basic chili recipe to work from. After setting the browned meat aside, I sautéed a few spoonfuls of store-bought chili powder, chopped onions, and minced garlic in the residual fat. Once the aromatics were softened, I returned the beef to the pot along with a can of pinto beans and a small can of whole tomatoes that I pureed in the food processor. Finally, I stirred in 2 cups of water. I brought the mixture to a boil, put the lid on the pot, and transferred it to a 275-degree oven where the ambient heat would cook it gently. After about an hour, the result was only mediocre: The flavors were no longer raw-tasting, but they were somewhat blah. Plus, the beef still had the dry, tough texture I was trying to avoid.

Sixty minutes of simmering clearly wasn't long enough to tenderize the meat. I put the chili back into the oven, pulling it out and sampling it every 15 minutes or so. The meat was fairly tender at the 90-minute mark, but it still wasn't living up to its full potential. Then I remembered: Muscle fibers tighten up when heated, squeezing out some of the liquid they contain, and the smaller the piece, the more liquid will be lost to the surrounding environment. Clearly my ground meat was shedding too much moisture during the browning step.

There are a few tricks to help keep ground beef tender and juicy. I was already employing one: using meat with a relatively high fat content. Another is to add salt and let the meat sit for about 20 minutes. In addition to seasoning the meat, salt alters the structure of the meat proteins to better allow it to retain moisture. Finally, you can raise the pH of the meat with a little baking soda to help the proteins attract more water and hold on to it.

Indeed, incorporating baking soda—¾ teaspoon plus 2 tablespoons of water to help it dissolve—not only kept the meat juicy and made it even more tender, but it also produced an unforeseen benefit: Since the beef now barely shed any moisture during cooking (not even the small amount of water that I added to dissolve the baking soda) and a higher pH significantly speeds up the Maillard reaction, the meat browned much more quickly. This meant that I could cook it in a single batch rather than in three—a major timesaver.

With that, I shifted my focus to giving the chili memorably spicy flavor. Store-bought chili powder is convenient, but it's not that much trouble to make a homemade blend that tastes significantly better. I started with six dried whole ancho chiles, toasted to bring out their raisin-like sweetness and fruity heat. But it was hard to grind the small quantity of chiles in a food processor, since the pieces just bounced around the workbowl. One trick we've used in the past is to add cornmeal to the mix to bulk it up. The cornmeal also serves to slightly thicken and add corn flavor to the chili. I used the same approach, but substituted a few tortilla chips for the cornmeal, since I always have them on hand to serve with chili.

For another layer of heat and smokiness, I stirred in minced chipotles in adobo. And to boost the chile notes without adding more heat, I threw in some sweet paprika. Of course, chili powder isn't made from just chiles. I also added a generous amount of ground cumin, plus garlic powder, ground coriander, dried oregano, black pepper, and dried thyme.

Finally, about that fat. After the chili came out of the oven, it was covered in a layer of bright orange grease. When I reflexively skimmed it off, my tasters complained that the chili tasted a little flat and lean. The DayGlo color should have been a giveaway that the fat was loaded with oil-soluble compounds from my spice blend. Discarding it robbed the chili of flavor. So for my next batch, instead of removing the fat, I just stirred it back in. Now the chili boasted deeply spiced complexity.

To cut some of its richness, I added 2 teaspoons of sugar and a couple of tablespoons of cider vinegar. I served the chili with lime wedges, fresh cilantro, chopped onion, and plenty of tortilla chips and steamed white rice. This chili was full-flavored and rich but certainly not so rich that my guests didn't come back for seconds.

—ANDREW JANJIGIAN, *Cook's Illustrated*

Best Ground Beef Chili

SERVES 8 TO 10

Garnish with diced avocado, sour cream, and shredded Monterey Jack or cheddar cheese. This intensely flavored chili should be served with tortilla chips or white rice.

- 2 pounds 85 percent lean ground beef
- 2 tablespoons plus 2 cups water
- Salt and pepper
- ¾ teaspoon baking soda
- 6 dried ancho chiles, stemmed, seeded, and torn into 1-inch pieces
- 1 ounce tortilla chips, crushed (¼ cup)
- 2 tablespoons ground cumin
- 1 tablespoon paprika
- 1 tablespoon garlic powder
- 1 tablespoon ground coriander
- 2 teaspoons dried oregano
- ½ teaspoon dried thyme
- 1 (14.5-ounce) can whole peeled tomatoes
- 1 tablespoon vegetable oil
- 1 onion, chopped fine
- 3 garlic cloves, minced
- 1–2 teaspoons minced canned chipotle chile in adobo sauce
- 1 (15-ounce) can pinto beans
- 2 teaspoons sugar
- 2 tablespoons cider vinegar
- Lime wedges
- Coarsely chopped cilantro
- Chopped red onion

1. Adjust oven rack to lower-middle position and heat oven to 275 degrees. Toss beef with 2 tablespoons water, 1½ teaspoons salt, and baking soda in bowl until thoroughly combined. Set aside for 20 minutes.

2. Meanwhile, place anchos in Dutch oven set over medium-high heat; toast, stirring frequently, until fragrant, 4 to 6 minutes, reducing heat if anchos begin to smoke. Transfer to food processor and let cool.

3. Add tortilla chips, cumin, paprika, garlic powder, coriander, oregano, thyme, and 2 teaspoons pepper to food processor with anchos and process until finely ground, about 2 minutes. Transfer mixture to bowl. Process tomatoes and their juice in now-empty workbowl until smooth, about 30 seconds.

4. Heat oil in now-empty pot over medium-high heat until shimmering. Add onion and cook, stirring

BEST GROUND BEEF CHILI

WHEN IT COMES TO COOK TIME, CHUCK IS CHUCK
You might think that because ground beef is made up of tiny pieces of meat, it doesn't need much time to cook. But ground chuck is exactly that—cut up pieces of chuck roast—and as such contains the same proteins and collagen that require adequate exposure to moist heat to properly break down. Many chili recipes cook the ground meat for 45 minutes or even less. For optimally tender results, we simmer ours for 1½ to 2 hours—almost as long as we do stew meat.

CUBED VERSUS GROUND
Both benefit from longer cooking.

BETTER BROWNING THROUGH CHEMISTRY
Browning ground beef is a challenge since it expels juices more rapidly than chunks of meat do, and most of that moisture needs to evaporate before browning can occur. To limit the amount of liquid, the usual solution is to brown in batches. We stick with one batch but toss the meat with baking soda before cooking, which helps lock in moisture. To quantify baking soda's impact, we ran a simple experiment.

EXPERIMENT
We cooked three batches of ground beef treated with baking soda and compared them with three otherwise identical untreated batches. We calculated the pre- and postcooking moisture level of each batch and compared degrees of browning.

RESULTS
On average, the untreated meat lost about 10 percent more moisture during cooking than the treated meat. That may not sound like much, but it makes a significant difference in how well ground meat browns: The treated batches were deeply browned, whereas the untreated batches didn't brown at all. (If we kept cooking the untreated meat, it would have eventually browned but would have been overdone.)

EXPLANATION
Raising the pH of meat increases its water-holding capacity, meaning that the proteins attract more water and are better able to hold on to it—not just during browning but throughout cooking. Besides keeping the meat from losing water that would make it steam versus brown, a higher pH also speeds up the Maillard reaction, making the treated meat brown even better and more quickly.

occasionally, until softened, 4 to 6 minutes. Add garlic and cook until fragrant, about 1 minute. Add beef and cook, stirring with wooden spoon to break meat up into ¼-inch pieces, until beef is browned and fond begins to form on pot bottom, 12 to 14 minutes. Add ancho mixture and chipotle; cook, stirring frequently, until fragrant, 1 to 2 minutes.

5. Add remaining 2 cups water, beans and their liquid, sugar, and tomato puree. Bring to boil, scraping bottom of pot to loosen any browned bits. Cover, transfer to oven, and cook until meat is tender and chili is slightly thickened, 1½ to 2 hours, stirring occasionally to prevent sticking.

6. Remove chili from oven and let stand, uncovered, for 10 minutes. Stir in any fat that has risen to top of chili, then add vinegar and season with salt to taste. Serve, passing lime wedges, cilantro, and chopped onion separately. (Chili can be made up to 3 days in advance.)

NEW ENGLAND FISH CHOWDER

✓ **WHY THIS RECIPE WORKS:** New England–style fish chowders are often loaded with heavy cream and potatoes, but we wanted a paleo-friendly version with the same creamy texture of the original. Pureeing cooked cauliflower into our base re-created the velvety consistency of dairy-based versions. We started by rendering bacon and sautéing onion and thyme in the fat before stirring in our cauliflower. We simmered sliced florets in a mixture of water and clam juice to reinforce the seafood flavor. Once the cauliflower began to break down, we transferred it to a blender and pureed the base to a smooth consistency. On returning the base to the pot, we added pieces of celery root, which were the perfect paleo stand-in for potatoes. Large chunks of cod were added last, allowing the fish to gently cook through. Before serving, we stirred fresh parsley and lemon juice into the soup for brightness.

Loaded with moist pieces of fish and chunks of potatoes in a lush, creamy base, a steamy bowl of fish chowder is a comforting New England classic with decidedly un-paleo ingredients—cream and potatoes—at the fore. Serving up a passable bowl of chowder without dairy seemed doable, but could I ever make it as rich and comforting as the real thing? I decided to find out.

The fish was the easy part. Firm, clean-tasting cod was the natural choice for this New England dish (though halibut or haddock worked, too) and I knew that cutting fillets into 2-inch pieces and adding them to the finished base would protect the fish from overcooking or flaking apart before serving.

My first big hurdle was creating a creamless creamy texture. With dairy out of the equation, I sought out a paleo-friendly ingredient that would lend body without overpowering the fish's delicate flavor. Working with the test kitchen's traditional fish chowder recipe, I tried removing the heavy cream and cornstarch (another non-paleo intruder) and bulking up the broth with arrowroot and tapioca flours, two go-to thickeners in paleo cooking. The arrowroot chowder was pleasingly thick, but it lacked the creamy quality I had in mind, and the tapioca flour turned my soup off-puttingly slimy. Looking to alternatives in the produce aisle, cauliflower seemed like a natural fit. I knew from the test kitchen's recipe for creamless cauliflower soup that this vegetable's low fiber content meant it could be blended into a smooth, velvety texture—no cream necessary. I simmered florets until they were tender and then gave them a spin in the blender. Just as I'd hoped, the texture was spot-on, but I would definitely need to hike up the flavor.

Every good chowder has a salty, smoky foil to balance out its richness, so I kicked off my next batch by rendering chopped-up strips of bacon for their flavorful fat. Keeping my aromatics simple, I browned chopped onion in the fat before adding in minced fresh thyme. I had my heart set on a seafood base, so a puree of water and cauliflower alone would not do. Any liquid the cod would shed would contribute only subtle fish flavor, so I turned to bottled clam juice to bolster the puree with some briny ocean flavor. I poured equal parts water and clam juice over the onions and thyme and let the pot simmer. As soon as the cauliflower was tender, I blended the whole mixture and was pleased to find my base was thick, creamy, and bursting with bright seafood flavor.

Before adding the fish, I wanted to give the chowder more heft. Potatoes are not part of a paleo diet, but root vegetables like rutabaga, parsnip, or celery root are great substitutes. Mellow celery root, cut into hearty chunks, paired well with my base, and it cooked to a tender texture in 15 minutes. With my chowder's flavors and textures hitting their mark, I added in the cod, which took mere minutes to cook. Parsley and lemon juice, added just before serving, gave my chowder a bright finish.

As I took my first spoonful of my reinvented New England classic I was pleased to find that my paleo version was, if anything, an upgrade.

—SEBASTIAN NAVA, *America's Test Kitchen Books*

New England Fish Chowder
SERVES 4

Halibut or haddock are good substitutes for the cod.

- 4 slices bacon, chopped
- 1 large onion, chopped
- 1 teaspoon minced fresh thyme or ¼ teaspoon dried
- 2 (8-ounce) bottles clam juice
- 2 cups water
- 8 ounces cauliflower florets cut into ½-inch pieces
- 1 celery root (14 ounces), peeled and cut into ½-inch pieces
  Kosher salt and pepper
- 1 bay leaf
- 1½ pounds skinless cod fillets, 1 inch thick, cut into 2-inch pieces
- 1 tablespoon minced fresh parsley
- 1 teaspoon lemon juice

1. Cook bacon in Dutch oven over medium heat until crisp, 5 to 7 minutes. Using slotted spoon, transfer bacon to paper towel–lined plate; set aside for serving.

2. Add onion to fat left in pot and cook over medium heat until softened, about 8 minutes. Stir in thyme and cook until fragrant, about 30 seconds. Stir in clam juice and water, scraping up any browned bits, and bring to simmer. Stir in cauliflower and cook until cauliflower falls apart easily when poked with fork, about 20 minutes.

3. Process cauliflower mixture in blender until smooth, about 1 minute; return to now-empty pot and bring to simmer over medium heat. Stir in celery root, 1 teaspoon salt, ¼ teaspoon pepper, and bay leaf and cook until celery root is tender, 15 to 20 minutes.

4. Season cod with salt and pepper and nestle into soup. Reduce heat to medium-low, cover, and simmer gently until cod flakes apart when gently prodded with paring knife and registers 140 degrees, 5 to 7 minutes.

5. Off heat, discard bay leaf. Stir in parsley and lemon juice and season with salt and pepper to taste. Break up any remaining large pieces of cod. Sprinkle individual portions with crisp bacon before serving.

CHAPTER 3

VEGETABLES AND SIDES

KIMCHI

✓ **WHY THIS RECIPE WORKS:** Kimchi is a Korean condiment of fermented vegetables, often cabbage and scallions, and sometimes leeks, radishes, and carrots. To make our own at home, we salted the cabbage to remove excess water. For flavor, we made a paste of garlic, ginger, Korean chili powder, sugar, fish sauce, and soy sauce for complexity and heat. We limited our vegetables to napa cabbage, scallions, and carrots. To eliminate air pockets and keep the cabbage submerged in its juices, we placed a plastic bag of water on top; we used two bags to prevent leaking. The fermentation process gives kimchi its signature flavor, and the ideal environment for fermenting is between 50 and 70 degrees (do not ferment above 70 degrees). After testing, we found that tasters preferred kimchi fermented at 65 degrees.

I have a weakness for kimchi. Whether I'm spooning it over a hot dog, stirring it into fried rice, using it to add some heat to my scrambled eggs, or, when it's really good, snacking on it plain, there is no shortage of ways to put this spicy, crunchy Korean condiment to good use. At its most basic, kimchi is a mix of pickled, fermented vegetables, often with napa cabbage at the fore—but with countless combinations of in-season vegetables to balance it out. Along with its potent blend of peppers, garlic, and spices, kimchi's signature tang and zippy effervescence comes from the careful process of fermentation. Having tasted a range of kimchis in the past, I had an idea of what I wanted from my own recipe: a somewhat thick, viscous, full-bodied brine with plenty of kick and vegetables that retained some fresh crunch. To turn out a jar of kimchi with my ideal characteristics, I needed to learn how to bring the science of fermenting home.

But before I tackled fermenting, I needed to pre-treat my vegetables. Tossing napa cabbage in pickling salt (the best option for clean-tasting pickled vegetables) removed excess water to maximize its crispness. After researching a number of kimchi recipes, I settled on a pungent paste of garlic, ginger, *kochukaru* (Korean chili powder), sugar, fish sauce, and soy sauce to deliver concentrated, authentic flavor. With all of these bold flavors present, and knowing that the fermentation would introduce more layers of complexity, I limited the rest of the roster to scallions and carrots.

To prevent any mold growth while my vegetables fermented, I pressed out air pockets as soon as I transferred my raw kimchi into jars. I further staved off any exposure to oxygen by laying parchment paper flush against the brine and creating a makeshift weighted seal by laying a water-filled zipper-lock bag (double-bagged to prevent leaks) on top of the parchment. I covered the jars with a triple layer of cheesecloth to allow gases to escape while protecting the kimchi against any dust or debris.

As my research taught me, when it comes to fermentation, maintaining the right temperature is paramount. The bacteria fermenting the cabbage would produce carbon dioxide (hence the effervescence) and various flavorful compounds. Temperature dictates how quickly this happens as well as which types of beneficial bacteria will ferment the vegetables and how long they will continue to do their work. These factors are key to determining the kimchi's depth of flavor, so I knew that finding my ideal kimchi would take some experimenting.

I prepared four identical batches of kimchi and stored them at four different temperatures—39 degrees (stored in my refrigerator), 50 degrees, 65 degrees, and 70 degrees, all of which were recommended by different recipes. After letting them ferment for just over a week, I found myself with four very different kimchis. The sample stored at 39 degrees proved unsafe. The cold slowed the fermentation so dramatically that the good bacteria couldn't preserve the vegetables before harmful bacteria moved in. At the other end of the spectrum, the 70-degree sample was effervescent, with very soft vegetables and a sharp, cheesy bite. The batch at 50 degrees was still crisp with complex, funky flavor, and a lightly thickened brine, but the 65-degree jar was my winning batch: Slightly softer than the 50-degree sample, it featured the most complex mix of bright acidity, pleasant fermented flavor, and a thickened brine. With that, I'd found my silver bullet.

With crunchy cabbage in a spicy, complex brine, my homemade kimchi was begging to be put to work in my next bowl of miso soup or alongside a plate of barbecue chicken. The best part: This recipe left room for kimchi lovers to adjust the flavor's intensity to their liking. As for me, with a recipe this simple, I plan on having a few jars of my potent pickled veggies on hand indefinitely.

—ANNE WOLF, *America's Test Kitchen Books*

Kimchi

MAKES ABOUT 2 QUARTS

You can find Korean chili powder (which has a mild, fruity flavor) at Asian markets and online. If Korean chili powder is unavailable, you can substitute ⅓ cup red pepper flakes.

- 1 (2½-pound) head napa cabbage, cored and cut into 2-inch pieces
- 2½ teaspoons canning and pickling salt
- 20 garlic cloves, peeled
- ½ cup Korean chili powder
- ⅓ cup sugar
- ¼ cup low-sodium soy sauce
- 3 tablespoons fish sauce
- 1 (2-inch) piece fresh ginger, peeled and chopped coarse
- 16 scallions, cut into 2-inch pieces
- 1 carrot, peeled and cut into 2-inch matchsticks

1. Toss cabbage with salt in bowl, cover, and let sit at room temperature for 1 hour. Transfer cabbage to colander, squeeze to drain excess liquid, and return to now-empty bowl. Cut out parchment paper round to match diameter of ½-gallon wide-mouth glass jar.

2. Process garlic, chili powder, sugar, soy sauce, fish sauce, and ginger in food processor until no large pieces of garlic or ginger remain, about 20 seconds. Add chili mixture, scallions, and carrot to cabbage and toss to combine. Tightly pack vegetable mixture into jar, pressing down firmly with your fist to eliminate air pockets as you pack. Press parchment round flush against surface of vegetables.

3. Fill 1-quart zipper-lock bag with 1 cup water, squeeze out air, and seal well. Place inside second zipper-lock bag, press out air, and seal well. Place bag of water on top of parchment and gently press down. Cover jar with triple layer of cheesecloth and secure with rubber band.

4. Place jar in 50- to 70-degree location away from direct sunlight and let ferment for 9 days; check jar daily, skimming residue and mold from surface and pressing to keep mixture submerged. After 9 days, taste kimchi daily until it has reached desired flavor. (This may take up to 11 days longer; cabbage should be soft and translucent with a pleasant cheesy, fishy flavor.)

5. When kimchi has reached desired flavor, remove cheesecloth, bag of water, and parchment, and skim off any residue or mold. Serve. (Kimchi and accumulated juice can be transferred to clean jar, covered, and refrigerated for up to 3 months; once refrigerated, kimchi will continue to soften and develop flavor.)

ROASTED TOMATOES

✓ **WHY THIS RECIPE WORKS:** When tomatoes are in season, oven roasting is a great way to intensify their flavor while increasing their shelf life. Many recipes call for a low oven and hours of cooking only to yield leathery tomatoes. By combining a couple of tricks, we were able to cut down on the cooking time without sacrificing quality of flavor. We sliced the tomatoes into thick rings for lots of exposed surface area. Oil transfers heat with great efficiency, so we poured some over the slices to help drive more moisture away and to concentrate the tomatoes' flavor. We started roasting the tomatoes in a 425-degree oven and then reduced the temperature to 300 degrees to finish cooking. The finished tomatoes had intense flavor and a garlicky, concentrated oil in which to preserve them.

If you've never roasted tomatoes, you should. It's a largely hands-off technique that yields the ultimate condiment: bright, concentrated tomatoes that are soft but retain their shape. They can be used right away or frozen, and they perk up just about any dish.

And yet I rarely roast tomatoes because most recipes take hours, which is no fun on a hot day. Faster recipes yield pulpy, bland results—an unappealing phase between raw and roasted. I wanted bright-tasting, soft-but-intact tomatoes in less time.

I started with larger round tomatoes, which boast a higher ratio of the flavorful "jelly" to skin than do the denser plum variety, and a lower ratio of chewy skin than smaller cherry or grape tomatoes. And since the main goal of roasting tomatoes is to burn off much of their moisture, I sliced them into ¾-inch-thick rounds—a shape that maximized their surface area for efficient evaporation and allowed me to fit 3 pounds in a single layer on a foil-lined rimmed baking sheet.

I drizzled the slices with a couple of tablespoons of extra-virgin olive oil, sprinkled them with kosher salt and pepper, and slid them into a 300-degree oven, hoping the low temperature would dry them out gradually without burning. But gradual was an understatement. They took about 5 hours to collapse

ROASTED TOMATOES

and shrivel sufficiently and made almost no progress during the first hour because in the low oven, the water inside them evaporated slowly.

What they needed was a blast of heat to get them hotter faster, so for the next batch I cranked the oven temperature to 425 degrees. Half an hour in, their edges were nicely dried out—good progress. Then to keep them from burning, I dropped the temperature back to 300 degrees, propped open the oven door so that the oven cooled quickly, and flipped them so they'd cook evenly. That brought the cooking time down to just under 4 hours, but I wanted to cut the time more.

I'd seen a few recipes that called for not just coating but submerging the tomatoes in oil. When I thought about it, I realized that because oil is more efficient than air at transferring heat, the tomatoes would probably cook faster. Sure enough, when I roasted the next batch in 1 cup of oil, they cooked up nicely concentrated and caramelized in about 2 hours. The only problem: A full cup of oil filled the sheet pan to the rim, making it difficult to maneuver. Scaling back to ¾ cup made handling easier and prolonged the roasting time by only about a half-hour.

A quick tweak—scattering the tomatoes with garlic cloves and dried oregano before roasting—added just enough fragrance and flavor. In fact, the results were so good with farmers' market tomatoes that I tried my method with supermarket specimens and was thrilled when it rendered even these blander fruits sweet-savory.

—LAN LAM, *Cook's Illustrated*

Roasted Tomatoes

MAKES 1½ CUPS

Avoid using tomatoes smaller than 3 inches in diameter, which have a smaller ratio of flavorful jelly to skin than larger tomatoes. To double the recipe, use two baking sheets, increase the baking time in step 2 to 40 minutes, and rotate and switch the sheets halfway through baking. In step 3, increase the roasting time to 1½ to 2½ hours.

- 3 pounds large tomatoes, cored, bottom ⅛ inch trimmed, and sliced ¾ inch thick
- 2 garlic cloves, peeled and smashed
- ¼ teaspoon dried oregano
  Kosher salt and pepper
- ¾ cup extra-virgin olive oil

NOTES FROM THE TEST KITCHEN

BIG SLICES FOR BIG FLAVOR

Trim off bottom of large tomato. Slice tomato into ¾-inch-thick slices, taking care to keep flavor-rich seeds and juices intact.

1. Adjust oven rack to middle position and heat oven to 425 degrees. Line rimmed baking sheet with aluminum foil. Arrange tomatoes in even layer on prepared sheet, with larger slices around edge and smaller slices in center. Place garlic cloves on tomatoes. Sprinkle with oregano and ¼ teaspoon salt and season with pepper to taste. Drizzle oil evenly over tomatoes.

2. Bake for 30 minutes, rotating sheet halfway through baking. Remove sheet from oven. Reduce temperature to 300 degrees and prop open door with wooden spoon to cool oven. Using thin spatula, flip tomatoes.

3. Return tomatoes to oven and continue to cook until spotty brown, skins are blistered, and tomatoes have collapsed to ¼ to ½ inch thick, 1 to 2 hours. Remove from oven and let cool completely, about 30 minutes. Discard garlic and transfer tomatoes and oil to airtight container. (Tomatoes can be refrigerated for up to 5 days or frozen for up to 2 months.)

Roasted Tomato Relish

MAKES 1¼ CUPS

Use this relish to top bruschetta, chicken, or pork tenderloin, or to dress up scrambled eggs or polenta.

- 1 cup Roasted Tomatoes, chopped coarse, plus 1 tablespoon reserved tomato oil
- 1 small shallot, minced
- ¼ cup chopped fresh cilantro
- ¾ teaspoon red wine vinegar
- ½ teaspoon capers, rinsed and minced
  Salt and pepper

Combine all ingredients in bowl and season with salt and pepper to taste.

Chunky Roasted Tomato Sauce
MAKES 1½ CUPS

Serve this chunky sauce over a short, tubular pasta like penne. This recipe makes enough sauce for 1 pound of pasta.

 2 tablespoons reserved tomato oil, plus 1½ cups Roasted Tomatoes (page 49)
 ½ small onion, chopped fine
    Salt and pepper
 2 garlic cloves, minced
 ½ teaspoon dried oregano
 ⅛ teaspoon red pepper flakes
 ¼ cup grated Parmesan cheese
 ¼ cup shredded basil
 1½ teaspoons red wine vinegar

Heat oil in 10-inch skillet over medium heat. When oil begins to shimmer, add onion and ¼ teaspoon salt and cook, stirring frequently until onion softens and begins to brown, 5 to 7 minutes. Add garlic, oregano, and pepper flakes and cook, stirring frequently, until fragrant, about 30 seconds. Add tomatoes and cook until warmed through, 3 to 4 minutes. Stir in Parmesan, basil, and vinegar. Season with salt and pepper to taste.

SAUTÉED SUMMER SQUASH WITH PARSLEY AND GARLIC

✔ **WHY THIS RECIPE WORKS:** We wanted an easy side that made the most of summer's abundant zucchini and summer squash. Hoping to highlight the crisp-tender texture of the squash, we needed a method that didn't involve salting, shredding, and draining but still allowed the squash to cook quickly. By peeling the squash with a vegetable peeler, we created thin, even strips of squash that cooked quickly and minimized knife work. Cooking the squash in a single batch encouraged the ribbons to become tender without browning, which masks their fresh flavor and dims their bright appearance. We paired the squash ribbons with a few bold but simple dressings to give our vibrant side a burst of extra flavor without weighing it down.

Summer squash has a lot going for it: It's inexpensive, its mild flesh pairs well with lots of flavors, and it cooks quickly. But it's also mostly water and full of seeds, meaning that unless you do some finagling, you're in for soggy, seedy results. Excess moisture is commonly addressed by cutting or shredding the vegetable, salting it, and then waiting for the liquid to drain off—a nonstarter on busy weeknights. Some recipes skip salting and call for simply sautéing over high heat. The goal is to tenderize the flesh before it breaks down and sheds liquid, but the technique is hardly foolproof. Thick pieces end up soft on the outside but firm in the middle, and while slicing the squash thin works, it doesn't eliminate seeds. I wanted nonwatery, seedless squash in a flash.

What if I removed the core altogether? Using a spoon to scrape the seeds from a halved squash left me with odd half-moon shapes. A better plan would be to work around the core, cutting the flesh first into thick vertical planks and then into thin, bite-size pieces. This was doable, but as I cut, I thought about a few recipes I'd seen that called for trading the knife for a vegetable peeler and shaving the squash into strips. I trimmed the ends from a colorful mix of summer squash and zucchini and grabbed a peeler. Using steady pressure and stopping when I reached the seeds, I quickly produced a pile of elegant ribbons. Time to move to the stove.

I placed a large nonstick pan over high heat and set out to cook the ribbons in a single batch. To prevent the strips from tangling, I tried coating them in extra-virgin olive oil before cooking, but this only made them greasy. Instead, I found that simply fluffing the squash with tongs as it hit the oil coated skillet and tossing it occasionally during cooking prevented clumping.

Normally, I want to develop as much browning as possible when cooking summer squash because of the rich flavor it adds. In this case, however, going over-board on browning detracted from the bright, colorful appearance of the ribbons, so I dialed down the heat. In less than 5 minutes, I had crisp-tender, beautifully trans-lucent squash that wasn't the least bit soggy or seedy.

Now I just needed to add some seasonings. A complex dressing would overpower the delicate squash flavor, so I kept it simple. I started by squeezing a lemon and adding minced garlic, extra-virgin olive oil, and lemon zest. As I tossed the dressing with the hot ribbons, they soaked it up and took on an attractive shimmer. With a final sprinkle of parsley, my work was done.

—ANNIE PETITO, *Cook's Illustrated*

Sautéed Summer Squash with Parsley and Garlic
SERVES 4

Be sure to start checking for doneness at the lower end of the cooking time.

- 1 small garlic clove, minced
- 1 teaspoon grated lemon zest plus 1 tablespoon juice
- 4 yellow squashes and/or zucchini (8 ounces each), ends trimmed
- 7 teaspoons extra-virgin olive oil
  Salt and pepper
- 1½ tablespoons chopped fresh parsley

1. Combine garlic and lemon juice in large bowl and set aside for at least 10 minutes. Using vegetable peeler, shave each squash lengthwise into ribbons. Peel off 3 ribbons from 1 side, then turn squash 90 degrees and peel off 3 more ribbons. Continue to turn and peel ribbons until you reach seeds. Discard core.

2. Whisk 2 tablespoons oil, ¼ teaspoon salt, ⅛ teaspoon pepper, and lemon zest into garlic mixture.

3. Heat remaining 1 teaspoon oil in 12-inch nonstick skillet over medium-high heat until just smoking. Add squash and cook, tossing occasionally with tongs, until squash has softened and is translucent, 3 to 4 minutes. Transfer squash to bowl with dressing, add 1 tablespoon parsley, and toss to coat. Season with salt and pepper to taste. Transfer to serving platter and sprinkle with remaining 1½ teaspoons parsley. Serve immediately.

VARIATIONS

Sautéed Summer Squash with Mint and Pistachios
Substitute 1½ teaspoons cider vinegar for lemon zest and juice. Substitute ⅓ cup chopped fresh mint for parsley and sprinkle squash with 2 tablespoons chopped toasted pistachios before serving.

Sautéed Summer Squash with Oregano and Red Pepper Flakes
Omit lemon zest. Add ¼ teaspoon red pepper flakes to heated oil in step 3 and substitute 2 teaspoons minced fresh oregano for parsley.

STUFFED ACORN SQUASH

✔ **WHY THIS RECIPE WORKS:** For stuffed acorn squash with clear squash flavor, we called on our key ingredient to fill more than one role. First, we cut squashes into wedges and roasted them to soften and brown their flesh. We chose apples and kale for a sweet-meets-savory stuffing. Roasted squash, scraped out of two spare wedges and mashed together with the cooked apple and kale, served as the "glue" to hold the stuffing in place. The mash also added a nutty, caramelized component to the filling while some minced rosemary and a splash of cider vinegar rounded out its robust flavor profile. A sprinkling of goat cheese added mild tang to contrast the sweet squash, and chopped almonds finished the wedges off with great crunch.

Acorn squashes are delicious simply roasted and mashed with butter, but around the holidays I like to gussy them up in a festive but not overburdened side dish. This year, I had my heart set on full-flavored stuffed squash with a filling that wouldn't spill all over my serving platter.

I started by doing some research into the test kitchen's previous squash recipes. My colleagues' rigorous tests demonstrated that to get flesh that was velvety and soft but still stable enough to hold its shape, I'd have to precook the wedges before adding any stuffing. Though this added an extra step, precooking did have a major perk: browning on the exposed squash created a sweet, caramelized note. To maximize that browning, I positioned the wedges on their sides on a rimmed baking sheet and slid them into the oven to roast at 400 degrees. Twenty minutes later I flipped them for even browning. Once they were soft enough that I could slip my knife easily into the flesh, I moved onto the stuffing.

I'd been considering a wide range of options for that stuffing. It wasn't difficult to take too-filling grains like rice and barley out of the potential lineup. Meat was

---

out, too—there would be more than enough of that on the holiday table. I decided to focus on vegetables. But which ones?

Spinach and Swiss chard were slippery and insubstantial here, so I turned to sturdy kale, cut into strips and sautéed until just wilted. After spooning the precooked kale into the squash wedges and baking them for another 5 minutes, the kale had a pleasant texture.

But when I went to set the squash on a platter, the kale just tumbled right off. I needed a glue to make it stick. But what? A bunch of grated cheese? Some beaten egg? No need. Instead, I found my glue right there on the sheet pan: roasted squash. For my next batch, I roasted eight wedges of squash (from two acorn squashes) and then scooped the flesh from two wedges and mashed it together with the kale. It baked up into a cohesive filling.

To round out the flavors, I added some bright chopped apple, a bit of garlic and rosemary, a splash of cider vinegar, tangy crumbled goat cheese, and some crunchy nuts. I had a rustic but elegant holiday side dish that would leave plenty of room for, among other things, dessert.

—ASHLEY MOORE, *Cook's Country*

Stuffed Acorn Squash

SERVES 6

Of the eight wedges of squash, use the two that are least attractive for the stuffing.

- 2 acorn squashes (1½ pounds each), quartered pole to pole and seeded
- ¼ cup extra-virgin olive oil, plus extra for drizzling
  Salt and pepper
- 6 ounces kale, stemmed and sliced into ¼-inch-thick strips
- 1 Fuji or Gala apple, peeled, cored, and cut into ¼-inch pieces
- 1 garlic clove, minced
- ½ teaspoon minced fresh rosemary
- 1 tablespoon cider vinegar
- 1 tablespoon unsalted butter
- 2 ounces goat cheese, crumbled (½ cup)
- 2 tablespoons coarsely chopped toasted almonds

1. Adjust oven rack to middle position and heat oven to 400 degrees. Toss squash wedges, 2 tablespoons oil,

1 teaspoon salt, and 1 teaspoon pepper in bowl until squash is thoroughly coated. Arrange wedges on rimmed baking sheet with 1 narrow cut side down. Roast until browned on first side, about 20 minutes. Flip wedges so other narrow cut side is down and continue to roast until browned on second side and tip of paring knife slips easily into flesh, about 15 minutes.

2. Remove sheet from oven and let wedges cool slightly. Once cool enough to handle, scoop flesh from 2 least attractive wedges into bowl; discard skins. (You should have about ¾ cup of scooped squash.) Turn remaining 6 wedges skin side down on sheet.

3. Heat 1 tablespoon oil in 12-inch nonstick skillet over medium heat until shimmering. Add kale, apple, and ¼ teaspoon salt and cook, covered, until kale is wilted, about 3 minutes. Uncover and continue to cook until any liquid has evaporated, about 30 seconds. Stir in scooped squash, mashing with spoon to incorporate, and cook until beginning to brown, about 1 minute.

4. Push squash mixture to sides of skillet. Add garlic, rosemary, and remaining 1 tablespoon oil to center of skillet and cook until fragrant, about 30 seconds. Stir garlic mixture into squash mixture. Stir in vinegar and cook until evaporated, about 1 minute. Off heat, stir in butter and season with salt and pepper to taste.

5. Divide filling evenly among wedges on sheet. Evenly sprinkle goat cheese and almonds over filling. Bake until cheese is softened and squash heated through, 5 to 7 minutes. Drizzle with extra oil before serving.

VARIATION

Stuffed Acorn Squash with Pear and Hazelnuts
Substitute 1 ripe pear for apple, fresh thyme for rosemary, and 2 tablespoons finely chopped toasted and skinned hazelnuts for almonds.

NOTES FROM THE TEST KITCHEN

CUTTING SQUASH SAFELY

Set squash on damp dish towel, position knife on rind of squash, and strike back of knife with rubber mallet to drive knife into squash. Continue to hit until knife halves squash.

STUFFED ACORN SQUASH

MODERN SUCCOTASH

✓ **WHY THIS RECIPE WORKS:** When most people think of succotash, an uninspiring side of frozen corn and lima beans springs to mind. We wanted a simple side dish made with crisp, sweet fresh corn and creamy beans. For the corn, crisp kernels fresh from the cob were the only option for this dish. For the beans, we used canned butter beans instead of limas as they kept prep simple and had a creamy consistency and pleasant mild flavor. We used some of the canning liquid from the beans to build a sauce that bound the succotash's ingredients together, creating a dish with a cohesive texture. A few nontraditional add-ins—crisp red bell pepper and a pinch of cayenne pepper—gave it distinct color and a bit of heat.

In 17th-century Plymouth, Massachusetts, Pilgrims and Native Americans frequently cooked up what was later referred to as "Plymouth succotash"—a stew of corn or hominy, dried beans, and bits of dried or fresh meat or fish. By the 19th century, succotash had evolved into the meatless side dish that we know today. But just because a dish boasts longevity doesn't mean that it's good. In fact, many folks crinkle their noses at the mention of succotash, since they have always known it as a dish of canned or frozen corn and lima beans swamped in a thick, dull cream sauce. This is a shame, since a quick, easy mix of crisp, sweet corn and creamy beans should be an easy summertime staple. I set out to modernize succotash by nixing the bland dairy and freshening up the lackluster vegetables.

The quality of the corn and beans would be crucial to success, so using fresh corn was a must. Fresh limas are hard to come by, so I tried a few alternatives—with no luck. Dried limas took hours to cook; frozen were inconsistent, as some cooked up creamy while others were grainy; and canned were unappealingly washed out in flavor and color. But canned limas did boast a pleasant creamy texture that made me wonder if other canned beans might fare even better.

After surveying the possibilities, I decided to try butter beans, which are closely related to limas. Sure enough, the larger butter beans offered mild flavor, decent looks, and the same appealing texture. After stripping the kernels from four ears of corn, I sautéed them in butter with the rinsed and drained beans. This warmed the beans through while retaining the crispness of the corn.

Purists say that true succotash contains only corn and beans. However, I found a lot of recipes that mixed in seasonal vegetables like eggplant, tomatoes, and squash. While the duo of beans and corn seemed too plain, a medley was too busy. Moderation was in order. An onion and two cloves of garlic provided a savory base; half a red bell pepper provided crispness and color; and final additions of minced parsley and lemon juice focused the freshness.

I was happy with the way the dish was shaping up but had one lingering concern: Without the traditional cream sauce to bind the ingredients, the dish resembled salsa instead of succotash. I tried "milking" the corn after removing the kernels by scraping the cob with the back of a knife, but there wasn't enough liquid to create even a light coating for the vegetables. Mixing chicken broth with a little cornstarch did a better job of giving the dish some cohesion, but the chicken flavor was distracting. The cornstarch gave me an idea, though: I could add a splash of the starchy "broth" from the canned beans—a sleeper ingredient we sometimes call on to lend body to bean soups and pasta dishes. Just 2 tablespoons delicately bound the ingredients and accentuated the bean taste without overpowering the other flavors.

With classic succotash flavors in place, I varied the recipe by swapping out the butter beans for a few alternative varieties—pink, pinto, and cannellini—as well as tweaking the vegetable and herb additions. The result is a handful of easy-to-prepare, fresh side dishes sure to restore the status of succotash.

—KEITH DRESSER, *Cook's Illustrated*

NOTES FROM THE TEST KITCHEN

HOW SMALL IS SMALL?
While we usually give weights for baking ingredients, we often call for vegetables in terms of size. Our default onion is a medium yellow onion, which is the approximate size of a tennis ball. For Modern Succotash, use a billiard ball–size onion weighing around 6 ounces.

Modern Succotash

SERVES 4 TO 6

Do not use frozen or canned corn in this dish.

- 1 (15-ounce) can butter beans, 2 tablespoons liquid reserved, rinsed
- 2 teaspoons lemon juice
- 3 tablespoons unsalted butter
- 1 small onion, chopped fine
- ½ red bell pepper, cut into ¼-inch pieces
  Salt and pepper
- 2 garlic cloves, minced
  Pinch cayenne pepper
- 4 ears corn, kernels cut from cobs (3 cups)
- 2 tablespoons minced fresh parsley

1. Stir reserved bean liquid and lemon juice together in small bowl; set aside. Melt butter in 12-inch nonstick skillet over medium-high heat. Add onion, bell pepper, and ½ teaspoon salt and cook, stirring frequently, until softened and beginning to brown, 4 to 5 minutes. Add garlic and cayenne and cook until fragrant, about 30 seconds.

2. Reduce heat to medium and add corn and beans. Cook, stirring occasionally, until corn and beans have cooked through, about 4 minutes. Add bean liquid mixture and cook, stirring constantly, for 1 minute. Remove skillet from heat, stir in parsley, and season with salt and pepper to taste. Serve.

VARIATIONS

Modern Succotash with Fennel and Scallions

Thinly slice white and green parts of 4 scallions on bias. Substitute cannellini beans for butter beans; 1 fennel bulb, cut into ¼-inch pieces, and scallion whites for onion and bell pepper; ¼ teaspoon ground fennel for cayenne; and scallion greens for parsley.

Modern Succotash with Leeks and Black Pepper

Substitute pink beans for butter beans; 1 leek, white and light green parts halved lengthwise, sliced thin, and washed, for onion and bell pepper; 1 teaspoon pepper for cayenne; and 3 tablespoons minced chives for parsley.

Modern Succotash with Poblano, Bacon, and Cilantro

Substitute pinto beans for butter beans and lime juice for lemon juice. Cook 2 slices chopped bacon in 12-inch nonstick skillet over medium-high heat, stirring occasionally, until crisp, 5 to 7 minutes. Using slotted spoon, transfer bacon to paper towel–lined plate and set aside. Reduce butter to 2 tablespoons and add it to fat in skillet. Proceed with recipe, substituting poblano chile for bell pepper, ¼ teaspoon ground coriander for cayenne, and cilantro for parsley. Sprinkle with reserved bacon before serving.

SKILLET-ROASTED CAULIFLOWER

✓ **WHY THIS RECIPE WORKS:** Roasted cauliflower has an irresistibly nutty, caramelized flavor, but we wondered if moving from the oven to the stovetop could get this simple side dish on the table more quickly. We began by cutting cauliflower into planks and then into flat-sided florets to maximize its exposed surface area for plenty of flavorful browning. Starting in a cold covered pan allowed the slices to gradually steam in their own moisture before we removed the lid and let them brown. To give our side dish some standout flavor, we finished cooking the slices with minced garlic, lemon zest, and fresh parsley. A final sprinkling of toasted bread crumbs delivered great crunch.

Roasting cauliflower is a good way to caramelize its sugars and transform this mild vegetable into something sweet and nutty-tasting. But between preheating the oven and the actual roasting time, the process can take up to an hour. Could a stovetop method deliver the same results in a time frame more suitable for a weeknight?

Following a standard sautéing method, I heated olive oil in a skillet until it started to shimmer and then added a head of cauliflower divided into florets. Cauliflower's dense texture means it can take a while to cook through, so it was no surprise when the craggy exteriors browned before the interiors had a chance to soften. I made another batch, this time pouring a little water into the pan and covering it. The trapped steam cooked the florets through, but now they looked anemic.

It was time to consider straying from the fundamentals. Since a hot pan browned the florets too quickly, how about starting with a cold one? I put a skillet with the cauliflower and oil on the stove, turned on the heat, and let it cook, covered, over medium-high heat for 5 minutes. I then removed the lid and let it continue to cook for another 12 minutes, stirring now and again. It was an unusual approach, but it delivered: Now I had tender florets with some deep brown, caramelized spots. Even better, it all happened in less than 20 minutes.

Why did it work? The cold start encouraged the cauliflower to release its moisture so that the florets steamed without any additional liquid and no dilution of flavor. That said, my florets still needed more browning. Because of their irregular, rounded shape, very few of their surfaces actually rested on the bottom of the pan. To fix that, I sliced the entire head of cauliflower into ¾-inch-thick planks and then cut around the core to divide each cross section into florets. These flat surfaces browned nicely, imparting a nutty flavor to each slice.

Finally, inspired by a classic gremolata, I found that a combination of sautéed garlic and lemon zest, with fresh chopped parsley added at the finish, perked up the cauliflower without overwhelming it. With a sprinkling of toasted fresh bread crumbs for crunch, my newfangled skillet-roasted cauliflower was complete.

—STEVE DUNN, *Cook's Illustrated*

Skillet-Roasted Cauliflower with Garlic and Lemon

SERVES 4 TO 6

During the first 5 minutes of cooking, the cauliflower steams in its own released moisture; do not lift the skillet lid during this time.

- 1 head cauliflower (2 pounds)
- 1 slice hearty white sandwich bread, torn into 1-inch pieces
- 5 tablespoons extra-virgin olive oil
  Salt and pepper
- 1 garlic clove, minced
- 1 teaspoon grated lemon zest, plus lemon wedges for serving
- ¼ cup chopped fresh parsley

1. Trim outer leaves of cauliflower and cut stem flush with bottom of head. Turn head so stem is facing down and cut head into ¾-inch-thick slices. Cut around core to remove florets; discard core. Cut large florets into 1½-inch pieces. Transfer florets to bowl, including any small pieces that may have been created during trimming, and set aside.

2. Pulse bread in food processor to coarse crumbs, about 10 pulses. Heat bread crumbs, 1 tablespoon oil, pinch salt, and pinch pepper in 12-inch nonstick skillet over medium heat, stirring frequently, until bread crumbs are golden brown, 3 to 5 minutes. Transfer crumbs to bowl and wipe out skillet.

3. Combine 2 tablespoons oil and cauliflower florets in now-empty skillet and sprinkle with 1 teaspoon salt and ½ teaspoon pepper. Cover skillet and cook over medium-high heat until florets start to brown and edges just start to become translucent (do not lift lid), about 5 minutes.

4. Remove lid and continue to cook, stirring every 2 minutes, until florets turn golden brown in many spots, about 12 minutes.

5. Push cauliflower to edges of skillet. Add remaining 2 tablespoons oil, garlic, and lemon zest to center and cook, stirring with rubber spatula, until fragrant, about 30 seconds. Stir garlic mixture into cauliflower and continue to cook, stirring occasionally, until cauliflower is tender but still firm, about 3 minutes longer.

6. Remove skillet from heat and stir in parsley. Transfer cauliflower to serving platter and sprinkle with bread crumbs. Serve, passing lemon wedges separately.

VARIATIONS

Skillet-Roasted Cauliflower with Curry, Raisins, and Almonds

Omit bread and lemon and reduce oil to ¼ cup. Substitute 2 tablespoons grated fresh ginger, ¾ teaspoon curry powder, and ⅛ teaspoon cayenne pepper for garlic. Substitute ¼ cup chopped fresh cilantro and 3 tablespoons golden raisins for parsley and sprinkle with ¼ cup toasted and finely chopped sliced almonds before serving.

Skillet-Roasted Cauliflower with Cumin and Pistachios

Omit bread and reduce oil to ¼ cup. Heat 1 teaspoon cumin seeds and 1 teaspoon coriander seeds in 12-inch nonstick skillet over medium heat, stirring frequently, until lightly toasted and fragrant, 2 to 3 minutes. Transfer to spice grinder or mortar and pestle and coarsely grind. Wipe out skillet. Substitute ground cumin-coriander mixture, ½ teaspoon paprika, and pinch cayenne pepper for garlic; lime zest for lemon zest; and 3 tablespoons

SKILLET-ROASTED CAULIFLOWER WITH CURRY, RAISINS, AND ALMONDS

chopped fresh mint for parsley. Sprinkle with ¼ cup toasted and chopped pistachios before serving with lime wedges.

Skillet-Roasted Cauliflower with Capers and Pine Nuts

Omit bread and reduce oil to ¼ cup. Reduce salt in step 3 to ¾ teaspoon. Substitute 2 tablespoons rinsed, minced capers for garlic. Substitute 2 tablespoons minced fresh chives for parsley and stir in ¼ cup toasted pine nuts with chives in step 6.

CHILES RELLENOS

✔ **WHY THIS RECIPE WORKS:** Authentic *chiles rellenos* (in English, "stuffed chiles") should be filled with just the right amount of melted cheese and enrobed in a delicate, crispy batter. Most versions however, fall flat and take hours to prepare. To make a better, quicker version we used soft, melty Muenster cheese for the filling. Cutting it into cubes made stuffing the chiles a breeze. Most recipes call for roasting and peeling the peppers before stuffing them, but we found this step unnecessary. We simply broiled the peppers to soften them and left their skins on. Instead of a fussy traditional egg white batter, we opted for a quick batter of flour, cornstarch, baking powder, and beer. For our quick sauce, we relied on pantry staples—chili powder, onion powder, garlic powder, chicken broth, and tomato sauce.

When I visit a Mexican restaurant, I rarely order *chiles rellenos* (cheese-stuffed chiles). Too many times I've been burned by an overloaded plate of soggy poblanos drowning in bland sauce and soggy cheese. This saddens me; for as much work as this dish requires (roasting, peeling, seeding, stuffing, battering, and frying chiles, for starters), shouldn't the resulting dish be beautiful and satisfying rather than gloppy and overwrought?

I set out to rescue chiles rellenos with a home version that featured a delicate and crispy coating, a complex sauce, and plenty of comforting cheesiness. My first stop was our cookbook library, where I uncovered a handful of existing recipes. But six hours and five recipes later, I had little to show for my work other than a sink full of dishes and a stovetop covered in batter, sauce, and cheese. I realized I had quite a task ahead.

Most recipes call for precooking the poblano peppers to ensure that they're tender at the table, and this step proved essential. When I tried to skip it, I had rigid peppers that were difficult to stuff and tasted raw. Setting the peppers on a baking sheet and putting them under the broiler for a few minutes was the best route to peppers with a structure just soft enough to stuff and fry without going mushy. And while most recipes call for the peppers to be peeled after that precook, I found (after a long series of tests) that the peel was a nonissue; tasters didn't mind it at all. And there was an added benefit—leaving the skin on gave the peppers extra stability and made stuffing them easier.

I slit a 3-inch-long opening into the side of each broiled pepper and, using a pair of scissors, snipped out the interior seed bulb. I then used a soupspoon to scrape out any remaining seeds. My poblanos were ready for cheese.

Recipes vary widely as to the type of cheese to use to fill the chiles, but after testing Monterey Jack, Muenster, and cheddar (and a few other types), my tasters voted for Muenster. The result surprised me, but my concern was assuaged by reading the advice of Diana Kennedy, a leading authority on Mexican cooking—soft, mellow, meltable Muenster is her choice of cheese, too.

But while Kennedy calls for long strips of cheese, I used cubes, which were easier to stuff into the peppers. I secured the stuffed chiles with wooden skewers and focused on the batter.

I tested an array of batters from the test kitchen arsenal—we have favorite coatings for everything from fried chicken to corn dogs. I settled on a light flour-and-beer-based batter that we use for frying pickles. It creates a light, crisp coating that enhances, rather than cloaks, what's inside.

With a few tweaks (including a dusting of flour to help the batter adhere), this batter coated the peppers just enough, and when fried in 375-degree oil on the stovetop, it created a crisp, light, golden-brown coating in the 4 minutes it took for the cheesy interior to melt.

Now for a sauce. I wanted something quick and easy made from pantry staples. A simple cooked mixture of chili powder, onion powder, garlic powder, chicken broth, and tomato sauce, bolstered with a teaspoon of smoky, rich sauce from a can of chipotles in adobo and brightened with lime juice, was just right.

A far cry from the dull and gloppy restaurant dishes I'd encountered in the past, my version was complex, delicate, refined, comforting, and easier than I imagined it would be.

—MORGAN BOLLING, *Cook's Country*

Chiles Rellenos

SERVES 4 TO 6

Use a Dutch oven that holds 6 quarts or more. You do not need to remove all of the chile seeds in step 3. Nonalcoholic lagers will also work in this recipe.

SAUCE

  1 tablespoon vegetable oil
  1 teaspoon chili powder
  ½ teaspoon onion powder
  ¼ teaspoon garlic powder
1½ cups chicken broth
  1 (15-ounce) can tomato sauce
  1 teaspoon adobo sauce from canned chipotle chiles in adobo sauce
  1 bay leaf
  1 tablespoon lime juice
   Salt and pepper

CHILES

  6 (4- to 5-ounce) poblano chiles
  8 ounces Muenster cheese, cut into 12 (1-inch) cubes
  6 (4-inch) wooden skewers
1½ cups (7½ ounces) all-purpose flour
1¼ cups (5 ounces) cornstarch
  2 teaspoons baking powder
   Salt
1½ cups mild lager, such as Budweiser
  3 quarts peanut or vegetable oil

NOTES FROM THE TEST KITCHEN

ASSEMBLING CHILES RELLENOS

1. Cut 3-inch long vertical slit in poblano, then cut out seed bulb with scissors. (Use spoon to scoop away remaining seeds.)

2. Place 2 cubes of Muenster cheese inside each poblano.

3. Overlap opening and thread with skewer to seal.

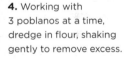

4. Working with 3 poblanos at a time, dredge in flour, shaking gently to remove excess.

5. Holding poblano by stem, dunk in batter to coat and transfer to hot oil.

1. FOR THE SAUCE: Heat oil in medium saucepan over medium-high heat until shimmering. Add chili powder, onion powder, and garlic powder and cook until fragrant, about 30 seconds. Add broth, tomato sauce, adobo sauce, and bay leaf and bring to boil. Reduce heat to medium and cook at vigorous simmer until reduced to 2 cups, 12 to 15 minutes. Stir in lime juice and season with salt and pepper to taste. Remove from heat, cover, and keep warm. (Discard bay leaf before serving.)

2. FOR THE CHILES: Meanwhile, adjust oven rack 6 inches from broiler element and heat broiler. Line rimmed baking sheet with aluminum foil. Evenly space poblanos on sheet and broil until skins just begin to blister on first side, 3 to 5 minutes. Flip and continue to broil until skins are just beginning to blister on second side, about 3 minutes longer. Let poblanos rest on sheet until cool enough to handle, about 10 minutes. Adjust oven to 200 degrees.

3. Peel off any loose skin from poblanos, if desired. Working with 1 poblano at a time, leaving stem intact and starting at top, make 3-inch-long vertical incision down 1 side of chile. Use scissors to cut away interior seed bulb, then use spoon to scoop out and discard bulb and seeds. (Some tearing may occur and is OK.)

4. Place 2 Muenster cubes inside each poblano. Overlap poblano opening and thread with skewer to seal. (Use 1 additional skewer per poblano if necessary.) Allow top of skewer to remain exposed by at least ½ inch for easy removal.

5. Place ½ cup flour in shallow dish. Combine remaining 1 cup flour, cornstarch, baking powder, and 1 teaspoon salt in medium bowl. Whisk lager into flour mixture until smooth.

6. Set wire rack in rimmed baking sheet and line rack with triple layer of paper towels. Add oil to large Dutch oven until it measures 2 inches deep and heat over medium-high heat to 375 degrees.

7. Working with three poblanos at a time, dredge in flour, shaking gently to remove excess. Holding each poblano by its stem, dunk in batter to evenly coat and then transfer to hot oil. Fry until golden and crispy, 4 to 5 minutes, turning frequently for even cooking. Adjust burner, if necessary, to maintain oil temperature between 350 and 375 degrees.

8. Transfer fried poblanos to prepared wire rack and let drain for 30 seconds. Season poblanos with salt, remove skewers, and transfer sheet to oven to keep poblanos warm. Return oil to 375 degrees and repeat with remaining poblanos and batter. Serve with sauce.

TO MAKE AHEAD: The poblanos can be broiled, seeded, and stuffed 24 hours in advance. The sauce can be made 2 days in advance and microwaved for 2 minutes until hot just before serving.

CHEESY CORN CASSEROLE

✓ **WHY THIS RECIPE WORKS:** With a texture falling somewhere between cornbread and creamed corn, this Southern and Midwestern holiday favorite usually relies on two convenience items: corn muffin mix and canned creamed corn. We wanted to revive this dish while still keeping it simple. First off, to control the casserole's sweetness, we ditched the muffin mix in favor of a pared-down blend of flour, cornmeal, and baking powder. Substituting frozen corn kernels for canned creamed corn yielded a far more fresh-tasting casserole, and pulsing half of the defrosted kernels in a food processor released extra corn flavor while also mimicking the lush texture of creamed corn. Scallions, cayenne pepper, and a mix of two cheeses— Monterey Jack and Parmesan—amped up the flavor.

Cheesy corn casserole is beloved in the South and Midwest, and its sweet corn flavor and impossibly easy prep have made it a holiday staple for generations. Most recipes involve stirring together corn muffin mix, canned creamed corn, canned corn kernels, sour cream, cheese, and eggs. You just dump it into a casserole dish and bake.

Sound too good to be true? It is. The worst of the handful of existing recipes I tried didn't even justify this minimal effort. They ranged from goopy to greasy and from appallingly bland to unappealingly dense. I knew this dish could do with a test kitchen makeover. I envisioned something substantial but light, with sweet corn and savory cheese flavors. Prefab corn muffin mixes are good in a pinch but they also make for an overly sweet casserole. Instead, I made a more savory from-scratch version, stirring together flour, cornmeal, and baking powder—definitely worth the 2 minutes it took to put together. I also ditched the canned corn kernels and creamed corn, which rarely have any flavor and are reliably mushy. Instead I turned to frozen kernels.

Pulsing half of them in the food processor released even more of their flavor and helped mimic the texture of creamed corn.

To these ingredients I added sour cream and a hefty dose of shredded cheddar. I stirred it all together and put it in the oven.

While the result was a substantive improvement, I found that the delicate corn was being drowned out by the cheddar. American cheese left me with the opposite problem: It was too mild. After casting about, I landed on a combination of Monterey Jack and Parmesan. Monterey Jack melts like a dream and gave me the creaminess I wanted, while the Parmesan added deep, nutty cheese flavor without becoming overwhelming. A colleague suggested cutting some of the Monterey Jack into cubes instead of shredding all of it to create excellent gooey cheese pockets throughout.

My casserole, though tasty, needed one more note. I gave it two: a little cayenne for heat and some scallions (white parts processed into the corn, green parts scattered on top) for bite. "A-maize-ing," one colleague joked. Talk about cheesy.

—MORGAN BOLLING, *Cook's Country*

Cheesy Corn Casserole

SERVES 8 TO 10

Two pounds of fresh corn kernels (from about eight cobs) can be substituted for the frozen corn.

- 8 ounces Monterey Jack cheese
- ½ cup (2½ ounces) all-purpose flour
- ⅓ cup (1⅔ ounces) cornmeal
- 2 teaspoons baking powder
- 1 teaspoon salt
- ¼ teaspoon pepper
- ¼ teaspoon cayenne pepper
- 2 pounds frozen corn, thawed
- 4 scallions, white and green parts separated and sliced thin
- 1 cup sour cream
- 1 ounce Parmesan cheese, grated (½ cup)
- 2 large eggs, lightly beaten
- 4 tablespoons unsalted butter, melted

1. Adjust oven rack to middle position and heat oven to 350 degrees. Grease 13 by 9-inch baking dish. Cut half of Monterey Jack into ½-inch cubes. Shred remaining half of Monterey Jack on large holes of box grater; set aside. Whisk flour, cornmeal, baking powder, salt, pepper, and cayenne together in large bowl.

2. Pulse half of corn and scallion whites in food processor to coarse puree, about 10 pulses. Stir pureed corn mixture into flour mixture. Stir in sour cream, ¼ cup Parmesan, eggs, melted butter, remaining half of corn, and cubed Monterey Jack until combined. Transfer mixture to prepared baking dish. Sprinkle with shredded Monterey Jack and remaining ¼ cup Parmesan.

3. Bake until casserole is slightly puffy and cheese is golden brown, 45 to 50 minutes. Transfer casserole to wire rack and let cool for 10 minutes. Sprinkle with scallion greens and serve.

VARIATION

Cheesy Corn Casserole with Jalapeños and Cilantro

Add ¼ cup minced pickled jalapeños to batter in step 2. Sprinkle with 2 tablespoons chopped fresh cilantro before serving.

NOTES FROM THE TEST KITCHEN

REVAMPING A PREFAB FAVORITE

Most memories of this rib-sticking classic are of bland, stodgy versions made with supermarket corn muffin mix and cans of creamed corn; when we cooked a handful of those versions we were totally unimpressed. To achieve a cleaner, more contemporary take, we ditched the corn muffin mix and canned corn and turned to frozen corn kernels, tangy sour cream, Monterey Jack cheese (cut into cubes for melty pockets inside and shredded for full coverage on top), nutty and flavorful grated Parmesan, and vibrant scallion greens and whites.

SOURDOUGH DRESSING

✓ **WHY THIS RECIPE WORKS:** We wanted to take an unconventional route for this holiday stuffing, opting for tangy, chewy sourdough bread as its base. Meaty shiitake mushrooms, chopped kale, sausage, sage, and golden raisins balanced out the bread's assertive flavor. To simplify the cooking, we roasted the vegetables and sausage in the oven while we toasted the bread into croutons. Then we tossed the lot with just enough broth and eggs to keep it moist and cohesive. Dotting the top of the casserole with butter and leaving it uncovered for the last 15 minutes of baking created a crisp, beautifully browned top.

Ordinary white sandwich bread gets its yearly brush with greatness in holiday dressing, coming to life when toasted and tossed with a savory mix of melted butter, onion, celery, and herbs. But what if I ditched the white bread in favor of complex, tangy sourdough?

I wasn't surprised to find several recipes for sourdough dressing in cookbooks from sourdough's home turf, California. What was unexpected, though, was their use of extra-flavorful vegetables like turnips and kale, presumably to stand up to the sourdough. I was inspired and headed into the kitchen right away.

The usual process for dressing is pretty simple. You first dry out cubed bread in the oven so the cubes can soak up the liquid without turning to mush. Next, you sauté onion and garlic with herbs and butter on the stovetop. Finally, you combine it all with a binder—broth, eggs, or a creamy custard—before baking in a casserole dish.

But since I was already tossing convention to the wind by exiling the white bread, why should I be tied to the usual process? I decided to roast my vegetables (including the onion and garlic) on a rimmed baking sheet rather than sauté them on the stovetop, since I could then toast up the bread simultaneously. I also auditioned a long list of vegetables. Though I liked the way sweet root vegetables like carrots and parsnips balanced the sour bread's tang, they took too long to cook. Meaty shiitake mushrooms and chopped curly kale, however, were a good fit in both flavor and texture—and they cooked perfectly in my allotted time.

The result was promising, but a bit wimpy. To give the dish some more muscle, I topped the tray of vegetables with small pieces of Italian sausage. As the sausage cooked, its fat rendered into the vegetables.

A few plumped golden raisins added after roasting contributed little bursts of sweetness and, in a nod to a more traditional Thanksgiving flavor profile, I kept sage and chopped onion in play.

After tossing the roasted vegetables and dried bread with chicken broth and three eggs, I scooped the dressing into a buttered casserole dish. I covered it with foil and baked it on the lower-middle rack for 15 minutes to brown the bottom and then removed the foil for the final 15 minutes needed to crisp the top. Dotting the top with butter ensured some nice brown bits.

Loaded top to bottom with savory, off-the-beaten-path flavors, my sourdough dressing was guaranteed to make a great first impression this Thanksgiving, and for years to come.

—CHRISTIE MORRISON, *Cook's Country*

Sourdough Dressing with Kale and Mushrooms

SERVES 8 TO 10

For a meatless variation, omit the sausage and use vegetarian broth. You will need two rimmed baking sheets for this recipe.

- 3½ tablespoons unsalted butter
- ½ cup golden raisins
- ½ cup water
- 1½ pounds sourdough bread, cut into 1-inch pieces
- ½ cup extra-virgin olive oil
  - Salt and pepper
- 12 ounces shiitake mushrooms, stemmed and sliced ¼ inch thick
- 8 ounces kale, stemmed and chopped coarse
- 1 onion, chopped
- 5 garlic cloves, smashed and peeled
- 2 tablespoons minced fresh sage
- 8 ounces sweet Italian sausage, casings removed
- 2½ cups chicken broth
- 3 large eggs, lightly beaten

1. Adjust oven racks to upper-middle and lower-middle positions and heat oven to 400 degrees. Grease 13 by 9-inch baking dish with 1 tablespoon butter. Grease one 15 by 11-inch sheet of aluminum foil with ½ tablespoon butter. Combine raisins and water in bowl and microwave for 30 seconds. Set aside and let raisins soften for at least 15 minutes; drain.

SOURDOUGH DRESSING WITH KALE AND MUSHROOMS

2. Meanwhile, toss bread, ¼ cup oil, and ½ teaspoon salt together in large bowl; spread evenly on rimmed baking sheet. Combine mushrooms, kale, onion, garlic, sage, remaining ¼ cup oil, ½ teaspoon salt, and ½ teaspoon pepper in now-empty bowl; spread on second rimmed baking sheet. Break sausage into ½-inch pieces and distribute evenly over vegetables.

3. Bake bread mixture on upper rack and vegetable mixture on lower rack until bread is golden brown but still tender inside and vegetables and sausage are golden, about 30 minutes, stirring halfway through baking. Transfer sheets to wire racks and let cool slightly, about 10 minutes. Combine toasted bread and vegetable mixture in large bowl.

4. Stir broth, eggs, and drained raisins into bread-vegetable mixture until liquid is absorbed. Transfer dressing to prepared dish. Cut remaining 2 tablespoons butter into ¼-inch pieces and sprinkle evenly over dressing. Cover tightly with prepared foil.

5. Bake dressing on lower rack for 15 minutes. Uncover and continue to bake until top is golden and crisp, about 15 minutes longer. Let cool for 10 minutes before serving.

TO MAKE AHEAD: Dressing can be made through step 4 and refrigerated for up to 24 hours. Increase covered baking time by 5 minutes.

BEST BAKED POTATOES

✓ WHY THIS RECIPE WORKS: To produce perfect baked potatoes—spuds with a fluffy interior, crispy skin, and even seasoning—we eliminated the usual guesswork in favor of a more precise approach. For starters, our tests pointed us to the ideal doneness temperature: 205 degrees. Baking russet potatoes in a hot (450-degree) oven prevented a leathery ring from forming underneath the peel, and taking the potato's temperature with an instant-read thermometer ensured we hit the 205-degree sweet spot every time. Coating the potatoes in salty water before baking was all the effort required to season the skin; brushing on vegetable oil once the potatoes were cooked through and then baking the potatoes for an additional 10 minutes promised the crispest skin possible. Potatoes this good deserve an accompaniment, so we came up with some simple but sophisticated toppings to serve with them.

Baking a potato is about as basic as cooking gets—so basic, in fact, that it doesn't even seem to require a recipe. Simply stick a russet in a moderately hot oven directly on the rack, and after about an hour, give it a squeeze. If it's still firm, bake it longer; if it gives to pressure, it's done.

The beauty of that method is its simplicity, but how often does it produce a truly great baked potato? In my experience, almost never. Whether the center is dense and gummy or the skin is soggy, shriveled, or chewy, the best I can do is slather on as much butter or sour cream as possible to cover up the flaws.

I wanted more from a baked potato than a dense or desiccated log of starch, and I was determined to examine every variable to nail down ideal results. That meant a fluffy interior encased in thin, crisp skin.

Russets are the classic choice for baked potatoes because they're a dry, floury variety, meaning they contain a relatively high amount (20 to 22 percent) of starch. (So-called in-between varieties like Yukon Golds, or waxy types like Red Bliss, contain 16 to 18 percent and about 16 percent starch, respectively.) The more starch a potato contains, the more water from inside the potato can be absorbed during baking. As the starch granules swell with water, they eventually force the cells to separate into clumps that result in the texture we perceive as dry and fluffy.

But when exactly does a potato reach that dry and fluffy stage—the point at which it is done? Taking a closer look at the bake-until-it's-squeezable approach would at least give me a baseline temperature to work from, so I pricked an 8-ounce russet a few times with a fork and placed it in a 400-degree oven. Once the exterior had softened, I cut slits to open up the potato and stuck an instant-read thermometer in several places. The outer ½ inch or so, which was soft enough to squeeze but not quite fluffy, registered 195 degrees, while the dense core, which was clearly underdone, was 175 degrees. From there, I baked off several more potatoes, placing probes at exterior points in each and removing them from the oven at different temperatures. At 200 degrees the outer edge was light and fluffy, while the core was just tender, but at 205 degrees the whites of the potatoes were at their best: fluffy from edge to center. A few more tests revealed that the method was somewhat forgiving; I could bake the potatoes as high as 212 degrees and still achieve perfectly light and fluffy results. The only hitch, I discovered, was that it was crucial to cut the potatoes open immediately after baking to let steam escape; if they sat for even 10 minutes, they retained more water than potatoes that were opened immediately and turned dense and gummy.

Now that I knew exactly when the potato was cooked through, I wanted to see how fast I could get it there. Microwaving the potatoes would surely speed up the cooking, I assumed. But further tests proved that this was actually the worst approach. Whether I used the microwave alone or in tandem with the oven, the potatoes always cooked unevenly and were often gummy and dense. Why? Because microwaves heat potatoes very unevenly, rendering some portions fully cooked while others are still rock hard. Back to the oven. The potatoes took between 60 and 80 minutes to cook through at 400 degrees, so I hoped that cranking the heat up to 500 would hasten things. Unfortunately, this caused the outer portion of the potato to overbrown and almost char in spots, leading to a slightly burned flavor. Going forward, I turned the oven temperature

NOTES FROM THE TEST KITCHEN

FINDING THE BEST—AND QUICKEST—WAY TO BAKE A POTATO
We found that if a baked potato reached between 205 and 212 degrees, the interior was uniformly fluffy—just the way we like it. The question was how quickly we could achieve that texture and if we could crisp the skin, too.

HOW FAST CAN WE COOK IT?

METHOD: Microwave for 6 minutes.

RESULT: Uneven cooking; gummy, stodgy interior; shriveled skin.

METHOD: Pressure-cook for 40 minutes.

RESULT: Fluffy inside, soggy skin; not much time savings.

METHOD: Bake at 500 degrees for 40 minutes.

RESULT: Overbrowned and slightly charred exterior; burned flavor.

SOLUTION: Bake at 450 degrees for 45 to 60 minutes—the sweet spot for evenly cooked potatoes.

WHAT IS THE BEST WAY TO CRISP THE SKIN?

METHOD: Deep-fry fully baked potato.

RESULT: Nicely crisped skin; too much work.

METHOD: Butter skin.

RESULT: Water in butter keeps skin from crisping.

METHOD: Oil skin before baking.

RESULT: Oil keeps moisture in skin from evaporating; soggy texture.

SOLUTION: Oil skin when almost done. Skin dehydrates during baking, then crisps in oil.

down notch by notch and eventually found 450 degrees for 45 minutes or so to be the sweet spot—the interior was soft and light, the skin nicely browned. Now I just had to see about crisping it up.

Since frying potatoes in oil crisps and browns their exteriors, I hoped that coating the russets' skin with oil might do the same as they baked. But as it turned out, painting the spuds with vegetable oil (1 tablespoon coated four potatoes nicely) and then baking them yielded disappointingly soft and chewy skins. The problem was that the oil created a barrier on the skin's exterior that prevented moisture from escaping, so the skins weren't able to dry out and crisp.

The better method was to apply the oil once the potatoes were cooked, by which point the skins had dehydrated considerably. Returning them to the oven for 10 more minutes rendered them deep brown and crisp (the extra time increases the interior temperature of the potatoes by just 2 or 3 degrees).

I was very pleased with my method, which really wasn't much more work than baking a potato without a recipe. But one variable lingered: seasoning. Sure, I'd sprinkle salt and pepper on the potato at the table, but what I really wanted was even seasoning all over. My first attempt, brining the potatoes for 1 hour before baking, delivered skins with fantastic flavor, but did I really have to add that much more time to the method? Instead, I tried simply wetting the raw potatoes and sprinkling them with salt—and when that failed (the salt crystals didn't stick), I simply dunked the potatoes in salty water. The flavor was just as full and even as that of the brined potatoes, but this step added mere seconds to my recipe. The last tweak I made, baking the potatoes on a rack set in a rimmed baking sheet, prevented drips of salt and water from staining the bottom of my oven and allowed the hot air to circulate evenly around the potatoes during baking.

Crisp and thoroughly seasoned on the outside and light and fluffy within, my baked potatoes were perfect as-is, though nobody disagreed that a pat of butter or sour cream was in order. And for the times when I wanted a real showstopper of a side dish (or even a main course with a salad), I put together a few simple toppings that could be made while the potatoes baked. Topped with a creamy egg salad–like mixture, herbed goat cheese, or smoked trout, these spuds were an unqualified hit at the dinner table.

—LAN LAM, *Cook's Illustrated*

NOTES FROM THE TEST KITCHEN

A SQUEEZE WON'T SUFFICE

It might sound fussy to take the temperature of a baked potato, but it's the only way to guarantee that you're getting a uniformly fluffy interior. The usual approach to checking for doneness by squeezing the potato doesn't work because while the outer edge might feel soft, the center can still be dense and firm. This cross section shows how different the texture (and temperature) can be from the surface to the center.

SOFT
195 degrees

FIRM
175 degrees

Best Baked Potatoes
SERVES 4

Open up the potatoes immediately after removal from the oven in step 3 so steam can escape. Top them as desired, or with one of our toppings (recipes follow).

> Salt and pepper
> 4 (7- to 9-ounce) russet potatoes, unpeeled, each lightly pricked with fork in 6 places
> 1 tablespoon vegetable oil

1. Adjust oven rack to middle position and heat oven to 450 degrees. Dissolve 2 tablespoons salt in ½ cup water in large bowl. Place potatoes in bowl and toss so exteriors of potatoes are evenly moistened. Transfer potatoes to wire rack set in rimmed baking sheet and bake until center of largest potato registers 205 degrees, 45 minutes to 1 hour.

2. Remove potatoes from oven and brush tops and sides with oil. Return potatoes to oven and continue to bake for 10 minutes.

3. Remove potatoes from oven and, using paring knife, make 2 slits, forming X, in each potato. Using clean dish towel, hold ends and squeeze slightly to push flesh up and out. Season with salt and pepper to taste. Serve immediately.

Creamy Egg Topping

MAKES 1 CUP

3	hard-cooked large eggs, chopped
¼	cup sour cream
1½	tablespoons minced cornichons
1	tablespoon minced fresh parsley
1	tablespoon Dijon mustard
1	tablespoon capers, rinsed and minced
1	tablespoon minced shallot
	Salt and pepper

Stir all ingredients together and season with salt and pepper to taste.

Herbed Goat Cheese Topping

MAKES ¾ CUP

4	ounces goat cheese, softened
2	tablespoons extra-virgin olive oil
2	tablespoons minced fresh parsley
1	tablespoon minced shallot
½	teaspoon grated lemon zest
	Salt and pepper

Mash goat cheese with fork. Stir in oil, parsley, shallot, and lemon zest. Season with salt and pepper to taste.

Smoked Trout Topping

MAKES 1 CUP

We prefer trout for this recipe, but any hot-smoked fish, such as salmon or bluefish, may be substituted.

5	ounces smoked trout, chopped
⅓	cup crème fraîche
2	tablespoons minced fresh chives
4	teaspoons minced shallot
1¼	teaspoons grated lemon zest
¾	teaspoon lemon juice
	Salt and pepper

Stir all ingredients together and season with salt and pepper to taste.

CANDIED SWEET POTATOES

✔ **WHY THIS RECIPE WORKS:** For candied sweet potatoes that wouldn't cause a toothache, we decided to keep this rustic side simple. Peeling and cutting sweet potatoes into ¾-inch rounds promised an even, soft texture. We tossed them in oil to promote browning and roasted them on a baking sheet. While the potatoes browned in the oven, we stirred together a mellow, sweet glaze, cutting maple syrup with some water to prevent it from overshadowing the potatoes' natural sweetness. A bit of cornstarch gave the glaze a clingy texture and briefly heating it thickened it up nicely. To ensure easy, mess-free serving, we transferred the sweet potatoes to a baking dish, arranging the rounds with the unbrowned sides facing up. We poured the glaze over the potatoes and finished them in the oven. Our candied sweet potatoes emerged beautifully browned and coated in a perfectly sweet glaze.

Candied sweet potatoes are a classic autumn side dish, but too often they border on dessert territory, clobbering you with sweetness (hello, marshmallows) and totally shortchanging the sweet potato's deep, earthy flavor. I set out to reclaim the pure flavors in this dish with a simple, balanced take in which the "candy" would provide a sweetly delicate counterpoint to the sweet potatoes.

I started with a handful of recipes found in our cookbook library, many of which called for baking or boiling whole sweet potatoes before slicing and glazing them—and then baking them again. And for all the work involved, too many of these recipes yielded mushy sweet potatoes cloaked in sticky, tooth-rattling syrups. Where was the subtle flavor of the potatoes themselves?

But these initial tests did make a number of things clear. For one thing, I learned that cutting the sweet potatoes too thin inevitably resulted in mush, but cutting them carefully into ¾-inch-thick rounds produced a soft texture that still held together. I also learned that roasting the cut pieces in a single layer on a rimmed baking sheet and then flipping them before glazing them and finishing them off produced attractively browned edges. Finally, I found that slathering the partially cooked sweet potato pieces with syrup for the last stretch of oven time gave them a richer flavor with a clingy glaze.

I tried out a long list of glaze flavors to see what would best complement the sweet potatoes without covering them up. I wanted sweetness, but it had to stay in balance. Tangy apple cider was too overpowering, whereas orange juice was distracting, too specifically citrusy. Brown sugar and warm holiday spices were too reminiscent of sweet potato pie and, of course, marshmallows were out.

Maple syrup and butter were the most promising, providing a woodsy sweetness and always-welcome butteriness, but the combo can be overly rich; I needed something to temper and restrain them. The fix? Water, the most neutral ingredient in the world. Cutting the maple syrup with an equal amount of water lightened the load without hijacking the flavor, and stirring in cornstarch helped absorb any unwanted wetness. While the spuds roasted, I simply combined the glaze ingredients in a saucepan and briefly boiled them to thicken up.

One last detail to smooth out: a neat appearance. Transferring the glazed sweet potatoes from the baking sheet to a serving dish made for a messy finish—potatoes fell apart as I was transferring them, leaving me with what resembled a mash. Though this is a dish of rustic flavors, it deserved an elegant presentation.

Since I was going into the oven to flip the sweet potatoes as soon as they'd browned on one side, why not flip them into a table-friendly, ovensafe baking dish? I arranged the medallions, added the glaze, and returned the sweet potatoes to the oven to finish. Glossy, glazy, earthy, rich, and just sweet enough—this was a holiday side dish to be proud of.

—CECELIA JENKINS, *Cook's Country*

NOTES FROM THE TEST KITCHEN

A BROILER-READY BAKING DISH

Our Candied Sweet Potatoes finish in a hot oven, so we needed an ovensafe dish that was up to the task. Lightweight and fitted with handles for safe maneuvering, the HIC Porcelain Lasagna Baking Dish is ideal for recipes that require high heat.

Candied Sweet Potatoes

SERVES 6 TO 8

Whisk the syrup frequently to keep it from boiling over. A broiler-safe dish (not Pyrex) is important because of the high heat.

- 3 pounds sweet potatoes, peeled, ends trimmed, and sliced ¾ inch thick
- 2 tablespoons vegetable oil
-    Salt and pepper
- ½ cup maple syrup
- ½ cup water
- 4 tablespoons unsalted butter
- 1 teaspoon cornstarch

1. Adjust oven rack to lowest position and heat oven to 450 degrees. Toss potatoes, oil, and 1 teaspoon salt together in bowl. Evenly space potatoes in single layer on rimmed baking sheet. Bake until potatoes are tender and dark brown on bottom, 18 to 22 minutes, rotating sheet halfway through baking.

2. Meanwhile, combine maple syrup, water, butter, cornstarch, and ⅛ teaspoon salt in small saucepan. Bring to boil over medium-high heat and cook, whisking frequently, until thickened and reduced to 1 cup, 3 to 5 minutes.

3. Place potatoes in broiler-safe 13 by 9-inch baking dish, browned side up, shingling as necessary if you have larger potatoes. Pour syrup mixture over potatoes and bake until bubbling around sides of dish, 8 to 10 minutes. Transfer dish to wire rack and let cool for 10 minutes. Season with pepper to taste. Serve.

TO MAKE AHEAD: Potatoes and syrup can be prepared through step 2, placed in baking dish, and kept at room temperature for up to 2 hours. In step 3, extend the baking time to 11 to 13 minutes.

CANDIED SWEET POTATOES

PERSIAN-STYLE RICE WITH GOLDEN CRUST (CHELOW)

PERSIAN-STYLE RICE WITH GOLDEN CRUST

✔ **WHY THIS RECIPE WORKS:** *Chelow* is a classic Iranian dish that marries fluffy rice pilaf with a golden-brown, crispy crust (known as *tahdig*). We found that rinsing the rice and then soaking it for 15 minutes in hot salted water was just as effective as the traditional 24-hour cold water soak in producing fluffy grains. Parboiling the rice and then steaming it to finish cooking was also essential to creating the best texture for the pilaf and the perfect crust. Steaming the grains for 30 minutes rather than the traditional hour was enough; we also wrapped the lid with a towel to absorb extra moisture and ensure fluffiness. Combining a portion of the rice with thick Greek yogurt and oil created a nicely browned, flavorful crust, while chunks of butter added during steaming enriched the pilaf portion. The yogurt also made the tahdig easier to remove from the pot, as did brushing the bottom of the pot with a little extra oil and letting the pot rest on a damp towel after cooking. Adding cumin seeds and parsley to the dish made for a more interesting and well-rounded flavor.

To Americans, rice is an everyday side dish made with minimal fuss. But for Iranians, a rice pilaf known as *chelow* ("CHEH-lo") is one of the most important dishes in their cuisine. What makes the dish so good is contrast: a marriage of unusually light and fluffy grains with a golden-brown, crispy crust that's so buttery, you can't help but go back for more. It's a showpiece pilaf.

The trade-off has always been the effort involved, as most shortcut recipes yield gummy, overcooked rice and pale, flavorless crusts. The best versions I've made call for rinsing the rice before soaking it for 24 hours, parboiling it, packing some of the rice down in hot oil to make a crust, and mounding the rest on top. The whole thing is then steamed for over an hour before being turned out onto a platter.

My goal was a middle-ground approach, where I'd streamline the best versions without sacrificing the pilaf's defining qualities.

Traditional recipes call for Persian rice, which isn't readily available in the United States, so nutty and aromatic long-grain basmati rice is the usual substitute. As for the cooking vessel, since the size of the pot's base determines the size of the crust and I wanted plenty to go around, I grabbed a large, wide Dutch oven.

I started by focusing on the pilaf portion of the rice—specifically, the rinsing and soaking steps. Starch granules are the primary component of rice; as the granules absorb water during cooking, they swell and can eventually burst, releasing gummy starch molecules that glue the grains together. Rinsing is a must to remove excess surface starch that would otherwise swell and burst. Soaking, meanwhile, helps hydrate the grains before cooking. But was it necessary here? A quick test comparing rice that was rinsed and then soaked for 24 hours with rice that was only rinsed confirmed that both rinsing and soaking yielded fluffier pilaf with more separate grains. After a few more tests and some analysis, I determined that a 15-minute bath in hot tap water provided almost as much hydration as a 24-hour soak—the grains' presoak weight increased by 25 percent and 29 percent respectively. Taste tests confirmed that there was little difference; a 15-minute hot soak and a 24-hour room-temperature soak produced grains that were equally fluffy and individual. I also discovered that adding salt to the water seasoned the grains for better flavor.

Besides the two-step prep process, the recipes from my research called for a two-stage cooking process: The rice is first parboiled in plenty of water and then drained and steamed in a well oiled pot. Eliminating the parboiling step wasn't an option, since the rice is steamed in too little water for the grains to cook fully and evenly. But accurately timing the parboiling step proved critical. I found that I needed to start timing from the moment I added the rice to the water. Thanks to the jump start that soaking had given the rice, it needed only 3 to 5 minutes in the pot to reach al dente. I also found that transferring the rice to a strainer and rinsing it under cool water before moving on to the steaming step helped avoid overcooking.

The second cooking stage is really a hybrid of steaming and frying. Recipes call for adding fat (I opted for oil) to the empty pot, packing in a layer of rice for the crust, and then adding the rest of the rice and drizzling it with water. After an initial blast of high heat to jump-start the crust formation, I reduced the heat and let the rice steam. In Iran, a special cloth "shower cap" is wrapped around the lid to pull excess moisture from the rice as it steams. The test kitchen does a similar thing with rice pilaf—we place a dish towel under the lid after cooking to absorb moisture—so I knew that a step like this would be worth it. Some recipes note that the longer the rice is steamed, the drier and fluffier the grains will be, but I found that 30 minutes did the trick—longer stints made a nominal difference. The pilaf portion of the rice was the fluffiest I'd ever made, so now I could move on to the crust, or *tahdig* ("ta-DEEG"), which needed some work.

I wanted a tahdig that was deep golden brown, with a crunchy—but not tough—texture and a rich, nutty, buttery, toasted flavor. But my results tasted somewhat lean and bland, the grains cooked a bit unevenly, and I also had some problems getting it out of the pot. I knew how to fix the uneven cooking problem. When packing the rice into the pot, the grains inevitably started cooking as soon as they hit the hot oil. So I moved the operation off the heat. I stirred the oil and rice together in a bowl, packed the mixture into the pot off the heat, and only then moved it onto the stove.

Some recipes called for mixing beaten egg or plain yogurt into the rice before spreading it into the pot to both enrich the flavor and bind the grains to help the crust come out more easily. The egg's flavor was a bit too distinct, but Greek yogurt added richness without identifying itself. What's more, the proteins in the yogurt helped facilitate browning for improved flavor.

But the crust was still not exactly easy to get out of the pot. Brushing a tablespoon of oil on the sides and bottom of the pot was helpful in this regard but still not perfect. In the end, tradition had the answer: Set the pot on a dampened dish towel or dip it into cool water after the rice finishes cooking. The rapid cooling causes the rice grains to contract, helping the crust release more easily. It seemed easier to let the pot sit on a damp towel, so I went with that approach. Just 5 minutes was all it took to get the rice to slip easily out of the Dutch oven with the help of a spatula.

Once the rice is cooked, some cooks flip the whole dish onto a platter. While this can look impressive, it's tricky to pull off. I found it much easier to scoop the rice onto a platter, use a thin metal spatula to break the crust into shards as I removed it from the pot, and then arrange the crispy pieces around the pilaf.

For my last tweak to the process, I considered how I'd been putting the parboiled rice back in the pot. After packing down the rice for the crust, traditional recipes call for mounding the remainder in a pyramid shape on top. Was this really necessary? As it turned out, yes. When I simply poured the rice into the pot and spread it out evenly, steam couldn't escape from the bottom of the pot as easily, and the crust cooked up chewy instead of crispy.

Both the pilaf portion and the crust looked impressive, and the flavor was close but needed a few tweaks. Some recipes call for pouring oil over the rice for enrichment, but I followed the lead of recipes that opted to use butter, poking holes into the mounded rice and inserting bits of butter into them. This added the flavor and richness the rice needed. (The water in the butter contributed a little extra steaming power, too.) For more complexity, I looked to the spice rack. Many recipes call for saffron, but I was satisfied with simple (and more affordable) whole cumin seeds, which added a distinct earthiness. Finally, some chopped parsley lent fresh, bright flavor and color.

The light, fluffy rice and golden, buttery shards of crust were a huge hit, immediately winning over those who weren't familiar with the dish. When I'm serving rice and want to impress, this is the recipe I'll turn to.

—ANNIE PETITO, *Cook's Illustrated*

Persian-Style Rice with Golden Crust (Chelow)

SERVES 6

We prefer the nutty flavor and texture of basmati rice, but Texmati or another long-grain rice will work. For the best results, use a Dutch oven with a bottom diameter between 8½ and 10 inches. It is important not to overcook the rice during the parboiling step, as it will continue to cook during steaming. Begin checking the rice at the lower end of the given time range. Do not skip placing the pot on a damp towel in step 7—doing so will help free the crust from the pot. Serve this pilaf alongside stews or kebabs.

2 **cups basmati rice**

  Salt

1 **tablespoon plus ¼ cup vegetable oil**

¼ **cup plain Greek yogurt**

1½ **teaspoons cumin seeds**

2 **tablespoons unsalted butter, cut into 8 cubes**

¼ **cup minced fresh parsley**

1. Place rice in fine-mesh strainer and rinse under cold running water until water runs clear. Place rinsed rice and 1 tablespoon salt in medium bowl and cover with 4 cups hot tap water. Stir gently to dissolve salt; let stand for 15 minutes. Drain rice in fine-mesh strainer.

2. Meanwhile, bring 8 cups water to boil in Dutch oven over high heat. Add rice and 2 tablespoons salt. Boil briskly, stirring frequently, until rice is mostly tender with slight bite in center and grains are floating toward top of pot, 3 to 5 minutes (begin timing from when rice is added to pot).

3. Drain rice in large fine-mesh strainer and rinse with cold water to stop cooking, about 30 seconds. Rinse and dry pot well to remove any residual starch. Brush bottom and 1 inch up sides of pot with 1 tablespoon oil.

4. Whisk remaining ¼ cup oil, yogurt, 1 teaspoon cumin seeds, and ¼ teaspoon salt together in medium bowl. Add 2 cups parcooked rice and stir until combined. Spread yogurt-rice mixture evenly over bottom of prepared pot, packing it down well.

5. Stir remaining ½ teaspoon cumin seeds into remaining rice. Mound rice in center of pot on top of yogurt-rice base (it should look like small hill). Poke 8 equally spaced holes through rice mound but not into yogurt-rice base. Place 1 butter cube into each hole. Drizzle ⅓ cup water over rice mound.

6. Wrap pot lid with clean dish towel and cover pot tightly, making sure towel is secure on top of lid and away from heat. Cook over medium-high heat until rice on bottom is crackling and steam is coming from sides of pot, about 10 minutes, rotating pot halfway through for even cooking.

7. Reduce heat to medium-low and continue to cook until rice is tender and fluffy and crust is golden brown around edges, 30 to 35 minutes longer. Remove covered pot from heat and place on wet kitchen towel set in rimmed baking sheet; let stand for 5 minutes.

8. Stir 2 tablespoons parsley into rice, making sure not to disturb crust on bottom of pot, and season with salt to taste. Gently spoon rice onto serving platter.

9. Using thin metal spatula, loosen edges of crust from pot, then break crust into large pieces. Transfer pieces to serving platter, arranging evenly around rice. Sprinkle with remaining 2 tablespoons parsley and serve.

A BLUEPRINT FOR THE BEST RICE YOU'LL EVER EAT

GREASED POT: Helps with crust removal.

PACKED RICE LAYER: Creates evenly browned, crispy crust.

MOUNDED RICE: Allows steam to escape so rice crust beneath cooks up crispy, not soggy.

POCKETS OF BUTTER: Add flavor and more steam during cooking for even fluffier rice.

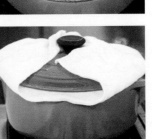

TOWEL-WRAPPED LID: Absorbs excess moisture for fluffy, not gummy, rice.

DAMP TOWEL: Makes grains contract to help tahdig release from pot.

CHAPTER 4

PASTA, PIZZA, SANDWICHES, AND MORE

PENNE ARRABBIATA

PENNE ARRABBIATA

✔ **WHY THIS RECIPE WORKS:** The fiery Italian pasta sauce known as *arrabbiata* should be complexly flavored, but many recipes rely on one-dimensional heat. To make sure ours had plenty of character, we started off the sauce with convenient canned tomatoes, pulsing them into a chunky puree. We looked beyond the standard practice of using only red pepper flakes and instead crafted a recipe with three forms of peppery flavor. We supplemented the flakes with paprika and pickled pepperoncini, adding depth while keeping the spiciness in check. Pecorino Romano, tomato paste, and anchovies, while difficult to detect in the sauce, added welcome umami notes and richness. Penne's tubular shape paired perfectly with this chunky sauce, and a sprinkling of extra Pecorino Romano gave this dish an authentic, rich finish.

Arrabbiata means "angry" in Italian, and one taste of this pasta sauce will confirm that it was aptly named. The simplest versions blend tomatoes, garlic, olive oil, and red pepper flakes to create the dish's signature fiery kick. While I appreciate simplicity, this template produces a thin, one-trick sauce dominated by mouth-searing heat. Recipes that look beyond this short ingredient list—to additions like onion, fresh hot chiles, tomato paste, fresh herbs, and grated cheese—seemed much more promising. After all, heat is much more enticing when it's one element of a more complex dish and not the sole attraction. Crafting a better version of this classic would require enhancing its body and boosting its complexity and depth of flavor while being careful to maintain the vibrancy and peppery kick that are its hallmarks.

I began with the tomatoes. Fresh tomatoes were a popular choice among the recipes I found, but given that this dish is a great cold-weather meal, I eliminated them from the running. Diced canned tomatoes didn't break down enough to thicken the sauce, and crushed tomatoes tasted overcooked. In the end, whole canned tomatoes had the brightest flavor. A few pulses in the food processor broke them down just enough.

Next, I focused on enhancing the savory depth and complexity of my arrabbiata. Dried oregano, though ubiquitous in Italian cooking, made the sauce taste like it came from a jar, so it was out. Fresh parsley and basil didn't add enough to warrant their purchase, and the texture and sweetness of onion distracted from the sauce's signature pepperiness. However, freshly grated Pecorino Romano did make the cut; stirring ¼ cup of the cheese into the sauce improved both its body and flavor. Another winning addition was tomato paste, which, like the cheese, is rich in glutamates—a couple of tablespoons gave the sauce savory, umami notes. Anchovies were a less obvious candidate because, while often found in Italian cooking, they are rarely seen in arrabbiata. Still, we use them often in the test kitchen as an umami booster, and a few minced fillets did just that.

With the body and flavor of the sauce much improved, it was time to focus on the heat. I wanted more complexity than the heat that comes from using red pepper flakes alone, but I didn't want to make the sauce overwhelmingly spicy. In addition to 1 teaspoon of red pepper flakes, I tried arbol chiles, the closest available substitute for the rehydrated dried Italian red chiles called for by some recipes I found. But while the arbols were mild enough, they added an out-of-place smoky flavor. I had better luck with sweet paprika. Made from dried sweet red pepper pods, it offered pepper flavor without upping the heat quotient.

The dish still lacked fresh bite, so I tried adding jalapeños, which appeared in a restaurant version of the dish that I'd tested early on; unfortunately, they added an off-putting grassy taste and too much heat, even when seeded. Fresh red cherry peppers, which appeared as an ingredient during my research, seemed promising, but I couldn't find them. As a substitute, I gave pickled cherry peppers a try and had surprisingly good results. The sauce was too spicy, but the vinegar from the peppers' bright pickling brine was a turning point.

The better option was pepperoncini. Also known as Tuscan peppers, these pickled peppers are much milder than cherry peppers but still delivered the acidity I wanted. Vinegar is often added as a finishing touch to recipes, bringing all the flavors together while retaining its brightness, but when I added the pepperoncini late in the cooking time, their flavor and vinegary punch were too dominant. Adding them at the beginning of the cooking process allowed their flavor to meld with the sauce. With that, the final piece of my arrabbiata puzzle fell into place.

I finally had what I was looking for: a quick pasta sauce that remained true to its "angry" roots but had a richness and complexity that offered more to love than just heat.

—STEVE DUNN, *Cook's Illustrated*

Penne Arrabbiata
SERVES 6

This recipe will work with other short tubular pastas like ziti or rigatoni.

1 (28-ounce) can whole peeled tomatoes
¼ cup extra-virgin olive oil
¼ cup stemmed, patted dry, and minced pepperoncini
2 tablespoons tomato paste
1 garlic clove, minced
1 teaspoon red pepper flakes
4 anchovy fillets, rinsed, patted dry, and minced to paste
½ teaspoon paprika
Salt and pepper
¼ cup grated Pecorino Romano, plus extra for serving
1 pound penne

1. Pulse tomatoes and their juice in food processor until finely chopped, about 10 pulses.

2. Heat oil, pepperoncini, tomato paste, garlic, pepper flakes, anchovies, paprika, ½ teaspoon salt, and ½ teaspoon pepper in medium saucepan over medium-low heat, stirring occasionally, until deep red in color, 7 to 8 minutes.

3. Add tomatoes and Pecorino and bring to simmer. Cook, stirring occasionally, until thickened, about 20 minutes.

4. Bring 4 quarts water to boil in large pot. Add pasta and 1 tablespoon salt and cook, stirring often, until al dente. Reserve ½ cup cooking water, then drain pasta and return it to pot. Add sauce and toss to combine, adjusting consistency with reserved cooking water as needed. Season with salt and pepper to taste. Serve, passing extra Pecorino separately.

NOTES FROM THE TEST KITCHEN

MAKING SAUCE YEAR-ROUND

For year-round arrabbiata, canned tomatoes are a great alternative to fresh. Pour canned whole tomatoes and their juice into food processor and pulse until finely chopped, about 10 pulses.

CAST-IRON SKILLET SAUSAGE LASAGNA

✔ **WHY THIS RECIPE WORKS:** A big, bubbling lasagna is the pinnacle of comfort food, but preparing one from scratch can seem daunting. We wanted a streamlined version that could be prepared and served all in a cast-iron skillet. Sautéed onion, garlic, and red pepper flakes kicked off the sauce's base before we added Italian sausage and canned whole tomatoes. Stirring an egg yolk and fresh thyme into the ricotta layer enriched it. Since even shorter no-boil lasagna noodles were too long to fit in the round skillet, we broke them in half, shingled them around the perimeter, and placed a single half in the center to keep the pasta layer gap-free. We then began layering—sauce, noodles, ricotta, and a blend of mozzarella and Parmesan. We topped off the third layer with extra cheese and, after a 30-minute bake in the oven, we had the bubbly, cheesy crust, meaty sauce, and perfectly cooked pasta we were looking for, all made in a single pan.

Is there any dish more satisfying than lasagna? From the bubbling, browned cheese crust to the tender noodles to the bright tomato sauce, this homey casserole is a mainstay at my family potlucks. When my fellow test cooks and I began working on a collection of cast-iron skillet recipes, I wondered if moving my Sunday dinner favorite from a baking dish to a cast-iron skillet could make a good thing even better.

If I was going to forgo the baking dish, I wanted the swap to be in favor of a simpler recipe. From making the sauce to browning the meat to boiling the pasta, most versions leave you with a pile of pots and pans to wash. To make my lasagna a more streamlined take on the original, I needed the skillet to be more than just a vessel. For starters, I would use it to prepare a fresh sauce, too. With convenience in mind, I started the sauce off by pulsing canned whole tomatoes in a food processor. This promised a juicy sauce I could crank out year-round. Turning to the skillet, I browned some chopped onion before adding spicy red pepper flakes and three minced garlic cloves. I added the processed tomatoes, let the mixture heat through, and dipped a spoon into the sauce to see how it tasted. I was pleased to find my simple ingredients had yielded a flavorful sauce, but I wanted this to be a hearty one-dish dinner; for my next batch I decided to bulk up the sauce with some protein.

Meatloaf mix—a combination of ground beef, pork, and veal—is a test kitchen favorite for introducing meaty flavor into cheesy lasagna, but the complex, seasoned flavors of Italian sausage sounded like an even quicker route. I removed a pound of hot Italian sausage from their casings and added the meat to the aromatic base, breaking up and browning it to add more flavor. I poured in the tomatoes and let the sauce thicken at a gentle simmer. Another taste, and I knew I'd nailed it: The sausage added just the depth the sauce needed. I found that sweet Italian sausage worked just as well. It was time to square away the remaining layers of my lasagna.

Since my sauce was full of big, meaty flavor, I was sure plain ricotta wouldn't fly. I gave this creamy layer new life by mixing in fresh thyme; adding an egg yolk gave it even more body and richness. A simple blend of shredded mozzarella and grated Parmesan promised plenty of melted, stretchy cheese and a browned, bubbly crust to top off the lasagna. For the pasta layer, no-boil noodles seemed like the right idea, since my goal was to avoid the extra pots and pans. They would cook right in the sauce as my lasagna baked. Because I was building my lasagna in a round skillet rather than the usual long rectangular dish, full-length noodles were a no-go. After spreading some of the sauce on the bottom of the skillet as my first layer, I broke the noodles in half and shingled them around the perimeter of the skillet; a single noodle half placed in the center filled the gap in the middle. From there I continued layering, spooning on the ricotta, sprinkling the cheese blend, and ladling on more sauce, repeating until the skillet was full. A final sprinkling of the cheese blend promised an appealing browned crust.

After only 30 minutes in the oven, my sausage lasagna was bubbling hot and ready to hit the table. A sprinkling of chopped basil brought in some fresh, herbal flavor before serving. The cast-iron skillet kept it warm from oven to table and, thanks to my streamlined prep, I could linger over dinner knowing there wasn't an evening of dish washing waiting for me when I was through.

—SARA MAYER, *America's Test Kitchen Books*

Cast-Iron Skillet Sausage Lasagna

SERVES 6

Do not use nonfat ricotta or fat-free mozzarella here.

- 3 (14.5-ounce) cans whole peeled tomatoes
- 2 tablespoons extra-virgin olive oil
- 1 onion, chopped fine
  Salt and pepper
- 3 garlic cloves, minced
- ¼ teaspoon red pepper flakes
- 1 pound hot or sweet Italian sausage, casings removed
- 12 ounces (1½ cups) whole-milk ricotta cheese
- 1 large egg yolk
- 1 teaspoon minced fresh thyme or ¼ teaspoon dried
- 8 ounces mozzarella cheese, shredded (2 cups)
- ¼ cup grated Parmesan cheese
- 12 no-boil lasagna noodles, broken in half
- 3 tablespoons chopped fresh basil

1. Adjust oven rack to middle position and heat oven to 400 degrees. Pulse tomatoes and their juice in food processor until coarsely ground, about 10 pulses.

2. Heat 12-inch cast-iron skillet over medium heat for 3 minutes. Add oil and heat until shimmering. Add onion and ½ teaspoon salt and cook until softened and lightly browned, 5 to 7 minutes. Stir in garlic and pepper flakes and cook until fragrant, about 30 seconds. Add sausage and cook, breaking up meat with wooden spoon, until no longer pink, about 5 minutes. Stir in processed tomatoes, bring to simmer, and cook until sauce is slightly thickened, about 10 minutes; transfer to bowl.

NOTES FROM THE TEST KITCHEN

LAYERING NOODLES FOR SKILLET LASAGNA

After spreading sauce layer, shingle 7 noodle halves around edge of skillet and place 1 noodle half in center.

3. In separate bowl, combine ricotta, egg yolk, thyme, ½ teaspoon salt, and ½ teaspoon pepper. Combine mozzarella and Parmesan in third bowl.

4. Spread ¾ cup sauce over bottom of now-empty skillet. Shingle 7 noodle halves around edge of skillet and place 1 noodle half in center. Dollop one-third of ricotta mixture over noodles, then top with one-quarter of mozzarella mixture and one-third of remaining sauce (in that order). Repeat layering process twice, beginning with noodles and ending with sauce. Top with remaining mozzarella mixture.

5. Transfer skillet to oven and bake until cheese is golden brown and lasagna is bubbling around edges, 30 to 40 minutes. Let lasagna cool for 10 minutes, then sprinkle with basil and serve.

FLUFFY BAKED POLENTA WITH RED SAUCE

✓ **WHY THIS RECIPE WORKS:** We had our hearts set on a creamy, light polenta but wanted it to be substantial enough to serve as an entrée. Cooking the cornmeal in water instead of dairy gave us clean, sweet corn flavor and an airy texture. Heating smashed garlic cloves in butter and oil left behind a flavorful garlic oil that boosted the polenta's savory quality, and adding half-and-half and nutty Pecorino Romano gave our lean polenta some welcome richness. While the polenta chilled, we pulled together a sweet-and-savory red sauce, processing canned whole tomatoes into a smooth, thick puree. Moving the sauce to the stovetop, we added olive oil, canned tomato sauce, Pecorino Romano, and garlic powder for complex flavor. Browning a halved onion and then letting it cook in the sauce allowed the onion's sharpness to subtly tame the sauce's sweetness. We sliced the polenta into blocks and baked them just long enough to brown and heat through. Topped with our homemade red sauce, this polenta can easily serve as a satisfying main course.

As I entered Cranston, Rhode Island, the lines in the center of the road changed from yellow to green, white, and red—an homage to the Italian flag. I suspected that following a road literally paved with Italian American pride would lead to excellent food. What I didn't know was that I'd find culinary treasure in a VFW (Veterans of Foreign Wars) dining hall.

Mike Lepizzera has run Mike's Kitchen out of the Tabor-Franchi VFW Post for more than three decades. The place is so popular that a line of eager diners wraps around the building at peak hours. A large chalkboard posted on the wood-paneled wall between military memorabilia and fading photos of soldiers serves as the menu. Sole Francaise, Gnocchi Sorrentino, Broccoli Rabe, Stuffed Squid . . . I wanted one of each, but the fluffy polenta and red sauce caught my eye. Was it a side dish? No, a waitress assured me. It's big enough for a meal.

A few minutes later, a 4-inch by 4-inch brick of golden polenta, swimming and smothered in a velvety red sauce, arrived at my table. It was light, airy, intensely flavorful, and substantial. The sauce was smooth, salty, and, while too sweet for my tastes on its own, was just right when combined with the cheesy polenta.

When I came back to the test kitchen to re-create this dish, I was stumped as to how to get the unique texture of that polenta. I had stealthily asked the waitress if the dish had any eggs in it, confident that this might be Lepizzera's secret ingredient, but her confused shake of the head confirmed that this was not a soufflé. How did he get the polenta so light and fluffy?

Based on the perfectly squared-off profile of the polenta on my plate, it was clear that the slice had been cut out of a larger tray of polenta. It must have had time to set up, probably in the refrigerator, transforming from a creamy porridge to something more solid. I assumed that the cooks would reheat it to order, one portion at a time. I tried applying this technique to several basic polenta recipes using rich half-and-half. It was not a turn-key solution. Some tests yielded polenta that was too soft, either from too much liquid or too much fat, and that turned into a goopy mess when sliced and baked. Others set up into dense bricks. I needed polenta that would hold its shape but still stay light.

I started by swapping out the half-and-half for a smaller amount of water, which was easier to control. I also added garlic-infused olive oil and a fair amount of butter. The flavor was much better; it seemed that the dairy had been muting the flavor of the polenta and weighing it down, while the switch to water allowed its corn flavor to stand out and kept the texture light, not dense. Stirring in a small amount of half-and-half at the end reintroduced just enough richness.

FLUFFY BAKED POLENTA WITH RED SAUCE

With that settled, I was ready to start adding cheese. Pecorino Romano, easily identifiable in Lepizzera's polenta, was the obvious choice. While wary that adding too much would weigh down the final product, I was happily surprised to find that I could add 3 ounces (1½ cups) of grated cheese to create a robust flavor without compromising the light and fluffy texture. The cheese also helped fortify the polenta so that once it chilled in an 8-inch square pan, I could slice it neatly into blocks before returning it to the oven to warm through and take on a bit of browning at the edges.

A simple tomato sauce, cooked with a halved onion for just a hint of sharpness and bolstered with a bit of sugar to amplify the polenta's slightly sweet corn flavor (and to mimic Lepizzera's sweeter sauce), plus some grated Pecorino Romano cheese completed the dish.

—KATIE LEAIRD, *Cook's Country*

Fluffy Baked Polenta with Red Sauce
SERVES 6

We developed this recipe using Quaker Yellow Corn Meal for its desirable texture and relatively short cooking time and recommend you use the same. The timing may be different for other types of cornmeal, so be sure to cook the polenta until it is thickened and tender. Whole milk can be substituted for the half-and-half. The polenta needs to be cooled for at least 3 hours before being cut, baked, and served.

POLENTA

    4 tablespoons unsalted butter
    2 tablespoons extra-virgin olive oil
    2 garlic cloves, smashed and peeled
    7 cups water
1½ teaspoons salt
    ½ teaspoon pepper
1½ cups cornmeal
    3 ounces Pecorino Romano cheese, grated (1½ cups)
    ¼ cup half-and-half

RED SAUCE

    1 (14.5-ounce) can whole peeled tomatoes
    ¼ cup extra-virgin olive oil
    1 onion, peeled and halved through root end
    1 (15-ounce) can tomato sauce
    1 ounce Pecorino Romano cheese, grated (½ cup)
1½ tablespoons sugar
    ¾ teaspoon salt
    ½ teaspoon garlic powder

1. FOR THE POLENTA: Lightly grease 8-inch square baking pan. Heat butter and oil in Dutch oven over medium heat until butter is melted. Add garlic and cook until lightly golden, about 4 minutes. Remove and discard garlic.

2. Add water, salt, and pepper to butter mixture. Increase heat to medium-high and bring to boil. Add cornmeal in slow, steady stream, whisking constantly. Reduce heat to medium-low and continue to cook, whisking frequently and scraping sides and bottom of pot, until mixture is thick and cornmeal is tender, about 20 minutes.

3. Off heat, whisk in Pecorino and half-and-half. Transfer to prepared pan and let cool completely on wire rack. Once cooled, cover with plastic wrap and refrigerate until completely chilled, at least 3 hours.

4. FOR THE RED SAUCE: Process tomatoes and their juice in blender until smooth, about 30 seconds. Heat 1 tablespoon oil in large saucepan over medium heat until shimmering. Add onion, cut side down, and cook without moving until lightly browned, about 4 minutes. Add pureed tomatoes, tomato sauce, Pecorino, sugar, salt, garlic powder, and remaining 3 tablespoons oil. Bring mixture to boil, reduce heat to medium-low, and simmer until sauce is slightly thickened, about 15 minutes. Remove from heat, discard onion, cover, and keep warm.

5. Adjust oven rack to middle position and heat oven to 375 degrees. Line rimmed baking sheet with parchment paper, then grease parchment. Cut chilled polenta into 6 equal pieces (about 4 by 2⅔ inches each). Place on prepared sheet and bake until heated through and beginning to brown on bottom, about 30 minutes. Serve each portion covered with about ½ cup red sauce.

FRIED PIZZA MONTANARA

✓ **WHY THIS RECIPE WORKS:** To make this crispy fried pizza a breeze to put together, we kept our ingredients convenient. We prepared a simple no-cook tomato sauce by whirring together canned tomatoes, olive oil, garlic, and red wine vinegar. For the crust, we split and rolled store-bought pizza dough into two 10-inch disks. Heating the oil in a high-sided Dutch oven kept frying safe as we added and submerged the disks of dough. Flipping the rounds halfway through frying made for even browning and setting the finished crusts on wire racks in baking sheets ensured that the bottoms of the pies stayed crisp. Warming up the sauce kept it from turning the puffy crust soggy. We sprinkled on shredded fresh mozzarella and Pecorino Romano and stuck the pizzas under the broiler for efficient browning. Torn fresh basil and a drizzle of extra-virgin olive oil finished the crispy pizzas perfectly.

Fried pizza, also called *pizza montanara* or *pizza fritta*, has become something of a sensation in New York pizzerias over the past several years. But, not unexpectedly, this pizza's roots run deeper, all the way back to Italy. In the rural, mountainous areas outside Naples, home cooks who lack ovens have been frying pizza for centuries. This tradition traveled with Italians as they came to the New World and has been passed down through generations.

When word spread through the test kitchen that I was making fried pizza, several staff members shared childhood memories of their grandmothers' New York or New Jersey kitchens. They described a puffed, golden-brown crust with a crisp, chewy texture. And despite being deep-fried, the crust wasn't greasy. This was something I'd have to see to believe.

I hit the books, where I found interesting stories about the dish itself but few instructions on how to make it. One thing I knew for sure: If I was going to fry the crust, I wanted the rest of the pizza to come together easily. With that in mind, I blitzed a few batches of a no-cook pizza sauce in the food processor, shredded some fresh mozzarella, tore a bunch of basil leaves, and grabbed some store-bought pizza dough.

While traditional pizza montanara is deep-fried, I was hoping to produce the same results—a puffed texture and crisp crust—using a shallower pool of oil. I heated ½ inch of vegetable oil (about ½ quart) to 350 degrees in a high-sided Dutch oven. In the meantime, I divided a pound of room-temperature pizza dough into two 8-ounce balls and began working them into 10-inch rounds on a floured counter.

Once the oil reached 350 degrees—hot enough to ensure the crust cooked up crisp, not greasy—I carefully added my first dough round. It began to puff immediately, and I had to press down on it with a spider skimmer to keep it submerged. Unfortunately, the oil didn't cover enough of the dough, so the middle stayed raw. I increased the oil depth until I was able to fully submerge the dough and found that 6 cups, which yielded a depth of about 1¼ inches, was sufficient (and 2 cups less oil than we usually use for deep frying). About 90 seconds per side gave me a golden-brown crust with a nice chew.

I spread ½ cup of my quick pizza sauce on each fried crust and scattered fresh mozzarella on top. Some recipes call for finishing the pizzas in the oven on a preheated pizza stone or in a cast-iron skillet to melt the cheese and heat the sauce, but both of those options meant I could finish only one pizza at a time, and I wanted two. I had better luck with a wire rack set in a rimmed baking sheet. Elevating the pies this way had the added benefit of allowing hot air to circulate underneath, ensuring that the bottoms of the pies stayed nice and crisp. Broiling the pizzas for about 5 minutes provided faster browning than baking, and warming the sauce first helped protect against sogginess.

If crowd reaction counts for anything, I had a hit on my hands. My sudden popularity among my colleagues made it clear, however, that two pizzas would not suffice for this recipe, so I tweaked my sauce and added a second ball of dough. I found that I could fry all four crusts in quick succession and then assemble the second two pies while the first two were broiling. No wonder my colleagues spoke so fondly of the pizza fritta from their childhoods.

—CHRISTIE MORRISON, *Cook's Country*

FRIED PIZZA MONTANARA

Fried Pizza Montanara

SERVES 4 TO 6

Room-temperature dough is much easier to shape than cold dough, so pull the dough from the fridge about 1 hour before you plan to start cooking. Shred the mozzarella on the large holes of a box grater.

SAUCE

- 1 (28-ounce) can whole peeled tomatoes, drained
- 1 tablespoon extra-virgin olive oil
- 2 garlic cloves, minced
- 1 teaspoon red wine vinegar
- 1 teaspoon dried oregano
- 1 teaspoon salt
- ¼ teaspoon pepper

PIZZA

- 2 (1-pound) balls pizza dough, room temperature
- 6 cups vegetable or peanut oil
- 1 ounce Pecorino Romano cheese, grated (½ cup)
- 8 ounces fresh mozzarella cheese, shredded (2 cups)
- ¼ cup fresh basil leaves, torn

  Extra-virgin olive oil for drizzling

1. FOR THE SAUCE: Process all ingredients in food processor until smooth, about 30 seconds. Transfer to small saucepan; cover and set over low heat to warm (sauce needn't be cooked, just warmed).

2. FOR THE PIZZA: Place 2 wire racks in 2 rimmed baking sheets. Cut four 12-inch squares of parchment paper.

3. Divide each dough ball into two 8-ounce balls and cover with greased plastic wrap. Press and roll 1 dough ball into 10-inch circle on lightly floured counter. Transfer to floured parchment square, dust top of dough round with flour, and set aside on counter. Press and roll second dough ball into 10-inch circle, transfer to floured parchment square, and stack on top of first dough round. Repeat with remaining 2 dough balls, creating second stack. Lightly cover dough round stacks with clean dish towel.

4. Add vegetable oil to large Dutch oven until it measures about 1¼ inches deep and heat over medium-high heat to 350 degrees. Gently lower 1 dough round into oil, keeping it as flat as possible as it enters oil. Fry first side, carefully pressing down with spider or slotted metal spatula to keep submerged, until puffed and golden brown, 1½ to 2 minutes. Adjust burner, if necessary, to maintain oil temperature between 325 and 350 degrees.

5. Using tongs, carefully flip dough round and continue to fry until second side is golden brown, 1½ to 2 minutes longer. Transfer to prepared wire rack. Repeat with remaining dough rounds. (You should have 2 fried crusts on each rack; crusts may extend slightly beyond edges of racks.)

6. Adjust oven rack 10 inches from broiler element and heat broiler. Spread ½ cup warm sauce over each crust, leaving 1-inch border. Sprinkle each crust with 2 tablespoons Pecorino, followed by ½ cup mozzarella. Broil 1 sheet of pizza until cheese melts and crusts begin to brown in spots, 4 to 6 minutes. Repeat with second sheet. Transfer pizzas to cutting board; sprinkle each with basil and drizzle with olive oil. Slice and serve.

NOTES FROM THE TEST KITCHEN

HOW TO MAKE FRIED PIZZA

1. SHAPE: Divide each dough ball in half. Roll each half into even 10-inch round.

2. FRY: Place each dough round in hot oil, pressing down to keep it submerged.

3. TOP AND BROIL: Ladle on sauce, add cheese, and broil 2 pizzas at a time.

WISCONSIN BUTTER BURGERS

✔ **WHY THIS RECIPE WORKS:** After a visit to Milwaukee, we wanted to re-create the most memorable meal we had there: butter burgers. Stewed onions are a required topping for butter burgers; we prepared ours in a saucepan, cooking a chopped onion in water and butter until just barely browned. To serve up burgers with a crisp exterior, we seasoned and formed ground beef into thin patties and cooked them in a hot skillet. Not moving the patties for the first 3 minutes of cooking helped develop the signature crust. We flipped them over to briefly cook the second side and then topped the burgers with American cheese. A slab of salted butter on the bun plus a small mound of buttery stewed onions made for the richest, butteriest burgers—what's better than that?

"Are you really putting butter on a burger?"

Questions like this came at me every time I made a batch of Wisconsin butter burgers in the test kitchen. But the minute the skeptics tried a bite, they were persuaded that the folks over at Solly's Grille in Glendale (a suburb of Milwaukee) were doing something right. Since 1936, when Kenneth "Solly" Salmon opened the joint, they've been serving these burgers for all three meals every day.

The small restaurant consists of two yellow U-shaped counters, an open kitchen, and, most important, a well-seasoned flat-top grill. Grab a stool and watch the cooks pull the well-done, crispy-edged burgers from the griddle; stack them onto bun bottoms; and top each with a slice of American cheese, a small pile of stewed onions, and a toasted bun top that's been lavishly slathered with butter. Even before you grab one, you know that butter is destined to run down your chin in the most satisfying way.

I was determined to create these burgers in the test kitchen, no flat-top required. I found a handful of recipes for butter burgers inspired by Solly's, but after cooking through a few of these, I determined that the test kitchen's tried-and-true recipe for the Best Old-Fashioned Burgers was my best inspiration for the burger base. I flattened each patty to ½ inch thick, sprinkled each with salt and pepper, and set them all in the fridge while I prepared the onions.

These "stewed" onions, softened and just barely taking on color (never caramelized), are a mandatory component. At Solly's, the onions are cooked slowly on the flat-top grill, but I approximated their color and texture in a saucepan with a bit of water, salt, and, naturally, butter. I covered the pot to let them stew until soft and then removed the lid and allowed them to cook a little longer until they were just barely beginning to brown.

Onions done, I seared my patties in a hot skillet for 3 minutes on the first side without moving them—a crucial step for those crisp edges. After a flip, just 1 minute on the other side finished them off. (I set a slice of American cheese on each and tacked on 30 seconds to give it time to melt.) These burgers were ready for their toppings.

I stacked a burger on each lightly toasted bun bottom and piled on some onions. I spread each bun top with 2 tablespoons of softened salted butter, capped each burger, and called my tasters. Together we huddled, hunched over our plates to prevent any butter dribbles, and devoured the burgers. Not one taster failed to ask for seconds.

—ASHLEY MOORE, *Cook's Country*

Wisconsin Butter Burgers

SERVES 4

Our favorite domestic salted butter is Kate's Homemade.

- 9 tablespoons salted butter, softened
- 1 onion, chopped
- 1 tablespoon water
  Salt and pepper
- 1 pound 90 percent lean ground beef
- 4 hamburger buns, toasted
- ½ teaspoon vegetable oil
- 4 slices American cheese

1. Melt 1 tablespoon butter in medium saucepan over medium heat. Add onion, water, and ¼ teaspoon salt and cook, covered, until tender, about 5 minutes. Remove lid and continue to cook until translucent and just beginning to brown, about 3 minutes. Cover and keep warm.

2. Transfer beef to rimmed baking sheet and separate into 4 equal mounds. Gently shape each mound into even ½-inch-thick patty, about 4½ inches in diameter. Combine ¾ teaspoon salt and ¾ teaspoon pepper in bowl and sprinkle both sides of patties with mixture. Refrigerate until ready to cook, up to 30 minutes.

3. Spread 2 tablespoons butter onto each bun top; set aside. Heat oil in 12-inch skillet over high heat until just smoking. Using spatula, transfer patties to skillet and cook without moving them for 3 minutes. Flip patties and cook for 1 minute. Top each burger with 1 slice of American cheese and continue to cook until cheese is melted, about 30 seconds longer.

4. Transfer burgers to bun bottoms. Divide onion mixture among burgers and cover with buttered bun tops. Serve immediately.

NOTES FROM THE TEST KITCHEN

MAKING BUTTER BURGERS

1. COOK ONIONS: "Stew" onions in butter and water in covered saucepan. Remove lid to brown onions.

2. SEAR BURGERS: Let burgers cook without moving for first 3 minutes to create flavorful browned crust.

3. BUTTER BUNS: Spread 2 tablespoons softened salted butter onto bun tops.

A BUN FOR EVERY BURGER

What good is a great burger without a bun to match? The tender, fluffy texture and rich sweetness of Martin's Sandwich Potato Rolls paired perfectly with our Wisconsin Butter Burgers.

GRILLED PORK BURGERS

✓ **WHY THIS RECIPE WORKS:** Burgers made from ground pork can be notoriously dry and crumbly. To serve up tender, mild-yet-savory grilled pork burgers, we created a bread and milk mixture (called a panade) to keep the ground pork moist and cohesive. Boosting the panade with minced shallot, Worcestershire and soy sauces, fresh thyme, and pepper injected the burgers with big, complex flavor. After working this flavorful mix into the ground pork, we formed it into patties and pressed divots into each to prevent the burgers from bulging on the grill. We cooked the patties over moderate heat to prevent them from drying out. We topped our moist, tender burgers with an easy horseradish sauce to complement the flavorful pork.

Pork usually shines on the grill, but there is one glaring exception: pork burgers, which tend to be tough, dry, and bland. This is because, due to lingering but outdated health concerns, the U.S. Department of Agriculture recommends cooking ground pork to 160 degrees, which wrings out the texture-enhancing juices from the meat, constricting it into an unappetizing hockey puck.

But pork burgers can be so much more. Pork has a nuanced, slightly sweet flavor that makes a fine canvas for seasonings, sauces, and add-ins. But to keep it tender, a successful pork burger needs an extra hit of moisture. Most recipes attempt to do just that by adding a host of flavorful, and typically fatty, ingredients. Bacon tops the list. While I rarely find fault with bacon, I did in this instance: Its smoky-sweet flavor, even when used judiciously, ran roughshod over the mild pork flavor; and its fat rendered out during grilling, causing serious flare-ups. Pork patties laden with cheese or butter suffered the same sooty fate.

Some recipes kept their ingredients simple—ground pork, salt, and pepper—but toyed with temperature to preserve moisture. High heat, low heat, and combo heat, I tried them all, but each yielded dry, bland burgers.

Looking beyond burgers for inspiration, I shifted my focus to their closest cousin, meatballs. The most obvious difference between the two is how meatballs are often enriched with a panade of bread mashed to a paste with a liquid, often milk, and sometimes egg. Simple, yes, but a panade works a minor miracle by both adding and trapping moisture (juices and fat), allowing meatballs to be thoroughly cooked without drying out. I whipped up a batch of burgers enhanced with a few spoonfuls of panade and was rewarded with the most moist, "porky" burgers to date. But the burgers were far from perfect. The texture was dense and the flavor was bland—they were veering into meatloaf territory. In successive batches, I abandoned the egg to loosen things up and made my next panade with just one slice of white sandwich bread mashed with 4 tablespoons of milk. This worked much better in terms of texture but did little for the flavor of my burgers. To build deeper flavor, I thought back to a recent test kitchen discovery in which we determined that you can use liquids more flavorful than milk in a panade to good effect. After days of testing various ratios of ingredients, I landed on keeping 2 tablespoons of milk for richness but replacing the rest with a combination of two of our favorite flavor enhancers: Worcestershire and soy sauces. Minced shallot, minced fresh thyme, and black pepper rounded out the seasonings.

As for grilling the burgers, a full chimney of briquettes spread in an even layer (or medium heat on a gas grill) provided just the right heat. To reach the necessary 150-degree internal temperature without burning their crusts, I found that I needed to flatten the burgers to about ¾ inch thick, or 4 inches in diameter (which perfectly fills out a standard hamburger bun). Pressing a dimple into the center of each burger ensured that the patties wouldn't bulge and be awkward to eat. To gild the lily, I made a quick burger sauce flavored with horseradish, whole-grain mustard, and garlic.

Sandwiched between toasted buns, these moist and juicy pork burgers can go toe-to-toe with any beef burger.

—MATTHEW CARD, *Cook's Country*

Grilled Pork Burgers

SERVES 4

We developed this recipe with whole milk, but low-fat will work, too.

- 1 slice hearty white sandwich bread, torn into pieces
- 1 shallot, minced
- 2 tablespoons milk
- 4 teaspoons soy sauce
- 1 tablespoon Worcestershire sauce
- 1¼ teaspoons minced fresh thyme
- 1 teaspoon pepper
- ½ teaspoon salt
- 1½ pounds 80 to 85 percent lean ground pork
- 4 hamburger buns, toasted and buttered
- 1 recipe Horseradish Burger Sauce (optional) (recipe follows)

1. Combine bread, shallot, milk, soy sauce, Worcestershire, thyme, pepper, and salt in large bowl. Mash to paste with fork. Using your hands, add pork and mix until well combined.

2. Divide pork mixture into 4 equal balls. Flatten balls into even ¾-inch-thick patties, about 4 inches in diameter. Using your fingertips, press centers of patties down until about ½ inch thick, creating slight divot.

3A. FOR A CHARCOAL GRILL: Open bottom vent completely. Light large chimney starter filled with charcoal briquettes (6 quarts). When top coals are partially covered with ash, pour evenly over grill. Set cooking grate in place, cover, and open lid vent completely. Heat grill until hot.

3B. FOR A GAS GRILL: Turn all burners to high and heat grill until hot, about 15 minutes. Turn all burners to medium.

4. Clean and oil cooking grate. Grill patties (covered if using gas), until browned on first side, 5 to 7 minutes. Flip and continue to grill until burgers register 150 degrees, 5 to 7 minutes longer. Serve burgers on buns with sauce, if using.

Horseradish Burger Sauce

MAKES ½ CUP

Buy refrigerated, prepared horseradish, not the shelf-stable kind, which contains preservatives and additives. Horseradish strength varies, so add it according to your taste.

- ¼ cup mayonnaise
- 2 tablespoons sour cream
- 1–2 tablespoons prepared horseradish
- 1 tablespoon whole-grain mustard
- 1 garlic clove, minced
    Pinch sugar
    Salt and pepper
    Hot sauce

Whisk mayonnaise, sour cream, horseradish, mustard, garlic, and sugar together in bowl. Season with salt, pepper, and hot sauce to taste.

GRILLED PORK BURGERS

Grilled Parmesan Pork Burgers

Add ½ cup grated Parmesan, 1 tablespoon minced fresh sage, 1 teaspoon ground fennel, and ½ teaspoon red pepper flakes to pork mixture in step 1.

Grilled Southwest Pork Burgers

Add 2 tablespoons minced jarred hot pepper rings, 1½ teaspoons chili powder, and ½ teaspoon minced fresh rosemary to pork mixture in step 1.

Grilled Thai-Style Pork Burgers

Substitute fish sauce for soy sauce. Add 3 tablespoons minced fresh cilantro, 2 teaspoons Sriracha sauce, and 1 teaspoon grated lime zest to pork mixture in step 1.

BLACK BEAN BURGERS

WHY THIS RECIPE WORKS: As with many meatless patties, black bean burgers often get their structure from fillers that rob them of their black bean flavor. We wanted that key ingredient to shine in our burgers. For convenient and reliable beans, we turned to canned. Eggs and flour served as our binding agents, and adding minced scallions, cilantro, and garlic delivered bright, fresh flavor. We stirred in some spices—cumin and coriander—and a hit of hot sauce. In keeping with our Latin American flavor profile, we turned to the corn flavor of tortilla chips to pull together our burger mix. After grinding the chips in a food processor, we added the beans and pulsed them into coarsely chopped pieces. We combined the beans with the flour-egg binder and refrigerated the mixture, which allowed the starches to absorb some of the eggs' moisture. After an hour, we formed patties and cooked the burgers in an oiled skillet. After a quick browning on each side, these burgers were ready to serve with all of our favorite fixings.

When it comes to vegetarian recipes, veggie burgers have never been high on my list. Most rely on a hodgepodge of ingredients with multiple grains and vegetables that need to be individually prepared before they go into the burger. Black bean burgers seemed more approachable. The earthy beans promised a hearty, satisfying meal, and because the beans themselves provide plenty of substance, ideally the process wouldn't be much more complicated than making an everyday beef burger—just mash up a couple of cans of beans, add a few complementary ingredients, shape into patties, and cook.

When I reviewed recipes, I found that there were a couple of approaches to handling the beans: They could be coarsely chopped, lightly mashed with a fork, or pureed until smooth. To bind the beans together, almost all recipes relied on eggs, and many also loaded up on starchy ingredients like bread crumbs or oats. Unfortunately, I wasn't impressed when I tried them. Lots of starch made it easy to shape chopped beans and eggs into patties, but these burgers turned dry and tasteless once cooked. At the other end of the spectrum were the recipes that called for mashed or pureed beans. The cohesive, hummus-like texture held together nicely even with minimal binders, but it also produced a burger with a gluey, pasty consistency.

As for add-ins, recipes tended to follow the lead of veggie burgers by throwing in everything from porcini mushrooms and soy sauce to poblano peppers and cashew nuts. I was after burgers that featured earthy bean flavor at their heart with just enough seasoning and mix-ins to give them a little zest and intrigue. I also wanted patties that weren't wet or gluey but rather just cohesive enough to hold together when flipped in the pan, with a little textural contrast from chunks of beans and a nice crust.

After draining and rinsing a couple of cans of beans, I spread the beans on paper towels to rid them of moisture. My thinking was the drier they were, the less starchy binder they might require. And to avoid a mushy texture, the beans would have to retain some of their shape. But they still needed to be broken down enough to incorporate well, so I pulled out the food processor. A couple of pulses produced nicely chopped pieces that would offer a bit of texture.

To transform the chopped beans into a cohesive burger mix, I tried stirring in a beaten egg along with a handful of panko bread crumbs. (I used only a small amount so as to let the bean flavor come to the fore.) Like tiny sponges, the bread crumbs did an excellent job of absorbing the egg's moisture, but even a little bit made the burgers taste bready. What's more, one egg seemed insufficient since each and every burger broke apart into crumbles as I flipped it.

Many recipes call for some sort of precooked grains, such as rice or bulgur, to bind the beans, but in the interest of simplicity, I opted to avoid that path. Instead, I experimented with a different sort of starch that would complement the Latin American provenance of black beans: tortilla chips. Since I already had the food processor out, I quickly blitzed a few chips before pulsing in the beans. Then I added two beaten eggs to help hold the burgers together. Everything seemed great—that is, until I tried to pack the burgers into patties. The mixture was so wet and sticky that shaping them was nearly impossible.

Adding more ground chips would only mute the flavor of the beans, so I took a lunch break, hoping that an hour of hands-off time would allow the starches in the beans and the tortilla chips to absorb the liquid from the egg. Just as I had hoped, the mixture was much easier to handle after it sat in the fridge for an hour. These patties were easy to form, held their shape fairly well, and developed a crisp, golden-brown crust when I fried them in a little bit of oil. Unfortunately, they still occasionally broke apart as I flipped them.

To glue the burgers together more effectively, I took the unorthodox step of adding a good sprinkling of flour. Sure enough, since wheat contains sticky starches, a mere 2 tablespoons all but guaranteed that the burgers would stay together, without negatively affecting flavor.

Now the burgers just needed some personality. Avoiding additions that were high in moisture or that needed to be cooked down ahead of time (such as onions and peppers), I landed on minced garlic and scallions and chopped fresh cilantro. They were quick and easy and fit my Latin American theme. For even more complexity, I spiked the mixture with citrusy coriander and smoky cumin. Finally, a dash of hot sauce added zip.

These burgers were ready to be topped with the usual fixings—gooey melted cheese, thinly sliced onion, lettuce, and tomato—or more deluxe toppings like a creamy avocado-feta spread, spicy chipotle mayonnaise, or a tangy roasted tomato–orange jam.

—ERIKA BRUCE, *Cook's Illustrated*

NOTES FROM THE TEST KITCHEN

KEYS TO AN IDEAL BLACK BEAN BURGER
Here's what we did to create a burger full of earthy bean flavor that wasn't muted by too much starchy binder.

GIVE 'EM A RINSE: Rinsing canned beans rids them of their starchy liquid, which can compromise the flavor and texture of our black bean burgers.

DRY BEANS: Removing excess moisture by draining on paper towels helps cut down on the need for absorbent binders.

BIND WITH BIG FLAVOR: Adding scallions, cilantro, and garlic to a mixture of eggs and flour promises burgers packed with Latin-inspired taste.

PULSE, DON'T PUREE: Pulsing the beans with tortilla chips (which we processed first) keeps the beans chunky for textural contrast.

LET IT REST: Letting the mixture sit gives the starches time to soak up the eggs so the burgers are easier to handle.

Black Bean Burgers

SERVES 6

The black bean mixture needs to be refrigerated for at least 1 hour or up to 24 hours prior to cooking. When forming the patties, it is important to pack them firmly together. Our favorite canned black beans are Bush's Best. Serve the burgers with your favorite toppings or with one of our spreads (recipes follow).

2 (15-ounce) cans black beans, rinsed
2 large eggs
2 tablespoons all-purpose flour
4 scallions, minced
3 tablespoons minced fresh cilantro
2 garlic cloves, minced
1 teaspoon ground cumin
1 teaspoon hot sauce (optional)
½ teaspoon ground coriander
¼ teaspoon salt
¼ teaspoon pepper
1 ounce tortilla chips, crushed coarse (½ cup)
8 teaspoons vegetable oil
6 hamburger buns

1. Line rimmed baking sheet with triple layer of paper towels and spread beans over towels. Let stand for 15 minutes.

2. Whisk eggs and flour in large bowl until uniform paste forms. Stir in scallions; cilantro; garlic; cumin; hot sauce, if using; coriander; salt; and pepper until well combined.

3. Process tortilla chips in food processor until finely ground, about 30 seconds. Add black beans and pulse until beans are roughly broken down, about 5 pulses. Transfer black bean mixture to bowl with egg mixture and mix until well combined. Cover and refrigerate for at least 1 hour or up to 24 hours.

4. Adjust oven rack to middle position and heat oven to 200 degrees. Divide bean mixture into 6 equal portions. Firmly pack each portion into tight ball, then flatten to 3½-inch-diameter patty. (Patties can be wrapped individually in plastic wrap, placed in a zipper-lock bag, and frozen for up to 2 weeks. Thaw patties before cooking.)

5. Heat 2 teaspoons oil in 10-inch nonstick skillet over medium heat until shimmering. Carefully place 3 patties in skillet and cook until bottoms are well browned and crisp, about 5 minutes. Flip patties, add 2 teaspoons oil, and cook second side until well browned and crisp, 3 to 5 minutes. Transfer burgers to wire rack set in rimmed baking sheet and place in oven to keep warm. Repeat with remaining 3 patties and 4 teaspoons oil. Transfer burgers to buns and serve.

Avocado-Feta Spread

MAKES ABOUT 1¼ CUPS

1 ripe avocado, cut into ½-inch pieces
1 ounce feta cheese, crumbled (¼ cup)
1 tablespoon extra-virgin olive oil
1 teaspoon lime juice
⅛ teaspoon salt
⅛ teaspoon pepper

Using fork, mash all ingredients in medium bowl until mostly smooth.

Chipotle Mayonnaise

MAKES ABOUT 1 CUP

3 tablespoons mayonnaise
3 tablespoons sour cream
2 teaspoons minced canned chipotle chile in adobo sauce
1 garlic clove, minced
⅛ teaspoon salt

Combine all ingredients. Cover and refrigerate for at least 1 hour.

Roasted Tomato–Orange Jam

MAKES ABOUT 1 CUP

Line the baking sheet with foil for easy cleanup.

12 ounces cherry tomatoes, halved
1 shallot, sliced thin
1 tablespoon extra-virgin olive oil
¼ teaspoon salt
⅛ teaspoon ground cinnamon
2 tablespoons orange marmalade

Adjust oven rack to middle position and heat oven to 425 degrees. Toss tomatoes, shallot, oil, salt, and cinnamon together in bowl. Transfer to aluminum foil–lined rimmed baking sheet and roast until edges of tomatoes are well browned, 15 to 20 minutes. Let cool slightly; transfer tomato mixture to food processor. Add marmalade and process until smooth, about 10 seconds.

PUFFY TACOS

✔ **WHY THIS RECIPE WORKS:** A San Antonio favorite, puffy tacos are traditionally made by deep-frying and shaping fresh *masa de maíz* (finely ground hominy) until it puffs into a light, crispy taco shell. We used more readily available dried masa harina and mixed it with warm water to form a pliable dough. Flattening the dough under a clear glass pie plate made it easy to gauge the size of our tortillas as we pressed them out. Frying in a saucepan required less oil, and the pan's smaller profile made the tacos easier to manage; we folded them into a wide U-shape using two spatulas. For a flavorful filling, a quick *picadillo* made with ground beef, potato, green bell pepper, onions, garlic, and cumin fit the bill.

Residents of San Antonio, Texas, have strong feelings about puffy tacos—deep-fried, light, crisp, emphatically corn-flavored shells that encase savory meat fillings. They're a regional take on tacos that deserves a spot on menus, and in home kitchens, everywhere.

Many San Antonio fans of the dish cite Diana Barrios-Treviño's restaurant, Los Barrios, as having the best in the city. So when our executive food editor, Bryan Roof, was in San Antonio, he visited Barrios-Treviño to see her technique firsthand. Barrios-Treviño started with fresh *masa de maíz*, or finely ground hominy, to create a moist dough. She used a tortilla press to stamp portions of masa dough into 6-inch tortillas and then dropped them one at a time into the deep-fryer. The tortillas puffed up, ballooning as Barrios-Treviño flipped and shaped them with two spatulas into the familiar taco-shell shape. She pulled the shells from the oil to drain upside down before stuffing them with a simple ground meat filling.

Back in the test kitchen, with Roof's guidance, I started to put together a working recipe. I knew this dish would require a number of steps, but I wanted to keep it as simple as possible. Since fresh masa is not available in most grocery stores, I made a dough using more widely available masa harina (dried masa), salt, and water. Rather than use a tortilla press, I pressed out disks using a clear pie plate; this simple technique produced tortillas of even thickness and was easier and more consistent than using a rolling pin. And since you can see through the plate, it's easy to gauge when you have a perfect 6-inch disk.

I brought some oil to 375 degrees in a Dutch oven (our go-to frying vessel) and dropped in my first masa disk. It puffed just as expected, but when I flipped it, the bottom burst and the shell split in two. I attempted again with both lower and higher oil temperatures but had the same result.

Realizing that I needed some expert advice, I reached out to Barrios-Treviño, who told me I probably had too much water in my dough. When frying, the heat of the oil rapidly pushes water out of the masa dough. The excess water was converting to steam rapidly, causing the shells to puff so much that they exploded. After a series of tests, I found the balance. A ratio of 1⅔ cups water to 2½ cups masa harina was the sweet spot for a workable dough that didn't explode.

I was using a hefty 3 quarts of oil to fully submerge the shells in a Dutch oven, but manipulating the shells in the deep Dutch oven was an awkward process. Would a shallower vessel make the process easier? I tried 2 cups of oil in an 8-inch skillet to see if shallow frying would be a feasible option, but the oil splattered and the oil temperature dropped almost 100 degrees after I added each tortilla. I switched to a large saucepan; by doing so I could get away with using just 2 quarts of oil, and the saucepan's smaller profile made shaping the tacos easier.

A favorite filling for San Antonio puffy tacos is a Texas take on *picadillo*—browned ground beef cooked with potatoes, onion, and green peppers and flavored with garlic, cumin, salt, and black pepper. I lined up 12 crisp, light puffy taco shells; stuffed them with my picadillo; and topped them with shredded lettuce, cheese, and tomatoes. Tasters tore into them with unbridled pleasure.

—MORGAN BOLLING, *Cook's Country*

PUFFY TACOS

Puffy Tacos

SERVES 6 TO 8

We used Maseca Brand Instant Masa Corn Flour for our taco shells. The dough should not be sticky and should have the texture of PlayDoh. If the dough cracks or falls apart when pressing the tortillas, just reroll and press again.

PICADILLO

- 12 ounces 85 percent lean ground beef
- ½ russet potato (4 ounces), peeled and cut into ¼-inch pieces
- Salt and pepper
- 1 onion, chopped fine
- 1 small green bell pepper, stemmed, seeded, and chopped fine
- 3 garlic cloves, minced
- 1½ teaspoons ground cumin
- 2 teaspoons all-purpose flour
- ¾ cup water

TACO SHELLS

- 2½ cups (10 ounces) masa harina
- 1 teaspoon salt
- 1⅔ cups warm water
- 2 quarts vegetable oil

- Shredded iceberg lettuce
- Chopped tomato
- Shredded sharp cheddar cheese
- Hot sauce
- Lime wedges

1. FOR THE PICADILLO: Combine beef, potato, 1 teaspoon pepper, and ¾ teaspoon salt in 12-inch nonstick skillet. Cook over medium-high heat until meat and potatoes begin to brown, 6 to 8 minutes, breaking up meat with spoon. Add onion and bell pepper and cook until softened, 4 to 6 minutes. Add garlic and cumin and cook until fragrant, about 30 seconds.

2. Stir in flour and cook for 1 minute. Stir in water and bring to boil. Reduce heat to medium-low and simmer until thickened slightly, about 1 minute. Season with salt and pepper to taste. Remove from heat, cover, and keep warm.

SUREFIRE TACO SHELLS
A few simple steps made shaping and frying authentic puffy taco shells a foolproof process.

1. Cut open sides of 1-gallon zipper-lock bag and place ball of dough inside. Fold plastic over top.

2. Press down on plastic with clear pie plate to flatten ball into 6-inch circle. Tortilla should be ⅛-inch thick.

3. Lower tortilla into hot oil. Don't splash, and watch carefully: In 15 to 20 seconds, tortilla will begin to puff up in middle.

4. Use 2 metal spatulas to grip tortilla and flip over in oil. Be careful not to pierce or tear tortilla.

5. Use spatulas to shape tortilla into wide-mouthed taco shell. Nudge shell down into oil and fry until golden brown.

3. FOR THE TACO SHELLS: Mix masa harina and salt together in medium bowl. Stir in warm water with rubber spatula. Using your hands, knead mixture in bowl until it comes together fully (dough should be soft and tacky, not sticky), about 30 seconds. Cover dough with damp dish towel and let rest for 5 minutes.

4. Divide dough into 12 equal portions, about ¼ cup each, then roll each into smooth ball between your hands. Transfer to plate and keep covered with damp dish towel. Cut sides of 1-gallon zipper-lock bag, leaving bottom seam intact.

5. Set wire rack in rimmed baking sheet and line rack with triple layer of paper towels. Add oil to large saucepan until it measures 2½ inches deep and heat over medium-high heat to 375 degrees.

6. When oil comes to temperature, enclose 1 dough ball at a time in split bag. Using clear pie plate (so you can see size of tortilla), press dough flat into 6-inch circle (about ⅛ inch thick).

7. Carefully remove tortilla from plastic and drop into hot oil. Fry tortilla until it puffs up, 15 to 20 seconds. Using 2 metal spatulas, carefully flip tortilla. Immediately press down in center of tortilla with 1 spatula to form taco shape, submerging tortilla into oil while doing so. Using second spatula, spread top of tortilla open about 1½ inches. Fry until golden brown, about 60 seconds. Adjust burner, if necessary, to maintain oil temperature between 350 and 375 degrees.

8. Transfer taco shell to prepared rack and place upside down to drain. Return oil to 375 degrees and repeat with remaining dough balls.

9. Divide picadillo evenly among taco shells, about ¼ cup each. Serve immediately, passing lettuce, tomato, cheddar, hot sauce, and lime wedges separately.

NOTES FROM THE TEST KITCHEN

MASA HARINA

Masa harina, the key ingredient for our Puffy Tacos' shells, is made of dried corn kernels that are hulled and then ground into a dough, called masa. This dough is washed, dried, and powdered into fine flour. Masa harina can be found in the Mexican foods section of your local grocery store.

PALEO SHREDDED BEEF TACOS

WHY THIS RECIPE WORKS: Robust, flavorful shredded beef tacos are a Mexican specialty. To turn out a bold version to suit paleo diners, we started with collagen-rich chuck-eye roast and braised it gently in a covered Dutch oven. We built a bold braising liquid with tomato paste, ancho chiles, and plenty of spices. The potent liquid infused the beef with big flavor, and it pulled double duty as a base for our sauce. Placing the beef on onion rounds elevated it above the braising liquid to allow it to brown. Once the beef had finished cooking, we pureed the liquid into a sauce. We made our own wraps using a batter of water, eggs, olive oil, and a paleo-friendly blend of almond, tapioca, and coconut flours. Cooked in a skillet like crêpes, the wraps were strong and pliable enough to fold around our meaty taco filling.

Carne deshebrada (Spanish for "shredded meat") is a slow-cooked taco filling of shredded beef napped with a rich sauce, but many of its key ingredients—including the corn tortilla in which the filling is served—do not align with the paleo diet. The test kitchen's recipe for this slow-braised beef gets its flavor from a sauce that stars, among other ingredients, store-bought broth and beer. Hoping to turn out an appealing paleo take on this taqueria classic, we needed to deliver flavorful beef in a homemade wrap.

Re-creating the pliable but strong structure of tortillas without wheat or corn seemed like the biggest hurdle, so we started there. During our research, a flourless dough of mashed green plantains sparked our interest. The process seemed easy—simply boil, peel, and mash plantains—but the resulting dough was sticky, tough, and impossible to roll into the thin rounds we had in mind. Next, we looked into the alternative flours employed in the paleo pantry and learned that high-protein almond flour was great for creating structure. To ensure that the dough also had some stretch to it, we blended almond flour with tapioca flour, a powder of pure starch that promised some elasticity. Unfortunately, once mixed with oil and water, this blend produced another sticky, hard-to-roll mass, and adding flour or reducing liquid only made it tougher. We were realizing that a rolled-out wrap wasn't in the cards and then we had our a-ha moment: What if we used a pourable, crêpe-like batter instead?

With a new vision in mind, we called on the same base ingredients and added three eggs for richness. Coconut flour is great at breaking up almond flour's density and absorbing extra moisture, so we added it to the mix, too. For the sake of ease, we combined all the ingredients in a blender and allowed the batter to rest so the flours could hydrate and the batter could thicken slightly. Once the mixture was ready, we poured some of the batter into a hot skillet and tilted gently to spread the batter over the bottom of the pan. These wraps looked the part but they were eggy-tasting and very delicate—not strong enough to stand up to any filling, let alone meaty carne deshebrada. For the next batch, we reduced the number of eggs to two and increased the amount of tapioca flour. This time, the egg flavor was muted and our wraps were much sturdier. The only lingering issue lay in the batter's tiny bubbles that turned into leak-causing holes in the wraps. We suspected the blender was to blame, injecting the batter with air as it whirred the ingredients together. As a final tweak, we tested to see if hand mixing would offer any improvements. Sure enough, this extra step cut back on air bubbles and avoided leaky wraps. With our batter at the ready, turning out sturdy 6-inch wraps was as easy as a few tilts of a skillet. We were now ready to tackle the taco filling.

Preparing the beef for carne deshebrada is pretty simple: Cover the cut of choice with water in a large pot, add some flavorings (onion, garlic, and cilantro, among others), and braise until tender. The meat is then removed, shredded, and combined with a sauce. Considering we would be building our sauce without the convenience of store-bought broth, working the flavorful cooking liquid into the sauce was a no-brainer. We chose a boneless chuck-eye roast for our beef—this collagen-rich cut would become tender and shred nicely and lend a lot of beefy flavor to the sauce. We then set about building our braising liquid.

We wanted a flavorful, multi-layered sauce, so we started at the spice rack. Cumin, cinnamon, cloves, and bay leaves promised plenty of authentic complexity. We wanted to add only as much liquid as we'd need to adequately sauce the beef, so we poured some water into the pot along with chopped onion, a little minced jalapeño, and garlic. We cooked the meat until tender before shredding it and returning it to the pot to toss with the sauce. Our choice of spices had done their job, but the sauce was just not meaty enough.

Browning is a surefire way to boost meat's flavor. To achieve plenty of browning without the added step of searing the meat, we aimed to raise the meat above the surface of the braising liquid for hands-off browning. We arranged the beef on thick rounds of onion and popped the pot in the oven. After about 2½ hours, the rounds had softened and sunk, but the beef had stayed afloat long enough to develop deep browning and tons of meaty flavor. And what about the sauce? We fished the onion slices out of the pot and gave it a taste. It was certainly good and meaty—but it wasn't much else.

Many deshebrada recipes lean on broth and beer for complexity, so we were tasked with finding flavorful paleo alternatives. Tomato paste is a test kitchen favorite for adding concentrated, meaty umami, so we spooned some in. This was an instant improvement and, as a bonus, it also yielded a smoother sauce. Cider vinegar delivered some fresh zing. For this new batch, we gave the cooking liquid a quick turn in the blender before combining it with the shredded meat. This sauce was better still, with a silky, unctuous texture.

Since we were already pureeing the sauce, there was no reason not to bring in some dried chiles. Recipes called for a wide variety, from fruity, moderately hot guajillos to mildly flavored, slightly spicy New Mexican reds to smoky-sweet anchos and earthy, raisiny pasillas. Each variety had its merits, but anchos came out on top. By the end of the cooking time, they were soft enough to be pureed into the sauce, giving it the punch it needed.

For paleo-friendly taco toppings, old standbys like cheese and sour cream were out of the question, but we felt that the filling's richness needed some contrast from a bright, crunchy topping. To that end, we looked to El Salvador and homed in on *curtido*, a crisp, tart cabbage-carrot slaw with a spicy kick. While the slaw is often fermented to develop flavor (a process that takes several days or even weeks), we found that a quick version tossed together while the meat was braising and then refrigerated for an hour was all our tacos required. The key was to marinate the shredded vegetables, onion, and jalapeño in a fruity cider vinegar–based pickling liquid before draining and serving them.

With that, we had beefy, rich, paleo-friendly tacos that could hold their own against the best of the rest.

—DANIELLE DESIATO AND LAWMAN JOHNSON, *America's Test Kitchen Books*

PALEO SHREDDED BEEF TACOS WITH CABBAGE SLAW

Paleo Shredded Beef Tacos with Cabbage Slaw

SERVES 4 TO 6

2 cups water, plus extra as needed

1¼ cups cider vinegar

4 teaspoons dried oregano

Kosher salt and pepper

4 cups shredded green cabbage

2 large carrots, peeled and shredded

1 jalapeño chile, stemmed, seeded, and minced

4 dried ancho chiles, stemmed, seeded, and torn into ½ inch pieces (1 cup)

3 tablespoons tomato paste

6 garlic cloves, lightly crushed and peeled

1 tablespoon ground cumin

¾ teaspoon ground cinnamon

½ teaspoon ground cloves

3 bay leaves

1 large onion, sliced into ½-inch-thick rounds

2 pounds boneless beef chuck-eye roast, pulled apart at seams, trimmed, and cut into 2-inch pieces

1 cup chopped fresh cilantro

12 (6-inch) Paleo Wraps, warmed (recipe follows)

Lime wedges

1. Whisk ½ cup water, ¾ cup vinegar, 1 teaspoon oregano, and 1 tablespoon salt together in large bowl until salt is dissolved. Add cabbage, carrot, and jalapeño and toss to combine. Cover and refrigerate until ready to serve. (Slaw can be refrigerated for up to 24 hours.)

2. Adjust oven rack to lower-middle position and heat oven to 325 degrees. Combine anchos, tomato paste, garlic, cumin, cinnamon, cloves, bay leaves, 1 tablespoon salt, ½ teaspoon pepper, remaining 1½ cups water, remaining ½ cup vinegar, and remaining 1 tablespoon oregano in Dutch oven. Arrange onion rounds in single layer on bottom of pot. Place beef on top of onion rounds in single layer.

3. Fit large piece of aluminum foil over pot, pressing to seal, then cover tightly with lid. Transfer pot to oven and cook until meat is well browned and tender, 2½ to 3 hours.

4. Using slotted spoon, transfer beef to large bowl and cover. Being careful of hot pot handles, strain cooking liquid through fine-mesh strainer into 2 cup liquid measuring cup (do not wash pot). Discard onion rounds and bay leaves, then transfer remaining solids to blender. Using wide, shallow spoon, skim excess fat from surface of liquid. Add water as needed to equal 1 cup. Add liquid to blender with solids and process until smooth, about 2 minutes; transfer to now-empty pot.

5. Using 2 forks, shred beef into bite-size pieces, discarding excess fat. Bring sauce to simmer over medium heat. Stir in shredded beef and season with salt to taste. Drain slaw and stir in cilantro. Serve shredded beef with warm wraps, slaw, and lime wedges.

Paleo Wraps

MAKES 12 (6-INCH) WRAPS

To allow for practice, the recipe yields extra batter. To make larger wraps, pour ⅓ cup of batter into a 10-inch skillet or ½ cup batter into a 12-inch skillet; cook as directed. To reheat, stack the wraps on a plate, sprinkle them with a little water, cover with a paper towel, and microwave until warm and soft, about 1 minute. Wraps can also be reheated one at a time in a skillet.

2 cups (6 ounces) almond flour

¾ cup (3 ounces) tapioca flour

¼ cup (1 ounce) coconut flour

2 teaspoons kosher salt

1¾ cups water

2 large eggs

3 tablespoons plus 1 teaspoon extra-virgin olive oil

1. Whisk almond flour, tapioca flour, coconut flour, and salt together in large bowl. In separate bowl, whisk water, eggs, and 3 tablespoons oil until combined. Whisk water mixture into almond flour mixture until thoroughly combined. Let batter rest for 15 minutes.

2. Meanwhile, place remaining 1 teaspoon oil in 8-inch nonstick skillet and heat over low heat for at least 5 minutes. Using paper towel, wipe out skillet, leaving thin film of oil on bottom and sides of skillet. Increase heat to medium and let skillet heat for 1 minute. After 1 minute, test heat of skillet by placing 1 teaspoon batter in center and cooking for 20 seconds. If mini test wrap is golden brown on bottom, skillet is properly heated; if too light or too dark, adjust heat accordingly and retest.

3. Whisk batter to recombine. Pour ¼ cup batter into far side of skillet and tilt and shake gently until batter evenly covers bottom of skillet. Cook wrap without moving it until top surface is dry and wrap starts to brown at edges, loosening wrap from side of skillet with rubber spatula, 1 to 3 minutes. Gently slide spatula underneath edge of wrap, grasp edge with your fingertips, and flip wrap. Cook until second side is lightly spotted, 1 to 3 minutes. Transfer cooked wrap to wire rack, inverting so spotted side is facing up.

4. Return skillet to medium heat for 10 seconds before repeating with remaining batter, whisking batter often to recombine. As wraps are done, stack on rack. Serve immediately or let cool to room temperature. (Cooled wraps can be wrapped tightly in plastic wrap and refrigerated for up to 1 week.)

CORNISH PASTIES

✔ **WHY THIS RECIPE WORKS:** At their best, the handheld turnovers known as pasties boast a rich and flaky crust and meaty filling; at their worst, they turn out dry and tough. To put our pasties on the right track, we started by making a sturdy but pliable dough. Using sour cream instead of water brought in extra tangy flavor, and plenty of butter promised a rich crust. The food processor made mixing the ingredients a breeze, and chilling the dough made it easier to handle. We wanted meaty, satisfying flavors in the filling, so we started by softening chopped onion in butter, deepening its flavor with fresh thyme and minced garlic. Hearty pieces of skirt steak, russet potatoes, rutabaga, and a little flour rounded out our filling. We rolled out the dough into ovals, mounded the filling in the middle of each, and folded the dough over to seal in the mixture. Vents cut into the top gave us some insurance against exploding pasties. As the pasties baked, the flour combined with the filling's exuded juices to create the gravy right inside the crust.

Cornish pasties should be great: tender beef and vegetables wrapped in a flaky crust. So I was surprised when one of our editors who ate these as a child told me, "The best thing about a pasty is the ketchup on the side."

Pasties do evoke strong feelings. Some fans adamantly oppose any vegetables in the filling other than potatoes and onions. Some, equally adamantly, endorse turnips, carrots, and rutabagas. Some recipes call for lard, while others use butter. Where to begin?

The mining industry in Michigan's Upper Peninsula attracted immigrants from Cornwall, England, in the 19th century and they brought their pasties with them. The miners' pasties were as big as dinner plates, filled with enough food to fuel an entire day's labor. The crust was sturdy enough for carrying and, some legends suggest, for protecting the contents even when dropped down the mine shaft.

A vibrant image, but I wanted a hand pie with a tender, not impact-resistant, crust. After trying flour doughs made with lard, shortening, and butter (and various combinations thereof), my tasters agreed that butter imparted the best flavor into the crust.

To make a pliable dough that would be easy to manipulate and shape, I added an egg and, instead of water, cold sour cream, which added a pleasant tangy flavor. The food processor allowed me to mix quickly and avoid overworking the dough. I pressed it into a disk, wrapped it, and refrigerated it; the cold dough was much easier to work with. In initial tests, my pasty fillings (beef, chopped onion, potato, and salt and pepper) were bland. I sautéed the onion in butter to deepen its flavor and added minced garlic and fresh thyme.

I chose cubed meat over ground (the latter gave me patties, not pasties), and after trying several cuts, I settled on skirt steak. It went, raw, into the cooled onions along with cubed potatoes and—after much testing and impassioned debate—earthy rutabaga. I seasoned the mixture with salt and pepper and then tossed it with flour to help the meat create its own gravy while it baked.

The final hurdle was construction. I rolled the pieces of dough into ovals and spooned some filling into the center of each. I brushed their edges with water to help them stick and folded the ovals over the filling to create half-moon shapes. I pressed the edges together, then trimmed and crimped for a neat finish.

To create an escape vent for steam (and forestall any leakage in the oven), I cut a small slit in the top of each pie. After 45 minutes, the pies were golden brown, with the filling just bubbling up through the vents.

Like the original miners' fare, these pasties are hearty, but the crust is more flaky than fortified. I'm as likely to fork-and-knife one as I am to eat it out of my hands. Ketchup optional.

—KATIE LEAIRD, *Cook's Country*

Cornish Pasties

SERVES 6

You can substitute turnips for rutabagas if you like. If you can't find skirt steak, you can use 1½ pounds of blade steak (the extra ¼ pound accounts for the trimming required with the blade cut). The pasties fit best on the baking sheet when placed crosswise in two rows of three. Serve the pasties with ketchup, if desired.

CRUST

- 1 cup sour cream, chilled
- 1 large egg, lightly beaten
- 3 cups (15 ounces) all-purpose flour
- 1¾ teaspoons salt
- 16 tablespoons unsalted butter, cut into ½-inch pieces and chilled

FILLING

- 1 tablespoon unsalted butter
- 1 onion, chopped fine
  Salt and pepper
- 1 tablespoon minced fresh thyme
- 2 garlic cloves, minced
- 1¼ pounds skirt steak, trimmed and cut into ½-inch pieces
- 10 ounces russet potatoes, peeled and cut into ½-inch pieces
- 10 ounces rutabaga, peeled and cut into ½-inch pieces
- ¼ cup all-purpose flour
- 1 large egg, lightly beaten with 2 teaspoons water

1. FOR THE CRUST: Whisk sour cream and egg together in small bowl. Process flour and salt in food processor until combined, about 3 seconds. Add butter and pulse until only pea-size pieces remain, about 10 pulses.

FORMING PASTIES
After the dough chills for at least 30 minutes, it's ready to shape and fill.

1. Divide dough into 6 equal pieces and roll each into oval shape.

2. Place filling in center of dough.

3. Brush edges of dough with water.

4. Fold dough over filling to create half-moon shape and press edges to seal.

5. Trim excess dough from sealed edges with pizza cutter and crimp with fork.

CORNISH PASTIES

Add half of sour cream mixture and pulse until combined, about 5 pulses. Add remaining sour cream mixture and pulse until dough begins to form, about 15 pulses.

2. Transfer mixture to lightly floured counter and knead briefly until dough comes together. Form dough into 6-inch disk, wrap tightly in plastic wrap, and refrigerate for 30 minutes. (Dough can be refrigerated for up to 24 hours; let chilled dough sit on counter for 15 minutes to soften before rolling.)

3. FOR THE FILLING: Melt butter in 10-inch skillet over medium heat. Add onion and ¼ teaspoon salt and cook until softened, about 5 minutes. Add thyme and garlic and cook until fragrant, about 30 seconds. Let cool slightly, about 5 minutes. Combine cooled onion mixture, steak, potatoes, rutabaga, 2 teaspoons salt, and ¾ teaspoon pepper in bowl. Add flour and toss to coat.

4. Adjust oven rack to upper-middle position and heat oven to 375 degrees. Line rimmed baking sheet with parchment paper. Remove dough from refrigerator and cut into 6 equal pieces (about 5 ounces each); cover with plastic wrap. Divide filling into 6 equal portions, about 1 heaping cup each.

5. Working with 1 piece of dough at a time, roll into 10 by 8-inch oval (about ⅛ inch thick) on lightly floured counter. Place 1 portion filling in center of dough. Moisten edges of dough with water, then fold narrow end of oval over filling to form half-moon shape. Press dough around filling to adhere.

6. Trim any ragged edges, then crimp edges with fork to seal; transfer to prepared sheet. (For more decorative edge, trim any ragged edges and, starting at 1 end, pinch and slightly twist dough diagonally across seam between your thumb and index finger. Continue pinching and twisting dough around seam.) Repeat with remaining dough and filling.

7. Using paring knife, cut 1-inch vent hole on top of each pasty. Brush pasties with egg wash. Bake until crust is golden brown and filling is bubbling up through vent hole, about 45 minutes, rotating sheet halfway through baking. Transfer pasties to wire rack and let cool for 10 minutes before serving.

TO MAKE AHEAD: Pasties can be prepared through step 6, then frozen on baking sheet. Once frozen, pasties can be stored in zipper-lock bag for up to 1 month. To cook from frozen, bake at 350 degrees for 1 hour 5 minutes to 1 hour 10 minutes.

POTATO-CHEDDAR PIEROGI

✔ **WHY THIS RECIPE WORKS:** Pierogi are traditional Polish dumplings that feature a mixture of mashed potatoes and cheese or sauerkraut tucked into a tender dough. Starting with the filling, we used a stand mixer to quickly and thoroughly combine our ingredients: boiled russet potatoes, shredded cheddar cheese, and butter. The heat from the potatoes melted the butter and cheese, ensuring an even consistency in the finished pierogi. While the filling chilled, we moved on to the dumpling dough. We found that we could bypass the usual blend of all-purpose and semolina flours by just using higher protein bread flour. Sour cream and egg helped bind the dough, making it pliable enough to roll out and stamp into rounds with a biscuit cutter. Pinching the edges of the filled pierogi sealed in the potato-cheddar mixture before we boiled them. A quick topping of caramelized onion, prepared in a skillet and then tossed with the pierogi before serving, made for an authentic finish.

When our executive food editor, Bryan Roof, returned from a trip to Pittsburgh, he was unabashedly enthusiastic about the pierogi he'd eaten in that city's historic Polish American quarter. The tender but chewy dumplings stuffed with potatoes, cheese, and sometimes sauerkraut won him over. I wanted to create a recipe that would win over the rest of us.

Pittsburgh, which rose to prominence as an industrial capital during the late 19th century, attracted thousands of Polish immigrants to work in steel mills and coal mines. By 1920, Polish Americans made up one-third of the city's workforce. Many settled in a steep, winding, hillside neighborhood overlooking the Allegheny River, now known as Polish Hill. There, Roof was invited into a Polish American home to make pierogi with Elaine Kitlowski, who generously shared her recipe with us.

It's a simple but exacting recipe, calling for equal parts all-purpose and hard durum semolina flour. Sour cream and egg bind the flours together into a supple dough that's easy to roll out thin, cut into circles, stuff with mashed potato, and seal up into dumplings for boiling. These pierogi had a faint bite, like the al dente quality of properly cooked pasta. They were excellent.

But I wondered about the semolina flour, which isn't always easy to find at the supermarket. Did I need it? I tried making the dough with just all-purpose flour. Unfortunately, the resulting pierogi were a flop.

The flour's protein content is one major factor in a dough's tenderness (water and the amount of kneading are others). Kitlowski's mix of all-purpose flour (with 11 grams of protein per cup) and semolina (about 21 grams) averaged out to roughly 16 grams of protein per cup, the same as in commonly available bread flour. Hopeful, I made a batch of pierogi using just bread flour and pitted the results against the pierogi made following Kitlowski's recipe. Tasters found both acceptable. Bread flour it would be.

Most Pittsburgh-style pierogi are stuffed with a simple mixture of mashed potatoes and cheddar cheese, plus salt and pepper. The trick lies in thoroughly combining the ingredients. After boiling slices of russet potatoes (chosen for their fluffiness) until soft, I used the stand mixer to quickly and completely incorporate butter and cheese into the still-hot potatoes. Some salt and pepper gave me a well-seasoned filling.

A happy result of all this testing was that it gave me a chance to develop an easy way to cut, fill, and shape the pierogi: I rolled the dough thin, to 1/8 inch, and then used a biscuit cutter to cut out 3-inch circles. I dropped a tablespoon of potato filling onto each circle and sealed the edges up and over the savory mound to form a half-moon shape. Once the pierogi were boiled, I tossed them in a topping of butter and caramelized chopped onion and offered them up. "Tastes like home," said one Pittsburgh-bred colleague.

—KATIE LEAIRD, *Cook's Country*

Potato-Cheddar Pierogi
MAKES ABOUT 30 PIEROGI

When rolling the dough in step 4, be sure not to dust the top surface with too much flour, as that will prevent the edges from forming a tight seal when pinched.

FILLING
- 1 pound russet potatoes, peeled and sliced 1/2 inch thick
  Salt and pepper
- 4 ounces sharp cheddar cheese, shredded (1 cup)
- 2 tablespoons unsalted butter

DOUGH
- 2½ cups (13¾ ounces) bread flour
- 1 teaspoon baking powder
  Salt
- 1 cup sour cream
- 1 large egg plus 1 large yolk

TOPPING
- 4 tablespoons unsalted butter
- 1 large onion, chopped fine
- ½ teaspoon salt

1. FOR THE FILLING: Combine potatoes and 1 tablespoon salt in large saucepan and cover with water by 1 inch. Bring to boil over medium-high heat; reduce heat to medium and cook at vigorous simmer until potatoes are very tender, about 15 minutes.

2. Drain potatoes in colander. While still hot, combine potatoes, cheddar, butter, ½ teaspoon salt, and ½ teaspoon pepper in bowl of stand mixer. Fit mixer with paddle and mix on medium speed until potatoes are smooth and all ingredients are fully combined, about 1 minute. Transfer filling to 8-inch square baking dish and refrigerate until fully chilled, about 30 minutes, or cover with plastic wrap and refrigerate for up to 24 hours.

3. FOR THE DOUGH: Whisk flour, baking powder, and ½ teaspoon salt together in clean bowl of stand mixer. Add sour cream and egg and yolk. Fit mixer with dough hook and knead on medium-high speed for 8 minutes (dough will be smooth and elastic). Transfer dough to floured bowl, cover with plastic, and refrigerate until ready to assemble.

4. Line rimmed baking sheet with parchment paper and dust with flour. Roll dough on lightly floured counter into 18-inch circle, about ⅛-inch thick. Using 3-inch biscuit cutter, cut 20 to 24 circles from dough. Place 1 tablespoon chilled filling in center of each dough round. Fold dough over filling to create half-moon shape and pinch edges firmly to seal. Transfer to prepared sheet.

5. Gather dough scraps and reroll to ⅛-inch thickness. Cut 6 to 10 more circles from dough and repeat with remaining filling. (It may be necessary to reroll dough once more to yield 30 pierogi.) Cover pierogi with plastic and refrigerate until ready to cook, up to 3 hours.

6. FOR THE TOPPING: Melt butter in 12-inch skillet over medium-low heat. Add onion and salt and cook until onion is caramelized, 15 to 20 minutes. Remove skillet from heat and set aside.

7. Bring 4 quarts water to boil in Dutch oven. Add 1 tablespoon salt and half of pierogi to boiling water and cook until tender, about 5 minutes. Using spider or slotted spoon, remove pierogi from water and transfer to skillet with caramelized onion. Return water to boil, cook remaining pierogi, and transfer to skillet with first batch.

8. Add 2 tablespoons cooking water to pierogi in skillet. Cook over medium-low heat, stirring gently, until onion mixture is warmed through and adhered to pierogi. Transfer to platter and serve.

TO MAKE AHEAD: Uncooked pierogi can be frozen for several weeks. After sealing pierogi in step 4, freeze them on baking sheet, about 3 hours. Transfer frozen pierogi to zipper-lock freezer bag. When ready to cook, extend boiling time in step 7 to about 7 minutes.

VARIATION

Potato-Sauerkraut Pierogi

Omit cheddar and pepper. In step 2, combine 1¼ cups sauerkraut, drained and chopped fine, and ¼ teaspoon white pepper with potatoes.

NOTES FROM THE TEST KITCHEN

PREPPING PIEROGI
For Pittsburgh-caliber pierogi, we needed the dumplings to stay sealed.

1. CUT: Using 3-inch biscuit cutter, cut 20 to 24 circles from dough. After cutting first batch, gather scraps, reroll dough, and cut 6 to 10 more circles.

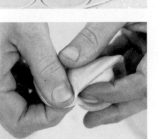

2. FILL AND FOLD: Place 1 tablespoon of filling in center of each dough round. Fold dough over filling to create half-moon shape. Pinch firmly to seal.

SUPERMARKET SAUERKRAUT
To find out which kraut is king, we tried six nationally available supermarket sauerkrauts plain and in pierogi. Slightly sweet with plenty of zing, Eden Organic Sauerkraut won us over. This jarred kraut lent a bright tanginess to our pierogi, and its small shreds were soft, with just a bit of chew for a perfect filling.

ZUCCHINI-SPAGHETTI AND MEATBALLS

✔ **WHY THIS RECIPE WORKS:** To turn spaghetti and meatballs into a paleo-friendly favorite, we wanted our recipe to be an upgrade, not just a series of substitutions. We needed to successfully replace the wheat pasta, bind the meatballs, and make a hearty sauce out of fresh tomatoes. Cooking a large batch of aromatics allowed us to divide them between the meatballs and the sauce. For a paleo panade (typically a combination of milk and bread) that would keep the meatballs moist, we turned to cashews, which in the paleo world are often boiled and pureed and used as a cheese substitute. We processed the aromatics, boiled cashews, basil, and an egg before kneading the mixture into ground beef. For the sauce, we processed fresh tomatoes and used the fat from browning the meatballs to sauté the aromatics for a superflavorful base. Tomato paste delivered concentrated tomato flavor along with the brightly flavored fresh tomato puree. Braising the meatballs right in the sauce allowed the sauce to pick up meaty flavor. Spiralized zucchini turned out to be the perfect spaghetti stand-in. After cranking out long strands, we tossed them with oil and salt and roasted them, eliminating any moisture that might compromise the sauce. After 20 minutes, our faux pasta was ready to be topped with fresh, flavorful sauce and tender, seasoned meatballs.

At first blush, converting spaghetti and meatballs to suit a paleo diet seemed daunting; classic recipes are fraught with nonpaleo ingredients. Wheat flour is on paleo's no-fly list, so I would need to find a suitable replacement for the pasta. In the test kitchen, we generally rely on a panade of milk and bread to help the meat stay moist and hold its shape, but both of those ingredients would have to go. Furthermore, convenient canned tomatoes, which often contain preservatives and sugar, were also ruled out. Eying my vegetable spiralizer, I decided to tackle the pasta first.

Paleo home cooks swear by spiralized vegetables as a substitute for spaghetti, so rather than reinvent the wheel, I started there. I wanted to find a vegetable with a pasta-like texture that wouldn't introduce any distracting flavors to the dish. I spun out a few different contenders. Sweet potatoes, carrots, parsnips, and celery root spiralized beautifully, but their flavors were too distinct and ill-suited for pairing with tomato sauce. Spiralized zucchini, however, had a mild, neutral flavor and its texture was just as tender as real spaghetti's. Leaving no stone unturned, I spiralized a few more vegetables and discovered that the slightly sweet flavor of butternut squash was yet another winner. I kept it in mind as a superb alternative to the zucchini.

On to the meatballs. My tender spiralized "spaghetti" deserved tender meatballs, so I knew I would need something to take the panade's place. I tested my way through a number of paleo-approved binding and tenderizing options that I'd seen in other recipes, including coconut flour, gelatin, and boiled, pureed cashews. Coconut flour and gelatin left the meat spongy, but the cashews created a creamy, paste-like base very similar to a traditional panade. This simple puree's neutral flavor promised to let the meatballs' flavorings shine, and its buttery texture held the meatballs together and kept the meat tender. To soften the cashews efficiently, I boiled them for 15 minutes, drained and rinsed them, and processed them with fresh basil and an egg for extra binding power.

To give the meat an aromatic boost, I browned chopped onion with some Italian-inspired flavors: minced garlic, oregano, and red pepper flakes. I doubled up my aromatics in order to use them in the sauce as well as in the meatballs. I pulsed half of the aromatics in with the cashew paste, reserving the other half for the sauce, and kneaded the paste into a pound of 85 percent lean ground beef, opting for a higher fat content for more richness. I rolled out a dozen meatballs and browned them in olive oil in a hot skillet. I was about to finish the meatballs by roasting them in the oven when I got an idea: What if I braised them right in the sauce? This simple step would make my paleo pasta dish a convenient one-pot meal, and adding the meatballs to the sauce would give it a meaty backbone. I left the rendered fat in the skillet and started on the sauce.

With canned tomatoes off the table, I grabbed ripe, fresh tomatoes and pulsed them in the food processor to a near-smooth consistency. I used the fat left in the skillet to brown the remaining aromatics a little more deeply and spooned in some tomato paste for deep tomato flavor. I poured in the bright tomato puree, stirred the sauce together, and braised the browned meatballs directly in the sauce, gently cooking the meatballs through.

My three essential components were ready to go, but I needed to find a way to gently cook the spiralized zucchini. Zucchini is loaded with lots of moisture, so it was clear that I'd need to dry it out before saucing it; otherwise, its exuded liquid would water down my robust sauce. I'd made enough sauce to top off four servings, so I needed to effectively dry a large amount of zucchini, ruling out any stovetop technique. A quick roasting in the oven proved the perfect solution. I tossed the strands with salt, to draw out excess liquid, and a bit of olive oil, which protected the strands from sticking to the baking sheet. A brief 20 minutes in the oven dried out the strands without compromising their tender texture.

NOTES FROM THE TEST KITCHEN

MAKING PALEO MEATBALLS

1. Process aromatics, basil, egg, boiled cashews, and salt to fine paste. In a separate bowl, knead ground beef with cashew paste until combined.

2. Pinch off and roll mixture into 1½-inch balls, then brown meatballs to enhance savory, meaty flavor.

3. Once tomato sauce has thickened, add browned meatballs to sauce and continue to simmer until meatballs cook through.

I served myself a heaping portion of my zucchini-spaghetti and much to my delight, this paleo take on a suppertime standard was as good as the real thing.
—DANIELLE DESIATO, *America's Test Kitchen Books*

Zucchini-Spaghetti and Meatballs
SERVES 4

If possible, use smaller, in-season zucchini, which have thinner skins and fewer seeds. For more information on spiralizing, see page 30. This recipe calls for a 12-inch nonstick skillet; however, a well-seasoned cast-iron skillet can be used instead.

¼ cup raw cashews
3 tablespoons extra-virgin olive oil
2 onions, chopped fine
6 garlic cloves, minced
1 tablespoon dried oregano
¼ teaspoon red pepper flakes
¼ cup plus 2 tablespoons chopped fresh basil
1 large egg
 Kosher salt and pepper
1 pound 85 percent lean ground beef
2 pounds tomatoes, cored and chopped
¼ cup tomato paste
3 pounds zucchini or yellow summer squash, trimmed

1. Bring 4 cups water to boil in medium saucepan over medium-high heat. Add cashews and cook until softened, about 15 minutes. Drain and rinse well.

2. Heat 1 tablespoon oil in 12-inch nonstick skillet over medium heat until shimmering. Add onions and cook until softened and lightly browned, 8 to 10 minutes. Stir in garlic, oregano, and pepper flakes and cook until fragrant, about 30 seconds. Transfer half of onion mixture to bowl and set aside.

3. Process remaining onion mixture, boiled cashews, ¼ cup basil, egg, and 1½ teaspoons salt in food processor to fine paste, about 1 minute, scraping down sides of bowl as needed; transfer to large bowl. Add ground beef and knead with your hands until well combined. Pinch off and roll mixture into 1½-inch meatballs (you should have 12 meatballs).

4. Process tomatoes in clean, dry workbowl until smooth, about 30 seconds. Heat 1 tablespoon oil in now-empty skillet over medium heat until just smoking. Brown meatballs on all sides, about 10 minutes; transfer to plate.

5. Add reserved onion mixture and tomato paste to fat left in skillet and cook over medium heat until tomato paste begins to brown, about 1 minute. Stir in processed tomatoes, bring to simmer, and cook until sauce is thickened, about 20 minutes.

6. Return browned meatballs and any accumulated juices to skillet. Reduce heat to medium-low, cover, and simmer gently until meatballs are cooked through, about 10 minutes. Adjust sauce consistency with hot water as needed. Stir in remaining 2 tablespoons basil and season with salt and pepper to taste. (Sauce and meatballs can be refrigerated for up to 3 days or frozen for up to 1 month; gently reheat before serving.)

7. Meanwhile, adjust oven rack to middle position and heat oven to 375 degrees. Using spiralizer, cut zucchini into ⅛-inch-thick noodles, then cut noodles into 12-inch lengths. Toss zucchini with 1 teaspoon salt, ½ teaspoon pepper, and remaining 1 tablespoon oil on rimmed baking sheet and roast until tender, 20 to 25 minutes. Transfer zucchini to colander and shake to remove any excess liquid. Transfer zucchini to large serving bowl, add several spoonfuls of sauce (without meatballs), and gently toss to combine. Serve zucchini with remaining sauce and meatballs.

VARIATION

Butternut Squash–Spaghetti and Meatballs

This recipe uses only the solid necks of the squash. Reserve the bulbs for another use. Cooked squash noodles will be delicate and may break when transferring to serving platter.

Using sharp vegetable peeler or chef's knife, remove skin and fibrous threads from two 3-pound butternut squashes. Trim off top of squash and cut squash in half where narrow neck and wide curved base meet; reserve squash bases for another use. Using spiralizer, cut squash necks into ⅛-inch-thick noodles, then cut noodles into 12-inch lengths (you should have 14 cups). Substitute squash noodles for zucchini noodles in step 7, covering tightly with aluminum foil for first 15 minutes of roasting; do not drain in colander. Gently transfer squash to serving platter and top with meatballs and several spoonfuls of sauce (do not toss). Serve with remaining sauce.

PAN-SEARED FLANK STEAK

✔ **WHY THIS RECIPE WORKS:** Flank steak is too long to fit in most skillets, and it's quite thin, so it often overcooks before the exterior is well browned. What's more, the long muscle fibers tend to contract when seared, causing the steak to buckle and resist browning. Since flank steak is thicker at one end, it has a tendency to cook unevenly. We were determined to find an indoor cooking method that produced a juicy, well-browned flank steak cooked to medium throughout. We cut the flank steak into four portions that would fit neatly in a 12-inch skillet and sprinkled them with salt for seasoning and sugar for browning. Then we baked the steaks in a very low oven until they reached 120 degrees. To develop a flavorful crust, we seared them in a hot skillet, flipping several times to even out the contraction of the muscle fibers on each side to prevent buckling. After enriching the lean steaks with compound butter, we sliced them thin against the grain for maximum tenderness.

In a perfect world, cooking a flank steak would be as simple as throwing it into a hot pan and searing it on each side. The outside would be crusty and brown by the time the inside was cooked to a rosy, even medium. But in the real world, flank steak can be too long to squeeze into a 12-inch skillet, so its ends reach up the sloped sides, making it awkward to cook. Plus, it's made up of long muscle fibers that contract when heated, causing the steak to buckle and therefore brown unevenly. The long muscle fibers also shrink unevenly as the meat cooks, so one end becomes thicker than the other. This means that the steak can turn out rare at the thick end and medium-well at the thin end. To top it off, the prolonged sear causes the meat just beneath the exterior to overcook and turn gray.

Moving outside to the grill solves most of these problems: There's no skillet to squeeze into (or smoke alarm to set off), and the more intense heat browns the steak better, even if it warps a bit. The uneven cooking and gray layer persist, but most cooks accept such imperfections as the price they pay for a quick grilled dinner.

But I wanted a year-round way to cook this beefy, lean steak—and a tolerance of imperfection is not among my more notable qualities. I was determined to find a reliable indoor method for producing a well-browned flank steak that was cooked medium throughout. (We like loose-textured, wide-fibered steaks like flank cooked to medium because at this degree of

PAN-SEARED FLANK STEAK WITH MUSTARD-CHIVE BUTTER

doneness the fibers shrink a bit more, which translates to greater tenderness.)

Hoping to limit smoke and spatter, I decided to try cooking the steak in the oven. To get any crust development, the meat was going to have to sit flat on a very hot, broad surface. But, alas, broiling the steak on a rimmed baking sheet was a failure. As it slowly heated up, moisture beaded on the wide, flat surface of the meat, inhibiting browning and leaving me with a gray steak that tasted steamed.

If I wanted that flavorful brown crust, I was going to have to use the direct heat of the stovetop. I started by dividing the steak into quarters. It was an unconventional move, but I had two reasons: First, doing so helped the steak fit neatly into the skillet. Second, it meant that I could remove the individual steaks from the skillet as they finished cooking, so they would all be cooked to a perfect medium.

I heated 2 tablespoons of oil in a skillet over medium-high heat until it was just smoking and added the steaks. Thinking that minimal interference would yield the best sear, I resolved to wait 3 minutes before moving them. The steaks buckled, though not as severely as the full steak had, and I hoped the warping would be reversed when I flipped them. Unfortunately, the damage was irreversible. The first sear had set a concave shape, so the steaks browned only around the edge of one side and only in the middle of the other.

I removed the two thinner steaks from the skillet after about 8 minutes when they reached 125 degrees. The thicker steaks took about 4 minutes longer. After resting, they were all cooked to medium, but there was a sizable band of gray, overcooked meat around the edges, and the browning—though better than my oven attempts—was still not up to par. As I wiped up the splatter on the stove, I knew there had to be a better way.

Cutting the steak into quarters gave me better control of the internal temperature of the meat and enabled me to fit it all in the pan, so I'd stick with that, but I had to reconsider the cooking method. Perhaps I had been hasty in eliminating the oven as a possibility.

One of the best methods for cooking thick steaks is the test kitchen's hybrid method that involves heating them gently in a 275-degree oven until they approach the perfect internal temperature and then transferring them to a hot skillet on the stovetop to brown. The oven step accomplishes three things: First, the precooked meat doesn't cool down a hot pan as drastically as a room-temperature steak would, so browning starts almost immediately. Second, some of the steak's surface moisture evaporates in the oven, so there's less to be converted to steam before browning can begin. Third, this accelerated browning means that the steak doesn't have to spend much time in the skillet, so the meat just below the crust doesn't overcook. There's also less time for splatter and smoke.

It's the best way to cook uniformly thick, hefty steaks like rib eyes or strip steaks, but would flank steak's irregular thinness be suited to this treatment? To find out, I divided my steak into quarters and seasoned them with salt. I also sprinkled on a teaspoon of sugar to assist in browning when the time came. I placed the meat on a wire rack set in a rimmed baking sheet and baked it in a 275-degree oven until the thickest steak reached 120 degrees, about 20 minutes. Then I seared the steaks in a hot skillet.

This time I was not as restrained about flipping the steaks. Reasoning that the buckling was caused not so much by the tightening of the fibers on each side of the steak as by the *unequal* tightening of those fibers, I flipped the steaks every minute to keep the surface tightening on each side pretty much equal. It worked. This time the steaks were much flatter, which meant that more of the meat stayed in contact with the cooking surface. This, combined with the caramelizing effect of the sugar, yielded the best browning thus far.

But the doneness varied. The thicker ends were cooked to a perfect medium, but the thinner ends were closer to medium-well.

During my next test I was hyper-vigilant, repeatedly temping each steak and removing each from the oven as it reached 120 degrees. But such frequent temperature taking meant opening the oven several times, and every time it lost heat and had little time to recover before I opened it again. The thinnest steak was done in 20 minutes, but it took almost 50 minutes before the thickest steak reached the target temperature, which was a lot of fuss.

And yet these steaks won me over. They browned beautifully in the skillet, and I was happy with their juicy, rosy interiors and lack of overdone gray meat just below the surface. Was there a hassle-free way to get all the meat to the target temperature at once?

It occurred to me that high-heat methods like grilling or searing in a skillet had resulted in the biggest doneness differential between the thick and thin steaks. Could I close the gap by using a very low-temperature oven?

I reduced the oven temperature to 250 degrees and inserted a probe thermometer into one of the thicker steaks. When the thermometer registered 120 degrees (since I wasn't opening the oven, this took only about 30 minutes), I transferred all the steaks to a skillet to brown. Sure enough, these steaks were closer in terms of doneness, but the thinner steaks were still a bit overcooked.

Lowering the oven temperature even more did the trick. Steaks that were warmed for 35 minutes in a 225-degree oven registered between 120 and 130 degrees, so that after searing and resting they were a perfect rosy medium.

Flank steaks this great deserved a bit of embellishment. I mixed up some flavorful compound butters and slathered them on the warm steaks to melt over them as they rested. I sliced the steaks thin across the grain for maximum tenderness and dotted them with just a bit more butter. Imperfection is no longer part of the flank steak bargain.

—ANDREA GEARY, *Cook's Illustrated*

Pan-Seared Flank Steak with Mustard-Chive Butter
SERVES 4 TO 6

Open the oven as infrequently as possible in step 1. If the meat is not yet up to temperature, wait at least 5 minutes before taking its temperature again. Slice the steak as thin as possible against the grain.

- 1 (1½- to 1¾-pound) flank steak, trimmed
- 2 teaspoons kosher salt
- 1 teaspoon sugar
- ½ teaspoon pepper
- 3 tablespoons unsalted butter, softened
- 3 tablespoons chopped fresh chives
- 2 teaspoons Dijon mustard
- ½ teaspoon grated lemon zest plus 1 teaspoon juice
- 2 tablespoons vegetable oil

1. Adjust oven rack to middle position and heat oven to 225 degrees. Pat steak dry with paper towels. Cut steak in half lengthwise. Cut each piece in half

crosswise to create 4 steaks. Combine salt, sugar, and pepper in small bowl. Sprinkle half of salt mixture on 1 side of steaks and press gently to adhere. Flip steaks and repeat with remaining salt mixture. Place steaks on wire rack set in rimmed baking sheet; transfer sheet to oven. Cook until thermometer inserted through side into center of thickest steak registers 120 degrees, 30 to 40 minutes.

2. Meanwhile, combine butter, 1 tablespoon chives, mustard, and lemon zest and juice in small bowl.

3. Heat oil in 12-inch skillet over medium-high heat until just smoking. Sear steaks, flipping every 1 minute, until brown crust forms on both sides, 4 minutes total. (Do not move steaks between flips.) Return steaks to wire rack and let rest for 10 minutes.

4. Transfer steaks to cutting board with grain running from left to right. Spread 1½ teaspoons butter mixture on top of each steak. Slice steak as thin as possible against grain. Transfer sliced steak to warm platter, dot with remaining butter mixture, sprinkle with remaining 2 tablespoons chives, and serve.

VARIATIONS

Pan-Seared Flank Steak with Sriracha-Lime Butter

Substitute 3 tablespoons chopped fresh cilantro, 1 tablespoon Sriracha sauce, and ½ teaspoon grated lime zest plus 1 teaspoon juice for chives, Dijon mustard, and lemon zest and juice in step 2.

Pan-Seared Flank Steak with Garlic-Anchovy Butter

Substitute 3 tablespoons chopped fresh parsley and 1 anchovy fillet, rinsed and minced to paste, for chives, Dijon mustard, and lemon zest and juice in step 2.

NOTES FROM THE TEST KITCHEN

FITTING A RECTANGLE INTO A CIRCLE

Squeezing a long flank steak into a 12-inch skillet usually means that the ends of the steak creep up the sloped sides of the pan, all but guaranteeing unevenly cooked meat. Cutting our flank steak into four pieces and warming it in the oven before searing (where it shrinks significantly) helps it fit neatly. Smaller pieces also have shorter muscle fibers, so the steaks don't buckle as much during searing.

STEAK DIANE

✅ **WHY THIS RECIPE WORKS:** This old-school restaurant favorite is often marked by a dramatic tableside flambé, but we wanted a steak Diane that favored flavor over flair. We ditched the traditional thin beef cutlets, which are prone to overcooking, and upgraded to filets mignons. Gently pounding these luxe steaks to a 1-inch thickness ensured that they cooked to medium-rare quickly. Even better: We were able to fit four steaks in the skillet at once. Searing the peppery steaks in a hot skillet produced a flavorful crust on the steaks and fond in the pan. We used the fond to make a rich sauce, adding beef broth and Worcestershire for deep flavor, cognac for boozy complexity, and butter and Dijon for a smooth texture. Chives, lemon juice, and an extra hit of cognac brightened the velvety sauce. The flambé did little to improve our steak Diane, so we skipped it, more than pleased with our vibrantly flavored steaks.

Originally conceived in the 19th century as an homage to Diana, the Roman goddess of the hunt, Steak Diane was first made with thin cutlets of venison cloaked in a rich, labor-intensive sauce based on veal stock. By the 1950s, the dish had become culinary dinner theater in restaurants from New York to Hollywood; tuxedoed waiters would wheel a cart up to your table, warm up thinly pounded beef filets in a chafing dish of cognac sauce, and set the whole thing aflame. Patrons were thrilled but, more often than not, the show overshadowed the supper. I set out to reclaim the essence of steak Diane—heavily peppered steaks under a cognac-rich sauce—with a contemporary version I could make at home.

I found many recipes in our cookbook library calling for pricey cuts of meat (rib eyes or New York strips) to be pounded ¼ inch thick, seasoned with salt and coarsely cracked pepper, and cooked quickly in butter before being doused in cognac sauce. I was skeptical. Surely such thin cuts of meat would overcook.

I watched disappointedly as my suspicions bore out: My thinly pounded steaks turned from pink to an unappetizing gray-brown in a matter of seconds in the skillet. I pressed on anyway, removing the steaks to create the sauce, sweating shallots, and then stirring together cognac, beef broth, Worcestershire sauce, and

accumulated meat juices to cook down. Once the sauce thickened, I whisked in butter and Dijon to create a velvety texture.

After balancing out the sauce with lemon juice and an extra splash of cognac, I stood back and stared at my finished dish. The sauce was excellent. The meat? Leather. Why was I pounding a thick, beautiful steak into an unappealing thin cutlet and sacrificing an opportunity for an attractive brown crust?

I worried at my own flirtation with steak Diane heresy, but I couldn't help wishing for a thicker cut of meat, one that would develop a flavorful crust. Creating that crust would also allow a fond (flavorful browned bits) to develop in the pan; in turn, this fond would deepen the complexity of the sauce. I tried four 1-inch-thick strip steaks for my next test, but these larger steaks required searing in two batches, leaving the first batch cold by the time the pan sauce was ready. I followed with a test using four filets mignons gently pounded with a rolling pin to a 1-inch thickness, slightly larger than the traditional ¼-inch thickness, but daintier than the typical 2-inch steakhouse size. This luxurious cut thrilled my tasters. (Since I was already getting out the rolling pin, I also decided to use it to pound and roll the peppercorns into a more authentic coarse crack.)

Ask a panel of people what they think defines steak Diane, and most will cite the dramatic flambé. But in my research I found several recipes, particularly older ones, that made no mention of torching the cognac. Now, don't get me wrong—I love a dramatic flambé as much as the next person, and the test kitchen has previously shown that this step can add a subtle depth to similar dishes. But because I was creating a recipe for home kitchens, I wanted to be certain that this eyebrow-singeing step was necessary.

I cooked up a batch of flambéed Diane and a batch of non-flambéed and served them, in a blind side-by-side test, to my tasters. Both got raves. Tasters found both sauces bright and complex. Given steak Diane's varied history, I was happy to know that skipping this step still produced an excellent dish, one in line with steak Diane's earliest roots.

With the peppery, boozy Diane flavors intact; a much better cut of meat; and a far easier (and safer) technique, I now had a rewarding home version of steak Diane that delivered vibrant flavor—no fire extinguisher necessary.

—CECELIA JENKINS, *Cook's Country*

Steak Diane

SERVES 4

Four well-trimmed (9- to 11-ounce) New York strip steaks may be substituted for the filets mignons, if desired. Cook them in two batches with an extra tablespoon of oil. Adding the cognac along with the beef broth helps reduce any potential flare-ups, but still use caution when bringing the sauce to a boil, especially if you have a gas stove.

1　teaspoon black peppercorns

4　(6- to 8-ounce) center-cut filets mignons,
　　1½ to 2 inches thick, trimmed

　　Salt

1　tablespoon vegetable oil

5　tablespoons unsalted butter, cut into 5 pieces

1　shallot, minced

¾　cup beef broth

½　cup plus 1 teaspoon cognac

1　tablespoon Worcestershire sauce

2　tablespoons minced fresh chives

1　teaspoon Dijon mustard

1　teaspoon lemon juice

1. Place peppercorns in zipper-lock bag, press out air, and seal. Pound and roll peppercorns with rolling pin until coarsely cracked. Pat steaks dry with paper towels and season with salt and cracked pepper. Place steaks between 2 sheets plastic wrap and roll and pound lightly with rolling pin to even 1-inch thickness.

2. Heat oil in 12-inch skillet over medium-high heat until just smoking. Place steaks in skillet and cook until well browned and meat registers 120 to 125 degrees (for medium-rare), 5 to 7 minutes per side. Transfer steaks to plate, tent with aluminum foil, and set aside.

3. Reduce heat to low and melt 1 tablespoon butter in now-empty skillet. Add shallot and cook until translucent, about 1 minute. Remove skillet from heat and add broth, ½ cup cognac, Worcestershire, and any accumulated meat juices from plate. Return skillet to medium-high heat and bring to boil, scraping up any browned bits. Cook until reduced to ⅓ cup, 5 to 7 minutes.

4. Off heat, whisk in 1 tablespoon chives, mustard, lemon juice, remaining 4 tablespoons butter, and remaining 1 teaspoon cognac until fully incorporated. Transfer steaks to platter, spoon sauce over top, and sprinkle with remaining 1 tablespoon chives. Serve.

HOME-CORNED BEEF WITH VEGETABLES

✔ **WHY THIS RECIPE WORKS:** We set our sights on a well-seasoned roast that made curing at home worthwhile. Wet curing, much like brining, proved the easiest, most hands-off option, so we submerged a flat-cut brisket in a solution of water, salt, and sugar. Pink salt, a specialty product that combines table salt and sodium nitrite, gives corned beef its distinct color, but we also found that it contributes to the meat's flavor, so we included it in the curing liquid. Adding garlic cloves, bay leaves, allspice berries, peppercorns, and coriander seeds promised complexly seasoned beef. The cure penetrated about ¼ inch per day, so a six-day soak was necessary for fully seasoned meat. Simmering the cured meat in the steady heat of the oven broke down its collagen, turning the meat perfectly tender, and a cheesecloth bundle of garlic, bay leaves, and peppercorns reinforced the flavors of the curing seasonings. We used the seasoned cooking liquid to simmer the vegetables, which took on the same complex flavors as the beef and provided an impressive, traditional presentation.

You can make a decent corned beef dinner by buying a corned beef brisket, simmering it in a big pot of water for a few hours, and adding carrots, potatoes, and cabbage at the end of cooking so they soak up some of the seasoned liquid. But you can make a superb corned beef if you skip the commercially made stuff and "corn" the meat yourself. (The Old English term refers to the "corns," or kernels of salt, used to cure the meat for preservation.) When this curing process is done properly, the meat isn't just generically salty (or overly salty, as commercial versions often are). It's seasoned but balanced, with complex flavor thanks to the presence of aromatics and spices. And although the process takes several days, it's almost entirely hands-off.

I'd never corned beef but had always wanted to try. In addition to having an easy one-dish meal for serving a crowd, I could use the leftover corned beef in sandwiches and hash. The trick would be figuring out just the right curing formula and length of time to produce tender, well-seasoned meat.

I knew I'd be using a flat-cut brisket, the most common cut for corned beef. As for the curing method, I had two options: wet or dry. Wet curing works much

HOME-CORNED BEEF WITH VEGETABLES

like brining: You submerge the meat in a solution of table and curing, or "pink," salt (more on that later) and water along with seasonings. Over time, the salt penetrates the meat, seasoning it and altering its proteins so that they retain moisture. Dry curing works more like salting: The meat gets rubbed with the salt mixture and seasonings, wrapped in plastic wrap, and weighed down with a heavy plate or pot. As the meat sits, the salt draws water out of it, creating a super-concentrated brine. To expose all of the meat to the brine, the meat is flipped daily. Whichever approach you use, the cured brisket gets simmered in water to break down its abundant collagen, the connective tissue that converts to gelatin during cooking and coats the meat fibers so that they appear more tender and juicy.

I tried both methods, wet curing one 5-pound flat-cut brisket for seven days and dry curing another for 10, the average length of time for each method that I found in recipes, to see how the flavor of the cured meats would differ. (For now, I left out the pink salt and seasonings.) I placed each in a Dutch oven with water and simmered them for 5 hours, which was a bit fussy since I had to adjust the stove dial to ensure gentle heat. The briskets tasted virtually the same, so I moved ahead with the wet cure, which was considerably faster and easier, with no need for daily flipping.

Now for the pink salt. This specialty product (which is dyed pink to distinguish it from conventional salt) is a mixture of sodium chloride (table salt) and sodium nitrite. Only a small amount, combined with conventional table salt, is needed for curing. Nitrites prevent the oxidation of fats, which would otherwise lead to off-flavors and certain types of bacterial growth. Hence, their preservative effect. They're also responsible for the attractive pink color of cured meats.

Since I wasn't relying on the pink salt for preservation, I wanted to confirm that it improved the flavor of the brisket, not just its color. I cured one with pink salt and one without and then offered both up to blindfolded tasters. The results were close, but the majority of tasters preferred the flavor of the pink salt batch. Plus, once the blindfolds came off, every single taster

preferred the rosy-hued meat. With that, I knew pink salt was a must. Finally, the seasonings: garlic cloves, allspice berries, bay leaves, coriander seeds, and brown sugar—the flavors of which truly put the meat a notch above commercial corned beef.

As for how long to cure the meat, I'd been following recipes from my research that called for seven days, but others called for as few as four—and both seemed rather arbitrary. I wanted a more precise method to determine when the meat was thoroughly cured, and I realized that the pink salt could help.

I started another batch and removed a sample of the core from the brisket each day, simmering them (the meat's color only changes when it's cooked) and looking for the point at which the center of the meat turned distinctly pink. The pink crept inward about ¼ inch per day. For the 2½- to 3-inch briskets I was using, that meant a six-day cure was the answer.

I wanted to try simmering the brisket in the oven, a method we often use when braising meat because the heat is more gentle and even. Waiting for the water to come to a boil in the oven would greatly prolong the cooking time, so I added the meat (rinsed first to remove the loose spices) and brought the water to a simmer on the stove before moving the pot to a 275-degree oven.

Three hours later, the brisket was fork-tender, at which point I transferred it to a platter to rest, ladling over some of the cooking liquid to keep it moist. Then I moved the pot back to the stove and cooked the vegetables in the meaty liquid: carrots and red potatoes (added first so they cooked through) as well as cabbage wedges. As they simmered, I sliced the brisket thin against the grain, which ensured that each bite was tender.

Texturally, the meat and vegetables were spot-on, but both components tasted a tad washed out, so I added a cheesecloth bundle of more garlic and curing spices to the cooking liquid (the cheesecloth meant I didn't have to pluck out any stray spices). This added subtle but clear depth to the dish, which was as impressive-looking as it had been easy to prepare—and so very worth making from scratch.

—LAN LAM, *Cook's Illustrated*

Home-Corned Beef with Vegetables

SERVES 8 TO 10

Pink curing salt #1, which can be purchased online or in stores specializing in meat curing, is a mixture of table salt and nitrites; it is also called Prague Powder #1, Insta Cure #1, or DQ Curing Salt #1. In addition to the pink salt, we use table salt here. If using Diamond Crystal kosher salt, increase the salt to 1½ cups; if using Morton kosher salt, increase to 1⅛ cups. This recipe requires six days to corn the beef, and you will need cheesecloth. Look for a uniformly thick brisket to ensure that the beef cures evenly. The brisket will look gray after curing but will turn pink once cooked.

CORNED BEEF

- 1 (4½- to 5-pound) beef brisket, flat cut
- ¾ cup salt
- ½ cup packed brown sugar
- 2 teaspoons pink curing salt #1
- 6 garlic cloves, peeled
- 6 bay leaves
- 5 allspice berries
- 2 tablespoons peppercorns
- 1 tablespoon coriander seeds

VEGETABLES

- 6 carrots, peeled, halved crosswise, thick ends halved lengthwise
- 1½ pounds small red potatoes, unpeeled
- 1 head green cabbage (2 pounds), uncored, cut into 8 wedges

1. FOR THE CORNED BEEF: Trim fat on surface of brisket to ⅛ inch. Dissolve salt, sugar, and curing salt in 4 quarts water in large container. Add brisket, 3 garlic cloves, 4 bay leaves, allspice berries, 1 tablespoon peppercorns, and coriander seeds to brine. Weigh brisket down with plate, cover, and refrigerate for 6 days.

2. Adjust oven rack to middle position and heat oven to 275 degrees. Remove brisket from brine, rinse, and pat dry with paper towels. Cut 8-inch square triple thickness of cheesecloth. Place remaining 3 garlic cloves, remaining 2 bay leaves, and remaining 1 tablespoon peppercorns in center of cheesecloth and tie into bundle with kitchen twine. Place brisket, spice bundle, and 2 quarts water in Dutch oven. (Brisket may not lie flat but will shrink slightly as it cooks.)

3. Bring to simmer over high heat, cover, and transfer to oven. Cook until fork inserted into thickest part of brisket slides in and out with ease, 2½ to 3 hours.

4. Remove pot from oven and turn off oven. Transfer brisket to large oven-safe platter, ladle 1 cup of cooking liquid over meat, cover, and return to oven to keep warm.

5. FOR THE VEGETABLES: Add carrots and potatoes to pot and bring to simmer over high heat. Reduce heat to medium-low, cover, and simmer until vegetables begin to soften, 7 to 10 minutes.

6. Add cabbage to pot, increase heat to high, and return to simmer. Reduce heat to low, cover, and simmer until all vegetables are tender, 12 to 15 minutes.

7. While vegetables cook, transfer beef to cutting board and slice ¼ inch thick against grain. Return beef to platter. Using slotted spoon, transfer vegetables to platter with beef. Moisten with additional broth and serve.

NOTES FROM THE TEST KITCHEN

CALCULATING A CURE TO THE CORE

By simmering a sample of the brisket each day, we found that the pink color moved inward ¼ inch per day on all sides. Our 2½- to 3-inch-thick brisket required six days to thoroughly cure.

BOTTOM ROUND ROAST BEEF WITH ZIP-STYLE SAUCE

✓ **WHY THE RECIPE WORKS:** For an inexpensive slow-roasted beef recipe, we set out to transform a bargain cut—bottom round roast—into a tender, juicy showstopper. By salting the meat and letting it rest before roasting we ensured that it was thoroughly seasoned. Sprinkling a woodsy mixture of thyme, rosemary, salt, and pepper over the roast delivered an herbal crust and contributed enough flavor to make browning the roast unnecessary. Instead of searing, we headed straight for the oven. Roasting the beef slowly in a 250-degree oven turned the meat supremely tender by slowly breaking down its tough connective tissue. After 2 hours, we turned off the oven and let the roast gradually reach medium doneness as the oven cooled. To round out and reinforce the roast's flavors, we served it with a Zip-style sauce, a winning combination of butter, Worcestershire sauce, garlic, rosemary, and thyme.

Pity the poor bottom round roast. Over the years, many cooks (including some of us in the test kitchen) have decried the cut, sometimes called rump roast, as unfit to serve as a special centerpiece—too tough, too livery, nothing at all like a tender, melty rib roast or eye round. But I wanted to find a way to serve this less-expensive cut from the usually tough rear leg as the main event—and not to have to apologize for it.

Several years ago, the test kitchen developed a recipe for slow-roasted beef that produced tender meat. To get it, we salted an eye round and set it aside for 18 to 24 hours before searing it in a skillet to jump-start a brown crust. We then slid it into a very low (225-degree) oven for a couple of hours and then turned off the heat, allowing the meat to finish cooking in the cooling oven. This low-and-slow method produced a tender, sliceable eye-round roast. I tried this method with a bottom round roast just to get a baseline for testing and found, much to my surprise, that it wasn't half bad—relatively tender with good beefy flavor. Still, it was a bit difficult to slice evenly and, more important, thinly. I wanted to solve this problem and, while I was at it, dress up the roast with some fresh herbs and streamline the hands-on part of the process. We often sear roasts on the stovetop to build a flavorful exterior before transferring them to the oven. But because I'd be adhering fresh herbs to the surface of the meat, I wondered if I could skip the searing step. After a few tests, I determined that searing the meat first added only a faint note of flavor, which was difficult to pick up amongst the rosemary and thyme.

We rarely recommend cooking a roast to medium, but after roasting many pounds of bottom round, I found that taking it to medium made a huge difference in my ability to slice it thin, which tasters determined was essential for a tender slice of meat on the plate. I set the oven to 250 degrees and roasted my herb-covered beef to an internal temperature of 120 degrees, which took about 2 hours. I then switched off the oven but left the roast inside until its interior reached 135 degrees, another 20 to 30 minutes. After letting it rest, I had a beautiful, flavorful roast that was easy to slice and looked much more elegant than any of us had expected.

With such a great roast, why not give it a great sauce? After trying several, I landed on a homemade version of herby, flavorful Zip Sauce, a favorite Detroit-area condiment. Zip Sauce lives up to its name—it comes together quickly by melting butter in a saucepan and then stirring in Worcestershire sauce, rosemary, thyme, garlic, salt, and pepper; once it comes to a simmer, it's done.

—ASHLEY MOORE, *Cook's Country*

Bottom Round Roast Beef with Zip-Style Sauce

SERVES 8

We recommend cooking this roast to medium for ease of slicing. Open the oven door as little as possible, and remove the roast from the oven when taking its temperature to prevent dropping the oven temperature too drastically. Because the sauce contains butter, it will solidify as it cools, so it's best kept warm for serving.

BEEF

1 (4-pound) boneless beef bottom round roast, trimmed
   Kosher salt and pepper

1 tablespoon minced fresh rosemary

1 tablespoon minced fresh thyme

2 tablespoons vegetable oil

ZIP-STYLE SAUCE

8 tablespoons unsalted butter

½ cup Worcestershire sauce

2 garlic cloves, minced

2 teaspoons minced fresh rosemary

1 teaspoon minced fresh thyme

½ teaspoon kosher salt

½ teaspoon pepper

1. FOR THE BEEF: Pat roast dry with paper towels and sprinkle with 2 teaspoons salt. Wrap in plastic wrap and refrigerate for at least 1 hour or up to 24 hours.

2. Adjust oven rack to middle position and heat oven to 250 degrees. Set wire rack in rimmed baking sheet. Combine rosemary, thyme, 2 teaspoons pepper, and 1 teaspoon salt in bowl.

3. Pat roast dry with paper towels. Brush roast all over with oil and sprinkle with herb mixture; place on prepared wire rack. Transfer to oven and cook until meat registers 120 degrees, 1¾ hours to 2¼ hours. Turn off oven and leave roast in oven, without opening door, until meat registers 135 degrees (for medium), 20 to 30 minutes longer. Transfer roast to carving board, tent with aluminum foil, and let rest for 30 minutes.

4. FOR THE ZIP-STYLE SAUCE: Bring butter, Worcestershire, garlic, rosemary, thyme, salt, and pepper to bare simmer in small saucepan over medium heat, whisking constantly. Remove from heat, cover, and keep warm.

5. Slice roast thin against grain and serve with sauce.

NOTES FROM THE TEST KITCHEN

ZIP SAUCE

Zip Sauce—a lively, butter based condiment for steak—was invented more than 75 years ago at Lelli's Inn, a northern Italian restaurant in Detroit. Customers couldn't get enough of the flavorful sauce, and it became so popular that neighboring restaurants concocted copycat versions. In 2006, Chef Michael Esshaki capitalized on a good thing when he started selling bottled Zip Sauce (just mix it with melted butter at home) online and in Detroit-area markets.

ULTIMATE CHARCOAL-GRILLED STEAKS

✔ WHY THIS RECIPE WORKS: For a steak that delivered a perfectly browned crust, even doneness, and charred flavor, we ditched the actual grill in favor of a superhot charcoal chimney. After trimming the fat caps to prevent flare-ups, we scored the steaks' surfaces for optimum browning. We cut our two steaks in half, creating four hefty servings, and skewered them in pairs for secure handling. We first baked the skewered steaks slowly in a low oven where the steady heat cooked the steaks evenly and dehydrated their surfaces for maximum char. To give the steaks a great browned crust, we lit coals in our chimney starter, creating an intense blast of heat. The skewers allowed us to suspend the meat over the hot coals, and the steaks quickly took on a beautiful crust and terrific charcoal-grilled flavor.

While it's hard to beat the smoky char of a grilled thick-cut steak, I have to admit that since I started using the test kitchen method for pan-searing steaks, the indoor version more often approaches perfection. Our pan-searing technique calls for first baking a thick steak in a low oven and then searing it in a smoking-hot preheated skillet. The initial baking not only evenly cooks the meat but also dries and warms the steak's surface, resulting in lightning-fast searing—just a minute or so per side. The result of this approach is the platonic ideal of a steak: a crisp, well-browned crust and medium-rare meat from edge to edge. The time is so fast that, unlike most methods, only a sliver of meat below the crust overcooks and loses its rosy hue.

But with grilling, though I've worked out some pretty hot grill setups over the years. Even with my best efforts, it takes so long to evenly brown the steak that I overcook a fair amount of meat below the surface. This summer I decided to hold grilled steak to a higher standard: perfectly cooked meat, a well-browned and crisp crust, and great charcoal-grilled flavor.

To reach perfection, I suspected that I'd need to think outside the box—or as it turned out, the grill. In my research I came across a novel technique for cooking over a live fire that relied on a charcoal chimney starter to not just light the coals but actually do the cooking.

To produce an amazing sear, celebrity chef and food science guru Alton Brown mimics the intensity of a steakhouse-caliber broiler by placing a porterhouse steak on the grill grate and then putting a lit chimney of coals right over it. I found other sources that took a similar approach but flipped the setup, placing the chimney on the grill's charcoal grate and then arranging the steak, set on the cooking grate, on top.

I gave both methods a try (I settled on strip over rib-eye steaks since the former don't have as much internal fat and would thus cause fewer flare-ups) and, variations aside, one thing was for certain: Searing over a chimney was faster than any traditional grill setup I'd ever used, browning one side of the steak in about 2 minutes. Why is it so fast? For much the same reason that a chimney is so effective at lighting a pile of coals: access to oxygen. In a chimney, the coals rest on a grate surrounded by big slits that let in lots of air, the sides of the chimney are perforated for additional airflow, and there is no bottleneck—both the top and bottom of the chimney have wide openings.

Together, these features allow a huge supply of oxygen to access the coals, which makes them burn hot. Plus, the cylindrical shape is ideal for focusing intense radiant heat toward the open ends.

But there was a downside to the chimney-based recipes. They all cooked the steaks start to finish over high heat, which inevitably led to an overcooked interior. To address this, I decided I would cook the interior of my steaks using our low-temperature oven method for pan-seared steaks and then move outside to sear them and give them that charcoal-grilled flavor.

After cooking a few steaks in a 275-degree oven for 30 minutes until they reached 105 degrees, I tried searing them both under and on top of a chimney. I quickly developed a preference for the latter. While putting the steak under the chimney avoided any chance of flareups because the fat dripped away from the heat source, ashes fell on the steak as it cooked and monitoring the browning required picking up the blazing-hot chimney. Putting the steak on top avoided both of these problems.

That said, the technique still had its issues. Placing a grill grate, which measures more than 20 inches in diameter, on top of a glowing-hot 6-quart chimney starter that was a mere 7½ inches in diameter was precarious to say the least. In addition, the grate itself posed a problem: The hot bars of the grill grate seared the parts of the steak touching it faster than the radiant heat from the coals could brown the rest of the steak's surface. The result was blackened grill marks over an unappealing background of gray meat—not exactly the thorough edge-to-edge browning I was after. And finally, flare ups were a problem, even with strip steaks. The intense heat of the chimney quickly rendered and torched the fat cap. Cutting off the fat cap was a simple way to extinguish the flareup issue, but I didn't have a simple solution for the grill grate. Or maybe it was that simple. What would happen if I just ditched the grate entirely?

There are many examples of cooking over a live fire without a grate—think of a pig suspended on a spit or even marshmallows toasted on sticks. But even with these precedents in mind, it felt a little odd as I ran two metal skewers, parallel to each other, lengthwise through the center of a 1¾-inch-thick strip steak. (One steak would easily serve two, so I figured that once I had my method down I could double the recipe.) After cooking my skewered steak through indoors, I moved outside and lit a chimney starter filled halfway with charcoal. As soon as the coals were ready, I set the skewered steak on top with the protruding ends of the skewers resting directly on the rim. I was finally onto something. In about 2 minutes the entire surface of the steak facing the coals turned a rich mahogany color and the edges charred beautifully. The gray band of overcooked meat was pretty small and the flavor was good. I just needed to make a few tweaks to reach perfection.

I had noticed that the steak charred best at the edges, which made sense because the edges have more exposed surface area and are thinner, making it easier for water to evaporate, a key factor for browning to occur. With that in mind, I sliced the steak in half crosswise before skewering to create two more edges and thus more browning. This worked well, with the added benefit of making serving a breeze—I simply slid the cooked steaks off the skewers and had two 8-ounce portions. Scoring the surface of the steaks in a crosshatch pattern before cooking provided additional edges to brown and char.

GRILLING OVER A CHIMNEY STARTER

We discovered that a chimney starter's cylindrical shape concentrates the heat—perfect for our innovative grilled steaks. Here's how to get your steaks ready to hit the chimney.

1. TRIM: Remove fat cap and divide strip steak in half. Crosshatch surface for maximum browned crust and sprinkle with salt.

2. SKEWER: To suspend steaks across chimney, pass two 12-inch metal skewers through steaks.

3. PRECOOK: Precook skewered steaks in oven to dry surfaces and guarantee extra browning on grill.

4. LIGHT COALS: Pour 3 quarts coals into chimney, filling halfway. Light coals and place steaks over chimney when top coals are covered in ash.

CHIMNEY CHAMP

A chimney starter is central to this recipe. Our favorite model, the Weber Rapidfire Chimney Starter, boasts sturdy construction, a generous 6-quart capacity, a heat-resistant handle, and plenty of ventilation holes, virtually guaranteeing that the coals ignite quickly.

Many tasters complained that the interiors of the steaks were bland, so I salted the meat and let it sit for an hour before putting it in the oven. This made a big flavor difference, but I saw a chance for greater improvement. I salted some more steaks and immediately popped them into a super-low 200-degree oven to cook for about an hour and a half (I cooked them to 120 degrees since carryover cooking would be minimal). My bet paid off. The steaks were well seasoned and cooked internally to perfection because of the even gentler cooking. And because the exterior had more time to dehydrate, these steaks browned and charred in just 60 seconds per side.

All that was left was to double the recipe to make four 8-ounce steaks on two sets of skewers. Since I was working with two strip steaks, each cut in half crosswise, I paired up the narrower ends from the two steaks on one set of skewers and the wider ends on another to ensure even cooking. I could only sear one pair at a time given the chimney's diameter, but it happened so fast that this didn't pose a problem.

With that, I had grilled steaks that lived up to the highest standards.

—DAN SOUZA, *Cook's Illustrated*

Ultimate Charcoal-Grilled Steaks

SERVES 4

Rib-eye steaks of a similar thickness can be substituted for strip steaks, although they may produce more flare-ups. You will need a charcoal chimney starter with a 7½-inch diameter and four 12-inch metal skewers for this recipe. If your chimney starter has a smaller diameter, skewer each steak individually and cook in four batches. It is important to remove the fat caps on the steaks to limit flare-ups during grilling.

2 (1-pound) boneless strip steaks, 1¾-inches-thick, fat caps removed
   Kosher salt and pepper

1. Adjust oven rack to middle position and heat oven to 200 degrees. Cut each steak in half crosswise to create four 8-ounce steaks. Cut ¹⁄₁₆-inch-deep slits on both sides of steaks, spaced ¼ inch apart, in crosshatch pattern. Sprinkle both sides of each steak with ½ teaspoon salt (2 teaspoons total). Lay steak halves with tapered ends flat on counter and pass two 12-inch metal skewers, spaced 1½ inches apart, horizontally through steaks, making sure to keep ¼-inch space between steak halves. Repeat skewering with remaining steak halves.

2. Place skewered steaks on wire rack set in rimmed baking sheet, transfer to oven, and cook until centers of steaks register 120 degrees, flipping steaks over halfway through cooking and removing them as they come to temperature, 1½ hours to 1 hour 50 minutes. Tent skewered steaks (still on rack) with aluminum foil.

3. Light large chimney starter filled halfway with charcoal briquettes (3 quarts). When top coals are completely covered in ash, uncover steaks (reserving foil) and pat dry with paper towels. Using tongs, place 1 set of steaks directly over chimney so skewers rest on rim of chimney (meat will be suspended over coals). Cook until both sides are well browned and charred, about 1 minute per side. Using tongs, return first set of steaks to wire rack in sheet, season with pepper, and tent with reserved foil. Repeat with second set of skewered steaks. Remove skewers from steaks and serve.

GRILLED SUGAR STEAK

✔ **WHY THIS RECIPE WORKS:** At its best, grilled sugar steak should boast a delicate, caramelized crust around a juicy center, but hitting that sweet spot was no simple feat. In order to get the sugar rub to cling, we patted our strip steaks dry and sprinkled them with a mixture of sugar and kosher salt—a ratio of 4 parts sugar to 3 parts salt ensured plenty of sweetness and just enough seasoning. After an hour's rest, the salt had drawn out enough moisture to help a second salt-sugar sprinkling, added right before grilling, cling to the steaks' surfaces. On the grill, we moved the steaks frequently to even out the browning. Letting the steaks rest before serving set the sweet crust in place.

Steak grilled with a sugar crust? Really? Really. At Bastien's, a historic family-owned restaurant in Denver, Colorado, grilled sugar steak has been the signature dish and a customer favorite for decades. Their strip steak is a juicy medium-rare on the inside (a note on the menu discourages ordering the steak cooked further)

and delicately crusty on the outside, delivering a fleeting moment of sweetness followed by a flood of meaty flavors. I set out to create an equally captivating version in the test kitchen.

Though famous for it, Bastien's doesn't have a lock on sugar steak: A little research turned up recipes from New Orleans, Kansas City, and California. Most called for rubbing the steaks with a combination of sugar and salt. Some used brown sugar, which I quickly discounted because of its strong molasses flavor. Others called for so much sugar that the steaks did nothing but burn and turn bitter. Some introduced ingredients like bourbon or cayenne pepper to the mix, but these additions muddied the waters. I wanted a clean, faintly sweet steak with a delicate crust. To get it, I'd need to find the right amount of sugar for sweetness, and just enough salt for seasoning. After cooking through five recipes and compiling notes from my tasters, I decided on a 2:1 ratio of sugar to salt as a good starting point.

My first problem revealed itself straight out of the gate: When I applied the sugar-salt mixture to the steaks (strips, just like Bastien's uses), it mostly just slid off the meat when it hit the grill. Whatever coating managed to stick melted off as it heated, leaving no trace of crust or flavor. This never happens with just salt; was the sugar creating an unexpected moisture problem?

Observing the coated steaks more closely, I saw that they started to moisten within a few minutes of being rubbed. The salt in the mixture pulled moisture out of the meat, which dissolved the sugar, creating a thin syrup. Not good. Moist steaks wouldn't give me the crust I wanted because once they were on the grill, the moisture would create steam, discouraging browning. (Patting them dry, our normal fix for too much moisture, would have removed the coating.)

I thought that maybe instead of fighting this natural process, I could put it to work in my favor. To find out, I sprinkled the sugar-salt mixture on my steaks and let them rest at room temperature for an hour. I removed them from the dish, applied more of the mixture, and found, to my delight, that the moisture on the steaks' surfaces allowed it to stick beautifully.

I reconsidered my 2:1 ratio of granulated sugar to salt. I hoped to forestall any burnt bitter flavors by switching to a 1:1 ratio, but then I couldn't detect sweetness at all. Adjusting the ratio to 4 parts sugar to 3 parts salt created the delicate crust and clean sweetness I wanted without any bitterness.

GRILLED SUGAR STEAK

One last detail needed smoothing out: heat. When I cooked steaks over a fire that was too cool, I never got a crust. Too hot, and the steaks just burned. I wanted char on the outside and juiciness on the inside.

To get it, I rotated the steaks once they started to caramelize and also swapped their positions over the coals (depending on how quickly some were coloring). We rarely suggest fussing with your steaks on the grill in this way, but keeping them moving helped me minimize the hot spots and even out the heavy browning caused by the sugar. Sweet success.

—CECELIA JENKINS, *Cook's Country*

Grilled Sugar Steak

SERVES 4 TO 6

These steaks need to sit for at least 1 hour after seasoning. You will have about 1 teaspoon of sugar mixture left over after the final seasoning of the steaks in step 3. If your steaks are more than 1 inch thick, pound them to 1 inch.

- ¼ cup sugar
- 3 tablespoons kosher salt
- 4 (9- to 11-ounce) boneless strip steaks, 1 inch thick, trimmed
- Pepper

1. Mix sugar and salt together in bowl. Pat steaks dry with paper towels and place in 13 by 9-inch baking dish. Evenly sprinkle 1½ teaspoons sugar mixture on top of each steak. Flip steaks and sprinkle second side of each steak with 1½ teaspoons sugar mixture. Cover with plastic wrap and let sit at room temperature for 1 hour or refrigerate for up to 24 hours.

2A. FOR A CHARCOAL GRILL: Open bottom vent completely. Light large chimney starter mounded with charcoal briquettes (7 quarts). When top coals are partially covered with ash, pour evenly over half of grill. Set cooking grate in place, cover, and open lid vent completely. Heat grill until hot, about 5 minutes.

2B. FOR A GAS GRILL: Turn all burners to high, cover, and heat grill until hot, about 15 minutes. Turn all burners to medium-high.

3. Clean and oil cooking grate. Transfer steaks to plate. (Steaks will be wet; do not pat dry.) Sprinkle steaks with 1 teaspoon sugar mixture on each side, then season with pepper.

4. Place steaks on hotter side of grill (if using charcoal) and cook (covered if using gas) until evenly charred on first side, 3 to 5 minutes, rotating and switching positions for even cooking. Flip steaks and continue to cook until meat registers 120 to 125 degrees (for medium-rare), 3 to 5 minutes, rotating and switching positions for even cooking.

5. Transfer steaks to wire rack set in rimmed baking sheet and let rest for 5 minutes. Slice and serve.

NOTES FROM THE TEST KITCHEN

HITTING THE SWEET SPOT
To get the right sweet-savory mix, we followed these steps.

1. Carefully trim excess fat from steaks.

2. Pat steaks dry with paper towel.

3. Sprinkle with sugar and salt mixture. Let steaks rest and sprinkle again.

4. Watch carefully and move steaks frequently on grill to prevent burning.

PORK AND RICOTTA MEATBALLS

✔ **WHY THIS RECIPE WORKS:** We wanted to showcase pork's sweet, mild flavor in a tender meatball, so we kept our accompanying flavors to a minimum. Because ground pork tends to dry out more easily than ground beef, a panade was essential to adding moisture and lightness to the meatballs; the rich body and slight tang of ricotta did just that. We combined the panade with ground pork and some bright, complementary flavorings: minced shallot, garlic, Parmesan, lemon zest, and a handful of parsley. Roasting the meatballs on a rack promoted even browning without the mess of a frying pan. While the meatballs roasted, we prepared a simple, garlicky sauce. Crushed canned tomatoes were an easy way to bring in bright tomato flavor. As soon as it had thickened, we braised the meatballs right in the sauce, which not only made the meatballs more tender but also infused the sauce with porky flavor.

What's not to love about meatballs? They're a staple in cuisines around the world. And the variations—meats, seasonings, binders—are endless. During a recent perusal of Italian cookbooks, I was reminded of an old trick for extra-tender meatballs: adding ricotta cheese.

Most meatball recipes include a mixture of milk and bread. Called a panade, this combination adds moisture to the mix and helps the meatballs stay tender. So why not ricotta cheese instead of milk? And why not all pork instead of a mix of meats? The combination of sweet, mild ground pork and fluffy, creamy ricotta suggested a meatball delicate in flavor and texture. I couldn't wait to give it a try and I quickly discovered a wealth of existing recipes to use for inspiration.

I gathered a handful of these recipes and got to work in the test kitchen. Many of them were fine (if not spectacular), but even the failures were instructive—I learned, for instance, that too much garlic nixed any porky flavors, that substituting chopped shallot for traditional onion helped highlight the meat's natural sweetness, and that sharp flavors like orange peel, which I found in a Sicilian-inspired recipe, were far too dominant a flavor for these comforting meatballs. Using what I'd learned, as well as past experience in the test kitchen, I stitched together a working recipe for pork and ricotta meatballs: a starting point.

To bolster the flavor of the pork, I added garlic, shallot, and Parmesan (not too much, as I didn't want to overwhelm the other flavors). Some chopped parsley and lemon zest provided a fresh note. I mixed in an egg and some fresh bread crumbs and formed balls. I seared a batch in a skillet, finishing them by pouring over some jarred tomato sauce (I'd work on the real thing later) and simmering until the meatballs were cooked through.

The results were impressive: These meatballs were tender, juicy, and flavorful, and they had an unexpected lightness that my tasters loved.

Why so tender and light? I asked our science editor to explain. He explained that the water in ricotta is tightly trapped in coagulated protein, so it doesn't leach out and make the bread crumbs soggy. Plus, the ricotta doesn't dissolve inside the meatballs, which means it forms lots of little barriers that keep the meat proteins from binding into a dense, tough ball. The result? An uncommonly tender meatball.

What's more, the ricotta added a savory richness that provoked comments of "More, please."

Traditional recipes often call for pan-frying the meatballs as I had done before adding the sauce, but this method can make a greasy mess of the stovetop. I found that assembling the meatballs on a wire rack set in a rimmed baking sheet and roasting them in the oven was an easier, cleaner option—elevating the meatballs this way allowed air to circulate around them, producing evenly browned (but still not fully cooked) meatballs in about 30 minutes. Plus, using the oven meant that I could double my recipe without having to brown the balls in batches.

Jarred tomato sauce has its merits, but I wanted a brighter, fresher take here. I kept things simple by gently cooking smashed garlic cloves in extra-virgin olive oil until just golden brown to infuse the sauce with subtle garlic flavor. I added some red pepper flakes and crushed tomatoes to the golden garlic and gently simmered the mixture while the meatballs browned in the oven. The sauce reduced slightly, bringing out the tomatoes' natural sweetness.

To finish the dish, I transferred the browned meatballs to my big pot of sauce and baked them at 300 degrees for 30 minutes so the flavors could meld. Gently braising the meatballs in the sauce made them even more tender and infused the sauce with sweet, meaty flavor. It also made the kitchen smell terrific.

—CHRISTIE MORRISON, *Cook's Country*

Pork and Ricotta Meatballs

SERVES 6 TO 8

It takes about 10 minutes of occasional mashing with a fork for the ricotta to fully wet the bread enough for the panade to achieve the desired paste consistency. Use a greased ¼-cup dry measuring cup or equal-size portion scoop to divvy up the meatballs, and use slightly wet hands when shaping them to minimize sticking. This recipe makes enough sauce to coat 1½ pounds of pasta.

MEATBALLS

4 slices hearty white sandwich bread,
   crusts removed, torn into small pieces
8 ounces (1 cup) whole-milk ricotta cheese
2 pounds ground pork
1 ounce Parmesan cheese, grated (½ cup),
   plus extra for serving
½ cup chopped fresh parsley
2 large eggs
2 shallots, minced
4 garlic cloves, minced
1 tablespoon salt
1½ teaspoons pepper
1 teaspoon grated lemon zest

SAUCE

¼ cup extra-virgin olive oil
10 garlic cloves, smashed and peeled
1 teaspoon red pepper flakes
2 (28-ounce) cans crushed tomatoes
   Salt and pepper
2 tablespoons chopped fresh basil

1. FOR THE MEATBALLS: Adjust oven rack to lower-middle position and heat oven to 450 degrees. Set wire rack in aluminum foil–lined rimmed baking sheet and spray evenly with vegetable oil spray. Combine bread and ricotta in large bowl and let sit, mashing occasionally with fork, until smooth paste forms, about 10 minutes.

2. Add pork, Parmesan, parsley, eggs, shallots, garlic, salt, pepper, and lemon zest to bread mixture and mix with your hands until thoroughly combined. Divide meat mixture into 24 portions (about ¼ cup each) and place on platter. Roll meat between your wet hands to form meatballs and space evenly on prepared wire rack. Roast meatballs until browned, 30 to 35 minutes, rotating sheet halfway through roasting. Remove from oven and reduce oven temperature to 300 degrees.

3. FOR THE SAUCE: Meanwhile, combine oil and garlic in Dutch oven set over low heat and cook until garlic is soft and golden on all sides, 12 to 14 minutes, stirring occasionally. Add pepper flakes and cook until fragrant, about 30 seconds. Stir in tomatoes and 1 teaspoon salt. Cover, with lid slightly ajar, and bring to simmer over medium-high heat. Reduce heat to medium-low and simmer until sauce has thickened slightly, about 30 minutes. Season with salt and pepper to taste.

4. Nestle meatballs into sauce, cover, and transfer pot to oven. Bake until meatballs are tender and sauce has thickened, about 30 minutes. Transfer meatballs and sauce to serving platter. Sprinkle with basil and serve, passing extra Parmesan separately.

NOTES FROM THE TEST KITCHEN

ROASTING AND BRAISING
Using a two-stage cooking process is the easiest way to guarantee tasty, tender meatballs.

Roast meatballs on wire rack set in rimmed baking sheet to brown in one batch. Finish cooking meatballs by braising directly in sauce.

SPOTLIGHT ON RICOTTA
Ricotta is a moist, semisolid cheese made from whey and milk. For these meatballs, we mash ricotta with small pieces of bread until the mixture, called a panade, is smooth. Since the ricotta is thicker than the milk usually used in panades, we found that it works best to mash occasionally over a 10-minute period until the panade is totally smooth. The ricotta adds richness and helps keep the meatballs moist and tender.

ITALIAN SAUSAGE WITH GRAPES AND BALSAMIC VINEGAR

ITALIAN SAUSAGE WITH GRAPES AND BALSAMIC

✔ **WHY THIS RECIPE WORKS:** Sausage with grapes is a humble Italian supper that celebrates the natural pairing of pork and fruit. To breathe new life into this dish, we set out to perfect the cooking technique. We used a combination of searing and steaming to produce sausages that were nicely browned but still moist and juicy. After sopping up some of the rendered fat, we scattered halved red grapes and thinly sliced onion around the sausages. We removed the cooked sausages and let the grapes and onion brown and soften a little more before stirring in white wine and oregano to balance the sweetness. Once the sauce had reduced, some balsamic vinegar drew all of the sweet and savory flavors into focus. A sprinkling of chopped mint leaves offered a fresh finishing touch.

I've always enjoyed the pairing of rich, salty pork and bright, sweet fruit—think pork chops and applesauce or prosciutto draped around cantaloupe. So naturally I'm intrigued by the Italian combination of pork sausage links with grapes and balsamic vinegar, a humble dish that originated in Umbria as a quick meal for vineyard laborers. Rich, juicy, and well browned, the sausages are a great match for the tangy-sweet vinegar-based sauce with grapes that soften and caramelize in the pan. Take into account that this dish can be on the table in less than 30 minutes, and it's no wonder it became an Italian classic.

But like most preparations based on just a couple of simple components, the fewer the ingredients, the more important the technique. I tried recipes that failed at every turn, starting with grapes that were barely cooked and bouncy and vinegar that tasted harsh instead of in balance with the meat's richness.

But the real problem was the sausage itself. Some recipes weren't explicit about how to cook the links—and as I discovered, you can't just throw them into a skillet and hope for the best. But even the recipes that did specify a method came up short: Cooked over high— and even somewhat over medium—heat, the sausages tended to burn in spots before they had cooked all the way through, or their casings split, allowing their flavorful juices to leak into the pan and leaving their interiors dry and mealy. Cooking them over a low flame solved those problems but introduced new ones—namely, tough, wrinkled exteriors and a pallid color.

In fact, these outcomes were all too familiar to me from other times I've tried to produce sausage that's both well-browned on the outside and juicy on the inside. If I could finally figure out the best way to cook the sausage, I'd have this dish, not to mention a host of others, at my disposal.

Those early tests proved that the sausages needed at least medium heat to develop color—and I hoped that with some adjustments to the searing method, I could prevent them from burning or splitting.

My first idea was to keep the links moving as they cooked so that no one spot would get too dark. I heated a little oil in the pan and added 1½ pounds of sweet Italian sausages, the kind most recipes called for, and proceeded to turn them constantly as they cooked so that their heat exposure was as even as possible. But while such careful monitoring did help prevent burning, the casings split and the meat dried out nonetheless. Plus, that method was way too fussy.

It turns out that sausages split when the links' natural casings, which are composed largely of collagen, lose moisture and thus become more rigid. At the same time, the moisture in the sausage turns to steam, causing the meat to expand and strain the casing so much that it eventually bursts.

Some recipes I found called for pricking the sausages with a fork before cooking them, which supposedly prevents the buildup of pressure that causes the casings to split. And it did. The downside was that the nicks gave the precious juices too many escape routes and yielded results that were only marginally moister than the sausages that had split.

As a last resort, I skipped the pricking and tried roasting the sausages on a baking sheet in a 400-degree oven—an attempt at developing good browning without the direct heat of searing. But it was another dead end, as the sausages lacked the deep browning I'd achieved with the stovetop's more direct heat.

Until now, I'd been avoiding moist-heat cooking methods because steaming or boiling the links would surely sacrifice flavorful browning. But I also knew that including some liquid would ensure that the meat cooked relatively gently and keep the casings hydrated and pliable. A combination of dry and moist heat seemed worth a shot.

I spent the next several tests fiddling with hybrid cooking methods: poaching or steaming followed by searing, or the reverse. The trouble with poaching or steaming first was that I had to use two vessels to cook the sausages, one with water and one without. Plus, introducing moisture from the get-go washed out the flavor of the links, so they never tasted as savory as they should have.

I had much better luck when I browned the links first. Borrowing the classic Chinese method for cooking potstickers, I cooked the sausages over medium heat, turning them once so that they browned on two sides, and then added ¼ cup of water to the pan. It was just enough to generate some steam but not so much that the water submerged the sausages and washed away their flavor. I immediately covered the pan so that the links could steam gently; after about 10 minutes, they hit their target temperature of 160 to 165 degrees. I let the links rest for about 5 minutes and then took a taste: Well browned outside and juicy within, they were ideal—and even better, this quick one-pan method would work for just about any stovetop sausage preparation.

With my sausage method settled, all I had left to do was plug the grapes and a quick pan sauce into the equation. I wanted the fruit to break down a little, so I halved 1 pound of red grapes lengthwise (their darker pigment would look nicer with the inky balsamic vinegar than paler green grapes would) and added them to the skillet with the browned links just before adding the water. Once the sausages were cooked through, I removed them from the pan but continued to cook the grapes, raising the heat to cook off excess moisture so that they would soften and caramelize but still retain their shape. Off heat, I stirred a couple of tablespoons of vinegar into the pan and promptly spooned the glazy sauce over the sausages.

The grapes were nicely cooked, but the sauce was a tad greasy, sweet, and one-dimensional. Removing some fat from the skillet before adding the grapes solved the first problem, while adding a thinly sliced onion along with the grapes lent the dish some savory-sweet backbone. Then, to loosen up the vinegar sauce's syrupy consistency and balance its sweetness, I deglazed the pan with ¼ cup of dry white wine (lighter and brighter than red) and added a tablespoon of chopped fresh oregano during the last minute of cooking. That way, the sauce would work as a dip for crusty bread or spooned over a heartier accompaniment like polenta. Sprinkling chopped mint over the finished dish added a touch of color and freshness.

—ANNIE PETITO, *Cook's Illustrated*

Italian Sausage with Grapes and Balsamic Vinegar
SERVES 4 TO 6

Our favorite supermarket balsamic vinegar is Bertolli Balsamic Vinegar of Modena (for more information, see page 282). Serve this dish with crusty bread and salad or over polenta for a heartier meal.

- 1 tablespoon vegetable oil
- 1½ pounds sweet Italian sausage
- 1 pound seedless red grapes, halved lengthwise (3 cups)
- 1 onion, halved and sliced thin
- ¼ cup water
- ¼ teaspoon pepper
- ⅛ teaspoon salt
- ¼ cup dry white wine
- 1 tablespoon chopped fresh oregano
- 2 teaspoons balsamic vinegar
- 2 tablespoons chopped fresh mint

1. Heat oil in 12-inch skillet over medium heat until shimmering. Arrange sausages in pan and cook, turning once, until browned on 2 sides, about 5 minutes. Tilt skillet and carefully remove excess fat with paper towel. Distribute grapes and onion over and around sausages. Add water and immediately cover. Cook, turning sausages once, until they register between 160 and 165 degrees and onions and grapes have softened, about 10 minutes.

2. Transfer sausages to paper towel–lined plate and tent with aluminum foil. Return skillet to medium-high heat and stir pepper and salt into grape-onion mixture. Spread grape-onion mixture in even layer in skillet and cook without stirring until browned, 3 to 5 minutes. Stir and continue to cook, stirring frequently, until mixture is well browned and grapes are soft but still retain their shape, 3 to 5 minutes longer. Reduce heat to medium, stir in wine and oregano, and cook, scraping up any browned bits, until wine is reduced by half, 30 to 60 seconds. Remove pan from heat and stir in vinegar.

3. Arrange sausages on serving platter and spoon grape-onion mixture over top. Sprinkle with mint and serve.

PORK SALTIMBOCCA

✓ WHY THIS RECIPE WORKS: While saltimbocca is most often associated with veal, we opted for more widely available (and cheaper) pork tenderloin. Aside from being easy to find, pork tenderloin is also extremely tender. We created our own cutlets by slicing each tenderloin into four portions and pounding them thin. Most recipes layer sage leaves under the prosciutto, but this yielded sage that tasted steamed rather than crisp, so we reversed the order. The prosciutto clung nicely to the pounded cutlets, and dipping sage leaves into beaten egg white helped them stick to the prosciutto. We gently pounded the cutlets again to ensure that the layers stayed put. To keep things simple, we prepared a quick pan sauce of chicken broth, white wine, garlic, more sage, and lemon juice to highlight the saltimbocca's flavors.

Saltimbocca, which roughly translates as "jumps in the mouth," is a traditional Roman dish popular in Italian American restaurants. In the classic version, thin veal cutlets are topped with prosciutto and sage, rolled into bundles, seared, and then finished in a bright white wine–butter sauce. More common today are deconstructed versions that lay the sage and prosciutto on top of a thin piece of veal (or chicken) before sautéing and saucing.

My goal was to reinvent this dish using pork tenderloin, a cut that, like veal and chicken, is mild and tender. I gathered and prepared a handful of recipes, and my tasters and I found plenty of problems to fix, including tough and chewy meat and out of balance flavors.

Different recipes call for various methods for getting the prosciutto to adhere to the pork. Using a toothpick is most common, but I wasn't keen on biting into a forgotten toothpick. Other recipes place the sage between the pork and prosciutto, but I found that this made the sage taste steamed and unpleasantly grassy. Another technique is to pound the prosciutto and sage into the meat, which has the added benefit of flattening the cutlets so they brown more evenly in the skillet. When I tried this approach, the pounding made the prosciutto adhere perfectly, but getting the sage to stay put was a bit of a challenge. Thankfully, a colleague suggested dipping the sage leaf into beaten egg white and lightly pounding it into the prosciutto. It worked.

Store-bought pork cutlets are often cut from the loin, which means they can be very lean and are easy to overcook. In the test kitchen, we prefer to make our own pork cutlets out of buttery-soft pork tenderloin (which has a similar texture to the more expensive veal)—just cut a 1-pound tenderloin into four pieces and then pound each one, cut side down, to a ¼-inch thickness. I was able to nail down the timing through a series of tests: I cooked the pork, prosciutto side down, in a hot skillet for 2 minutes, flipped, and cooked for just another minute. This resulted in tender, juicy pork and perfectly crisp prosciutto.

A quick, traditional saltimbocca pan sauce made of chicken broth, white wine, garlic, and lemon juice highlighted the pork and sage flavors. To bump up the flavor even more, I started the sauce by blooming a bit of extra minced sage with garlic in hot oil.

—ASHLEY MOORE, *Cook's Country*

Pork Saltimbocca

SERVES 4

Cutlets longer than 5 inches will crowd the skillet; trim large pieces as necessary.

- 2 (1-pound) pork tenderloins, trimmed
  Salt and pepper
- 8 thin slices prosciutto (3 ounces)
- 8 large fresh sage leaves, plus 1 teaspoon minced
- 1 large egg white, lightly beaten
- 3 tablespoons olive oil
- 2 garlic cloves, sliced thin
- 1 cup chicken broth
- ¼ cup dry white wine
- 4 tablespoons unsalted butter, cut into 4 pieces and chilled
- 2 teaspoons lemon juice

1. Cut each tenderloin crosswise into 4 equal pieces. Working with 1 piece at a time, place pork, cut side down, between 2 pieces of plastic wrap. Using meat pounder, gently pound to even ¼-inch thickness. (Pieces should be about 5 inches long.) Pat pork dry with paper towels and season with pepper.

2. Place 1 prosciutto slice on top of each cutlet, folding as needed to prevent overhang. Dip 1 side of each sage leaf in egg white and place 1 leaf, egg side down, in center of each prosciutto slice. Cover with plastic and pound lightly until prosciutto and sage adhere to pork.

3. Heat 2 tablespoons oil in 12-inch skillet over medium-high heat until shimmering. Add half of pork to skillet, prosciutto side down, and cook until lightly browned, about 2 minutes. Using tongs, carefully flip pork and cook until second side is light golden brown, about 1 minute. Transfer to platter and tent with aluminum foil. Repeat with remaining pork.

4. Add remaining 1 tablespoon oil to now-empty skillet and heat over medium-high heat until shimmering. Add garlic and minced sage and cook until fragrant, about 30 seconds. Stir in broth and wine and simmer until reduced to ½ cup, 5 to 7 minutes, scraping up any browned bits. Reduce heat to low and whisk in butter, 1 piece at a time. Stir in lemon juice and any accumulated meat juices from platter. Season with salt and pepper to taste. Spoon sauce over pork and serve.

NOTES FROM THE TEST KITCHEN

MAKING SALTIMBOCCA

1. Divide each tenderloin into 4 even pieces and place cut side down on plastic wrap.

2. Pound to ¼-inch thickness using meat pounder.

3. Top each cutlet with prosciutto and egg white–dipped sage leaf, pounding gently to adhere.

FRIED BROWN RICE WITH PORK AND SHRIMP

WHY THIS RECIPE WORKS: We learned that using brown rice instead of white in traditional pork fried rice offers two main advantages. First, because of its bran, brown rice holds up well if cooked aggressively in boiling water, which meant it needed just 25 minutes of cooking to turn tender. (We opted to cook it for an extra 10 minutes to give it the right soft texture.) Second, the bran layer also prevents freshly cooked brown rice from clumping, so we could use freshly cooked rice (our favorite fried white rice recipes call for leftover rice). While the rice cooked, we prepared a quick batch of sweet and spicy Chinese barbecue pork, and cooked a half pound of shrimp before frying an egg in the same skillet. With our mix-ins at the ready, we finalized the fried rice profile by blooming a combination of sliced scallion whites, minced garlic, and fresh ginger before adding in the cooked rice and soy sauce. Along with the pork and shrimp, we stirred in some peas for an added pop of color and sweetness.

Traditional fried rice recipes vary widely in terms of ingredients, but there's one component that's common to all of them: leftover (as in cold and stale) white rice. Take it from someone who's tried to rush the process: moist, freshly cooked white rice doesn't hold up to frying. It quickly absorbs oil, leaving you with a mushy, greasy mass. In addition, recently cooked white rice naturally clumps; it needs to stale a bit (a process known as retrogradation) to firm up so that the grains will stay separate when stir-fried. The problem for me is that I almost never have leftover white rice in the fridge—so I rarely make fried rice. However, since brown rice takes longer to cook, I sometimes make big batches of it so I will have leftovers. Curious one evening to see how brown rice would fare in lieu of traditional white rice, I took a chance and improvised a simple fried-rice supper.

I noticed a promising difference as soon as I began cooking: Because each grain is encased in bran, these grains stayed much more separate than white rice. And that meant I could use a lot less oil—less than half the amount, in fact—than I would have used to stir-fry white rice. In the finished dish, the brown rice added an appealingly robust nuttiness that blank slate white rice can't match; I'd just need to bump up the other flavors to balance it out. I also found that it was a bit too chewy and dry, so I wanted to tone that down. And lastly, while I often have leftover brown rice in my fridge, I know many people are put off by its long cooking time—it can take about 45 minutes on the stovetop or over an hour in the oven—so they simply don't make it very often. But I had an idea about how to address that.

One reason it takes so long to cook brown rice is that the bran hinders the hydration of the rice. Another reason is that most cooks make brown rice using the absorption method—that is, they cook it over low heat in just enough water to allow for hydration and a bit of evaporation, no stirring permitted.

This ultragentle method is the best way to cook delicate white rice because boiling the grains over high heat in a lot of water would cause them to tumble around, break up, and become mushy and sticky. That's because white rice is mostly unprotected starch. But we've found that since the starch in brown rice is enclosed and protected by the bran, it can actually be cooked like pasta, with plenty of water and plenty of heat. Preparing it this way whittled the cooking time down to 25 minutes. So much for brown rice's time-consuming reputation.

But here's the possibility that really interested me: If brown rice's bran coating had prevented clumping enough to allow me to cook the rice using the pasta method and to fry it in very little oil, might the bran also allow me to skip the chilling step that traditional white rice recipes require? In fact, I had to wonder if refrigerating the brown rice was the cause of the too-chewy and dry texture that I'd found objectionable in that first test.

To find out, I boiled and drained a pot of brown rice and then immediately moved ahead with the recipe. To keep the focus on the rice's texture, I kept things simple. I heated some oil in a nonstick skillet, scrambled a couple of eggs until they were just cooked, and added the warm, just-cooked rice to the pan. Then I mixed the eggs into the rice (breaking the curds into smaller pieces), seasoned it with salt, and stirred in some chopped scallions.

The difference between this sample and that initial batch I'd made with my leftover brown rice was significant. This freshly cooked rice was pliable and moist. It still had a bit more texture than was ideal, but ditching the chilling was definitely a step in the right direction.

I wondered if I might not even notice the extra chew once I'd incorporated the add-ins, so I moved on.

I needed to incorporate some heartier flavors and textures to balance the brown rice, so I decided to model my recipe on a more elaborate Chinese restaurant version, which augments the rice and egg with Chinese barbecued pork, shrimp, and vegetables to make the dish into a main course.

Once I started stir-frying, things would move quickly, so I got all my ingredients together while the rice boiled. For a quick version of Chinese barbecued pork, I cut some boneless country-style pork ribs across the grain into bite-size slices and tossed them in hoisin sauce, honey, and five-spice powder. I chopped some scallions and shrimp, beat some eggs, grated some ginger, and minced some garlic, and I was ready to go.

For even cooking and because the skillet would be quite full by the end, I cooked the components in batches: first the shrimp and eggs and then the pork. I kept these off to the side in a bowl while I browned the scallion whites in sesame oil along with a good amount of garlic and ginger. I then added half the warm rice, which left me plenty of space in the skillet to break up the clumps of aromatics. Because I'd learned in my early experiments that fried brown rice would need a bit more seasoning than white, I added some soy sauce even though it's not traditional in fried rice. Then I added the remainder of the rice, the cooked proteins, and some frozen peas for color and sweetness. I finished it all off by stirring in the scallion greens.

The new flavors worked really well with the brown rice, but the firm texture of the bran still stood out too much. I wanted grains that were a bit smoother and plumper.

I use all kinds of white rice: long-grain for pilaf, medium-grain for paella, and short grain for risotto, so why was I limiting myself to long-grain brown rice for this recipe? With their rounder, plumper shapes, shorter-grain rices, I realized, were a much better option than long-grain rice for this recipe. Medium-grain brown rice was a bit hard to find, but I bought some short-grain and boiled up a batch. Though it was fully cooked after 25 minutes like the long-grain brown rice, I found that it actually benefited from a little extra cooking. While long-grain rice is prone to blowing out and turning mushy if overcooked, giving the short-grain rice an extra 10 minutes made it just a bit softer. So how did short-grain brown rice work in the fried rice? Beautifully. The smooth, rounded grains had a pleasantly resilient texture that melded well with the other components. Now that I know I can make fried rice with brown rice, less oil, and less forethought, I'll be making it a lot more often.

—ANDREA GEARY, *Cook's Illustrated*

Fried Brown Rice with Pork and Shrimp

SERVES 6

Freshly boiling the short-grain rice gives it the proper texture for this dish. Do not use leftover rice, and do not use a rice cooker. The stir-fry portion of this recipe moves quickly, so be sure to have all your ingredients in place before starting. This recipe works best in a nonstick skillet with a slick surface. Serve with a simple steamed vegetable, if desired.

NOTES FROM THE TEST KITCHEN

BENEFITS OF THE BRAN

Unlike refined grains of white rice, brown rice grains are still surrounded by the bran. We found that this is a big advantage when it comes to making fried rice.

NO LEFTOVERS NEEDED: Unlike white rice, brown rice's bran helps prevent clumping, so it can be used immediately after cooking.

QUICK COOKING METHOD: The bran protects the starch within each grain, so brown rice can be cooked aggressively and quickly.

LESS OIL REQUIRED: Because bran helps brown rice grains stay separate, half as much oil is used as in white rice applications.

2 cups short-grain brown rice
Salt
10 ounces boneless country-style pork ribs, trimmed
1 tablespoon hoisin sauce
2 teaspoons honey
⅛ teaspoon five-spice powder
Small pinch cayenne pepper
4 teaspoons vegetable oil
8 ounces large shrimp (26 to 30 per pound), peeled, deveined, tails removed, and cut into ½-inch pieces
3 eggs, lightly beaten
1 tablespoon toasted sesame oil
6 scallions, white and green parts separated and sliced thin on bias
2 garlic cloves, minced
1½ teaspoons grated fresh ginger
2 tablespoons soy sauce
1 cup frozen peas

1. Bring 3 quarts water to boil in large pot. Add rice and 2 teaspoons salt. Cook, stirring occasionally, until rice is tender, about 35 minutes. Drain well and return to pot. Cover and set aside.

2. While rice cooks, cut pork into 1-inch pieces and slice each piece against grain ¼ inch thick. Combine pork with hoisin, honey, five-spice powder, cayenne, and ½ teaspoon salt and toss to coat. Set aside.

3. Heat 1 teaspoon vegetable oil in 12-inch nonstick skillet over medium-high heat until shimmering. Add shrimp in even layer and cook without moving them until bottoms are browned, about 90 seconds. Stir and continue to cook until just cooked through, about 90 seconds longer. Push shrimp to 1 side of skillet. Add 1 teaspoon vegetable oil to cleared side of skillet. Add eggs to clearing and sprinkle with ¼ teaspoon salt. Using rubber spatula, stir eggs gently until set but still wet, about 30 seconds. Stir eggs into shrimp and continue to cook, breaking up large pieces of egg, until eggs are fully cooked, about 30 seconds longer. Transfer shrimp-egg mixture to clean bowl.

4. Heat remaining 2 teaspoons vegetable oil in now-empty skillet over medium-high heat until shimmering. Add pork in even layer. Cook pork without moving it until well browned on underside, 2 to 3 minutes. Flip pork and cook without moving it until cooked through and caramelized on second side, 2 to 3 minutes. Transfer to bowl with shrimp-egg mixture.

FRIED BROWN RICE WITH PORK AND SHRIMP

5. Heat sesame oil in now-empty skillet over medium-high heat until shimmering. Add scallion whites and cook, stirring frequently, until well browned, about 1 minute. Add garlic and ginger and cook, stirring frequently, until fragrant and beginning to brown, 30 to 60 seconds. Add soy sauce and half of rice and stir until all ingredients are fully incorporated, making sure to break up clumps of ginger and garlic. Reduce heat to medium-low and add remaining rice, pork mixture, and peas. Stir until all ingredients are evenly incorporated and heated through, 2 to 4 minutes. Remove from heat and stir in scallion greens. Transfer to warmed platter and serve.

ONE-PAN PORK TENDERLOIN

WHY THIS RECIPE WORKS: For an easy weeknight dinner, we envisioned an all-in-one meal centered around pork tenderloin and prepared on a single baking sheet. We looked for vegetables that would cook through at the same rate as the pork; halved fingerling potatoes and crunchy green beans were just the ticket. We arranged the beans down the middle of the pan and placed the pork on top of them to create steam, which helped the beans cook through without drying out; the drippings from the meat also helped flavor the green beans. This step insulated the pork and prevented overcooking. Brushing the meat with hoisin sauce added both color and flavor. An easy garlic-chive butter melted over the resting pork and tossed with the vegetables made for a rich finish.

Mild-flavored, lean pork tenderloin makes a great weeknight meal because it is relatively inexpensive, cooks quickly, and takes well to a wide variety of flavors. I set out to make an easy but flavorful dinner of two pork tenderloins and a few vegetables on a single baking sheet—easy cooking, easy cleanup.

To start my testing, I looked for two vegetables that would cook at a similar rate to the pork. Since pork tenderloins can reach their optimal temperature of 140 degrees in as little as 20 minutes at 450 degrees, most root vegetables, which take much longer to cook, were out. Thin fingerling potatoes (halved lengthwise),

however, worked well, cooking through in the same time it took to cook the pork. Now I needed a green vegetable to complete the meal.

Green beans, which are great roasted, came to mind; I was disappointed, then, when the green beans that I roasted with the pork and potatoes became tough and chewy from the intense dry heat. For my next test, I tried insulating the beans by positioning the tenderloins directly on top of them. This method effectively steamed the green beans to a crisp-tender texture.

When I removed the tenderloins from the baking sheet, however, I noticed that while the potatoes and beans had cooked through, they hadn't picked up much tasty browning. To remedy this lack of color, I returned the vegetables to the oven while the pork rested (a necessary post-roast step that ensures juiciness). Ten minutes later, both the spuds and the green beans were browned and tender, and the pork was ready for slicing.

But while the pork was moist and juicy, it needed a little help in the flavor department. It also looked a little pale without a browned crust. I could give it one by cooking it more (either under the broiler or in a sauté pan), but I knew that, while it would be brown, it would also be dry.

My fix: a sweet glaze. Since sugars caramelize and brown faster than meat, I knew that coating the meat with one would improve its appearance and flavor. I came up short with maple syrup (too sweet), honey (too sticky), and brown sugar (too molassesy). What's more, each provided sweetness but not much else. Inspiration appeared in a jar of hoisin sauce. This thick, dark, potent Chinese sauce is made of soybeans, ginger, chiles, garlic, and sugar—it's a staple ingredient in stir-fries. I brushed some of it on the tenderloins. After 25 minutes in the oven, the pork picked up just the right amount of sweetness and a rounded, unexpected complexity from the hoisin. Tasters couldn't quite identify the secret flavor, but they sure liked it.

To give this dinner a little extra oomph, I mashed together softened butter, chives, and minced garlic and dotted the hot pork with this flavored butter while the meat was resting and the vegetables were finishing up in the oven. I saved some to toss with the browned potatoes and green beans, too.

—CHRISTIE MORRISON, *Cook's Country*

One-Pan Pork Tenderloin with Green Beans and Potatoes

SERVES 4 TO 6

Buy tenderloins that are of equal size and weight so they cook at the same rate. A rasp-style grater makes quick work of turning the garlic into a paste. Our favorite hoisin sauce is Kikkoman's.

    4   tablespoons unsalted butter, softened
    2   tablespoons minced fresh chives
    1   garlic clove, minced to paste
        Salt and pepper
    2   (1-pound) pork tenderloins, trimmed
   ¼   cup hoisin sauce
    1   pound green beans, trimmed
    3   tablespoons extra-virgin olive oil
   1½ pounds fingerling potatoes, unpeeled,
        halved lengthwise

1. Adjust oven rack to lower-middle position and heat oven to 450 degrees. Combine butter, chives, garlic, ¼ teaspoon salt, and ¼ teaspoon pepper in bowl; set aside. Pat pork dry with paper towels and season with pepper. Brush tenderloins all over with hoisin sauce.

2. Toss green beans, 1 tablespoon oil, ¼ teaspoon salt, and ¼ teaspoon pepper together in large bowl. Arrange green bean mixture crosswise down center of rimmed baking sheet, leaving room on both sides for potatoes. Toss potatoes, remaining 2 tablespoons oil, ¼ teaspoon salt, and ¼ teaspoon pepper together in now-empty bowl. Arrange potatoes, cut side down, on both sides of green beans.

3. Lay tenderloins, side by side without touching, lengthwise on top of green beans. Roast until pork registers 140 degrees, 20 to 25 minutes. Transfer tenderloins to carving board and dot each with 1 tablespoon reserved herb butter. Tent with aluminum foil and let rest while vegetables finish cooking.

4. Gently stir vegetables on sheet to combine. Return sheet to oven and roast until vegetables are tender and golden brown, 5 to 10 minutes longer. Remove from oven, add remaining 2 tablespoons herb butter to sheet, and toss vegetables to coat. Transfer vegetables to platter. Cut pork into ½-inch-thick slices and place over vegetables, pouring any accumulated juices over top. Serve.

TUSCAN-STYLE ROAST PORK

✔ **WHY THIS RECIPE WORKS:** The Tuscan roast pork dish known as *arista* promises to turn lean, mild pork loin into a juicy roast flavored with garlic and rosemary with a deeply browned crust. Unfortunately, most versions turn out dry and bland. To boost both flavor and juiciness, we salted the meat before cooking, having double-butterflied the roast for thorough seasoning and to maximize the distribution of the filling. For a rich, porky boost to the herbal flavoring, we processed pancetta and combined it with the garlic-rosemary mixture. After spreading the paste over the pork, we rolled it tightly and refrigerated it for an hour, just enough time for the seasoning to penetrate the meat. Roasting the pork in a low oven allowed it to cook through gently. We prepared a simple sauce by combining the seasoned oil (reserved from cooking the garlic and rosemary) with the juice from half a lemon. After searing the roast on all sides to create a crisp crust, we served the deeply seasoned pork with its lively vinaigrette.

Boneless pork loin is a popular cut for good reason. It's widely available and affordable, and its uniform shape lends itself to even cooking and easy serving. But it has its flaws, too. Pork loin is lean and mild, and it's prone to overcooking. That's why I recently became intrigued by a classic Tuscan roast pork dish, *arista*, which derives its name from the Greek word *aristos*, meaning "the best." It promises to transform the loin into a flavorful roast with a deeply browned crust and plenty of rosemary and garlic in every bite. Though it can be made with a bone-in or boneless roast, I was drawn to the simplicity of using a boneless loin and the opportunity to turn this everyday cut into something more special.

Despite the simple concept, no two recipes I found were alike. Oven temperatures varied (anywhere from 325 to 475 degrees) as did roasting times (45 minutes to 4 hours) and ways to incorporate the garlic and rosemary (from simply rubbing the seasonings over the exterior to making a tunnel through the middle of the roast in which to deposit them). Regardless of the approach—and I tried them all—the outcome was the same: not good. The meat was usually underseasoned, dry, and tough. And it didn't stop there. The "crusts" were closer to beige than brown, and the rosemary and garlic flavors came across as either fleeting or aggressively harsh.

Something had obviously been lost in translation, and I was determined to find an approach that would deliver a version of arista that lived up to its name.

American pork contains little marbling, and pork loin is one of the leanest cuts of pork, so avoiding overcooking can be a challenge. And overcooking is only compounded by attempts to deeply brown the exterior, which typically leads to overcooking the meat just below the surface. But we've dealt with this issue before in the test kitchen; our solution is to reverse-sear. Cooking the meat through very gently in a low-temperature oven ensures that it cooks evenly from edge to center, and browning it in a hot skillet on the stovetop gets the job done so quickly that it avoids overcooking much of the meat beneath the surface. The long time in the oven also helps dry the exterior, encouraging a nicely browned, crisp crust. It's a technique we've used with flank steak, rack of lamb, and strip steaks, so I felt confident that it would work here, too.

I cooked the loin through in a 275-degree oven, pulling it out when it was just below the medium mark (135 degrees), knowing that carryover cooking would continue to raise the temperature to 145 to 150 degrees, my target for doneness. Then I browned the roast over high heat in a few tablespoons of oil. To guard against overcooking, I browned just three sides (no one would see the unbrowned fourth side). Now I had a pork loin roast with a perfectly cooked interior, but I was surprised to find that the browning was patchy. Also, the meat was still bland and could stand to be a bit juicier. The solution to the latter two problems was pretreating the meat. Salting the roast before cooking would draw the seasoning into the meat and help it retain moisture during cooking by changing the protein structure. And unlike brining, salting wouldn't add excess liquid that might impede browning.

In the past we found that simply salting the exterior of a pork loin doesn't season deeply enough. Instead, we double-butterfly the roast. Making two cuts into the meat allows you to essentially unroll the loin, exposing lots of surface area. I rubbed each side with 1½ teaspoons of kosher salt and then rolled it back up and tied it with twine. After refrigerating it for an hour, I roasted it as before. Tasters confirmed: The meat was now well seasoned and far juicier.

Next up: how to incorporate the garlic and rosemary. Recipes I'd tried called for applying the garlic and rosemary in such a way that the flavor was either superficial (on the exterior only) or unevenly dispersed. But no matter the method, the flavor was spotty; I wanted garlic and rosemary in every bite. Given how well the double butterflying method allowed me to season the meat with salt, it seemed like the obvious way to also distribute the garlic and rosemary. Rubbing a mixture made with a hefty amount of chopped garlic, rosemary, and a bit of red pepper flakes and lemon zest for some brightness into one side of the salted butterflied pork before rolling it up definitely distributed the flavors well, but tasters noted that the garlic and rosemary tasted raw and harsh. They were basically steaming inside the pork. Simmering the mixture in some oil before spreading it over the meat helped mellow its flavor; and because I wanted a clean garlic flavor, I used plenty of oil and opted for a nonstick skillet to cook the minced garlic until soft while avoiding browning. Then I simply strained off the oil. And because the pork loin tasted a bit lean, I decided to add some meaty reinforcement to the mixture. Minced in the food processor, pancetta's concentrated pork flavor and richness did the trick.

It was time to circle back to the issue of uneven browning. I realized that the problem was that the pork wasn't making even contact with the oil. I'd been using a 12-inch skillet with a couple of tablespoons of oil. This setup works fine when browning cuts of meat that fill up most of the pan, but here the skinny, cylindrical roast covered only the center of the skillet, leaving the oil to pool around the edges. Downsizing to a 10-inch skillet created a more snug setup, with an even layer of oil across the surface of the pan. This was also a good chance to use the oil I'd strained off from the rosemary and garlic.

After browning, I let the meat rest for 20 minutes, tented with foil to keep it warm, before serving it to my tasters. The meat was juicy and flavorful, and the crust certainly looked the part, but it had turned soggy. It had been steaming under the foil. The fix was quick: I simply changed the order of things. After removing the roast from the oven, I let it rest, and then I patted away any excess moisture, browned it on the stove, and served it immediately.

Traditionally arista is served with just juices from the pan, but I decided that it wouldn't be much more work to put together a more polished sauce. I made a quick vinaigrette-style sauce with the remainder of the infused olive oil strained from the herb mixture and the juice from the lemon I had zested earlier. This tasted a little too acidic, so I tried halving the lemon and, before browning the pork, cooking it cut side down in the skillet over high heat until it softened and browned. I squeezed this caramelized juice into the oil. Bright, slightly sweet, and perfumed with garlic and rosemary, this quick sauce was the perfect finishing touch for the pork.

—ANNIE PETITO, *Cook's Illustrated*

Tuscan-Style Roast Pork with Garlic and Rosemary (Arista)

SERVES 4 TO 6

We strongly prefer natural pork in this recipe, but if you use enhanced pork (injected with a salt solution), reduce the salt to 2 teaspoons (1 teaspoon per side) in step 3. After applying the seasonings, the pork needs to rest, refrigerated, for 1 hour before cooking.

    1 lemon
  ⅓ cup extra-virgin olive oil
    8 garlic cloves, minced
  ¼ teaspoon red pepper flakes
    1 tablespoon chopped fresh rosemary
    2 ounces pancetta, cut into ½-inch pieces
    1 (2½-pound) boneless center-cut pork
        loin roast, trimmed
        Kosher salt

1. Finely grate 1 teaspoon zest from lemon. Cut lemon in half and reserve. Combine lemon zest, oil, garlic, and pepper flakes in 10-inch nonstick skillet. Cook over medium-low heat, stirring frequently, until garlic is sizzling, about 3 minutes. Add rosemary and cook for 30 seconds. Strain mixture through fine-mesh strainer set over bowl, pushing on garlic-rosemary mixture to extract oil. Set oil aside and let garlic-rosemary mixture cool. Using paper towels, wipe out skillet.

2. Process pancetta in food processor until smooth paste forms, 20 to 30 seconds, scraping down sides of bowl as needed. Add garlic-rosemary mixture and continue to process until mixture is homogeneous, 20 to 30 seconds longer, scraping down sides of bowl as needed.

3. Position roast fat side up. Insert knife one-third of way up from bottom of roast along 1 long side and cut horizontally, stopping ½ inch before edge. Open up flap.

Keeping knife parallel to cutting board, cut through thicker portion of roast about ½ inch from bottom of roast, keeping knife level with first cut and stopping about ½ inch before edge. Open up this flap. If uneven, cover with plastic wrap and use meat pounder to even out. Sprinkle 1 tablespoon kosher salt over both sides of roast (½ tablespoon per side) and rub into meat to adhere. Spread inside of roast evenly with pancetta-garlic paste, leaving about ¼-inch border on all sides. Starting from short side, roll roast (keeping fat on outside) and tie with twine at 1-inch intervals. Set wire rack in rimmed baking sheet and spray with vegetable oil spray. Set roast fat side up on prepared rack and refrigerate for 1 hour.

4. Adjust oven rack to middle position and heat oven to 275 degrees. Transfer roast to oven and cook until meat registers 135 degrees, 1½ to 2 hours. Remove roast from oven, tent with aluminum foil, and let rest for 20 minutes.

NOTES FROM THE TEST KITCHEN

DOUBLE-BUTTERFLYING FOR FLAVOR
To ensure an even distribution of the garlic-rosemary filling, we double-butterfly the pork loin roast.

1. Insert knife one-third of way up bottom of roast along 1 long side and cut horizontally, stopping ½ inch before edge. Open flap.

2. Keeping knife parallel to cutting board, cut through thicker portion of roast about ½ inch from bottom of roast, keeping knife level with first cut.

3. Sprinkle both sides with kosher salt, rub salt into meat to adhere, and spread filling over inside of roast.

CIDER-BRAISED PORK ROAST

5. Heat 1 teaspoon reserved oil in now-empty skillet over high heat until just smoking. Add reserved lemon halves, cut side down, and cook until softened and cut surfaces are browned, 3 to 4 minutes. Transfer lemon halves to small plate.

6. Pat roast dry with paper towels. Heat 2 tablespoons reserved oil in now-empty skillet over high heat until just smoking. Brown roast on fat side and sides (do not brown bottom of roast), 4 to 6 minutes. Transfer roast to carving board and remove twine.

7. Once lemon halves are cool enough to handle, squeeze into fine-mesh strainer set over bowl. Press on solids to extract all pulp; discard solids. Whisk 2 tablespoons strained lemon juice into bowl with remaining reserved oil. Slice roast into ¼-inch-thick slices and serve, passing vinaigrette separately.

CIDER-BRAISED PORK ROAST

✓ **WHY THIS RECIPE WORKS:** For this recipe, we paired pork butt roast with sweet-tart apple flavor. Rubbing the pork butt with a brown sugar–salt mixture and refrigerating it overnight thoroughly seasoned the meat and helped keep it juicy. Before braising, we seared the roast in a Dutch oven for some flavorful browning and added sliced onion and minced garlic, allowing them to soften before we poured in some cider. Thyme, a bay leaf, and a cinnamon stick added a savory counterpoint to the braising liquid. We transferred the pot to the oven where the roast braised to a supertender texture. To reinforce the apple flavor, we strained the braising liquid and used the fat to brown Braeburn apple wedges. As a final fruity flourish, we reinforced the flavor of the braising liquid with apple butter and cider vinegar. A slurry of cornstarch and reserved cider thickened the liquid into a beautiful sauce.

Whether it's applewood-smoked bacon or pork chops served with applesauce, pork and apples are an unbeatable combination. With this in mind, I set out to create a recipe for a pork roast slowly braised in cider.

I collected several recipes to test drive. They featured different cuts, different cooking times and temperatures, and supporting ingredients that ranged from onions and celery to orange and caraway. Out of the six recipes I prepared, not one was a success. The meat was bland and leathery in recipes that called for lean tenderloin or loin. Recipes that called for fattier cuts were greasy and produced tough, chewy meat. And they all had muddied flavors that didn't taste much like either pork or apples. I wanted a flavorful, tender roast infused with clean, bright, sweet-tart cider flavor.

I knew from experience that pork shoulder (also known as Boston butt or pork butt, the cut called for in recipes for pulled pork) is a good cut for braising—its fat and connective tissue break down over the long cooking time, resulting in silky, tender, flavorful meat. I tested bone-in versus boneless shoulder roasts, and my tasters preferred the moister meat that came off the bone-in roast; this made sense, because there is a lot of connective tissue around the bone that breaks down during cooking, keeping the meat moist.

I rubbed the roast with a mixture of salt and brown sugar and refrigerated it overnight so the seasoning could penetrate it. This not only made the meat taste better, but the salt helped the muscle fibers hold on to moisture, which made the meat juicier, too. I seared the seasoned pork in a Dutch oven, poured in enough cider (1¾ cups) to come about halfway up the sides of the roast, and gently cooked it in a 300-degree oven until the meat registered 190 degrees and was completely tender. This pork was pretty good, but it was a little dry. Reducing the oven temperature to 275 degrees made for gentler cooking that kept the meat juicier. After about 2½ hours, the pork was perfect.

It was time to fine-tune. I tested cutting the cider with other flavorful ingredients like chicken broth, wine, apple juice, and apple liqueur. Each one diluted or distracted from the clean taste of the cider. Onions, garlic, bay leaf, cinnamon (for a subtle warm note that goes well with cider), and thyme were welcome additions that built a baseline of savory flavor without muting the cider. But when the pork was done, the braising liquid—which, after defatting, becomes the sauce—wasn't thick enough for serving.

Boiling the sauce down on the stovetop worked but took more effort than I wanted to expend. I tried stirring a cup of apple butter into the braising liquid to thicken it and reinforce the apple flavor; my tasters loved the flavor but not the slippery texture. I decided to keep ¼ cup of the apple butter for flavor. As for thickening, cornstarch worked better here. I reserved ¼ cup of cider and, once the roast was done, whisked it together with 1 tablespoon of cornstarch. I then added this mixture, called a slurry, to the pot. It thickened the sauce beautifully.

I was almost at the end of my journey but felt that something was missing. How about actual apples? I tried adding wedges of apples to the braise at various points—from the get-go, in the middle, at the end—but the apples were consistently too hard, too soft, or too mealy. Simply searing the apples in the flavorful pork fat that I'd separated out of the braising liquid was the solution. This made for deliciously porky-sweet apples that held their shape and texture alongside the sliced roast.
—CECELIA JENKINS, *Cook's Country*

Cider-Braised Pork Roast

SERVES 8

Pork butt roast is often labeled Boston butt in the supermarket. This roast needs to cure for 18 to 24 hours before cooking. If you can't find Braeburn apples, substitute Jonagold. If you don't have a fat separator, strain the liquid through a fine-mesh strainer into a medium bowl in step 4 and wait for it to settle.

NOTES FROM THE TEST KITCHEN

THE SAUCE'S SECRET

Though straining through a fine-mesh strainer works well in a pinch, a fat separator is the best tool for removing excess fat. In our Cider-Braised Pork Roast, this is the key to a silky, not greasy, sauce. Our favorite model is the Cuisipro Fat Separator.

REMOVING THE BONE

Using a long knife and holding onto the tip of the T-shaped bone, cut the meat away from all sides of the bone until it is loose enough to pull out of the roast.

---

1 **(5- to 6-pound) bone-in pork butt roast**
¼ **cup packed brown sugar**
   Kosher salt and pepper
3 **tablespoons vegetable oil**
1 **onion, halved and sliced thin**
6 **garlic cloves, smashed and peeled**
2 **cups apple cider**
6 **sprigs fresh thyme**
2 **bay leaves**
1 **cinnamon stick**
2 **Braeburn apples, cored and cut into 8 wedges each**
¼ **cup apple butter**
1 **tablespoon cornstarch**
1 **tablespoon cider vinegar**

1. Using sharp knife, trim fat cap on roast to ¼ inch. Cut 1-inch crosshatch pattern in fat cap. Place roast on large sheet of plastic wrap. Combine sugar and ¼ cup salt in bowl and rub mixture over entire roast and into slits. Wrap roast tightly in double layer of plastic, place on plate, and refrigerate for 18 to 24 hours.

2. Adjust oven rack to middle position and heat oven to 275 degrees. Unwrap roast and pat dry with paper towels, brushing away any excess salt mixture from surface. Season roast with pepper.

3. Heat oil in Dutch oven over medium-high heat until just smoking. Sear roast until well browned on all sides, about 3 minutes per side. Turn roast fat side up. Scatter onion and garlic around roast and cook until fragrant and beginning to brown, about 2 minutes. Add 1¾ cups cider, thyme sprigs, bay leaves, and cinnamon stick and bring to simmer. Cover, transfer to oven, and braise until fork slips easily in and out of meat and meat registers 190 degrees, 2¼ to 2¾ hours.

4. Transfer roast to carving board, tent with aluminum foil, and let rest for 30 minutes. Strain braising liquid through fine-mesh strainer into fat separator; discard solids and let liquid settle for at least 5 minutes.

5. About 10 minutes before roast is done resting, wipe out pot with paper towels. Spoon 1½ tablespoons of clear, separated fat from top of fat separator into now-empty pot and heat over medium-high heat until shimmering. Season apples with salt and pepper. Space apples evenly in pot, cut side down, and cook until well browned on both cut sides, about 3 minutes per side. Transfer to platter and tent with foil.

6. Wipe out pot with paper towels. Return 2 cups defatted braising liquid to now-empty pot and bring to boil over high heat. Whisk in apple butter until incorporated. Whisk cornstarch and remaining ¼ cup cider together in bowl and add to pot. Return to boil and cook until thickened, about 1 minute. Off heat, add vinegar and season with salt and pepper to taste. Cover sauce and keep warm.

7. To carve roast, cut around inverted T-shaped bone until it can be pulled free from roast (use clean dish towel to grasp bone if necessary). Slice pork and transfer to serving platter with apples. Pour 1 cup sauce over pork and apples. Serve, passing remaining sauce separately.

ROASTED RACK OF LAMB

✓ **WHY THIS RECIPE WORKS:** Roasting a rack of lamb is a simple process, but there's a fine line between a show-stopper and a dried-out disappointment. For a rack that would do us proud at our next fête, the seasoning needed to be spot-on, the meat had to be juicy, and we'd want a bold relish to serve alongside it. Carving a shallow cross-hatch into the fat cap and rubbing the racks' surfaces with a blend of kosher salt and ground cumin promised lamb loaded with flavor. Roasting the meat was as simple as heating the oven and arranging the lamb on a wire rack set in a baking sheet. While the racks roasted, we put together an easy relish to dress up the lamb, combining chopped roasted red pepper, minced parsley, olive oil, fresh lemon juice, and minced garlic. To brown the exterior of the racks, we quickly seared them in a skillet before serving.

For many, hosting company at the holidays means pulling out all the stops to present a centerpiece-worthy entrée. Old standbys like turkey or prime rib are great choices—except that they are only for crowds. Plus, they eat up precious time and energy: From salting and trussing to roasting, resting, and carving, it can take hours or even days to get them from supermarket to table.

Enter rack of lamb. With elegantly curved rib bones attached to a long, lean loin, it is as grand as any beef roast or whole bird—but it cooks a whole lot faster and its small size makes it ideal for fewer guests. What's more, its tenderness and delicate but distinctive flavor make it approachable for those who have not tried lamb (and may surprise those who think they dislike it). Because the loin muscle of the animal gets little exercise, the meat doesn't get tough or develop much of a strong, gamy flavor. The fact that this particular cut is so lean also plays a role in its mild taste.

A single rack of domestic lamb weighs about 2 pounds and contains seven or eight rib bones that arc from the loin. Traditionally, the racks are spiffed up via "french-ing," a process that involves cutting away the sinew, fat, and small bits of meat that cover the bones. It can be tedious work, but happily, butchers often take care of this so it's easy to find a roast that is just about oven-ready. Given the small size of a single rack, I decided to cook two frenched racks, which would ably serve four to six guests.

Since lamb fat is the primary source of the musky flavor that some shy away from, I trimmed the fat cap to ¼ inch. Next, I scored crosshatch marks into the fat and sprinkled the racks all over with kosher salt. Cutting slits in the fat would allow the salt to quickly penetrate the meat as well as help the fat render.

With the meat ready to go, I got down to the business of cooking. There are a lot of recipes out there promising "simple but spectacular" results, with the usual recommendation being to roast the meat in a hot oven for about 30 minutes. Using this approach, the racks didn't brown very well; plus, they were pink only at the very center—the outer portion was a dry, dusty gray. If I was going to splurge on rack of lamb, I wanted dazzling results. That meant rosy, juicy, and tender meat surrounded by a rich mahogany exterior.

And yet, abandoning the so-called simple approach resulted in only minor advancements. Slow-roasting the racks in a more moderate oven meant that every bite was juicy, but this lamb wasn't full-flavored because there was zero browning on its exterior. In the test kitchen, we often turn to dual-temperature techniques to achieve both great browning and even cooking. The question was, how should I apply this approach to rack of lamb?

A sear-then-roast routine made sense. I fired up the stove and seared the racks in a skillet until they were good and brown, which took about 5 minutes per rack (and made a pretty good mess of my stovetop). I then placed the seared lamb on a wire rack set in a rimmed baking sheet and slipped it into a 250-degree oven to finish cooking.

The racks emerged gorgeously brown from the pan searing, but when I carved them into chops, frustration set in: Because the loin is relatively small, all that time in the skillet had overcooked most of the meat. I cleaned up and started over, this time placing a roasting pan in the oven and heating the oven to 500 degrees. My hope was that the racks would rapidly brown when they hit the preheated pan. Then I could dial down the oven and let the meat gently finish cooking. But this was another disappointment: The preheated pan wasn't hot enough to sufficiently brown the racks, and the initial high oven temperature overcooked the meat.

Searing followed by roasting was a no-go. How about the reverse? I placed the seasoned racks in a 250-degree oven and let them roast gently until they reached 120 degrees, or just shy of medium-rare. There were a couple of possible approaches for browning the exterior in the oven: Crank the heat as high as it would go or enlist the broiler. I tried both. The broiler browned the fat cap more quickly than the hot oven, so the rack overcooked less. But it still overcooked. Perhaps a skillet was the way to go after all.

I slow-roasted two more racks, this time pulling them from the oven when they were somewhat underdone. I then seared the fat caps one at a time in a hot skillet. To my surprise, each rack browned in less than 2 minutes. When I cut into the meat, I was again surprised, this time by how uniformly rare it was. The explanation was simple. I had assumed that the racks would require a substantial amount of time to brown and would therefore finish cooking in the skillet. But the browning happened so fast—there wasn't even time for the stovetop to get messy—that I clearly needed to let them roast all the way to their serving temperature, 125 degrees for medium-rare. Sure enough, using this method, I finally got the oohs and ahhs I sought: These racks had deeply browned exteriors and perfectly rosy interiors.

But why had they browned so quickly? The slow roasting time had warmed up the fat cap. This allowed it to immediately jump to the temperature necessary for stovetop browning to occur.

With a foolproof cooking method at hand, it was time to try salting the racks ahead of time to see if the treatment, which changes the meat's structure to help it hold on to more juices, was necessary. I salted two racks and let them sit for 1 hour. Then I asked tasters to compare their flavor and texture to racks that were seasoned and then immediately cooked. Tasters reported that the seasoned racks were just as juicy as the salted ones. That's because salt's ability to help meat retain juices is most apparent when meat is exposed to high temperatures, and my lamb was being cooked at only 250 degrees. That meant that it never got hot enough for much moisture to be squeezed out. It had one other thing going for it: Unlike steaks or many other roasts, rack of lamb is protected by a moisture-retaining fat cap on one side and bones on the other side. Given these factors, it was unnecessary to give the lamb a salt treatment. What it did need was a little dressing up, so I went ahead and mixed some ground cumin with kosher salt. I used some of this cumin salt to season the racks; the rest I saved for garnishing the lamb. And while the roasts cooked, I mixed together a quick relish of roasted red peppers, fresh parsley, minced garlic, lemon juice, and extra-virgin olive oil. With the relish spooned alongside the cumin-scented chops, I knew I had a hit. I loved the depth and texture that the cumin salt added, so I whipped up an anise salt and paired it with a mint-almond relish. With these simple recipes, lamb will surely be at the center of my holiday table more often.

—LAN LAM, *Cook's Illustrated*

Roasted Rack of Lamb with Roasted Red Pepper Relish

SERVES 4 TO 6

We prefer the milder taste and bigger size of domestic lamb, but you may substitute lamb imported from New Zealand or Australia. Since imported racks are generally smaller, in step 1 season each rack with ½ teaspoon of the salt mixture and reduce the cooking time to 50 to 70 minutes.

LAMB

2 (1¾- to 2-pound) racks of lamb, fat trimmed to ⅛ to ¼ inch and rib bones frenched
    Kosher salt

1 teaspoon ground cumin

1 teaspoon vegetable oil

RELISH

½ cup jarred roasted red peppers,
   rinsed, patted dry, and chopped fine

½ cup minced fresh parsley

¼ cup extra-virgin olive oil

¼ teaspoon lemon juice

⅛ teaspoon garlic, minced to paste
   Kosher salt and pepper

1. FOR THE LAMB: Adjust oven rack to middle position and heat oven to 250 degrees. Using sharp knife, cut slits in fat cap, spaced ½ inch apart, in crosshatch pattern (cut down to, but not into, meat). Combine 2 tablespoons salt and cumin in bowl. Rub ¾ teaspoon salt mixture over entire surface of each rack and into slits. Reserve remaining salt mixture. Place racks, bone side down, on wire rack set in rimmed baking sheet. Roast until meat registers 125 degrees for medium-rare or 130 degrees for medium, 1 hour 5 minutes to 1 hour 25 minutes.

2. FOR THE RELISH: While lamb roasts, combine red peppers, parsley, olive oil, lemon juice, and garlic in bowl. Season with salt and pepper to taste. Let stand at room temperature for at least 1 hour before serving.

3. Heat vegetable oil in 12-inch skillet over high heat until just smoking. Place 1 rack, bone side up, in skillet and cook until well browned, 1 to 2 minutes. Transfer to carving board. Pour off all but 1 teaspoon fat from skillet and repeat browning with second rack. Tent racks with aluminum foil and let rest for 20 minutes. Cut between ribs to separate chops and sprinkle cut side of chops with ½ teaspoon salt mixture. Serve, passing relish and remaining salt mixture separately.

VARIATION

Roasted Rack of Lamb with Sweet Mint-Almond Relish

Substitute ground anise for cumin in salt mixture. Omit red pepper relish. While lamb roasts, combine ½ cup minced fresh mint; ¼ cup sliced almonds, toasted and chopped fine; ¼ cup extra-virgin olive oil; 2 tablespoons red currant jelly; 4 teaspoons red wine vinegar; and 2 teaspoons Dijon mustard in bowl. Season with salt and pepper to taste. Let stand at room temperature for at least 1 hour before serving.

NOTES FROM THE TEST KITCHEN

EASY AS 1-2-3

Putting an impressive roast on the table doesn't have to be stressful or take all day. Our rack of lamb is ready in less than 2 hours.

SEASON

There's no need to salt ahead of time. Because of the insulating bones and thin layer of fat, rack of lamb sprinkled with salt right before roasting is just as juicy as meat salted an hour in advance.

SLOW-ROAST

For juicy meat that's a rosy medium-rare from center to edge, we simply roast the racks until they reach 125 degrees, 1 hour 5 minutes to 1 hour 25 minutes.

SEAR

The fat cap warms up in the oven, so when it hits a hot skillet, it quickly reaches the temperature necessary for browning. Because the rack browns in 2 minutes, none of the meat overcooks during this step.

CHAPTER 6

POULTRY AND SEAFOOD

BETTER CHICKEN MARSALA

BETTER CHICKEN MARSALA

WHY THIS RECIPE WORKS: To make a restaurant-caliber chicken Marsala, we started by revisiting the usual approach to preparing chicken cutlets. Pounding whole breasts can tear the meat, so we cut them into three evenly sized pieces before pounding. Dredging them in flour promoted better browning and helped thicken the sauce. For a flavorful sauce to coat the chicken, we softened and simmered umami-rich dried porcini mushrooms in Marsala wine to concentrate their rich flavors, adding gelatin for a silky texture. Pancetta, shallot, tomato paste, and garlic reinforced the dish's savory profile. A bit more Marsala and some lemon juice added near the end of cooking brightened the sauce's flavor without making it taste overly boozy.

Everyone knows chicken Marsala, a menu staple at virtually every Italian American restaurant in the United States. But despite its wide-ranging appeal, the dish is rarely made at home. That's too bad, because it's relatively simple to prepare and—when done right—truly satisfying: thin chicken cutlets, dusted lightly with flour, pan-seared until golden brown but still tender and juicy, and napped with a sumptuous sauce of Marsala wine and thinly sliced mushrooms. What's not to like?

Well, as it turned out, quite a bit. When I prepared a handful of recipes, not one dish could hold a candle to the best restaurant versions. For starters, the thin cutlets tended to dry out by the time they browned. What's more, their flour coating turned gummy as soon as I spooned the sauce on top. Then there was the sauce itself, which ranged from thin and watery to syrupy and sweet. Clearly there was lots of room for improvement.

My first step was to streamline the preparation of the cutlets themselves. I knew of two approaches: Either use a meat pounder to flatten a whole breast, or cut the breast in half horizontally into two thinner pieces. The problem with the former method is that all that pounding virtually guarantees tearing the meat. On the other hand, it's difficult to evenly halve a breast horizontally since the meat becomes thinner as you approach the tapered end.

Eventually, I came up with a better way: First, halve the breast crosswise. Then, split the thick side horizontally, leaving three similarly sized pieces that require only a minimum of pounding to become cutlets. To season the cutlets and help them stay moist, I tossed them with salt and set them aside for 15 minutes.

Normally in this dish the cutlets are dredged in flour before they're seared. The flour serves a few purposes. First, it absorbs any surface moisture (a plus since moisture inhibits browning), and then it browns. It also gives the Marsala-mushroom sauce something to grab on to, so the cutlets become nicely coated. The problem was that the flour didn't cook through in the short time that the cutlets were in the pan, causing that gummy mess once the sauce (for now, a placeholder recipe) was introduced.

I wondered if cornstarch would fare better, but it behaved similarly. I even tried using precooked starch in the form of ground saltines. The resulting cutlets were less sticky, but the coating had a gritty texture instead of a smooth one. I also tried cooking the cutlets bare, but that was a dead end: Without a flour coating, the sauce slid right off the chicken; plus, since flour offers the chicken some protection from the heat, it was tricky to get bare cutlets fully browned before they overcooked.

I needed to reconsider the approach of arranging the seared cutlets on a platter and spooning the sauce on top. Did the sauce and cutlets need more time together?

Back at the stove, I returned the browned flour-coated cutlets to the skillet after preparing the sauce and let it bubble gently for a few minutes. Problem solved: During simmering, any excess flour sloughed off into the sauce where it gelatinized, leaving the coating thin, silky, and not the least bit gummy. And because the salting step was effective at maintaining moisture, this additional gentle cooking didn't harm the meat.

With perfectly cooked cutlets at hand, I turned my attention to the sauce. White mushrooms, sliced thin and sautéed, are typically used. They are fine but subtle, and I wanted more complexity. Switching to earthier cremini mushrooms and adding garlic, shallot, and tomato paste was a good start. I had seen recipes that also included pancetta, and indeed, I liked the meatiness it contributed.

As for the Marsala, this Sicilian fortified wine is produced in both sweet and dry styles. Obviously, sweet Marsala tastes sweeter than dry, but I also found that the dry type offered more depth of flavor. In addition, I came to prefer the complexity of moderately priced Marsala, rather than the super-cheap bottles.

Most recipes rely on a combination of chicken broth and Marsala; I liked a 1:1 ratio. I reduced both before adding them to the mushroom mixture, starting with the Marsala and then adding the broth. As we have found in previous recipes, reducing the wine and broth together prevented sufficient alcohol evaporation, producing a boozy taste. However, last-minute additions of ¼ cup of raw Marsala, lemon juice, and chopped oregano brightened the sauce without making it taste like alcohol. Finally, adding dried porcini mushrooms to the reduction rounded out the flavor.

Reducing the wine and broth helped intensify the sauce but did little to add body. (The flour from the cutlets contributed some viscosity but not nearly enough.) A few tablespoons of butter, whisked in at the very end, helped a bit more. Then, as I was thinking about the way a restaurant chef might give the sauce some heft, reduced veal stock (demi-glace) crossed my mind. This spoonable, gelatinous ingredient can provide a luxurious consistency. I wasn't about to buy (or make) demi-glace for this recipe, but I knew of a good stand-in: gelatin. Four teaspoons added to the reducing wine gave the sauce velvety body.

After a sprinkle of parsley, everything was in its place in my new and improved classic.

—ANDREW JANJIGIAN, *Cook's Illustrated*

Better Chicken Marsala

SERVES 4 TO 6

It is worth spending a little extra for a moderately priced dry Marsala ($10 to $12 per bottle). Serve the chicken with potatoes, white rice, or buttered pasta.

2¼   cups dry Marsala
4   teaspoons unflavored gelatin
1   ounce dried porcini mushrooms, rinsed
4   (6- to 8-ounce) boneless, skinless chicken
    breasts, trimmed
    Kosher salt and pepper
2   cups chicken broth
¾   cup all-purpose flour
¼   cup plus 1 teaspoon vegetable oil
3   ounces pancetta, cut into ½-inch pieces
1   pound cremini mushrooms, trimmed and sliced thin
1   shallot, minced
1   tablespoon tomato paste
1   garlic clove, minced
2   teaspoons lemon juice
1   teaspoon minced fresh oregano
3   tablespoons unsalted butter, cut into 6 pieces
2   teaspoons minced fresh parsley

1. Bring 2 cups Marsala, gelatin, and porcini mushrooms to boil in medium saucepan over high heat. Reduce heat to medium-high and vigorously simmer until reduced by half, 6 to 8 minutes.

2. Meanwhile, cut each chicken breast in half crosswise, then cut thick half in half again horizontally, creating 3 cutlets of about same thickness. Place cutlets between sheets of plastic wrap and pound gently to even ½-inch thickness. Place cutlets in bowl and toss with 2 teaspoons salt and ½ teaspoon pepper. Set aside for 15 minutes.

3. Strain Marsala reduction through fine-mesh strainer, pressing on solids to extract as much liquid as possible; discard solids. Return Marsala reduction to saucepan, add broth, and return to boil over high heat. Lower heat to medium-high and simmer until reduced to 1½ cups, 10 to 12 minutes. Set aside.

4. Spread flour in shallow dish. Working with 1 cutlet at a time, dredge cutlets in flour, shaking gently to remove excess. Place on wire rack set in rimmed baking sheet. Heat 2 tablespoons oil in 12 inch skillet over medium-high heat until smoking. Place 6 cutlets in skillet and lower heat to medium. Cook until golden brown on 1 side, 2 to 3 minutes. Flip and cook until golden brown on second side, 2 to 3 minutes. Return cutlets to wire rack. Repeat with 2 tablespoons oil and remaining 6 cutlets.

5. Return now-empty skillet to medium-low heat and add pancetta. Cook, stirring occasionally, scraping pan bottom to loosen browned bits, until pancetta is brown and crisp, about 4 minutes. Add cremini mushrooms and increase heat to medium-high. Cook, stirring occasionally and scraping pan bottom, until liquid released by mushrooms evaporates and mushrooms begin to brown, about 8 minutes. Using slotted spoon, transfer cremini mushrooms and pancetta to bowl. Add remaining 1 teaspoon oil and shallot to pan and cook until softened, 1 minute. Add tomato paste and garlic and cook until fragrant, 30 seconds. Add reduced Marsala mixture, remaining ¼ cup Marsala, lemon juice, and oregano and bring to simmer.

6. Add cutlets to sauce and simmer for 3 minutes, flipping halfway through simmering. Transfer cutlets to platter. Off heat, whisk in butter. Stir in parsley and cremini mushroom mixture. Season with salt and pepper to taste. Spoon sauce over chicken and serve.

ROASTED BONE-IN CHICKEN BREASTS

✔ **WHY THIS RECIPE WORKS:** To serve up perfect roasted bone-in breasts, we adapted a cooking technique commonly used for steaks: reverse searing. We started by applying salt under the skin to season the meat and help it retain moisture. Gently baking the breasts promised juicy, evenly cooked meat and dried out the skins so that a quick sear was all we needed for a crackly, burnished crust. Starting the chicken over low heat allowed excess moisture to evaporate, preventing splattering. Best of all, our hands-off method left us enough time to prepare a flavorful sauce while the chicken cooked.

Choosing boneless, skinless chicken breasts over less-expensive bone-in breasts is like paying extra for a car that has had its air bags removed: You're spending more for less protection. Boneless, skinless breasts are entirely exposed to the heat during cooking, and the bare meat turns leathery as it dries out. But bone-in chicken breasts, with skin on one side and bone on the other, have protection built right in. What's more, the crispy, nicely browned skin of roasted chicken adds flavor and textural contrast.

Bone-in breasts have only one problem that I can see: People view the bone and skin as a complication rather than an asset. In fact, in my research I couldn't find a single recipe for how to actually cook them well. I resolved to devise an easy method that would deliver juicy, well-seasoned meat and crispy brown skin.

I started with the simplest approach. I placed four bone-in breasts on a rimmed baking sheet, sprinkled them with salt, and roasted them in a 425-degree oven. In 25 minutes, they had reached the target temperature of 160 degrees, and the skin was crackly and brown. But the meat was quite dry, especially at the narrow end of each breast, and the seasoning had not penetrated beyond the surface. Lowering the oven temperature to 375 helped: The narrow ends of the breasts weren't as dry, and the chicken was slightly juicier. The skin was still flabby and pale, but I'd deal with that later.

Since the more moderate oven had produced juicier meat, how about dropping the temperature more drastically? I decided to try the reverse-sear technique, a method we often use with steaks. We cook the meat in a low oven until it reaches the desired temperature and then sear it in a skillet on the stovetop. The interior stays incredibly juicy, while the oven-dried exterior browns quickly, with little mess and minimal chance of overcooking the meat just beneath the surface.

After poking holes in the skin to help the fat render, I baked the next batch of chicken in a 250-degree oven. When it reached 160 degrees, I placed the pieces skin side down in a hot skillet. After 3 minutes, the skin was brown and supercrispy. The meat was terrifically moist, too. I noted just two problems: There was zero seasoning once you got past that beautiful skin. And that stint in the oven? It was 1 hour and 45 minutes long.

A cooking time approaching 2 hours was not an option, so I ran through several tests to find the temperature that would produce juicy chicken in a reasonable amount of time. The sweet spot was 325 degrees for about 40 minutes.

The meat was juicy and the skin was crispy, but the chicken still tasted bland. I had hoped to forgo pretreatments like salting and brining because I didn't want to add time to the recipe. My technique was working so well that I could get away with skipping the salt for its moisture-retaining effect, but I realized that I did need it for seasoning. Before putting the next batch in the oven, I carefully peeled back the skin on each breast and sprinkled 1½ teaspoons of kosher salt over all four before smoothing the skin back into place. After 40 minutes in the oven and a quick sear on the stovetop, this was the juiciest and most flavorful batch yet.

As for the searing, I found that there was often a small amount of collected moisture hiding underneath the skin, which caused the chicken to splatter alarmingly when I placed it in a smoking-hot skillet. Rather than try to remove the moisture (and possibly mar the skin in the process), I kept the heat low until the chicken was safely transferred and then turned it up. By the time the pan was hot enough to splatter, the hidden water had evaporated.

Except for the salting at the beginning and the quick sear at the end, my method was pretty much hands-off. That left me with time to pull together a few flavorful sauces while the chicken was in the oven. With that, I had a sauce that was as uncomplicated to prepare as the chicken.

—ANDREA GEARY, *Cook's Illustrated*

Roasted Bone-In Chicken Breasts

SERVES 4

Be sure to remove excess fatty skin from the thick ends of the breasts when trimming. You may serve these chicken breasts on their own or prepare a sauce (recipes follow) while the chicken roasts.

- 4 (10- to 12-ounce) bone-in chicken breasts, trimmed
- 1½ teaspoons kosher salt
- 1 tablespoon vegetable oil

1. Adjust oven rack to lower-middle position and heat oven to 325 degrees. Line rimmed baking sheet with aluminum foil. Working with 1 breast at a time, use your fingers to carefully separate chicken skin from meat. Peel skin back, leaving it attached at top and bottom of breast and at ribs. Sprinkle salt evenly over all chicken, then lay skin back in place. Using metal skewer or tip of paring knife, poke 6 to 8 holes in fat deposits in skin. Arrange breasts skin side up on prepared sheet. Roast until chicken registers 160 degrees, 35 to 45 minutes.

2. Heat 12-inch skillet over low heat for 5 minutes. Add oil and swirl to coat surface. Add chicken, skin side down, and increase heat to medium-high. Cook chicken without moving it until skin is well browned and crispy, 3 to 5 minutes. Using tongs, flip chicken and prop against side of skillet so thick side of breast is facing down; continue to cook until browned, 1 to 2 minutes longer. Transfer to platter and let rest for 5 minutes before serving.

Jalapeño and Cilantro Sauce

MAKES 1 CUP

For a spicier sauce, reserve and add some of the chile seeds to the blender.

- 1 cup fresh cilantro leaves and stems, trimmed and chopped coarse
- 3 jalapeño chiles, stemmed, seeded, and minced
- ½ cup mayonnaise
- 1 tablespoon lime juice
- 2 garlic cloves, minced
- ½ teaspoon kosher salt
- 2 tablespoons extra-virgin olive oil

Process cilantro, jalapeños, mayonnaise, lime juice, garlic, and salt in blender for 1 minute. Scrape down sides of blender jar and continue to process until smooth, about 1 minute longer. With blender running, slowly add oil until incorporated. Transfer to bowl.

Tahini and Honey Sauce

MAKES ½ CUP

A rasp-style grater makes quick work of turning the garlic into a paste.

- ¼ cup tahini
- 2 tablespoons lemon juice
- 2 tablespoons extra-virgin olive oil
- 1 tablespoon water
- 2 teaspoons honey
- 1 garlic clove, minced to paste
- ¾ teaspoon kosher salt
- ⅛ teaspoon ground cumin
    Pinch cayenne pepper
- 2 tablespoons chopped fresh cilantro

Whisk tahini, lemon juice, oil, water, honey, garlic, salt, cumin, and cayenne in bowl until smooth. Stir in cilantro.

Spicy Butter Sauce

MAKES ⅓ CUP

Our favorite conventional hot sauce is Frank's RedHot Original Cayenne Pepper Sauce.

- 3 tablespoons hot sauce
- 1 teaspoon cornstarch
- 3 tablespoons cold butter, cut into 3 pieces

Whisk hot sauce and cornstarch together in small saucepan. Cook over medium-low heat, whisking constantly, until mixture is bubbly and thick, about 2 minutes. Off heat, whisk in butter, 1 piece at a time, until melted. Serve warm.

RANCH FRIED CHICKEN

✔ **WHY THIS RECIPE WORKS:** To create a fried chicken recipe with all the tangy, herbal flavors of ranch dressing, we incorporated the three hallmark herbs—dill, cilantro, and chives—into buttermilk and flour coatings for the chicken and into a flavorful dipping sauce. To keep the fresh herb flavor at the fore, we needed the chicken to spend as little time as possible in the hot oil; opting for small, quick-cooking thighs was the best solution. For authentic ranch flavor, we enhanced the buttermilk's tang with some vinegar; garlic gave it even more flavor and cayenne added a touch of heat. Using the seasoned buttermilk mixture both as a coating for the chicken and as a base for the sauce kept the recipe streamlined.

Savory, crunchy crust and irresistibly juicy meat make fried chicken one of our favorite foods in the test kitchen. For a summery twist, I set out to make fried chicken with all its beloved attributes, plus the aroma and flavor of bright, lively fresh herbs.

First, I had to pick a flavor lane. The woodsy herbs traditionally paired with poultry—rosemary, thyme, and sage—reminded me of winter. But chive, dill, and cilantro recalled a summery American flavor: ranch. Buttermilk, already one of fried chicken's best friends, would provide ranch's signature tang.

To start, I brined my chicken pieces, as we usually do in the test kitchen, and then dipped them in buttermilk and a few different herbed coatings (flour, cornstarch, bread crumbs, and combinations thereof) and used our tried-and-true frying methods. But batch after batch tasted more or less the same—fried. The herbs were undetectable in the final product.

I tried treating the chicken to a bath in an herby marinade. I tried rubbing dried spices directly on the chicken before coating it with flour. I even infused the frying oil with herbs. But still I had only faintly green chicken to prove that I had used any fresh herbs at all.

Why were the herb flavors disappearing? Our science editor explained that the flavor compounds in herbs become unstable and volatile when exposed to heat. Some compounds start to chemically break down while others simply evaporate at hot temperatures. The breading helped protect the herbs from the heat but for only a short time.

Aha: So the issue wasn't how I introduced the herbs to the chicken, but rather how long I let them stay in the hot oil. With this knowledge, I tried precooking the chicken, poaching it before coating it with the herbs. Less than a minute in the hot oil and this chicken was crispy. And, at last, I could taste the herbs. But I lost the juicy decadence. And who wants to cook chicken twice?

Another look at the cut of chicken I was using revealed a loophole. If I used smaller boneless thighs instead of thicker bone-in parts, I could reduce the frying time by half. And with the increased surface area on boneless, skinless thighs, I could increase the amount of herby coating per piece. What's more, thigh meat is naturally juicier than breast meat so I could forgo the standard brining step and shave off an hour of prep time. Plus, chicken thighs are cheaper. After a few tests, I settled on a three-part technique for the chives, dill, and cilantro. I whisked them into buttermilk along with the other ranch components (vinegar, garlic, salt, pepper, and mayonnaise) to make an herby liquid coating. I mixed the herbs into the flour coating along with some cornstarch for extra crunch. And I used the herbs in a ranch-style dipping sauce. The final analysis? Not one, but two American classics found a place at my summer table.

—KATIE LEAIRD, *Cook's Country*

Ranch Fried Chicken

SERVES 4 TO 6

Use a Dutch oven that holds 6 quarts or more for this recipe.

CHICKEN
- 8 (5- to 7-ounce) boneless, skinless chicken thighs, trimmed
  Salt and pepper
- 2 quarts peanut or vegetable oil

BUTTERMILK MIXTURE
- 1 cup buttermilk
- 2 tablespoons minced fresh chives
- 2 tablespoons minced fresh cilantro
- 2 teaspoons minced fresh dill
- 2 teaspoons distilled white vinegar
- 1 garlic clove, minced
- ½ teaspoon salt
  Pinch cayenne pepper

1¼ cups all-purpose flour

½ cup cornstarch

3 tablespoons minced fresh chives

3 tablespoons minced fresh cilantro

1 tablespoon minced fresh dill

1½ teaspoons garlic powder

1½ teaspoons salt

¾ teaspoon pepper

RANCH SAUCE

½ cup mayonnaise

Salt and pepper

1. FOR THE CHICKEN: Pat chicken dry with paper towels and season with salt and pepper.

2. FOR THE BUTTERMILK MIXTURE: Whisk all ingredients together in bowl. Set aside ¼ cup buttermilk mixture for ranch sauce.

3. FOR THE COATING: Whisk all ingredients together in large bowl.

4. Set wire rack in rimmed baking sheet. Set second wire rack in second rimmed baking sheet and line half of rack with triple layer of paper towels.

5. Working with 1 piece at a time, dip chicken in remaining buttermilk mixture to coat, letting excess drip back into bowl; then dredge in coating, pressing to adhere. Transfer chicken to first wire rack (without paper towels). (At this point, coated chicken may be refrigerated, uncovered, for up to 2 hours.)

6. Heat oil in large Dutch oven over medium-high heat until it reaches 350 degrees. Add half of chicken to hot oil and fry until golden brown and registers 175 degrees, 7 to 9 minutes. Adjust burner, if necessary, to maintain oil temperature between 325 and 350 degrees.

7. Transfer chicken to paper towel–lined side of second wire rack to drain on each side for 30 seconds, then move to unlined side of rack. Return oil to 350 degrees and repeat with remaining chicken.

8. FOR THE RANCH SAUCE: Whisk mayonnaise into reserved buttermilk mixture. Season with salt and pepper to taste.

9. Transfer chicken to platter and serve with ranch sauce.

SPANISH BRAISED CHICKEN WITH SHERRY AND SAFFRON

✔ WHY THIS RECIPE WORKS: Starring ultratender chicken in a rich, slightly coarse sherry sauce, *pollo en pepitoria* is a classic Spanish braise. For a version we could make at home, we started with collagen-rich chicken thighs, which we browned to build a savory base. This cut of chicken takes well to braises, turning supremely tender and moist. To the sauce's base of sherry and broth, we added a touch of cinnamon, bay leaf, and chopped canned tomatoes for some contrasting acidity. After braising the chicken in the sauce, we blended a portion of the cooking liquid with chopped hard-cooked egg yolks, toasted slivered almonds, and aromatics (known as a *picada*) to give the sauce its signature texture. Fresh parsley and chopped hard-cooked egg whites promised an authentic presentation.

At a Spanish restaurant not long ago, a chicken dish called *pollo en pepitoria* caught my attention. The meat, which had been braised until it was incredibly tender, arrived covered in a creamy, fragrant, subtly coarse sauce that featured three of the cuisine's star ingredients: sherry, saffron, and almonds. Scattered over the chicken were chopped egg whites and fresh parsley. The flavors and lush consistency were so appealing that I sopped up the extra sauce on the plate with pieces of crusty bread. I then hurried home to find recipes so that I could make the dish myself.

I quickly learned that the dish, which some sources note is a great specialty of the saffron producing Castilla–La Mancha region of Spain, gets its creamy-but-not-quite-smooth consistency from a *picada*. This nut-based paste seasoned with garlic and herbs or spices is commonly used in Spanish cuisine to thicken soups, stews, and sauces. Interestingly, the picada for pollo en pepitoria is made even more rich by mashing hard-cooked egg yolks with the nuts. That explained the chopped egg white garnish.

But as stunning as this dish was in the restaurant, the versions I tried were not. Every one had richness in spades, but the creamy sauce usually came off as cloying and even a bit one-dimensional. With some work, though, I was sure I could produce a luxurious, complex-flavored sauce that was as rich and satisfying as it was balanced.

Most Spanish cookbook authors note that the dish is traditionally made with a whole chicken (in those cases, it's called *gallina en pepitoria*), but plenty of modern recipes call for chicken parts—particularly thighs. The dark meat is especially nice for braising because it contains abundant connective tissue, which melts into gelatin as the chicken cooks, leaving the meat nicely tender. In fact, when we braise chicken thighs in the test kitchen, we maximize that texture by cooking them slowly and not just until they hit their target doneness temperature of 175 degrees, but well beyond that to 195 degrees; at that point, they're not just tender but downright silky.

The cooking method starts as does any classic braise: with browning the meat. I chose skin-on thighs, since the rendered fat from the skin would contribute big savory flavor to the dish. I would remove and discard the skin before serving since a long simmer makes chicken skin soggy.

From there, I softened a chopped onion with a couple of minced garlic cloves and salt in the rendered fat and saw to the sherry. We avoid "cooking sherry," which contains salt and preservatives that distract from the wine's nutty flavor. Sweet sherries and cream sherries would also taste cloying in a savory braise. Instead, I reached for a dry, light-bodied variety called *fino* that's equally widely available. I poured a generous ⅔ cup into the pan, scraped up the flavorful browned bits known as fond, added chicken broth and brought the pot up to a simmer, and placed the parcooked thighs in the liquid. I simmered the thighs with the lid on for the better part of an hour, by which point the meat just barely clung to the bone. Then came the picada, which is made like a pesto: Nuts—almonds are most traditional—get blitzed in the blender with more garlic, a pair of hard-cooked egg yolks, and a pinch of saffron (a little goes a long way) until the mixture is as smooth as possible. After stirring the thick paste into the pan, you simmer everything for another few minutes to meld the flavors and thicken it further.

To brighten the rich almond-egg sauce, I finished it with a spritz of fresh lemon juice, which turned out to be a good move, albeit too subtle. I couldn't add much more lemon juice before the sauce would turn distinctly citrusy, but tomatoes also contain acid and were worth trying. Unlike in Italian sauces, where they're often the focal point, tomatoes are sometimes introduced in Spanish sauces to complement other flavors. Going forward, I experimented with chopped and grated fresh and canned whole tomatoes. I found that a small can of whole peeled tomatoes, drained and chopped fine, offered the necessary brightness along with nice savory sweetness. While I was making flavor tweaks, I also added a bay leaf and a dash of cinnamon—elements I'd seen in a handful of published recipes—when I sautéed the garlic, which made the sauce just a bit more fragrant.

The sauce was just about there, but I had two quibbles with the almonds. Most recipes I found didn't call for toasting them, so I hadn't up until now, but not surprisingly this quick step noticeably deepened their flavor and, thus, the flavor of the sauce. The bigger issue was their texture; pepitoria is meant to have a rustic, slightly coarse consistency, but here the picada was too gritty to integrate well in the braising liquid. I tried simply buzzing the ingredients for longer in the blender, but even after 3 full minutes, they didn't break down sufficiently. I also tried replacing the nuts themselves with almond butter—an admittedly odd move that unfortunately did away with the sauce's pleasantly coarse texture.

NOTES FROM THE TEST KITCHEN

SHOPPING FOR SHERRY

Dry sherries come in a variety of subclassifications that represent degrees of aging and fortification—from drier, lighter-bodied, and less expensive *fino* to nuttier, heavier, and pricier *oloroso*. We've found that it's fine to cook with an inexpensive fino, such as Taylor Dry Sherry, but if you want a bottle that's as good to drink as it is to cook with, consider Lustau Palo Cortado Península Sherry.

COOKING ONLY   COOKING AND DRINKING

I finally realized that the way to make a smoother picada was to treat it like soup and blend it with some of the braising liquid. The liquid not only saturated and smoothed out the dry nut mixture but also increased the volume of food in the blender jar, making it easier for the ingredients to engage the blade and process the picada more thoroughly. The resulting sauce was thick, creamy, and just shy of smooth—ideal for coating the moist chicken or swiping up with a piece of good crusty bread.

—ADAM RIED, *Cook's Illustrated*

Spanish Braised Chicken with Sherry and Saffron (Pollo en Pepitoria)

SERVES 4

Any dry sherry, such as fino or Manzanilla, will work in this dish. Serve with crusty bread.

  8 (5- to 7-ounce) bone-in chicken thighs, trimmed
     Salt and pepper
  1 tablespoon extra-virgin olive oil
  1 onion, chopped fine
  3 garlic cloves, minced
  1 bay leaf
  ¼ teaspoon ground cinnamon
  ⅔ cup dry sherry
  1 cup chicken broth
  1 (14.5-ounce) can whole peeled tomatoes, drained and chopped fine
  2 hard-cooked large eggs, peeled and yolks and whites separated
  ½ cup slivered blanched almonds, toasted
     Pinch saffron threads, crumbled
  2 tablespoons chopped fresh parsley
  1½ teaspoons lemon juice

1. Adjust oven rack to middle position and heat oven to 300 degrees.

2. Pat thighs dry with paper towels and season both sides of each with 1 teaspoon salt and ½ teaspoon pepper. Heat oil in 12-inch skillet over high heat until just smoking. Add thighs and brown on both sides, 10 to 12 minutes. Transfer thighs to large plate and pour off all but 2 teaspoons fat from skillet.

3. Return skillet to medium heat, add onion and ¼ teaspoon salt, and cook, stirring frequently, until just softened, about 3 minutes. Add 2 teaspoons garlic, bay leaf, and cinnamon and cook until fragrant, about 1 minute. Add sherry and cook, scraping up any browned bits, until sherry starts to thicken, about 2 minutes. Stir in broth and tomatoes and bring to simmer. Return thighs to skillet, cover, transfer to oven, and cook until chicken registers 195 degrees, 45 to 50 minutes. Transfer thighs to serving platter, remove and discard skin, and cover loosely with aluminum foil to keep warm. While thighs cook, finely chop egg whites.

4. Discard bay leaf. Transfer ¾ cup chicken cooking liquid, egg yolks, almonds, saffron, and remaining garlic to blender jar. Process until smooth, about 2 minutes, scraping down jar as needed. Return almond mixture to skillet. Add 1 tablespoon parsley and lemon juice; bring to simmer over medium heat. Simmer, whisking frequently, until thickened, 3 to 5 minutes. Season with salt and pepper to taste.

5. Pour sauce over chicken, sprinkle with remaining 1 tablespoon parsley and egg whites, and serve.

PERI PERI GRILLED CHICKEN

✔ WHY THIS RECIPE WORKS: To bring this bold East-meets-West grilled chicken home, we started with a complex spice paste, blending garlic, shallot, bay leaves, lemon zest and juice, pepper, and plenty of salt. The addition of five-spice powder alluded to the Asian-inspired versions of this dish we uncovered during our research, and tomato paste delivered some richness to balance out the spices' potency. Arbol chiles and cayenne pepper took the place of hard-to-find peri peri peppers, mimicking their distinct hot yet fruity flavor. We chose chicken parts over a whole bird for the promise of more surface area to char. Poking the skin and tossing the parts in the paste helped the flavors penetrate the meat, seasoning it and helping it stay juicy on the grill, and chopped peanuts delivered subtle sweetness and extra texture. We followed the grill setup used for barbecue recipes, with a hotter side to build flavorful browning and a cooler side where the chicken could finish cooking gently. Placing a pan of water on the cooler side also helped regulate the grill's heat.

The spicy grilled dish known as peri peri chicken has old African roots and a meandering history, but the basic idea is this: Chicken is marinated overnight in a paste of garlic, herbs, spices, lemon juice, and peri

peri chiles—fiery local peppers whose name means "pepper pepper" in Swahili. The next day the chicken is grilled over a hot fire until the meat is tender and the skin is crisp and charred. The result is a dish packed with complex, spicy flavor.

While doing some initial research, I found that published recipes for this dish vary greatly, but given its backstory, I wasn't all that surprised. Portuguese travelers brought the peri peri pepper from South America to East Africa, where it met up with the ancient tradition of cooking chicken over a live fire. When the sailors picked up and moved on to the next conquest, they took the pepper and the cooking method with them. With each landing, the dish assumed some of the flavors and character of its adopted homes, including India and the former Portuguese colony of Macao, located near Hong Kong.

The first time I ever had peri peri chicken was at a Chicago restaurant called Fat Rice that features the melting-pot cuisine of Macao. The meat was tender, the skin was perfectly crisped, and, most notably, the dish hit me with undeniable heat, yes, but also layers of complexity and richness. This chicken set the bar for my own adaptation.

Traditional versions described in African cookbooks used merely chiles, lemon juice, and a few herbs like oregano and ground bay leaves for seasoning. Macanese versions incorporated five-spice powder, which lent the dish a more Asian flavor. Recipes that had few ingredients yielded chicken with little more than grill flavor; more successful were those that used a lot of chiles and a generous amount of spice paste to ensure that the seasonings weren't overpowered by the smoke and char of grilling. But none of them really hit the mark for the spicy yet complex taste I was after. Since peri peri peppers (fresh or dried) are hard to come by in the States, I'd need to find a good substitute. I also wanted to iron out the cooking method for my version; most recipes simply said "grill over a hot fire."

Because peri peri chicken is really a type of barbecued chicken with a different flavor profile, I decided to use the test kitchen's foolproof approach to that dish: We spread charcoal evenly over half the grill, providing a hotter area where char is developed, while leaving the other half of the grill free of coals, creating a place to finish the cooking gently over indirect heat. We also put an aluminum pan filled with water on the grill to absorb heat and eliminate hot spots. This method calls for chicken parts for two reasons: They provide more surface area for charring and sauce (or in my case, spice paste), and they allow for more even cooking since the more delicate breast pieces can be placed farther from the fire. Finally, we salt the chicken overnight. While salt might not have been a major component in the peri peri chicken recipes I'd tried (they called for ½ to 2 teaspoons at most), I'd use quite a bit more—2 tablespoons, in fact, based on our barbecued chicken recipe. During marinating, the salt not only penetrates the meat and seasons it throughout but also alters the proteins in the chicken so that the meat more tenaciously holds on to water during cooking—one more guarantee that it would come off the grill tender and juicy.

With the cooking method settled, I could focus on flavor. My spice paste started with a few ingredients whizzed together in the food processor: garlic, shallots, lemon zest and juice, bay leaves, paprika, and black pepper. I also added a generous amount of five-spice powder for complexity. Olive oil would help extract the fat-soluble components in the spices, while sugar would enhance all the flavors.

Now for the peri peri peppers. I was able to track down peri peri hot sauce, so I at least had a sense of the pepper's character: hot, but also fruity and complex. For the best available substitute, I settled on dried arbol chiles. But I quickly learned that tasters' tolerance for spiciness, and to some degree the spiciness of the chiles themselves, varied. If I added a little cayenne for baseline heat, I could use a range of arbols (from four to 10) and still get plenty of fruity chile flavor. I also sorted out an easy way to adjust the heat midstream. I began with a judicious amount of arbols and then tasted the paste before applying it to the chicken, adding more arbols until it was just past the point of being as hot as I wanted the finished chicken to be. The heat of the grill took the edge off, leaving the spiciness at just the right level.

I was close, but my recipe still lacked the richness and complexity of the version I'd had at Fat Rice. Stumped as to what to do next, I called the chef. Although he wouldn't reveal all his secrets, he did generously describe his technique, which he learned from a chef in Macao. He told me that once the chicken was cooked, he

PERI PERI GRILLED CHICKEN

applied a sauce made from coconut milk, tomato paste, and finely chopped peanuts and then returned the chicken to the grill to char it further.

I didn't want to complicate my recipe by adding a sauce, but I was game to try incorporating these ingredients into my spice paste. Coconut milk left the exterior of the grilled chicken pasty, but tomato paste and the chopped peanuts gave my dish the balancing richness and hint of sweetness it had been missing. This was a grilled chicken recipe I'd be turning to time and again; it's as delicious as it is easy to make.

—ANDREW JANJIGIAN, *Cook's Illustrated*

Peri Peri Grilled Chicken

SERVES 6 TO 8

This recipe requires refrigerating the spice paste–coated chicken for at least 6 hours or up to 24 hours prior to cooking. When browning the chicken, move it away from the direct heat if any flare-ups occur. Serve the chicken with white rice.

4–10 arbol chiles, stemmed

3 tablespoons extra-virgin olive oil

2 tablespoons salt

8 garlic cloves, peeled

2 tablespoons tomato paste

1 shallot, chopped

1 tablespoon sugar

1 tablespoon paprika

1 tablespoon five-spice powder

2 teaspoons grated lemon zest plus ¼ cup juice (2 lemons)

1 teaspoon pepper

½ teaspoon cayenne pepper

3 bay leaves, crushed

6 pounds bone-in chicken pieces (breasts, thighs, and/or drumsticks), trimmed

½ cup dry-roasted peanuts, chopped fine

1 (13 by 9-inch) disposable aluminum pan (if using charcoal) or 2 (9-inch) disposable aluminum pie plates (if using gas)

Lemon wedges

1. Process 4 arbols, oil, salt, garlic, tomato paste, shallot, sugar, paprika, five-spice powder, lemon zest and juice, pepper, cayenne, and bay leaves in blender until smooth, 10 to 20 seconds. Taste paste and add up to 6 additional arbols, depending on desired level of heat (spice paste should be slightly hotter than desired heat level of cooked chicken), and process until smooth. Using metal skewer, poke skin side of each chicken piece 8 to 10 times. Place chicken pieces, peanuts, and spice paste in large bowl or container and toss until chicken is evenly coated. Cover and refrigerate for at least 6 hours or up to 24 hours.

2A. FOR A CHARCOAL GRILL: Open bottom vent halfway and place disposable pan filled with 3 cups water on 1 side of grill. Light large chimney starter filled with charcoal briquettes (6 quarts). When top coals are partially covered with ash, pour evenly over other half of grill (opposite disposable pan). Set cooking grate in place, cover, and open lid vent halfway. Heat grill until hot, about 5 minutes.

2B. FOR A GAS GRILL: Place 2 disposable pie plates, each filled with 1½ cups water, directly on 1 burner of gas grill (opposite primary burner). Turn all burners to high, cover, and heat grill until hot, about 15 minutes. Turn primary burner to medium-high and turn off other burner(s). (Adjust primary burner as needed to maintain grill temperature between 325 and 350 degrees.)

3. Clean and oil cooking grate. Place chicken, skin side down, on hotter side of grill and cook until browned and blistered in spots, 2 to 5 minutes. Flip chicken and cook until second side is browned, 4 to 6 minutes. Move chicken to cooler side of grill and arrange, skin side up, with legs and thighs closest to fire and breasts farthest away. Cover (positioning lid vent over chicken if using charcoal) and cook until breasts register 160 degrees and legs and thighs register 175 degrees, 50 to 60 minutes.

4. Transfer chicken to serving platter, tent with aluminum foil, and let rest for 10 minutes before serving, passing lemon wedges separately.

SKILLET-ROASTED CHICKEN IN LEMON SAUCE

✔ **WHY THIS RECIPE WORKS:** Inspired by the lemon roast chicken served at Rao's restaurant in New York City, we set out to re-create the dish at home. Rather than cut up hard-to-find young chickens as they do at Rao's, we turned to bone-in parts and brined them for thorough seasoning. To create the burnished skin we wanted, we adopted a two-step cooking technique, first searing the parts in a hot skillet and then finishing them in the oven. A flour-thickened braising liquid, fortified with both lemon juice and lemon zest to maximize lemon flavor later made for a potent serving sauce. We arranged the chicken in the skillet so the skin stayed above the liquid—this setup allowed the meat to cook through while the skin's browning deepened. The addition of parsley, oregano, and extra zest made for a fresh finish.

Even if you've never landed a table at Rao's, New York City's legendary Italian restaurant, you may have heard of its famous roast lemon chicken. The dish is a take on *pollo al limone* in which two small chickens are cut in half and cooked under the restaurant's powerful broiler (called a salamander). The deeply bronzed birds are then cut into pieces and bathed in a simple, pungent sauce of lemon juice (a full cup per bird), olive oil, red wine vinegar, garlic, and dried oregano before being briefly broiled again and served with crusty bread for dipping.

With its simple, bold preparation, the dish is undeniably appealing, and the restaurant's recipe (published in its cookbook and on the Internet) is hugely popular. But it's not perfect. When I tried to replicate it, I hit a number of snags. First: The small, quick-cooking birds used at Rao's are not available in most supermarkets, and home broilers are not nearly as powerful or even-heating as restaurant broilers. As a result, the skin on the larger supermarket birds (which has more fat than the skin on the younger birds used at Rao's) browned unevenly and was flabby since it didn't fully render. Then there was the sauce. Pouring it over the chicken made the skin soggy, and marrying the two components at the last minute made the flavor transfer between them superficial. Plus, the sauce was thin—fine as a bread dipper but not viscous enough to cling to the meat—and downright puckery.

The good news was that all of these flaws seemed fixable, so I set my sights on making a more accessible version of the Rao's classic and refining its flavors.

My first task: picking the right chicken. As an easy alternative to the small birds, I decided to use bone-in chicken parts; 3 pounds of mixed white and dark meat would roughly approximate the yield of two small chickens and would serve four. The Rao's recipe doesn't call for brining or salting the chicken, but we've found that both methods season the meat and help keep it moist. To make this a weeknight-friendly dish, I chose brining, which can be done in 30 minutes (salting bone-in chicken pieces takes at least 6 hours to have an impact). I dried the brined meat's exterior well so as not to inhibit browning.

As for the cooking method, a comparison of conventional home broilers to salamanders explained why the former was yielding such uneven results. Most salamanders comprise multiple closely aligned parallel elements that disperse heat evenly over the surface of the food. With home broilers, the design of the heating element can vary considerably: Some models have a single bar running down the middle of the oven, others a serpentine coil—and neither projects widespread, even heat. Plus, the heat output and the distance you can put between the element and the food vary; I needed to lower the oven rack 10 inches from the element in our test kitchen ovens to ensure that the chicken pieces cooked through before burning, but not every home oven offers that option.

The more foolproof approach would be to sear the chicken on the stovetop and then finish cooking it in the oven in the sauce. Doing so meant I could incorporate the flavorful fond left in the pan after searing the chicken pieces into the sauce, and I could also maximize the flavor transfer between the chicken pieces and the sauce.

After patting the chicken parts dry, I browned them in a 12-inch ovensafe skillet, transferred them to a plate, and briefly sautéed minced garlic and shallot in the rendered chicken fat. To balance the acidity, I reduced the amount of lemon juice to ¼ cup and skipped the vinegar (we couldn't taste it with all the citrus). To this mixture I added 1 cup of chicken broth—which was just enough liquid to submerge the bottom halves of the chicken pieces while leaving the skin exposed. In essence, I'd be braising the meat—but uncovered so that the exposed skin could crisp in the oven's heat.

In less than 15 minutes, the skin was crisp and the white meat was cooked through; the downside was that I had to remove the breasts from the pan before the legs and thighs, which took longer to cook, were done. As for the sauce, cooking the lemon juice had weakened the fruit's flavor, and the consistency was still too thin.

The easiest way to synchronize the doneness of the white and dark meats in the oven was to extend the cooking time of the dark meat on the stovetop, browning it on both sides rather than just the skin side so that it went into the oven at a higher temperature than the white meat. Problem solved.

Since I was cooking the lemon juice, I knew that adding more of it to the sauce would only increase the acidity, not the flavor. Added at the end of cooking, it made the sauce sour. But the aromatic compounds in lemon zest are more stable and retain more fruity lemony flavor when heated. After trying various amounts of zest, I settled on introducing 1 tablespoon right before I added the chicken, for the bright, citrusy boost I was after.

As for thickening the sauce, I first tried the most conventional tactic—removing the cooked chicken from the liquid and tenting it with foil to keep it warm, whisking some cornstarch into the sauce, and briefly simmering it. It worked, but at the expense of the chicken's skin, which steamed under the foil and lost its crispiness. But what if I thickened the sauce at the beginning instead by adding flour, which is more heat-stable than cornstarch, to the aromatics? The tricky part was that as the chicken cooked, it shed juices that thinned the sauce, so it took a few tests before I determined that 4 teaspoons of flour made for full-bodied, lemony gravy. I also swapped in butter for the chicken fat because I found that the rendered fat varied from batch to batch. Two tablespoons of butter gave me a perfectly rich sauce. After transferring the chicken to a serving platter, I gave the mixture a whisk to smooth it out and scrape the flavorful fond from the sides of the pan back into the sauce.

A combination of chopped oregano, parsley, and more lemon zest—stirred into the sauce and sprinkled over top—added fruity brightness that complemented the crisp skin; moist, flavorful meat; and silky, lemony sauce. This wasn't exactly Rao's chicken, but in the spirit of New York, I could say I did it my way.

—ANNIE PETITO, *Cook's Illustrated*

Skillet-Roasted Chicken in Lemon Sauce

MAKES 4 SERVINGS

Serve with crusty bread, rice, potatoes, or egg noodles. To ensure crisp skin, dry the chicken well after brining and pour the sauce around, not on, the chicken right before serving.

½ cup salt
3 pounds bone-in chicken pieces (2 split breasts cut in half crosswise, 2 drumsticks, and 2 thighs), trimmed
1 teaspoon vegetable oil
2 tablespoons unsalted butter
1 large shallot, minced
1 garlic clove, minced
4 teaspoons all-purpose flour
1 cup chicken broth
4 teaspoons grated lemon zest and ¼ cup juice (2 lemons)
1 tablespoon fresh parsley leaves
1 teaspoon fresh oregano leaves

1. Dissolve salt in 2 quarts cold water in large container. Submerge chicken in brine, cover, and refrigerate for 30 minutes to 1 hour. Remove chicken from brine and pat dry with paper towels.

2. Adjust oven rack to lower-middle position and heat oven to 475 degrees. Heat oil in ovensafe 12-inch skillet over medium-high heat until just smoking. Place chicken skin side down in skillet and cook until skin is well browned and crisp, 8 to 10 minutes. Transfer breasts to large plate. Flip thighs and legs and continue to cook until browned on second side, 3 to 5 minutes longer. Transfer thighs and legs to plate with breasts.

3. Pour off and discard fat in skillet. Return skillet to medium heat; add butter, shallot, and garlic and cook until fragrant, 30 seconds. Sprinkle flour evenly over shallot-garlic mixture and cook, stirring constantly, until flour is lightly browned, about 1 minute. Slowly stir in broth and lemon juice, scraping up any browned bits, and bring to simmer. Cook until sauce is slightly reduced and thickened, 2 to 3 minutes. Stir in 1 tablespoon zest and remove skillet from heat. Return chicken, skin side up (skin should be above surface of liquid), and any accumulated juices to skillet and transfer to oven. Cook, uncovered, until breasts register 160 degrees and thighs and legs register 175 degrees, 10 to 12 minutes.

4. While chicken cooks, chop parsley, oregano, and remaining 1 teaspoon zest together until finely minced and well combined. Remove skillet from oven and let chicken stand for 5 minutes.

5. Transfer chicken to serving platter. Whisk sauce, incorporating any browned bits from sides of pan, until smooth and homogeneous, about 30 seconds. Whisk half of herb-zest mixture into sauce and sprinkle remaining half over chicken. Pour some sauce around chicken. Serve, passing remaining sauce separately.

CAST-IRON SKILLET ROASTED CHICKEN

✓ **WHY THIS RECIPE WORKS:** We set out to produce perfectly cooked crisp-skinned chicken that could be on the table in less than an hour. We started by heating a cast-iron skillet in a very hot oven; butterflying the chicken ensured that the skin would be evenly exposed to the pan's hot surface. We flipped the chicken partway through cooking so that the skin wouldn't get soggy sitting in the exuded juices. A simple mixture of extra-virgin olive oil, rosemary, and garlic brushed on the chicken during roasting elevated the flavor and crisped the skin even further.

When I think of my ideal roast chicken, I picture a golden-brown bird with juicy, perfectly cooked meat and enough crisp skin to share with the whole table. Here in the test kitchen, we've mastered the weeknight roast chicken—a simple technique that calls for roasting a whole bird in a preheated skillet—but the skin is not always crisp enough for me. On the other hand, our recipes that guarantee the burnished skin I love require over an hour of brining or letting the chicken dry overnight in the refrigerator, making them impractical for a weeknight dinner. I wanted the best of both worlds: a perfectly cooked roast chicken with crackling browned skin that I could easily prepare after a long day at work.

I began by looking into the test kitchen's archives, trying to decode the secrets behind supremely crisp skin. In all cases, high heat proved critical, delivering intense browning and rendering away the fat that would otherwise make the skin soggy. Butterflying the chicken—that

is, removing the backbone, then opening and flattening the bird—is another one of our go-to techniques, as it maximizes the meat's contact with the oven's heat and the cooking surface. The missing part in the equation was the vessel. That's when I spied my cast-iron skillet.

Having cooked my fair share of steaks in this versatile vessel, I knew that no other skillet can match the sear imparted by ripping-hot cast iron. This is because, unlike traditional and nonstick skillets, cast-iron skillets boast incredible heat retention. If I subbed it in for my traditional skillet, the initial temperature drop when the chicken hit the preheated skillet would be minimal. Translation: A hot cast-iron skillet would start browning the bird immediately. Thanks to the oven's intense heat and the skillet's efficient sear, I had no qualms about skipping out on brining. While this step usually serves to protect the chicken from overcooking, I was confident that my superhot skillet and oven combo would get the job done before the meat was compromised.

To start, I placed my skillet in the oven and set it to a blazing 500 degrees. Readying the chicken was as simple as butterflying it and rubbing its skin with extra-virgin olive oil. A bit of salt and pepper took care of the seasoning. As soon as the oven hit its mark, I placed the chicken in the skillet. I turned the temperature down to 450, confident that the skillet would retain the high heat on its own. The lively sizzle when the chicken hit the cast iron tipped me off that I was on the right track. After about 30 minutes I checked the chicken's progress. The breast was browning beautifully, but I was wary of the rendered juices pooling in the bottom of the skillet. This liquid would certainly compromise the skin's texture, so I carefully flipped the chicken so the skin could continue to crisp in the oven's dry heat while the thighs cooked through. This step was a game-changer: A mere 10 minutes more and my chicken was fully cooked, juicy, and boasting a beautiful golden skin.

I carved up the impressive-looking bird and was pleased with the results. The meat was moist and there was no soggy skin to speak of, but I was dismayed to find the crisp skin just a bit bland. To give the skin a little flavor without compromising its texture, I prepared a mixture of olive oil, minced rosemary, and minced garlic. Since fresh herbs would burn in the high heat, I waited until after I flipped the chicken to apply the flavored oil, allowing the aromatics to bloom but not scorch. This small change seasoned the skin and helped deepen its browning even further.

I now had a juicy, flavorful roast chicken I could easily prepare any day of the week. Plus, the butterflied bird was a cinch to carve. Jackpot.

—LAWMAN JOHNSON, *America's Test Kitchen Books*

Cast-Iron Skillet Roasted Chicken

SERVES 4

The chicken may slightly overhang the skillet at first, but once browned it will shrink to fit; do not use a chicken larger than 4 pounds. Serve with lemon wedges.

 2 tablespoons extra-virgin olive oil
 1 teaspoon minced fresh rosemary
 1 garlic clove, minced
 1 (3½ to 4-pound) whole chicken, giblets discarded
 Salt and pepper

1. Adjust oven rack to lowest position, place 12-inch cast-iron skillet on rack, and heat oven to 500 degrees. Meanwhile, combine 1 tablespoon oil, rosemary, and garlic in bowl; set aside.

2. With chicken breast side down, use kitchen shears to cut through bones on either side of backbone; discard backbone. Flip chicken over, tuck wingtips behind back, and press firmly on breastbone to flatten. Pat chicken dry with paper towels, then rub with remaining 1 tablespoon oil and season with salt and pepper.

3. When oven reaches 500 degrees, place chicken breast side down in hot skillet. Reduce oven temperature to 450 degrees and roast chicken until well browned, about 30 minutes.

4. Using potholders, remove skillet from oven. Being careful of hot skillet handle, gently flip chicken breast side up. Brush chicken with oil mixture, return skillet to oven, and continue to roast chicken until breast registers 160 degrees and thighs register 175 degrees, about 10 minutes. Transfer chicken to carving board, tent loosely with aluminum foil, and let rest for 15 minutes. Carve chicken and serve.

CAST IRON CLEANUP

If your skillet has stubborn stuck-on food or is a little rusty, the best fix is to scrub it with kosher salt.

1. Wipe out loose dirt with cloth and pour in vegetable oil to ¼ inch depth. Heat pan over medium-low for 5 minutes. Remove from heat and add ¼ cup kosher salt.

2. Using potholder to grip handle, scrub pan with thick cushion of paper towels (hold paper towels with tongs). Rinse pan under hot running water and dry well. Repeat, if necessary.

BUTTERFLYING A WHOLE CHICKEN

1. Using kitchen shears, cut through bones on either side of backbone and trim away any excess fat or skin at neck. Discard backbone.

2. Flip chicken over, tuck wingtips behind back, and use heel of your hand to flatten breastbone.

TWO-HOUR TURKEY AND GRAVY

✔ **WHY THIS RECIPE WORKS:** To turn out a showstopping turkey with gravy in under 2 hours, we came up with a few clever techniques. Buying a prebrined turkey saved us extended brining time and ensured moist and seasoned meat. To encourage the bird to cook through evenly and efficiently, we sliced the skin between the turkey thighs and breasts, exposing more of the slower-cooking dark meat to the oven's heat. Roasting the turkey in a hot oven crisped the skin and accelerated cooking. Halved onions, hearty pieces of carrot and celery, and the reserved turkey neck, arranged in the bottom of the roasting pan helped us build a quick gravy while the turkey rested.

Here in the test kitchen, we've cooked turkey in dozens of ways: We've brined, glazed, smoked, spatchcocked, and even fired up the deep-fryer. And we've cooked some marvelous turkeys. But I wanted a recipe that many home cooks, particularly those who cook turkey just once a year, might find helpful during the busy holiday season. Besides juicy, flavorful meat and crisp skin, I also wanted ease, with a side of speed.

In a perfect world, all you'd do is tie on an apron, slide a whole turkey into the oven, and a couple of hours (and a glass of sherry) later, pull out a beautiful, golden-brown, Norman Rockwell–esque centerpiece. And since it'd be done so quickly, you'd set it aside to rest—a necessary step for juicy meat—and fill the now-empty oven with dressing, green bean casserole, dinner rolls, and the rest of the requisite side dishes. Wishful thinking? Perhaps. But I was determined.

I bought a 14-pound turkey, big enough for a 10-person feast. To save time and effort, I chose a prebrined bird, meaning that it was already injected with a salt water solution to help season the meat and keep it moist. I nestled the bird into a roasting rack, and since I wanted it to cook quickly, I started it in a high 450-degree oven.

The breast reached 160 degrees—our test kitchen target for juicy white meat—in just 1 hour and 35 minutes. However, large roasts continue to cook after they come out of the oven, a phenomenon known as carryover cooking, and in this case, the breast meat climbed to 180 degrees: cardboard.

I kept closer tabs on the temperature during my next test, checking it every few minutes. Once the breast meat hit 120 degrees I turned my oven down to a low 250 degrees, hoping that the reduction would finish cooking the bird more gently and stave off overcooking during the resting phase. It worked, mostly: I had juicy breast meat under lovely, crackly skin. And the bird was still in and out of the oven in less than 2 hours.

But the crux of all turkey woes loomed: White meat cooks faster than dark meat, and my dark meat wasn't done. Dark meat (legs and thighs) needs to reach at least 175 degrees to be fully cooked—long after the point at which the white meat goes dry.

We have a few techniques in the test kitchen to help keep the breast from overcooking, including icing down the breast before it cooks or flipping the turkey over partway through cooking—but while these tricks helped, they were more work than I was willing to do. I tried covering the breast with aluminum foil, but the difference was minimal.

I flipped my thinking. Rather than protecting the breast meat, I wondered, could I expose the dark meat to more heat more quickly? For my next test, I cut into the skin on both sides of the bird, just between the breast and the thigh, to open up that area. This caused the legs to spread away from the breast, giving them more surface area and exposing them to more oven heat faster. Success: The thighs reached 175 degrees at approximately the same time as the breast hit 160. I set the turkey aside to rest (uncovered, to keep the skin crisp).

What's turkey without gravy? A prom queen without a date, that's what. So I tossed some vegetables and the turkey neck under the turkey while it roasted, letting them take on deep, caramelized flavors. After the bird came out, I used these roasting pan goodies, along with white wine, sage, thyme, and water, to make a simple, flavorful gravy.

—MORGAN BOLLING, *Cook's Country*

TWO-HOUR TURKEY AND GRAVY

Two-Hour Turkey and Gravy

SERVES 10 TO 12

If you can't find a self-basting turkey (Butterball makes our favorite self-basting bird), a kosher turkey can be substituted. Avoid opening the oven too frequently to take the turkey's temperature. If your turkey is on the smaller side of the weight range, follow the lower end of the time ranges given, and vice versa.

- 2 onions, quartered through root end
- 2 carrots, peeled and cut into 3-inch pieces
- 1 celery rib, cut into 3-inch pieces
- 1 (12- to 14-pound) pre-brined turkey, neck reserved, giblets discarded
- 3 tablespoons extra-virgin olive oil
  Kosher salt and pepper
- 3 cups water, plus extra as needed
- 1 tablespoon unsalted butter
- ¼ cup dry white wine
- ¼ cup all-purpose flour
- 4 sprigs fresh thyme
- 1 sprig fresh sage

1. Adjust oven rack to lowest position and heat oven to 450 degrees. Scatter onions, carrots, celery, and turkey neck in bottom of large roasting pan. Set V-rack over vegetables in roasting pan. Pat turkey dry with paper towels and tuck wingtips behind back. Transfer turkey, breast side up, to V-rack.

2. Using sharp knife, slice through skin between breast and leg on each side of turkey to expose entire underside of thigh without cutting into meat. Combine oil, 1 tablespoon salt, and 1½ teaspoons pepper in small bowl. Brush turkey all over with oil mixture.

3. Roast turkey until thickest part of breast registers 120 degrees and thickest part of thighs registers at least 135 degrees, 60 to 70 minutes.

4. Reduce oven temperature to 250 degrees and continue to roast turkey until breast registers 160 degrees and thighs register 175 degrees, 35 to 45 minutes longer. Transfer turkey to carving board and let rest for 45 minutes.

5. While turkey rests, transfer vegetables and turkey neck from roasting pan to bowl, leaving turkey juices behind. Add water to roasting pan with turkey juices and scrape up any browned bits from pan bottom.

Transfer deglazed juices to 4-cup liquid measuring cup; add extra water, if needed, to equal 4 cups.

6. Melt butter in Dutch oven over medium-high heat. Add vegetables and turkey neck and cook until any liquid has evaporated and browned bits begin to form on bottom of pot, 3 to 5 minutes. Add wine and cook until nearly evaporated, about 2 minutes, scraping up any browned bits.

7. Sprinkle flour over top and cook, stirring constantly, for 1 minute. Add thyme sprigs, sage sprig, deglazed pan juices, ½ teaspoon salt, and ½ teaspoon pepper. Bring to boil, then reduce heat to medium-low and simmer until thickened to gravy consistency, 12 to 15 minutes.

8. Strain gravy through fine-mesh strainer set over medium saucepan; discard solids. Season with salt and pepper to taste. Keep warm over low heat until serving. Carve turkey and serve with gravy.

NOTES FROM THE TEST KITCHEN

PREPPING TURKEY FOR FASTER COOKING

A little up-front prep helps ensure that the dark meat (thighs and legs) cooks at the same rate as the white meat (breasts).

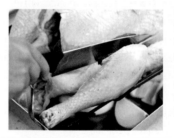

Use sharp knife to slice through skin (not meat) between breast and leg on each side. This cut loosens leg so it splays out slightly, exposing more dark meat to direct heat, accelerating its cooking.

RATING ROASTING RACKS

A good roasting rack securely holds a turkey, elevating it so it doesn't sit in fat while cooking. It should allow hot air to circulate around the meat—key for accurate cooking and a perfectly crisp skin. After testing out a number of models, we found our favorite: All-Clad's Nonstick Large Rack. This broad rack felt supremely secure, even when holding a 22-pound turkey.

It handled everything we set inside it and had nice pronounced handles that were easy and secure to grab. It allowed for proper 360-degree air circulation, so its food was always perfectly browned and evenly rendered.

MISO-MARINATED SALMON

✓ **WHY THIS RECIPE WORKS:** Marinating salmon with miso promises firm, flavorful fish, but some recipes require three days of marinating time. We wanted salmon with all of the depth of flavor that this dish is known for, but with a streamlined approach. A simple marinade of miso, sugar, sake, and mirin clung nicely to the surface of the salmon, and the sugar promised deep browning. After testing a host of marinating times, we discovered that the ideal range was between 6 and 24 hours, delivering fillets that were thoroughly seasoned and slightly firm around the outer edges. Broiling the salmon 8 inches from the heating element allowed the fillets to cook through while the surface caramelized.

The Japanese technique of marinating fish in miso started as a way to preserve a fresh catch without refrigeration during its long journey inland. In the last few years, however, after its introduction by chef Nobu Matsuhisa at his namesake restaurant, it has become a popular restaurant preparation in this country. The technique itself is quite simple. Miso is combined with sugar, sake, and mirin (sweet Japanese rice wine) to make a marinade that is typically applied to oily fish like salmon or black cod and left to sit for about three days; during that time, the marinade seasons the fish and draws moisture out of its flesh so that it becomes quite firm and dense. The fish is then scraped clean and broiled, producing meaty-textured, well-seasoned fillets with a lacquered savory-sweet glaze.

Those flavors pair particularly well with a rich fish like salmon, and the marinade takes minutes to make. But to me, three days is just too long to wait for such a simple dish—and frankly, I don't prefer the salmon to be quite so dense. I wondered if I could tweak the traditional technique to produce miso-marinated salmon just to my liking: moist, well-seasoned fillets that were slightly firmer than usual and evenly burnished on the surface.

I started by applying a riff on the Nobu marinade to the salmon and was happy with its flavor balance and consistency: A loose paste made from ½ cup of white miso, ⅓ cup of sugar, and 3 tablespoons each of sake and mirin clung nicely to the fillets. The question was how long to let the fish marinate. To find out, I made several more batches of the marinade, coated four skin-on salmon fillets with each, and let the fish sit for 30 minutes, 1 hour, 6 hours, and 24 hours—the longest I was willing to wait. After wiping off the excess paste, I placed the fillets on a foil-covered wire rack set in a baking sheet and broiled them 6 inches from the element. To confirm that there was a benefit to marinating, not just glazing, the fish, I also coated another four unmarinated fillets with the marinade mixture just before cooking.

The results were convincing: The flavor of the glazed fillets was merely skin-deep, while the batch that had been marinated for 24 hours delivered deep, complex seasoning throughout. There was a textural bonus to marinating, too: The salmon had firmed up just a bit at the surface, which made for a nice contrast to its silky interior. There was some flexibility with the marinating time; I could achieve largely the same effect when I marinated the fish for anywhere from 6 to 24 hours.

The only remaining problem was that the glaze was overbrowning before the interior was cooked. Reducing the sugar to ¼ cup helped (and nobody missed the extra sweetness), but the real fix was lowering the oven rack. When I positioned the rack 8 inches from the element, the fillets cooked up tender and silky just as the glaze took on an attractively deep bronze color—and if the edges started to burn, I simply pulled up the foil underneath to act as a shield. It was just the result I wanted in a fraction of the time.

—ANNIE PETITO, *Cook's Illustrated*

NOTES FROM THE TEST KITCHEN

MARINATING WITH MISO

A miso marinade works much like a typical curing technique. The miso (a paste made by fermenting soybeans and sometimes other grains with salt and a grain- or bean-based starter called *koji*), sugar, and alcohol all work to season and pull moisture out of the flesh, resulting in a firmer, denser texture. Miso also adds flavor benefits: sweetness, acidity, and water-soluble compounds such as glutamic acid that, over time, penetrate the proteins and lend them deeply complex flavor.

Miso-Marinated Salmon

SERVES 4

Note that the fish needs to marinate for at least 6 or up to 24 hours before cooking. Use center cut salmon fillets of similar thickness and be sure to check for pinbones. Yellow, red, or brown miso paste can be used instead of white.

½ cup white miso paste

¼ cup sugar

3 tablespoons sake

3 tablespoons mirin

4 (6- to 8-ounce) skin on salmon fillets

Lemon wedges

1. Whisk miso, sugar, sake, and mirin together in medium bowl until sugar and miso are dissolved (mixture will be thick). Dip each fillet into miso mixture to evenly coat all flesh sides. Place fish skin side down in baking dish and pour any remaining miso mixture over fillets. Cover with plastic wrap and refrigerate for at least 6 hours or up to 24 hours.

2. Adjust oven rack 8 inches from broiler element and heat broiler. Place wire rack in rimmed baking sheet and cover with aluminum foil. Using your fingers, scrape miso mixture from fillets (do not rinse) and place fish skin side down on foil, leaving 1 inch between fillets.

3. Broil salmon until deeply browned and centers of fillets register 125 degrees, 8 to 12 minutes, rotating sheet halfway through cooking and shielding edges of fillets with foil if necessary. Transfer to platter and serve with lemon wedges.

NOTES FROM THE TEST KITCHEN

A BONE TO PICK

Before preparing Miso-Marinated Salmon or Cedar-Planked Salmon, check the salmon for pinbones. Draping the fillet over an inverted mixing bowl helps pinbones protrude. Locate pinbones by running your fingers along length of fillet.

Use tweezers to grasp tip of bone and pull slowly but firmly at slight angle in direction bone is naturally pointing. Repeat until all pinbones are removed.

CEDAR-PLANKED SALMON

✓ **WHY THIS RECIPE WORKS:** To achieve cedar-planked salmon with balanced cedar flavor, we found that it was essential to remove the salmon's skin before grilling. The direct contact with the plank ensured that the finished fish had pronounced (but not overwhelming) cedar flavor. We rubbed the fish with salt, sugar, and dill and let the seasoning penetrate while we soaked the cedar plank in water (a necessary step to keep it from catching fire). A tangy cucumber-yogurt sauce was the perfect complement to our smoky fish.

To those who have never tried it, grilling salmon on a cedar plank may seem unnecessarily showy. That's what we used to think, too. But in recent years the test kitchen has experimented with this technique, and we've found that it just may be the best way to grill salmon. Soft fish, big flavor, easy cleanup. A stellar midsummer supper.

The planks aren't showy; they're practical. Because of salmon's delicate flesh, it can easily stick to the grill or, worse, fall through the grate. But inserting a wooden plank between the fish and the grill grate defuses these dangers because—wait for it—the fish never actually touches the grill.

What's more, the subtle smoky flavor that cedar smoke contributes—woodsy, earthy, outdoorsy, summery—is just plain fantastic. And the rustic presentation is a knockout at the table.

Untreated cedar planks for cooking used to be an expensive specialty item that was difficult to procure in many parts of the country, but today you can find planks in supermarkets, hardware stores, and big-box stores coast to coast (look near the charcoal and other grilling supplies). I picked up a dozen packages of planks, ordered in 20 pounds of salmon, poured myself a big cup of coffee, and sat down in our cookbook library to pore over recipes for cedar-planked salmon.

The recipes I found called for all sorts of cures, sauces, marinades, and rubs for the fish and a multitude of different set-ups for the grill. And while all called for me to soak the planks for an hour or so before cooking to help forestall any flare-ups over the fire, they otherwise treated the planks very differently. Some called for preheating the plank before laying the fish fillets on it. One even required you to place the plank directly on the hot coals to jump-start its smoking process, a daunting option that took just one flame-filled test for me to eliminate. (Thankfully I had my fire extinguisher nearby when I took this one for a spin.)

After a few hours at the grill, I concluded that while some of these recipes showed promise, there was one common shortcoming: The cedar, so rich and rewarding as an aroma during the cooking process, was barely discernible once the salmon reached the plate. I didn't want a piece of fish that tasted like a campfire, but I did want to get some character out of the planks I'd picked up.

I decided to tone down my approach on the front end, skipping the elaborate rubs and marinades I found in my initial research and instead taking a quieter approach with a simple mixture of brown sugar, salt, and dill rubbed onto four ½-pound skin-on fillets (enough to feed four). The salt helped season the fish, while the sugar would add flavor and, I hoped, would help the fillets achieve a nice lightly browned color. I let the seasoned fish rest while I soaked my plank for an hour.

Based on my initial tests, I knew that preheating the soaked plank on the grill before adding the fish was important for a present but balanced cedar flavor, one that complemented, rather than clobbered, the fish. Without this step, it would take 5 minutes before the cedar would even start smoking. Because the fish is done within 12 to 15 minutes, by the time the cedar flavor had sufficiently infused the fish, the fillets would be tragically overcooked and my dinner would go straight to the cat.

Preheating the plank on the grill made a big difference in my next couple of rounds, but I still wasn't satisfied. The fish wasn't taking on quite as much cedar flavor as I wanted.

I tried covering the salmon and plank with an inverted disposable aluminum pan to help trap the smoke. But this took me too far in the other direction; the intense cedar flavor was so strong that the fillets tasted like a moth-proof closet; the delicate salmon flavor didn't stand a chance. I started wondering whether chasing this cedar flavor was just an exercise in futility.

A fellow test cook saw my distress and, after closely inspecting my work, wondered whether the skin on the salmon was inhibiting the development of smoky flavor. I was skeptical. I worried that removing it was removing a thin layer of protection, and I might end up with dried-out salmon, more like smoked or cured fish than a fresh fillet.

But I tried a side-by-side test with skin-on versus skinless fillets. My coworker was right: Removing the skin had little effect on the moistness of the salmon, while concurrently opening the door for just enough cedar flavor.

To seal the deal, I served my tender, smoky salmon with a classic Greek tzatziki sauce of yogurt and cucumber. The acidity of the yogurt and lemon in the sauce balanced the richness of the fish, and the herbs echoed the cure. The cucumber added texture without overwhelming the fish's delicate nature. Score.

After rigorous testing and plenty of trial and error, my tasters were finally satisfied. Rich, deeply seasoned, and full of earthy, woodsy cedar flavor, this salmon was a hit. Even avowed fish-haters liked it.

And perhaps the best part of all, especially for cooks who've lived through the misery of cleaning up after grilling fish at home: I spent exactly zero minutes scouring my pristine grill grate.

—MORGAN BOLLING, *Cook's Country*

Cedar-Planked Salmon

SERVES 4

Be sure to buy an untreated cedar plank specifically intended for cooking. You can find cedar planks near the charcoal in most grocery, big box, and hardware stores; one plank will easily hold four portions. To ensure uniform pieces of fish, we prefer to purchase a whole center-cut salmon fillet and cut it into four equal pieces. Note that the seasoned fillets must be refrigerated for at least 1 hour before grilling. When preheating the cedar plank, you will know it's ready when it is just giving off wisps of smoke. It should not ignite. Serve with lemon wedges and Cucumber-Yogurt Sauce (recipe follows).

1   (2-pound) center-cut, skinless salmon fillet, about 1½ inches thick
2   tablespoons packed brown sugar
1½ tablespoons kosher salt
1   tablespoon chopped fresh dill
1   teaspoon pepper
1   (16 by 7-inch) cedar plank
1   teaspoon vegetable oil
    Lemon wedges

CEDAR-PLANKED SALMON

1. Cut salmon crosswise into 4 equal fillets and pat dry with paper towels. Combine sugar, salt, dill, and pepper in bowl. Sprinkle salmon all over with sugar mixture, place on plate, and refrigerate, uncovered, for at least 1 hour or up to 24 hours. One hour before grilling, soak cedar plank in water for 1 hour (or according to manufacturer's directions).

2A. FOR A CHARCOAL GRILL: Open bottom vent completely. Light large chimney starter filled with charcoal briquettes (6 quarts). When top coals are partially covered with ash, pour evenly over grill. Set cooking grate in place. Place cedar plank in center of grill. Cover and open lid vent completely. Heat grill until plank is lightly smoking and crackling (it should not ignite), about 5 minutes.

2B. FOR A GAS GRILL: Place cedar plank in center of grill. Turn all burners to medium-low, cover, and heat grill until plank is smoking and crackling (it should not ignite), about 15 minutes. Leave all burners on medium-low. Adjust burners as needed to maintain grill temperature between 300 and 325 degrees.

3. Brush skinned side of salmon fillets with oil, then place skinned side down on plank. Cover grill and cook until center of salmon is translucent when checked with tip of paring knife and registers 125 degrees (for medium-rare), 12 to 15 minutes. Using tongs, transfer plank with salmon to baking sheet, tent with aluminum foil, and let rest for 5 minutes. Serve with lemon wedges.

NOTES FROM THE TEST KITCHEN

HOW TO SOAK A CEDAR PLANK
To keep your cedar plank from catching fire, you must soak it for an hour before grilling. We set the plank in a rimmed baking sheet, covered it with water, and weighed it down with a measuring cup to keep the plank submerged.

Cucumber-Yogurt Sauce
MAKES ABOUT ¾ CUP

Don't substitute regular plain yogurt for Greek or the sauce will be watery.

- ½ cucumber, peeled, halved lengthwise, and seeded
- ½ cup plain whole-milk Greek yogurt
- 1 tablespoon extra-virgin olive oil
- 1 tablespoon chopped fresh mint
- 1 tablespoon chopped fresh dill
- 1 small garlic clove, minced
- ¼ teaspoon pepper
- ⅛ teaspoon salt

Shred cucumber on large holes of box grater. Combine yogurt, oil, mint, dill, garlic, pepper, salt, and shredded cucumber in bowl. Cover and refrigerate until chilled, about 20 minutes. Serve.

GRILLED WHOLE TROUT

WHY THIS RECIPE WORKS: When it comes to grilling trout, getting a whole fish off the grill in one piece can be a challenge. To get the trout from grill to serving platter before the interior overcooked, we applied a mayonnaise-honey mixture to the exterior. This coating encouraged browning without adding competing flavors. A sprinkling of marjoram and lemon zest ensured subtly flavored fish. We discovered that the hotter the grill, the easier the fish released from the grate. We placed the trout on the grill and after a few minutes per side, we had beautifully browned trout that released with ease.

I'm always surprised that more people don't grill whole fish. The grill infuses fish with smoky flavor, while the intense heat crisps the skin beautifully, lending contrast to the moist flesh beneath. And because the skin acts as a buffer during cooking, it helps ensure that the interior cooks through gently. The skin also keeps the delicate flesh contained, making a whole fish easier to handle than fillets.

So why don't more people grill them? One reason might be that the idea of cleaning and scaling whole fish sounds like a chore; plus, they need to be boned at the table or before serving. But there's an easy answer to those obstacles: Choose whole trout. Not only are whole trout almost always sold cleaned and scaled, but their backbones and pinbones are also removed. And they're small, weighing about 10 ounces each, so one fish can serve one person—no need to fuss with portioning.

There's just one problem with grilling whole trout: The skin is prone to sticking to the cooking grate (as it is with any fish), which can cause the flesh to come off in ragged pieces. It was time to tackle this challenge.

When I researched recipes, I realized that there was a dearth of promising solutions. Most recipes called for wrapping the whole fish in things like foil, wet newspaper, or banana leaves or in something edible like bacon or prosciutto. Since all these approaches would prevent the skin from crisping—one of the key selling points to me of grilling whole fish in the first place—they were of no use. My best bet would be to just start grilling and see what inspiration came to me. Before I fired up the grill, I prepped the trout, simply snipping off the quick-to-burn fins, seasoning the interior with salt and pepper, and brushing the exterior with oil.

When grilling fish in the past, I've noticed that sticking is more of an issue on gas grills than on charcoal grills, so I decided to start there, figuring that adapting to charcoal afterward wouldn't be a problem. I also settled on cooking over high heat. This might seem like the

wrong tactic for delicate fish, but I knew that it could be beneficial to prevent sticking. Foods stick to the cooking grate when bonds form between sulfur-containing amino acids in the food's proteins and the iron atoms in the cooking grate. Fortunately, these bonds break when exposed to high enough heat for a long enough time.

I proceeded to cook my fish, flipping them just once as soon as they'd browned (a clear sign that the grill had reached a temperature hot enough to release the fish). After 10 minutes, the fish were beautifully browned on both sides and released nicely. But there was a problem: The flesh had reached 150 degrees, about 20 degrees higher than the target for perfect doneness. I needed the skin to brown more quickly.

For food to brown, heat must break down its proteins into amino acids and its carbohydrates into simpler sugars known as reducing sugars, freeing these molecules to recombine into hundreds of new compounds that bring darker color and more complex flavor. To speed up this reaction, my first thought was to boost the amount of reducing sugars present. In past similar situations, we've used honey, which is basically a solution of the reducing sugars fructose and glucose. I figured that it wouldn't take much—just ⅛ teaspoon or so per fish—but evenly coating the fish with a small amount of honey was a messy, difficult task. I tried whisking the honey into the oil I was already brushing on the fish, but because honey is water-based, the two wouldn't combine. After a conversation with our science editor, I had an unusual but effective answer: ditching the oil in favor of mayonnaise. Mayonnaise is an emulsion of oil droplets suspended in water, so when I stirred the honey into the mayo, the honey dissolved into the water portion, allowing it to evenly disperse. I found that ½ teaspoon of honey combined easily with 2 tablespoons of mayonnaise.

It was time to fire up the grill and try again. My fish browned beautifully on the first side after just 3 minutes—2 minutes sooner than in my previous test. Using fish spatulas, I had no trouble flipping the fish, and after another 3 minutes, they were ready. The skin was perfect, with great grill flavor without a hint of honey or mayo, and the fish itself was moist, tender, and perfectly cooked.

It was time to move on to charcoal. I understood now why sticking was less of a problem on charcoal: A charcoal grill can get hotter than a gas grill, in part because you can manipulate the heat output by varying charcoal setups and using the vents to make the charcoal burn hotter and faster. Still, I'd keep my mayo coating in play

HOW TO FLIP A WHOLE FISH

Given whole trout's long shape and delicate skin, you can't just push a spatula under it and flip it over like a burger. You need two spatulas and a little maneuvering.

1. Slide spatula scant 1 inch under backbone edge and lift edge up. Slide second spatula under, then remove first spatula, allowing fish to ease onto second spatula.

2. Place first spatula on top of fish so it's oriented in same direction as second spatula and flip fish over.

for added insurance. And to concentrate the heat of the coals for maximum heat output, I corralled the coals in the center of the grill with the help of a disposable aluminum pan that I'd poked a few holes in to increase airflow. Using a chimney filled two-thirds of the way with charcoal delivered perfectly cooked fish in minutes.

My recipe just lacked a little flavor boost. In addition to serving the fish with lemon wedges, I used lemon zest and marjoram, an herb that goes well with char-grilled flavor. This recipe is so quick, easy, and flavorful that it's sure to win many converts to grilling whole fish.

—LAN LAM, *Cook's Illustrated*

Grilled Whole Trout with Marjoram and Lemon

SERVES 4

We prefer marjoram in this recipe, but thyme or oregano can be substituted. Do not flip the fish over in one motion. Instead, use two thin metal spatulas to gently lift the fish from the grate and then slide it from the spatula back onto the grate. The heads can be removed before serving, if desired.

    2   teaspoons minced fresh marjoram
    1   teaspoon grated lemon zest, plus lemon
        wedges for serving
        Kosher salt and pepper
    4   (10- to 12-ounce) whole trout, gutted,
        fins snipped off with scissors
    2   tablespoons mayonnaise
    ½   teaspoon honey
    1   (13 by 9-inch) disposable aluminum pan
        (if using charcoal)

1. Place marjoram, lemon zest, and 2 teaspoons salt on cutting board and chop until finely minced and well combined. Rinse each fish under cold running water and pat dry with paper towels inside and out. Open up each fish and sprinkle marjoram mixture evenly over flesh of fish. Season each fish with pepper. Close up fish and let stand for 10 minutes. Stir mayonnaise and honey together. Brush mayonnaise mixture evenly over entire exterior of each fish.

2A. FOR A CHARCOAL GRILL: Using kitchen shears, poke twelve ½ inch holes in bottom of disposable pan. Open bottom vent completely and place disposable pan in center of grill. Light large chimney starter two-thirds filled with charcoal briquettes (4 quarts). When top coals

are partially covered with ash, pour into even layer in disposable pan. Set cooking grate over coals with bars parallel to long side of disposable pan, cover, and open lid vent completely. Heat grill until hot, about 5 minutes.

2B. FOR A GAS GRILL: Turn all burners to high, cover, and heat grill until hot, about 15 minutes. Leave all burners on high.

3. Clean and oil cooking grate. Grill fish (directly over coals if using charcoal and with lid closed if using gas) until skin is browned and beginning to blister, 2 to 4 minutes. Using thin metal spatula, lift bottom of thick backbone edge of fish from cooking grate just enough to slide second thin metal spatula under fish. Remove first spatula, then use it to support raw side of fish as you use second spatula to flip fish over. Grill until second side is browned, beginning to blister, and thickest part of fish registers 130 to 135 degrees, 2 to 4 minutes. Transfer fish to platter and let rest for 5 minutes. Serve with lemon wedges.

COCONUT SHRIMP WITH MANGO DIPPING SAUCE

✓ WHY THIS RECIPE WORKS: We sought to upgrade coconut shrimp with a crisp, flavorful coconut coating and tender shrimp. A bound breading (flour, batter, crumbs) worked best. After tossing the shrimp in flour to stave off excess moisture, we focused on building a flavorful batter and crisp coating. Beer and baking powder gave the egg dip extra crisping power, and adding coconut milk introduced some coconut flavor. Cayenne brought in some heat and flour helped the mixture cling to the shrimp. To infuse our coating with bright coconut flavor, we mixed sweetened shredded coconut with panko bread crumbs; adding lime zest kept the sweetness in check. Chilling the breaded shrimp before frying set the coating. A sweet and spicy quick dipping sauce made with frozen mango and peach preserves made a perfect accompaniment.

Coconut shrimp has an image problem. Too many dive bars serve prefab, dried-out, overcooked shrimp encased in soggy coatings. I wanted sweet, tender shrimp in crispy jackets with vivid coconut flavor.

I did some research into this South Florida favorite and tried a few existing recipes. Some used a simple batter with coconut stirred in, others a bound breading with added coconut. Some were baked, others deep-fried.

The results were disheartening: sandy breadings, flimsy coatings, rubbery shrimp. My only takeaway was that the deep-fried versions were best. Other than that, I'd have to start from scratch.

Often, when we want to add a crunchy coating to fish, we start with a flour dusting to absorb its moisture, dunk the fish in beaten egg to create a glue, and press the pieces in bread crumbs. I took this route, adding unsweetened coconut shreds to the bread crumbs. The result? Shrimp with a sandy, not-very-coconutty coating.

For my next round, I kept the initial light flour dusting and then added beer and a bit of baking powder—two ingredients we often turn to for extra-crispy coatings—to the beaten egg. I pressed the shrimp into the bread-crumb mixture and fried them up.

My shrimp were crispy, but while I could see the coconut shreds in the coating, I couldn't taste them. I went for broke with a three-pronged attack: I added a bit of coconut milk to the beer, upped the ratio of coconut flakes to bread crumbs to 2 to 1, and swapped in sweetened coconut flakes. For zing, I added lime zest.

The flavor was there, but I had inconsistent crispiness and a coating that slid off. Was my oil temperature off? I tried higher temps, which burned the coconut, while low temps kept the coating from sticking. Oil heated to 350 degrees gave me the best results; frying the shrimp in three batches helped ensure that the oil maintained its temperature. For added insurance, I found that chilling the coated shrimp in the fridge for 20 minutes (or up to 2 hours) helped the coating stay on.

My tasters were happy munching on these shrimp as is, but I wanted a tropical dipping sauce to take them over the top. After experimenting with chili sauces and various chopped fruit sauces, I decided that mango was the way to go. I blended convenient frozen mango chunks with peach preserves for sweetness and stability. Finally, a squeeze of lime juice and some minced cilantro, shallot, and jalapeño added a pop of freshness and mild heat.

—LEAH COLINS, *Cook's Country*

Coconut Shrimp with Mango Dipping Sauce
SERVES 6 TO 8

Gently press the coconut mixture onto the shrimp to help it adhere. Frying in small batches ensures a consistent oil temperature and even browning. Zest the lime before juicing it for the sauce.

DIPPING SAUCE

6 ounces (¾ cup) frozen mango chunks, thawed
¼ cup peach preserves
2 tablespoons lime juice
  Salt and pepper
2 teaspoons minced fresh cilantro
2 teaspoons minced shallot
2 teaspoons minced jalapeño chile

SHRIMP

1⅓ cups all-purpose flour
2 cups sweetened shredded coconut
1 cup panko bread crumbs
2 teaspoons grated lime zest
  Salt and pepper
1½ teaspoons baking powder
¼ teaspoon cayenne pepper
½ cup mild lager, such as Budweiser
¼ cup canned coconut milk
1 large egg
1½ pounds extra-large shrimp (21 to 25 per pound), peeled and deveined
3 quarts peanut or vegetable oil

1. FOR THE DIPPING SAUCE: Process mango, preserves, lime juice, pinch salt, and pinch pepper in blender until completely smooth, about 1 minute, scraping down sides of blender jar as needed. Transfer to bowl and stir in cilantro, shallot, and jalapeño. Season with salt and pepper to taste; set aside.

2. FOR THE SHRIMP: Adjust oven rack to middle position and heat oven to 200 degrees. Line rimmed baking sheet with parchment paper. Set wire rack in second rimmed baking sheet and line with triple layer of paper towels.

3. Spread ⅔ cup flour in shallow dish. Combine coconut, panko, lime zest, 1 teaspoon salt, and 1 teaspoon pepper in second shallow dish. Whisk baking powder, cayenne, and remaining ⅔ cup flour together in medium bowl; then whisk in lager, coconut milk, and egg until fully incorporated and smooth.

4. Pat shrimp dry with paper towels and season with salt and pepper. One at a time, dredge shrimp in flour, shaking off excess; dip into beer batter, letting excess drip back into bowl; then coat with coconut-panko mixture, pressing gently to adhere. Arrange breaded shrimp on parchment-lined sheet. Refrigerate for at least 20 minutes or up to 2 hours.

5. Add oil to large Dutch oven until it measures about 2 inches deep and heat over medium-high heat to 350 degrees. Add one-third of shrimp, 1 at a time, to hot oil. Fry, stirring gently to prevent pieces from sticking together, until shrimp are golden brown, 1½ to 2 minutes. Adjust burner as necessary to maintain oil temperature between 325 and 350 degrees.

6. Transfer shrimp to prepared wire rack and place in oven to keep warm. Return oil to 350 degrees and repeat in 2 more batches with remaining shrimp. Serve with dipping sauce.

SHRIMP SCAMPI

✔ **WHY THIS RECIPE WORKS:** Shrimp scampi should be garlicky and buttery with tender shrimp in the starring role, but many attempts at this seemingly simple dish turn out bland. We started by brining the shrimp in a salt and sugar solution to keep them moist and reinforce their natural sweetness. For sauce with great seafood flavor, we created a quick stock by browning the shells before pouring in white wine. After straining out the shells we were left with a bright, concentrated stock. For big garlic flavor, we sliced eight cloves and browned them in oil with some red pepper flakes for heat. We poured the stock over the browned garlic and poached the shrimp in the liquid, infusing them with flavor. A cornstarch and lemon juice slurry helped to thicken the sauce and added tang. A sprinkling of parsley delivered a fresh pop of color.

Shrimp scampi is rarely awful—it's unusual for things to go terribly wrong when garlic, wine, and butter are involved—but restaurant versions always make me wish I'd ordered differently. I have never been presented with the ultimate scampi, the one that I can almost taste when I peruse the menu: perfect briny beauties in a garlicky, buttery (not greasy) white wine sauce.

It was time to realize this ideal scampi vision at home. Shrimp are susceptible to overcooking, turning them dry and tough, so I gave my shrimp a short dunk in a saltwater solution to season them and help preserve moisture. I heated extra-virgin olive oil in a skillet, sautéed a few cloves of minced garlic and a dash of red pepper flakes, and added the shrimp. Once the shrimp turned opaque, I poured in dry white wine followed by a chunk of butter, a squeeze of lemon juice, and a sprinkle of parsley.

I didn't go hungry that night, but the scampi was far from perfect. One problem was that the sauce separated into a butter-and-oil slick floating on top of the wine—not ideal for dunking bread into. (Some serve shrimp scampi over a pile of spaghetti, but I think it's best with a crusty loaf.) Then there were the shrimp: Some were a bit overdone, while others were still translucent. Finally, the overall dish lacked both seafood and garlic flavors. For results that I'd be truly satisfied with, some adjustments were in order.

Back in the test kitchen, I thought about ways to improve the shrimp. Flavorful crustaceans are often thought of as sweet, so would adding sugar to the brine be beneficial? Sure enough, my colleagues agreed that when used judiciously (2 tablespoons of sugar along with 3 tablespoons of salt in 1 quart of water), the sugar subtly boosted the natural flavor of the shrimp. I also found that using untreated shrimp, with no added salt or preservatives, produced the best results.

Another detail to consider was the cooking method. The inconsistent doneness of my first batch had come from crowding the skillet, so I needed to sauté the shrimp in batches. Or did I? What if, instead of sautéing the shrimp and then adding the wine, I gently poached the shrimp in the wine? As it turned out, this approach cooked all of the shrimp just right and in unison, as long as the skillet was covered with a lid to trap steam.

Now that I had flavorful, properly cooked shrimp, it was time to tackle the sauce. I had three items on my to-do list. First: Seriously bump up the flavor. (I'd found that the 5 minutes or so that it took to cook the shrimp wasn't long enough to impart much of a seafood taste to the dish.) Second: Add extra garlic for a more robust punch. Third: Fix the separated consistency of the sauce.

A few ladles of stock made from trimmings, bones, or other ingredient scraps can be a great way to infuse flavor into a sauce. Here I could make a stock from the shrimp shells, so I started buying shell-on shrimp instead of the prepeeled type (to save time, I started using the jumbo size so I'd have fewer to peel). I first browned the shells in a little olive oil and then simmered them in the wine for 30 minutes with a few sprigs of thyme for a little more complexity. But the stock didn't taste all that shrimpy. I had assumed that simmering the shells for a longer period of time would extract more flavor from them, but a timing test debunked that myth. In fact, you get more flavor from shells simmered for only 5 minutes. This was an easy change to implement.

SHRIMP SCAMPI

Next, I doubled the amount of garlic. It worked to boost the garlic flavor but not without a cost: The minced pieces gave the sauce a gritty quality. I switched from mincing the cloves to slicing them into thin rounds. But since sliced garlic is milder than minced, the switch required that I up the number of cloves to eight.

All that remained was to bind the fats and wine together into a rich sauce. Flour, gelatin, and pectin would work, but cornstarch seemed like the best option since it required no cooking. I could hydrate it in the wine, but I decided that it would be more convenient to use the lemon juice I was adding to the sauce. A teaspoon of cornstarch worked like a charm. I stirred the mixture into the sauce before adding butter, which easily whisked into the sauce, giving it a creamy texture. In fact, it was so rich and creamy that I was able to scale back the amount of butter to 4 tablespoons without it turning too lean. And there it was: the scampi I'd been looking for.

—ANDREW JANJIGIAN, *Cook's Illustrated*

Shrimp Scampi

SERVES 4

Extra-large shrimp (21 to 25 per pound) can be substituted for jumbo shrimp. If you use them, reduce the cooking time in step 3 by 1 to 2 minutes. We prefer untreated shrimp, but if your shrimp are treated with sodium or preservatives like sodium tripolyphosphate, skip the brining in step 1 and add ¼ teaspoon of salt to the sauce in step 4. Serve with crusty bread.

- 3 **tablespoons salt**
- 2 **tablespoons sugar**
- 1½ **pounds shell-on jumbo shrimp (16 to 20 per pound), peeled, deveined, and tails removed, shells reserved**
- 2 **tablespoons extra-virgin olive oil**
- 1 **cup dry white wine**
- 4 **sprigs fresh thyme**
- 3 **tablespoons lemon juice, plus lemon wedges for serving**
- 1 **teaspoon cornstarch**
- 8 **garlic cloves, sliced thin**
- ½ **teaspoon red pepper flakes**
- ¼ **teaspoon pepper**
- 4 **tablespoons unsalted butter, cut into ½-inch pieces**
- 1 **tablespoon chopped fresh parsley**

1. Dissolve salt and sugar in 1 quart cold water in large container. Submerge shrimp in brine, cover, and

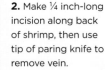
refrigerate for 15 minutes. Remove shrimp from brine and pat dry with paper towels.

2. Heat 1 tablespoon oil in 12-inch skillet over high heat until shimmering. Add shrimp shells and cook, stirring frequently, until they begin to turn spotty brown and skillet starts to brown, 2 to 4 minutes. Remove skillet from heat and carefully add wine and thyme sprigs. When bubbling subsides, return skillet to medium heat and simmer gently, stirring occasionally, for 5 minutes. Strain mixture through colander set over large bowl. Discard shells and reserve liquid (you should have about ⅔ cup). Wipe out skillet with paper towels.

3. Combine lemon juice and cornstarch in small bowl. Heat remaining 1 tablespoon oil, garlic, pepper flakes, and pepper in now-empty skillet over medium-low heat, stirring occasionally, until garlic is fragrant and just beginning to brown at edges, 3 to 5 minutes. Add reserved wine mixture, increase heat to high, and bring to simmer. Reduce heat to medium, add shrimp, cover, and cook, stirring occasionally, until shrimp are just opaque, 5 to 7 minutes. Remove skillet from heat and, using slotted spoon, transfer shrimp to bowl.

4. Return skillet to medium heat, add lemon juice–cornstarch mixture, and cook until slightly thickened, 1 minute. Remove from heat and whisk in butter and parsley until combined. Return shrimp and any accumulated juices to skillet and toss to combine. Serve, passing lemon wedges separately.

BLOOD ORANGE MARMALADE

✔ **WHY THIS RECIPE WORKS:** With their blush-tinged skin, crimson-colored flesh, and berry-like flavor notes, blood oranges are ideal for making an intensely flavored marmalade. We tested several methods of preparing the fruit and found that the simplest method—simmering them whole before chopping the peels and mashing the pulp—worked best. We added a whole lemon for its bright flavor and natural pectin, plus just the right amount of sugar to balance the tartness. Tightly sealing our pot with aluminum foil and a lid prevented any of the liquid from evaporating as it simmered. To achieve the proper consistency, our marmalade needed to reach between 220 and 222 degrees. It was only within this range that our marmalade passed the "wrinkle test," indicating that the liquid had gelled properly.

I've always had somewhat mixed feelings about marmalade. Unlike the juicy, sweet fruit flavors of jams and jellies that I happily smear on toast and scones, marmalades have always been my worst-case-scenario spread, pulled into rotation only when there are no other options. Much as I love the bright flavors of citrus, most marmalades take a hard turn at "tart" and veer straight towards "sour." But winter in New England meant that my favorite summer fruits were still a distant dream. With citrus available in abundance, I wondered if I could make a marmalade that could change my mind about this classic preserve.

Authentic marmalades enjoyed in Scotland are made with bitter Seville oranges, but I wanted to tone down the sourness without relying too heavily on sugar. Blood oranges are far sweeter than Sevilles, boasting a fruity, almost berry-like flavor, and their striking red flesh would give the marmalade a warm rosy hue. As soon as I began my research I was pleased to discover a number of recipes using a mostly hands-off process: Whole oranges are simmered and then the entire fruit, from peel to pulp, is used to create a luminous gel with bits of candied peel suspended in it. The process appeared easy, but nailing the amounts of fruit, sugar, and water would be essential. I cobbled together a recipe and headed into the kitchen.

For my first batch, I combined 5 cups of water with a pound of blood oranges in a large saucepan. Commercial pectin is used in many jelly recipes, but because oranges are naturally rich in this gelling agent, I hoped I could skip this store-bought ingredient. I also added a lemon for flavor and extra pectin. After bringing the pot to a boil, I sealed it tightly with foil (to prevent any escaping steam) and put on the lid. After simmering for some 2½ hours, the fruit was plenty soft and almost broken down—perhaps the lengthy simmer was a little excessive considering blood oranges have much thinner skins than the traditional Sevilles. I proceeded anyhow, scraping the soft pulp from the peels, mashing it with a potato masher, and returning it to the pot to cook down further. As soon as the mixture had concentrated and broken down further, I strained out the stringy bits of pulp, leaving behind the intensely flavored liquid. Into the concentrated liquid I stirred ½-inch bits of peel (I had sliced them while the pulp boiled) and, anticipating the need to tamp down the cooking liquid's tartness, I added a hefty 4½ cups of sugar and cooked the mixture more to thicken it. The outcome? A far-too-sweet marmalade that took almost an hour to thicken. I'd anticipated a relatively quick, easy recipe, and this wasn't it.

Starting from the beginning, I ran a few tests to see how much time was needed to soften the oranges. Starting with the simmering time, I found that the fruit turned perfectly tender after 1½ hours, shaving an hour off my original timing. To speed up the thickening and intensify the gel's flavor, I reduced the amount of water from 5 cups to 4—just enough to boil the fruit, but not so much that it would weaken the pectin's bonds and hinder gelling. My heavy-handed use of sugar also needed to be scaled back. Sugar serves two purposes in fruit preserving—to draw water away from the pectin, allowing it to gel the liquid, and to sweeten the marmalade—and I found that 3½ cups was just enough to accomplish both tasks.

To ensure that my marmalade was absolutely foolproof, I relied on a couple of simple tests. Because marmalade thickens as it cools, using a "chilled plate" test makes it possible to judge the texture while the marmalade is still warm. To do this, I placed two plates in the freezer as the marmalade cooked. When the marmalade appeared ready, I spooned a small amount onto a chilled plate and, after freezing for 2 minutes, I gently pushed the cooled marmalade with my index finger. If it wrinkled around the edges, it was ready; if it was still runny, then the liquid needed to be cooked a little longer. Keeping a second plate in the freezer allowed me to retest if necessary. As another safeguard, I kept my instant-read thermometer handy, monitoring at what temperature the marmalade reached its ideal thickness and passed the wrinkle test. Around 222 degrees the marmalade hit its mark squarely.

Finishing off my marmalade for long-term storage was as easy as following standard boiling water canning procedures. I readied the jars by immersing them in water (covering the lids with about an inch of water), bringing the pot to a simmer, turning off the stove, and covering the pot to seal in the heat. Once the marmalade was ready, I carefully portioned it into the hot jars, poking out air pockets and leaving a little headspace in which the gel could expand.

Once the jars were sealed—whether for short- or long-term storage—I knew that marmalade would be my new go-to toast topper. My jars of sunset-red gel were so appealing, I could hardly wait to crack one open.

—NICOLE KONSTANTINAKOS,
America's Test Kitchen Books

Blood Orange Marmalade

MAKES FOUR 1-CUP JARS

Blood oranges are available from November to May. In their absence, use navel, Valencia, or Seville oranges.

    4   cups water
    1   pound blood oranges, scrubbed
    1   lemon, scrubbed
    3½ cups sugar

1. Bring water, oranges, and lemon to boil in large saucepan over high heat. Reduce heat to low and cover pot with heavy-duty aluminum foil and lid. Simmer gently until fruit is easily pierced with skewer, about 1½ hours. Off heat, let mixture cool, covered, for at least 5 hours or up to 24 hours.

2. Set canning rack in large pot, place four 1-cup jars in rack, and add water to cover by 1 inch. Bring to simmer over medium-high heat, then turn off heat and cover to keep hot.

3. Place 2 small plates in freezer to chill. Transfer oranges and lemon to cutting board; cut fruits into quarters. Using paring knife, scrape pulp with most of pith from peels; reserve pith and peels separately. Return pulp to pot with liquid, mash lightly with potato masher, bring to simmer over medium heat, and cook

for 10 minutes. Meanwhile, slice peels into thin strips, then cut crosswise into ¼-inch pieces.

4. Strain liquid through fine-mesh strainer into Dutch oven, pressing firmly on solids; discard solids. Stir in chopped peels and sugar. Bring to vigorous boil over medium-high heat, stirring and adjusting heat as needed, until thickened and registers 220 to 222 degrees, 15 to 25 minutes. (Temperature will be lower at higher elevations; see Notes from the Test Kitchen for more information.) Remove pot from heat.

5. To test consistency, place 1 teaspoon marmalade on chilled plate and freeze for 2 minutes. Gently push cooled marmalade with your finger; marmalade should wrinkle around edges when set. If runny, return pot to heat and simmer for 1 to 3 minutes longer before retesting. Skim any foam from surface of marmalade using large spoon.

6. Place dish towel flat on counter. Using jar lifter, remove jars from pot, draining water back into pot. Place jars upside down on towel and let dry for 1 minute. Using funnel and ladle, portion hot marmalade into hot jars, leaving ¼ inch headspace. Slide wooden skewer along inside edge of jar and drag upward to remove air bubbles.

NOTES FROM THE TEST KITCHEN

MARMALADE SET TEMPERATURES BY ELEVATION

TEMPERATURE	ELEVATION
220–222 degrees	sea level
218–220 degrees	1,000 ft
216–218 degrees	2,000 ft
214–216 degrees	3,000 ft
212–214 degrees	4,000 ft
211–212 degrees	5,000 ft
209–211 degrees	6,000 ft

TESTING MARMALADE TEXTURE

To test marmalade's consistency, place 1 teaspoon of marmalade on chilled plate and freeze for 2 minutes.

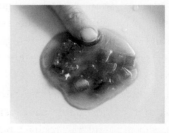

Gently push cooled marmalade with finger. Marmalade should wrinkle around edges when set. If runny, return pot to heat and simmer marmalade for 1 to 3 minutes longer before retesting.

7A. FOR SHORT-TERM STORAGE: Let marmalade cool to room temperature, cover, and refrigerate until marmalade is set, 12 to 24 hours. (Marmalade can be refrigerated for up to 3 months).

7B. FOR LONG-TERM STORAGE: While jars are hot, wipe rims clean, add lids, and screw on rings until fingertip-tight; do not overtighten. Return pot of water with canning rack to boil. Lower jars into water, cover, bring water back to boil, then start timer. Cooking time will depend on your altitude: Boil 10 minutes for up to 1,000 feet, 15 minutes for 1,001 to 3,000 feet, 20 minutes for 3,001 to 6,000 feet, or 25 minutes for 6,001 to 8,000 feet. Turn off heat and let jars sit in pot for 5 minutes. Remove jars from pot and let cool for 24 hours. Remove rings, check seals, and clean rims. (Sealed jars can be stored for up to 1 year.)

VARIATION

Grapefruit Marmalade

Any grapefruit variety can be used in this recipe; the flavor and color of the marmalade will vary only slightly.

Substitute 2 grapefruits (12 ounces each), scrubbed, for blood oranges; simmer as directed in step 1, turning grapefruits over halfway through cooking. Cut each grapefruit into 8 pieces in step 3.

ALMOND YOGURT PARFAITS

✔ **WHY THIS RECIPE WORKS:** For a nondairy parfait with supremely creamy dairy-free yogurt, we began by making our own nut milk, blending softened almonds with water and straining the mixture to separate the milk from the pulp. To turn the milk into yogurt, we brought it to a simmer and stirred in agar-agar, an algae-based thickener. Emptying a probiotic capsule into the mixture was an easy way to incorporate healthy bacteria and give the yogurt pleasant tang. The warmth of the oven light was enough to encourage the yogurt to set up, and once it had reached the desired consistency, a whir in the blender smoothed it out nicely. To turn our yogurt into a luscious parfait, we sweetened it with some honey and layered it with the bright flavor of fresh fruit. We also added nuts and seeds, toasted to bring out their flavor and crunch.

Yogurt layered with crunchy nuts and fresh fruit makes a great healthy breakfast option, but for anyone avoiding dairy, this morning treat is off the table. Most store-bought dairy-free yogurts are laden with stabilizers and leave much to be desired in both flavor and texture. We wanted to elevate nondairy yogurt to a level where anyone—dairy-free, gluten-free, paleo, or otherwise—would enjoy a spoonful with their morning coffee or as an afternoon snack any day of the week.

Seeking inspiration, we started by perusing the yogurt aisle at our nearby supermarket and we were struck by the range of nondairy yogurts available. From soy to chia seed to coconut to almond, there is no shortage of options—unless you want yogurt that actually tastes good. When we tasted them, these alternatives ran the gamut from watery and bland to gritty and overly sweet. It was clear that we'd have to make our own yogurt, starting with a homemade nondairy milk.

Coconut and almond milks seemed like the most accessible options since nut milks are easy to make at home. Coconut milk was the faster option: We blended unsweetened shredded coconut with hot water and then strained out the liquid through a cheesecloth-lined fine-mesh strainer. Almond milk, though equally easy, required some waiting: We had to soak the nuts overnight before whirring them with water and extracting the liquid through the same strainer setup. To determine which would star in our parfaits, we had to turn our milks into yogurts.

Traditional yogurt is made by heating and cooling milk, denaturing its proteins, and fermenting the lactose with live cultures (healthy bacteria). This process creates yogurt's distinct creamy texture. Without milk proteins present, we needed to find a different, and paleo-friendly, way to thicken our yogurt. Gelatin, tapioca flour, and agar-agar were our top contenders at the outset, but the first two let us down: Gelatin produced a springy, Jell-O-like texture, and tapioca flour turned the yogurts slimy. Agar-agar, an algae-based thickener, did the trick, creating a rich, smooth texture in the almond milk. Despite our best efforts, the coconut milk wasn't working. Once it was thickened, we were put off by grainy, lumpy spoonfuls, the result of the coconut fat solidifying into small granules suspended in the yogurt. While some of our tasters didn't mind this, the consensus was that the almond milk yogurt was superior.

But the live cultures in dairy yogurt do more than just thicken—they also provide the signature tangy flavor. It's nearly impossible to replicate that taste without using cultures, so even though our almond yogurt got its texture elsewhere, we still needed those healthy

ALMOND YOGURT PARFAITS

bacteria for flavor. The easy solution? Adding in the contents of a probiotic capsule. Both the agar-agar and the bacteria require an incubation period to do their work, and the warmth from the oven light was just enough. We left the bowl of yogurt in the oven overnight and then transferred it to the refrigerator to thicken up. A few hours later, our yogurt emerged perfectly smooth, rich, and creamy—a far cry from the ho-hum products we found in the supermarket. We were finally ready to make our parfaits.

A touch of honey promised subtle sweetness to contrast the earthy, crunchy nuts and bright fresh fruit. Almonds were a natural choice for the accompanying nuts, but walnuts were also appealing. Toasting them heightened their earthy flavor and boosted their crunch. Tossing in some toasted sunflower seeds added even more contrast. For fruit, the juicy flavors of fresh berries seemed like the perfect contrast to our lush yogurt. Layered in tall glasses, our homemade parfaits outshone the store-bought versions by leaps and bounds.

—DANIELLE DESIATO AND LAWMAN JOHNSON,
America's Test Kitchen Books

Almond Yogurt Parfaits

SERVES 4

Almost any combination of fruits, nuts, and seeds will work well here. Do not substitute frozen fruit. Serve the parfaits within 15 minutes of assembling or the nuts and seeds will begin to turn soggy. We prefer to use homemade almond yogurt; however, you can substitute 3 cups of your favorite unsweetened store-bought brand.

  1 **recipe Almond Yogurt (recipe follows)**
  2 **tablespoons honey**
  1 **cup whole almonds or walnuts, toasted and chopped**
  ½ **cup raw sunflower seeds, toasted**
 20 **ounces (4 cups) blackberries, blueberries, raspberries, and/or sliced strawberries**

Whisk yogurt and honey in bowl until thoroughly combined. In separate bowl, combine almonds and sunflower seeds. Using four 16-ounce glasses, spoon ¼ cup yogurt-honey mixture into each glass, then top with ⅓ cup berries, followed by 2 tablespoons nut mixture. Repeat layering process 2 more times with remaining yogurt, berries, and nut mixture. Serve.

TOASTING NUTS AND SEEDS

To toast 1 cup or less of nuts or seeds, toast in dry skillet over medium heat, stirring occasionally, until fragrant, 3 to 8 minutes.

VARIATIONS

Almond Yogurt Parfaits with Pineapple and Kiwi

Add 1 teaspoon ground ginger to yogurt with honey. Substitute ½ cup toasted pepitas for sunflower seeds and 3 cups ½-inch pineapple pieces and 3 kiwis, peeled and cut into ½-inch pieces, for mixed berries.

Almond Yogurt Parfaits with Dates, Oranges, and Bananas

Microwave 1 cup chopped dates with 1 cup water in bowl for 30 seconds; drain and let cool. Cut away peel and pith from 2 oranges. Quarter oranges, then slice crosswise into ¼-inch-thick pieces. Add ½ teaspoon ground cinnamon and ¼ teaspoon ground nutmeg to yogurt with honey. Substitute softened dates, orange pieces, and 3 thinly sliced bananas for mixed berries.

Almond Yogurt

MAKES ABOUT 3 CUPS

You can find agar-agar and probiotic capsules at your local natural foods store. The flavor of the yogurt may vary depending on the brand of probiotic used; we developed this recipe using Renew Life Ultimate Flora Critical Care 50 Billion probiotic capsules. Do not substitute agar-agar flakes for the agar-agar powder.

1¾ **teaspoons agar-agar powder**
  ¼ **cup water**
  3 **cups Almond Milk (recipe follows)**
  1 **50-billion probiotic capsule**

1. Adjust oven rack to middle position. Sprinkle agar-agar over water in small bowl and let sit until softened, about 10 minutes.

2. Heat milk in large saucepan over medium-low heat until just simmering. Add softened agar-agar and cook, whisking constantly, until fully dissolved. Transfer mixture to bowl and let cool, stirring occasionally, until mixture registers 110 degrees, about 20 minutes.

3. Twist open probiotic capsule and whisk contents into cooled milk mixture; discard capsule's casing. Cover bowl tightly with plastic wrap, place in oven, and turn on oven light. Let yogurt sit undisturbed for at least 12 hours or up to 24 hours. (Yogurt will not thicken while sitting.)

4. Refrigerate yogurt until completely chilled and set, about 4 hours. Process yogurt in blender until smooth, about 30 seconds. (Yogurt can be refrigerated for up to 1 week.)

Almond Milk

MAKES ABOUT 4 CUPS

Honey gives the almond milk a subtly sweet, rounded flavor. This recipe can be doubled.

- 1¼ cups whole blanched almonds
- 2 teaspoons honey (optional)
- ¼ teaspoon kosher salt

1. Place almonds in bowl and add cold water to cover by 1 inch. Soak almonds at room temperature for at least 8 hours or up to 24 hours. Drain and rinse well.

2. Line fine-mesh strainer with triple layer of cheesecloth that overhangs edges and set over large bowl. Process soaked almonds and 4 cups water in blender until almonds are finely ground, about 2 minutes. Transfer mixture to prepared strainer and press to extract as much liquid as possible. Gather sides of cheesecloth around almond pulp and gently squeeze remaining milk into bowl; discard spent pulp. Stir in honey, if using, and salt until dissolved. (Almond milk can be refrigerated for up to 2 weeks.)

EGGS IN PURGATORY

✔ **WHY THIS RECIPE WORKS:** Pairing poached eggs and a spicy red sauce in a single pan, eggs in purgatory is an appealingly simple meal. To ensure perfectly cooked eggs nestled in a bracing sauce, we needed a cooking technique that suited both elements. Starting on the stovetop, we cooked a combination of aromatics to create an intensely flavored base. We wilted basil leaves in the mixture for a savory herbal note before stirring in crushed tomatoes and simmering to thicken the sauce. We cleared eight wells in the sauce and slid a cracked egg into each, covering the skillet so the whites could begin to set. Finishing the cooking in the oven ensured fully cooked whites enveloping perfectly runny yolks. A sprinkling of Parmesan, chopped fresh basil, and a few crunchy slices of toast turned this simple dish into a satisfying meal.

Eggs in purgatory is a simple dish of quivering eggs poached directly in a spicy red sauce, equally good as a rousing breakfast or a satisfying meatless supper.

At least, I thought this popular Italian American dish would be simple. And indeed, tests of existing recipes showed that making the tomato sauce was a breeze. But achieving eight perfectly poached large eggs (enough to serve four) with set whites and runny yolks? That was a different story.

First, the sauce: In a 12-inch skillet, I cooked some garlic in oil; added grated onions, tomato paste, red pepper flakes, and dried oregano; and cooked it just until the tomato paste started to brown, about 5 minutes. I stirred in a can of crushed tomatoes and a few basil leaves. After a 15-minute simmer, it was ready for eggs.

I cracked eight eggs over the sauce, covered the skillet, and waited 4 minutes. How wrong could things go? Very. I had a skillet full of totally unevenly cooked eggs: The parts of the eggs that had sunk deeper into the sauce were rubbery and tough, while the whites up top were still watery. A mess.

I tried a few work-arounds, including separating the eggs and cooking the whites first before adding the yolks later. This was too complicated. I tried warming the eggs in hot tap water before cracking them; this proved unreliable. I nestled the eggs deeper into the sauce and then covered the pan to reflect heat back onto the floating whites. Nope: The yolks overcooked, and the whites were still watery. I felt as if I were the one in purgatory.

Next, I tried cooking the eggs in groups of two and four, covered and uncovered, and over varying levels of heat. While some methods came close, nothing gave me even results every time.

I turned to a more reliable source of overhead heat: the broiler. After cooking the eggs for just a couple of minutes on the stovetop, I slid the skillet under the broiler to finish. No dice: The whites were overcooked and rubbery.

But salvation was close. By flipping the oven control from "broil" to "bake," I took advantage of the gentler heat that reflected off the oven walls. This coddled, rather than blasted, the eggs, finishing them to tender-but-set whites and perfectly runny yolks in about 5 minutes. Rotating the pan halfway through ensured even cooking.

Victory. I had a bright tomato sauce, fully cooked whites, and silky yolks, plus a reminder that sometimes the simplest recipes are the hardest to nail down.

—CECELIA JENKINS, *Cook's Country*

Eggs in Purgatory

SERVES 4

Our preferred brands of canned crushed tomatoes are Tuttorosso and Muir Glen. Grate the onion on the large holes of a box grater. This dish should be a little spicy, but if you're averse to heat, we've provided a range for the red pepper flakes. When adding the eggs to the sauce, take care to space them evenly so the whites don't run together.

8	(¾-inch-thick) slices rustic Italian bread
7	tablespoons extra-virgin olive oil, plus extra for drizzling
4	garlic cloves, sliced thin
¼	cup grated onion
1	tablespoon tomato paste
¾–1¼	teaspoons red pepper flakes
	Salt and pepper
½	teaspoon dried oregano
1	cup fresh basil leaves plus 2 tablespoons chopped
1	(28-ounce) can crushed tomatoes
8	large eggs
¼	cup grated Parmesan cheese

1. Adjust oven rack to middle position and heat broiler. Arrange bread slices on baking sheet and drizzle first sides with 2 tablespoons oil; flip slices and drizzle with 2 tablespoons oil. Broil until deep golden brown, about 3 minutes per side. Set aside and heat oven to 400 degrees.

2. Heat remaining 3 tablespoons oil in ovensafe 12-inch skillet over medium heat until shimmering. Add garlic and cook until golden, about 2 minutes. Add onion, tomato paste, pepper flakes, 1 teaspoon salt, and oregano and cook, stirring occasionally, until rust-colored, about 4 minutes. Add basil leaves and cook until wilted, about 30 seconds. Stir in tomatoes and bring to gentle simmer. Reduce heat to medium-low and continue to simmer until slightly thickened, about 15 minutes, stirring occasionally.

3. Remove skillet from heat and let sit 2 minutes to cool slightly. Crack 1 egg into bowl. Use rubber spatula to clear 2-inch-diameter well in sauce, exposing skillet bottom. Using spatula to hold well open, immediately pour in egg. Repeat with remaining eggs, evenly spacing 7 eggs in total around perimeter of skillet and 1 in center.

4. Season each egg with salt and pepper. Cook over medium heat, covered, until egg whites are just beginning to set but are still translucent with some watery patches, about 3 minutes. Uncover skillet and transfer to oven. Bake until egg whites are set and no watery patches remain, 4 to 5 minutes for slightly runny yolks or about 6 minutes for soft-cooked yolks, rotating skillet halfway through baking.

5. Sprinkle with Parmesan and chopped basil and drizzle with extra oil. Serve with toasted bread.

NOTES FROM THE TEST KITCHEN

MAKING WELLS FOR EGGS

Use spatula to clear 2-inch-long well, exposing skillet bottom. Quickly pour 1 egg into each well.

100 PERCENT WHOLE-WHEAT PANCAKES

✓ **WHY THIS RECIPE WORKS:** We wanted hearty pancakes that allowed whole-wheat flour's nutty, wholesome flavor to shine. Because whole-wheat flour contains fewer gluten-forming proteins than white, we found that we did not have to worry about overmixing the batter. We also discovered that our pancakes tasted best when made with fresh flour (old flour can give off bitter notes). Keeping the batter simple, we combined whole-wheat flour, sugar, baking powder, baking soda, and salt before whisking in a mixture of tangy buttermilk, oil, and eggs. We ladled the thick batter into a hot skillet and cooked the pancakes until golden brown, flipping after about 2 minutes.

I've always liked the nutty flavor and slightly rustic texture of whole-wheat flour, so I'm glad to see it being added to everything from muffins to pizza crusts. But where, I wondered, were all the pancake recipes? A pancake would be a perfect place to swap whole-wheat flour for white flour because its robust flavor would be an ideal foil for the caramel-y sweetness of maple syrup—and the health benefits of eating whole grains don't hurt either.

Pancake recipes that feature a portion of whole-wheat flour do exist, of course, but those that call for 100 percent whole-wheat flour are surprisingly rare. Most cut the whole-wheat flour with an equal amount of white flour, while others call for grains like oats or buckwheat. Many recipes also call for fruit juice, fruit, vanilla, or cinnamon.

I wanted something different: a no-frills, all whole-wheat pancake that was simple to prepare and as light, tender, and fluffy as a pancake made with white flour.

I was puzzled by most cooks' reluctance to use all whole-wheat flour in a pancake recipe. Maybe its nutty flavor was too strong for some; that would explain all the flavor additions. And I've experienced enough brick-like loaves of whole-wheat bread to suspect that it might also have something to do with concerns about the structure: 100 percent whole-wheat flour is notorious for producing squat, dense, tough baked goods.

Erring on the side of caution, I made one of the straightforward half wheat–half white recipes I had

found. Except for the whole-wheat flour, this recipe was just like most other pancake recipes: I whisked the two flours with baking powder, baking soda, salt, and sugar in one bowl, and I whisked buttermilk (which I chose over milk since its tangy flavor would better complement the whole wheat), eggs, and vegetable oil in another. Then I folded the two mixtures together very carefully since the recipe, like most, cautioned that overmixing would lead to dense, tough pancakes.

Despite my concerns, there were no structural issues: These pancakes were as tender and fluffy as any white-flour pancakes I had ever made. But the taste was another story. Even using only 50 percent whole-wheat flour, the pancakes had a bitter flavor that overpowered the nuttiness. It wasn't terrible, but it didn't bode well for my 100 percent whole-wheat goal.

Before making any rash decisions, I did some research and learned that what we think of as "whole-wheat flavor" is actually two different flavors. That toasty, slightly tannic flavor comes from phenolic acid in the bran. This flavor is constant over time. The second is a bitter flavor that comes from the small amount of fat in the flour—specifically, the oxidation of that fat. This bitterness will build over time as the fat is exposed to air during storage (storing the flour in the freezer will slow oxidation).

No wonder I'd been put off by the results of that first test. I had used an open bag of flour I'd been keeping in my cupboard. For my next batch of pancakes, I made sure to use a fresh bag of flour (just opened and well within its expiration date). The results tasted much better. These pancakes were nutty and sweet.

Their surprisingly soft, light texture convinced me to try increasing the whole wheat, so I made the recipe again, this time using 75 percent whole-wheat flour and 25 percent white. As I had hoped, these pancakes had a bit more earthy, nutty whole-wheat flavor, but the real surprise was that they were even lighter and more tender than the previous batch. This pointed me to a really interesting discovery: Using all whole-wheat flour doesn't make pancakes tougher or denser. In fact, it makes them more foolproof. To understand why, it's helpful to understand a little about gluten.

Both white and whole-wheat flours contain proteins that bond together in the presence of moisture to form

100 PERCENT WHOLE-WHEAT PANCAKES

an elastic network called gluten. Stirring or kneading a batter or dough builds and strengthens that gluten network. That's a good thing when you're making yeasted bread because it is this network that captures the gases given off by the yeast, enabling a loaf to swell and maintain its shape during its lengthy rise and baking time. The gluten network is also what gives the final baked bread its satisfyingly resilient chew.

But for quick breads such as pancakes, gluten is a liability. The foamy, delicate batter is leavened by fast-acting chemical leaveners (baking powder and baking soda), which create tiny air bubbles throughout the batter, and the viscosity of the batter is enough to hold the bubbles in place in the brief time between mixing and setting. A strong gluten network will actually restrict the air bubbles' expansion in a delicate pancake batter and thus hinder rise. Also, the resilient texture of gluten isn't desirable in a pancake, hence the dire warnings about overmixing.

But I realized that logic applies only to pancakes made with white flour. Whole-wheat flour behaves differently for two reasons. First, unlike white flour, whole-wheat flour contains the bran and germ, and these do not contribute gluten-forming proteins, so a cup of whole-wheat flour contains fewer gluten-forming proteins than does a cup of white flour. Second, those bits of bran are quite sharp, and they slice across any gluten strands that do form, shortening them and weakening the network.

So whole-wheat flour is bad for gluten development. That makes it bad for yeasted loaves but ideal for pancakes. When I mixed the mostly whole-wheat pancake batter, the bran was weakening the gluten structure. Using whole-wheat flour meant that I could be much less cautious about my mixing technique and still produce perfectly tender, fluffy pancakes.

So what was stopping me from making a 100 percent whole-wheat version? Nothing. In my next batch, I used all whole-wheat flour and ended up with exactly what I'd been wanting. These pancakes had nutty, earthy flavor and they were as tall and tender as any white-flour pancake I'd ever had.

—ANDREA GEARY, *Cook's Illustrated*

100 Percent Whole-Wheat Pancakes

MAKES 15 PANCAKES

An electric griddle set at 350 degrees can be used in place of a skillet. If substituting buttermilk powder and water for fresh buttermilk, use only 2 cups of water to prevent the pancakes from being too wet. To ensure the best flavor, use either recently purchased whole-wheat flour or flour that has been stored in the freezer for less than 12 months. Serve with maple syrup and butter.

2 cups (11 ounces) whole-wheat flour
2 tablespoons sugar
1½ teaspoons baking powder
½ teaspoon baking soda
¾ teaspoon salt
2¼ cups buttermilk
5 tablespoons plus 2 teaspoons vegetable oil
2 large eggs

NOTES FROM THE TEST KITCHEN

WHISKING WITHOUT RISK
Recipes for white-flour pancakes always warn against overmixing. That's because it will create a strong, restrictive gluten network, and that makes for tough, dense cakes. But we discovered that the same rule doesn't apply to pancakes made with whole-wheat flour for two reasons. The first is that cup for cup, whole-wheat flour has fewer gluten-forming proteins than white flour. Second, whole-wheat flour contains bran, which is sharp and will cut through gluten strands that do form. When the gluten strands are shorter, the gluten network is weakened and the pancakes become even more tender.

WHITE-FLOUR PANCAKES

25 stirs   100 stirs

WHOLE-WHEAT PANCAKES

25 stirs   100 stirs

1. Adjust oven rack to middle position and heat oven to 200 degrees. Spray wire rack set in rimmed baking sheet with vegetable oil spray; place in oven.

2. Whisk flour, sugar, baking powder, baking soda, and salt together in medium bowl. Whisk buttermilk, 5 tablespoons oil, and eggs together in second medium bowl. Make well in center of flour mixture and pour in buttermilk mixture; whisk until smooth. (Mixture will be thick; do not add more buttermilk.)

3. Heat 1 teaspoon oil in 12-inch nonstick skillet over medium heat until shimmering. Using paper towels, carefully wipe out oil, leaving thin film on bottom and sides of pan. Using ¼-cup dry measuring cup or 2-ounce ladle, portion batter into pan in 3 places. Gently spread each portion into 4½-inch round. Cook until edges are set, first side is golden brown, and bubbles on surface are just beginning to break, 2 to 3 minutes. Using thin, wide spatula, flip pancakes and continue to cook until second side is golden brown, 1 to 2 minutes longer. Serve pancakes immediately or transfer to wire rack in oven. Repeat with remaining batter, using remaining 1 teaspoon oil as necessary.

VARIATION

Wheat Berry Pancakes
MAKES 12 PANCAKES

This recipe is for mixing only. For cooking directions refer to steps 1 and 3 of 100 Percent Whole-Wheat Pancakes and be sure to have extra vegetable oil on hand for the skillet. For efficient blending of the buttermilk and wheat berry mixture, it's important for the blender to create and maintain a vortex, which looks like a whirlpool. Watch the batter as it is mixing; if the vortex closes (or does not form), changing the blender speed or adding more buttermilk will bring it back. Because pulverizing the wheat berries creates some stress on a blender's motor, we recommend using a machine with at least a 450-watt motor and ice-crushing capability. If you are using a high-end blender like a Vitamix or Blendtec, the blending times will be shorter.

1½ cups wheat berries
2 tablespoons sugar
¾ teaspoon salt

1½ cups buttermilk
5 tablespoons vegetable oil
2 large eggs
1½ teaspoons baking powder
½ teaspoon baking soda

Process wheat berries, sugar, and salt in blender on high speed until as fine as possible, about 3 minutes. Transfer mixture to bowl. Add 1 cup buttermilk to blender and pour wheat berry mixture on top. Blend on high speed, adding additional buttermilk and changing speed as necessary to maintain vortex, until mixture is thick and has only small lumps, about 3 minutes. Add oil, eggs, and any remaining buttermilk and continue to blend until fully incorporated, about 30 seconds longer. With blender running, add baking powder and baking soda, and blend until incorporated, about 15 seconds.

ALABAMA ORANGE ROLLS

✔ **WHY THIS RECIPE WORKS:** To make Alabama's famous citrus-infused rolls at home, we needed to figure out how to pack big orange flavor into every bite. Using a yeasted cinnamon roll dough as our starting point, we replaced the milk with a combination of orange juice and cream for clean orange taste void of sourness. We kneaded the simple dough together and let it rise before rolling it into a rectangle, coating the surface with butter for richness, and sprinkling it with a mixture of orange zest and sugar. We rolled the dough into a tight log and sliced it into eight rolls, arranging them in a greased cake pan. After a second rise, the rolls baked to a gorgeous golden brown. A rich, balanced glaze of orange juice, cream, sugar, and butter reinforced the rolls' unmistakable orange flavor and gave them an appealing glossy finish.

For years, friends from Alabama have been telling me about the famous orange rolls served at All Steak restaurant in Cullman, Alabama. Crowds go crazy for the sweet spirals that deliver an outsized punch of citrus flavor, so I headed south to join in the fray.

Small and spiraled, like baby cinnamon rolls, these glazy rolls filled with orange-flavored sugar and topped with a citrusy icing filled the room with aromas of yeast, butter, and orange. I loved them, but I couldn't help wondering what they'd smell like while baking and what they'd taste like straight out of the oven. I determined right then to create a version to make at home.

Their soft, chewy texture indicated that these rolls were leavened with yeast, like the doughs we use for cinnamon rolls and other similar pastries. I started with one of our in-house cinnamon roll recipes, mixing together flour, sugar, yeast, and salt. Butter was a must, but instead of the milk we normally use, I swapped in orange juice, hoping this would amp up the orange flavor.

After kneading, resting, shaping, and nestling the dough into a cake pan for a second rise, I baked the rolls and gave them a try. The orange juice definitely increased the citrus presence, but maybe too much: This batch took on a distinctly sour flavor. I tried adding dairy back into the mix in various amounts; after testing different combinations, I found that ½ cup of orange juice and ¼ cup of cream was as far as I could go without introducing sourness.

But the reintroduction of cream, while allowing a bit of subtle orange flavor to come through, still muted the full impact of citrus's signature good-morning zing. To bring it back, I grated the zest from a couple of oranges and tossed it with a bit of sugar to fill the rolls. But once this batch baked off, I realized I'd gone too far; now my filling was bitter, not bright.

A few follow-up tests showed me that the line between bold and bitter was very fine; just 2 teaspoons of orange zest (from a single orange) gave me the right level of vibrancy and virtually no bitterness.

Going into the glaze portion of my testing, I assumed that just stirring together powdered sugar and liquid (in this case, orange juice, of course) would settle things. But this method just made a mess. Too much orange juice and the mixture ran off and pooled at the bottom of the pan rather than clinging to the rolls; too much sugar and the glaze was chalky and sickeningly sweet. I'd have to take a new tack.

After testing a wide range of methods, I found the solution in a quickly cooked glaze based on granulated, not powdered, sugar. When heated, granulated sugar liquefies and becomes smooth and free from chalkiness. Boiling sugar and orange juice, plus some heavy cream to hold the sharp citrus in check, for just 4 minutes allowed any excess moisture to evaporate, leaving a thick, syrupy, flavorful glaze that didn't overwhelm the rolls.

Just a couple of tablespoons of the sweet, vibrant glaze brushed on the rolls after they came out of the oven gave them a lovely sheen. I had a winner.

—KATIE LEAIRD, *Cook's Country*

Alabama Orange Rolls

MAKES 8 ROLLS

Be sure to zest the orange before juicing. When zesting the orange, remove just the outer part of the peel—the inner white pith is very bitter. We bake these rolls in a dark-colored cake pan because they brown better. If you only have a light-colored pan, increase the baking time to 45 to 50 minutes. Note that the dough needs to rise for a total of 2½ to 3½ hours.

DOUGH

- 3 cups (15 ounces) all-purpose flour
- ¼ cup (1¾ ounces) sugar
- 2¼ teaspoons instant or rapid-rise yeast
- 1 teaspoon salt
- ½ cup warm orange juice (110 degrees)
- ¼ cup heavy cream
- 6 tablespoons unsalted butter, cut into 6 pieces and softened
- 1 large egg plus 1 large yolk

FILLING

- ½ cup (3½ ounces) sugar
- 2 teaspoons grated orange zest
- 2 tablespoons unsalted butter, softened

GLAZE

- ¼ cup heavy cream
- ¼ cup (1¾ ounces) sugar
- 2 tablespoons orange juice
- 2 tablespoons unsalted butter
- ⅛ teaspoon salt

MAKING ALABAMA ORANGE ROLLS

1. Roll dough into 16 by 8-inch rectangle with long side parallel to counter's edge. Spread butter over surface of dough, then sprinkle buttered surface evenly with sugar mixture.

2. Roll dough away from you into tight, even log. Pinch seam between your forefinger and thumb along entire length of log to seal tightly.

3. Use serrated knife to cut log into eight 2-inch-thick slices.

4. Arrange slices in cake pan, 1 roll in center and remaining rolls around perimeter, with seam sides facing inwards.

ZESTING ORANGES

Zest's oils add vibrancy to our Alabama Orange Rolls. Here's how to get bright—not bitter—orange flavor with ease.

Swipe rinsed and dried fruit along grater in 1 direction—not back and forth—to remove only flavorful zest. Avoid grating bitter white pith.

1. FOR THE DOUGH: In bowl of stand mixer, whisk flour, sugar, yeast, and salt together. Add orange juice, cream, butter, and egg and yolk. Fit mixer with dough hook and knead on medium speed until dough comes together, about 2 minutes. Increase speed to medium-high and continue to knead dough until smooth and elastic, about 8 minutes longer. Dough will be soft.

2. Transfer dough to lightly floured counter and knead until smooth ball forms, about 30 seconds. Place dough in greased large bowl, cover tightly with plastic wrap, and let rise in warm place until doubled in size, 1½ to 2 hours.

3. FOR THE FILLING: Combine sugar and zest in small bowl. Transfer dough to lightly floured counter. Roll dough into 16 by 8-inch rectangle with long side parallel to counter's edge. Spread butter over surface of dough using small offset spatula, then sprinkle evenly with sugar mixture. Roll dough away from you into tight, even log and pinch seam to seal.

4. Grease dark-colored 9-inch cake pan, line bottom with parchment paper, then grease parchment. Roll log seam side down and cut into eight 2-inch-thick slices using serrated knife. Place 1 roll in center of prepared pan and others around perimeter of pan, seam sides facing center. Cover with plastic and let rise in warm place until doubled in size, 1 to 1½ hours. Adjust oven rack to middle position and heat oven to 325 degrees.

5. Discard plastic and bake rolls until golden brown on top and interior of center roll registers 195 degrees, 40 to 45 minutes. Let rolls cool in pan on wire rack for 30 minutes.

6. FOR THE GLAZE: Once rolls have cooled for 30 minutes, combine all ingredients in small saucepan and bring to boil over medium heat. Cook, stirring frequently, until large, slow bubbles appear and mixture is syrupy, about 4 minutes.

7. Using spatula, loosen rolls from sides of pan and slide onto platter; discard parchment. Brush glaze over tops of rolls and serve warm.

MIXED BERRY SCONES

✓ **WHY THIS RECIPE WORKS:** For mixed berry scones with a light, crumbly texture and berries in every bite, we incorporated the butter in two different ways. We processed half of the chilled butter with flour, sugar, baking powder, and salt, which distributed it evenly through the dry ingredients and created a rich crumb. We then pulsed the remaining butter into pea-sized pieces to achieve buttery pockets throughout the scones. Tossing the frozen berries in confectioners' sugar before folding them into the flour mixture prevented them from bleeding into the dough. A honey-butter glaze, brushed on partway through baking, gave the scones a sweet sheen.

A cook's inspiration can strike in unlikely spots. Case in point: Freight House Antiques in Erving, Massachusetts. Turns out that the place has an attached coffee shop, where each day proprietor Rita Dubay sets out a display of pies, muffins, and more baked goods—including massive, sweet, crumbly mixed berry scones. I loved her scones so much I raced back to the test kitchen determined to create a version for myself.

We have company recipes for scones that vary from traditional, dense English scones to cakey, sweet American styles. I baked and sampled my way through several American-style recipes trying to imitate Dubay's scones, to no avail. So I reached out to Dubay to learn her tricks, but like many great cooks, while she gave me some clues, she kept the recipe itself a secret.

Determined nonetheless, I started grating frozen butter into flour, sugar, salt, and baking powder—several recipes agreed that this technique helps produce a flaky scone—and then mixed in milk, eggs, and frozen berries before shaping the dough into scones and baking them off.

The frozen berries were causing me issues right off the bat, bleeding into my batter and leaving me with blue-marbled scones. Plus, the berry flavor was more tart than sweet. I found that tossing the frozen berries with confectioners' sugar before mixing them into the other dry ingredients controlled the bleed and beat back the tartness.

I still had some issues, though. The grated butter left nice buttery pockets in my scones, but grating frozen sticks of butter was a pain. I wondered if I could get the same effect with the food processor. I pulsed the chilled butter into the dry ingredients, leaving pea-size chunks, but when I baked this batch, the butter pieces didn't fully incorporate into the dough and leached out onto the baking sheet. I tried processing in the butter until it was fully incorporated, but these scones lacked richness.

Another cook in the kitchen suggested combining the two methods, processing in half the butter until fully incorporated and then pulsing in the second half for larger chunks. Now I had rich scones packed with biscuit-like butter pockets. A brushing of honey butter on top of the scones before the final 5 to 8 minutes of baking gave them a nice sheen and sweet finish.

With a few adjustments I found that I could freeze the unbaked scones without sacrificing flavor or texture. I could make a batch of dough on Sunday, freeze the shaped scones, and bake them off one at a time throughout the week.

—MORGAN BOLLING, *Cook's Country*

Mixed Berry Scones
MAKES 8 SCONES

Work the dough as little as possible, just until it comes together. Work quickly to keep the butter and berries as cold as possible for the best results. Note that the butter is divided in this recipe. An equal amount of frozen blueberries, raspberries, blackberries, or strawberries (halved) can be used in place of the mixed berries.

SCONES
- 1¾ cups (8¾ ounces) frozen mixed berries
- 3 tablespoons confectioners' sugar
- 3 cups (15 ounces) all-purpose flour
- 12 tablespoons unsalted butter, cut into ½-inch pieces and chilled
- ⅓ cup (2⅓ ounces) granulated sugar
- 1 tablespoon baking powder
- 1¼ teaspoons salt
- ¾ cup plus 2 tablespoons whole milk
- 1 large egg plus 1 large yolk

GLAZE
- 2 tablespoons unsalted butter, melted
- 1 tablespoon honey

1. FOR THE SCONES: Adjust oven rack to upper-middle position and heat oven to 425 degrees. Line rimmed baking sheet with parchment paper. If your berry mix contains strawberries, cut them in half. Toss berries with confectioners' sugar in bowl; freeze until needed.

2. Combine flour, 6 tablespoons butter, granulated sugar, baking powder, and salt in food processor and process until butter is fully incorporated, about 15 seconds. Add remaining 6 tablespoons butter and pulse until butter is reduced to pea-size pieces, 10 to 12 pulses. Transfer mixture to large bowl. Stir in berries.

3. Beat milk and egg and yolk together in separate bowl. Make well in center of flour mixture and pour in milk mixture. Using rubber spatula, gently stir mixture, scraping from edges of bowl and folding inward until very shaggy dough forms and some bits of flour remain. Do not overmix.

4. Turn dough out onto well-floured counter and, if necessary, knead briefly until dough just comes together, about 3 turns. Using your floured hands and bench scraper, shape dough into 12 by 4-inch rectangle, about 1½ inches tall. Using knife or bench scraper, cut dough crosswise into 4 equal rectangles. Cut each rectangle diagonally into 2 triangles (you should have 8 scones total). Transfer scones to prepared sheet. Bake until scones are lightly golden on top, 16 to 18 minutes, rotating sheet halfway through baking.

5. FOR THE GLAZE: While scones bake, combine melted butter and honey in small bowl.

6. Remove scones from oven and brush tops evenly with glaze mixture. Return scones to oven and continue to bake until golden brown on top, 5 to 8 minutes longer. Transfer scones to wire rack and let cool for at least 10 minutes before serving.

TO MAKE AHEAD: Unbaked scones can be frozen for several weeks. After cutting scones into triangles in step 4, freeze them on baking sheet. Transfer frozen scones to zipper-lock freezer bag. When ready to bake, heat oven to 375 degrees and extend cooking time in step 4 to 23 to 26 minutes. Glaze time in step 6 will remain at 5 to 8 minutes.

CINNAMON SWIRL BREAD

☑ **WHY THIS RECIPE WORKS:** For a bread that was reminiscent of cinnamon buns but more elegant in presentation, we started with a slightly sweet base that was rich enough to stand up to a hearty cinnamon filling. Incorporating some cinnamon into the dough boosted its flavor. For the filling, we opted for a simple combination of cinnamon, brown sugar, and melted butter. Getting the filling to stay put and not ooze out of our bread required a special braiding technique that exposed the attractive swirls of cinnamon. We found that a cast-iron skillet was the perfect vessel for baking this indulgent bread, since its high sides helped to shape the loaf and give it a distinct bottom crust.

When someone is baking cinnamon rolls in the test kitchen, you can bet I'm the first taster to volunteer. The aromas of yeasted dough and warm cinnamon wafting from the kitchen are irresistible. But, much to my dismay, cinnamon rolls fall squarely in the category of special treats, not everyday fare. That's where cinnamon bread comes in to fill the void.

In theory, cinnamon swirl bread should deliver similarly alluring results, but that's rarely been the case in my experience. My ideal is a fluffy, delicate crumb beneath a distinct browned crust with a substantial swirl of gooey cinnamon sugar. But most versions I've sampled are either austere white sandwich loaves rolled up with a scant sprinkling of cinnamon and sugar or overly sweet breads ruined by gobs of filling oozing from the cracks. After a little research, I realized that the closest thing to what I was looking for was babka, New York's Jewish bakery specialty that boasts a rich yeasted bread layered with a sweet, gooey cinnamon-sugar filling. Today's versions are usually loaf-shaped, but traditional Eastern European babkas are always round. Envisioning a tall, multilayered, coiled bread—think oversized cinnamon bun—I sought out a circular vessel and settled on my trusty cast-iron skillet. I was sure its heat retention would produce a distinct crust that would put my cake pan to shame.

CAST-IRON SKILLET CINNAMON SWIRL BREAD

Creating a shape that held the filling in place would be key, but before worrying about that I'd need a dough strong enough to withstand plenty of twisting and pulling. I began by whisking yeast with warm water and warm milk (an addition typical of enriched cinnamon roll doughs) to activate it and help it dissolve. Butter and sugar ensured a rich, sweet bread. After adding flour and a bit of salt, I kneaded the dough together and let it rise. When it came time to create my swirls, I had a couple of techniques in mind to try out. I rolled the dough into a rectangle, spread it with melted butter, and sprinkled on a mixture of cinnamon and sugar. The test kitchen's babka recipe calls for rolling the filled dough into a cylinder and then folding and twisting it before nestling it into a loaf pan. Translating this trick for use in a round skillet was a hassle, leaving me with a lumpy, unevenly shaped bread. I wanted my cinnamon bread to be a beauty, and the simple babka technique was not working.

Another cinnamon bread recipe in our archives seemed promising: Though the bread bakes in a loaf pan, the recipe relies on a braiding technique that guarantees a stunning presentation: You roll the dough into a cylinder, cut the log in half lengthwise to expose the inner layers, then wind the two halves together, creating dramatic swirls of cinnamon filling. I wound the braid into a spiral and placed it in the skillet where I let it rise a second time before baking. As the dough rose, it nuzzled up against the high sides of the skillet, gaining great height and creating an impressive dome shape.

As the bread baked, the kitchen filled with those familiar, magnetic aromas of yeasted bread and sweet cinnamon. After letting the finished loaf cool, I cut myself a slice. The bread boasted a perfect even crumb and had beautiful swirls throughout, but I felt let down by its flavor. The cinnamon's overall impact fell short of what I wanted and the filling was too sugary-sweet. I couldn't deny that the cast-iron skillet had made a real difference, though. Where many cinnamon breads bake up like tender coffee cakes or overly sweet sandwich breads, the cast iron had acted much like a baking stone, producing a gorgeous browned crust. If I could just improve the bread's flavor, I'd have a showstopper on my hands.

Revisiting my dough, I decided to stir 2 teaspoons of cinnamon right into the flour, ensuring that the dough

reinforced the filling's spiced flavor. To tone down the overly sweet filling and impart a caramelized flavor more suited to the cinnamon, I swapped granulated sugar for brown. I proceeded to knead, rest, fill, and braid the dough as before. My cinnamon swirl bread was still a visual stunner, but to really push it over the top, I brushed it with an egg wash before baking to give it some sheen.

The loaf baked to a gorgeous golden brown with balanced, sweet cinnamon flavor throughout. My tasters loved the dramatic cinnamon streaks and golden crust. Best part of all? It tasted even better than it looked.

—SARA MAYER, *America's Test Kitchen Books*

Cast-Iron Skillet Cinnamon Swirl Bread

MAKES 1 LOAF

- 1 cup warm whole milk (110 degrees)
- 8 tablespoons unsalted butter, melted
- ¼ cup (1¾ ounces) granulated sugar
- 2 tablespoons warm tap water
- 2¼ teaspoons instant or rapid-rise yeast
- 3¼ cups (16¼ ounces) all-purpose flour, plus extra as needed
- 2 teaspoons salt
- 2 teaspoons ground cinnamon
- ½ cup packed (3½ ounces) light brown sugar
- 1 large egg, lightly beaten

1. Whisk milk, 6 tablespoons melted butter, granulated sugar, water, and yeast together in 2-cup liquid measuring cup until yeast dissolves. Whisk flour, salt, and 1 teaspoon cinnamon together in bowl of stand mixer. Using dough hook with mixer on low speed, slowly add milk mixture and mix until dough comes together, about 2 minutes. Increase speed to medium and continue to mix until dough is smooth and elastic, about 10 minutes. (If after 5 minutes dough is still very sticky, add 1 to 2 tablespoons extra flour; dough should clear sides of bowl but stick to bottom.)

2. Transfer dough to lightly floured counter and knead by hand to form smooth, round ball, about 1 minute. Place dough in large, lightly greased bowl, cover tightly with greased plastic wrap, and let rise until doubled in size, about 1 hour.

3. Combine brown sugar and remaining 1 teaspoon cinnamon in bowl. Transfer dough to lightly floured counter and roll into 16 by 12-inch rectangle with long side facing you. Brush remaining 2 tablespoons melted butter over dough, leaving ½-inch border at edges. Sprinkle cinnamon-sugar mixture over butter, leaving ¾-inch border at top edge, and press lightly to adhere. Roll dough away from you into firm cylinder, keeping roll taut by tucking it under itself as you go. Pinch seam and ends closed. If necessary, gently reshape log to be 16 inches in length with even diameter.

4. Grease 10-inch cast-iron skillet. With short side of dough log facing you, cut log in half lengthwise, using bench scraper. Turn dough halves cut sides up and arrange side by side. Pinch top ends together. Lift and place 1 dough half on opposite side of second half. Repeat, keeping cut sides up, until dough halves are tightly braided. Pinch remaining ends together. Twist braided dough into spiral and tuck end underneath. Transfer loaf to prepared skillet, cover with greased plastic, and let rise until doubled in size, 45 minutes to 1 hour.

5. Adjust oven rack to lower-middle position and heat oven to 325 degrees. Brush loaf with beaten egg, transfer skillet to oven, and bake until loaf is deep golden brown and filling is melted, 45 to 55 minutes, rotating skillet halfway through baking.

6. Using potholders, transfer skillet to wire rack and let loaf cool for 10 minutes. Being careful of hot skillet handle, remove loaf from skillet, return to rack, and let cool to room temperature, about 2 hours, before serving.

NOTES FROM THE TEST KITCHEN

BRAIDING CINNAMON SWIRL BREAD

After pinching top ends of dough halves together, lift and place 1 dough half on opposite side of second half. Repeat, keeping cut sides up, until dough halves are tightly braided.

FLAKY BUTTERMILK BISCUITS

✔ **WHY THIS RECIPE WORKS:** We set out to bake the ultimate flaky biscuits with minimal fuss. First, for an even distribution of butter, and, as a result, plenty of small air pockets, we froze whole sticks and grated all but 1 tablespoon from each into a mixture of flour, sugar, baking powder, baking soda, and salt. Opting for high-protein King Arthur flour promised more gluten and therefore a more structured, stable crumb. Buttermilk gave the biscuits pleasant tang, which the sugar balanced out nicely. To produce the maximum number of layers, we rolled out and folded the dough a total of five times, turning the dough from shaggy to smooth. To make the most of our multi-layered dough, we bypassed the biscuit cutter in favor of square biscuits; this switch protected us against wasted scraps or tough rerolled biscuits. Letting the dough rest for 30 minutes and trimming away the creased edges ensured that these biscuits rose up tall in the oven. A bit of melted butter brushed on before baking reinforced the biscuits' butter flavor and ensured a lovely golden brown hue.

From the enormous soft and fluffy Southern cat head to the simple drop, I love biscuits of all kinds. But my current obsession is a specimen I've recently found in several restaurants. It's crisp and crunchy on the outside but tender and light as air inside, with flaky strata that peel apart like sheets of buttery paper in a way that rivals a croissant. No, this is not an everyday biscuit; it's an ethereal, once-in-a-while treat rich enough that there's no need to spread on any extra butter, just a slathering of jam, if that. But when I tried recipes billed as "rich and tender flaky biscuits," very few lived up to the promise, and those that did required a lengthy process of folding the dough and letting it rest that was as much work as making croissants. I set out to see what I could do to produce my ideal flaky biscuit with considerably less fuss.

Despite the failures, those early tests did help sort out a few things. First, I'd use only butter rather than a mixture of butter and shortening. Shortening lacks flavor, and I also found that it inhibited the formation of distinct layers. Similar to pie crusts, leaving distinct pieces of fat in the dough (what many recipes refer to as "pea-size" pieces) is key to producing flakiness. As the biscuits cook, the bits of fat melt into the dough, leaving small voids. Then, as the water in the dough turns to steam, it expands these gaps and creates layers. The problem with shortening is that it has a soft texture and tends to combine with the flour rather than stay distinct like butter. Most recipes I found called for 2 to 4 tablespoons of fat per cup of flour; I suspected that I could squeeze in more. I settled on 16 tablespoons butter to 3 cups flour—a little more than 5 tablespoons per cup.

As for the type of flour, unlike ultratender, fluffy Southern-style biscuits that demand a specialty low-protein flour (generally 7 to 8 percent) like White Lily, my early tests confirmed that flaky biscuits are better off made with all-purpose flour. This is because all-purpose flour has a little more protein (10 to 12 percent), and when combined with water, the protein in flour produces gluten. The more protein, the more gluten, which translates to a biscuit dough with more strength that can bake up with distinct, structured layers rather than cakey and fluffy. I tried bread flour (which is closer to 13 percent protein) but found that it created an overly strong gluten network that produced tough biscuits. The best results came from using King Arthur all-purpose flour, which is 12 percent protein.

I also determined that I'd use buttermilk rather than milk for its distinctive tang, a touch of sugar for complexity, a little baking soda to enhance browning and add some lift, and, finally, baking powder for additional lift. As for shaping, I settled on square biscuits. Round biscuits were pretty, but they left too much scrap dough and rerolling those scraps produced biscuits that were tough. Shaping the dough into a square slab and then cutting that into squared-off biscuits was fast and meant no rerolling—and no waste.

I moved on to the heart of the matter: mixing and shaping. Many biscuit recipes require that you spend a lot of effort getting the butter into small, even, pea-size pieces by cutting it into the dry ingredients using a dough cutter, a pair of knives, a food processor, or your hands. The problem with most of these approaches is that it's far too easy to over- or under-do it, both of which hamper flakiness. I found that the most consistent method was to grate the butter using the large holes of a box grater, a trick I picked up from our recipe for blueberry scones.

Of course, the effort is moot if these shreds of butter soften during mixing and shaping. To avoid that, I froze the butter for 30 minutes before grating it. And to get around the awkwardness of grating the stubs, I saved the last tablespoon of each stick to melt and brush on the tops of the biscuits just before baking them, which would improve crisping and browning.

The grated butter helped create some layering but not nearly what I was after. In a pie dough, leaving the butter in small pieces is sufficient to get the right flaky effect, but that's because pie dough contains far less liquid (and far more butter) and is rolled out thin, a pair of factors that inherently smears the butter into thin sheets among floury layers. But in a wet, minimally rolled-out slab of biscuit dough, the butter pieces just float randomly in the mixture like raisins in a muffin batter. And that's where folding comes in. This process starts with rolling out the dough into a large, thin rectangle and then folding it into thirds like a letter. You then press the dough together to seal the package tightly, turn it 90 degrees, and repeat. The special thing about folding dough is that the technique works by multiplication, not addition. Each fold doesn't simply give you one more layer; it creates an exponentially greater number of layers because it's a trifold every single time, not a single fold.

Folding my biscuit dough, at least in the early stages, was a messy affair: It started out shaggy and crumbly—anything but a cohesive mass—and it seemed like I wasn't really doing anything useful. But slowly and surely, the dry bits and the wet bits came together; by the fourth fold, the process was pretty tidy. The interesting thing was, I found in subsequent tests that the messier—and less mixed—the dough was in the beginning, the better. Even in those first few messy "folds," the slivers of butter were getting pressed and stretched into thinner and thinner sheets among clumps of wet and dry dough. If I mixed the dough in the bowl to the point where it was uniform before I folded it (which is what most recipes call for) or if I added more liquid to help bring the dough together, I ended up with layers that were less defined.

Some recipes call for letting the dough rest for as long as 30 minutes after every set of folds. This is because with each set the gluten in the dough gets stronger, making the dough increasingly harder to roll out. But because my dough wasn't cohesive for the first few sets of folds, gluten didn't develop at the same pace, and I could make five folds without any resting.

When I cut this dough into squares, each biscuit looked like the side view of a book, with layers that pulled away from one another dramatically during baking—just the effect I'd hoped for. There was only one problem: Most of the biscuits were coming out of the oven lopsided. In fact, of the nine biscuits the recipe produced, only the one cut from the center of the dough came out square and level.

I realized that the edges of the dough slab were being compressed during the rolling and folding process. Trimming away ¼ inch from the perimeter of the dough before cutting the biscuits took care of that, but the biscuits were still a bit wonky. By the fifth fold, the layers of dough were taut like stretched rubber bands. Once the layers started to separate in the oven, this tension caused them to slip and slide in different directions, leaving the biscuits lopsided. A single 30-minute rest in the refrigerator—a far cry from the multiple rests other recipes required—gave them time to relax. With that, I had buttery, superflaky biscuits that consistently rose up tall and true.

—ANDREW JANJIGIAN, *Cook's Illustrated*

Flaky Buttermilk Biscuits

MAKES 9 BISCUITS

We prefer King Arthur all-purpose flour for this recipe, but other brands will work. Use sticks of butter. In hot or humid environments, chill the flour mixture, grater, and work bowls before use. The dough will start out very crumbly and dry in pockets but will be smooth by the end of the folding process; do not be tempted to add extra buttermilk. Flour the counter and the top of the dough as needed to prevent sticking, but be careful not to incorporate large pockets of flour into the dough while folding.

FOLDING FOR A SMOOTH FINISH

At the outset, this dough appears scraggly, but folding it repeatedly allows the slivers of butter to be stretched into thinner and thinner sheets among the wet and dry clumps, creating more layers. By the last fold, it will smooth out.

1. REALLY SHAGGY: Dough barely gets mixed before being transferred to counter.

2. STILL SHAGGY: After first fold, dough remains very dry and crumbly.

3. GETTING LESS SHAGGY: By third fold, dough is starting to smooth out and look more like typical dough.

4. MOSTLY SMOOTH: After fourth fold, dough is only a little rough around edges; folds look distinct.

5. ALL SQUARED AWAY: After fifth fold, dough is rolled out, rests for 30 minutes, and is cut into squares for baking.

3 cups (15 ounces) King Arthur all-purpose flour

2 tablespoons sugar

4 teaspoons baking powder

½ teaspoon baking soda

1½ teaspoons salt

16 tablespoons (2 sticks) unsalted butter, frozen for 30 minutes

1¼ cups buttermilk, chilled

1. Line rimmed baking sheet with parchment paper and set aside. Whisk flour, sugar, baking powder, baking soda, and salt together in large bowl. Coat sticks of butter in flour mixture, then grate 7 tablespoons from each stick on large holes of box grater directly into flour mixture. Toss gently to combine. Set aside remaining 2 tablespoons butter.

2. Add buttermilk to flour mixture and fold with spatula until just combined (dough will look dry). Transfer dough to liberally floured counter. Dust surface of dough with flour; using your floured hands, press dough into rough 7-inch square.

3. Roll dough into 12 by 9-inch rectangle with short side parallel to edge of counter. Starting at bottom of dough, fold into thirds like business letter, using bench scraper or metal spatula to release dough from counter. Press top of dough firmly to seal folds. Turn dough 90 degrees clockwise. Repeat rolling into 12 by 9-inch rectangle, folding into thirds, and turning clockwise 4 more times, for total of 5 sets of folds. After last set of folds, roll dough into 8½-inch square about 1 inch thick. Transfer dough to prepared sheet, cover with plastic wrap, and refrigerate for 30 minutes. Adjust oven rack to upper-middle position and heat oven to 400 degrees.

4. Transfer dough to lightly floured cutting board. Using sharp, floured chef's knife, trim ¼ inch of dough from each side of square and discard. Cut remaining dough into 9 squares, flouring knife after each cut. Arrange biscuits at least 1 inch apart on sheet. Melt reserved butter; brush tops of biscuits with melted butter.

5. Bake until tops are golden brown, 22 to 25 minutes, rotating sheet halfway through baking. Transfer biscuits to wire rack and let cool for 15 minutes before serving.

FLUFFY DINNER ROLLS

✔ **WHY THIS RECIPE WORKS:** Moist, fluffy dinner rolls are great when fresh but they lose those qualities as they cool. In order to bake rolls with a longer shelf life, we applied a method called *tangzhong*, a Japanese bread-making technique which adds extra moisture to dough using a flour paste. The added liquid in the dough helps the rolls maintain their optimum texture for more than a day. We prepared the paste in the microwave, heating and whisking a mixture of flour and water in 20-second increments until it had a pudding-like texture. We gradually worked the remaining ingredients into the paste, incorporating cold milk, an egg, flour, and yeast one after the other. A strong gluten network was necessary to support the extra moisture in this dough, so we let it rest before adding the salt, sugar, and butter to encourage strong gluten formation. Flattening each portion of dough and rolling it up in a spiral organized the gluten strands into coiled layers, which baked up into feathery sheets. These rolls were incredibly light, and, best of all, they were just as good when reheated a day later.

I used to think that the Old Testament adage "There is nothing new under the sun" could be applied to bread baking. Most "new" bread recipes are actually just modern twists on established recipes or resurrections of bygone techniques. So I was intrigued when I read about *tangzhong*, an oddball bread-making technique that originated in Japan and was popularized by pastry chef Yvonne Chen in the early 2000s.

Instead of simply combining the dry and wet ingredients and kneading as you would to make a conventional loaf, you begin by cooking a portion of the flour and liquid to form a pudding-like paste that you then let cool and mix into the dough. Fans of the method claim not only that it produces bread with a particularly moist, airy, feathery crumb but also that the loaf remains fresh and soft longer than conventional bread.

Curious, I made a popular published Japanese milk bread recipe (a soft, rich sandwich loaf with a snow-white crumb that's a staple in Asian bakeries) that employs the tangzhong method and was immediately won over: The dough was soft and silky, and its pillowy

FLUFFY DINNER ROLLS

crumb was made up of delicate, almost croissant-like sheets. Eating it gave me the kind of satisfaction I get from a really good dinner roll—except that this bread was even fluffier and, as promised, maintained its impressively moist, plush crumb over the next couple of days.

So, what if I applied this Japanese technique to my usual pull-apart dinner roll recipe? If it worked, it could potentially yield the best dinner rolls I'd ever made and give them a perk that most rolls don't have: make-ahead potential.

In the recipes I found that employ the tangzhong method, the paste is about 5 parts liquid to 1 part flour and makes up 15 to 20 percent of the total dough weight. My standard dinner roll recipe yields 25 ounces of dough, so to make about 5 ounces of paste, I whisked together ½ cup of water and 3 tablespoons of bread flour in a saucepan. As I stirred the mixture over medium heat, its consistency went from heavy cream to thick pudding. I set the paste aside to cool while I added the remaining ingredients to the stand mixer bowl: 2 cups of bread flour, instant yeast, a little sugar and salt, 4 tablespoons of softened butter, an egg, and ¼ cup milk. Then I added the cooled paste and started mixing. But after 3 minutes, I knew something was wrong: The dough, which is usually slightly sticky and workable was dry and tight.

I knew this wasn't typical for a tangzhong dough, because the Japanese milk loaf dough I'd made had been soft and smooth. It wasn't until I compared the hydrations of the two doughs that I discovered the discrepancy: My standard dough had a hydration of 60 percent (meaning there were 6 parts liquid to every 10 parts flour), while the hydration of the Japanese milk bread was 80 percent, which I later learned was typical for a dough using the tangzhong method. Ordinarily, that much liquid would make a dough slack, sticky, and hard to shape, but not so with my milk bread.

I made another batch of rolls with a hot-water paste, but this time I added extra milk (½ cup total) to the dough to bring the hydration to 80 percent. Sure enough, the dough was soft and silky, not sticky, and held its shape nicely after kneading.

So why wasn't it a sticky mess? In a standard dough, where you mix cold water and flour, most of the water is not absorbed, so the stickiness you feel is so-called free water. But as I learned making Mandarin pancakes for mu shu pork, flour can absorb twice as much hot water as cold water. Heating the water for the paste allows it to be fully absorbed by the flour; in essence, a portion of what would be free water in a standard dough gets locked away. Thus, when the flour paste is mixed with the rest of the ingredients, the dough is smooth, not sticky.

From there, I knocked the air out of the doubled dough to eliminate large air bubbles and encourage a fine crumb, portioned it into 12 pieces, rolled each into a taut ball, and arranged the rolls in a greased cake pan to rise. Baked at 375 degrees until they were deep golden brown, these rolls were moist and flavorful— but they were a bit squat and the crumb was coarse.

A close look at some tangzhong recipes revealed my mistake: I had added more moisture to my dough without building any additional structure to support the greater expansion of steam produced by the extra water. So I made a few changes. First, I added an autolyse—a brief resting period between mixing and kneading the dough that alters the gluten-forming proteins so they can link up more effectively. Withholding sugar and salt until after the autolyse makes this little power nap even more effective, since those ingredients would otherwise slow the alteration of the proteins. Second, I waited until the second half of the kneading period— when the gluten was well established—to add the butter, since fat makes the gluten strands slippery and unable to "grab" each other to form a network. I also streamlined my method by microwaving the flour paste; roughly 60 seconds on high did the trick. And rather than wait for the hot paste to cool (so it wouldn't kill the yeast on contact), I added it to cold milk and whisked them together until the mixture was merely warm.

With those changes, my rolls were lighter and boasted a finer crumb, so I was definitely on the right track. But those gossamer-thin layers were still missing, and I wondered if altering my shaping method might help.

When dough is kneaded, the flour proteins link up in a fairly random way. Rounding each portion of dough into a tight ball, as you typically would when shaping dinner rolls, organizes the proteins on the exterior into a kind of membrane (bakers call this a "gluten cloak") but does not affect the proteins on the interior, which remain random. The Japanese milk bread's shaping method was elaborate, and now I suspected that it was the key to the bread's delicate vertical layers. To shape that loaf, I had divided the dough into four pieces, rolled each one into a rectangle, and folded each rectangle into thirds like a business letter; I then flattened each piece of dough out again and rolled it up again like a jelly roll before nestling it into the loaf pan with the others.

Because I was shaping 12 dinner rolls instead of four larger dough pieces, I tried a simplified version, flattening each piece into a long, narrow rectangle before rolling it up and placing it in the pan. When the rolls had doubled, they looked especially smooth and plump, thanks to the strong gluten development. I baked them to a deep golden brown, removed them from the pan, and brushed them with ½ tablespoon of melted butter.

When I pulled one roll from the round, it separated from the others cleanly, and I delightedly peeled away layer after delicate layer. The combined effect of the added liquid in the flour paste, the well-developed gluten, and the unusual shaping had given me the ideal dinner roll: moist, tender, and particularly fluffy. The most convincing part of all: The rolls were great the next day when I refreshed them in the oven, a real bonus when making them for a holiday dinner.

—ANDREA GEARY, *Cook's Illustrated*

Fluffy Dinner Rolls

MAKES 12 ROLLS

We strongly recommend weighing the flour for the dough. The slight tackiness of the dough aids in flattening and stretching it in step 5, so do not dust your counter with flour. This recipe requires letting the dough rest for at least 2 hours before baking. The rolls can be made a day ahead. To refresh them before serving, wrap them in aluminum foil and heat them in a 350-degree oven for 15 minutes.

FLOUR PASTE
- ½ cup water
- 3 tablespoons bread flour

DOUGH
- ½ cup cold milk
- 1 large egg
- 2 cups (11 ounces) bread flour
- 1½ teaspoons instant or rapid-rise yeast
- 2 tablespoons sugar
- 1 teaspoon salt
- 4 tablespoons unsalted butter, softened, plus ½ tablespoon, melted

NOTES FROM THE TEST KITCHEN

CREATING A LAYERED LOOK
Rolling the dough into balls causes the gluten to organize randomly and the crumb to be sponge-like. Stretching and rolling the dough into tight spirals organizes the gluten into sheets, and the rolls develop delicate, distinct layers.

1. FORM: Gently stretch and press dough into 8 by 2-inch strip.

2. ROLL: Starting at 1 end, roll strip into snug cylinder.

3. ARRANGE: Place cylinders seam side down in prepared pan.

1. **FOR THE FLOUR PASTE:** Whisk water and flour together in small bowl until no lumps remain. Microwave, whisking every 20 seconds, until mixture thickens to stiff, smooth, pudding-like consistency that forms mound when dropped from end of whisk into bowl, 40 to 80 seconds.

2. **FOR THE DOUGH:** In bowl of stand mixer, whisk flour paste and milk together until smooth. Add egg and whisk until incorporated. Add flour and yeast. Fit stand mixer with dough hook and mix on low speed until all flour is moistened, 1 to 2 minutes. Let stand for 15 minutes.

3. Add sugar and salt and mix on medium-low speed for 5 minutes. With mixer running, add softened butter, 1 tablespoon at a time. Continue to mix on medium-low speed 5 minutes longer, scraping down dough hook and sides of bowl occasionally (dough will stick to bottom of bowl).

4. Transfer dough to very lightly floured counter. Knead briefly to form ball and transfer, seam side down, to lightly greased bowl; lightly coat surface of dough with vegetable oil spray and cover with plastic wrap. Let rise until doubled in volume, about 1 hour.

5. Grease 9-inch round cake pan and set aside. Transfer dough to counter. Press dough gently but firmly to expel all air. Pat and stretch dough to form 8 by 9-inch rectangle with short side facing you. Cut dough lengthwise into 4 equal strips and cut each strip crosswise into 3 equal pieces. Working with 1 piece at a time, stretch and press dough gently to form 8 by 2-inch strip. Starting on short side, roll dough to form snug cylinder and arrange shaped rolls seam side down in prepared pan, placing 10 rolls around edge of pan, pointing inward, and remaining 2 rolls in center. Cover with plastic and let rise until doubled, 45 minutes to 1 hour.

6. When rolls are nearly doubled, adjust oven rack to lowest position and heat oven to 375 degrees. Bake rolls until deep golden brown, 25 to 30 minutes. Let rolls cool in pan on wire rack for 3 minutes; invert rolls onto rack, then reinvert. Brush tops and sides of rolls with melted butter. Let rolls cool for at least 20 minutes before serving.

DUTCH CRUNCH

WHY THIS RECIPE WORKS: The hallmarks of San Francisco's famous Dutch crunch rolls are their chewy crumb and their mottled, crackly appearance that gives rise to its signature crunch. For the dough, we opted for a simple combination of all-purpose flour, water, butter, sugar, and yeast, which produced the delicate flavor and soft texture we wanted. To make the traditional yeasted rice flour topping, we combined our ingredients and let the mixture rest before brushing it onto the risen rolls. Resting ensured the most dramatically crackled topping.

Back when I lived in San Francisco, the foundation of my daily lunch was a Dutch crunch roll. A soft, slightly sweet submarine-size roll with a distinctive mottled, crunchy top, it was the basis for nearly every sandwich I ate during those years. Since it was readily available everywhere in the city, I actually had no idea it was a regional specialty until I moved back to the East Coast and suddenly found myself unable to locate it. I realized that I was going to have to create my own recipe.

There are two parts to these sandwich rolls: the dough and the signature craggy topping. I tackled the dough first. While I wanted a soft, chewy crumb inside, the flavor of the bread needed to be unobtrusive, since the roll is merely a backdrop used to showcase sliced meats, cheeses, and other sandwich accoutrements. To achieve the right texture and flavor, I ran a long series of tests. Knowing that different flours have different protein levels that may affect the final texture, I experimented with different varieties before settling on good old all-purpose. I also tried adding an egg to the dough (common in bread recipes), but this made the final product gummy. For liquid, I tested water against milk; water won for its cleaner flavor. A few side-by-side tests led me to choose sugar over honey for a sweet component, and after testing varying amounts of melted butter, I found that 3 tablespoons contributed just the right texture and flavor.

Now that I was happy with the dough, it was time to take on this bread's real distinguishing factor, the crunchy crust. In the Netherlands, Dutch crunch is

DUTCH CRUNCH

known as *tijgerbrood,* or "tiger bread," named for the way the bread's patterned crust resembles the striped cat's coat. In England, fans often refer to it as "giraffe bread." Regardless of the name, the majority of recipes for Dutch crunch agree on the ingredients for the trademark topping: water, oil, sugar, salt, and—most important—rice flour and yeast. It's these last two ingredients that are the keys to that crunchy, mottled crust.

Just to establish what function the yeast was serving in the topping, I tried baking two batches of Dutch crunch simultaneously, one with the yeasted rice paste topping and the other with an otherwise-identical topping in which I had left out the yeast. The former had large raised blotches of browned topping in the desired giraffe pattern. The latter had a crackly coating, but it was flush with the bread's surface, and the spots were much smaller and very delicate. So the yeast was definitely in.

I played with the amount of water in the paste until I got the right texture. If the paste was too thick, it weighed down the bread and inhibited the dough from rising properly; if it was too thin, it ran down the sides of the loaves and pooled into a sticky mess on the baking sheet. I eventually found that 10 tablespoons of water created a paste that could easily be brushed onto the bread.

In the process of making loaf after loaf to test my topping, it occurred to me that the yeasted topping should really be treated, in essence, like a second bread. So for my next test, instead of just painting the paste onto the rolls and baking them immediately, I let the topping rise before applying it. Sure enough, the resulting loaves had even more dramatic patterns, and their crusts were crunchier and more flavorful than before. Through a series of tests, I settled on a 20-minute rise for the yeasted topping before applying it to the rolls and baking. Perfect.

—KATIE LEAIRD, *Cook's Country*

Dutch Crunch

MAKES 8 SANDWICH ROLLS

The topping's consistency is thick (like pancake batter); be sure to use it all. Don't worry if the topping runs down the sides of the rolls (forming a "foot" at the base of each roll) while brushing. Don't use sweet white rice flour in this recipe.

DOUGH

3½ cups (17½ ounces) all-purpose flour
1¼ cups warm water (110 degrees)
 3 tablespoons unsalted butter, melted
 4 teaspoons sugar
2¼ teaspoons instant or rapid-rise yeast
 1 teaspoon salt

TOPPING

 ½ cup plus 2 tablespoons warm water (110 degrees)
 ¾ cup (4 ounces) white rice flour
 2 tablespoons vegetable oil
 2 tablespoons sugar
2¼ teaspoons instant or rapid-rise yeast
 ½ teaspoon salt

NOTES FROM THE TEST KITCHEN

CREATING THE SIGNATURE CRACKLE

1. LAY IT ON THICK: Spoon 2 tablespoons of topping over each roll.

2. BRUSH TO COAT: Working quickly, brush to evenly coat top and sides of each roll.

1. FOR THE DOUGH: Using stand mixer fitted with dough hook, mix all ingredients together on low speed until cohesive mass starts to form, about 2 minutes. Increase speed to medium and knead until dough is smooth and elastic, 5 to 7 minutes.

2. Grease large bowl and line rimmed baking sheet with parchment paper. Turn dough onto lightly floured counter and knead briefly to form smooth ball, about 30 seconds. Transfer dough to prepared bowl and turn to coat. Cover with plastic wrap and let rise at room temperature until almost doubled in size and fingertip depression in dough springs back slowly, 1 to 1½ hours.

3. Gently press down on center of dough to deflate. Place dough on clean counter and divide into 8 equal pieces (about 3½ ounces each). Form each piece into rough ball by pinching and pulling dough edges under so that top is smooth.

4. Flip each ball onto smooth side and pat into 4-inch circle. Fold top edge of circle down to midline, pressing to seal. Fold bottom edge of circle up to meet first seam at midline and press to seal. Fold in half so top and bottom edges meet and pinch together to form seam. Flip dough seam side down and gently roll into 6-inch log. Arrange rolls into 2 staggered rows of 4 on prepared sheet; set aside to rise at room temperature until almost doubled in size, about 45 minutes. Adjust oven rack to middle position and heat oven to 400 degrees.

5. FOR THE TOPPING: Twenty-five minutes before rolls are finished rising, whisk all ingredients together in medium bowl. Cover bowl and let topping rise until doubled in size, about 20 minutes. Stir risen topping to deflate. Spoon 2 tablespoons topping over each roll and quickly brush to evenly coat top and sides.

6. Transfer sheet to oven and bake until golden brown and craggy and centers register 210 degrees, 22 to 25 minutes, rotating sheet halfway through baking. Transfer rolls to wire rack and let cool completely before serving.

CREATING THE SIGNATURE SHAPE
To form the dough into oblong sandwich rolls, start by dividing it into 8 equal pieces.

1. Form each piece into rough ball by pinching and pulling dough edges under so that top is smooth.

2. Flip each ball onto smooth side and pat into 4-inch circle.

3. Fold top edge of circle down to midline, pressing to seal. Fold bottom edge of circle to meet first seam at midline and press to seal.

4. Fold in half so top and bottom edges meet and pinch together to form seam. Flip dough seam side down. Gently roll dough into 6-inch log.

5. Arrange rolls in 2 staggered rows of 4 on prepared baking sheet.

SWEET POTATO CORNBREAD

✔ **WHY THIS RECIPE WORKS:** To ensure that our sweet potato cornbread had great flavor and a tender, not mushy, crumb, we started by precooking the potatoes in the microwave. This simple step streamlined the prep. We mashed the potatoes and whisked in the rest of our wet ingredients; incorporating the mixture into a 3:1 ratio of cornmeal to flour gave our bread the best flavor and a sturdy texture. Brown sugar provided deep complementary sweetness.

Sweet potato cornbread marries two Southern staples—sweet potatoes and cornbread—to take the latter in a colorful, flavorful new direction. But introducing cooked sweet potatoes to cornbread affects the bread's texture, and not always in a good way. I wanted sweet potato flavor and no soggy mess.

After experiments with a handful of recipes, I learned that precooking the sweet potato is a must. My test recipes varied in their precooking methods (boiling, roasting, microwaving), but I found that drier methods of cooking made it easier to control the added moisture in the cornbread. Microwaving won out for ease and efficiency. After poking each potato to allow steam to escape (I was using 1½ pounds of potatoes to start), I zapped them for about 15 minutes, flipping them every 5 minutes for even cooking. I let them cool a bit before scooping the softened flesh from the skins.

After several tests with different ratios of cornmeal and flour, I landed on 1½ cups cornmeal to just ½ cup flour for a light-yet-sturdy bread.

Tasters preferred samples made with whole milk to those with buttermilk. They also shied away from warm spices like cinnamon and nutmeg. And just ¼ cup of brown sugar helped the bread develop deeper color and enhanced the delicate sweet potato flavor.

Cast-iron cornbread is great, but I found that an ovensafe nonstick skillet was a low-fuss replacement. I melted a tablespoon of butter in the skillet until the foaming subsided (nonstick or not, fat is essential for crisp brown edges), poured in the batter, and transferred the operation to a 425-degree oven for 30 minutes. I let the cornbread cool in the pan for about an hour before sliding it from the skillet. At once crumbly and cohesive, savory and sweet, this sweet potato version—with a browned crust and brilliant orange-gold interior—was in a league of its own.

—CHRISTIE MORRISON, *Cook's Country*

Sweet Potato Cornbread
SERVES 10 TO 12

You can make this cornbread in a 10-inch cast-iron skillet or in an ovensafe nonstick skillet. Light or dark brown sugar works equally well in this recipe. Note that the cornbread needs to cool for 1 hour before being removed from the pan.

- 1½ pounds sweet potatoes, unpeeled
- ½ cup whole milk
- 8 tablespoons unsalted butter, melted, plus 1 tablespoon unsalted butter
- 4 large eggs
- 1½ cups (7½ ounces) cornmeal
- ½ cup (2½ ounces) all-purpose flour
- ¼ cup packed (1¾ ounces) brown sugar
- 1 tablespoon baking powder
- ½ teaspoon baking soda
- 1¾ teaspoons salt

1. Adjust oven rack to middle position and heat oven to 425 degrees. Prick potatoes all over with fork. Microwave on large plate until potatoes are very soft and surfaces are slightly wet, 10 to 15 minutes, flipping every 5 minutes. Immediately slice potatoes in half to release steam.

2. When potatoes are cool enough to handle, scoop flesh into bowl and mash until smooth (you should have about 1¾ cups); discard skins. Whisk in milk, melted butter, and eggs. Whisk cornmeal, flour, sugar, baking powder, baking soda, and salt together in separate large bowl. Stir sweet potato mixture into cornmeal mixture until combined.

3. Melt remaining 1 tablespoon butter in 10-inch ovensafe nonstick skillet over medium-high heat until bubbling, about 3 minutes. Swirl butter to coat bottom and sides. Pour batter into hot skillet and smooth top with rubber spatula. Bake until cornbread is golden brown and toothpick inserted in center comes out clean, 25 to 30 minutes. Let cornbread cool in skillet on wire rack for 1 hour. Loosen edges of cornbread from skillet with spatula and slide out onto cutting board. Cut into wedges and serve.

SPICY CHEESE BREAD

✔ **WHY THIS RECIPE WORKS:** This chewy, cheesy snack bread is legendary in Wisconsin, and replicating it in our kitchen was no small task. Preparing a challah-like dough for an eggy, soft bread was the easy part—our stand mixer kneaded the dough together in minutes. To get a cheese-loaded bread without bogging it down with grease, we distributed cubes of provolone and Monterey Jack cheeses and spicy red pepper flakes over the rolled-out dough after its first rise. Working with room-temperature cheese proved essential, as cold cheese hindered the dough's rise. We rolled the dough into a cylinder and then coiled the long log into a round spiral before transferring it to a greased cake pan for a second rise. A coating of beaten egg and more red pepper flakes promised a golden, spicy crust. Tenting the bread with foil for the latter half of its baking time prevented an overbrowned crust, and brushing its surface with butter just after baking ensured a soft, rich crust.

Don't be angry if you're bumped in the back when wandering through the farmers' market in Madison, Wisconsin. It is likely that the person who walked into you has his or her attention on a giant loaf of steaming, fragrant bread and is pulling off chunks and gobbling them down as he or she strolls. Stella's bakery sells dozens of loaves of their famous spicy cheese bread at the market, where the soft, sweet, chewy, cheesy, spicy snack is legendary.

Since not everyone has easy access to Stella's and the market in Madison, I set out to create a similarly delicious bread back in the test kitchen—one that took minimal active work and yielded a substantial reward. No small task.

I experimented with various breads, including brioche and country-style, but quickly settled on challah as the best. The eggy dough baked up soft, with a thin golden crust, and, as I was thrilled to discover, took just 5 minutes of kneading in a stand mixer. That's zero minutes by hand.

A much tougher nut to crack was how to add in the cheese. I wanted it to be fully incorporated, but I didn't want to lose the little bits of ooze. I started with the easiest option: simply tossing shredded cheese into the stand mixer while the bread was kneading.

Sadly, when I set the dough aside to rise, not much happened. I placed it on a baking sheet and baked it anyway. What a greasy bust that was. When incorporated this way, the cheese bogged down the dough and prevented it from rising.

I skipped the cheese on my next round and allowed the dough to rise for 2 hours on its own. Then, I rolled the rested, risen dough into an 18 by 12-inch rectangle with the long side facing the counter's edge and sprinkled cheese cubes and pepper flakes evenly over the top. I formed the dough into a tight cylinder and then gently rolled it back and forth on the counter until it measured 30 inches long. I spiraled the dough log and placed it on a baking sheet. After letting it rest and rise a second time, it baked into an even loaf with well-distributed pockets of cheese. (My tasters and I chose a combination of Monterey Jack and provolone for a mild, melty mix.)

But unfortunately the bread was too dense—nowhere near as soft and airy as the cheeseless challah that I'd baked before. I worried that I'd added too much cheese, so I dialed it back and tried again, to no avail.

On the way to the fridge to gather cheese for yet another experiment, it hit me: Yeast is most active in a warm, moist environment. Perhaps the cheese I was taking straight from the refrigerator was bringing down the temperature of the dough and inhibiting the yeast. So I let the cheese come to room temperature before adding it to the dough. Sure enough, it rose visibly more this time, and after an egg wash and a generous sprinkle of red pepper flakes (that's the spicy part), the light, chewy, stretchy bread was just right.

Except for one thing: It was losing its shape as it baked. I put together another loaf, this time baking it in a cake pan rather than on a sheet. Bingo. My spiral shape was intact, and covering it with foil halfway through its time in the oven protected the top from getting too dark and the sprinkled pepper flakes from burning.

The final step was key: A generous brush of melted butter applied shortly after the loaf came out of the oven helped the crust stay supple and gave it a shine.

—KATIE LEAIRD, *Cook's Country*

SHAPING SPICY CHEESE BREAD

Achieving an even distribution of spice and cheese takes careful shaping.

1. SPRINKLE FILLINGS: After rolling dough into rectangle, cover surface with cheese cubes and red pepper flakes.

2. ROLL INTO LOG: Starting with longer side, roll dough into tight cylinder, trapping cheese cubes inside.

3. CREATE SPIRAL: Use gentle pressure to roll dough log back and forth until it is 30 inches long. Then, create spiral shape.

4. PLACE IN PAN: Nestle spiral into greased cake pan, cover with towel, and let dough rise for 1 to 1½ hours.

5. ADD SPICE: Once dough has doubled in size, brush the top with beaten egg and sprinkle with red pepper flakes.

Spicy Cheese Bread

MAKES 1 LOAF

Take the cheese out of the refrigerator when you start the recipe to ensure that it comes to room temperature by the time you need it. Cold cheese will retard rising. The dough needs to rise for several hours before baking.

BREAD

3¼ cups (16¼ ounces) all-purpose flour

¼ cup (1¾ ounces) sugar

1 tablespoon instant or rapid-rise yeast

1½ teaspoons red pepper flakes

1¼ teaspoons salt

½ cup warm water (110 degrees)

2 large eggs plus 1 large yolk

4 tablespoons unsalted butter, melted

6 ounces Monterey Jack cheese, cut into ½-inch cubes (1½ cups), room temperature

6 ounces provolone cheese, cut into ½-inch cubes (1½ cups), room temperature

TOPPING

1 large egg, lightly beaten

1 teaspoon red pepper flakes

1 tablespoon unsalted butter, softened

1. FOR THE BREAD: Whisk flour, sugar, yeast, pepper flakes, and salt together in bowl of stand mixer. Whisk warm water, eggs and yolk, and melted butter together in liquid measuring cup. Add egg mixture to flour mixture. Fit mixer with dough hook and knead on medium speed until dough clears bottom and sides of bowl, about 8 minutes.

2. Transfer dough to unfloured counter, shape into ball, and transfer to greased bowl. Cover with plastic wrap and let rise in warm place until doubled in size, 1½ to 2 hours.

3. Grease 9-inch round cake pan. Transfer dough to unfloured counter and press to deflate. Roll dough into 18 by 12-inch rectangle with long side parallel to counter's edge. Distribute Monterey Jack and provolone evenly over dough, leaving 1-inch border around edges. Starting with edge closest to you, roll dough into log. Pinch seam and ends to seal, then roll log so seam side is down. Roll log back and forth on counter, applying gentle, even pressure, until log reaches 30 inches in length. If any tears occur, pinch to seal.

4. Starting at one end, wind log into coil; tuck end underneath coil. Place loaf in prepared cake pan and cover loosely with clean dish towel. Let rise in warm place until doubled in size, 1 to 1½ hours. Adjust oven rack to lower-middle position and heat oven to 350 degrees.

5. FOR THE TOPPING: Brush top of loaf with egg, then sprinkle with pepper flakes. Place cake pan on rimmed baking sheet. Bake until loaf is golden brown, about 25 minutes. Rotate loaf, tent with aluminum foil, and continue to bake until loaf registers 190 degrees, 25 to 30 minutes longer.

6. Transfer pan to wire rack and brush bread with butter. Let cool for 10 minutes. Run knife around edge of pan to loosen bread. Slide bread onto wire rack, using spatula as needed for support. Let cool for 30 minutes before slicing. Serve warm.

FLOURLESS NUT AND SEED LOAF

✔ **WHY THIS RECIPE WORKS:** Hoping to turn out a hearty, naturally gluten-free bread, we set our sights on a flourless nut and seed loaf. To start, we toasted the nuts and seeds to enhance their flavor. To hold the loaf together, we looked to oats to create a binding porridge. Flaxseeds and powdered psyllium husk, when hydrated, create a gel with strong binding properties, so we included them as well. For flavor, we liked the combination of sunflower seeds, sliced almonds, and pepitas; maple syrup added a subtle sweetness. Coconut oil complemented the nutty flavor of the loaf. We allowed everything to fully hydrate in the pan before baking. Baking this bread in a loaf pan did not allow for enough evaporation, so we baked it for 20 minutes to allow the outside to set before turning it out onto a wire rack set in a rimmed baking sheet and returning it to the oven for 35 to 45 minutes. After letting it cool for a few hours before cutting, we had a rich, nutty loaf perfect for snacking or toasting.

As someone who has lived gluten-free for many years, I am very aware that finding appealing flourless baked goods is a challenge. Here in the test kitchen, we defer to our own flour blends for homemade breads, cakes, and cookies with the taste and chew we love, but naturally gluten-free foods hold their own appeal. I set out to bake a hearty flourless loaf that relied on nuts and seeds for flavor and some test kitchen know-how to hold it all together. I couldn't wait to get started.

Nut and seed loaves aren't a new idea—I've spied them on every gluten-free and paleo blog I've ever visited, all hailing it as a revelation in a loaf pan, loaded with protein and fiber and full of hearty flavor. During my research, the striking photos of these loaves enticed me, revealing cross-sections of dense slices packed with toasted nuts and seeds, but what really grabbed my attention was the promise of an almost effortless recipe. Many recipes called for simply mixing ingredients together and transferring the "dough" into a pan. Indeed, these nut and seed loaves were sounding more appealing the more I read. I gathered some potential ingredients and got to work.

Existing recipes call for combinations of up to six nuts and seeds and a host of obscure binding agents, but I wanted my loaf to be on the simpler side, so I aimed for a pared-down list. Almonds boast a mild flavor and are loaded with heart-healthy fats, so they were my nut of choice. The flavor of vitamin-rich sunflower seeds paired well with the almonds, as did the subtle sweetness of pepitas. Since the nuts and seeds would be the stars of my loaf, I heightened their flavors by toasting them, streamlining this step by spreading them on a baking sheet to toast in the oven.

With my three star ingredients at the ready, I needed to settle on a binder. Considering this loaf's rustic flavor profile, I looked to powdered psyllium husk first. I've had success using this ingredient in gluten-free breads because it binds well with water, creating a strong structure. It also has an earthy flavor that would pair beautifully with the toasted nuts and seeds. But I suspected that psyllium, strong as it is, wouldn't be quite enough on its own, so I looked for reinforcements. Chia seeds came to mind because they're widely available and, when soaked, turn liquids into a dense gel. Sweet, wheat-flavored flaxseeds have a similar gelling effect and are rich with the essential fatty acid alpha-linolenic acid (ALA), an added bonus. With an eye toward enjoying my loaf for breakfast, I also gave rolled oats a shot.

I mixed and matched these binders with a few batches of the toasted nuts and seeds, and, in the end, only chia didn't cut it. While dry chia seeds are crunchy and reminiscent of poppy seeds, once soaked they took on a sweetness that seemed out of line with the other flavors. When I hydrated the flaxseeds along

FLOURLESS NUT AND SEED LOAF

with the psyllium husk, the two formed a sturdy gel and the rolled oats created a perfectly thick binding porridge. A bit of maple syrup promised a subtle sweetness to balance out the other ingredients, and melted coconut oil was an easy, flavor-enhancing substitute for vegetable oil.

To build my loaf, I combined the toasted nuts and seeds with my three binders before stirring in a mixture of water, maple syrup, and coconut oil. This large, wet mass looked nothing like any dough I'd ever seen, but that was to be expected. The binders needed to be fully hydrated to serve their purpose, so I transferred the mixture to a loaf pan and left it alone. After about 2 hours, the binders were fully hydrated and the loaf was ready to bake. After 45 minutes in a hot oven, the loaf felt firm and dry to the touch, but I was disappointed to find that it was still quite soggy on the inside. I suspected the loaf pan was hindering some of the evaporation in this densely packed mixture, but I knew the pan was necessary to help the dough hold its shape.

I decided to try a two-stage bake, allowing the surface to dry and set up in the pan for the first 20 minutes, and then tipping the partially baked loaf out onto a baking sheet to finish. After about 35 minutes, I pulled the loaf from the oven, let it cool briefly, and cut a slice—clearly too soon. The center was still steaming and my slice was slimy. I left the rest of the loaf alone for a few hours and sure enough, once it completely cooled, I was proudly serving up hearty slices of my flourless bread. With smears of butter and jam, a single slice had the makings of a simple but supersatisfying breakfast. I finally saw what those bloggers were on to—this loaf was so good, and so effortlessly gluten-free, I couldn't wait to share it.

—MEAGHEN WALSH, *America's Test Kitchen Books*

Flourless Nut and Seed Loaf

MAKES 1 LOAF

This recipe calls for an 8½ by 4½-inch loaf pan; if using a 9 by 5-inch loaf pan, the loaf will not be quite as tall. Do not use quick oats; their dusty texture doesn't work in this recipe. Make sure to buy old-fashioned rolled oats that have been processed in a gluten-free facility. Both brown and golden flaxseeds work well here. Vegetable oil or olive oil can be substituted for the coconut oil.

1 cup raw sunflower seeds
1 cup sliced almonds
½ cup raw pepitas
1¾ cups (5¼ ounces) old-fashioned rolled oats
¼ cup whole flaxseeds
3 tablespoons powdered psyllium husk
1½ cups water
3 tablespoons coconut oil, melted and cooled
2 tablespoons maple syrup
¾ teaspoon salt

1. Adjust oven rack to middle position and heat oven to 350 degrees. Combine sunflower seeds, almonds, and pepitas on rimmed baking sheet and bake, stirring occasionally, until lightly browned, 10 to 12 minutes.

2. Line bottom of 8½ by 4½-inch loaf pan with parchment paper and spray with vegetable oil spray. Transfer toasted nut-seed mixture to bowl, let cool slightly, then stir in oats, flaxseeds, and psyllium. In separate bowl, whisk water, coconut oil, maple syrup, and salt together until well combined. Using rubber spatula, stir water mixture into nut-seed mixture until completely incorporated.

3. Scrape mixture into prepared pan. Using your wet hands, press dough into corners and smooth top. Cover loosely with plastic wrap and let sit at room temperature until mixture is fully hydrated and cohesive, about 2 hours.

4. Adjust oven rack to middle position and heat oven to 350 degrees. Remove plastic and bake loaf for 20 minutes.

5. Invert loaf onto wire rack set in rimmed baking sheet. Remove loaf pan and discard parchment. Bake loaf (still inverted) until deep golden brown and loaf sounds hollow when tapped, 35 to 45 minutes.

6. Let loaf cool completely on rack, about 2 hours. Serve. (Loaf can be stored at room temperature, uncovered, for up to 3 days; do not wrap. It can also be wrapped in double layer of plastic and frozen for up to 1 month.)

WHOLE-GRAIN GLUTEN-FREE BROWN SUGAR COOKIES

✓ **WHY THIS RECIPE WORKS:** Featuring slightly crisp edges, chewy centers, and toffee-like sweetness, brown sugar cookies offer a sophisticated alternative to their white sugar cousins. To make our cookies gluten-free while also heightening their deep, nutty flavor, we used our own whole-grain gluten-free flour blend which includes teff flour, brown rice flour, ground golden flaxseeds, and sweet rice flour for a flavor, color, and texture similar to whole-wheat flour. Fully hydrating the cookie dough eliminated grittiness and dryness in the cookies, and adding plenty of butter kept them nice and chewy. We rolled the dough into balls and tossed them in sugar to give them a sweet, crisp coating. Pulling the cookies out of the oven when the edges were just barely set also helped keep them chewy.

There is a time and place for classic sugar cookies, but sometimes I want a treat with a little more depth. Brown sugar cookies are a sophisticated upgrade, boasting sweet toffee flavor with the same appealing chew. Sugar cookies may seem simple, but getting the right chewy-meets-crispy texture can be a challenge. When you're baking with gluten-free flours, that challenge is even greater.

Using the ATK Whole-Grain Gluten-Free Flour Blend seemed like a surefire way to deliver deep, nutty flavors to back up the brown sugar. For my first batch, I followed the traditional creaming method (whipping softened butter with sugar until it's fluffy, beating in an egg, and then adding the dry ingredients), but unfortunately this old standby produced cakey, overly tender cookies. Melting the butter worked better—these cookies had a texture much closer to what I was after—but they were still a little too soft and cakey for my taste. I wanted more chew. In traditional recipes, the gluten structure would contribute to that dense, chewy texture, but in the absence of wheat flour, I would need to figure out a different route. After a little research, I landed on xanthan gum, a go-to ingredient in gluten-free baking that helps strengthen the protein network, creating elasticity and chewiness. Adding just a small amount into the dry ingredients delivered the texture I was looking for. Adding an extra yolk further improved the cookies' structure and boosted the dough's richness.

The deep, molasses-y flavors of dark brown sugar beat out mellower light brown, making it possible to sweeten the cookies without adding a ton of sugar. Vanilla extract and a healthy dose of salt balanced the sweetness and accentuated the nuances of the brown sugar. After experimenting with varying amounts of baking powder and baking soda, I found that ½ teaspoon of baking powder and ¼ teaspoon of baking soda gave my cookies a nice, tight crumb and a craggy top.

My structural fixes produced a great-looking batch of cookies, but when I bit into one, the downside of my new flour blend reared its ugly head: Even though my cookies had a chewy softness to them, they were still unappealingly gritty. This problem was an easy fix, though. For the next batch, after mixing everything together, I let the dough rest for a good 30 minutes. This waiting period was just enough time for my hearty flour blend to hydrate and soften. Underbaking the cookies just slightly—removing them from the oven as soon as the edges had begun to set—offered an added layer of textural insurance. This batch baked up chewy and subtly sweet, but my tasters were clamoring for even more brown sugar flavor. Rolling the balls of dough in brown sugar seemed like the answer, but this sugar's tendency to clump made this step a chore. Combining it with granulated sugar and breaking apart any clumps ahead of time made it much easier.

At long last, I had my grown-up take on a lunch box favorite, and the fact that it was gluten-free didn't stop anyone from reaching for seconds. These cookies had a deep, sophisticated sweetness, a perfectly chewy crumb, and a crisp sugar crust that was impossible to resist.

—STEPHANIE PIXLEY, *America's Test Kitchen Books*

Whole-Grain Gluten-Free Brown Sugar Cookies

MAKES 24 COOKIES

Do not substitute other whole-grain blends for the ATK Whole-Grain Gluten-Free Flour Blend; they will not work in this recipe. The xanthan can be omitted, but the cookies will spread more and will be less chewy. Do not shortchange the dough's 30-minute rest or the cookies will spread more and taste gritty. To make these cookies dairy free, substitute vegetable oil for butter, and unsweetened soy or almond milk for milk. Do not use rice milk.

ROLLING SUGAR
¼ cup packed dark brown sugar

¼ cup granulated sugar

COOKIES
10½ ounces (2⅓ cups) ATK Whole-Grain Gluten-Free Flour Blend (recipe follows)

½ teaspoon salt

½ teaspoon baking soda

¼ teaspoon baking powder

¼ teaspoon xanthan gum

10½ ounces (1½ cups packed) dark brown sugar

14 tablespoons unsalted butter, melted and cooled

1 large egg plus 1 large yolk

1 tablespoon milk

1 tablespoon vanilla extract

1. FOR THE ROLLING SUGAR: Combine sugars in shallow dish and crumble with your fingers until no large clumps remain; set aside to dry out.

2. FOR THE COOKIES: Whisk flour blend, salt, baking soda, baking powder, and xanthan gum together in medium bowl. In large bowl, whisk sugar and melted butter until sugar dissolves and no lumps remain. Whisk in egg and yolk, milk, and vanilla until mixture is very smooth and glossy. Stir in flour mixture with rubber spatula until dough is completely homogeneous. Cover bowl with plastic wrap and let dough rest for 30 minutes. (Dough will be sticky and soft.)

3. Adjust oven rack to middle position and heat oven to 350 degrees. Line 3 baking sheets with parchment paper. Working with 2 tablespoons of dough at a time, roll dough into balls and drop into rolling sugar. Coat each dough ball with sugar and space 2½ inches apart on prepared sheets.

4. Bake cookies, 1 sheet at a time, until edges have begun to set but centers are still soft (cookies will look raw between cracks and seem underdone), 12 to 14 minutes, rotating sheet halfway through baking.

5. Let cookies cool on sheet for 5 minutes, then transfer to wire rack. Serve warm or at room temperature. (Cookies can be stored in airtight container at room temperature for up to 1 day.)

ATK Whole-Grain Gluten-Free Flour Blend
MAKES 45 OUNCES (ABOUT 10 CUPS)

We had the best results using Bob's Red Mill brown rice flour and sweet white rice flour. We used Flax USA 100% Natural Flax, Cold Milled Ground Golden Flax Seed during our testing. We don't recommend using Bob's Red Mill ground golden flaxseeds because they are too coarsely ground and will taste gritty in the baked goods. Do not substitute ground brown flaxseeds because their flavor will be too strong. Do not attempt to grind flaxseeds yourself because you will not be able to grind them fine enough. Be sure to bring flour to room temperature before using.

24 ounces (5¼ cups) teff flour

8 ounces (1¾ cups) brown rice flour

8 ounces (2⅓ cups) ground golden flaxseeds

5 ounces (1 cup) sweet white rice flour

Whisk all ingredients in large bowl until well combined. Transfer to airtight container and refrigerate for up to 3 months or freeze for up to 6 months. Bring to room temperature before using.

BUILDING OUR WHOLE-GRAIN BLEND

Inspired by the success of our ATK All-Purpose Gluten-Free Flour Blend (page 220), we set out to create a whole-grain blend that loosely mimicked the flavor, color, and texture of whole-wheat flour. We set a few parameters: We wanted to use five ingredients or less, we didn't want to include any binders such as xanthan or guar gum, and we wanted to keep the blend as allergen-friendly as possible, avoiding nuts, milk powder, oat flour, and potato starch. Finally, we wanted whole-grain flours to make up more than 50 percent of our blend. After baking dozens of muffins using combinations of amaranth, brown rice, millet, sorghum, and teff, we eliminated sorghum, millet, and amaranth from the running—the sorghum consistently made muffins taste dry and tough, while the millet and amaranth added an unwelcome aftertaste and a grainy texture.

As we moved through more focused rounds of testing, teff flour consistently came out on top for its hearty chew, darker color, and wheat-like flavor. Brown rice flour also ranked well because its mild flavor and texture smoothed out the rough edges of the teff. Working with a ratio of 3 parts teff flour to 1 part brown rice flour, we put starch under the spotlight and tasted muffins made with tapioca starch, arrowroot, sweet white rice flour, and cornstarch. Tasters unanimously preferred the clean flavor and smooth texture of sweet white rice flour over the others, so we settled on 3 parts teff flour and 1 part brown rice flour to ⅔ part sweet white rice flour. Ground golden flaxseeds added a well-rounded, wheaty flavor and richness. After 126 tests and more muffins than any one person could consume in a year, we were finally confident we had the perfect whole-grain blend.

GLUTEN-FREE PEANUT BUTTER SANDWICH COOKIES

✓ **WHY THIS RECIPE WORKS:** To create a gluten-free peanut butter sandwich cookie that was packed with peanut flavor, we started with our homemade all-purpose gluten-free flour blend. Cutting the flour with chopped peanuts provided lots of flavor and prevented our cookies from becoming cakey. To get the best texture, we used extra leavener so that the cookies would puff and then collapse in the oven. Resting the batter before portioning and baking the cookies hydrated the flour, staving off a gritty texture, and adding xanthan gum kept them from spreading too thin. A simple filling made with peanut butter, butter, and confectioners' sugar offered a rich, creamy counterpoint to the crunchy cookies. We microwaved the filling before spooning it onto the cookies, which made spreading easy.

To a peanut butter obsessive like me, that distinguishing crosshatch on top of a traditional peanut butter cookie feels like a cheat, allowing flavorless cookies to parade under the peanut butter title. And when it comes to the gluten-free variety, recipes for crumbly, gritty cookies prevail. I wanted a straightforward gluten-free cookie, and I didn't want to shortchange the peanut flavor just because I wasn't using a traditional flour.

Traditional or gluten-free, many peanut butter cookies suffer the same fate: The raw dough has more peanut flavor than the baked cookies. This is because in the presence of heat, the starch granules in flour soak up peanut flavor molecules like a sponge, reducing their aroma and limiting their ability to interact with our taste buds. As I mulled over this fact, it occurred to me that a sandwich cookie—that is, two peanut butter cookies enclosing a filling made primarily with uncooked (read: full-flavored) peanut butter—might be the ideal delivery system for the strong flavor that I craved.

The cookies themselves would have to be quite thin and flat (so you could comfortably eat two of them sandwiched with filling) as well as crunchy, to contrast with the creamy center. As for that smooth filling, it had to be substantial enough that it wouldn't squish out the sides of the cookies with each bite. I also wanted my cookies to have the simplicity of a drop cookie: no chilling of the dough, no slicing, no rolling, and no cutting.

Because a good sandwich cookie is all about balanced flavors and textures, I knew that the filling would influence my cookie and vice versa. I chose to start with the filling since it would be simpler. Most recipes call for blending peanut butter and confectioners' sugar (granulated sugar remains too gritty and doesn't provide much thickening power) with a creamy element, such as butter, cream cheese, heavy cream, or even marshmallow crème. I settled on butter, which provided the silkiest consistency and allowed for the purest peanut butter flavor. I softened 3 tablespoons of butter with ¾ cup of creamy peanut butter in the microwave and then, to keep the peanut flavor in the forefront, stirred in a modest ½ cup of confectioners' sugar.

This filling tasted great, but it was far too soft, squirting out from my placeholder cookies as soon as I pressed them together. To thicken things up, I ultimately found that I had to double the sugar amount, making for a very sweet filling. For a perfectly balanced whole, I would have to counter the filling with significantly less sweet cookies.

Setting the filling aside, I stirred together a dough using our ATK All-Purpose Gluten-Free Flour Blend and a good scoop of peanut butter. After portioning the dough and baking it, I had cookies that weren't bad for a first try, offering just the right degree of sweetness to complement the sugary filling. But they were too thick and soft. I wanted more spread, more crunch, and—if I could pack it in—more peanut flavor.

My first change was to scrap one of the two eggs I was using (they contribute protein that traps air and makes baked goods cakey), replacing it with 3 tablespoons of milk to keep the cookies from drying out. But I knew that other factors also influence how much cookie dough will spread in the oven: sugar (more sugar equals more spread) and moisture level (more moisture leads to a looser dough that spreads more readily). I'd already established that I couldn't make the dough any sweeter, so my only option was to increase the moisture level by cutting back on flour. Since my goal was also a supernutty-tasting cookie, I decided to replace a full cup of the

GLUTEN-FREE PEANUT BUTTER SANDWICH COOKIES

flour blend with finely chopped peanuts, which would absorb far less moisture as well as add welcome crunch and peanut flavor. These changes helped, but the cookies still weren't spreading enough.

What would happen if I took out all of the flour? Flourless peanut butter cookie recipes abound, and I'd always been curious about them. I eliminated the flour and, to my surprise, found that the resulting cookies were not that much thinner or flatter, though they tasted great. Unfortunately, they were also far too crumbly. I added flour back incrementally, finding that a ratio of just over ¾ cup flour blend to the ½ cup of peanut butter and 1¼ cups of finely chopped peanuts created relatively thin, nutty-tasting cookies that were still sturdy enough to serve as a vehicle for the filling. I knew from previous experience with gluten-free baking that my blend would yield a gritty cookie if not properly hydrated, but that was an easy fix: Leaving the dough to rest for 30 minutes allowed the blend to fully hydrate and soften. Finally, to get them thinner, I relied on brute force: After portioning the dough on the baking sheet, I used my wet hand to squash it into even 2-inch rounds.

ATK All-Purpose Gluten-Free Flour Blend
MAKES 42 OUNCES (ABOUT 9⅓ CUPS)

We had the best results using Bob's Red Mill white rice flour and brown rice flour. Be sure to use potato starch, not potato flour. Alternatively, 7 ounces (1¼ cups plus 2 tablespoons) sweet white rice flour, or 7 ounces (1¾ cups) arrowroot starch/flour/powder can be substituted for the potato starch. Tapioca starch is also sold as tapioca flour; they are interchangeable. You can omit the milk powder, but the cookies won't brown as well and they will taste less rich. Alternatively, you can substitute soy milk powder. Bring the flour to room temperature before using.

- **24** ounces (4½ cups plus ⅓ cup) white rice flour
- **7½** ounces (1⅔ cups) brown rice flour
- **7** ounces (1⅓ cups) potato starch
- **3** ounces (¾ cup) tapioca starch
- **¾** ounce (3 tablespoons) nonfat milk powder

Whisk all ingredients in large bowl until well combined. Transfer to airtight container and refrigerate for up to 3 months or freeze for up to 6 months. Bring to room temperature before using.

I was almost there, but I had one final trick up my sleeve: tinkering with the baking soda. In other cookie recipes, we have found that adding extra soda causes the bubbles within the dough to inflate so rapidly that they burst before the cookies set, leaving the cookies flatter than they would be with less soda. A mere ¼ teaspoon of baking soda would be sufficient to leaven the ¾ cup of flour in my recipe; when I quadrupled that amount to a full teaspoon, the cookies quickly puffed up in the oven and then deflated. Voilà: greater spread, just as I had hoped. In addition, these cookies boasted a coarser, more open crumb, which provided extra routes through which moisture could escape. This left the cookies even crunchier—a better foil for the creamy filling.

With my creamy, peanutty filling and ultracrunchy cookies ready to go, it was time to put the two components together. But on my first few maddening attempts, the cookies shattered into pieces as I tried to spread the firm filling. I resisted the urge to loosen the filling with more butter, lest it squish out from between the cookies, making the package impossible to eat with any degree of decorum. Then I realized that it was a matter of timing: If I prepared the filling right before assembly, it could be easily scooped and pressed between the cookies while it was still warm from the microwave—no painstaking spreading necessary—after which it would cool and set to an ideal firm texture. At last, I had a gluten-free cookie with a simple, understated appearance that delivered the powerful peanut wallop promised (but rarely provided) by those pretenders sporting the traditional fork marks.

—SARA MAYER, *America's Test Kitchen Books*

Gluten-Free Peanut Butter Sandwich Cookies
MAKES 24 SANDWICH COOKIES

Using salted peanut butter is important; do not use unsalted peanut butter for this recipe. You can substitute King Arthur Gluten-Free Multi-Purpose Flour (4 ounces equals ¾ cup) or Betty Crocker All-Purpose Gluten Free Rice Blend (4 ounces equals ½ cup plus ⅓ cup). Cookies made with Betty Crocker will taste similar, but the dough will be soft, wet, and more difficult to handle. Xanthan gum is crucial to the structure of the cookies. Do not shortchange the dough's 30-minute rest or the cookies will spread more and taste gritty. To make these cookies dairy free, substitute vegetable oil for butter, and unsweetened soy or almond milk for milk. Do not use rice milk.

COOKIES

1¼ cups unsalted dry-roasted peanuts

4 ounces (¾ cup plus 2 tablespoons) ATK All-Purpose Gluten-Free Flour Blend (page 220)

1 teaspoon baking soda

½ teaspoon salt

¼ teaspoon xanthan gum

3 tablespoons unsalted butter, melted

½ cup creamy peanut butter

3½ ounces (½ cup) granulated sugar

3½ ounces (½ cup packed) light brown sugar

3 tablespoons whole milk

1 large egg

FILLING

¾ cup creamy peanut butter

3 tablespoons unsalted butter

3 ounces (¾ cup) confectioners' sugar

1. FOR THE COOKIES: Pulse peanuts in food processor until finely chopped, about 8 pulses. Whisk flour blend, baking soda, salt, and xanthan gum together in bowl. In separate bowl, whisk butter, peanut butter, granulated sugar, brown sugar, milk, and egg together. Stir flour mixture into peanut butter mixture with rubber spatula until combined. Stir in peanuts until evenly distributed. Cover bowl with plastic wrap and let dough rest for 30 minutes.

2. Adjust oven racks to upper-middle and lower-middle positions and heat oven to 350 degrees. Line 2 baking sheets with parchment paper. Working with half of dough, keeping other half covered, scoop out 2 heaping teaspoons of dough, roll into balls, and space 3 inches apart on prepared sheets; dough will be very sticky. Using your damp hands, press dough balls into 2-inch cookies. Repeat with remaining dough.

3. Bake cookies until deep golden brown and firm to touch, 12 to 15 minutes, switching and rotating sheets halfway through baking. Let cookies cool on sheets for 5 minutes, then transfer to wire rack and let cool completely before assembling.

4. FOR THE FILLING: Microwave peanut butter and butter until melted and warm, about 40 seconds. Stir in confectioners' sugar until combined.

5. While filling is warm, place 24 cookies upside down on counter. Place 1 tablespoon filling in center of each cookie. Top each with one of remaining cookies, right side up, and press gently until filling spreads to edges. Let filling set for 1 hour before serving. (Assembled cookies can be stored in airtight container for up to 3 days.)

ULTRANUTTY PECAN BARS

✔ **WHY THIS RECIPE WORKS:** For a streamlined pecan bar recipe that put the nuts center stage, we cut back on sweetness and increased the amount of pecans to a full pound. Toasting the nuts brought out their rich flavor, and tossing them with a thick uncooked glaze of corn syrup, brown sugar, and melted butter promised deep caramel notes without muting the pecans' flavor. We prepared an easy press-in crust reminiscent of buttery shortbread and simply scooped the filling over it; we found that we could skip parbaking the crust by baking the bars on the lowest rack in the oven. A final sprinkling of sea salt balanced out the caramel flavor in these bars.

Most pecan bars take their cue from pecan pie, with a single layer of nuts dominated by a thick, gooey, ultrasweet filling sitting atop a pat-in-the-pan crust. I'm not opposed to that style, but it's mainly about the filling and only a little about the nuts. As a lover of nuts (pecans especially), I've always thought it would be great to have a bar that emphasized the star ingredient, especially as a choice for a holiday cookie tray.

The closest I've come are recipes that ditch the rich, egg-based custard in favor of a toffee-like topping. These call for heating sugar and butter together until thickened, stirring in the nuts, and spreading the mixture over a parbaked crust before popping it into the oven. But when I tried a few such approaches, I found that the resulting bars still had a one-note sweetness that distracted from the pecans—and there were never enough pecans in the first place. My ideal was a pecan bar featuring a buttery crust piled high with nuts held in place not by a filling, per se, but by a not-too-sweet glaze whose only jobs were to enhance the flavor of the pecans and glue them to the crust. For that kind of a bar, I was on my own.

I started with a placeholder crust, a food processor–blended mixture of flour, sugar, salt, and cold butter that I borrowed from our archives and scaled up to fit a 13 by 9-inch pan (you can never have too many cookies on hand during the holidays). I patted the sandy dough into the pan and parbaked it for 20 minutes at 350 degrees until the crust was light brown—standard procedure to prevent a wet filling from seeping in and making it soggy.

Since I wanted a topping that was all about the nuts, I wondered what would happen if I simply tossed the pecans with corn syrup, which is one-third less sweet than granulated sugar, before spreading them over the crust. I tried this, stirring ½ cup into a relatively modest 2 cups of chopped pecans, which I toasted first to enhance their rich flavor. But it was a bust, as the corn syrup's flat taste did nothing to bring out the flavor of the nuts, and now the bar wasn't sweet enough overall. Next, I experimented with maple syrup, thinking its caramel-like flavors might complement the pecans, heating it with some butter to cut some of the sweetness and bring extra nuttiness to the glaze. Its flavors matched nicely with the pecans, but the syrup dried out and crystallized in the oven, making the topping crusty with an unappealing matte finish. Honey didn't work either. Though it produced a moist, glossy, slightly chewy topping that my tasters liked for its texture, its prominent flavor was a distraction from the pecans. Ultimately, I landed on a combination of corn syrup and brown sugar, the latter's molasses-like notes a good match for the pecans. I heated ½ cup of corn syrup and ¾ cup of brown sugar with 7 tablespoons of butter on the stove until the mixture was bubbly and syrupy; I then took the glaze off the heat and stirred in vanilla extract to add complexity, followed by the pecans. This glaze had a lot going for it: It was glossy

and stayed slightly moist and chewy in the oven. But its sweetness still dominated the pecans. I wondered if I could fix that simply by increasing the amount of nuts, which had been my goal anyway.

I upped the nuts from 2 cups to 3 cups and left them in halves, which gave them a more impressive presence. This worked so well to offset the glaze's sweetness that I added another cup. The nuts were now the main event of the topping, enhanced but not overpowered by the glaze. There was another bonus: With this many pecans, the nuts did not sit neatly in a single layer on the crust but were more haphazardly layered on top of one another, allowing for a variety of textures—some nuts were chewy, sitting directly in a slick of glaze, while those sitting on the very top were crisp.

With the topping settled, I turned my attention back to the crust. I'd been using the food processor to cut the cold butter into the flour, but it occurred to me that there was an even easier crust I could use. In our French apple tart recipe, we make an easy press-in crust using melted butter instead of chilled, stirring it right into the dry ingredients. Buttery and sturdy, this shortbread-like crust was ideal for the pecan topping and a snap to make.

I had an additional thought: Now that the topping was barely wet at all, did I even need to parbake the crust? I tried skipping this step, spreading the hot topping over the unbaked crust and baking it for 20 minutes. When I turned the bars out of the pan, I found that the bottom of the crust was still pale and slightly pliable. Baking the bars on the bottom rack and for a little longer produced a crust that was evenly golden, but it also created a new problem: Since the bars were closer to the heat source, more moisture was evaporating from the topping, which was getting crunchy and brittle in parts, especially at the edges.

Up until now I had been boiling the glaze on the stove before adding the nuts. If I didn't do that, I thought, maybe enough moisture would stay in the glaze to keep the topping more pliable. Plus, it would make the recipe even quicker. It was worth trying.

For my next test, I combined the brown sugar, corn syrup, vanilla, and salt in a bowl. I melted the butter separately and then stirred it, piping hot, into the mixture so the sugar would melt, continuing to stir until the mixture was homogeneous and glossy. But it was so thick that after I stirred in the nuts, there was no question of spreading it evenly across the crust. All I could do was push it to the edges as best I could, leaving patches of crust bare. I was sure this was a dead end, but as I watched the bars cook, I could see the thick brown sugar mixture begin to melt. After 25 minutes, the topping was bubbling across the crust, and all the empty spots were completely coated.

Once the bars were cooled, I turned them out of the pan. They were golden brown on the bottom, with a glossy, even sheen on top. I trimmed the edges to neaten them up and cut them into squares. The bars were chewy and moist, not overly sweet, and loaded with pecans. For a final touch, I sprinkled the bars with flake sea salt as they came out of the oven.

—ANNIE PETITO, *Cook's Illustrated*

Ultranutty Pecan Bars

MAKES 24 BARS

It is important to use pecan halves, not pieces. The edges of the bars will be slightly firmer than the center. If desired, trim ¼ inch from the edges before cutting into bars. Toast the pecans on a rimmed baking sheet in a 350-degree oven until fragrant, 8 to 12 minutes, shaking the sheet halfway through toasting.

CRUST

1¾ cups (8¾ ounces) all-purpose flour
 6 tablespoons (2⅔ ounces) sugar
 ½ teaspoon salt
 8 tablespoons unsalted butter, melted

TOPPING

 ¾ cup packed (5¼ ounces) light brown sugar
 ½ cup light corn syrup
 7 tablespoons unsalted butter, melted and hot
 1 teaspoon vanilla extract
 ½ teaspoon salt
 4 cups (1 pound) pecan halves, toasted
 ½ teaspoon flake sea salt (optional)

1. FOR THE CRUST: Adjust oven rack to lowest position and heat oven to 350 degrees. Make foil sling for 13 by 9-inch baking pan by folding 2 long sheets of aluminum foil; first sheet should be 13 inches wide and second sheet should be 9 inches wide. Lay sheets of foil in pan perpendicular to each other, with extra foil hanging over edges of pan. Push foil into corners and up sides of pan, smoothing foil flush to pan. Lightly spray foil with vegetable oil spray.

2. Whisk flour, sugar, and salt together in medium bowl. Add melted butter and stir with wooden spoon until dough begins to form. Using your hands, continue to combine until no dry flour remains and small portion of dough holds together when squeezed in palm of your hand. Evenly scatter tablespoon-size pieces of dough over surface of pan. Using your fingertips and palm of your hand, press and smooth dough into even thickness in bottom of pan.

3. FOR THE TOPPING: Whisk sugar, corn syrup, melted butter, vanilla, and salt together in medium bowl until smooth (mixture will look separated at first but will become homogeneous), about 20 seconds. Fold pecans into sugar mixture until nuts are evenly coated.

4. Pour topping over crust. Using spatula, spread topping over crust, pushing to edges and into corners (there will be bare patches). Bake until topping is evenly distributed and rapidly bubbling across entire surface, 23 to 25 minutes.

5. Transfer pan to wire rack and lightly sprinkle with flake sea salt, if using. Let bars cool completely in pan on rack, about 1½ hours. Using foil overhang, lift bars out of pan and transfer to cutting board. Cut into 24 bars. (Bars can be stored at room temperature for up to 5 days.)

NOTES FROM THE TEST KITCHEN

STREAMLINING PECAN TOPPING

We skipped the step of heating the topping on the stovetop, instead combining the ingredients off the heat and spreading the thick mixture over the crust. The topping melted during baking, distributing itself evenly over the crust.

WHOLE-GRAIN GLUTEN-FREE CARROT CUPCAKES

WHOLE-GRAIN GLUTEN-FREE CARROT CUPCAKES

✓ **WHY THIS RECIPE WORKS:** We set out to transform an old-time favorite, classic carrot cake, into a gluten-free cupcake. We wanted a tender, open crumb and slightly domed tops—which can be quite challenging in gluten-free baked goods. We started with our whole-grain gluten-free flour blend because we thought that its earthy flavor would pair well with the natural sweetness of carrots. Using both white and brown sugars promised cupcakes with balanced sweetness and deep toffee-like notes to complement the nutty flour blend. Thinning the batter with some milk loosened it up for taller, more tender cupcakes. Shredded carrots tend to shed their liquid during baking, so to prevent soggy cakes we stirred the carrots into the batter and then let it rest for 30 minutes. A good stir incorporated the moisture into the batter. Lush cream cheese frosting is carrot cake's classic finishing touch, and we kept ours simple. After combining cream cheese, butter, sour cream, and vanilla, we incorporated a cup of confectioners' sugar for a balance of sweetness and tang.

In the hierarchy of cakes, carrot cake falls squarely in the dump-and-stir camp, typically baked in a 13 by 9-inch pan and topped off with a generous smear of vanilla or cream cheese frosting. This humble snack cake has always been a favorite of mine, its moist crumb and spiced, subtly sweet carrot flavor routinely beating out every other dessert on the table. I wanted to turn this classic sheet cake into an individual-sized treat I could share with my friends, including those avoiding gluten, so I readied the test kitchen's two gluten-free blends and headed into the kitchen.

Most carrot cake recipes follow a simple formula: Flour, baking powder, salt, cinnamon, and nutmeg are whisked together in one bowl, and eggs, brown sugar, vanilla extract, and vegetable oil (oil, not butter, is almost always used) in another. Shredded carrots are folded into the wet ingredients with any number of crunchy mix-ins before the dry ingredients are added and the cake is baked for upwards of 35 minutes (the carrots add moisture so the cake requires a longer baking time). Since cupcakes meant baking cakes on a smaller scale, I nixed the nuts and raisins right off the bat—the shredded carrots would offer enough textural interest on their own. For the flour, I had a choice between the gluten-free all-purpose blend,

which mimics white flour, and our recently developed whole-grain blend. Since I was eliminating nuts from the batter, the whole-grain blend seemed like the clear choice—its naturally nutty flavor would add an earthy dimension to the cupcakes, and it would play well with the nutmeg, cinnamon, and brown sugar. I prepared my first batter, mixing the dry ingredients and shredded carrots into the wet ingredients, portioned it out into a muffin tin lined with paper liners, and slid the tin into the oven.

After 20 minutes of baking, it was clear this simple recipe needed some extra attention. Because the cupcakes required less baking time than a traditional cake, the carrot shreds hadn't had a chance to soften. They had, however, shed a good deal of liquid into the cakes, leaving them soggy in the middle even as the surfaces began to overbrown. I needed to take a closer look at the carrots, so I ran a couple more tests.

Hoping to tackle the excess moisture head on, my first instinct was to dry the shredded carrots with a quick spin in the microwave. No dice: The batch I baked with microwaved shreds turned out unpalatably dry cupcakes. Next I tried approaching from the opposite angle, working the carrots into the batter so the exuded liquid became part of the mixture itself. In two separate tests, I used pureed carrots and then finely ground carrots, but both disappeared into the batter, leaving the star of the dessert unidentifiable. I didn't want crunchy carrots, but I did like the orange streaks against the toffee-colored crumb.

I decided to give shredded carrots another shot. Hoping to use the exuded moisture to my cupcakes' benefit, in this round I let the batter rest after stirring in the dry ingredients and carrots. Before portioning, I gave the batter a stir, incorporating the carrots' liquid into the mixture. This batch was the closest to perfect so far: The crumb was moist, not sodden, and the carrot shreds were visible but tender.

The final sticking points: Without gluten's binding proteins, my cupcakes were a little too crumbly, and my whole-grain blend's earthy flavors were overpowering the brown sugar's sweetness—my cupcakes were veering towards hearty when I wanted them to be understatedly sweet.

These were easy fixes. For my final batch, I added a hefty scoop of granulated sugar to reinforce the more subtle brown sugar. This switch also tightened the crumb while the remaining brown sugar still kept the cake moist. To perfect the cupcakes' texture, I also added a small amount of xanthan gum to the dry ingredients—a go-to in gluten-free baking for adding lift and gluten-like elasticity. To ensure a more open, tender crumb, I also thinned the batter slightly by adding a few tablespoons of milk to the wet ingredients. At last, these cupcakes had it all: The bright, sweet carrots perfectly complemented the nutty whole-grain and molassesy brown sugar flavors. Paired with a moist, fragrantly spiced crumb, these cupcakes were ready to take their place on the dessert tray—all that remained was a complementary frosting to top them off.

The simple, sophisticated sweetness of my carrot cupcakes called for an indulgent finishing touch, and cream cheese frosting seemed like just the ticket. Since I'd upped the sweetness in the cake, I decided to double down on tang here, beating softened butter and a tablespoon of sour cream into cream cheese. A touch of vanilla and salt rounded out the flavor before I gradually added in plenty of confectioners' sugar for a smooth, airy frosting. I piped the frosting onto my cooled cupcakes and called in my tasters. Their reaction was unanimous: Gluten-free or not, these cupcakes were a hit—sweet carrot flavor, nutty complexity, a perfectly moist crumb, and an irresistible sweet-meets-tangy frosting.

—AMANDA RUMORE, *America's Test Kitchen Books*

Whole-Grain Gluten-Free Carrot Cupcakes

MAKES 12 CUPCAKES

Do not substitute other whole-grain blends for the ATK Whole-Grain Gluten-Free Flour Blend; they will not work in this recipe. The xanthan can be omitted, but the cupcakes will be more crumbly. Do not short-change the batter's 30-minute rest or the cupcakes will taste wet and mushy. To make the cupcakes dairy free, substitute unsweetened soy milk or almond milk for milk. Do not use rice milk.

- 7½ ounces (1⅔ cups) ATK Whole-Grain Gluten-Free Flour Blend (page 217)
- 1 teaspoon baking powder
- ½ teaspoon baking soda
- ¼ teaspoon ground nutmeg
- ¼ teaspoon salt
- ⅛ teaspoon xanthan gum
- ⅛ teaspoon ground cinnamon
  Pinch ground cloves
- 3½ ounces (½ cup) granulated sugar
- 1¾ ounces (¼ cup packed) light brown sugar
- 2 large eggs
- 3 tablespoons 1 or 2 percent low-fat milk
- ⅓ cup vegetable oil
- 8 ounces carrots, peeled and shredded (1½ cups)
- 1 recipe Cream Cheese Frosting (recipe follows)

1. Whisk flour blend, baking powder, baking soda, nutmeg, salt, xanthan gum, cinnamon, and cloves together in bowl.

2. In separate bowl, whisk granulated sugar, brown sugar, eggs, milk, and oil until thoroughly combined. Using rubber spatula, stir in shredded carrots and flour blend mixture until thoroughly incorporated. Cover bowl with plastic wrap and let batter rest at room temperature for 30 minutes.

3. Adjust oven rack to middle position and heat oven to 350 degrees. Line 12-cup muffin tin with paper liners. Stir batter to recombine and portion evenly into prepared muffin tin. Bake until toothpick inserted in center of cupcakes comes out clean, 18 to 22 minutes, rotating muffin tin halfway through baking.

4. Let cupcakes cool in muffin tin for 10 minutes, then transfer to wire rack and let cool completely, about 1 hour. (Unfrosted cupcakes can be stored in airtight container at room temperature for up to 1 day.) Spread or pipe frosting onto cupcakes before serving.

Cream Cheese Frosting

MAKES ABOUT 2 CUPS

Do not substitute low-fat or nonfat cream cheese in this recipe; they will make the frosting soupy. If the frosting becomes too soft to work with, refrigerate it until firm. To make a vanilla bean frosting (with specks of vanilla), substitute seeds from 1 small vanilla bean for vanilla extract. To make this frosting dairy free, use dairy-free cream cheese and dairy-free sour cream; substitute Earth Balance Vegan Buttery Sticks for butter.

8 ounces cream cheese, softened

5 tablespoons unsalted butter, softened

1 tablespoon sour cream

¾ teaspoon vanilla extract

⅛ teaspoon salt

4 ounces (1 cup) confectioners' sugar

Using stand mixer fitted with whisk, whip cream cheese, butter, sour cream, vanilla, and salt on medium-high speed until smooth, 1 to 2 minutes. Reduce mixer speed to medium-low, slowly add sugar, and whip until incorporated and smooth, 1 to 2 minutes. Increase speed to medium-high and whip frosting until light and fluffy, 3 to 5 minutes.

HONEY CAKE

✔ WHY THIS RECIPE WORKS: For a holiday-worthy honey cake with bold honey flavor, we wanted a cake that was moist, not greasy. We cut back on the large amount of oil used in most recipes, turning instead to unsweetened applesauce to keep the crumb well hydrated. Orange juice helped boost the baking soda and baking powder's leavening power, keeping the cake light. To ensure that the cake would have unmistakable honey flavor, we used a whopping 1¾ cups and lowered the oven temperature to prevent the natural sugars from overbrowning. Generously coating the Bundt pan with baking spray with flour ensured that this sticky cake released cleanly once baked, and drizzling a sweet vanilla glaze over the cooled cake made for a festive presentation.

Honey cake, besides being a sweet treat as good for breakfast as it is for dessert, is a staple at dinners celebrating Rosh Hashanah, the Jewish New Year, as a symbol of a sweet new year. As I found in my research, traditions and recipes for this yearly treat vary from family to family—and cooks have very strong opinions about what makes a good one (or a bad one).

To learn more about this cake firsthand, I headed into our cookbook library, found six promising recipes, and baked samples. The cakes smelled great coming out of the test kitchen ovens, so as soon as they were cool, I eagerly grabbed a slice of each.

My enthusiasm quickly dwindled. These cakes were not pleasant to eat, as they were by turns greasy, gummy, or dry. The biggest problem, though, was that even the ones with passable textures had dominant flavors of warm spices, citrus, or liquor—everything but honey. They all had honey in them, all right, but we just couldn't taste it.

I decided to hit the reset button and start from scratch with a simple Cook's Country Bundt cake (though honey cakes come in all shapes and sizes, from loaves to sheets, Bundt cakes are big and festive, perfect for the holidays). For my first test, I replaced half the sugar with honey and, to make the cake compatible with kosher dietary laws, used vegetable oil instead of butter (most honey cake recipes do the same). A straight swap of oil for butter didn't work, though, as it made for exactly the kind of greasy cake I'd rejected in the initial testing.

I tried reducing the oil in various amounts, but my tasters were never satisfied with the results: Cakes were still either too greasy, gummy, or dry, with no apparent sweet spot. Trying to brainstorm other ingredients that could add moisture, I considered applesauce. Could this trick, usually reserved for "healthier" desserts, work here?

After trying various amounts in combination with a bit of oil, I landed on 6 tablespoons of applesauce and 4 tablespoons of vegetable oil. The applesauce lent moisture and a subtle, fruity background sweetness but, I was happy to discover, didn't make the cake taste like apples at all. This combination, along with both baking soda and baking powder, gave me a tender, tall cake with plenty of moisture.

On to the honey. All the recipes I tried early on called for at least some sugar in addition to the honey, but I was determined to use honey as the cake's sole source of sweetness. I baked through a slew of sticky tests where I slowly subbed honey for sugar ¼ cup at a time. I was pleased that the cake that traded all the sugar for honey turned out to be the tasters' favorite—it had a strong honey flavor.

But as is often the case in cooking (and particularly in baking), solving one problem created another. Honey is sweeter than sugar and browns more quickly, so now the cake was turning too brown, too quickly, in the oven. After several tests at various temperatures, I found that

HONEY CAKE

backing down just slightly from my 350-degree baking temperature, to 325 degrees, evened out the cooking for the best well-browned but moist cake.

I whisked together a simple vanilla-flavored glaze to dress up the cake with minimal effort.

When I cut a slice, I knew I'd achieved the holiday-worthy cake I had initially envisioned. Most important, it tasted how I thought honey cake should taste: like honey.

—MORGAN BOLLING, *Cook's Country*

Honey Cake

SERVES 12

Make sure to use unsweetened applesauce in this cake. If you plan to make this cake ahead of time, hold off on glazing it until 30 minutes before serving. You'll need 20 ounces of honey for this recipe. This cake is sticky; baking spray with flour provides the cleanest release, but if you have only regular cooking spray, apply a heavy coat and then dust the inside of the pan with flour.

CAKE

2½   **cups (12½ ounces) all-purpose flour**

1¼   **teaspoons salt**

  1   **teaspoon baking powder**

½   **teaspoon baking soda**

½   **cup water**

  4   **large eggs**

¼   **cup plus 2 tablespoons unsweetened applesauce**

¼   **cup vegetable oil**

¼   **cup orange juice**

  1   **teaspoon vanilla extract**

1¾   **cups honey**

GLAZE

  1   **cup (4 ounces) confectioners' sugar**

4½   **teaspoons water**

  1   **teaspoon vanilla extract**

    Pinch salt

1. FOR THE CAKE: Adjust oven rack to middle position and heat oven to 325 degrees. Heavily spray 12-cup non-stick Bundt pan with baking spray with flour. Whisk flour, salt, baking powder, and baking soda together in large bowl. Whisk water, eggs, applesauce, oil, orange juice, and vanilla in separate bowl until combined. Whisk honey into egg mixture until fully incorporated.

2. Whisk honey mixture into flour mixture until combined. Scrape batter into prepared pan. Bake until skewer inserted into middle of cake comes out clean, 45 to 55 minutes, rotating pan halfway through baking.

3. Let cake cool in pan on wire rack for 30 minutes. Using small spatula, loosen cake from sides of pan and invert onto rack. Let cool completely, about 2 hours. (Cooled cake can be wrapped with plastic wrap and stored at room temperature for up to 3 days.)

4. FOR THE GLAZE: Whisk together all ingredients. Drizzle glaze evenly over top of cake. Let sit until glaze is firm, about 30 minutes. Serve.

NOTES FROM THE TEST KITCHEN

THE BUZZ ABOUT HONEY

To find the best supermarket honey, we selected five top-selling honeys—three traditional and two raw—and tasted each product plain and in Honey Cake. In both tastings, we universally preferred the two raw honeys, calling them "complex," with "slight bitterness" and "strong floral notes." After doing some research, we learned that while traditional honey is usually heated to thin it to strain out its pollen for a clear appearance, raw honey is usually heated only high enough (about 120 degrees) to prevent it from crystallizing on store shelves. This gentler heat helps preserve the honey's delicate, nuanced flavors. Pollen contains alkaloids and phenolics—chemicals that add complex, slightly bitter flavors, and tasters liked how these tempered the honey's sweetness. Flavor is also influenced by what the bees feed on, and while the traditional honeys in our lineup were primarily sourced from clover-eating bees, the raw brands were mixtures from bees that feasted on all sorts of grasses and flowers, resulting in strong floral and grassy notes. Our favorite product, Nature Nate's 100% Pure Raw and Unfiltered Honey, sources its honey from bees that feed on a blend of wildflowers, clover, Chinese tallow, and vetch; it is slightly bitter and floral, with a deep, balanced sweetness.

SWISS HAZELNUT CAKE

☑ **WHY THIS RECIPE WORKS:** To re-create this Philadelphia bakery specialty, we first needed to bake a layer cake with unmistakable hazelnut flavor. Tasters disliked cakes made with artificial flavoring, so we added toasted, ground hazelnuts to delicate cake flour for nuanced nut flavor. We whisked together a rich batter before folding in whipped egg whites for an airy texture. Making this cake's traditional Swiss meringue buttercream frosting is quite an undertaking, but we found we could simply beat butter, confectioners' sugar, and marshmallow crème to create an equally rich, pillowy frosting. We added hazelnut liqueur to reinforce the cake's flavor. The signature finishing touch to Swiss hazelnut cake is a layer of chocolate shavings, and we made quick work of preparing them using a food processor fitted with a shredding disk. Chilling the disk in the freezer and freezing the delicate shavings before applying them to the frosted cake kept them from melting, making for an impressive presentation.

A Philadelphia grandmother places a weathered black-and-white photograph on top of the bakery case at the Swiss Haus Bakery in the Center City neighborhood of Philadelphia. The faded picture shows her as a young bride a half-century ago, cutting through her Swiss Haus wedding cake. The woman wants to know if the bakery, which has been making the same recipes in the same building since 1923, can re-create this dessert for an upcoming celebration. The bakery can proudly fill this order, as a piece of Swiss Haus cake is a piece of living history.

When I visited the Swiss Haus Bakery to taste their famous hazelnut sponge cake, I found a beautiful cake frosted with a fluffy vanilla icing and covered in chocolate shavings. The cake itself was light and airy with a subtle nut flavor, the frosting delicate and sweet. I wanted to translate this local favorite into a cake anyone could make at home.

I started with the base cake. The Swiss Haus pastry chef, Donna Feldman, was trained decades ago by the founding family's baker and would not disclose the recipe. She did, however, give me a valuable tip: "It's all about the egg whites." I surmised that the cake was either a sponge or chiffon cake, as both of these use whipped egg whites to achieve their light, fluffy texture.

After testing, I settled on a chiffon base because it's simpler and more reliable than sponge: You just combine your wet and dry ingredients, fold in beaten egg whites, and bake. To get the signature nutty flavor, I tried adding hazelnut extract, but it tasted like hazelnut flavoring, not hazelnuts. I had better luck substituting toasted hazelnuts ground in a food processor into a flour-like texture for a portion of the flour. And there was no need to remove the nut skins after toasting, as they contributed to the cake's signature speckled look.

Swiss meringue buttercream, which is made by heating and whipping egg whites and sugar and then beating in softened butter, was the obvious frosting choice for its satiny texture. But this buttercream is a project and then some. Searching for a quicker path to a creamy, sweet frosting, I had a wacky idea: What if I replaced the Swiss buttercream's meringue base with marshmallow crème? Though it was intensely sweet at first, adjusting the amounts of butter and powdered sugar and adding some hazelnut liqueur tempered the sweetness and made a perfectly pillowy frosting. This simple one-bowl method was a much easier approach.

Speaking of easy, shaving a block of chocolate to make the curls that adorn the cake was anything but. Watching me shake the cramps out of my hand, a colleague suggested trying the food processor. I fitted the machine with the shredding disk and fed a standard chocolate bar through the top tube. It was the loudest noise in the kitchen that day, but it worked. However, by the time I processed a second bar, the mechanical friction started to melt the chocolate. So I slipped the shredding disk into the freezer for a bit. This temperature tweak allowed me to shave down two chocolate bars in mere seconds with no messy melting, at least until I went to apply those curls to the cake. The heat from my hands instantly softened the delicate shards, ruining the look of the cake. Freezing the shaved chocolate and using a folded piece of parchment paper like a flexible putty knife to press the curls onto the cake solved the problem.

This tender, hazelnut-freckled cake is a tasty, beautiful reflection of its Philadelphia-born inspiration.

—KATIE LEAIRD, *Cook's Country*

Swiss Hazelnut Cake

SERVES 12 TO 16

We grind the toasted hazelnuts with their skins on for better color and flavor. We developed this recipe with Fluff brand marshmallow crème. When working with the marshmallow crème, grease the inside of your measuring cup and spatula with vegetable oil spray to prevent sticking. Note that the shredding disk should be placed in the freezer for 15 minutes before shaving the chocolate. You may use a vegetable peeler or the large holes of a box grater to shave the chocolate. In step 9, it's important to handle the chocolate shavings using the folded parchment paper so they don't melt from the heat of your hands.

CAKE

- ½ cup (2 ounces) skin-on hazelnuts, toasted and cooled
- 1¼ cups (5 ounces) cake flour
- 1 cup (7 ounces) granulated sugar
- 1½ teaspoons baking powder
- ½ teaspoon salt
- ½ cup vegetable oil
- ¼ cup water
- 3 large eggs, separated, plus 2 large whites
- 2½ teaspoons vanilla extract
- ¼ teaspoon cream of tartar

FROSTING

- 24 tablespoons (3 sticks) unsalted butter, softened
- ¼ teaspoon salt
- 1¾ cups (7 ounces) confectioners' sugar
- 12 ounces (2⅔ cups) marshmallow crème
- 2 tablespoons hazelnut liqueur
- 6 ounces bittersweet bar chocolate

1. FOR THE CAKE: Adjust oven rack to middle position and heat oven to 350 degrees. Line 2 light-colored 9-inch round cake pans with parchment paper; grease parchment but not pan sides.

2. Process hazelnuts in food processor until finely ground, about 30 seconds. Whisk flour, sugar, baking powder, salt, and ground hazelnuts together in large bowl. Whisk oil, water, egg yolks, and vanilla together in separate bowl. Whisk egg yolk mixture into flour-nut mixture until smooth batter forms.

3. Using stand mixer fitted with whisk, whip egg whites and cream of tartar on medium-low speed until foamy, about 1 minute. Increase speed to medium-high and whip until soft peaks form, 2 to 3 minutes. Gently whisk one-third of whipped egg whites into batter. Using rubber spatula, gently fold remaining egg whites into batter until incorporated.

4. Divide batter evenly between prepared pans and gently tap pans on counter to release air bubbles. Bake until tops are light golden brown and cakes spring back when pressed lightly in center, 25 to 28 minutes, rotating pans halfway through baking.

5. Let cakes cool in pans for 15 minutes. Run knife around edges of pans; invert cakes onto wire rack. Discard parchment and let cakes cool completely, at least 1 hour. (To prepare to make chocolate shavings, place food processor shredding disk in freezer.)

NOTES FROM THE TEST KITCHEN

PRODUCING PERFECT CHOCOLATE SHREDS
Temperature and timing are key factors in creating uniform chocolate shavings.

1. Place food processor's shredding disk in freezer for 15 minutes.

2. Quickly feed chocolate bar through shredder, then freeze shavings.

3. Use parchment to gently press frozen chocolate shreds into frosting.

6. FOR THE FROSTING: Using clean stand mixer fitted with whisk, whip butter and salt on medium speed until smooth, about 1 minute. Reduce speed to low and slowly add sugar. Increase speed to medium and whip until smooth, about 2 minutes, scraping down sides of bowl as needed. Add marshmallow crème, increase speed to medium-high, and whip until light and fluffy, 3 to 5 minutes. Reduce speed to low, add hazelnut liqueur, return speed to medium-high, and whip to incorporate, about 30 seconds.

7. Line rimmed baking sheet with parchment paper. Fit food processor with chilled shredding disk. Turn on processor and feed chocolate bar through hopper. Transfer shaved chocolate to prepared baking sheet and spread into even layer. Place in freezer to harden, about 10 minutes.

8. Place 1 cake layer on cake stand. Spread 2 cups frosting evenly over top, right to edge of cake. Top with second cake layer, pressing lightly to adhere. Spread remaining 2 cups frosting evenly over top and sides of cake.

9. Fold 16 by 12-inch sheet of parchment paper into 6 by 4-inch rectangle. Using parchment rectangle, scoop up half of chocolate shavings and sprinkle over top of cake. Once top of cake is coated, scoop up remaining chocolate shavings and press gently against sides of cake to adhere, scooping and reapplying as needed. Serve.

NOTES FROM THE TEST KITCHEN

FINDING A GREAT CAKE STAND

You can decorate a cake on a plate, but a good cake stand makes it faster and easier by elevating the cake for better visibility and by rotating for quick and even frosting application. When it comes time to decorate, we turn to the Winco Revolving Cake Decorating Stand. This model provides excellent visibility and comfort, rotating quickly and smoothly yet stopping precisely as needed. Its attached base makes for easy transporting, and centering guides on its surface make it easy to frost like a pro.

FLOURLESS CHOCOLATE CAKE

WHY THIS RECIPE WORKS: Recipes for flourless chocolate cake abound, but they tend be very complicated. For our take on this indulgent dessert, we wanted to bypass fancy techniques without sacrificing flavor or texture. We gently melted chocolate and butter in the microwave before incorporating the remaining ingredients. In the absence of flour, we called on eggs for structure and cornstarch for body, and water promised a moist, smooth texture. Vanilla and espresso powder added depth to the chocolate flavor. Ensuring a crack-free cake was as easy as straining and resting the batter, followed by tapping out any bubbles that rose to the surface. Baking the cake in a low oven produced a perfectly smooth surface.

Swing a cat in the city of your choice, and you're likely to hit a restaurant that serves flourless chocolate cake. Rich, smooth, and dense, with deep chocolate flavor, this once-uncommon dessert is now ubiquitous.

Ubiquitous, that is, except in most home kitchens, where recipes employing complicated techniques keep nonprofessionals away. I set out to create an easy and approachable recipe for flourless chocolate cake that used only straightforward techniques and basic equipment.

I tried making versions using six existing recipes of varying levels of difficulty (one especially easy one was named "Chocolate Idiot Cake"), including our celebrated company recipe from 1998. Some were dense like a brownie, while others reminded me of thick chocolate soup. Since flour was out of contention, some recipes called for ground nuts for structure, but these were too gritty. One used eggs for structure, and it worked beautifully; this cake was delicious, like a soft yet dense chocolate truffle. But this approach, though totally successful, required several bowls and some tricky techniques. I wanted a dump-and-stir version.

I cobbled together a working recipe and hit the kitchen. My first order of business was the easiest: melting the chocolate (we use good-quality bittersweet chocolate) and butter (two sticks for maximum richness). While most recipes call for a double boiler for this task, I turned to the microwave, where zapping the two

FLOURLESS CHOCOLATE CAKE

ingredients gently in a glass bowl saved me a couple of dirty pots. Letting the combination cool for about 5 minutes allowed me to add it to a mixture of eggs, sugar, cornstarch (for body), and vanilla without curdling the eggs.

Interestingly, a few of my initial recipes called for water in the egg-sugar mixture. Intrigued, I tried one cake with ½ cup added water and one without. The cake with the water was much more moist, while the one without was very chalky and dry. Clearly, the water was helping hydrate the mix and give it a more tender chew. For my next test, I tried incorporating the water in two different ways: with a stand mixer, which incorporates a lot of air into the batter, and in a bowl whisked by hand. The results were drastically different: The cake from the stand mixer souffléed so high that it fell over the springform pan and onto the oven floor (a mess I'd be happy never to make again), while the hand-mixed version baked clean and even.

This was welcome news, because it meant I could make this cake from start to finish by hand. But my cake had some minor appearance issues—namely, a small crack and dozens of visible air bubbles on the top. These are minor problems (once you put a bite of this rich, buttery cake in your mouth, the last thing you'll worry is an imperfect top), but I wanted to minimize them.

Earlier test kitchen experiments have taught us that one major culprit in creating cracks in similar cakes (such as cheesecakes) is a high oven temperature—if the cake bakes too quickly or unevenly, it tends to crack. To avoid this, we often set the springform pan into a larger pan with a couple of inches of water in it; the gentler heat created by this water bath helps the cake come to temperature more gradually without developing cracks. But I wanted to avoid the awkwardness of a water bath. Could I achieve a crack-free cake by simply lowering the oven temperature? As it turned out, I could. After a few experiments, I found that a relatively tame 275-degree oven, with the oven rack smack in the middle, kept cracks at bay.

As for the air bubbles, I found that straining my fully mixed batter through a strainer and into the springform pan removed much of the trapped air, significantly reducing the number of bubbles on top. It also removed any errant pieces of coagulated egg, further

ensuring a supersmooth texture. A gentle tap on the counter followed by a 10-minute rest nudged out even more air. (A few bubbles are inevitable and are a small price to pay for a cake this good.)

After baking it for about 50 minutes and then letting it cool and chill until firmly set (about 6 hours, a major test of patience), I had a great cake. To make sure it wasn't a fluke (and to quiet my still-hungry tasters), I made four more cakes in four different ovens, using the same straining technique. Much to my tasters' delight, all four worked.

—ASHLEY MOORE, *Cook's Country*

Flourless Chocolate Cake

SERVES 10 TO 12

This cake needs to chill for at least 6 hours, so we recommend making it the day before serving. An accurate oven thermometer is essential here. Our preferred bittersweet chocolate is Ghirardelli 60% Cacao Bittersweet Chocolate Premium Baking Bar. Top the cake with chocolate shavings, if desired; to make shavings, simply shave bittersweet bar chocolate with a vegetable peeler.

CAKE

- 12 ounces bittersweet chocolate, broken into 1-inch pieces
- 16 tablespoons unsalted butter
- 6 large eggs
- 1 cup (7 ounces) sugar
- ½ cup water
- 1 tablespoon cornstarch
- 1 tablespoon vanilla extract
- 1 teaspoon instant espresso powder
- ½ teaspoon salt

WHIPPED CREAM

- ½ cup heavy cream, chilled
- 2 teaspoons sugar
- ½ teaspoon vanilla extract

1. FOR THE CAKE: Adjust oven rack to middle position and heat oven to 275 degrees. Spray 9-inch springform pan with vegetable oil spray. Microwave chocolate and butter in bowl at 50 percent power, stirring occasionally with rubber spatula, until melted, about 4 minutes. Let chocolate mixture cool for 5 minutes.

2. Whisk eggs, sugar, water, cornstarch, vanilla, espresso powder, and salt together in large bowl until thoroughly combined, about 30 seconds. Whisk in chocolate mixture until smooth and slightly thickened, about 45 seconds. Strain batter through fine-mesh strainer into prepared pan, pressing against strainer with rubber spatula or back of ladle to help batter pass through.

3. Gently tap pan on counter to release air bubbles; then let sit on counter for 10 minutes to allow air bubbles to rise to top. Use tines of fork to gently pop any air bubbles that have risen to surface. Bake until edges are set and center jiggles slightly when cake is shaken gently, 45 to 50 minutes. Let cake cool for 5 minutes, then run paring knife between cake and sides of pan.

4. Let cake cool on wire rack until barely warm, about 30 minutes. Cover cake tightly with plastic wrap, poke small hole in top, and refrigerate until cold and firmly set, at least 6 hours.

5. FOR THE WHIPPED CREAM: Using stand mixer fitted with whisk, whip cream, sugar, and vanilla on medium-low speed until foamy, about 1 minute. Increase speed to high and whip until stiff peaks form, 1 to 3 minutes.

6. To unmold cake, remove sides and slide thin metal spatula between cake bottom and pan bottom to loosen, then slide cake onto serving platter. Let cake stand at room temperature for 30 minutes. Slice with warm, dry knife. Dollop slices with whipped cream and serve.

NOTES FROM THE TEST KITCHEN

AVOIDING SUNKEN CAKE

Baking our Flourless Chocolate Cake too quickly at too high a temperature will cause it to soufflé and subsequently fall and crack. For an even, smooth cake, bake it at exactly 275 degrees. To make sure your oven is at the right temperature, place an oven thermometer in the center of the middle rack and heat the oven to 275 degrees. As soon as the oven indicates that it is preheated, check the thermometer reading, then adjust the temperature setting as necessary.

CHOCOLATE-CARAMEL LAYER CAKE

✔ **WHY THIS RECIPE WORKS:** For a decadent dessert that paired dark chocolate cake and gooey caramel, we needed our star flavors to be rich and distinct. For moist cake with deep chocolate taste, we mixed together a simple batter, adding extra water for a moist crumb and replacing butter with neutral-tasting vegetable oil to draw more focus to the chocolate. For a not-too-sweet caramel that was thick but spreadable, we cooked a mixture of sugar, corn syrup, and water until it turned dark. Stirring in cream, vanilla, and some salt promised a lush, salty-sweet flavor, and plenty of butter ensured that the filling would be spreadably soft without oozing. A sweet chocolate frosting balanced out the deep flavors of the cake and filling.

I love tall, imposing layer cakes that make a splash at parties. The components should be pitch-perfect and strike that balance between kid birthday nostalgia and adult sophistication—a moist, tender crumb; distinct, spreadable filling that's just thick enough to glue the layers together; and frosting that's silky and full-bodied but not so sweet or rich that a forkful is overwhelming.

Chocolate cake is my favorite, and I've made plenty layered with buttercream, ganache, and mousse. But this time I wanted to home in on chocolate and caramel—a combination that has a kind of visceral appeal. A quick search turned up plenty of recipes with a wide range of profiles. Maybe all I had to do was bake off a few and find one I liked.

Wishful thinking. It wasn't that every recipe was a total failure; there were cakes with solid chocolate flavor, gooey caramels, and smooth frostings. And many of them had at least four layers so that the whole package looked rather majestic. But not one delivered the trifecta I had in mind: layers of dark, truly chocolaty cake separated by pleasantly bitter, soft but not runny caramel and generously covered with glossy chocolate frosting that was a notch less rich than the cake itself.

Deep chocolate flavor was a must for the cake but so was getting the crumb just right. In addition to being moist and tender, it needed to be sturdy enough to hold up under the weight of the caramel and frosting. And given that this was a three-component dessert, I wanted to keep the cake-making process as simple as possible.

Those textural considerations would be affected by the mixing method, so I reviewed the two basic options.

First—and most traditional for layer cakes—there was the creaming method. This involves beating softened butter with sugar in a stand mixer until it becomes light and fluffy, adding eggs one by one, and then gradually beating in the dry and liquid components alternately until just combined.

I was more keen on the second option, the dump-and-stir method, which involves simply whisking together the dry and wet ingredients in separate bowls and then whisking the wet into the dry until a smooth batter forms. This would be much faster and easier than hauling out my stand mixer, and stirring the liquid directly into flour that has not been coated with butter would create more gluten. This in turn would make for a sturdier but sufficiently tender cake that could be halved to make four layers (I'd cut each cake into two rounds) able to stand up to the filling and frosting.

I threw together a basic chocolate cake batter and divided it between two 9-inch round cake pans that I greased, floured, and lined with parchment paper. After baking for 25 minutes in a 325-degree oven, the cakes emerged nicely resilient, albeit tighter and drier than I wanted. The chocolate flavor was also a tad dull. Adding ½ cup of water moistened the crumb (more buttermilk would have increased the acidity in the cake and potentially compromised the leaveners), and swapping the melted butter for more neutral-tasting vegetable oil allowed the chocolate flavor to shine.

Making caramel sauce is a two-stage process. First, you heat sugar until it melts; some cooks also add a little water, which helps the sugar caramelize evenly without burning, and light corn syrup, which helps prevent crystallization. The degree to which you cook the sugar after melting determines the flavor of the caramel; the higher the final temperature, the more complex and bitter it will be. Next, cream, butter, and other flavorings (like salt and vanilla) are added, which creates a fluid caramel sauce. As the mixture cooks, the temperature increases, water evaporates, and the caramel sauce stiffens—eventually turning into hard candy.

Thus, the key to making a faintly bitter and spreadable but not runny caramel was to zero in closely on its temperature at the two different stages. I boiled 1¼ cups of sugar with ¼ cup each of water and light corn syrup in a saucepan until the mixture turned amber, which took about 10 minutes. Then I lowered the heat and continued to caramelize the sugar mixture until it turned dark amber and its temperature registered between 375 and 380 degrees—a good indication that its flavor would be just a touch bitter but not burnt. Off the heat, I stirred in 1 cup of heavy cream, 6 tablespoons of butter, 1 teaspoon of vanilla, and a generous ¾ teaspoon of salt (salty caramel would be a great complement to the sweeter frosting).

Now for the tricky part—figuring out just how much to reduce the liquidy caramel. I returned the heat to medium and simmered the mixture (stirring frequently to ensure even cooking) until it hit about 240 degrees; at that point, it looked a bit runny, but I hoped it would stiffen up a bit as it cooled. I poured it into a greased baking pan—spreading it out would help it cool faster—and waited until it was just warm to the touch.

But it didn't stiffen up enough, so when I went to spread it on the prepared cakes, some of the caramel soaked into the cake while more of it gently oozed from between the layers. The obvious next test was to cook the caramel to a higher temperature—250 degrees—but that overdid it, producing a mixture too firm to spread.

I briefly changed course and made a dulce de leche–type caramel with sweetened condensed milk, since its thick, viscous consistency would be close to what I was after. But its duller, milkier flavor didn't offer the same complexity and depth as a traditional caramel.

What my filling needed, I realized, was something that is both solid and soft at room temperature—like butter. I made a couple more batches of caramel with increasing amounts of butter and found that adding 2 extra tablespoons produced a cooled caramel that was soft enough to spread but solid enough that it didn't soak into or leak out of the cake.

Tasting the deep chocolate cake spread with the caramel filling confirmed that the frosting could stand to be a bit sweeter than the cake—and I had just the thing in mind. In the test kitchen archives is a chocolate frosting that has just the right rich body and glossy sheen; even better, it is a cinch to make since it comes together in the food processor in just minutes.

I followed the recipe, processing softened butter with confectioners' sugar, cocoa powder, corn syrup (its moisture helps dissolve the confectioners' sugar and prevents unpleasant graininess), vanilla, and melted milk chocolate. It spread beautifully over the cake—thick and smooth. But my tasters and I agreed that the milk chocolate flavor was a few notches sweeter than it should be, so I swapped it for bittersweet.

The darker chocolate coat made the cake look and taste more sophisticated, but the whole package still had a touch of whimsy and birthday party charm—exactly the type of cake I couldn't wait to make for my next dinner party. And for the salted caramel fans, I sprinkled on a bit of coarse sea salt, which gave it a delicate crunch.

—LAN LAM, *Cook's Illustrated*

Chocolate-Caramel Layer Cake

SERVES 12

Baking spray that contains flour can be used to grease and flour the pans. Both natural and Dutch-processed cocoa will work in this recipe. When taking the temperature of the caramel in steps 3 and 4, remove the pot from the heat and tilt the pan to one side. Use your thermometer to stir the caramel back and forth to equalize hot and cool spots and make sure you are getting an accurate reading.

CAKE

- 1½ cups (7½ ounces) all-purpose flour
- ¾ cup (2¼ ounces) unsweetened cocoa powder
- 1½ cups (10½ ounces) granulated sugar
- 1¼ teaspoons baking soda
- ¾ teaspoon baking powder
- ¾ teaspoon salt
- ¾ cup buttermilk
- ½ cup water
- ¼ cup vegetable oil
- 2 large eggs
- 1 teaspoon vanilla extract

CARAMEL FILLING

- 1¼ cups (8¾ ounces) granulated sugar
- ¼ cup light corn syrup
- ¼ cup water
- 1 cup heavy cream
- 8 tablespoons unsalted butter, cut into 8 pieces
- 1 teaspoon vanilla extract
- ¾ teaspoon salt

FROSTING

- 16 tablespoons unsalted butter, softened
- ¾ cup (3 ounces) confectioners' sugar
- ½ cup (1½ ounces) unsweetened cocoa powder
-   Pinch salt

- ½ cup light corn syrup
- ¾ teaspoon vanilla extract
- 6 ounces bittersweet chocolate, melted and cooled
- ¼–½ teaspoon coarse sea salt (optional)

1. FOR THE CAKE: Adjust oven rack to middle position and heat oven to 325 degrees. Grease two 9-inch round cake pans, line with parchment paper, grease parchment, and flour pans. Sift flour and cocoa into large bowl. Whisk in sugar, baking soda, baking powder, and salt. Whisk buttermilk, water, oil, eggs, and vanilla together in second bowl. Whisk buttermilk mixture into flour mixture until smooth batter forms. Divide batter evenly between prepared pans and smooth tops with rubber spatula.

2. Bake until toothpick inserted in center comes out clean, 22 to 28 minutes, rotating pans halfway through baking. Let cakes cool in pans on wire rack

---

NOTES FROM THE TEST KITCHEN

FROSTING CAKES WITH FLAIR

Giving cakes a polished look need not require years of practice. Here are three easy techniques for finishing layer cakes.

C-SHAPED SWIRL

Beginning on side of cake, use small spoon to make C-shaped swirl. Make second swirl next to first about ¾ inch away, orienting C in different direction. Make more swirls, oriented in different directions, over sides and top of cake until frosting is completely covered.

ZIG-ZAG

Gently run spatula (offset works best) over sides and top of cake to smooth frosting. Holding 12-inch-long serrated knife at both ends with blade facing down and centered over top of cake, gently move knife from side to side to create zigzag pattern.

SPIRAL

Set cake on turntable-style cake stand. Place tip of offset spatula or spoon at center of cake. Slowly rotate cake while dragging tip of spatula or spoon toward edge to create spiral.

for 15 minutes. Remove cakes from pans, discarding parchment, and let cool completely on wire rack, at least 2 hours.

3. FOR THE CARAMEL FILLING: Lightly grease 8-inch square baking pan. Combine sugar, corn syrup, and water in medium saucepan. Bring to boil over medium-high heat and cook, without stirring, until mixture is amber colored, 8 to 10 minutes. Reduce heat to low and continue to cook, swirling saucepan occasionally, until dark amber, 2 to 5 minutes longer. (Caramel will register between 375 and 380 degrees.)

4. Off heat, carefully stir in cream, butter, vanilla, and salt (mixture will bubble and steam). Return saucepan to medium heat and cook, stirring frequently, until smooth and caramel reaches 240 to 245 degrees, 3 to 5 minutes. Carefully transfer caramel to prepared pan and let cool until just warm to touch (100 to 105 degrees), 20 to 30 minutes.

5. FOR THE FROSTING: Process butter, sugar, cocoa, and salt in food processor until smooth, about 30 seconds, scraping down sides of bowl as needed. Add corn syrup and vanilla and process until just combined, 5 to 10 seconds. Scrape down sides of bowl, then add chocolate and pulse until smooth and creamy, 10 to 15 seconds. (Frosting can be made 3 hours in advance. For longer storage, cover and refrigerate frosting. Let stand at room temperature for 1 hour before using.)

6. Using long serrated knife, score 1 horizontal line around sides of each cake layer; then, following scored lines, cut each layer into 2 even layers.

7. Using rubber spatula or large spoon, transfer one-third of caramel to center of 1 cake layer and use small offset spatula to spread over surface, leaving ½-inch border around edge. Repeat with remaining caramel and two of remaining cake layers. (Three of your cake layers should be topped with caramel.)

8. Line edges of cake platter with 4 strips of parchment to keep platter clean. Place 1 caramel-covered cake layer on platter. Top with second caramel-covered layer. Repeat with third caramel-covered layer and top with final layer. Spread frosting evenly over sides and top of cake. Carefully remove parchment strips. Let cake stand for at least 1 hour. (Cake can be made 2 days in advance and refrigerated. Let stand at room temperature for at least 5 hours before serving.) Sprinkle with coarse sea salt, if using. Cut and serve.

REFINED STRAWBERRY SHORTCAKE

✓ WHY THIS RECIPE WORKS: For an elegant take on classic strawberry shortcake, we decided to use a light and airy genoise cake as our base. Since this cake gets its structure from whipped eggs, we ensured that our cake was foolproof by first whisking the sugar and eggs together over a pot of simmering water to melt the sugar and stabilize the egg mixture. A stand mixer made quick work of whipping the egg mixture into a foam. Transferring the foam to a wider bowl made for easier mixing, and gently folding in the remaining ingredients kept the batter light. Picturing a tall dessert piled high with berries, we baked two layers: One layer would serve as the base and the other we would cut into a ring which, when placed atop the base, would contain the berries. Thickening some of the exuded berry juice with cornstarch ensured that our cake sliced beautifully, and brushing the rest of the berry juice onto the cakes gave every bite big strawberry flavor.

Plenty of juicy, sweet berries and whipped cream are a must for strawberry shortcake, but what about the shortcake itself? Some opt for biscuits, but I've always been drawn to the style featuring light, fluffy cake, since it seems better suited to soaking up the berry juice. For my ideal version, a flavorful cake that wouldn't fall apart when soaked with the juice was a must, and I liked the idea of a whole cake since it would offer a more elegant presentation. As for the strawberries, I wanted to pack in as many as possible.

What kind of cake would be best? Recipes were split between butter and sponge cakes. Butter cakes practically dissolved when soaked with juice. Sponge cakes, which rely on whipped eggs or egg whites for leavening and structure, held up much better. I settled on a type of sponge called genoise, which has a rich flavor from whole eggs and melted butter.

But genoise isn't without problems. Recipes call for whipping the eggs and sugar until the mixture has more than tripled in volume and then gently folding in the dry ingredients (just cake flour and salt) followed by the melted butter and any flavorings. But since the batter contains no chemical leaveners, if the eggs aren't fully aerated or if the batter is deflated during folding, the cake turns out dense, flat, and rubbery.

REFINED STRAWBERRY SHORTCAKE

First I considered how the eggs were whipped. Most recipes call for whisking the eggs and sugar over a pan of simmering water until the sugar is dissolved and then whipping this mixture in a stand mixer until it reaches the ribbon stage, so called because it forms a ribbon that holds its shape when dribbled down into the bowl from the whisk, indicating that it's stable.

Some recipes skip heating the mixture, but I found that in these cases the whipped eggs deflated very quickly. Why? When eggs are whipped, their proteins unwind, link up, and trap both the air introduced by whipping and the water in the eggs. The water provides support to the network, or foam, but over time the water seeps out, weakening the foam, and air escapes. Heating the sugar and water as opposed to just stirring them together ensures that all of the sugar dissolves, which makes for a more viscous mixture. And the more viscous a liquid, the slower the water it contains escapes. This leads to a more stable foam.

So the heating step was key. I put my sugar and eggs in the bowl of the stand mixer and placed the bowl over a saucepan of simmering water. I found that heating the mixture to 115 to 120 degrees before whipping it fully dissolved the sugar and delivered the sturdiest egg foam.

One key to maximizing airiness is minimizing the number of strokes used to fold in the dry ingredients. Sifting them over the foam and folding them into it in batches, which many recipes call for, was a must, ensuring that there were no clumps of flour that needed aggressive mixing. Transferring the egg foam from the narrow mixer bowl to a wide, shallow bowl made the folding process even more efficient since fewer strokes were required.

Last to go into the batter were the butter, vanilla extract, and lemon zest. Just folding them in didn't work well, however. Because the mixture was more dense than the egg foam, it took a lot of strokes to incorporate it. To address this, I whisked ¾ cup of the egg foam into the melted butter mixture and then folded this lightened mixture into the batter. The resulting cake was perfectly airy with a uniform crumb—and, best of all, I got these same results cake after cake.

Now I just needed to figure out how to corral the berries, which would tumble off if I simply arranged them on top. One approach I read about cut a well in the cake. To simplify this idea, I divided the batter between two 9-inch cake pans. I'd cut the center from one of the baked layers and set the ring on top of the uncut layer. The ring would act like a retaining wall, securely holding the strawberries in place.

As for the strawberries, I hulled 2 pounds and, instead of quartering them as some recipes call for, I sliced them thin. Slices would lie flatter, not only allowing me to pack in more berries but also giving the filling a neater appearance. Slices were also more helpful for the macerating step.

I assembled my cake, placing the cake ring on the uncut layer, scooping the berries into the well, and topping it off with lightly sweetened whipped cream, which also included a little crème fraîche for tang. This cake looked the part, but when I sliced into it, I saw that the juice wasn't evenly distributed, and the berries slipped and slid as I sliced.

I tried again. To make the berry filling more cohesive, I strained the juice from the macerated berries, thickened a small portion with cornstarch, and then combined this gelled mixture with the berries. I brushed the remaining juice evenly over the cake before adding the berries and tangy whipped cream.

This cake looked elegant and sliced easily, and each bite delivered that perfect combination of fresh strawberries, light-as-air cake, and tangy whipped cream. I knew even the staunchest biscuit-style shortcake fans wouldn't be able to resist it.

—LAN LAM, *Cook's Illustrated*

Refined Strawberry Shortcake

SERVES 8

For the best texture, mix the cake batter quickly but gently, and have your equipment ready and ingredients measured before beginning. Cool the melted butter only slightly, to between 95 and 110 degrees. This recipe was written for light-colored cake pans; if your pans are dark, reduce the baking time in step 7 to 10 to 13 minutes.

STRAWBERRIES

- 2 pounds strawberries, hulled and sliced vertically ¼ inch thick (6 cups)
- ¼ cup (1¾ ounces) granulated sugar
- 2 teaspoons lemon juice
   Pinch salt
- ½ teaspoon cornstarch

CAKE

- 4 tablespoons unsalted butter, melted and cooled slightly
- 1 teaspoon vanilla extract
- ½ teaspoon grated lemon zest
- 1¼ cups (5 ounces) cake flour
- ¼ teaspoon salt
- 5 large eggs
- ¾ cup (5¼ ounces) granulated sugar

WHIPPED CREAM

- 1 cup heavy cream
- ⅓ cup crème fraîche
- 3 tablespoons confectioners' sugar, plus extra for dusting

1. FOR THE STRAWBERRIES: Toss strawberries with sugar, lemon juice, and salt in large bowl. Set aside for at least 1½ hours or up to 3 hours.

2. FOR THE CAKE: Adjust oven rack to middle position and heat oven to 350 degrees. Spray two 9-inch round cake pans with baking spray with flour. Line with parchment paper and spray parchment with baking spray with flour. Combine melted butter, vanilla, and lemon zest in medium bowl. Whisk flour and salt together in second bowl.

3. Combine eggs and sugar in bowl of stand mixer; place bowl over medium saucepan filled with 2 inches simmering water, making sure that water does not touch bottom of bowl. Whisking constantly, heat until sugar is dissolved and mixture registers 115 to 120 degrees, about 3 minutes.

4. Transfer bowl to stand mixer fitted with whisk. Beat on high speed until eggs are pale yellow and have tripled in volume, about 5 minutes. (Egg foam will form ribbon that sits on top of mixture for 5 seconds when dribbled from whisk.) Measure out ¾ cup egg foam, whisk into butter mixture until well combined, and set aside.

5. Transfer remaining egg foam to large, wide bowl and sift one-third of flour mixture over egg foam in even layer. Using rubber spatula, gently fold batter 6 to 8 times until small streaks of flour remain. Repeat folding 6 to 8 times with half of remaining flour mixture. Sift remaining flour mixture over batter and gently fold 10 to 12 times until flour is completely incorporated.

6. Pour butter mixture over batter in even layer. Gently fold until just incorporated, taking care not to deflate batter. Divide batter evenly between prepared pans.

7. Bake until centers of cakes are set and bounce back when gently pressed and toothpick inserted in center comes out clean, 13 to 16 minutes, rotating

NOTES FROM THE TEST KITCHEN

KEEPING THE AIR IN AIRY CAKE

For our Refined Strawberry Shortcake, we use a style of sponge cake known as a genoise. Like any sponge, a genoise should have an airy, springy texture—but if the whipped eggs intended to give it this texture aren't fully aerated or deflate during folding, the cake turns out dense, flat, and rubbery. Here's how we made it foolproof.

1. HEAT EGGS WITH SUGAR: Fully dissolving sugar in eggs makes mixture more viscous and better able to hold in air when whipped.

2. WHIP TO RIBBON STAGE: A ribbon of foam that holds for 5 seconds when dribbled from whisk indicates stable structure that will hold air.

3. LIGHTEN UP MELTED BUTTER: Whisking some egg foam into butter mixture lightens mixture and makes it easier to incorporate into batter.

4. FOLD IN FLOUR IN WIDE BOWL: Sifting flour over a broad area means fewer strokes are needed to mix it in—minimizing risk of deflating foam.

pan halfway through baking. Remove cakes from pans, discarding parchment, and let cool completely on wire rack, about 2 hours.

8. Drain berries in fine-mesh strainer over bowl. Measure out 2 tablespoons juice into small bowl (reserve remaining juice in bowl) and stir in cornstarch until well combined. Microwave, stirring every 10 seconds, until mixture is very thick and translucent, 30 to 45 seconds. Set aside.

9. Place 1 cake layer right side up on platter. Place second layer upside down on cutting board. Using paring knife, cut circle from center of cake on board, leaving 1-inch-wide ring of cake. (Reserve circle for another use.) Place upside-down cake ring on top of layer on platter. Using pastry brush, brush all of unthickened strawberry juice onto bottom cake layer and inner sides of cake ring. Gently combine berries and reserved thickened juice in now-empty bowl. Spoon berry mixture into cake ring, forming even layer.

10. FOR THE WHIPPED CREAM: Using stand mixer fitted with whisk, whip cream and crème fraîche on low speed until foamy, about 1 minute. Add sugar, increase speed to medium-high, and whip until soft peaks form, about 2 minutes. Dollop 2 tablespoons whipped cream onto center of cake. Transfer remaining whipped cream to serving bowl. Dust cake ring with confectioners' sugar. Cut and serve, passing extra whipped cream separately.

BAKED ALASKA

✔ WHY THIS RECIPE WORKS: Baked Alaska should be an impressive trifecta of toasty meringue, smooth ice cream, and tender cake, but most recipes are cloyingly sweet, since they call for a thick layer of insulating meringue. For a more nuanced dessert, we encased coffee ice cream (the coffee flavor's slight bitterness balanced out the sweetness) in a sturdy-yet-light chocolate chiffon cake. This helped insulate the ice cream, allowing us to use less meringue overall. To simplify preparation and serving, we skipped the traditional bombe shape in favor of a halved cylinder.

Baked Alaska is the unicorn of the dessert world; everyone has heard of it, but few have seen one in real life. Maybe that's because its three components—a circle

of cake topped with a dome of ice cream and covered in meringue—make it sound too fussy to cobble together at home. Or maybe baked Alaska seems intimidating since it appears to defy the laws of thermodynamics: Baking this dessert in a very hot oven browns and crisps the billowy meringue exterior while leaving the ice cream core frozen and firm. Some restaurants further heighten the drama by lowering the lights, dousing the creation with liqueur, and setting it ablaze at the table.

Nevertheless, the dessert is still basically a dressed-up ice cream cake, and it's no more difficult to make than any other version. My own reasons for not throwing one together more often have always been that baked Alaska is very sweet, and the traditional bombe shape—while visually impressive when whole—is difficult to slice and serve neatly. Even if you do manage to cut neat slices, the meringue and ice cream invariably part company when you move the slices from the platter to dessert plates. My goal was to re-engineer baked Alaska so it would be as enjoyable to eat as it is impressive to behold.

My first move was to pick a style of meringue: French, Italian, or Swiss. With the French kind, the egg whites don't fully cook, and the result is relatively coarse and foamy. I prefer the other styles because the sugar completely dissolves. The results are creamier, denser, and more stable.

Ultimately, I chose the Swiss version, which is a bit easier to make. The basic method is to gently whisk egg whites and sugar in a bowl over simmering water (I cook it until the mixture reaches 160 degrees for food safety) and then whip it in a stand mixer until stiff peaks form.

As for the cake, baked Alaska can be made with anything from a lean and airy genoise to a rich and tender pound cake to a brownie. I thought that the brownie sounded like a nice flavor and visual contrast to the meringue. Sticking with the traditional bombe shape for now, I baked a basic brownie in an 8-inch round pan and packed softened vanilla ice cream into a plastic wrap–lined bowl with the same diameter. To form the ice cream cake, I pressed the cooled brownie round onto the ice cream and popped the whole thing in the freezer. Once it was firm, I unmolded the cake and covered the surface with a thick layer of meringue (which was tricky, because it tended to slip down the surface of the ice cream). Finally, I baked the Alaska

BAKED ALASKA

in a 500-degree oven for just a few minutes until the exterior was brown and crisp.

I was right—everyone liked the chocolate flavor and visual contrast of the brownie, but in combination with the ice cream and that thick coat of meringue, the whole package was much too sweet. Plus, the ice cream turned icy when I refroze it before baking. Decreasing the amount of meringue reduced some of that sweetness, but doing so came at a cost. When I baked off another Alaska covered with about half as much meringue, the ice cream core turned to soft-serve.

Lesson learned: That voluminous meringue coat isn't there just for aesthetics. Its primary function is insulation. The meringue protects the ice cream at the center from melting in the heat of the oven.

Here's how it works: When egg whites are beaten, they form a foam—a liquid (egg whites are primarily water) that traps millions of tiny air bubbles and holds them together in a solid shape. Foams make great insulators because the air bubbles contain relatively few molecules and thus conduct heat energy poorly. The more meringue I used, the better the insulation would be.

If I couldn't reduce the amount of meringue, maybe I could at least make it less sweet by replacing one-quarter of the sugar with corn syrup, which is less sweet. But recalibrating the meringue only marginally reduced the dessert's overall sweetness. To really make a difference, I would need to reduce the amount of meringue, too, which would bring me back to my compromised insulation problem. Or so I thought.

Up until that point, I'd been relying almost exclusively on the meringue for insulation. But cakes are also foams with the ability to insulate, so maybe I could make better use of that component. I'd actually seen a couple of baked Alaska recipes in which the ice cream was completely encased in cake and had dismissed them as overkill. Now I recognized this as a potentially genius move that would allow me to cut way back on the meringue while keeping the ice cream well insulated.

But in order to do so, I had to make some changes—starting with the type of cake. The brownie was not only too sweet but also too inflexible to encase the ice cream, so I switched to a chiffon cake. Because this cake is made with whipped egg whites, it's not only spongier and more flexible than a brownie but also contains much more air, making it a better insulator. (Its plain flavor wasn't an incentive, but I'd revisit that later.)

Using the more resilient chiffon cake also allowed me to change the way I assembled my baked Alaska. Rather than line a bowl with cake pieces and soft ice cream, which always resulted in icy ice cream and messy slicing, I abandoned the bombe shape and instead turned the ice cream into a cylinder and wrapped cake around it.

First, I cut the cardboard off two pint containers of ice cream, pressed them together to form a cylinder, and stashed it in the freezer. To make a wide, flat cake that could be wrapped around the cylinder, I baked the chiffon batter in a rimmed baking sheet, cutting the cake into pieces that I used to encase the ice cream. I halved the ice cream cylinder lengthwise, placed the halves cut side down on a piece of cake, and placed my creation on a wire rack set in a rimmed baking sheet (to separate it from the sheet's surface, which would get hot in the oven). I wrapped the remaining cake pieces around the ice cream, spread the cake with just 2 inches of meringue, appreciating how much better it clung to the surface of the cake than it had to the ice cream, and baked it.

The final results were even more encouraging: Not only were there no drips of melted ice cream, but the slices I cut were tidy and intact and the cross-section view was striking: a half-circle of ice cream surrounded by cake and just enough meringue.

All I had left to revisit was the flavor. Since the chocolate brownie had been a good match for the meringue, I made the chiffon cake chocolate by substituting cocoa for some of the cake flour.

To make the flavors even more complex, I tried a series of tart sorbets in place of the plain old vanilla ice cream; they had good flavor but were too lean. Instead, I used a premium coffee ice cream that was rich, creamy, and had just the right hint of bitterness—a great match for the other components.

My version of baked Alaska wasn't just an edible science project about insulation; it was a showpiece dessert that tasted every bit as good as it looked.

—ANDREA GEARY, *Cook's Illustrated*

Baked Alaska

SERVES 8

Coffee ice cream provides the best contrast with sweet meringue in this recipe, but other flavors may be substituted, if desired. A high-quality ice cream such as Häagen-Dazs works best because it is slower to melt. To ensure the proper texture when serving, it is necessary to remove the cake from the freezer before making the meringue. This recipe leaves just enough leftover cake and ice cream to make an additional for-two version, Bonus Baked Alaska (recipe follows).

2 (1-pint) containers coffee ice cream

CAKE

1 cup (4 ounces) cake flour
⅓ cup (1 ounce) unsweetened cocoa powder
⅔ cup (4⅔ ounces) sugar
1½ teaspoons baking powder
¼ teaspoon salt
½ cup vegetable oil
6 tablespoons water
4 large eggs, separated

MERINGUE

¾ cup (5¼ ounces) sugar
⅓ cup light corn syrup
3 large egg whites
2 tablespoons water
Pinch salt
1 teaspoon vanilla extract

1. Lay 12-inch square sheet of plastic wrap on counter and remove lids from ice cream. Use scissors to cut cardboard tubs from top to bottom. Peel away cardboard and discard. Place ice cream blocks on their sides in center of plastic with wider ends facing each other. Grasp each side of plastic and firmly press blocks together to form barrel shape. Wrap plastic tightly around ice cream and roll briefly on counter to form uniform cylinder. Place cylinder, standing on end, in freezer until completely solid, at least 1 hour.

2. FOR THE CAKE: Adjust oven rack to middle position and heat oven to 350 degrees. Lightly grease 18 by 13-inch rimmed baking sheet, line with parchment paper, and lightly grease parchment. Whisk flour, cocoa, ⅓ cup sugar, baking powder, and salt together in large bowl. Whisk oil, water, and egg yolks into flour mixture until smooth batter forms.

3. Using stand mixer fitted with whisk attachment, whip egg whites on medium-low speed until foamy, about 1 minute. Increase speed to medium-high and whip whites to soft, billowy mounds, about 1 minute. Gradually add remaining ⅓ cup sugar and whip until glossy, soft peaks form, 1 to 2 minutes. Transfer one-third of egg whites to batter; whisk gently until mixture is lightened. Using rubber spatula, gently fold remaining egg whites into batter.

4. Pour batter into prepared sheet; spread evenly. Bake until cake springs back when pressed lightly in center, 10 to 13 minutes. Transfer cake to wire rack and let cool for 5 minutes. Run knife around edge of sheet, then invert cake onto wire rack. Carefully remove parchment, then re-invert cake onto second wire rack. Let cool completely, at least 15 minutes.

5. Transfer cake to cutting board with long side of rectangle parallel to edge of counter. Using serrated knife, trim ¼ inch off left side of cake and discard. Using ruler, measure 4½ inches from cut edge and make mark with knife. Using mark as guide, cut 4½-inch-wide rectangle from cake. Trim piece to create 11 by 4½-inch rectangle and set aside. (Depending on pan size and how much cake has shrunk during baking, it may not be necessary to trim piece to measure 11 inches.) Measure 4 inches from new cut edge and make mark. Using mark as guide, cut 4-inch rectangle from cake. Trim piece to create by 10 by 4-inch rectangle, wrap rectangle in plastic, and set aside. Cut 3½-inch round from remaining cake and set aside (biscuit cutter works well). Save scraps for Bonus Baked Alaska (recipe follows).

6. Unwrap ice cream. Trim cylinder to 4½ inches in length and return remainder to freezer for Bonus Baked Alaska. Place ice cream cylinder on 4½ by 11-inch cake rectangle and wrap cake around ice cream. (Cake may crack slightly.) Place cake circle on one end of cylinder. Wrap entire cylinder tightly in plastic. Place cylinder, standing on cake-covered end, in freezer until cake is firm, at least 30 minutes.

7. Unwrap cylinder and place on cutting board, standing on cake-covered end, and cut in half lengthwise. Unwrap reserved 10 by 4-inch cake rectangle and place halves on top, ice cream side down, with open ends

BUILDING A NEW BAKED ALASKA

1. Cut ice cream tubs from top to bottom and peel away cardboard. Place blocks on plastic wrap on their sides with wider ends facing each other.

2. Wrap plastic tightly around ice cream and roll on counter to form even cylinder. Place in freezer, standing on end, for 1 hour.

3. Trim ¼ inch off left side of cake. Cut 4½ by 11-inch rectangle, 4 by 10-inch rectangle, and 3½-inch round. Save scraps for Bonus Baked Alaska.

4. Unwrap ice cream and trim cylinder to 4½ inches in length. Return remainder to freezer.

5. Place ice cream on 11 by 4½-inch cake rectangle and wrap cake around ice cream. Place cake circle on 1 end of cylinder. Wrap in plastic. Freeze, standing on cake-covered end, for 30 minutes.

6. Unwrap cylinder, stand on cake-covered end, and cut in half lengthwise. Place halves on 10 by 4-inch rectangle, ice cream side down, with open ends meeting in middle.

meeting in middle. Wrap tightly with plastic and press ends gently to close gap between halves. Return to freezer for at least 2 hours and up to 2 weeks.

8. FOR THE MERINGUE: Adjust oven rack to upper-middle position and heat oven to 500 degrees. Spray wire rack set in rimmed baking sheet with vegetable oil spray. Unwrap cake and place on rack. Combine sugar, corn syrup, egg whites, water, and salt in bowl of stand mixer; place bowl over saucepan filled with 1 inch simmering water, making sure that water does not touch bottom of bowl. Whisking gently but constantly, heat until sugar is dissolved and mixture registers 160 degrees, 5 to 8 minutes.

9. Place bowl in stand mixer fitted with whisk attachment. Beat mixture on medium speed until bowl is only slightly warm to touch, about 5 minutes. Increase speed to high and beat until mixture begins to lose its gloss and forms stiff peaks, about 5 minutes. Add vanilla and beat until combined.

10. Using offset spatula, spread meringue over top and sides of cake, avoiding getting meringue on rack. Use back of spoon to create peaks all over meringue.

11. Bake until browned and crisp, about 5 minutes. Run offset spatula or thin knife under dessert to loosen from rack, then use two spatulas to transfer to serving platter. To slice, dip sharp knife in very hot water and wipe dry after each cut. Serve immediately.

Bonus Baked Alaska

SERVES 2

Our Baked Alaska recipe leaves just enough leftover cake and ice cream to make an additional for-two version.

From remaining cake, cut two 3⅓-inch rounds and one 11 by 2-inch strip. Place leftover ice cream disk on top of 1 cake round. Wrap strip of cake around sides of disk. Place remaining cake round on top, wrap tightly in plastic, and freeze. Following step 10, spread meringue over cake and bake as directed.

CAST-IRON SKILLET APPLE PIE

✔ **WHY THIS RECIPE WORKS:** When it's done well, there is nothing quite as perfect as apple pie, and for apple lovers, deep-dish pies are the ultimate dessert. However, this pie is often plagued with unevenly cooked fruit, and the exuded juices tend to turn the crust pale and soggy, making it impossible to slice the pie neatly. We discovered that a cast-iron skillet can solve all of these problems. We started by precooking the apples in the skillet, driving off some of the extra juice while adding deep caramelized flavor. We enriched our filling with complex, complementary flavors, adding apple cider, maple syrup, lemon zest and juice, and cinnamon. The high sides of the skillet were perfect for a deep-dish pie. Greasing the skillet before lining it with dough ensured a golden brown crust and made the pie easy to slice and serve.

It's hard to find fault in apple pie. From the buttery, flaky crust to the tender, sweet-tart cinnamon apples, there's much to love about this classic American dessert. But while a basic double-crust pie has its charms, I wanted to make something more impressive this year—without veering too far from tradition. Since there's an abundance of apples available in New England in the fall, why not pile as many as possible into a deep-dish pie? It seemed an achievable feat, but as I began to research existing recipes, I was cautioned by my fellow test cooks that, more often than not, deep-dish pies are downright flooded with liquid, producing a soggy crust and fillings that range from mushy and applesaucey to simply uncooked. With their warnings in mind, I raised the stakes: This fruit-packed pie also needed to have a crisp, sliceable crust and tender, caramelized apples.

Achieving a crisp crust seemed like the greatest challenge, but I had a sneaking suspicion that a change in vessel could be my pie's saving grace. Where most other deep-dish pies use a standard pie plate and simply pile in the filling, a high-walled option promised to better contain the apples. A cast-iron skillet seemed like the perfect solution. For years I've proudly served up my fair share of centerpiece roasts and rustic cornbreads in this rugged skillet, so I knew it could handle the volume—and the hot cast iron would deepen my crust's browning in the process. I decided to use one of the test kitchen's favorite, go-to recipes for pie crust, which uses vodka in place of some water to ensure the crust doesn't turn tough. It's simple, foolproof, and tastes great. Now, I just needed to make sure that the apples didn't make my crust into a sodden mess.

Though apple pies often veer toward sweeter apples, I like mine with a balance of sweet and tart varieties. For this pie, I peeled, cored, and sliced a few pounds each of sweet Golden Delicious and crisp Granny Smiths. To stave off the crust-compromising excess liquid I'd been warned about, I decided to precook the apples. Microwaving seemed like a quick solution, but it didn't add much in the way of flavor. Instead, I decided to put my skillet to good use. I heated up the pan and dumped in my apple slices. This technique quickly proved overly hasty, as the crowded skillet yielded unevenly cooked apples, with some slices steaming to a soggy mess and just a smattering caramelizing nicely. I decided to pump the brakes, melting butter in the skillet and cooking the apples in batches. Precooking also made the slices shrink down a little, meaning I could bump up my apple haul to a full 4 pounds.

The syrupy cinnamon liquid that ties the filling together is what turns humble apples into a decadent dessert, and since my deep-dish pie was an over-the-top affair already, I wanted to introduce plenty of complementary flavor here. Cinnamon was a given, but from there I created a slurry with apple cider and cornstarch to help loosely bind the apples together. Lemon juice would reinforce the apples' natural pectin, thickening the juices further while lemon zest offered some contrasting zing. The filling needed some sweetness, and adding maple syrup instead of sugar gave me just that plus more complex flavor.

I rolled out the bottom crust and pressed it into my skillet before piling in the apples. Once I'd laid on the top crust (cutting vents in the top for escaping steam and sealing the top and bottom edges together), I slid my pie into the oven to bake. After just under an hour, I was ready to sample my sky-high pie. My mistake made itself obvious immediately: As I tried to serve up my first slice, the bottom crust wouldn't come out neatly and was far paler than expected. Well-seasoned cast-iron skillets should boast a perfectly nonstick surface, but in my case—with the crust weighed down by layers of apples—it clearly behooved me to grease

CAST-IRON SKILLET APPLE PIE

the pan before building my pie. I started over, and was happy to find that my revised deep-dish pie was more than worth the rehash—this time the bottom crust was a crisp golden brown and it lifted cleanly from the pan. I'd also gussied this one up, adding a simple decorative edge to the top crust and brushing on an egg wash for an attractive sheen.

My tasters were all impressed with the rustic presentation—the cast-iron skillet alone won a lot of fans—and when I began plating slices, they were in awe of the sheer volume of apples I'd managed to pack between the two crusts. I agreed that the pie was a stunner, and when they took a bite, their reaction was unanimous: The filling was perfect, with tender, caramelized, sweetly spiced apples, and the cast iron's positive impact on the crust—browning it deeply and imparting rich, buttery flavor into every bite—was unmistakable.

—LEAH COLINS, *America's Test Kitchen Books*

Cast-Iron Skillet Apple Pie

SERVES 8

We like a mix of tart and sweet apples; you can also use Empires or Cortlands (tart) and Fuji, Jonagolds, or Braeburns (sweet). If you use an enameled skillet, we recommend placing a baking sheet underneath while baking to catch any juices that might bubble over. You can use our Foolproof Double-Crust Pie Dough (recipe follows) or store-bought pie dough in this recipe.

- 2 **tablespoons unsalted butter**
- 2 **pounds Golden Delicious apples, peeled, cored, halved, and sliced ½ inch thick**
- 2 **pounds Granny Smith apples, peeled, cored, halved, and sliced ½ inch thick**
- 1 **recipe Foolproof Double-Crust Pie Dough (recipe follows), top and bottom crusts rolled out into 12-inch rounds**
- ¼ **cup apple cider**
- ¼ **cup maple syrup**
- 1 **tablespoon cornstarch**
- ½ **teaspoon salt**
- ½ **teaspoon grated lemon zest plus 1 tablespoon juice**
- ⅛ **teaspoon ground cinnamon**
- 1 **large egg, lightly beaten with 2 tablespoons water**
- 2 **teaspoons sugar**

1. Heat 10-inch cast-iron skillet over medium heat for 3 minutes. Melt 1 tablespoon butter in skillet. Add half of apples, cover, and cook until apples begin to release their juice, about 4 minutes. Uncover and continue to cook, stirring occasionally, until apples are tender and golden brown, about 5 minutes. Transfer apples and their juice to rimmed baking sheet. Repeat with remaining 1 tablespoon butter and remaining apples; transfer to sheet. Spread apples into even layer and let cool to room temperature, about 30 minutes.

2. Adjust oven rack to lowest position and heat oven to 400 degrees. Grease clean, dry, cooled skillet. Loosely roll 1 crust around rolling pin and gently unroll it onto prepared skillet. Ease crust into skillet by gently lifting and supporting edge of dough with your hand while pressing into skillet bottom and corners with your other hand. Leave any overhanging dough in place.

3. Whisk cider, maple syrup, cornstarch, salt, lemon zest and juice, and cinnamon together in large bowl until smooth. Add cooled apples and any accumulated juices and toss to combine. Transfer apple mixture to dough-lined skillet, mounding apples slightly in middle. Loosely roll remaining crust around rolling pin and gently unroll it onto filling.

4. Trim any overhanging dough to ½ inch beyond lip of skillet, then ease edge of top crust into skillet until flush with bottom crust. Gently press top and bottom crusts together to seal. Roll in edge of crust, then press rolled edge against sides of skillet using index finger to create attractive fluted rim. Using paring knife, cut eight 2-inch vents in top crust in circular pattern. Brush crust liberally with egg wash and sprinkle with sugar.

5. Transfer skillet to oven and bake until crust is deep golden brown and filling is bubbling, 40 to 50 minutes, rotating skillet halfway through baking. Transfer skillet to wire rack and let pie cool until filling is set, about 2 hours. Serve slightly warm or at room temperature.

Foolproof Double-Crust Pie Dough

MAKES ENOUGH FOR ONE 10-INCH PIE

Vodka is essential to the tender texture of this crust and imparts no flavor—do not substitute water. This dough is moister than most standard pie doughs and will require lots of flour to roll out (up to ¼ cup). A food processor is essential for making this dough—it cannot be made by hand.

2½ cups (12½ ounces) all-purpose flour

2 tablespoons sugar

1 teaspoon salt

12 tablespoons unsalted butter, cut into ¼-inch pieces and chilled

8 tablespoons vegetable shortening, cut into 4 pieces and chilled

¼ cup vodka, chilled

¼ cup ice water

1. Process 1½ cups flour, sugar, and salt in food processor until combined, about 5 seconds. Scatter butter and shortening over top and continue to process until incorporated and mixture begins to form uneven clumps with no remaining floury bits, about 15 seconds.

2. Scrape down bowl and redistribute dough evenly around processor blade. Sprinkle remaining 1 cup flour over dough and pulse until mixture has broken up into pieces and is evenly distributed around bowl, 4 to 6 pulses.

3. Transfer mixture to large bowl. Sprinkle vodka and ice water over mixture. Stir and press dough together, using stiff rubber spatula, until dough sticks together.

4. Divide dough into 2 even pieces. Turn each piece of dough onto sheet of plastic wrap and flatten each into 4-inch disk. Wrap each piece tightly in plastic and refrigerate for 1 hour. Before rolling out dough, let it sit on counter to soften slightly, about 10 minutes. (Dough can be wrapped tightly in plastic and refrigerated for up to 2 days or frozen for up to 1 month. If frozen, let dough thaw completely on counter before rolling it out.)

NOTES FROM THE TEST KITCHEN

PIE CRUST IN A PINCH

Hands down, homemade pie crust is worth the effort, but when time is of the essence, premade pie crust is a great alternative. Aside from being tasty, we looked for a store-bought crust that could be rolled out and fitted into a larger pan. Subtly sweet, rich, and tender, Wholly Wholesome 9″ Certified Organic Traditional Bake at Home Pie Dough is a strong substitute when there isn't time to make a homemade crust.

CHERRY CLAFOUTI

WHY THIS RECIPE WORKS: Cherry clafouti is at its best when it boasts a smooth yet sliceable custard loaded with juicy cherries in every bite. For concentrated cherry flavor and to stave off any liquid that might compromise the custard, we roasted pitted and halved cherries in a hot oven for 15 minutes. Tossing the cherries with a mixture of flour and cinnamon absorbed any excess juices and replaced the slightly spicy, floral flavor the pits contribute in traditional recipes. Preparing the custard with a moderate amount of dairy and flour made for a tender yet slightly resilient texture with just enough richness. We switched from a casserole dish to a preheated 12-inch skillet for better browning, pouring the custard batter in before sprinkling on the cherries. As it baked, the clafouti puffed and browned to a beautiful golden hue. Once the clafouti had cooled we sprinkled on some sugar for a touch of sweetness and a delicate crunch.

When I have a surplus of summer fruit and not much time to make dessert, I usually throw together a crisp or cobbler—easy, satisfying, and crowd-pleasing. But I've often admired France's answer to those simple desserts: clafouti, a rustic yet graceful baked custard that is studded with fresh fruit such as apricots, plums, or—most classic and my favorite—cherries. To make it, you mix up a batter without any chemical leaveners (similar to that used for crêpes) using flour, sugar, eggs, milk and/or heavy cream, and a touch of vanilla or almond extract; pour it into a buttered baking dish; scatter the cherries (usually unpitted) on top; and bake it for the better part of half an hour. When finished, the custard should be rich and tender but resilient enough to be neatly sliced and the fruit plump enough to disrupt the custard with bright, sweet-tart flavor.

But as simple as clafouti is, the texture of the custard is tricky to get right: It can easily end up either pasty and bready or loose and creamy like crème brûlée. It can turn out too thin to sink a fork into or so tall that it overwhelms the cherries. As for the fruit, whole cherries never integrate well in the custard and often burst, leaking juices into the custard that render it soggy and (thanks to the acid in the fruit juice) curdled in isolated patches. Plus, I've always found the inclusion of pits curious; spitting them out when snacking is one thing, but doing so at the dinner table seems indecorous. I hoped that with a little work, I could come up with a recipe that consistently turned out a rich, tender custard punctuated with bright cherry flavor.

Whether a custard bakes up bready, creamy, or somewhere in between depends largely on the ratio of dairy and flour to eggs. Why? Well, the proteins in whole eggs provide structure; adding fat (from heavy cream, milk, or egg yolks alone) and starch (from flour) dilutes that structure as each buffers the proteins and keeps them from linking up too tightly. The more the protein network is diluted, the looser the custard will be.

For the tender but set texture I wanted, I analyzed the quantities of these core components in a dozen published clafouti recipes and compared the textures they produced. Not surprisingly, the flour-heavy recipes (which called for as much as 1 cup) were the ones that baked up tough and bready, while richer batters (which called for up to 2¼ cups heavy cream) produced custards that were too tender and creamy to slice.

It took several more rounds of tinkering before I hit on the ideal: four whole eggs, 1 cup of heavy cream plus ⅔ cup of whole milk (a combination that lent the batter more than double the amount of fat that an equal amount of half-and-half would have but considerably less than heavy cream alone), and a modest ½ cup of flour. Baked at 350 degrees for about 20 minutes, this custard could be sliced into neat wedges but still yielded to the pressure of a fork.

But as nice as its texture was, this custard was a tad dull, and my tasters and I agreed that some browning on the top and bottom would go a long way toward creating more complex flavor. So I started cranking up the oven temperature. By the time I got to 425 degrees, the very top edge was browning nicely, but the underside remained pale—which made me wonder if the glass baking dish I was using wasn't transferring heat quickly enough to the bottom of the custard.

A 12-inch metal skillet would surely conduct heat faster, I thought. And I was right—the browning improved in the pan. But what really helped was preheating the skillet on the oven's lower rack (close to the heat source), removing it from the oven and adding a pat of butter, and then pouring the batter over the top. The butter browned quickly, adding rich flavor to the custard's underside, and the blast of heat souffléed the

edges for a dramatic appearance and nicely browned crust. A bonus: It was much easier to cut and serve neat slices from the skillet, with its flared sides, than from the straight-sided baking dish.

Most classic clafouti recipes call for whole, unpitted cherries because, they claim, the pits add stronger cherry flavor; not pitting the cherries also saves prep time. But I wondered if the pits made a real flavor difference in clafouti. Even if they did, they made it difficult to slice (and eat) the dessert.

A side-by-side tasting of custards baked with pitted and unpitted cherries proved that the flavor difference was real—my tasters noted a pleasantly warm, cinnamon-like flavor in the unpitted batch. And as it turned out, they were onto something: Cherry pits and cinnamon share a fragrant, floral compound called linalool.

This got me thinking: Why not simply add a touch of cinnamon to pitted cherries? Removing the pits would, of course, add time to the recipe, but the results were well worth the effort. Not only did the cinnamon-dusted pitted cherries taste virtually identical to the unpitted ones, but doing away with the fruits' stones meant that I could halve the cherries, which would prevent them from bursting during baking.

But simply tossing halved cherries into the clafouti didn't prevent them from shedding juice that created those damp, curdled pockets. To fix that, I'd need to drive off some of their moisture before incorporating them into the custard. I tried both microwaving the halved cherries and roasting them (cut side up) on a foil-lined rimmed baking sheet for about 15 minutes. I found that the latter did a better job of driving off moisture; roasting also nicely concentrated the fruits' flavor. As they cooled briefly, I splashed the cherries with fresh lemon juice for a jolt of bright flavor. Then, to sop up any of their residual juices, I added a couple of teaspoons of flour to the cinnamon I was already tossing with the fruit. My final tweak, sprinkling granulated sugar over the baked custard, added just a hint of sweet crunch that contrasted nicely with the tender custard.

This clafouti—with its creamy but set interior, rich-tasting crisp crust, and bursts of concentrated cherry flavor—was an improvement on classic renditions but still simple enough to stand in for a casual cobbler.

—DAN SOUZA, *Cook's Illustrated*

Cherry Clafouti

SERVES 6 TO 8

We prefer whole milk in this recipe, but 1 or 2 percent low-fat milk may be substituted. Do not substitute frozen cherries for the fresh cherries.

1½	pounds fresh sweet cherries, pitted and halved
1	teaspoon lemon juice
2	teaspoons all-purpose flour, plus ½ cup (2½ ounces)
⅛	teaspoon ground cinnamon
4	large eggs
⅔	cup (4⅔ ounces) plus 2 teaspoons sugar
2½	teaspoons vanilla extract
¼	teaspoon salt
1	cup heavy cream
⅔	cup whole milk
1	tablespoon unsalted butter

1. Adjust oven racks to lowest and upper-middle positions; place 12-inch skillet on lower rack and heat oven to 425 degrees. Line rimmed baking sheet with aluminum foil and place cherries, cut side up, on sheet. Roast cherries on upper rack until just tender and cut sides look dry, about 15 minutes. Transfer cherries to medium bowl, toss with lemon juice, and let cool for 5 minutes. Combine 2 teaspoons flour and cinnamon in small bowl; dust flour mixture evenly over cherries and toss to coat thoroughly.

2. Meanwhile, whisk eggs, ⅔ cup sugar, vanilla, and salt in large bowl until smooth and pale, about 1 minute. Whisk in remaining ½ cup flour until smooth. Whisk in cream and milk until incorporated.

3. Remove skillet (skillet handle will be hot) from oven and set on wire rack. Add butter and swirl to coat bottom and sides of skillet (butter will melt and brown quickly). Pour batter into skillet and arrange cherries evenly on top (some will sink). Transfer skillet to lower rack and bake until clafouti puffs and turns golden brown (edges will be dark brown) and center registers 195 degrees, 18 to 22 minutes, rotating skillet halfway through baking. Transfer skillet to wire rack and let cool for 25 minutes. Sprinkle clafouti evenly with remaining 2 teaspoons sugar. Slice into wedges and serve.

SWEET GLAZED PEACHES

✔ **WHY THIS RECIPE WORKS:** Fresh summer peaches are always a treat, but to turn them into a lovely dessert, we wanted to pair them with a lightly sweet glaze. We peeled, pitted, and halved a half-dozen peaches and tossed them in a mixture of lemon juice, sugar, and salt to season the fruit and draw out some of the flavorful juices to begin the glazing process. Sliding them under the broiler for an intense blast of heat warmed and lightly browned the peaches, and adding some water to the skillet before broiling kept the fruit from sticking. Brushing on a mixture of red currant jelly and butter partway through broiling gave the peaches more nuanced flavor, and, once they were well browned, we reduced the juices left in the skillet into a thick glaze to pour over the fruit. Chopped, toasted pistachios added a contrasting crunch to the dessert.

How do you eat your way through an overabundance of ripe, in-season peaches? Some folks grill them for a side dish; others chop them into a fruit salad. I wanted something different: a warm, summery dessert with just enough added sweetness to amplify the peaches' complex, summery flavors.

I found dozens of recipes for glazed peaches, and after a few days in the kitchen, I'd learned that most cover up fruit with cloyingly sweet syrup. What's more, some peaches turned to mush in the oven. None had the light-handed sweetness or velvety texture I wanted.

I gathered another pile of peaches and hit the kitchen. I peeled several peaches (a serrated vegetable peeler made this a breeze), halved and pitted them, tossed the halves with sugar, and baked them at 300 degrees for 40 minutes, thinking that the low temperature would gently caramelize the sugar into a sticky-sweet glaze.

Wrong. By the time the peaches took on any color, there was nothing but mush in the dish. And the sugar had turned bitter during its long stay in the dry heat. I needed a complete rethink.

For my next round, I tossed the peaches with sugar and a little lemon juice for balance and tried a 450-degree oven. The peaches held their shape, but by the time they were warm all the way through, the sugar had burned. I switched to broiling, thinking that the direct heat might give me a little color on top before the peaches overcooked. Adding a bit of water to the pan helped prevent sticking.

SWEET GLAZED PEACHES

I was right. The three small adjustments gave me the soft-but-firm texture I wanted after about 18 minutes in the oven. To boost the flavor, I took the next batch of peaches out after about 11 minutes and brushed them with a mixture of melted butter and red currant jelly before returning them to the broiler. Five more minutes was all it took to get a beautiful, lightly browned batch of peaches with a sticky glaze. A bit more glaze drizzled over, plus a few nuts for texture, and I had a simple, sweet summertime dessert.

—DIANE UNGER, *Cook's Country*

Sweet Glazed Peaches

SERVES 6

Use a serrated peeler to peel the peaches. These peaches are best served warm with vanilla ice cream or frozen custard.

- 2 tablespoons lemon juice
- 1 tablespoon sugar
- ¼ teaspoon salt
- 6 firm, ripe peaches, peeled, halved, and pitted
- ⅓ cup water
- ¼ cup red currant jelly
- 1 tablespoon unsalted butter
- ¼ cup pistachios, toasted and chopped

1. Adjust oven rack 6 inches from broiler element and heat broiler. Combine lemon juice, sugar, and salt in large bowl. Add peaches and toss to combine, making sure to coat all sides with sugar mixture.

2. Transfer peaches, cut side up, to 12-inch oven-safe skillet. Pour any remaining sugar mixture into peach cavities. Pour water around peaches in skillet. Broil until peaches are just beginning to brown, 11 to 15 minutes.

3. Combine jelly and butter in bowl and microwave until melted, about 30 seconds, then stir to combine. Remove peaches from oven and brush half of jelly mixture over peaches. Return peaches to oven and continue to broil until spotty brown, 5 to 7 minutes.

4. Remove skillet from oven, brush peaches with remaining jelly mixture, and transfer peaches to serving platter, leaving juices behind. Bring accumulated juices in skillet to simmer over medium heat and cook until syrupy, about 1 minute. Pour syrup over peaches. Sprinkle with pistachios and serve.

VARIATIONS

Honey-Glazed Peaches

Substitute honey for red currant jelly and toasted, skinned, and coarsely chopped hazelnuts for pistachios.

Raspberry-Glazed Peaches

Substitute seedless raspberry jelly for red currant jelly and toasted, coarsely chopped walnuts for pistachios.

BANANAS FOSTER

✔ **WHY THIS RECIPE WORKS:** Bananas Foster is widely known for its presentation—a dramatic tableside flambé—but for our version, we wanted its boozy, caramelized flavor to be the most memorable part. We skipped the flambé altogether, dissolving dark brown sugar in gold rum for deep caramel flavor. Barely ripe bananas made for peak banana flavor, and they held their shape through cooking, turning just tender during browning. For a perfectly smooth and creamy sauce, we approached it as we would a pan sauce, browning the bananas in the rum-sugar mixture, setting them aside, and then whisking butter into the sauce at the end. An extra hit of rum and some lemon juice, added just before serving, gave this rich, indulgent dessert a fresh finish.

Iconic American dishes come from every corner of the map, but no city's food has more flourish than that of New Orleans. Take bananas Foster, which chef Paul Blangé of Brennan's restaurant conceived in 1951 for Richard Foster, a regular customer who also happened to be chairman of the New Orleans Crime Commission.

This dessert of bananas sautéed in butter, sugar, cinnamon, banana liqueur, and rum was prepared tableside and then, for a bit of dining room theater, set aflame to mute its boozy edges. Served over vanilla ice cream, it quickly became, and remains, a mainstay at many New Orleans restaurants.

But oh, the crimes it has been subjected to since. In my experiments with existing recipes I found mushy bananas, harsh alcohol flavors, and greasy, sickly-sweet sauces. My biggest challenge would be balancing the elements to keep the sweetness in check and the butter amount generous but not greasy.

I omitted the banana liqueur right off the bat; my tasters and I thought it unnecessarily sweet, not to mention tough to find. After several tests, I settled on ripe but not too-ripe bananas, which held up nicely without turning to mush. And I chose dark brown sugar over white or light brown; its rich caramel flavor was just right.

With my ingredients settled, I focused on technique. My biggest question concerned the flambé. While dramatic and exciting, it's also tricky and potentially dangerous, so I wanted to know if it was absolutely necessary. In a series of side-by-side tests, tasters detected only a minuscule difference, but when they were pressed to vote, I was surprised but pleased that a majority preferred the non-flambéed version. Courting heresy, I nixed this eyebrow-singeing step.

For my first post-flambé test, I melted 4 tablespoons of butter in a skillet over medium heat, but I had problems getting all of the sugar dissolved without the butter breaking into a greasy, separated mess, especially after sautéing the bananas and finishing off the sauce. I'd fixed the same problem in other pan sauces, though, so I decided to flip the 65-year-old script and add the butter at the end, off the heat, hoping this would help maintain the butter's creamy emulsion. Would it work?

NOTES FROM THE TEST KITCHEN

TASTING RUM FOR BANANAS FOSTER
The rum-making process starts by fermenting sugar cane juice, sugar cane syrup, or molasses and then distilling the resulting liquid. The clear distillate is then aged—almost always in oak barrels—a process whereby tannins in the wood impart flavor and color. Generally speaking, the longer a rum is aged, the darker it becomes.

LIGHT (WHITE OR SILVER)	**MEDIUM (GOLD OR AMBER)**	**DARK**
Aged 6 to 12 months; clean, straightforward flavor.	Typically aged about 3 years; nuanced caramel flavor.	Typically aged 5 to 7 years; bold molasses flavor.

I set the butter aside and started a fresh batch, whisking together the brown sugar, rum, and cinnamon over medium heat. I also added a couple of tablespoons of water, which loosened the sauce without adding more rum. When the mixture started to steam, I added bananas that I'd quartered into logs and cooked them until they were soft and lightly golden. I moved them to a serving dish and then removed the skillet from the heat and whisked in the butter 1 tablespoon at a time. An extra 2 teaspoons of rum at the end freshened its presence, and a bit of lemon juice offered a burst of brightness.

The resulting sauce was rich, creamy, sweet, buttery, and full of rum flavor. I draped a few pieces of golden sautéed banana on a scoop of vanilla ice cream and drizzled the silky sauce over the top. Tasters were too busy gobbling it up to miss the flambé flourish.

—CHRISTIE MORRISON, *Cook's Country*

Bananas Foster
SERVES 4

Look for yellow bananas with few spots; overly ripe bananas will fall apart during cooking. We prefer the flavor of gold rum, but you can substitute white or dark rum if desired.

½   cup packed (3½ ounces) dark brown sugar
¼   cup plus 2 teaspoons gold rum
2   tablespoons water
1   cinnamon stick
¼   teaspoon salt
3   ripe bananas, peeled, halved crosswise, then halved lengthwise
4   tablespoons unsalted butter, cut into 4 pieces
1   teaspoon lemon juice
    Vanilla ice cream

1. Combine sugar, ¼ cup rum, water, cinnamon stick, and salt in 12-inch skillet. Cook over medium heat, whisking frequently, until sugar is dissolved, 1 to 2 minutes.

2. Add bananas, cut side down, to skillet and cook until glossy and golden on bottom, 1 to 1½ minutes. Flip bananas and continue cooking until tender but not mushy, 1 to 1½ minutes longer. Using tongs, transfer bananas to rimmed serving dish, leaving sauce in skillet.

3. Remove skillet from heat and discard cinnamon stick. Whisk butter into sauce, 1 piece at a time, until incorporated. Whisk in lemon juice and remaining 2 teaspoons rum. Pour sauce over bananas. Serve over vanilla ice cream.

LEMON POSSET WITH BERRIES

✓ **WHY THIS RECIPE WORKS:** Lemon posset is a rich, citrusy dessert that transforms cream, sugar, and lemon juice into a mousse-like treat. For a posset that set up to a firm, dense texture, we reduced a mixture of cream and sugar to evaporate some of the cream's water. A tablespoon of lemon zest added to the cream ensured bright citrus flavor that wouldn't diminish when heated. We added a generous amount of lemon juice to help thicken the mixture and counteract the sweetness of the sugar. Letting the mixture rest for 20 minutes allowed the flavors to meld, and straining it into ramekins ensured a silky-smooth consistency in every serving. Fresh berries offered bright bursts of flavor and kept the posset from feeling overly rich.

It may sound like a small mammal, but posset is actually an old-time English dessert that most Americans have never encountered. Until fairly recently, even most English cooks would likely have associated the name with a tart, creamy drink dating back to the Middle Ages.

But today's posset, which has been taken up by English celebrity chefs and cookbook writers and is starting to appear on American restaurant menus, is something altogether different: a chilled dessert with the marvelously plush texture of a mousse or pudding that comes together almost by magic from nothing more than sugar, cream, and citrus juice. There are no temperamental egg yolks or add-ins like gelatin, flour, or cornstarch needed to help the mixture thicken and set—or to interfere with the clean, bright taste of citrus.

Eager to bring this supremely simple dessert into the test kitchen, I gave a few recipes a whirl, choosing to focus on classic lemon versions (lime, orange, grapefruit, and combinations thereof are also common). The technique rarely varied: Heat cream with sugar until the sugar dissolves, add lemon juice, and chill as you wait for the mixture to gel to a velvety texture. As for the results, every single one appealed to my weakness for creamy, buttery-smooth desserts. But that didn't mean there wasn't room for improvement. Some possets were a bit too thin and almost runny, while others turned out firm but overly sweet, lacking enough citrusy tang to cut the cream's richness. And I wondered if I could make the lemon flavor a bit more complex. With a little finessing, I was sure I could transform these three ingredients into a silky, creamy dessert (think crème brûlée) with enough bright-tart flavor to balance the richness of the cream.

My first step was to understand the magic behind how the dessert works. Here's how it goes: When acid is added to milk (or when milk turns sour over time), the change in pH causes the milk's casein proteins to lose the negative charge that ordinarily keeps them separate. Instead, they bond together in clusters, and the milk becomes grainy, or curdled. When acid is added to cream—which is a more viscous liquid than milk thanks to its smaller amount of water and greater amount of fat (at least 36 percent fat as opposed to whole milk's 3.25 percent)—the effect is different. The fat in cream outweighs the casein proteins 10 to 1 (in milk they are about equal) and so interferes with the proteins' ability to form tight curds. As a result, a smooth, creamy consistency develops instead of a grainy one. Heating the cream for posset also has an effect: It causes the whey proteins in the dairy to unwind and attach themselves to the casein molecules and so helps stabilize the gelled liquid.

With that in mind, I realized that the key to perfect posset would simply be determining the optimal ratio of ingredients to achieve the ideal texture as well as flavor. I decided to nail down sweetness first. I simmered 2-cup batches of heavy cream with different amounts of sugar (from ¼ cup up to ⅔ cup) for 5 minutes, stirred 4 tablespoons of lemon juice into each batch, and then portioned and chilled the mixtures until they were set. Tasting the samples, it was clear that the sugar's role in the dessert was more critical than I initially realized: The less sugar in the mix, the thinner and looser the dessert was. That's because dissolved sugar binds water molecules, increasing viscosity, and therefore gives the gel structure as well as a velvety mouthfeel.

LEMON POSSET WITH BERRIES

(Think of how thick a sugar syrup is compared with plain water.) I decided to move forward using ⅔ cup of sugar, which produced a nicely set consistency. However, I would need to compensate for the sweetness since this amount of sugar made the posset somewhat cloying.

That meant adding more lemon juice. After some fiddling, I found that 6 tablespoons of freshly squeezed juice provided a sharp, tangy—but not harsh—flavor. But that amount of juice also produced a slightly looser set than I liked. I had thought that more lemon juice might create a firmer texture. But by adding more juice, I was also adding more water—just enough, it seemed, to hamper the acid's ability to fully gel the cream.

I had a thought: Cream also contains water, so what if I reduced the cream to remove some of its water? That might get the overall liquid in the mix closer to what it had been with 2 cups of cream and 4 tablespoons of lemon juice, which in turn might let me use a full 6 tablespoons of lemon juice and still have the firm set I wanted. For my next batch, instead of simmering the cream and sugar, I turned up the heat and boiled it hard for a few minutes. I stirred in 6 tablespoons of lemon juice and put the mixture in the refrigerator. When I checked it a few hours later, it was not only firm but also had the most dense, luxuriously creamy texture of any posset I'd made yet. Was there something else going on besides the removal of water?

As it turns out, yes. Our science editor explained that by boiling, I was also concentrating the proteins and fats in the cream, which would lead to a firmer set. Additionally, the vigorous action of boiling the cream instead of simmering it breaks up the fat into more numerous, smaller droplets. This has a twofold effect: There are more of the droplets to get in the way of the casein proteins forming tight curds, which leads to an even creamier texture. At the same time, the increase in the number of fat droplets leads to a thicker consistency. This is because cream is an emulsion of fat and water, and the more fat droplets present to break up the water, the more viscous the mixture.

To ensure consistent results, I elected to boil the cream and sugar not for a certain period of time but to a particular volume. With some experimentation, I found that reducing the cream and sugar to 2 cups (about a 30 percent reduction) before adding the lemon juice produced dense, ultraplush results.

I had the texture of my posset exactly right, but its flavor needed to be a little brighter and more complex. The obvious thing to do was to incorporate some of

NOTES FROM THE TEST KITCHEN

THREE-INGREDIENT MAGIC
Lemon juice, cream, and sugar practically make themselves into posset. Here's how it works.

LEMON JUICE
Lemon juice acidifies the cream, causing the casein proteins in the cream to clump.

HEAVY CREAM
Fat in the cream prevents the casein from clumping tightly; instead of curdling as milk would, the mixture thickens.

SUGAR
The sugar adds viscosity, giving the posset structure and a creamy texture.

the zest, which contains oils that are more resistant to breaking down under heat than the juice and would impart a more well-rounded lemon flavor than the juice alone. I added a full tablespoon of finely grated zest to the cream-sugar mixture before boiling it. Then, after I poured in the lemon juice, I let the mixture steep off the heat for 20 minutes before straining out the zest as well as any skin that formed, ensuring that there would be no skin on the final dessert. The result was a livelier flavor and just the right amount of lemony punch to cut through the sweetness and richness of the cream.

Pleased with my results, I portioned the posset into ramekins (portioning was key; spooning the set dessert from one large serving bowl caused the texture to suffer). After 3 hours in the fridge, the possets were cold, fully set, and ready to be garnished with a handful of fresh mixed berries. This British classic was so easy and elegant that I knew it would become a staple in my repertoire.

—ANNIE PETITO, *Cook's Illustrated*

Lemon Posset with Berries

SERVES 6

This dessert requires portioning into individual servings. Reducing the cream mixture to exactly 2 cups creates the best consistency. Transfer the liquid to a 2-cup heatproof liquid measuring cup once or twice during boiling to monitor the amount. Do not leave the cream unattended, as it can boil over easily.

- 2 cups heavy cream
- ⅔ cup (4⅔ ounces) granulated sugar
- 1 tablespoon grated lemon zest plus 6 tablespoons juice (2 lemons)
- 1½ cups blueberries or raspberries

1. Combine cream, sugar, and lemon zest in medium saucepan and bring to boil over medium heat. Continue to boil, stirring frequently to dissolve sugar. If mixture begins to boil over, briefly remove from heat. Cook until mixture is reduced to 2 cups, 8 to 12 minutes.

2. Remove saucepan from heat and stir in lemon juice. Let sit until mixture is cooled slightly and skin forms on top, about 20 minutes. Strain through fine-mesh strainer into bowl; discard zest. Divide mixture evenly among 6 individual ramekins or serving glasses.

3. Refrigerate, uncovered, until set, at least 3 hours. Once chilled, possets can be wrapped in plastic wrap and refrigerated for up to 2 days. Unwrap and let sit at room temperature for 10 minutes before serving. Garnish with berries and serve.

OLD-FASHIONED VANILLA FROZEN CUSTARD

✓ **WHY THIS RECIPE WORKS:** Frozen custard is ice cream's richer, creamier cousin, but many homemade versions turn icy in the freezer. We wanted a smooth texture, indulgent flavor, and a mostly hands-off approach, so we started with the custard's base. We heated a mixture of heavy cream, whole milk, and a vanilla bean, adding corn syrup to stave off ice crystals. Slowly whisking the warm cream mixture into a rich mixture of egg yolks, sugar, and some dry milk powder helped prevent the eggs from curdling. We also strained the custard to remove any stray solid bits of egg. After chilling the custard, we thoroughly whipped it in a stand mixer, injecting it with plenty of air for a silky texture.

Frozen custard isn't just a fancy name for ice cream; it's actually a lovely frozen treat in its own right—as refreshing on a hot summer afternoon as it is soothing on a cool autumn evening. The popular regional sweet treat (Wisconsin, New York, and Arkansas all claim versions as their own) takes its name from a custard base that includes egg yolks and heavy cream for a luxurious texture.

Commercial frozen custard—the thick, soft serve–like treat made famous by the Kohr Brothers in Coney Island and Kopp's in Milwaukee—requires an industrial condenser to produce its almost taffy-like consistency. But through research, I found recipes for frozen custard in cookbooks written as far back as the late 19th century, long before ice cream makers. I decided to pursue this old-fashioned technique.

Taking a cue from several of these old recipes, I started my testing with a custard: specifically, *crème anglaise*, a classic French cooked custard of cream, milk, sugar, egg yolks, and vanilla. After the mixture reached 180 degrees, I transferred it to a bowl set inside a bigger bowl of ice to quickly cool. Then I followed an approach common in early ice cream recipes and poured the mixture into a baking dish for freezing (the extra surface area this vessel creates helps it freeze quickly). The flavor was excellent. But the texture? Riddled with ice crystals.

The key to supersmooth frozen custard is limiting the buildup of ice crystals as it freezes. How do you do this? Incorporating and churning air reduces the effect of ice crystals—the enemy of smooth ice cream or frozen custard—on the tongue. Machines add this air, and break down the ice crystals, by constantly churning the mixture as it freezes. Most machine-free recipes mimic this action by asking the cook to stir or whisk the mixture periodically during freezing. But I wanted a mostly hands-off approach. What would happen, I wondered, if I incorporated air into the mixture before I froze it? I whipped my custard in a stand mixer, testing varying lengths of whipping time, and achieved a relatively smooth custard after about 3 minutes.

But I wanted better than "relatively" smooth. I wanted perfect. I experimented with different amounts and combinations of dairy ingredients, including heavy cream, half-and-half, whole milk, sweetened condensed milk, and evaporated milk. I found that a combination of heavy cream and whole milk was best. (A little nonfat dry milk powder enhanced the dairy flavor.)

Sugar plays a dual role in frozen custard: as a sweetener and as further insurance against ice crystals. So does corn syrup, but because it's only 40 percent as sweet as white sugar, corn syrup does the job without adding unneeded sweetness. After whipping in plenty of air and freezing the custard, I found its texture silky and creamy.

With a freezer full of baking dishes, I was delighted to find that the custard froze just perfectly in a quart-size plastic container.

—CHRISTIE MORRISON, *Cook's Country*

Old-Fashioned Vanilla Frozen Custard

MAKES ABOUT 1 QUART

One teaspoon of vanilla extract can be substituted for the vanilla bean; stir the extract into the strained custard in step 3. Use an instant-read thermometer for the best results.

6 large egg yolks
¼ cup (1¾ ounces) sugar
2 tablespoons nonfat dry milk powder
1 cup heavy cream
½ cup whole milk
⅓ cup light corn syrup
⅛ teaspoon salt
1 vanilla bean

1. Whisk egg yolks, sugar, and milk powder in bowl until smooth, about 30 seconds; set aside. Combine cream, milk, corn syrup, and salt in medium saucepan. Cut vanilla bean in half lengthwise. Using tip of paring knife, scrape out vanilla seeds and add to cream mixture, along with vanilla bean. Heat cream mixture over medium-high heat, stirring occasionally, until it steams steadily and registers 175 degrees, about 5 minutes. Remove saucepan from heat.

2. Slowly whisk heated cream mixture into yolk mixture to temper. Return cream-yolk mixture to saucepan and cook over medium-low heat, stirring constantly, until mixture thickens and registers 180 degrees, 4 to 6 minutes.

3. Immediately pour custard through fine-mesh strainer set over large bowl; discard vanilla bean. Fill slightly larger bowl with ice and set custard bowl in bowl of ice. Transfer to refrigerator and let chill until custard registers 40 degrees, 1 to 2 hours, stirring occasionally.

4. Transfer chilled custard to stand mixer fitted with whisk and whip on medium-high speed for 3 minutes, or until mixture increases in volume to about 3¾ cups. Pour custard into airtight 1-quart container. Cover and freeze until firm, at least 6 hours, before serving. (Frozen custard is best eaten within 10 days.)

VARIATION

Old-Fashioned Chocolate Frozen Custard
Omit vanilla bean. Add ½ ounce finely chopped 60 percent cacao bittersweet chocolate and 1 tablespoon Dutch-processed cocoa to cream mixture in step 1 before cooking. Add ½ teaspoon vanilla extract to strained custard in step 3.

SO·CAL CHURROS

✓ **WHY THIS RECIPE WORKS:** The fried pastries known as churros should be crisp on the outside and soft on the inside, but piping thick *pâte à choux* dough into hot oil is no easy feat. We began by preparing a simple dough, precooking a mixture of water, butter, sugar, vanilla, and salt before stirring in flour and beating in eggs. The dough proved easier to work with when still warm, so we transferred it to a pastry bag right away. Piping all of the dough onto a baking sheet and then frying the churros in batches made it easier to monitor the their doneness. A roll in cinnamon sugar gave our churros a sweet, authentic finish, and a simple chocolate sauce made for a perfect accompaniment.

The kitchen was stuffy and hot, a pot of oil sizzled on the stove, and dough stuck in clumps to my fingers as I fumbled with a pastry bag. An acrid smell filled the air as one churro started to burn while I was still trying to pipe out the rest of the batch. Were my California dreams—of breezy Pacific seaside evenings eating fluted, fried fritters coated in sweet cinnamon sugar and dunked in chocolate sauce—at a disappointing end? No way. I don't go down that easily. I was determined to succeed.

People often think of churros as Latin American doughnuts, but they are actually more closely related to French cream puffs. Both cream puffs and churros start from the same dough, *pâte à choux*. It's a simple affair: A mix of water, flour, and butter is precooked in a saucepan and then enriched with whole eggs before being shaped and cooked. This dough has a high moisture content, so when portions of it hit the heat (in this case, very hot oil), steam forms and puffs up the pastries. The result: delicately crispy exteriors and soft, airy interiors.

I started with a simple dough: 2 cups each of flour and water, a little butter, and an egg. I spooned the stiff stuff into a pastry bag and, employing a fair amount of muscle and a metal star-shaped tip, piped short logs into a Dutch oven filled with oil shimmering at 375 degrees.

In minutes, I had beautiful golden-brown churros. They looked very nice, but once cooled and tasted, they revealed themselves to be one-dimensional: no crispy-soft contrast in textures, no depth of flavor.

I commenced tinkering. I tried an eggless dough, just to see what would happen, but this resulted in crunchy, not crispy, churros. I tried one egg, two eggs, three eggs. Too few and there was no delicate interior; too many and

the centers were undercooked and soggy. Two eggs plus 2 tablespoons of butter for richness (without weighing things down) was the right ratio. I added 2 tablespoons of sugar and a teaspoon of vanilla for sweetness and flavor, plus a little salt for balance, and my dough was settled. But it still wasn't easy to squeeze through the bag.

A *churrería*, a traditional churro-making shop, would, of course, be outfitted with heavy-duty motorized machinery to extrude the stiff dough through grooved cylinders directly into vats of frying oil. I'd been trying to mimic this process by piping cooled dough directly into the oil, using kitchen scissors to snip churros off at the tip. But as each one dropped into the 375-degree oil, it caused a scary splash. I tried to pipe closer to the oil surface, but keeping a steady hand so close to the hot oil was unnerving. Timing was tricky, too: By the time I'd piped in my sixth churro, the first one had burned. What's more, my danger-ridden piping procedure produced inconsistent lengths and shapes.

The string of failures all added to my mounting anxiety (and waning will, as noted earlier).

Churros are meant to be fun, not fraught. I needed to divide and conquer, breaking down the process into smaller, distinct stages. Could I somehow give all of my attention to piping first and then focus on frying?

Warily optimistic, I piped 6-inch lines of prepared and cooled dough onto a parchment-lined baking sheet, taking my time to make each one perfect. To my delight, they held their shape and were easy to just pick up and slip into the hot oil by hand; I could do it quickly enough to ensure that all six finished at about the same time.

But it took a lot of strength to force the cooled dough out of the bag; I pushed so hard in one test that my piping bag split open. I found that if I piped the dough while it was still slightly warm from the saucepan, I could press it out of the bag with relative ease.

This created another minor challenge: When I went to pick up the warm dough logs, they squished in my hands. But this was easily solved by giving the dough time to cool off a bit. Refrigerating the dough logs for 15 minutes helped even more.

Once they were chilled, I could easily slip six churros into the oil at once without rushing or splashing. After 5 minutes in the oil, they were puffed, crispy, and browned. A light coating of cinnamon-sugar and a simple chocolate sauce for dunking were the perfect finishing touch.

—KATIE LEAIRD, *Cook's Country*

SO-CAL CHURROS

So-Cal Churros

We used a closed star #8 pastry tip, ⅝ inch in diameter, to create deeply grooved ridges in the churros. However, you can use any large, closed star tip of similar diameter, though your yield may vary slightly. It's important to mix the dough for 1 minute in step 2 before adding the eggs to keep them from scrambling.

DOUGH

- 2 cups water
- 2 tablespoons unsalted butter
- 2 tablespoons sugar
- 1 teaspoon vanilla extract
- ½ teaspoon salt
- 2 cups (10 ounces) all-purpose flour
- 2 large eggs
- 2 quarts vegetable oil

CHOCOLATE SAUCE

- ¾ cup heavy cream
- 4 ounces semisweet chocolate chips
- Pinch salt
- ¼ teaspoon vanilla extract

COATING

- ½ cup (3½ ounces) sugar
- ¾ teaspoon ground cinnamon

1. FOR THE DOUGH: Line 1 rimmed baking sheet with parchment paper and spray with vegetable oil spray. Combine water, butter, sugar, vanilla, and salt in large saucepan and bring to boil over medium-high heat. Remove from heat; add flour all at once and stir with rubber spatula until well combined, with no streaks of flour remaining.

2. Transfer dough to bowl of stand mixer. Fit mixer with paddle and mix on low speed until cooled slightly, about 1 minute. Add eggs, increase speed to medium, and beat until fully incorporated, about 1 minute.

3. Transfer warm dough to piping bag fitted with ⅝-inch closed star pastry tip. Pipe eighteen 6-inch lengths of dough onto prepared sheet, using scissors to snip dough at tip. Refrigerate, uncovered, for at least 15 minutes or up to 1 hour.

4. Adjust oven rack to middle position and heat oven to 200 degrees. Set wire rack in second rimmed baking sheet and place in oven. Line large plate with triple layer of paper towels. Add oil to large Dutch oven until it measures about 1½ inches deep and heat over medium-high heat to 375 degrees.

5. Gently drop 6 churros into hot oil and fry until dark golden brown on all sides, about 6 minutes, turning frequently for even cooking. Adjust burner, if necessary, to maintain oil temperature between 350 and 375 degrees. Transfer churros to paper towel–lined plate for 30 seconds to drain off excess oil, then transfer to wire rack in oven. Return oil to 375 degrees and repeat with remaining dough in 2 more batches.

6. FOR THE CHOCOLATE SAUCE: Microwave cream, chocolate chips, and salt in bowl at 50 percent power, stirring occasionally, until melted, about 2 minutes. Stir in vanilla until smooth.

7. FOR THE COATING: Combine sugar and cinnamon in shallow dish. Roll churros in cinnamon sugar, tapping gently to remove excess. Transfer churros to platter and serve warm with chocolate sauce.

NOTES FROM THE TEST KITCHEN

CHURNING OUT CHURROS

1. Stir flour into boiled mixture of water, butter, sugar, vanilla, and salt until no streaks remain.

2. Transfer dough to stand mixer; beat on low speed for 1 minute, then add eggs and beat until incorporated.

3. Pipe eighteen 6-inch lengths of warm dough, snipping at tip. Refrigerate 15 minutes to 1 hour to firm up before frying.

TEST KITCHEN RESOURCES

* Every product tested may not be listed in these pages. Please visit CooksIllustrated.com to find complete listings and information on all products tested and reviewed.

CHAPTER 9

BEST KITCHEN QUICK TIPS

STAMPING OUT PINEAPPLE RINGS

Lisa Gillian of Sugar Grove, Ill., doesn't own a pineapple corer but likes to cut rings from the fruit for serving.

1. After slicing off the skin, slice the fruit into disks.

2. Stamp out the core with a small biscuit cutter.

STACKING POTS WITH LIDS

Sheila Shapiro of West Tisbury, Mass., doesn't have much room to store her lidded pots but has found an easy way to maximize her cabinet space. By upturning the lids on her pots, she can stack them on top of one another. This works especially well for enameled cookware (like a Dutch oven), because it prevents the lid from getting scratched.

SPRITZING MEAT WITH FLAVOR

Joe Hild of Tampa, Fla., spritzes the food he smokes with apple juice to achieve extra flavor. Instead of filling a spray bottle with the juice, he inserts the tube from the sprayer directly into a juice box. That way, he uses just as much as he needs and doesn't need to store an entire bottle of leftover juice.

CLEAN CUPCAKE CARRIER

Expanding on our recent tip about transporting a single cupcake in an upside-down deli container (which also allows you to pick up the cupcake without smearing the frosting), Marni Fylling of Hoboken, N.J., devised a way to transport a whole batch: She flips a plastic storage container upside down, places the cupcakes on the lid, and then snaps the container on top.

SCALING FISH WITH A COOKIE CUTTER

Occasionally when she buys whole fish, Darlene Brunswick of Springfield, Mass., finds that some scales are still intact. To remove them, she grabs her scalloped cookie cutter. The curved edges easily remove the scales when she drags the cutter against them along the length of the fish.

AERATING ONE GLASS OF WINE

Recalling that we had good results aerating a bottle of wine in a blender, Diane Kiino of Kalamazoo, Mich., turned to her electric milk frother when she needed to aerate just one glass. Buzzing the wine with the tiny whisk for just a few seconds improved its flavor.

REMOVING EGGSHELL BITS

Bits of broken eggshell can be hard to remove from a bowl of cracked eggs. Franklin English of Atlanta, Ga., suggests wetting two fingers. Because the water molecules naturally cling to the fingers and the shells, the water acts as a weak glue that makes it easy to pick out the pieces.

COOL CONTAINER FOR BACON GREASE

Many cooks pour bacon grease into a lidded container, such as an old tin can, to let it cool before disposing of it or storing it, but the hot grease makes the metal container too hot to handle. Matt Donnelly of Los Angeles, Calif., instead uses an insulated disposable coffee cup with a lid to contain the grease when discarding it.

SAVING PASTA SCRAPS

Mimicking the bags of mixed pasta scraps commonly sold in Italy, Pauline Fanuele of Nesconset, N.Y., saves unused strands and pieces of short store-bought pastas to use in soups and stews.

SMOOTH CAKE FROSTING

When frosting the sides of a cake, Antonia Chandler of Houston, Texas, finds that her bench scraper is the best tool for smoothing the sides. She spins the cake on a turntable-style stand, holding the edge of the scraper steady against the side of the cake so that it smooths any uneven patches.

SLOW-COOKER WARMING TRAY

Janet McCarron of Seattle, Wash., likes to set up a station for making candy or decorating cookies during the holidays and has found that her slow cooker comes in handy as a warming tray. She places glass jars of chocolate in the vessel and pours in enough water to come partially up their sides, creating a warm bath, which keeps the chocolate warm and fluid for as long as she needs while assembling her treats.

A NEW WAY TO MAKE FUDGE

Rather than fashioning a parchment sling to prevent homemade fudge from sticking to a traditional baking pan, Amy Baranek of Randolph, Mass., uses a springform pan. After removing the sides, she slides an offset spatula under the prepared fudge to pop it onto a cutting board. (To create square pieces for serving, simply trim the rounded edges.)

NO-MESS NUT CHOPPER

Chopping nuts can be messy, as they tend to scatter all over the counter. Chris Wilson of Laurel, Miss., contains them by loading the nuts into a manual citrus juicer, squeezes to break them up, shakes to redistribute the contents, and repeats the method until all the nuts are evenly chopped.

A GRATE IDEA FOR ALMOND PASTE

Pat Wood of Broomfield, Colo., has found that stiff almond paste is difficult to incorporate into other ingredients, even if you crumble it. To break it up even more, she shreds it into fine pieces on a box grater.

MAKESHIFT FREEZER SHELVES

Rather than sift through her freezer to find hidden smaller items, Marsha Wianecki of Okemos, Mich., created shelves using plastic magazine holders. By arranging the holders on their sides with the openings facing forward, she's able to easily see and reach their contents.

BEST KITCHEN QUICK TIPS

MOVING THE MIXER

It was hard for Fran Curtis of Eugene, Ore., to move her heavy stand mixer out of the corner when she wanted to use it until she put the mixer on top of a cotton place mat. Now she is able to easily slide the mixer across the counter when needed.

FRUIT CUSHION

When shopping for delicate pieces of fruit, Brian Solomon of Narberth, Pa., puts the fruit in a plastic bag and blows air into it before tying a knot to seal the opening. The air creates a protective cushion that allows him to put the fruit in his shopping cart or in a bag for the trip home without fear of bruising.

CABBAGE "BOWLS"

When making cabbage-based recipes, like coleslaw, Bonnie Powers of Dublin, N.H., uses the discarded outer leaves as disposable bowls for collecting vegetable peels and scraps. When she's done prepping, she simply tosses the leaves into the garbage or compost.

TRUSSING A CHICKEN WITHOUT TWINE

Helas Wolf of New York, N.Y., discovered that you don't need kitchen twine to truss a chicken. Instead, she uses the pocket of extra fat near the opening of the bird, cutting two slits in the pocket and then crossing the legs and pulling the ankles through the slits.

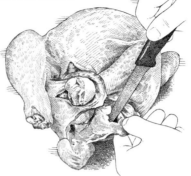

1. Cut slit in fat pocket on 1 side of cavity and thread leg opposite it into and through flap.

2. Cut second slit in fat pocket on other side of cavity and thread second leg into and through slit.

FASTER FOOD WRAPPING

To avoid repeatedly cutting plastic wrap to individually seal up multiple portions of foods like muffins or raw burger patties, Jennifer Siegel of Westfield, N.J., uses this more efficient method.

1. Tear off very long piece of plastic wrap. Place individual portions evenly along bottom half of wrap and fold top half over portions. Press down between them and on ends to seal.

2. Cut between portions to create individual packets, folding edges under to close. (Wrapped foods can be placed in zipper-lock bag or stored individually.)

SECURING POT LIDS

Needing to transport a large pot of hot soup to a potluck, Pat Short of West Lafayette, Ind., came up with the following trick to keep the lid tightly shut. Using large rubber bands (like those wrapped around bunches of broccoli or leeks), she looped two bands around the lid's handle on opposite sides and then stretched the bands over the outer handles on the sides of the pot.

A STEADIER POUR OF SYRUP

Because it's easy to pour out too much maple syrup over pancakes or waffles, Mara Morgan of Boise, Idaho, controls the pour and creates a steady stream by affixing a spare liquid pourer (the kind she uses for cruets of oil and vinegar) to the top of the syrup bottle. The pourer does get sticky, so she removes and washes it between uses.

SAVING SPENT LEMONS FOR ZEST

Instead of tossing out her spent lemon halves after juicing, Susan Lacy of Miamisburg, Ohio, freezes them for zesting later. The halves can be easily stacked and stored in a zipper-lock bag, and the freezer firms them up for easy zesting.

SECURING A DIP BOWL ON A PLATTER

To keep a dip bowl from sliding around on a platter, Janet Tarrant of Prescott, Ariz., folds a piece of plastic wrap into a small square and places it on the platter before placing the bowl on top, pressing on the bowl to secure it. The plastic is virtually invisible, and the bowl of dip stays securely anchored to the platter.

TACO SHELL PREP

Roger Cummings of Olympia, Wash., garnishes four hard-shell tacos at a time by steadying them in an empty egg carton. Any garnishes that fall off drop into the egg carton and are easily discarded afterward.

NOODLE KNIFE BLOCK

Brad Mumsford of St. Louis, Mo., has a surprising use for uncooked spaghetti: a homemade knife block. He packs a tall container with the dried strands and then slides the knives in point side down to store them.

EASY-TO-RECOGNIZE HARD-COOKED EGGS

When Megan Homan of Rockwood, Mich., makes a few hard-cooked eggs for the coming week, she marks their spaces on the cardboard carton with the letter H so she doesn't confuse them with the uncooked eggs.

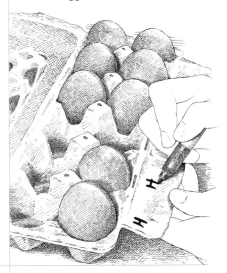

CONTAINING MARINATING MEAT

Miriam Miltenberger of St. David, Ariz., found that an empty plastic salad greens container (one with no holes in the bottom) works well for marinating smaller cuts or chunks of meat. The plastic top snaps tightly to keep the meat contained; the container is flat, so it stacks easily in the fridge; and the container can be rinsed and recycled after use.

CAKE STAND ORGANIZER

When she's not using her cake stand for displaying desserts, Stephanie Kohn of Jacksonville, Fla., discovered that it can do double duty as an organizer for core ingredients like salt, pepper, and olive oil, or even for soap dispensers and sponges. The stand's elevation keeps countertop clutter to a minimum.

FRUGAL FRUIT INFUSION

Rather than throwing them in the trash, Alexis Patrissi of Ardsley, N.Y., saves strawberry tops for flavoring water. Steeping the tops from 1 pound of strawberries in 4 cups of water for 1 hour yields a lightly sweet, fruity beverage, and because the strawberries have already been washed, there is no extra prep. (Spent citrus halves also work well.)

MAKING THE BURGER LOVER'S BURGER

Nothing is more satisfying than a juicy burger. After making hundreds over the years, we've sorted out the ingredients and techniques that produce the perfect patty.

GRIND THE MEAT YOURSELF

Grinding your own meat leads to a burger that's far superior to those made from commercially ground beef because it allows you to control the cut and how finely you grind it. And you don't need special equipment to do it—just a food processor. The trick is to grind the meat fine enough to ensure tenderness but coarse enough that the patty will stay loose.

USE THE BEST CUT

Chuck is often used for commercial ground beef, but it contains lots of connective tissue that must be removed before grinding. Instead, we use sirloin steak tips (or "flap meat"), which are well marbled and require little trimming.

TRIM AND CUT

After removing any excess fat and gristle, cut the steak tips into ½-inch chunks, which will process evenly during grinding.

ADD BUTTER FOR JUICINESS

The fat in butter helps burgers cook up superjuicy, and the butter's protein encourages browning. To ensure that the butter pieces are consistent and evenly distributed, cut the butter into small cubes.

FREEZE THE BEEF AND BUTTER

To firm up the meat and butter before grinding, freeze the pieces on a plate or rimmed baking sheet in a single layer for about 30 minutes. That way, the food processor cuts them cleanly instead of smashing them, which leads to pasty, dense results.

WORK IN BATCHES

Process the beef and butter in small batches, stopping to redistribute them around the bowl as necessary, to ensure a precise, even grind.

INSPECT THE GRIND

After grinding, spread the mixture on a rimmed baking sheet and discard any long strands of gristle or large chunks of hard meat or fat.

FORM THE PATTIES

Careful seasoning and handling will result in flavorful, tender burgers.

WAIT TO SEASON

Salting ground beef before forming patties seasons the meat and keeps it juicy. But don't season the meat until you're ready to form the patties and don't oversalt; over time, salt dissolves meat proteins, causing them to bind together, making for dense, tough patties. Mixing ¾ teaspoon of kosher salt into 1½ pounds of meat produces juicy, tender burgers.

SHAPE WITH A LIGHT TOUCH

The more you handle ground meat, the more its proteins will link together and the tougher the burger will be. Handle the meat gently when forming burgers.

PORTION Divide ground beef into equal-size balls.

PACK Toss each ball between your hands until lightly packed.

PRESS Flatten into patties ¾ inch thick and 4½ inches in diameter.

FOR WELL-DONE BURGERS, ADD A PANADE

If you prefer burgers well-done, a panade can help keep the meat moist and tender. This paste of starch and liquid gets between the meat proteins so that they don't bind together tightly and forms a gel that lubricates the proteins, keeping them moist.

FORMULA: For 1½ pounds of beef, combine 1 slice of hearty white sandwich bread, torn into pieces, with 2 tablespoons of milk. Let mixture sit for about 5 minutes until bread is soaked and mash it to paste with fork; you'll have about ¼ cup. Gently mix panade into meat before forming burgers.

IF YOU DON'T GRIND YOUR OWN MEAT

When you don't have time to grind the meat yourself, follow these guidelines for buying the best possible commercial ground beef.

DO buy ground beef labeled 80 percent lean, ideally "ground chuck," which is well marbled and cooks up relatively tender, juicy, and flavorful (preground chuck contains little gristle).

DON'T buy packages labeled "ground round," a lean, tough cut that lacks beefy flavor, or "ground beef," which can contain cuts from any part of the cow and might be livery or tough.

DON'T buy ground beef that looks brown or that has leached juices into the package—signs that it may not be freshly ground and that it may have been previously frozen, respectively.

DON'T splurge on grass-fed ground beef. It costs about 50 percent more than grain-fed beef, and we've found that the leaner meat lacks the flavor and juiciness we expect in a burger.

DO consider cooking commercial ground beef to 160 degrees, per U.S. Department of Agriculture guidelines.

Burger Lovers' Burgers
SERVES 4

When stirring the salt and pepper into the ground meat and shaping the patties, take care not to overwork the meat or the burgers will be dense. Sirloin steak tips are also sold as flap meat. If desired, toast the buns while the cooked burgers rest. Serve the burgers with your favorite toppings.

- 1½ **pounds sirloin steak tips, trimmed and cut into ½-inch chunks**
- 4 **tablespoons unsalted butter, cut into ¼-inch pieces**
  Kosher salt and pepper
- 1 **(13 by 9-inch) disposable aluminum pan (if using charcoal)**
- 1 **teaspoon vegetable oil (if using stovetop)**
- 4 **hamburger buns**

1. FREEZE MEAT Place beef chunks and butter on large plate or rimmed baking sheet in single layer. Freeze until meat is very firm and starting to harden around edges but still pliable, about 35 minutes.

2. GRIND MEAT Place one-quarter of meat and one-quarter of butter pieces in food processor and pulse until finely ground into rice grain–size pieces (about 1/32 inch), 15 to 20 pulses, stopping and redistributing meat around bowl as necessary to ensure beef is evenly ground. Transfer meat to baking sheet. Repeat grinding with remaining meat and butter in 3 batches. Spread mixture over sheet and inspect carefully, discarding any long strands of gristle or large chunks of hard meat, fat, or butter.

3. FORM PATTIES Sprinkle 1 teaspoon pepper and ¾ teaspoon salt over meat and gently toss with fork to combine. Divide meat into 4 balls. Toss each between your hands until uniformly but lightly packed. Gently flatten into patties ¾ inch thick and about 4½ inches in diameter.

DONENESS CHART

To take the temperature of burgers without breaking them apart, leave them in the pan (or on the grill), slide the tip of the thermometer into the top edge, and push it toward the center, making sure to avoid hitting the pan (or grill grate) with the probe.

GRILL METHOD

4. Using your thumb, make 1-inch-wide by ¼-inch-deep depression in center of each patty. Transfer patties to platter and freeze for 30 to 45 minutes.

5A. FOR A CHARCOAL GRILL: Using skewer, poke 12 holes in bottom of disposable pan. Open bottom vent completely and place disposable pan in center of grill. Light large chimney starter two-thirds filled with charcoal briquettes (4½ quarts). When top coals are partially covered with ash, pour into disposable pan. Set cooking grate in place, cover, and open lid vent completely. Heat grill until hot, about 5 minutes.

5B. FOR A GAS GRILL: Turn all burners to high, cover, and heat grill until hot, about 15 minutes. Leave all burners on high.

6. Clean and oil cooking grate. Season 1 side of patties liberally with salt and pepper. Using spatula, flip patties and season other side. Grill patties (directly over coals if using charcoal), without moving them, until browned and meat easily releases from grill, 4 to 7 minutes. Flip patties and continue to grill until browned on second side and meat registers 120 to 125 degrees (for medium-rare) or 130 to 135 degrees (for medium), 4 to 7 minutes longer.

7. Transfer burgers to plate and let rest for 5 minutes. Transfer burgers to buns and serve with toppings.

STOVETOP METHOD

4. Season 1 side of patties liberally with salt and pepper. Using spatula, flip patties and season other side. Heat oil in 12-inch skillet over high heat until just smoking. Using spatula, transfer burgers to skillet and cook, without moving them, for 3 minutes. Using spatula, flip burgers and continue to cook until burgers register 120 to 125 degrees (for medium-rare) or 130 to 135 degrees (for medium), 2 to 3 minutes longer.

5. Transfer burgers to plate and let rest for 5 minutes. Transfer burgers to buns and serve with toppings.

	DEGREES (BEFORE REST)
MEDIUM-RARE	120–125
MEDIUM	130–135
MEDIUM-WELL	140–145
WELL-DONE	160+

FOR FLAT BURGERS, MAKE AN IMPRESSION

Making a slight dimple in the center of a raw patty can prevent it from bulging as it cooks, which happens when the meat's protein exceeds 140 degrees and shrinks, squeezing the edges of the patty like a belt. But only grilled burgers need to be dimpled. Why? Because while grilled burgers will be exposed to high heat all over even without direct contact with the cooking surface, only the portions of pan-seared burgers that make contact with the cooking surface will get very hot. Plus, pan-seared burgers cook more quickly, so the meat is less susceptible to shrinking.

DIMPLE DOS AND DON'TS
Dimple burgers cooked on the grill, but don't bother dimpling burgers in a skillet.

MAKE IT A CHEESEBURGER

Adding cheese at the right time and trapping heat around the burgers help the slices melt quickly and evenly.

WAIT TO ADD CHEESE

When the burgers are nearly done—about 2 minutes to go on the grill and 90 seconds on the stove—top them with sliced cheese (we like cheddar or American).

ADD A LID

Cover grilled burgers with an overturned disposable aluminum roasting pan and stovetop burgers with a lid.

TIP: TRACK DONENESS WITH TOOTHPICKS

When cooking for a crowd, it can be tricky to distinguish well-done burgers from medium-rare at a glance. Assign each level of doneness a particular number of toothpicks (e.g., one for rare, two for medium, three for well-done) and peg the proper marker(s) into the patties as they come off the heat.

GUIDE TO FREEZING INGREDIENTS

Too often, that extra half-can of tomato paste or handful of chopped onion gets thrown away. We tested dozens of ingredients to see which we could freeze for future use.

FREEZE IT RIGHT

When freezing food, air is the enemy. Freezer burn, indicated by ice crystals and brownish-white discoloration, happens when frozen food is exposed to air and dehydrates and oxidizes. Here's how to ensure the best texture and flavor.

KEEP YOUR FREEZER COLD

The quicker foods freeze, and the fewer temperature fluctuations once frozen, the better. Your freezer should register 0 degrees Fahrenheit or colder; use a thermometer to check.

KEEP A RECORD!

Freezing leftovers is great—until you forget about them. To keep track of what you have, affix a dry-erase board to the freezer and make notes when you add items. This also reminds you to use up older items.

PORTION LIQUIDS

Liquids can be frozen in ice cube trays and then transferred to a zipper-lock bag.

MINIMIZE HEADROOM

In hardsided containers, fill to ½ inch from the top and place plastic wrap on the food's surface before attaching the lid.

DOUBLE WRAP

For solid foods you're wrapping in zipper-lock bags, first wrap in plastic wrap and then put the food in the bag, pressing out as much air as possible before sealing.

PANTRY

These pantry ingredients can be frozen and thawed with virtually no noticeable change in quality.

ANCHOVIES, BACON
Coil up individually, freeze on plate, and transfer to zipper-lock bag.

APPLESAUCE
Portion in ½- to 1-cup containers to freeze; transfer to zipper-lock bag.

BEANS (SOAKED AND CANNED)
Rinse soaked dried beans and drain canned beans. Pat beans dry with paper towels, transfer to zipper-lock bag.

BREAD
Wrap sliced loaves in plastic wrap; wrap unsliced loaves in foil and seal in zipper-lock bag. Thaw slices at room temperature; no need to thaw slices for toast. Place foil-wrapped loaves in 450-degree oven for 10 to 15 minutes; remove foil and return to oven for 1 to 2 minutes.

BROTH
Freeze small amounts in ice cube trays or muffin tin cups; transfer to zipper-lock bag. Pour large portions broth into zipper-lock bag, seal, and lay flat to freeze.

CANNED TOMATO PASTE
Open ends of can, push out paste, and freeze in zipper-lock bag.

CHIPOTLE CHILES IN ADOBO SAUCE
Freeze spoonfuls of chiles and sauce on parchment paper–lined baking sheet; transfer to zipper-lock bag.

COCONUT MILK
Portion into ½- to 1-cup containers to freeze; transfer to zipper-lock bag. After thawing, process with immersion blender for 30 seconds to re-emulsify before use.

COOKED GRAINS
Spread cooked grains on baking sheet to cool, transfer to zipper-lock bag, and lay flat to freeze. No need to thaw before use.

TORTILLAS (CORN AND FLOUR)
Separate tortillas with waxed or parchment paper and place in zipper-lock bag. To thaw, defrost stacks of 3 to 4 tortillas in microwave at 50 percent power, 10 to 20 seconds per stack.

WINE
Freeze 1-tablespoon portions in ice cube tray; transfer to zipper-lock bag. Use only in cooking since freezing causes many of wine's organic compounds to precipitate out as solids (heat reintegrates them).

DAIRY AND EGGS

We found that freezing dairy products and eggs didn't affect flavor, only texture. Liquids seemed thinner and separated; yogurts and some cheeses were grainy. That's because freezing causes the water and proteins to separate; the water then forms ice crystals while the proteins clump. Blending liquids with an immersion blender will eliminate some but not all clumps, so it's best to use thawed dairy in baked goods where it's not a primary ingredient. (Freezing also separates water and protein in egg yolks. But we came up with a great fix: stirring a simple syrup into the yolks. The dissolved sugar interferes with ice crystal formation and also prevents clumping.)

CREAM CHEESE

Seal in zipper-lock bag. Don't use as spread or in recipes where grainy texture will be noticeable, such as in cheesecake. Fine for biscuits and pound cake.

CULTURED DAIRY (BUTTERMILK, SOUR CREAM, YOGURT)

Portion in ½- to 1-cup containers to freeze; transfer to zipper-lock bag. Not good for custards, puddings, or most uncooked applications. (Greek yogurt is the exception—since freezing thins its texture, it can be swapped for regular yogurt in uncooked recipes.) Thawed buttermilk mixes well in salad dressings that include emulsifying agents (e.g., mayonnaise).

EGG WHITES

Freeze individually in ice cube trays; transfer to zipper-lock bag. Thawed whites will whip more quickly than fresh since freezing begins the process of unwinding their proteins that whipping continues.

EGG YOLKS

Prepare syrup of 2 parts sugar to 1 part water; stir into yolks using ¾ teaspoon syrup per 4 yolks. Syrup will not impart noticeable sweetness; yolks are fine even for savory applications such as hollandaise sauce.

HARD AND SEMISOFT CHEESES

Wrap cheese (cheddar, Brie, Pecorino Romano, mozzarella, and Parmesan all freeze well) tightly in foil; seal in zipper-lock bag. Cheddar turns crumbly after thawing; use only in melted applications.

MILK AND CREAM

Portion in ½- to 1-cup containers to freeze; transfer to zipper-lock bag. Avoid using in uncooked applications; custards and puddings; and coffee, cocoa, and other hot beverages. Fine for baked goods and mashed potatoes. Thawed heavy cream can be whipped, but use it immediately or it will start to weep.

PRODUCE

Freezing alters the texture of many types of produce, but their flavors can remain intact.

BANANAS

Peel and seal in zipper-lock bag. Best for quick breads (thaw first) and smoothies (keep frozen). Avoid pies, puddings, or recipes where bananas needs to hold their shape.

CITRUS ZEST

Freeze in packed ½-teaspoon mounds on baking sheet; transfer to zipper-lock bag. Avoid using as garnish since color fades.

CHOPPED ONIONS

Seal in zipper-lock bag. Freezing turns onions mushy. Use only in cooked applications (no need to thaw first).

FRESH HERBS

Chop parsley, basil, tarragon, or cilantro; transfer by spoonful to ice cube trays, top with water, and freeze. Transfer to zipper-lock bag. Add frozen cubes directly to soups, sauces, and stews. Herb flavor won't be quite as strong as fresh.

GARLIC

Mince garlic, combine with ½ teaspoon vegetable oil per clove, and freeze in heaping teaspoons on baking sheet. Transfer to zipper-lock bag.

GINGER

Grate ginger, freeze 1-teaspoon portions on baking sheet, and transfer to zipper-lock bag.

SCIENCE: CUT GARLIC AND ONIONS BEFORE FREEZING

Cut garlic and onions release the same enzyme that reacts with their sulfur compounds to produce their pungent flavors. Freezing reduces the enzyme's activity, so garlic and onions should be cut before freezing to preserve their flavors. One difference in how we freeze them: We coat garlic in oil to protect its flavor compounds from oxidation. Onions contain an extra enzyme that does this job, so there's no need for oil.

FIVE TO ALWAYS FREEZE

There are a few ingredients that we always put directly in the freezer to preserve freshness and flavor and prevent spoilage.

BAY LEAVES

Stored in the freezer for three months, bay leaves were far more flavorful than those stored at room temperature for the same amount of time.

EXTRA BUTTER

If kept in the fridge longer than a month, even unopened sticks of butter can pick up off-flavors. Freeze extra sticks sealed in a zipper-lock bag.

EXTRA COFFEE BEANS

Unless coffee beans are sealed in unopened, airtight containers, their flavor deteriorates noticeably after 10 days at room temperature. Before freezing, portion extra beans in one-day allotments to minimize exposure to air and moisture.

NUTS

The high fat content of nuts means that they can turn rancid surprisingly fast at room temperature. There's no need to thaw them before use.

WHOLE-GRAIN FLOURS, OATS, AND CORNMEAL

Freezing prevents fats in whole grains from oxidizing and producing off-flavors; transfer items to airtight containers first. Bring them to room temperature before baking with them.

ESSENTIAL GUIDE TO TURKEY

Turkey can look and taste great, or it can be a dry, pale disaster. Even if this is your first turkey, our guide will help you buy, prepare, and roast the perfect bird.

SHOPPING

Around the holidays, turkeys come fresh and frozen, large and small, and often stamped with confusing package labels. Here's what to look for—and what to avoid.

FRESH ISN'T ALWAYS BEST

Unless you're buying a turkey fresh from a local farm, a frozen turkey is a better bet. Why? Frozen turkeys are frozen quickly and completely, which prevents large ice crystals from forming and damaging the meat. Turkeys labeled "fresh" may be chilled to as low as 26 degrees, a temperature at which tiny ice crystals can still form in the meat. If these crystals melt (which can happen if the temperature fluctuates during transport or thawing), they can merge with neighboring crystals, refreeze, and puncture the meat, allowing juices to escape during cooking and the meat to cook up dry and tough.

DON'T BUY BIG

The bigger the bird, the harder it is to get the white and dark meat to cook evenly. Plus, some ovens can't accommodate large turkeys. We recommend birds that weigh between 12 and 14 pounds. If you're feeding a crowd, consider supplementing the whole bird with turkey parts.

BUYER BEWARE

The terms below aren't always plainly stamped on package labels, so be sure to check the fine print for notations about water retention or added ingredients.

WATER-CHILLED

Most poultry is water-chilled—that is, dunked in a cold chlorinated bath, which causes it to retain water, diluting flavor and inflating cost. We've found that these birds can taste bland and spongy compared with air-chilled poultry. (Air-chilling is typically noted on labels.) The only water-chilled poultry we do buy is kosher, since the process saves you the trouble of brining.

PRE- OR SELF-BASTED

Pre- or self-basted (also called "enhanced") turkeys are water-chilled birds injected with a solution (look for turkey broth, oil, sugar, or sodium phosphate on the label) to enhance flavor and moisture. We've found them to be somewhat wet with a mild, almost bland flavor.

OUR FAVORITE TURKEYS

We prefer air-chilled poultry, which is hung from a conveyor belt and circulated around a cold room, because the process produces birds with better flavor and texture than water-chilled birds. However, air-chilled turkeys can be hard to find, so we have two alternatives.

TIMESAVER: KOSHER

Per Jewish dietary law, kosher turkey carcasses are covered in kosher salt and then rinsed multiple times in cold water, which seasons the meat and helps it retain moisture. As a result, kosher turkeys do not need to be brined or salted.

- Our favorite: **Empire Kosher Turkey** ($2.49 per lb)

SPLURGE: HERITAGE

Because heritage turkeys are conceived naturally and allowed to live longer than conventional birds, they have longer legs and wings, more fat and dark meat, and richer flavor. The downside: They can cost 10 times more than conventional turkeys.

- Our favorite: **Mary's Free-Range Heritage Turkey** ($166.72 for 7- to 14-lb bird, plus shipping)

MUST-HAVE TURKEY TOOLS

INSTANT-READ THERMOMETER:

- Our favorite: **ThermoWorks Splash-Proof Super-Fast Thermapen** ($96.00)

We love this thermometer's accuracy, how rapidly it registers temperatures, and its large, easy-to-read display.

ROASTING RACK:

- Our favorite: **All-Clad Non-Stick Roasting Rack** ($24.95)

This durable rack has conveniently located handles and is large enough to hold a 14-pound turkey.

ROASTING PAN:

- Our favorite: **Calphalon Contemporary Stainless Roasting Pan with Rack** ($99.99)

The sturdy construction of this pan and its roomy, secure handles earned it our top rating. It comes with a U-shaped rack.

DON'T BOTHER:

- **Covered Oval Roasting Pans**
  Problems: narrow, crowded, small handles

- **Disposable Aluminum Roasting Pans**
  Problems: flimsy construction, no handles

- **Bulb Baster**
  Problems: basting prevents skin from drying and crisping (see "Six Roasting Rules")

BEFORE YOU COOK

DEFROST EARLY

Whole turkeys take several days to thaw. Plan on one day for every 4 pounds—and if your bird isn't kosher or prebasted, factor in at least 6 hours to brine or at least 24 hours to salt.

- **Emergency Quick-Thaw:** Place turkey in its wrapper in bucket filled with cold water and thaw for 30 minutes per pound. Change water every half-hour to prevent bacteria growth.

BRINE OR SALT FOR BETTER FLAVOR AND TEXTURE

Brining and salting both season and enhance juiciness in turkey meat. Which method you use depends on how much time and space you have and how much you care about having really crisp skin.

BRINING

PROS: faster (6 to 12 hours)

CONS: requires a lot of fridge space; extra moisture can prevent skin from crisping

- Our favorite brining bag: **Ziploc Big Bags XL** ($5.79 for four 2 by 1.7-foot foodsafe bags)

SALTING

PROS: requires less fridge space; helps skin dry out and crisp

CONS: slower (24 to 48 hours)

SAVE (MOST OF) THE GIBLETS

Turkey cavities often contain the neck, heart, and gizzard—flavor powerhouses that should be used for gravy. Brown and sweat them to extract flavor and then discard. Just don't use the liver (large, shiny, dark red); its strong flavor ruins gravy.

TAKING TURKEY'S TEMPERATURE

The most reliable way to gauge the doneness of turkey is to take its temperature with an instant-read thermometer.

BREAST: Insert the thermometer from the neck end, holding it parallel to the bird. (Avoid hitting the bone, which can give an inaccurate reading.) It should register 160 degrees.

THIGH: Insert the thermometer at an angle into the area between the drumstick and breast away from the bone. It should register 175 degrees.

REHEATING LEFTOVER TURKEY

Our gentle method helps ensure moist meat and crisp skin.

1. Wrap all leftovers in aluminum foil, stacking any slices, and place on wire rack set in rimmed baking sheet. Heat in 275-degree oven until meat registers 130 degrees.

2. Place any skin-on pieces skin side down in lightly oiled skillet over medium-high heat, heating until skin recrisps.

1. WARM GENTLY:
Heat all leftovers in 275-degree oven.

2. RECRISP SKIN:
Recrisp any skin-on pieces in oiled skillet.

SIX ROASTING RULES

1. DON'T STUFF

Stuffing cooked in the turkey cavity tastes great, but by the time the stuffing reaches a safe temperature (165 degrees), the meat is overcooked.

2. ROAST ON A RACK

Roasting a turkey on a V-rack allows air to circulate around the bird, which helps the meat cook evenly and the skin dry out and crisp.

3. FLIP DURING COOKING

Start the bird breast side down to shield the white meat from the heat and then turn it breast side up halfway through cooking to crisp the skin. Use clean paper towels to grab the turkey at the top and bottom ends, tip it so the juices in the cavity run into the pan, and flip it breast side up.

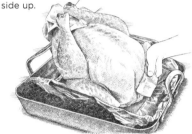

4. DON'T BASTE

Basting does nothing to moisten dry breast meat. The liquid runs off the turkey, and it prevents the skin from crisping.

5. DON'T RELY ON POP-UP THERMOMETERS

If your turkey comes with a pre-inserted thermometer, ignore it (but don't remove it). These devices can pop up above or below a foodsafe temperature.

6. LET REST BEFORE CARVING

Resting the turkey for about 30 minutes allows its muscle fibers to reabsorb juices; skip this step and that liquid will run all over your carving board, leaving the meat dry. No need to tent the turkey with aluminum foil; as long as it's intact, it will cool slowly.

PINK TURKEY IS OK

Pink-tinted turkey isn't necessarily undercooked. Often, the color is simply an indication that the pH of the meat is high, which stabilizes the meat's pink pigment so that it doesn't break down when exposed to heat. (We've observed that pork with a high pH can also remain pink when fully cooked.) As long as the meat registers the prescribed temperature, it's safe.

ESSENTIAL TOOLS (AND INGENIOUS GADGETS)

Decades of testing have taught us what every well-equipped kitchen should have. Here are our favorite tools—plus a handful of other useful gadgets.

THE MUST-HAVES

These models are the best of the best in their respective categories.

BENCH SCRAPER

DexterRussell 6" Dough Cutter/Scraper—Sani-Safe Series

Its sharp beveled edge cuts, scrapes, and scoops with ease.

CAN OPENER

Fissler Magic SmoothEdge Can Opener

It tidily removes lids; plus, its long handle offers great leverage.

COARSE GRATER

Rösle Coarse Grater

This flat paddle with grippy feet can grate over any surface or bowl.

COLANDER

RSVP International Endurance Precision Pierced 5 Qt. Colander

Tiny, allover perforations drain water quickly but don't allow food to slip through.

DRY MEASURING CUPS

Amco Houseworks Professional Performance 4-Piece Measuring Cup Set

Long, clearly marked handles make the "dip and sweep" method easy.

GARLIC PRESS

Kuhn Rikon Stainless Steel Epicurean Garlic Press

Conical holes produce a fine, uniform mince for even flavor. Easy to squeeze and clean.

INSTANT-READ THERMOMETER

ThermoWorks SplashProof SuperFast Thermapen

So fast and easy to use, you'll wonder how you ever lived without it.

KITCHEN SHEARS

Kershaw Taskmaster Shears/Shun Multi-Purpose Shears

These shears are sharp enough to butcher chicken yet nimble enough to trim pie dough.

LADLE

Rösle Hook Ladle with Pouring Rim

The Rösle's angled handle offers control when reaching into any pot.

LIQUID MEASURING CUP

Pyrex 2-Cup Measuring Cup

It's everything you need: sturdy tempered glass etched with clear, fade-resistant markings.

MANDOLINE/V-SLICER

Swissmar Börner Original V-Slicer Plus Mandoline

It can slice faster and more precisely than a skilled chef with a knife.

MEASURING SPOONS

Cuisipro Stainless Steel Measuring Spoon Set

The oval bowls of these spoons fit in small jars and are flush with the handles for level measuring.

RASP GRATER

Microplane Classic Zester Grater

With minimal effort, it grates wisps of cheese or citrus zest and makes paste of garlic or ginger.

SALAD SPINNER

OXO Good Grips Salad Spinner

The OXO dries greens more thoroughly than any other model.

SILICONE SPATULA

Rubbermaid Professional 13½-Inch High-Heat Scraper

Its firm-but-flexible edge scrapes as well as it stirs.

TONGS

OXO Good Grips 12-Inch Locking Tongs

The shallow pincers grip heavy roasts as easily as they do slender asparagus spears.

VEGETABLE PEELER

Kuhn Rikon Original Swiss Peeler

This lightweight, cheap peeler skins anything from butternut squash to ginger.

WHISK

OXO Good Grips 11" Balloon Whisk

This lightweight model features a long handle that won't slip into bowls or pots.

CLEVER USES FOR CORE TOOLS

Some of our favorite tools have hidden talents.

SALAD SPINNER
Thoroughly but gently dry berries and herbs by spinning them in a paper towel–lined salad spinner.

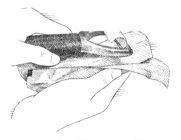

VEGETABLE PEELER
Peel cold butter into thin ribbons that are easy to spread.

FISH SPATULA
Slide the thin edge under delicate cookies.

COARSE GRATER
Break down a rock-hard block of brown sugar by shaving it along the grater's sharp holes.

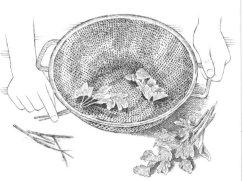

COLANDER
Pluck herbs by pulling the stems through the colander's tiny holes.

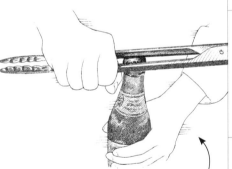

TONGS
Open a bottle by sandwiching the cap between the handles and gently pulling to pop it off.

Extract citrus juice by holding the tongs closed, sticking the pincers into the halved fruit, and twisting.

GADGETS WORTH BUYING

We've tested hundreds of quirky gadgets over the years, but only a handful have stood out as useful.

ADJUSTABLE MEASURING CUP: KITCHENART ADJUST-A-CUP PROFESSIONAL SERIES, 2-CUP

WHY IT'S WORTH OWNING: This clear plastic barrel with measurement markings and a plunger makes it easy to measure and extract semi-solid or sticky ingredients like honey or peanut butter. Simply draw back the plunger to the desired marking, fill the cup, and push forward to eject the ingredient—no fussy scraping needed.

BOIL-OVER PREVENTION: KUHN RIKON SPILL STOPPER

WHY IT'S WORTH OWNING: This bowl-shaped flexible silicone lid (which doubles as a splatter guard) has flaps that open just enough to let milk foam flow over its surface, where it is contained by curved edges.

BOWL ANCHOR: STAYBOWLIZER

WHY IT'S WORTH OWNING: This two-sided silicone gadget solves the problem of mixing bowls that spin or rock on the counter, leaving our hands free to whisk oil into vinaigrette or mix cookie dough.

JAR OPENER: AMCO SWING-A-WAY JAR OPENER

WHY IT'S WORTH OWNING: Using a combination of traction and pressure, this model releases the vacuum on jars of all sizes and loosens tight threads on plastic lids.

WINE AERATOR: NUANCE WINE FINER

WHY IT'S WORTH OWNING: This long, tube-like aerator improves wine's flavor and aroma without the usual wait for the wine to breathe. It slides into the neck of the bottle, leaving only a pouring spout for neat, hands-free aerating.

HOMEMADE CHICKEN BROTH THREE WAYS

Homemade broth brings everything to a higher level. With these simple recipes and tips, you may never go back to the commercial stuff.

BUILDING BLOCKS OF GOOD BROTH

Great chicken broth is like culinary liquid gold: a backbone of savory cooking that can transform even the simplest soup, sauce, rice, or pasta into something flavorful and satisfying. To work in a variety of applications, the broth should taste rich yet balanced and neutral—not assertive, vegetal, sour, or sweet. And unlike watery commercial broths, good homemade versions should boast gelatin-rich body. The trick to a good broth is choosing the right ingredients.

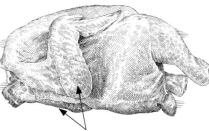

WINGS AND BACK
Good sources of collagen and meat (and some fat)

WHAT PARTS GO IN THE POT?

Historically, thrifty cooks made chicken broth with leftover carcasses or older hens that were too tough for eating. Today, most homemade versions use anything from a whole bird to scraps like backs and wings. To see which parts make the best broth, we compared four batches of broth made with 4 pounds of all wings, all backs, all legs, and a combination of backs and wings, choosing these parts because they contain relatively high levels of collagen. We deliberately left out breasts, since they offer little collagen, are not a well-exercised muscle, and are expensive; whole birds, since they contain a high proportion of breast meat; and thighs, which offer similar traits to legs but cost more.

All four broths were flavorful and full-bodied, but the batch made with the combination of backs and wings offered the richest flavor and the most viscous consistency. The backs are full of collagen that breaks down into gelatin during cooking; they also contain a little muscle and fat. Wings boast a large amount of skin and multiple joints, both of which are abundant sources of collagen as well as flavorful meat, making them a better choice than legs, which contain fewer joints. Chicken backs are often available at supermarket butcher counters during colder months. You can also freeze backs if you butcher a whole chicken at home.

TWO HANDY TOOLS

A good pot is critical for making broth—we use our favorite, Le Creuset 7¼-Quart Round French Oven ($349.99)—and these two tools make the process easier and more efficient.

LAMSONSHARP 7-Inch Meat Cleaver ($48.00)
This reasonably priced model offers a comfortable handle and a sharp blade.

CIA Masters Collection Fine-Mesh Strainer ($27.49)
This model sits securely on most bowls, thanks to a wide bowl rest.

SAVE THE FAT

Flavorful chicken fat makes a great substitute for butter or oil in a number of savory applications, such as sautéing aromatics, roasting root vegetables, and frying eggs. Store it in an airtight container in the refrigerator for up to one month or in the freezer for up to six months, adding more fat as desired.

BODY BUILDER FOR QUICK BROTHS

Because our Quick and Cheater Chicken Broths don't call for a long simmering time, they lack the body of our Classic Chicken Broth. But there's a quick fix: unflavored gelatin. Adding 1 tablespoon per cup of liquid gives these broths surprisingly good body.

MINIMIZE OTHER FLAVORS

Because we want our broths to taste as chicken-y as possible, we skip the traditional *mirepoix*—the mixture of chopped onions, carrots, and celery used as a base for soups and stews—as well as other popular additions like garlic and thyme. Instead, we use only chopped onion and bay leaves, which add just enough dimension and flavor to the broth without making it taste too vegetal.

KEEP IT SIMPLE
For the best flavor, we add only onion and bay leaves.

FOR CLEARER BROTH, SIMMER; DON'T BOIL

Boiling will cause soluble proteins and rendered fat from the meat to emulsify into the cooking liquid, turning it greasy and cloudy. By simmering, you minimize the amount of fat that gets emulsified, so the broth is clearer, and the scum simply settles to the bottom of the pot, where it can be avoided.

SIMMERING: Fine bubbles constantly breaking at the surface; wisps of steam.

BOILING: Large bubbles constantly breaking at the surface; heavy steam.

CLASSIC CHICKEN BROTH
Makes about 8 cups

This classic approach to making chicken broth calls for simmering chicken backs and wings in water for several hours but requires almost no hands-on work. The long, slow simmer helps the bones and meat release both deep flavor and gelatin.

Why Make This Broth: Rich flavor and body with very little hands-on work.

> **Prep time:** about 5 minutes
> **Cook time:** about 5 hours

If you have a large pot (at least 12 quarts), you can easily double this recipe to make 1 gallon.

- 4 **pounds chicken backs and wings**
- 3½ **quarts water**
- 1 **onion, chopped**
- 2 **bay leaves**
- 2 **teaspoons salt**

1. Heat chicken and water in large stockpot or Dutch oven over medium-high heat until boiling, skimming off any foam that comes to surface. Reduce heat to low and simmer gently for 3 hours.

2. Add onion, bay leaves, and salt and continue to simmer for another 2 hours.

3. Strain broth through fine-mesh strainer into large pot or container, pressing on solids to extract as much liquid as possible. Allow broth to settle for about 5 minutes, then skim off fat.

AN ALTERNATE FAT-REMOVAL METHOD

If you do not plan to use the broth right away, you can refrigerate it and let the fat solidify. Use a wide, shallow spoon to skim the solidified fat from the surface and deposit it into another container to save for another use.

QUICK CHICKEN BROTH
Makes about 8 cups

When time is limited, this method ekes out remarkably rich flavor in a little over an hour. We chop the chicken into small pieces (more surface area means faster flavor extraction) and then brown and sweat them to draw out their flavorful juices before adding the cooking liquid.

Why Make This Broth: Great flavor for the time it takes.

> **Prep time:** about 20 minutes
> **Cook time:** about 60 minutes

A meat cleaver makes quick work of chopping the chicken into small pieces, but a hefty, sharp chef's knife will also work.

- 1 **tablespoon vegetable oil**
- 1 **onion, chopped**
- 4 **pounds chicken backs and wings, cut into 2-inch pieces**
- 8 **cups water**
- 8 **teaspoons unflavored gelatin**
- 2 **bay leaves**
- 2 **teaspoons salt**

1. Heat oil in large stockpot or Dutch oven over medium-high heat until shimmering. Add onion and cook until lightly browned and softened slightly, 2 to 3 minutes; transfer to large bowl.

2. Add half of chicken pieces and cook on both sides until lightly browned, 4 to 5 minutes. Transfer cooked chicken to bowl with onions. Repeat with remaining chicken pieces. Return onion and chicken pieces to pot, reduce heat to low, cover, and cook until chicken releases its juices, about 20 minutes.

3. Increase heat to high and add water, gelatin, bay leaves, and salt. Bring to simmer, then cover and barely simmer until broth is rich and flavorful, about 20 minutes, skimming off any foam that comes to surface.

4. Strain broth through fine-mesh strainer into large pot or container, pressing on solids to extract as much liquid as possible. Allow broth to settle for about 5 minutes, then skim off fat.

CHEATER CHICKEN BROTH
Makes about 8 cups

To quickly improve the flavor of commercial broth, we skip the bones and start by browning ground chicken, which has lots of surface area and thus gives up its flavor fast. Simmering the sautéed ground meat in the broth for just 30 minutes gives the broth a significant chicken-y boost.

Why Make This Broth: An upgrade to commercial stock that's fast and easy.

> **Prep time:** about 5 minutes
> **Cook time:** about 40 minutes

Commercial chicken broth contains little fat, so leave some on the broth's surface when skimming to boost its flavor. Both dark and white meat ground chicken will work here.

- 1 **tablespoon vegetable oil**
- 1 **pound ground chicken**
- 1 **onion, chopped**
- 4 **cups water**
- 4 **cups chicken broth**
- 8 **teaspoons unflavored gelatin**
- 2 **bay leaves**
- 2 **teaspoons salt**

1. Heat oil in large saucepan over medium-high heat until shimmering. Add chicken and onion and cook, stirring frequently, until chicken is no longer pink, 5 to 10 minutes.

2. Reduce heat to medium-low. Add water, broth, gelatin, bay leaves, and salt and bring to simmer. Reduce heat to medium-low, cover, and cook for 30 minutes. Strain broth through fine-mesh strainer into large pot or container, pressing on solids to extract as much liquid as possible. Allow broth to settle for about 5 minutes, then skim off fat.

BEST WAY TO COOL BROTH

The best way to cool hot liquid—without risking the spoilage of other food in your refrigerator—is to let the liquid cool to 85 degrees on the counter, which takes about an hour. It's then safe to transfer to the fridge, where it takes about 4 hours and 30 minutes to cool to 40 degrees—well within the FDA's recommended range.

THE ASIAN PANTRY

While the universe of Asian ingredients is vast, we turn to these staple ingredients to bring authentic flavor to Asian recipes. And in some cases, the right product can be critical.

CHILI-GARLIC SAUCE

A puree of chiles, garlic, vinegar, and salt, this complex, spicy sauce adds brightness and heat to countless stir-fries, sauces, and glazes. The popular Huy Fong, or "Rooster" brand, is available in many supermarkets. If you can't find chili-garlic sauce, Sriracha sauce, which contains similar ingredients, makes a spicier, less acidic stand-in. For 1 tablespoon of chili-garlic sauce, use 2 teaspoons of Sriracha.

CHINESE EGG NOODLES

There are countless varieties of egg noodles, both dried and fresh. Wavy fresh ones (sometimes labeled "lo mein noodles") offer just the right springy chew for stir-fries. Many supermarkets stock them alongside tofu. Avoid vacuum-packed "Chinese-style" fresh noodles, which can be gummy. If you can't find Chinese egg noodles, use dried linguine: Though it's not authentic, we've found that it offers a similar firm chew.

CHINESE RICE WINE (SHAOXING)

Like Japanese mirin, Shaoxing is made from fermented rice, but its flavor is deeper, more aromatic, and not as sweet. It's a staple in stir-fries, sauces, and glazes. If you can't find Shaoxing, use dry sherry.

COCONUT MILK

The sweet, rich liquid strained from shredded raw coconut meat that's been steeped in water, coconut milk is used extensively in Thai and Vietnamese cooking. Our favorite brand is **Chaokoh Coconut Milk**. We found that products with relatively low amounts of sugar (less than 1 gram per ⅓ cup) boasted more coconutty flavor. Light coconut milk is far less creamy, and we found that it can ruin the texture of desserts. It's acceptable in soups and curries.

DRIED RICE NOODLES

Made from ground rice and water, rice noodles are cut into myriad shapes and thicknesses, but when cooked, all should taste like fresh rice with a tender, pleasantly resilient bite. Unlike other dried noodles, dried rice noodles are usually just soaked in hot water until tender before being added to stir-fries or salads. Our favorite brand is **A Taste of Thai Straight Cut Rice Noodles**.

FISH SAUCE

This liquid product of fermented anchovies, which is used as both an ingredient and a condiment, boasts a rich and savory saltiness that adds depth to countless Thai and Vietnamese dishes. It's strong stuff with an intense aroma. We use this sauce not just in Asian dishes but also to season marinades. Used judiciously, it adds savoriness, not fishy flavor. Our favorite brand is **Red Boat 40°N Fish Sauce**.

MAKING FRIED RICE WITHOUT LEFTOVERS

Chilled, hardened leftover rice is crucial in fried rice since fresh rice turns mushy. But we don't always have leftovers on hand. Here's our work-around: Heat 2 tablespoons vegetable oil in large saucepan over medium heat until shimmering. Add 2 cups jasmine or long-grain white rice; stir to coat. Add 2⅔ cups water and bring to boil. Reduce heat to low, cover, and simmer until liquid is absorbed, about 18 minutes. Off heat, remove lid and place dish towel over saucepan. Let stand, covered, until rice is just tender, about 8 minutes. Spread cooked rice onto rimmed baking sheet. Let cool for 10 minutes, then refrigerate for 20 minutes. Makes 6 cups.

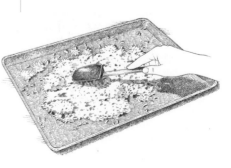

GOCHUJANG

This moderately spicy, salty, savory paste made from chiles, glutinous rice, fermented soybeans, and salt makes a powerful base for Korean sauces and marinades. Stir it into soup, barbecue sauce, ketchup, mayonnaise, or butter, or thin it with water to a drizzling consistency and use it as a condiment for eggs, vegetables, rice, noodles, or dumplings.

HOISIN SAUCE

A thick, reddish-brown mixture of soybeans, sugar, vinegar, garlic, and chiles, hoisin sauce is used in many classic Chinese dishes, including barbecued pork, Peking duck, and *mu shu* pork. Hoisin should pack a punch, but some products taste flat. The best sauces balance sweet, salty, pungent, and spicy elements so that no one flavor dominates. Our favorite brand is **Kikkoman Hoisin Sauce.**

JASMINE RICE

This rice variety's delicate floral, buttery scent is the result of a flavor compound common to all rice varieties, which occurs in high levels in aromatic rices such as jasmine and basmati. Look for packages stamped with a green seal from Thailand's Department of Foreign Trade, an indication that at least 92 percent of the rice is the purest form called Hom Mali ("good smelling"). Our favorite brand is **Dynasty Jasmine Rice.**

MIRIN

This Japanese rice wine adds sweetness and acidity to sauces and glazes like teriyaki. Hard-to-find traditional mirin contains no added ingredients; supermarket brands usually contain sweeteners and salt. Our favorite brand is **Mitoku Organic Mikawa Mirin Sweet Rice Seasoning.** If you can't find mirin, replace 1 tablespoon of mirin with an equal amount of white wine plus 1 teaspoon of sugar.

OYSTER SAUCE

Made from a reduction of boiled oysters, this condiment adds salty-sweetness (not fishiness) and body to stir-fries. Oyster sauce should taste deeply savory with a hint of sweetness. Lesser brands can taste like little more than gloppy soy sauce. Our favorite brand is **Lee Kum Kee Premium Oyster Flavored Sauce.**

RICE VINEGAR

Not to be confused with rice wine, rice vinegar (sometimes incorrectly called rice wine vinegar) has malty sweetness and mild acidity. It's primarily used to season sushi rice and stir-fries and makes a less-sharp alternative to other vinegars in dressings. It's sold seasoned or unseasoned.

The latter contains no added salt or sugar, so it can be used in a variety of dressings and sauces. Use the seasoned kind for applications like quick pickles where you want both acidity and sweetness.

SICHUAN PEPPERCORNS

Not actually peppercorns but dried fruit rinds from a Chinese citrus tree, these contribute a unique tingling sensation and a piney, citrusy aroma. We bloom them in oil or grind them and sprinkle them over Chinese dishes like *ma pao* tofu and salt and pepper shrimp. They don't actually contribute any heat, so they shouldn't be subbed in for black or red pepper. Our favorite brand is **Dean & DeLuca Szechuan Peppercorns.**

SOY SAUCE

Made from soybeans fermented in a brine with roasted wheat, this savory condiment is used globally in Asian cuisines to season and add depth. Different types serve different purposes: We use a more robust-tasting brand in cooked applications and reserve pricier long-aged soy sauce for dipping. **Lee Kum Kee Tabletop Premium Soy Sauce** is our favorite for cooking; **Ohsawa Nama Shoyu Organic Unpasteurized Soy Sauce** is our favorite for dipping. Tamari, a byproduct of miso production, has a similarly salty-savory flavor to soy sauce; the two can be used interchangeably. Many tamaris are also gluten-free.

TOASTED SESAME OIL

While plain sesame oil has very little color, smell, or flavor, toasted (or roasted) sesame oil boasts deeper color and much stronger, richer flavor. We've found that a little goes a long way in dressings, dipping sauces, and stir-fries in Chinese, Korean, and Japanese recipes. Due to its potent flavor and relatively low smoke point, it shouldn't be used as a primary cooking oil. But try adding a few drops to neutral vegetable or peanut oil when stir-frying to give food a mildly nutty flavor boost. To keep flavor fresh, store it in the refrigerator.

WHITE PEPPERCORNS

These are simply skinned black peppercorns, which taste less spicy and more floral than black pepper since skinning removes much of the spicy compound piperine. They're a common seasoning in Chinese and Thai dishes; we also use them in non-Asian applications like spaetzle, mayonnaise, and spice rubs. Only substitute black pepper if the amount called for is less than 1 teaspoon—otherwise, the pepper may mask other flavors.

STAPLE FRESH FLAVORS

In addition to everyday aromatics and herbs like garlic, shallots, scallions, and cilantro, lemon grass and ginger are also worth keeping on hand.

LEMON GRASS

Native to India and tropical Asia, this grassy herb imparts citrusy, floral flavors to South Asian soups, curries, and stir-fries. Look for stalks that are green, firm, and fragrant.

STRIP TO THE CORE: Remove the dry outer layers to expose the tender inner stalk before mincing.

SUB DRIED FOR FRESH?: Dried lemon grass works well in soups and curry paste but it falls short in stir-fries, where there isn't enough liquid to rehydrate the pieces.

GINGER

A rhizome grown largely in Jamaica, China, and India, ginger is bright and floral but also packs heat thanks to its pungent gingerol, a relative of the spicy compounds in chiles.

OLD IS OK: Ginger dries out and loses its distinct pungency as it ages. So if your ginger is older, use more of it than a recipe calls for and add it toward the end of cooking (heat also dulls its pungency).

SCRAPE, DON'T PEEL: Scraping off the knotty skin with a spoon is easier than peeling with a knife or vegetable peeler.

SUPERMARKET BALSAMIC VINEGAR

Since we last tasted supermarket balsamic vinegar, a new certification limits which products can call themselves "balsamic vinegar of Modena" and bear an *Indicazione Geografica Protetta* seal. Curious if certification would improve our options, we tasted supermarket balsamics bearing this new seal. Our tasting revealed a range of textures and flavors, from thick to watery, pleasantly fruity to harshly acidic. After a little investigating, we discovered that the guidelines governing the use of the seal are pretty loose, and while production must take place within Reggio Emilia or Modena and certain varieties of grapes must be used, those grapes can be grown anywhere. In the end, six of the products were perfectly acceptable used in a vinaigrette or reduced and drizzled over asparagus. While each of our top picks balance fruity sweetness with bright acidity, our winner had an almost drinkable flavor with notes of apple, molasses, and dried fruit. Balsamic vinegars are listed in order of preference.

RECOMMENDED

BERTOLLI Balsamic Vinegar of Modena
PRICE: $3.49 for 8.5 fl oz ($0.41 per fl oz)
COMMENTS: Served plain, this balsamic vinegar tasted of dried fruit like figs, raisins, and prunes. Some nuances disappeared once it was reduced or whisked into vinaigrette, but it was still pleasantly sweet. While its texture was fairly thin, its flavor earned high marks in the dressing and the glaze.

MONARI FEDERZONI Balsamic Vinegar of Modena
PRICE: $2.50 for 16.9 fl oz ($0.15 per fl oz)
COMMENTS: Tasters praised the consistency of this vinegar, which was viscous but not too thick to coat greens or asparagus. It had a bright acidity and "nice fruit flavor" that made for a sweet glaze and boasted hints of blueberries and wine when served plain.

COLAVITA Balsamic Vinegar of Modena
PRICE: $2.99 for 17 fl oz ($0.18 per fl oz)
COMMENTS: Although some tasters noted harshness in this vinegar when sampling it plain, this was tempered to a "nice bite" in vinaigrette and glaze. In those applications, a fruity sweetness came to the forefront. As one taster said, "It's perfectly balanced."

ORTALLI Balsamic Vinegar of Modena
PRICE: $6.69 for 16.9 fl oz ($0.40 per fl oz)
COMMENTS: Tasters approved of the full and "balanced" flavors of this balsamic. Plain, it tasted of cooked fruit; in vinaigrette and glaze, it showcased flavors of plum, honey, and molasses. Although it was a little thin in body even when reduced, its rich flavor and pleasant acidity more than made up for it.

BELLINO Balsamic Vinegar of Modena
PRICE: $5.49 for 16.9 fl oz ($0.32 per fl oz)
COMMENTS: This vinegar consistently scored in the middle of the lineup. Although it was both sweet and acidic, it lacked complexity and was deemed "not outstanding." It showed to its best advantage in the vinaigrette, where its sweet start and pleasantly bright finish made it a crowd pleaser.

RECOMMENDED *(continued)*

LUCINI AGED Balsamic Vinegar of Modena
PRICE: $13.99 for 8.5 fl oz ($1.65 per fl oz)
COMMENTS: The only aged product in our lineup, this vinegar was so viscous and thick when tasted plain that tasters compared it to port and dessert wine. Whisked in vinaigrette and reduced to a glaze, it became sticky and syrupy—appealing to some tasters, but overwhelming to others.

RECOMMENDED WITH RESERVATIONS

STAR Balsamic Vinegar of Modena
PRICE: $2.99 for 8.5 fl oz ($0.35 per fl oz)
COMMENTS: Though this vinegar earned some favorable reviews, we still have reservations. Namely: It was too sharp and "puckery" when tasted plain and maintained its harshness even when reduced to a glaze. What we did like: a consistency that was pleasantly thick in vinaigrette and became "syrupy" when reduced.

CENTO Balsamic Vinegar of Modena
PRICE: $3.49 for 16.9 fl oz ($0.21 per fl oz)
COMMENTS: Tasted plain and in a vinaigrette, the berry notes of this vinegar drew comparisons to candy, juice, and even KoolAid. It was also panned for being harsh and "astringent," with "an assertive and unpleasant bite." It mellowed to an acceptable level of fruitiness when reduced to a glaze. As for the consistency, it scored in the middle of the pack straight from the bottle and became "nice and thick" when reduced or whisked in vinaigrette.

DE NIGRIS Balsamic Vinegar of Modena, White Eagle
PRICE: $5.49 for 16.9 fl oz ($0.32 per fl oz)
COMMENTS: This sample consistently fell to the bottom of our rankings. Although it lent acidic brightness to vinaigrette and glaze, it had a one-note flavor that bordered on "tannic," and some tasters noticed a "harsh" aftertaste. It remained thin and mild-tasting even when reduced.

SUPERMARKET EXTRA-VIRGIN OLIVE OIL

Good extra-virgin olive oil is lively, bright, and full-bodied, with flavors ranging from peppery to buttery. But like all fresh fruit, olives are highly perishable, and their complex flavors degrade quickly, which makes producing a top-notch oil a time-sensitive, labor-intensive, and expensive process. Could we find a reasonably priced supermarket oil that would live up to its pricier counterparts? Of the brands we tasted, one oil stood out for its "fragrant," "complex," and "fruity" flavors. Because its olives are grown within 150 miles of the pressing and bottling facility (six of the 10 brands we tasted are sourced from multiple regions and countries), this company maximizes its harvest's efficiency and reduces the risk of spoiled olives or oxidized oil. Its price is so reasonable that we can use it as a condiment, but we won't feel bad about also using it in cooking. Olive oils are listed in order of preference.

RECOMMENDED

CALIFORNIA OLIVE RANCH EVERYDAY Extra Virgin Olive Oil
PRICE: $9.99 for 500 ml ($0.59 per oz)
SOURCE: Northern California
BOTTLED IN: Artois, California
COMMENTS: "Fruity," "fragrant," and "fresh" with a "complex finish," this top-ranked oil is a supermarket standout. In fact, its flavor rivaled that of our favorite high-end brand, Columela Extra-Virgin Olive Oil.

LUCINI PREMIUM SELECT Extra Virgin Olive Oil
PRICE: $20.99 for 500 ml ($1.24 per oz)
SOURCE: Tuscany and Central Italy
BOTTLED IN: Tuscany
COMMENTS: Drizzled over tomatoes and mozzarella and as a dip for bread, this pricey Italian oil—our former supermarket favorite—tasted "incredibly rich," "bright," and "buttery" with a pleasantly "peppery aftertaste," though those flavors became somewhat muted in vinaigrette. There, it was deemed "subtle."

RECOMMENDED WITH RESERVATIONS

COLAVITA Extra Virgin Olive Oil, Premium Italian
PRICE: $18.99 for 34 oz ($0.56 per oz)
SOURCE: Italy
BOTTLED IN: Pomezia, Italy
COMMENTS: With a "fresh, light, green taste" and a "mildly peppery finish," this oil earned acceptable but not stellar scores. Several tasters deemed it "mild—just OK," especially in vinaigrette, where it was a little too "neutral."

GOYA Extra Virgin Olive Oil
PRICE: $5.99 for 17 oz ($0.35 per oz)
SOURCE: Andalusia, Spain
BOTTLED IN: Andalusia
COMMENTS: Notes for this oil ranged from "balanced, but mild" and "middle-of-the-road" to just plain "boring." In vinaigrette, it made a "mellow and balanced dressing, but has no real distinct EVOO flavor."

RECOMMENDED WITH RESERVATIONS *(continued)*

BOTTICELLI Extra Virgin Olive Oil
PRICE: $8.99 for 25.3 oz ($0.36 per oz)
SOURCE: Italy, Spain, Greece, Tunisia
BOTTLED IN: Italy
COMMENTS: On its own, this blended oil tasted "mild" and "not that fresh" with a "bitter aftertaste"; in vinaigrette, it came across as "fine" but "heavy" and without "much character to it." As one taster summed it up, "it could be any old regular oil off the shelf."

FILIPPO BERIO Extra Virgin Olive Oil
PRICE: $5.99 for 16.9 oz ($0.35 per oz)
SOURCE: Italy, Spain, Greece, and Tunisia
BOTTLED IN: Massarosa (Lucca), Italy
COMMENTS: While a few tasters appreciated this oil's "slight peppery aftertaste" and found it "smooth" in vinaigrette, many detected "vinegary" notes and a "greasy consistency"—possible signs that the olives weren't processed quickly enough after picking or that the oil was on the verge of going rancid.

OLIVARI Extra-Virgin Olive Oil
PRICE: $6.99 for 17 oz ($0.41 per oz)
SOURCE: Italy, Greece, Spain, Turkey, Tunisia, and Morocco
BOTTLED IN: New York
COMMENTS: Disappointingly, this oil's "bright [and] fruity" aroma gave way to a "flat," "thin" flavor that "dissipates quickly." Over tomatoes and mozzarella, it tasted more "punchy" but still "a little stale," even though the "best by" date was more than a year away.

POMPEIAN Extra Virgin Olive Oil
PRICE: $12.99 for 32 oz ($0.41 per oz)
SOURCE: May include Italy, Greece, Spain, Argentina, Tunisia, Turkey, Morocco, Chile, United States, Uruguay, Portugal
BOTTLED IN: Maryland
COMMENTS: This oil was "neutral" and "timid" at best; one taster even said, "Nothing. I've got nothing here." But the more alarming comments were about its off-flavors—"metallic," "soapy," and "acidic" among them.

GRADE A DARK AMBER MAPLE SYRUP

Anyone who's tasted real maple syrup on pancakes, in desserts, or even in savory glazes or dressings knows that there is no cheap substitute. We decided to home in on Grade A Dark Amber since it's the most widely available grade, tasting eight brands to find our favorite. We immediately noticed a range of colors among the different syrups—some were dark like molasses while others were only faintly golden. We learned that the color deepens over the course of sugaring season, but surprisingly these differences did not correlate to the syrups' flavors: Most of the lighter colored products tasted just as robust as darker ones. After some research, we found that most producers sell their syrup to packagers that blend and bottle hundreds of different producers' syrups under a brand name. To us, there's a distinct advantage to blending: It means that all Grade A Dark Amber syrups sold in supermarkets are going to taste very similar. After two blind tastings—plain and in maple syrup pie—we found all the syrups to be very similar and recommend them all. We don't have a winner; instead, they appear in order of price per fluid ounce.

RECOMMENDED

UNCLE LUKE'S Pure Maple Syrup, Grade A Dark Amber

PRICE: $20.69 for 32 fl oz ($0.65 per fl oz)
COMMENTS: The least expensive product we tried, which looked particularly dark and "molasses-y," boasted "rich caramel flavor" that tasted "pleasantly toasty" in pie.

MAPLE GROVE FARMS Pure Maple Syrup, Grade A Dark Amber

PRICE: $6.99 for 8.5 fl oz ($0.82 per fl oz)
COMMENTS: With "bold," "concentrated maple flavor," this syrup worked well in the pie's custard filling, where tasters deemed it "toasty," "caramelized," and "balanced."

HIGHLAND SUGARWORKS Pure Organic Maple Syrup, Grade A Dark Amber

PRICE: $23.87 for 32 fl oz ($0.75 per fl oz)
COMMENTS: This "very light" colored syrup was "buttery," "smooth," and "sweet." Some tasters picked up on "fruity" or even "coffee" flavors.

MAPLE GOLD Pure Maple Syrup, Grade A Dark Amber

PRICE: $16.50 for 12 fl oz ($1.38 per fl oz)
COMMENTS: Tasters picked up on this dark-colored syrup's "toasty," "woodsy," "assertive vanilla" flavors and even noticed some "tanginess."

COOMBS FAMILY FARMS Pure Maple Syrup, Grade A Dark Amber

PRICE: $24.54 for 32 fl oz ($0.77 per fl oz)
COMMENTS: "Butter and vanilla" flavors stood out in this dark brown syrup, which some tasters likened to "maple sugar candy."

SPRING TREE Pure Maple Syrup, Grade A Dark Amber

PRICE: $18.49 for 12.5 fl oz ($1.48 per fl oz)
COMMENTS: This "balanced," "complex" syrup had flavor notes that ranged from "bright and tangy" to "woodsy," with a "sweet finish."

ANDERSON'S Pure Maple Syrup, Grade A Dark Amber

PRICE: $26.19 for 32 fl oz ($0.82 per fl oz)
COMMENTS: This syrup, which boasted the deepest "caramelized brown color," delivered "rich," "woody" smokiness and strong "caramel" notes that stood out particularly well in maple syrup pie.

CAMP Pure Maple Syrup, Grade A Dark Amber

PRICE: $19.95 for 12.7 fl oz ($1.57 per fl oz)
COMMENTS: This "light-colored syrup" impressed tasters with its "good balance of maple depth and tang" and range of complex flavors—from "smoky" to a "hint of orange."

BEEF BROTH

A slew of new products have hit the beef broth market since our last tasting seven years ago, and we wanted to see if a truly beefy broth had finally come along. We rounded up some options from top-selling brands that contained at least 450 milligrams of sodium per serving (in previous broth tastings, we've found that products with less sodium taste underseasoned) and sampled them warmed, simmered in beef stew, and reduced in gravy. At best, the broths contributed a savory taste. The worst, however, were either bland, overwhelmingly salty, or plagued by "bitter" or "burnt" off-notes. The problem is that in lieu of adding actual meat to their products, broth manufacturers often use chemical flavorings to amp up flavor. However, we found that what really benefited these products was the presence of savory yeast extract, which contains glutamates and nucleotides that together amplify umami flavors. In the end, we had one product to recommend. Though lacking in actual beefy taste, our winner delivered "fuller" flavor than any of the other products. Broths are listed in order of preference.

RECOMMENDED

BETTER THAN BOUILLON Beef Base
PRICE: $6.99 for 8 oz ($0.02 per reconstituted fl oz)
STYLE: Paste
SODIUM: 680 mg per cup
COMMENTS: Though lacking in actual beefy taste, a good amount of salt and multiple powerful flavor enhancers delivered "fuller flavor than other samples." The paste is economical, stores easily, and dissolves quickly in hot water.

RECOMMENDED WITH RESERVATIONS

WYLER'S Reduced Sodium Beef Flavor Cubes
PRICE: $2.00 for 2 oz ($0.02 per reconstituted fl oz)
STYLE: Cubes
SODIUM: 540 mg per cup
COMMENTS: With little actual beef and four different forms of hydrolyzed vegetable protein, monosodium glutamate, and yeast extract, these bouillon cubes delivered savory flavor that was more "mushroomy" than beefy.

KITCHEN ACCOMPLICE Reduced Sodium Beef Style Broth Concentrate
PRICE: $4.99 for 12 oz ($0.02 per reconstituted fl oz)
STYLE: Liquid concentrate
SODIUM: 480 mg per cup
COMMENTS: Although soup and gravy tasted "meaty," the flavors were generically "savory" instead of distinctly beefy.

RACHAEL RAY STOCK-IN-A-BOX All-Natural Beef Flavored Stock (made by Colavita)
PRICE: $3.49 for 32 oz ($0.11 per fl oz)
STYLE: Liquid
SODIUM: 480 mg per cup
COMMENTS: This broth didn't have the off-flavors that we found in other products, but compared to more seasoned broths, our top-rated liquid broth tasted "watery" and "flat."

RECOMMENDED WITH RESERVATIONS (continued)

SWANSON Cooking Stock, Beef
PRICE: $2.99 for 32 oz ($0.09 per fl oz)
STYLE: Liquid
SODIUM: 500 mg per cup
COMMENTS: Yeast extract gave this stock a boost of savory flavor, but tasters found it made soup and gravy that tasted "bitter" and "charred."

NOT RECOMMENDED

COLLEGE INN Bold Stock Tender Beef Flavor
PRICE: $2.99 for 17.6 oz ($0.17 per fl oz)
STYLE: Liquid
SODIUM: 750 mg per cup
COMMENTS: This broth was marred by "weird," "tinny" flavors that were "bitter" and "metallic." This is most likely due to the inclusion of potassium chloride—known to add off-flavors.

KNORR Homestyle Beef Stock
PRICE: $3.99 for 4.66 oz ($0.04 per reconstituted fl oz)
STYLE: Paste (1 tub per 3½ cups of water, makes 14 cups)
SODIUM: 710 mg per cup
COMMENTS: Six ingredients—including salt—precede the mention of beef, so it's no wonder that this concentrate had one of the highest perceived salt levels. Each tub of concentrate yields 3½ cups of broth, an amount that doesn't match up with most recipes.

ORRINGTON FARMS Beef Broth Base & Seasoning
PRICE: $2.79 for 12 oz ($0.01 per reconstituted fl oz)
STYLE: Powder
SODIUM: 950 mg per cup
COMMENTS: This powdery concentrate made stew and gravy "taste more of salt than anything else." No surprise, given that each serving contains a whopping 950 milligrams.

WHOLE-MILK GREEK YOGURT

High in protein and indulgently creamy, whole-milk Greek yogurt fills many roles, serving as a satisfying snack, a key ingredient in savory dips and sauces, and an easy substitute for sour cream or cream cheese in baking. In tasting different brands both plain and in *tzatziki* (a Greek sauce of yogurt, shredded cucumber, garlic, and dill), we discovered that textures ranged from thick enough to hold a spoon upright to as thin and runny as non-Greek yogurt. Some were weighty and dense, others as airy as whipped cream. When it came to flavor, our favorites offered clean, milky sweet flavor with mild but definite tang, and they were nicely thick. Though fat levels varied widely, that detail didn't matter as much as the perceived richness of the yogurt. Our favorite contained 11 grams of fat per cup—only half the fat of our highest-fat yogurt—but, bolstered by the thickest density in the lineup, it satisfied our tasters. Yogurts are listed in order of preference.

RECOMMENDED

FAGE TOTAL Classic Greek Yogurt
PRICE: $8.49 for 35.3 oz ($0.24 per oz)
FAT: 11 g per cup
PROTEIN: 20 g per cup
COMMENTS: With a "faintly sweet," "super-rich, fresh dairy taste," "like cream" or "butter," and "not terribly tangy, just enough to know it's yogurt," this "dense" and "decadent" yogurt was the thickest of the lineup. High protein and no added stabilizers or thickeners listed on the label indicate that this is traditionally strained yogurt. It held its own against the garlic's sharpness in tzatziki sauce.

DANNON OIKOS Traditional Plain Greek 4% Yogurt
PRICE: $5.39 for 32 oz ($0.17 per oz)
FAT: 9 g per cup
PROTEIN: 20 g per cup
COMMENTS: With a "yogurt taste that is more assertive" than our winner's, this brand was on the tangy side, but tasters felt that "the richness balances it." Its "whipped texture" offered "less body" than tasters expected, but it had "great, fresh dairy taste." It won the top spot in our tzatziki tasting.

WALLABY ORGANIC Organic Greek Whole Milk Yogurt Plain
PRICE: $7.79 for 32 oz ($0.24 per oz)
FAT: 10 g per cup
PROTEIN: 19 g per cup
COMMENTS: With a "supersmooth," "creamy," even "velvety" texture, this yogurt won fans, especially among those who don't like sour flavor in their yogurt. Tasters said it had a "very mild taste," though for some it "borders on bland." In tzatziki sauce, it was "good all around, but not very tangy" and "a little loose."

RECOMMENDED WITH RESERVATIONS

THE GREEK GODS Greek Yogurt Traditional Plain
PRICE: $4.29 for 24 oz ($0.18 per oz)
FAT: 14 g per cup
PROTEIN: 9 g per cup
COMMENTS: This "stiff," "bland" yet watery yogurt adds pectin to simulate traditional yogurt's thick, strained consistency, which explains why it has one of the lowest levels of protein per serving in our lineup. The flavor was "pretty neutral" in tzatziki. It was also sweet, not from added sugar but as a result of not straining (lactose, milk's natural sugar, is normally removed when yogurt is strained).

CHOBANI Greek Yogurt Whole Milk Plain
PRICE: $6.59 for 32 oz ($0.21 per oz)
FAT: 9 g per cup
PROTEIN: 20 g per cup
COMMENTS: With the one of the tangiest tastes and one of the thinnest textures, Chobani slid toward the bottom of the pack. "Almost like regular yogurt," complained one taster. While a few enjoyed its "sour cream"–like tang, others just called it "very sour." In tzatziki it was "watery—both in texture and flavor."

NOT RECOMMENDED

MAPLE HILL CREAMERY Greek Whole Milk Yogurt Plain
PRICE: $2.29 for 5.3 oz ($0.43 per oz)
FAT: 9 g per cup
PROTEIN: 18 g per cup
COMMENTS: This yogurt, made with milk from grass-fed cows, has a strong, savory flavor. A few tasters loved it, but most found the "barnyard funk" too challenging. It was also much looser than our preferred Greek yogurt.

BAKING POWDER

Using the right baking powder can mean the difference between a show-stopping cake or a dense dud. To find an all-purpose baking powder that yielded tall, airy cakes and chewy cookies, we rounded up six widely available products and started baking. Baking powder contains a combination of baking soda, starch, and powdered acid(s). Plus, modern baking powders are double acting, meaning they release some carbon dioxide when moistened and the rest when heated. During testing, we found that single-acid baking powders released only 30 percent of their overall gas in the oven while those with two acids released 60 percent or more. Our cakes rose highest with the latter, but single acid powders produced chewier cookies. We wanted an all-purpose powder, though, so top honors went to the product that turned out great cakes and cookies in equal measure. None of the brands we tested ruined a baking project, but our favorite excelled at producing tender cakes, soft biscuits, and perfectly chewy cookies. Baking powders are listed in order of preference.

HIGHLY RECOMMENDED

ARGO DOUBLE ACTING Baking Powder
PRICE: $1.73 for 12 oz ($0.14 per oz)
INGREDIENTS: Sodium acid pyrophosphate, sodium bicarbonate, cornstarch, and monocalcium phosphate
AVERAGE CAKE HEIGHT: 1.09 in
GAS RELEASED,
ROOM TEMPERATURE: 30%
GAS RELEASED, OVEN: 70%
COMMENTS: This brand performed well in every test we threw at it, making "chewy" cookies, "fluffy" biscuits, and "moist" but "airy" cakes. Its easy-to-use plastic tub helped it edge out the competition.

RECOMMENDED

BOB'S RED MILL Baking Powder
PRICE: $3.29 for 16 oz ($0.21 per oz)
INGREDIENTS: Sodium acid pyrophosphate, sodium bicarbonate, cornstarch, and monocalcium phosphate
AVERAGE CAKE HEIGHT: 1.19 in
GAS RELEASED,
ROOM TEMPERATURE: 10%
GAS RELEASED, OVEN: 90%
COMMENTS: Cakes made with this baking powder were among the tallest and "fluffiest" of the bunch. Biscuits and cookies emerged from the oven "tender" and "airy." Unfortunately, this brand's frustrating plastic-bag packaging got it booted from the top spot.

CALUMET Baking Powder
PRICE: $2.49 for 7 oz ($0.36 per oz)
INGREDIENTS: Baking soda, cornstarch, sodium aluminum sulfate, calcium sulfate, monocalcium phosphate
AVERAGE CAKE HEIGHT: 1.24 in
GAS RELEASED,
ROOM TEMPERATURE AND OVEN:
Proprietary
COMMENTS: This brand made "taller," "airier," and "more tender" cakes and biscuits than any other brand, but the extra oomph produced cookies that were a little "too cakey." Some tasters detected a slight "metallic" taste in biscuits.

RECOMMENDED (continued)

CLABBER GIRL Baking Powder
PRICE: $2.27 for 8.1 oz ($0.28 per oz)
INGREDIENTS: Cornstarch, sodium bicarbonate, sodium aluminum sulfate, monocalcium phosphate
AVERAGE CAKE HEIGHT: 1.1 in
GAS RELEASED,
ROOM TEMPERATURE: 40%
GAS RELEASED, OVEN: 60%
COMMENTS: "Pillowy" cakes and "tender" cookies earned this brand high marks for texture, but 30 percent of tasters picked up on an off, "metallic" flavor in biscuits from the addition of sodium aluminum sulfate.

RECOMMENDED WITH RESERVATIONS

RUMFORD Baking Powder
PRICE: $3.47 for 8.1 oz ($0.43 per oz)
INGREDIENTS: Monocalcium phosphate, sodium bicarbonate, cornstarch (made from non-genetically modified cornstarch)
AVERAGE CAKE HEIGHT: 1.02 in
GAS RELEASED,
ROOM TEMPERATURE: 70%
GAS RELEASED, OVEN: 30%
COMMENTS: This brand, which releases 70 percent of its carbon dioxide at room temperature, made "shallower," "heavier" cakes. While not our preferred baking powder for cakes, this product produced "chewy" crinkle cookies and "fluffy" biscuits.

HAIN PURE FOODS FEATHERWEIGHT Baking Powder
PRICE: $5.39 for 8 oz ($0.67 per oz)
INGREDIENTS: Monocalcium phosphate, potato starch, potassium bicarbonate
AVERAGE CAKE HEIGHT: 0.89 in
GAS RELEASED,
ROOM TEMPERATURE: 70%
GAS RELEASED, OVEN: 30%
COMMENTS: This brand uses an atypical combination of ingredients to produce a salt-free and corn-free baking powder, but it comes at a price. While cookies were perfectly "fudgy," cakes were "dense" and biscuits had a "speckled" appearance (but tasted fine).

PRESHREDDED PARMESAN

The savory saltiness of Parmigiano-Reggiano is hard to beat, but it can be pricey. Cheese made in the same style but with less exacting standards is just called "Parmesan," and we wanted to find a preshredded Parmesan cheese that would provide a suitable shortcut when topping off a plate of pasta or using in a cheese-heavy dish like polenta. Texture was the biggest issue: Compared with the fluffy strands of freshly shredded cheese, some preshredded Parmesans were stiff and fibrous and our lowest-ranked cheeses were very bland. We were surprised to learn that the size of the shreds impacted tasters' opinions; we preferred Parmesan that had one-third small shreds and two-thirds large. When we pitted our winner against the real thing, most tasters still preferred the subtle tang and nutty flavor of Parmigiano-Reggiano, but our new winner held its own, especially in polenta, where tasters found it "rich," "cheesy," and "creamy." After sending our favorite preshredded product to a lab for analysis, our preference made sense: This cheese had a nearly identical proportion of fat to moisture as the real Parmigiano-Reggiano, which translated into the firm, crystalline bite and complex buttery richness we associate with real Parm. Cheeses are listed in order of preference.

RECOMMENDED

SARGENTO Artisan Blends Shredded Parmesan Cheese
PRICE: $3.99 for 5 oz ($0.80 per oz)
SODIUM: 336 mg per oz   FAT: 7.9 g per oz
MOISTURE: 8.6 g per oz
SIZE OF SHREDS: 34% small, 66% large
COMMENTS: A mix of small and large shreds lent this blend of 10- and 18-month-aged Parmesan a "fluffy," "lighter" texture that was "perfectly smooth" and "creamy" in polenta. On pasta, this cheese's "nutty" flavor was reminiscent of freshly shredded Parmesan.

KRAFT Natural Cheese Shredded Parmesan Cheese
PRICE: $4.08 for 7 oz ($0.58 per oz)
SODIUM: 400 mg per oz   FAT: 7.8 g per oz
MOISTURE: 7.8 g per oz
SIZE OF SHREDS: 40% small, 60% large
COMMENTS: The more refined cousin of the ubiquitous green can, this Parm was "bold" and "tangy," with a "slightly salty" kick. This product's smaller shreds distributed well in pasta and made for "silky" polenta.

RECOMMENDED WITH RESERVATIONS

DIGIORNO Shredded Parmesan
PRICE: $3.84 for 5.04 oz ($0.76 per oz)
SODIUM: 400 mg per oz   FAT: 7.6 g per oz
MOISTURE: 8.0 g per oz
SIZE OF SHREDS: 30% small, 70% large
COMMENTS: In polenta, these moderately sized strands produced a "sharp," "distinctly Parmesan" flavor and "creamy" texture. While many tasters appreciated their "buttery," "nutty" notes on pasta, a few remarked that their texture was "a bit plasticky."

4C Homestyle Shredded Parmesan
PRICE: $4.99 for 6 oz ($0.83 per oz)
SODIUM: 392 mg per oz   FAT: 4.1 g per oz
MOISTURE: 6.9 g per oz
SIZE OF SHREDS: 50% small, 50% large
COMMENTS: These small, "waxy" shreds were "chewy" and "stiff" on pasta but melted easily in polenta for a "silky," "even" texture. Most found this cheese was "sweet" and "nutty;" others noted a "slight sour" aftertaste.

RECOMMENDED WITH RESERVATIONS *(continued)*

FRIGO Shredded Parmesan Cheese
PRICE: $2.44 for 5 oz ($0.49 per oz)
SODIUM: 380 mg per oz   FAT: 7.6 g per oz
MOISTURE: 8.8 g per oz
SIZE OF SHREDS: 23% small, 77% large
COMMENTS: These "softer," "fluffy" strands had the ideal Parmesan texture but fell flat on flavor. Tasters found these shreds "tart" and "slightly sour," with an aftertaste reminiscent of "Swiss cheese." Off-flavors were muted when mixed into polenta.

STELLA Shredded Parmesan Cheese
PRICE: $3.99 for 5 oz ($0.80 per oz)
SODIUM: 380 mg per oz   FAT: 7.5 g per oz
MOISTURE: 9.0 g per oz
SIZE OF SHREDS: 17% small, 83% large
COMMENTS: While some tasters enjoyed the "mild," "slightly sweet" flavor of these shreds, others found them "bland" and "boring." Most agreed that the strands were too large and "stiff," making for "clumpy" polenta.

NOT RECOMMENDED

BELGIOIOSO Shredded Parmesan
PRICE: $2.91 for 4.24 oz ($0.69 per oz)
SODIUM: 252 mg per oz   FAT: 8.7 g per oz
MOISTURE: 6.8 g per oz
SIZE OF SHREDS: 7% small, 93% large
COMMENTS: While this product is made from our favorite domestic wedge Parmesan, these "long" and "chewy" strands were compared to "candle wax" and "twigs" when sampled on pasta. They were no better in polenta, where they congealed into "gloppy," "stringy" masses. Tasters also noted that this cheese was "a little too bland," a result of its lower salt level.

SHERRY VINEGAR

We are big fans of sherry vinegar's nutty, savory flavors, so we wanted to find a favorite that we could use in applications across the board. We tasted a host of different vinegars, purchasing most of them at conventional supermarkets with a few coming from specialty stores and online. We first tasted the vinegars plain to see if we could detect any nuances that might not carry through when the vinegars were combined with food. Not only did most deliver the "bright," "punchy" acidity that we demand from a good vinegar, but many also elicited descriptions more in line with fine wine. When we stirred them into gazpacho and in vinaigrette drizzled over salad greens, many of their complex flavors were still evident. In the end, we had something positive to say about all of the vinegars and loved six enough to recommend them. Vinegars are listed in order of preference.

RECOMMENDED

NAPA VALLEY NATURALS Reserve Sherry Vinegar
PRICE: $5.49 for 12.7 oz ($0.43 per fl oz)
SOURCE: Spain
COMMENTS: Our slightly sweet winner had "just the right amount of tang" and boasted flavors ranging from "lemony" to "smoky." In gazpacho, it added "nice depth" that highlighted the fresh flavors.

O Sherry Vinegar
PRICE: $9.99 for 6.8 oz ($1.47 per fl oz)
SOURCE: California
COMMENTS: With a sweet boost from apricot wine vinegar, this "rich," "smooth" vinegar contributed fruity depth to the vinaigrette and gazpacho, where the tomato flavor was "prominent" and "bright."

GRAN CAPIRETE 50 Years Aged Sherry Vinegar
PRICE: $16.99 for 8.45 oz ($2.01 per fl oz)
SOURCE: Spain
COMMENTS: This pricey vinegar's "rich," "dark" flavors made for an "earthy" but "vibrant" dressing and rounded out the soup with a "nice, easy finish."

COLUMELA Sherry Vinegar Solera 30
PRICE: $14.00 for 12.7 oz ($1.10 per fl oz)
SOURCE: Spain
COMMENTS: In both applications, this vinegar delivered a "nice kick" but offered a "smooth" finish and "fruitiness" that kept it from being too sharp or acidic.

COLUMELA Classic Sherry Vinegar
PRICE: $6.99 for 12.7 oz ($0.55 per fl oz)
SOURCE: Spain
COMMENTS: Though "sharper" and more "bracing" than its pricier older sibling, this vinegar's "woody," "spicy, complex" notes were especially nice in vinaigrette.

RECOMMENDED (continued)

MAITRE JACQUES Sherry Vinegar
PRICE: $4.13 for 16.9 oz ($0.24 per fl oz)
SOURCE: Spain
COMMENTS: With "just enough tartness," this vinegar allowed the soup's tomato flavor to "come through" and made for a "bright" vinaigrette, even if the complexity was lacking a bit.

RECOMMENDED WITH RESERVATIONS

ROMULO Sherry Vinegar (also sold as Pons Sherry Vinegar)
PRICE: $7.99 for 12.7 oz ($0.63 per fl oz)
SOURCE: Spain
COMMENTS: Some tasters enjoyed the "punchy vinaigrette" made with this vinegar; others found its "bracing acidity" too strong. It fared best in gazpacho, where it was "tangy and very bright" but not overly so.

DON BRUNO Sherry Vinegar
PRICE: $5.99 for 12.67 oz ($0.47 per fl oz)
SOURCE: Spain
COMMENTS: Even tasted plain, this vinegar was surprisingly mellow. It remained steadfastly "in the middle of the pack" in both applications, where tasters expected more vibrancy and complexity.

POMPEIAN Sherry Vinegar
PRICE: $9.99 for 16 oz ($0.62 per fl oz)
SOURCE: Spain
COMMENTS: Though plagued by the aroma of "acetone" and "cheap alcohol" when tasted plain, this vinegar's flaws (likely due to an excess of the compound ethyl acetate) weren't noticeable once it was added to the dressing and soup. Generally, it fared best among those who liked a "punchy" vinegar.

MILD JARRED RED SALSA

Salsa ranks among America's favorite dips, and nothing beats the jarred varieties for convenience. Still, many jarred salsas prove mushy, bland, and overcooked. For people who prefer their salsa less fiery, we wanted to find a mild option that got the ratios of heat, salt, acidity, and tomato flavor just right. We tasted seven mild salsas, first plain and then with tortilla chips. Off the bat, two were deemed too hot when eaten on their own; the very mildest salsa was entirely too bland. Our top brand had a bit of a kick but didn't overwhelm sensitive palates. Sweetness was also critical, and brands that had 2 grams of sugar per serving rated higher than those with less. In terms of texture, salsas that used either tomato puree or tomato concentrate gave the base full, natural body. Our winning salsa boasted even ½-inch onion and pepper pieces that still had some crunch to them—an element that really set it apart. Salsas are listed in order of preference.

RECOMMENDED

CHI-CHI'S Thick & Chunky Salsa
PRICE: $1.50 for 16 oz ($0.09 per oz)
SUGAR: 2 g
COMMENTS: Our winning salsa was praised for its "hint of heat," "good balance," and "sweet," "satisfying tomato flavor." But with a "thick," "smooth" base fortified with concentrated crushed tomatoes and studded with "crunchy," "ideal-size chunks" of vegetables, it was the salsa's texture that really won over our panel.

RECOMMENDED WITH RESERVATIONS

TOSTITOS Chunky Salsa
PRICE: $3.39 for 15.5 oz ($0.22 per oz)
SUGAR: 2 g
COMMENTS: A few tasters found this salsa "chunky," "balanced," and "mellow" with "a decent amount of spice." But there was little to distinguish it, either. Overall, we found it "unremarkable," and "not deeply exciting," especially when eaten with chips.

LA VICTORIA Thick'n Chunky Salsa
PRICE: $3.04 for 16 oz ($0.19 per oz)
SUGAR: 1 g
COMMENTS: "Surprisingly spicy" on its own, this salsa was "better with chips," where tasters generally noted only "a little heat" and found the salsa's high ratio of chunks to liquid "good for dipping." While we liked its "vibrant" color and "very tomato-y" taste, many tasters thought this salsa was "very acidic," marred by a "pickle-y," "vinegar-y" flavor.

PACE Chunky Salsa
PRICE: $2.49 for 16 oz ($0.16 per oz)
SUGAR: 2 g
COMMENTS: This salsa had "nice tomato flavor" and "tang" but a "soupy" base. Worse, tasters consistently found it "too oniony." Indeed, it was the only salsa to use both fresh and dehydrated onions, which may have imparted "canned" or "chemical" overtones. After straining the salsa, we saw that more than half the solids were cut onions that our tasters found "tough" and "raw."

NOT RECOMMENDED

HERDEZ Salsa Casera
PRICE: $2.18 for 16 oz ($0.14 per oz)
SUGAR: 1 g
COMMENTS: The only product to include serrano peppers (instead of the milder jalapeños favored by the other brands), this salsa had a heat that "kick[ed] you in the face." Although a few liked this salsa's "fresh," "bright" flavor, most disliked its "thin," "runny" base, which made "dipping a challenge."

NEWMAN'S OWN Mild Salsa
PRICE: $2.99 for 16 oz ($0.19 per oz)
SUGAR: 1 g
COMMENTS: Though "visually appealing" with large vegetable chunks, this salsa lost on flavor. Tasters found the cilantro in this salsa to be "weird," "bitter," and "harsh," characterized by "a detergent aftertaste." With only 65 milligrams of salt per serving and not enough acidity, this salsa was also deemed "flat."

MRS. RENFRO'S Mild Salsa
PRICE: $3.32 for 16 oz ($0.21 per oz)
SUGAR: less than 1 g
COMMENTS: Thickened with cornstarch, this salsa had a "slimy," "gelatinous," "viscous" consistency. Flavorwise, the salsa's "bland," "tomato-y," "too sweet" taste prompted comparisons to "baby food," "children's spaghetti sauce," and "Chef Boyardee."

TORTILLA CHIPS

Tortilla chips are gaining popularity in American supermarkets, so we set out to find which one was best. Although they're traditionally made with white or yellow corn, we noticed a variety of blue corn chips as well, so we included several bags in our line up. We tasted all of the tortilla chips plain and with salsa and guacamole. To our surprise, blue corn chips universally sank to the bottom of the pack when tasters detected "slightly bitter," "burnt," or "bean-y" notes that stood in stark contrast to the "sweet," "mild" flavor of white and yellow corn chips. Saltier chips tasted "fresh" and "bright," which tasters appreciated. While most chips were great for dipping, a few turned soggy under salsa or crumbled on a drag through guacamole. Our favorite chip boasted large air pockets that made it structurally strong while still maintaining a crispy, flaky texture. Chips are listed in order of preference.

RECOMMENDED

ON THE BORDER Café Style Tortilla Chips
PRICE: $3 for 12 oz ($0.25 per oz)
TYPE OF CORN: Yellow and white
SODIUM: 110 mg
COMMENTS: This recently reformulated product was praised for its "traditional," "buttery" sweetness and "bright corn flavor." Tasters found these big "flaky" chips "light and airy," with a "bubbly," "crisp" exterior that was "the perfect counterpart to salsa."

TOSTITOS Original Restaurant Style Tortilla Chips
PRICE: $4.29 for 13 oz ($0.33 per oz)
TYPE OF CORN: White
SODIUM: 115 mg
COMMENTS: Many tasters identified this top-selling product's "familiar," "very salty" seasoning and "large," "sturdy" shape. These "coarse," "crunchy" chips were "built for heavy dipping" and had "simple, straightforward flavor" that tasters loved.

SANTITAS White Corn Tortilla Chips
PRICE: $2 for 11 oz ($0.18 per oz)
TYPE OF CORN: White
SODIUM: 115 mg
COMMENTS: Our former favorite, this product was "very salty" and "grainy," with "mellow corn flavor" and "light roasted notes." Though a little too thin for some tasters, these chips were "crisp but strong," with "satisfying crunch" and a "slightly bubbly" exterior.

RECOMMENDED WITH RESERVATIONS

GARDEN OF EATIN' Blue Corn Tortilla Chips
PRICE: $3.99 for 8.1 oz ($0.49 per oz)
TYPE OF CORN: Blue
SODIUM: 60 mg
COMMENTS: With the lowest levels of salt in our lineup, these blue corn chips were "a little bland" for some tasters, though most appreciated their "mild" earthiness. Tasters also liked the "dense," "thick" texture of these chips, perfect for "sturdy," "supported dipping."

RECOMMENDED WITH RESERVATIONS *(continued)*

MISSION Tortilla Triangles
PRICE: $3.49 for 13 oz ($0.27 per oz)
TYPE OF CORN: White
SODIUM: 90 mg
COMMENTS: This product, made from all white corn, was "sweet," "mild," and "inoffensive" but was "bordering on too bland" for some tasters. Though these chips could hold a good scoop of dip, tasters noted that the chips turned "soft" and "soggy" under the weight of salsa.

FOOD SHOULD TASTE GOOD Blue Corn Tortilla Chips
PRICE: $3.29 for 5.5 oz ($0.60 per oz)
TYPE OF CORN: Blue
SODIUM: 80 mg
COMMENTS: These "hearty" chips are made from blue corn, quinoa, rice flour, and flaxseeds. While many tasters appreciated this product's "slight sweetness" and "sturdy" texture, others were turned off by its "smoky," "earthy" flavor.

NOT RECOMMENDED

XOCHITL Blue Corn Chips
PRICE: $5.29 for 12 oz ($0.44 per oz)
TYPE OF CORN: Blue
SODIUM: 103 mg
COMMENTS: These "fragile," "paper-thin" chips had "razor-sharp" edges that cut tasters' mouths and shattered in salsa. Most tasters couldn't get past the "burnt toast" bitterness and "bean-y" blue corn flavor, but those that could noted unpleasant "stale" and "cardboardy" aftertastes.

HOT DOGS

With the goal of finding the best supermarket all-beef hot dogs, we cooked up the seven top-selling varieties of skinless dogs, and the tasters' favorites were clear. Our top dogs were almost 20 percent heavier than the thinner low-scoring products, but heft wasn't as important as a juicy, tender texture and pleasant bouncy snap. Those with corn products listed as primary ingredients were too sweet; our favorites contained very few to no corn products, letting the smoky beefy flavor and strong saltiness take center stage. Hot dogs are listed in order of preference.

RECOMMENDED

NATHAN'S FAMOUS Skinless Beef Franks
PRICE: $6.99 for 8 ($0.87 per hot dog)
WEIGHT OF ONE DOG: 50 g
COMMENTS: This product emerged as top dog for its "supersmoky" meatiness and "juicy," "snappy" texture. Tasters thought these "plump" hot dogs were the "perfect size" and gave a "nice contrast to the bun." "This is my ideal dog," said one happy taster.

KAYEM Skinless Beef Hot Dogs
PRICE: $5.99 for 8 ($0.75 per hot dog)
WEIGHT OF ONE DOG: 50 g
COMMENTS: Another "big and substantial" dog, this "juicy" sausage was "meaty" and "tender" with "just the right amount of smoke." Tasters thought the "mild," "subtle" spice blend used in this product was "classic" and "familiar."

RECOMMENDED WITH RESERVATIONS

BAR-S Premium Beef Franks
PRICE: $3.25 for 8 ($0.41 per hot dog)
WEIGHT OF ONE DOG: 41 g
COMMENTS: These sausages were plenty "meaty" and "juicy," with a "firm," "springy" texture, though a few tasters noted a "sour," "chemical" aftertaste. While these dogs were too "small" for some tasters, most agreed that they had a "salty" kick and a "hint of smoke" that stood up against the bun.

HEBREW NATIONAL Beef Franks
PRICE: $6.49 for 7 ($0.93 per hot dog)
WEIGHT OF ONE DOG: 49 g
COMMENTS: Tasters liked the "intensely savory" beefiness and "springy" texture of these dogs, but most thought these "slim," "skinny" sausages weren't big enough for a standard bun. Still, many praised their "juicy" tenderness and "slightly spicy" flavor.

RECOMMENDED WITH RESERVATIONS *(continued)*

OSCAR MAYER Classic Beef Franks
PRICE: $5.99 for 10 ($0.60 per hot dog)
WEIGHT OF ONE DOG: 42 g
COMMENTS: These "very skinny" sausages were among the smallest in our lineup, and while tasters liked their "smoky" meatiness, most thought these "slim" dogs got "lost in the bun." "I might put two of these in the same bun," said one taster. Some also thought this product, which lists corn syrup as its third ingredient, was a little too sweet, with a "maple," "barbecue sauce" flavor.

NOT RECOMMENDED

BALL PARK Beef Franks
PRICE: $4.99 for 8 ($0.62 per hot dog)
WEIGHT OF ONE DOG: 53 g
COMMENTS: "Mush mush mush!" said one taster complaining about these "spongy," "flabby" sausages, which were likened to "school cafeteria hot dogs." The few tasters that could get past the "creepy soft" texture found these dogs dominated by a "sweet," "bologna-y" flavor with a "chemical," "plastic" aftertaste.

APPLEGATE The Great Organic Uncured Beef Hot Dog
PRICE: $6.49 for 8 ($0.81 per hot dog)
WEIGHT OF ONE DOG: 56 g
COMMENTS: Tasters came up with a hodgepodge of descriptions for the "odd," "tart" flavors in this hot dog, from "cabbage" and "broccoli" to "sea water" and "low tide." "I have never had a hot dog with this taste," remarked one unhappy taster. Equally unimpressive was this dog's "crumbly," "mealy" texture that left a "cottony" dryness in tasters' mouths.

SUPERMARKET BLACK TEA

Coffee may get all the buzz, but tea is still hot stuff among American consumers. To find a favorite black tea, we chose seven of the most popular or widely available black teas and tasted them both plain and with milk and sugar, evaluating them for flavor, astringency, complexity, and overall appeal. In general, the brands that scored high when tasted plain tanked when tasted with milk and sugar, and vice versa. Tea's astringency and bitterness is linked to tannins, compounds that dry the mouth as you sip. Tannic teas pair well with milk because milk's proteins, called caseins, bind with the tannins and soften their characteristic astringency. If a tea isn't tannic enough, the caseins can overwhelm its flavor, which is why most low-tannin teas tasted flat with milk. Another telling trend: The teabags packed with more tea were more tannic and were best served with milk. Because these differences didn't point us to a single brand, we had a winner for black tea enjoyed plain and another best served with milk and sugar. Teas are listed in order of preference.

If You Like It Plain

RECOMMENDED

TWININGS English Breakfast Tea
PRICE: $3.49 for 20 bags ($0.17 per bag)
WEIGHT PER TEA BAG: 1.95 g
TANNIN LEVEL: 789 mg per liter
COMMENTS: Our tasters crowned this black tea the plain tasting winner because it was "mellow" and "well-balanced" with "honey and floral" notes. It was "a bit sharp but pleasantly so," marked by its straightforward, clean flavors.

LIPTON Black Tea
PRICE: $4.99 for 100 bags ($0.05 per bag)
WEIGHT PER TEA BAG: 2.17 g
TANNIN LEVEL: 1,264 mg per liter
COMMENTS: Our tasters liked the "floral smell" and "nutty," "toasted" flavors in this black tea blend. While the measured tannins were high, tasters nonetheless found this tea to be "warm" and "pleasant" when tasted plain.

BIGELOW English Teatime
PRICE: $2.50 for 20 bags ($0.13 per bag)
WEIGHT PER TEA BAG: 2.33 g
TANNIN LEVEL: 1,061 mg per liter
COMMENTS: This black tea fell neatly in the middle of the pack, with "good base flavors" that were not particularly distinctive but had "a hint of bitterness" and a "citrus finish" that made for a pleasant drinking experience.

STASH English Breakfast
PRICE: $3.69 for 20 bags ($0.18 per bag)
WEIGHT PER TEA BAG: 2.10 g
TANNIN LEVEL: 941 mg per liter
COMMENTS: Our tasters called this reliable tea an "acceptable" blend that "sneaks up on you." It "didn't have much personality," but most agreed that the tea didn't offend the palate either. Summarized one taster: "Your regular ol' tea."

If You Take Milk and Sugar

RECOMMENDED

TETLEY British Blend
PRICE: $3.99 for 80 bags ($0.05 per bag)
WEIGHT PER TEA BAG: 2.63 g
TANNIN LEVEL: 1,265 mg per liter
COMMENTS: With milk and sugar, our tasters preferred this blend's "caramel notes," "pleasant bitterness," and "full, deep, smoky flavors." They also praised its boldness and fruity flavor.

CELESTIAL SEASONINGS English Breakfast Estate Tea
PRICE: $4.99 for 20 bags ($0.25 per bag)
WEIGHT PER TEA BAG: 2.41 g
TANNIN LEVEL: 835 mg per liter
COMMENTS: When milk and sugar were added, tasters loved this brand's "strong, true tea taste." It had "appropriate tannins" that made it "interesting" and "balanced" in flavor.

RECOMMENDED WITH RESERVATIONS

TAZO AWAKE English Breakfast Tea
PRICE: $4.99 for 20 bags ($0.25 per bag)
WEIGHT PER TEA BAG: 2.58 g
TANNIN LEVEL: 1,234 mg per liter
COMMENTS: This black tea tasted "nutty" and "woodsy" when we added milk and sugar. While the tea "wasn't thrilling," it did deliver a pleasant aftertaste that tasters preferred to other brands.

LIPTON Black Tea
PRICE: $4.99 for 100 bags ($0.05 per bag)
WEIGHT PER TEA BAG: 2.17 g
TANNIN LEVEL: 1,264 mg per liter
COMMENTS: This tea lost some complexity when we added milk and sugar, but it was still "pleasant" and "clean." "My British father-in-law wouldn't approve," one taster noted.

GLUTEN-FREE WHITE SANDWICH BREADS

Giving up gluten in one's diet can be a life-altering change. We wanted to see if the sandwich breads on supermarket shelves (or, more often, in the freezer cases) could make the transition easier. To find out if the options had improved since our last gluten-free bread tasting, we gathered a selection of loaves and called in our tasters. We offered the breads in three forms: plain, toasted with butter, and baked with eggs in a strata. Among the new brands of white sandwich bread, two were subpar in every application. Even toasting and buttering them could not make these samples palatable. The other three breads were acceptable, though tasters still had quibbles with texture or flavor. In the end, we did find three loaves we could recommend with reservations, though even these, like our bottom-ranking loaves, had a strange sweetness. Breads are listed in order of preference.

RECOMMENDED WITH RESERVATIONS

CANYON BAKEHOUSE Mountain White Gluten Free Bread
PRICE: $5.00 for 18-ounce loaf
COMMENTS: "I like this most of all," one taster wrote. "Amazingly close to regular bread!" agreed another. "Slightly sweet" and "nutty," it had a texture that was "softer," "the best chew of the bunch," albeit "a hint mushy," or "gummy/slimy," even when it was toasted. Baked in strata, it "holds its shape well," though some found it "spongy."

UDI'S Gluten Free White Sandwich Bread
PRICE: $6.29 for 12-ounce loaf
COMMENTS: "Dry, cottony, bland," with "subtle sweetness," our former winner, newly reformulated with less sodium and less protein, didn't rock our world, but made a "nice blank canvas" as a "pretty good approximation of white sandwich bread."

THREE BAKERS Whole Grain White Bread, Gluten Free
PRICE: $6.79 for 17-ounce loaf
COMMENTS: "This doesn't have much flavor," one taster wrote, which was the consensus of our panel. As for texture, it was "sandy," "crumbly," and "very chewy, not in a good way, almost marshmallow-y" when served plain; "very disappointing." Baked in strata, its flavor was "neutral, mildly sweet," but "the bread dissolved too much" and became "pasty."

NOT RECOMMENDED

KATZ White Bread, Gluten Free
PRICE: $6.19 for 21-ounce loaf
COMMENTS: With "no structure," this "crumbly," "sponge-like," "starchy" bread "disintegrates quickly" in the mouth: "It starts off moist but fades to gritty," a taster wrote. Some tasters complained of "fishy" or "fake butter" off-flavors. In strata, it was too "firm" and "absorbed liquid unevenly," and tasters noted a "weird, almost plastic" flavor.

THE ESSENTIAL BAKING COMPANY Sunny Seeded White Bread, Gluten Free
PRICE: $5.50 for 14-ounce loaf
COMMENTS: "Sweet, incredibly dry, so weird for white bread"—tasters agreed about this loaf whose crust is solidly studded with whole sunflower seeds. While tasters felt the seeds gave the crust a pleasing nutty flavor, they gave thumbs down to the interior crumb. "Hack! I need the Heimlich maneuver. So sandy and dusty." In strata, it was "wet" and "pasty."

GLUTEN-FREE MULTIGRAIN SANDWICH BREADS

At first glance you might assume the multigrain breads would beat out the white variety because they boast an abundance of hearty grains and fiber, but in most instances, these breads looked a lot like their counterparts (with the exception of those with a smattering of seeds or grains that were visible in the crust or floating within the mostly white interiors). To be labeled "multigrain," breads only have to contain more than one type of grain—and that can be in the form of refined flours. In fact, our favorite "multigrain" gluten-free bread contained no fiber or protein at all, a sign that it contains no whole grains. Our two recommended brands are our favorite gluten-free sandwich breads overall. Despite being labeled as multigrain and whole-grain, in our opinion these breads are so much like white bread that they are interchangeable whether you are simply making a sandwich or using them as part of a recipe. Breads are listed in order of preference.

RECOMMENDED

GLUTINO Gluten Free Multigrain Bread
PRICE: $5.49 for 14.1-ounce loaf
COMMENTS: With the most salt of all the breads, and with one of the highest fat contents (at 3.5 grams per slice), this loaf had a flavor advantage. "It has chew and some structure," with an interior that was "fluffy and light, almost like challah," though some noted that it "doesn't seem very multigrain." Overall, as one taster wrote, "Miles better than the others."

THREE BAKERS 7 Ancient Grains Whole Grain Bread, Gluten-Free
PRICE: $5.99 for 17-ounce loaf
COMMENTS: With "a yeasty, rich flavor," "crust that is very chewy," and "seeds and grains that add interest," this bread was appealing to tasters. Toasted, this loaf had "nice crunch" but became "gummy in the middle."

RECOMMENDED WITH RESERVATIONS

CANYON BAKEHOUSE 7-Grain Bread, Gluten-Free
PRICE: $5.49 for 18-ounce loaf
COMMENTS: "Nutty" and "slightly sweet," this loaf had "normal bread flavor." Toasted, it was much less successful: "a little off—sort of sweet and turns mushy quickly in my mouth" noted one taster.

KINNIKINNICK SOFT Multigrain Bread, Gluten-Free
PRICE: $4.99 for 16-ounce loaf
COMMENTS: This bread was deemed "very light" with "no chew" to the interior but a "substantial" crust.

RECOMMENDED WITH RESERVATIONS (continued)

UDI'S Gluten Free Whole Grain Bread
PRICE: $5.99 for 12-ounce loaf
COMMENTS: "Woof. Dry," wrote one taster, who summed up the comments of many. "No chewy pull; it just breaks," with a flavor that is "nice, but not very complex." Toasted, it was dry, with a texture "like Styrofoam."

NOT RECOMMENDED

SCHAR Gluten-Free Hearty Grain Bread
PRICE: $4.99 for 15-ounce loaf
COMMENTS: "Dry, dry, dry," complained a taster. "Leaves pasty coating of sand/mud in my mouth." "Dense," "stiff," and "compact," the bread had "no chew or air," and tasters found it "a bit sour," "like old beer." Toasted, it was much the same.

THE ESSENTIAL BAKING COMPANY Super Seeded Multi-Grain Bread
PRICE: $5.99 for 14-ounce loaf
COMMENTS: Many tasters noted "overly sweet," "molasses-y" flavors, "like bad cinnamon raisin bread." It also featured "lots and lots of sunflower seeds," which contributed to its high fat content. As toast, it still had problems: It was "very sweet" and "off-putting."

KATZ Whole Grain Bread, Gluten-Free
PRICE: $6.19 for 21-ounce loaf
COMMENTS: Tasters disliked this bread's "dry, rock-like texture." It was "stiff," "brittle," and "foamy." "Truly awful," wrote one. "I would give up bread if this were my only option."

KNIFE SHARPENERS

We wanted a sharpener that could sharpen both ultrathin Asian-style chef's knives with narrow 15-degree blade angles as well as the 20-degree edge of more traditional blades. To find one model that fit the bill, we rounded up manual and electric sharpeners and dulled nine of our favorite chef's knives. Some sharpeners came with unintuitive directions and designs or fussy cleaning requirements; others made jarring vibrations or grinding noises. With diamond abrasives, supportive chambers, and intuitive design, our favorite models put razor-sharp edges on dull knives (our winner left knives sharper than they were out of the box) and were easy to use. Whether you buy a manual or electric model depends on personal preferences: Manual sharpeners are smaller, lighter, cheaper, and easier to use, while electric sharpeners are great for repairing extensive damage. Products appear below in order of preference.

Electric

HIGHLY RECOMMENDED

		PERFORMANCE		TESTERS' COMMENTS
CHEF'SCHOICE Trizor XV Knife Sharpener MODEL: 15 PRICE: $149.99 ABRASIVE: Diamond		ROUTINE SHARPENING NOTCH REMOVAL DESIGN	★★★ ★★★ ★★★	With diamond abrasives and a spring-loaded chamber that precisely guided the blade, this sharpener produced edges that were sharper than on brand-new knives from edge to tip, even converting a 20-degree edge to 15 degrees.

RECOMMENDED

CHEF'SCHOICE Diamond Sharpener for Asian Knives MODEL: 316 PRICE: $79.99 ABRASIVE: Diamond		ROUTINE SHARPENING NOTCH REMOVAL DESIGN	★★½ ★★ ★★★	Fitted with diamond abrasives and a chamber that "cradled" the blade, this electric sharpener was quick and easy to use. It wasn't quite as effective at sharpening as our winner, but results were comparable to a factory sharpened edge. It removed nicks in 30 minutes.

NOT RECOMMENDED

SHUN Electric Sharpener MODEL: AP0119 PRICE: $79.95 ABRASIVE: Ceramic		ROUTINE SHARPENING NOTCH REMOVAL DESIGN	★½ ★★ ★★	This model put a reasonably sharp edge on the knife, but it worked too aggressively, removing 3 grams of metal from the blade after four rounds of sharpening. Its wheels sprayed dust as it worked and left a zipper-like pattern on the blade.

Manual

RECOMMENDED

CHEF'SCHOICE Pronto Manual Diamond Hone Asian Knife Sharpener MODEL: 463 PRICE: $49.99 ABRASIVE: Diamond		ROUTINE SHARPENING NOTCH REMOVAL DESIGN	★★½ N/A ★★★	Our favorite manual sharpener quickly restored a razor-sharp edge to blades that had no serious damage. Its high guides ensured that the blade met the abrasive at a precise and secure angle so we could put even pressure along the entire edge. The handle was grippy and comfortable, and it fit easily in a drawer.

RECOMMENDED WITH RESERVATIONS

VICTORINOX SwissSharp MODEL: 49002 PRICE: $32.40 ABRASIVE: Carbide		ROUTINE SHARPENING NOTCH REMOVAL DESIGN	★★ N/A ★★	This sharpener put a decent edge on the knife, was quick to operate, and was compact enough to stow in a drawer. The blade teetered back and forth in the V-shaped chamber; when we looked at it microscopically, it showed a wavy, irregular edge.

NOT RECOMMENDED

WÜSTHOF Two Stage Hand-Held Sharpener MODEL: 2922 PRICE: $19.99 ABRASIVE: Carbide		ROUTINE SHARPENING NOTCH REMOVAL DESIGN	★½ N/A ★	This sharpener was sturdy to hold but didn't secure the knife: Extra space at the top of its chamber allowed the knife to teeter as it slid over the abrasives. We had to ease up on pressure as we pulled the knife through the chamber, which made for an inconsistent edge.
KUHN RIKON Dual Knife Sharpener MODEL: 2949 (black) PRICE: $19.50 ABRASIVE: Ceramic		ROUTINE SHARPENING NOTCH REMOVAL DESIGN	★ N/A ★	Because this model didn't support even pressure along the length of the blade, the knife never got very sharp; under a microscope, it looked jagged and rutted at the tip and heel. Instructions were unintuitive, and pronounced ridges on the handle dug into our hands.

SLICING KNIVES

Slicing knives are long and straight for smooth, even slicing, and for years our favorite has been a 12-inch slicing knife from Victorinox. To see if it still stood out, we pitted it against new models, slicing turkey breast and roast beef and rating each knife on its handle, blade, sharpness, and agility. Comfortable handles and subtle flexibility allowed for control and strength. Length mattered, too. Shorter blades caused our knuckles to brush against the meat as we sliced, while longer blades gave us room to work. Narrower blades were preferred, as were those with the friction-reducing divots called Grantons along their sides. In the end the Victorinox wowed us all over again. It was long, sharp, and just flexible enough to give us utter control and perfect slices. Products appear below in order of preference.

HIGHLY RECOMMENDED	PERFORMANCE		TESTERS' COMMENTS
VICTORINOX 12" Fibrox Pro Granton Edge Slicing/Carving Knife MODEL: 47645 PRICE: $54.65 BLADE LENGTH: 12 in BLADE HEIGHT: 1.5 in WEIGHT: 5.6 oz BLADE ANGLE: 15° GRANTONS: Yes	HANDLE BLADE SHARPNESS AGILITY	★★★ ★★★ ★★★ ★★★	Our previous winner turned in another gold-medal performance: "Every slice is perfect," said one tester. It was supersharp and had a long, tall blade that kept our hands out of the way and was "just flexible enough so you feel like it's doing what you tell it to." It was perfectly balanced, and the handle was comfortable and grippy any way we held it.

RECOMMENDED

	PERFORMANCE		TESTERS' COMMENTS
MERCER RENAISSANCE 11" Granton Slicer MODEL: M23720 PRICE: $32 BLADE LENGTH: 11 in BLADE HEIGHT: 1.25 in WEIGHT: 5.6 oz BLADE ANGLE: 15° GRANTONS: Yes	HANDLE BLADE SHARPNESS AGILITY	★★½ ★★★ ★★★ ★★½	This blade felt "good and sharp," "nicely weighted," and "slightly flexible, but not too much." Though a few testers who preferred to choke up disliked the particularly pronounced tab on its underside, its rounded handle felt "intuitive" to most, and a few noted that the classic black riveted design was particularly confidence-inspiring and elegant for tableside slicing.
WÜSTHOF PRO 11-Inch Hollow Edge Slicing Knife MODEL: 4859 PRICE: $44.95 BLADE LENGTH: 11 in BLADE HEIGHT: 1.13 in WEIGHT: 5.6 oz BLADE ANGLE: 14° GRANTONS: Yes	HANDLE BLADE SHARPNESS AGILITY	★★ ★★★ ★★★ ★★½	This agile, semiflexible blade was long and sharp and moved through meat with a controlled, even stroke. The handle was made of tacky plastic and felt pleasingly grippy and secure, but its underside had a full, rounded belly that tucked into a deep divot, which put some testers' index fingers in an "awkward" position, like "I'm angled backwards," according to one.

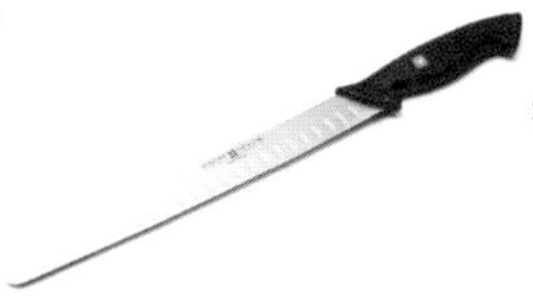

RECOMMENDED WITH RESERVATIONS

	PERFORMANCE		TESTERS' COMMENTS
MESSERMEISTER Four Seasons 12-Inch Round Tip Kullenschliff Slicer MODEL: 501812K PRICE: $50 BLADE LENGTH: 12 in BLADE HEIGHT: 1.25 in WEIGHT: 5.6 oz BLADE ANGLE: 20° GRANTONS: Yes	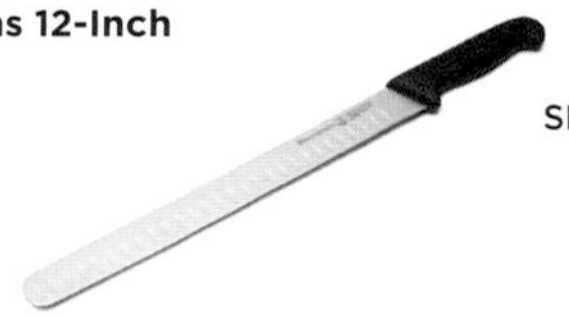 HANDLE BLADE SHARPNESS AGILITY	★★½ ★★½ ★★ ★★	This knife was nice and long but felt "duller for sure." It had a wider blade angle, at 20 degrees, and the second thickest spine, at 1.91 millimeters, which likely explains why, while we were able to get "nice intact pieces," it felt like "more work." The handle felt comfortable for most testers, but some found it slightly too fat for comfort.
ZWILLING J.A. HENCKELS Professional S Hollow Edge Slicing Knife MODEL: 31121263 PRICE: $79.95 BLADE LENGTH: 10 in BLADE HEIGHT: 1.07 in WEIGHT: 4.8 oz BLADE ANGLE: 15° GRANTONS: Yes	HANDLE BLADE SHARPNESS AGILITY	★★ ★★ ★★ ★★	This knife felt "well constructed" and "sharp," but at 10 inches, the blade was a bit short lengthwise for most; it wasn't so short that our knuckles touched the meat while we were slicing, but we had to take extra care. Its handle was a bit small, and the blade was short heightwise, too, so as we finished each slice, even small-handed testers banged their knuckles on the cutting board.

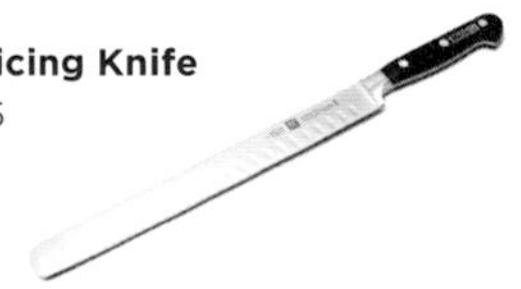

NOT RECOMMENDED

	PERFORMANCE		TESTERS' COMMENTS
VICTORINOX 10" Fibrox Pro Slicing/Carving Knife MODEL: 47542 PRICE: $36.69 BLADE LENGTH: 10 in BLADE HEIGHT: 1.17 in WEIGHT: 4 oz BLADE ANGLE: 15° GRANTONS: No	HANDLE BLADE SHARPNESS AGILITY	★★ ★ ★★ ★½	Unlike our winning knife from the same maker, this model lacked a Granton edge, which may explain why even though they shared the same 15-degree blade angle and slimmer spine, this one felt duller; testers had to "work harder" to get a decent slice. At 10 inches long and 1 inch high, it was too small; testers had to take care not to touch the meat or bang their knuckles on the cutting board.

CARBON-STEEL SKILLETS

In restaurant kitchens, carbon-steel skillets are a chef's secret weapon—a utilitarian vessel that produces incredible browning on a slippery nonstick surface. We wondered if this pan could make all our other skillets more of an option than a necessity, so we tasked a few models with frying eggs, pan-searing steaks, and baking tarte Tatin. Focusing on 12-inch models, we evaluated the skillets' shape, weight, handle comfort, and maneuverability. Carbon steel requires seasoning, and we were astonished at how nonstick even the initial seasoning made these pans. The deep, even browning these pans produced was easily on par with cast iron, but because carbon-steel pans are lighter and thinner, they heated up in half the time. Acidic food stripped off most of the pan's dark patina, but it was restored after a few rounds of stovetop heating and wiping the skillet with oil. In the end, we were impressed. These skillets offer the versatility of a traditional pan, the heat retention of cast iron at a lighter weight, and the slick release of a good nonstick skillet without the synthetic coating or the lack of durability. Products appear below in order of preference.

HIGHLY RECOMMENDED

	PERFORMANCE	TESTERS' COMMENTS
MATFER BOURGEAT Black Steel Round Frying Pan, 11⅞" MODEL: 062005 PRICE: $44.38 WEIGHT: 4.7 lb COOKING SURFACE: 9 in	COOKING ★★★ NONSTICK ★★★ EASE OF USE ★★★	This affordable pan had it all: thick, solid construction; a smooth interior; an ergonomically angled handle; and sides flared for easy access but high enough to contain splashes.
BLU SKILLET Ironware 13" Fry Pan MODEL: SQ2281937 PRICE: $230 WEIGHT: 5.5 lb COOKING SURFACE: 10 in	COOKING ★★★ NONSTICK ★★★ EASE OF USE ★★★	This beautifully designed pan arrived preseasoned, with the metal heat-treated to a shade of slate blue that darkened with use. Its broad cooking surface, flared sides, and perfect release made it a pleasure to use. Our only quibble (besides price): It's heavy.

RECOMMENDED

	PERFORMANCE	TESTERS' COMMENTS
MAUVIEL M'STEEL Round Fry Pan, Steel Handle 12.5" MODEL: 3651.32 PRICE: $79.95 WEIGHT: 5.1 lb COOKING SURFACE: 10 in	COOKING ★★★ NONSTICK ★★★ EASE OF USE ★★½	Very spacious and sturdy, with low sides and a reliably slick surface, this pan browned evenly but felt slightly heavier than ideal and lacked a helper handle to share the weight.
TURK Heavy Steel Frying Pan 11" MODEL: 66228 PRICE: $79 WEIGHT: 4.3 lb COOKING SURFACE: 8 in	COOKING ★★★ NONSTICK ★★★ EASE OF USE ★★	Solidly built and well-designed—with low flaring sides, a nicely angled handle, and a seasoned surface that never stuck—this pan was maneuverable and easy to use. Its only flaw: a too-small cooking surface that made the pan feel cramped.
DE BUYER Mineral B Frypan, 12.6" MODEL: 5610.32 PRICE: $79.95 WEIGHT: 5.75 lb COOKING SURFACE: 9¼ in	COOKING ★★★ NONSTICK ★★★ EASE OF USE ★½	This roomy pan browned foods well. The seasoning instructions had us coat just the cooking surface with oil, so the untreated sides stuck until the pan had been used a number of times. Its high-angled handle and heft made it difficult to maneuver.
PADERNO World Cuisine Heavy Duty Polished Carbon Steel Frying Pan, 12½" MODEL: A4171432 PRICE: $42.34 WEIGHT: 6.2 lb COOKING SURFACE: 9½ in	COOKING ★★½ NONSTICK ★★½ EASE OF USE ★½	With enough cooking space and the lower-angled handle we prefer, this pan had plenty of promise. But it provided a slightly less slippery release than the top pans, and its sides were a bit too shallow. Its weight made it hard for testers to maneuver.

RECOMMENDED WITH RESERVATIONS

	PERFORMANCE	TESTERS' COMMENTS
LODGE 12" Seasoned Steel Skillet MODEL: CRS12 PRICE: $39.95 WEIGHT: 4.2 lb COOKING SURFACE: 9¼ in	COOKING ★★ NONSTICK ★★ EASE OF USE ★★	This comparatively light pan was comfortable to lift and handle. Its slick preseasoned surface deteriorated as we cooked, and food began to stick. Slightly thinner, it ran a little hot with a tendency toward hot spots.

NOT RECOMMENDED

	PERFORMANCE	TESTERS' COMMENTS
VOLLRATH 12½" Carbon Steel Fry Pan MODEL: 58930 PRICE: $45.01 WEIGHT: 3.3 lb COOKING SURFACE: 9¼ in	COOKING ★★ NONSTICK ★★ EASE OF USE ★	This thin pan became superhot superfast, and hot spots made our tarte Tatin's apples caramelize unevenly. High, cupped sides made it hard to get a spatula beneath foods, and the bottom warped by the end of testing.

OVEN THERMOMETERS

For reliable, consistent results with recipes, a good oven thermometer is critical. We gathered nine models, rating them on accuracy as well as the legibility of their faces and ease of use. We checked for consistency by arranging four copies of each alongside a high-tech digital thermometer. Out of the gate, three products faltered, registering temperatures 10 to 25 degrees off the real temperature. Most models had thin, flat bases designed to sit atop an oven rack, but those under 2¼ inches wide were prone to tipping; we also disliked models with clamp-like bases designed to clip onto grates. Faces with minimal markings beyond 25-degree increments were easiest to read, but we knocked off points for casings that obscured or cast long shadows on the numbers. In the end, nearly half our lineup failed to meet our criteria for legibility and stability. Add to that the three models that faltered in our accuracy tests, and we were left with just four recommended thermometers. Products appear below in order of preference.

RECOMMENDED		PERFORMANCE		TESTERS' COMMENTS
CDN Pro Accurate Oven Thermometer MODEL: DOT2 PRICE: $8.70 TEMPERATURE RANGE: 150–550°F		ACCURACY EASE OF USE LEGIBILITY	★★★ ★★★ ★★½	This model aced our accuracy tests. It sports a sturdy base and clear markings with large numbers at boldly visible 50- and 25-degree increments. Its face is prone to glare, but is still fairly easy to read.
TAYLOR TruTemp Thermometer MODEL: 3506 PRICE: $6.10 TEMPERATURE RANGE: 100–600°F		ACCURACY EASE OF USE LEGIBILITY	★★★ ★★★ ★★	As with our winner, this model gave consistently accurate readings. Testers appreciated the large display, but its tiny dashes denoting increments of less than 25 degrees were distracting.
POLDER Commercial Oven Thermometer MODEL: THM 550N PRICE: $7.19 TEMPERATURE RANGE: 50–500°F		ACCURACY EASE OF USE LEGIBILITY	★★★ ★★★ ★½	This small thermometer provided readings that matched the oven's temperature in test after test. Frustratingly, at certain angles its metal casing obscured some numbers entirely and cast shadows on others.
COOPER-ATKINS Dial Oven Thermometer MODEL: 24HP 011 PRICE: $4.63 TEMPERATURE RANGE: 100–600°F		ACCURACY EASE OF USE LEGIBILITY	★★★ ★★★ ★½	Our old winner continued to impress us with consistently accurate readings and a wide, sturdy base. But the metal casing hid some numbers from view, and the food safety instructions printed on the bottom of the face were distracting.
NOT RECOMMENDED				
WILLIAMS-SONOMA Oven Thermometer MODEL: 21 4024691 PRICE: $19.95 TEMPERATURE RANGE: 150–600°F		ACCURACY EASE OF USE LEGIBILITY	★★★ N/A ★★	We found no faults with the accuracy or readability of this thermometer, but its clamp-like clip was incompatible with every oven rack we tried. It was hard to clip on, and it often swiveled or fell over.
NORPRO Oven Thermometer MODEL: 5973 PRICE: $7.97 TEMPERATURE RANGE: 150–600°F		ACCURACY EASE OF USE LEGIBILITY	★★★ ★ N/A	This model's accuracy couldn't offset its flaws: Its base is barely bigger than the gaps between the bars on our oven racks. The numbers appearing between temperature increments were hard to read at a glance.
TAYLOR Connoisseur Oven Use Thermometer MODEL: 503 PRICE: $13.22 TEMPERATURE RANGE: 150–600°F		ACCURACY EASE OF USE LEGIBILITY	★★★ N/A ½	Though this thermometer gave accurate readings, its clamp-like clip was hard to slide onto oven rack bars. It routinely fell over, making its otherwise easy-to-read face illegible. The silicone backing melted and warped when it fell onto the oven floor.
TAYLOR Oven Thermometer MODEL: 5932 PRICE: $6.90 TEMPERATURE RANGE: 100–600°F		ACCURACY EASE OF USE LEGIBILITY	★ ★★★ ★★★	One unit of this model was off by 25-degree variations in two accuracy tests. It's too bad, because the temperature markings are easy to read, and its wide base easily supports its extra-large face.
MAVERICK Oven Thermometer MODEL: OT01 PRICE: $12 TEMPERATURE RANGE: 100–600°F		ACCURACY EASE OF USE LEGIBILITY	★ ★★★ ★	One copy of this thermometer gave readings 10 to 25 degrees below the actual oven temperature during testing. The model is also quite small, with tiny, often obscured numbers. Its one pro: It did sit securely on the oven rack.
MAVERICK Large Dial Oven Thermometer MODEL: OT02 PRICE: $20.94 TEMPERATURE RANGE: 100–600°F		ACCURACY EASE OF USE LEGIBILITY	★ ★ ★★★	Like its sibling, this thermometer faltered in accuracy. The base also couldn't support the weight of its oversized face, and it toppled over enough times to crack one unit's glass front.

SPRINGFORM PANS

All too often, a faulty springform pan is to blame for crumbled, mushy, or cracked cheesecakes. Springform pans' two-piece design often leaves small gaps where water from a water bath seeps in and butter from the crust leaks out, all but guaranteeing a disappointing dessert. Hoping to find a reliable pan, we gathered eight models and used each to make no-bake, oven-baked, and water bath–baked cheesecakes. Off the bat, silicone pans were disastrous, and glass bottoms made for pallid crusts that were practically glued into the pan. We favored pans with light-colored nonstick finishes, which browned slowly and released readily. Springforms with flat or recessed bases were difficult to maneuver a spatula or knife along, whereas those with raised bases gave us more room to leverage our tools for picture-perfect slices. Wide bases were best, giving us something to grab on to throughout baking while also tempering leaking. While none of the pans were completely leakproof (we always recommend wrapping your pan in foil before baking in a water bath), we found one that turned out attractive cakes every time. Products appear below in order of preference.

RECOMMENDED

	PERFORMANCE		TESTERS' COMMENTS

WILLIAMS-SONOMA Goldtouch Springform Pan, 9"
MODEL: 782898203
PRICE: $49.95
MATERIAL: Nonstick metal
BASE WIDTH: 10.65 in

DESIGN ★★★
BROWNING ★★★
RELEASE ★★★
SEAL ★★
DURABILITY ★★½

This pan produced pristine cheesecakes with golden, evenly baked crusts. Its tall sides gave us something to grab when turning the pan and though not completely leakproof, its wide, raised base caught leaking butter and provided support when cutting slices or removing cake.

NORDIC WARE 9" Leakproof Springform Pan `BEST BUY`
MODEL: 55742 (gray ProForm)
PRICE: $16.22
MATERIAL: Nonstick metal
BASE WIDTH: 9.74 in

DESIGN ★★½
BROWNING ★★½
RELEASE ★★★
SEAL ★★
DURABILITY ★★½

Our old favorite, this springform made beautiful, evenly browned cheesecakes that were easy to release from the pan. Leaking was minimal, and most butter pooled along its base, though a few drops overflowed onto the oven floor. This pan's base had a few minor scratches after testing.

KAISER LA FORME PLUS 9" Springform Pan
MODEL: 70.0637.0200
PRICE: $37.98
MATERIAL: Nonstick metal
BASE WIDTH: 10.00 in

DESIGN ★★½
BROWNING ★★
RELEASE ★★½
SEAL ★★
DURABILITY ★★½

The darkest pan of the bunch, this springform slightly overbrowned crusts in spots but not enough to make a big difference in flavor. Cakes were mostly easy to release, and any leaking was corralled along the pan's wide base.

CALPHALON Nonstick Bakeware 9-in Springform Pan
MODEL: 1826048
PRICE: $21.95
MATERIAL: Nonstick metal
BASE WIDTH: 8.89 in

DESIGN ★★
BROWNING ★★★
RELEASE ★★
SEAL ★★
DURABILITY ★★½

This pan's lighter finish produced gorgeous, evenly browned crusts. Though cakes were fairly easy to release, its flat base required more finessing and leaked butter onto the oven floor. A few scratches remained after testing.

NOT RECOMMENDED

ZENKER BY FRIELING Handle-It Glass Bottom Springform with Handles, 9"
MODEL: Z3850
PRICE: $34.95
MATERIALS: Nonstick metal and glass
BASE WIDTH: 8.92 in

DESIGN ★★
BROWNING ★★
RELEASE ★½
SEAL ★½
DURABILITY ★

Though handles made this pan easy to maneuver, its small glass bottom was fussy to align with the collar and made unevenly browned crusts. Ridges along the pan's collar crumbled delicate crusts. By the end of testing, this pan had large scratches all along its collar and base.

LÉKUÉ Springform Pan
MODEL: 2412323R01M017
PRICE: $26.99
MATERIAL: Silicone and ceramic
BASE WIDTH: 9.38 in

DESIGN ★
BROWNING ★
RELEASE ★
SEAL ★
DURABILITY ★

We had to wrestle this pan's silicone collar around its ceramic bottom plate and our efforts were fruitless: The pan leaked butter all over the oven and turned cheesecake cooked in a water bath to mush.

KITCHEN TIMERS

There's nothing like a spectacular kitchen failure to drive home the importance of timing in cooking. From smartphones to ovens to microwaves, home cooks have no shortage of time keepers, but a good kitchen timer is still valuable: more durable and moisture-resistant than other electronics and more versatile than appliance timers. We rounded up 13 digital timers that could track from two to four events at once. We first tested each timer against the official time kept by the National Institute of Standards and Technology and were pleasantly surprised to find that all of our models were accurate. They also all emerged from our durability testing intact. One model had everything we wanted plus a unique innovation: Where most timers had hours, minutes, and seconds buttons that you press and scroll through to set, our winner was the only one with a keypad, allowing users to type in the exact time they want without scrolling or resetting. Products appear below in order of preference.

RECOMMENDED	PERFORMANCE	TESTERS' COMMENTS
OXO Good Grips Triple Timer MODEL: 1071501 PRICE: $19.99 NUMBER OF TIMERS: 3	INTUITIVENESS ★★★ EASE OF USE ★★★ DESIGN ★★½ VERSATILITY ★★★ DISPLAY & ALERTS ★★½ CLEANUP & DURABILITY ★★★	This timer was simple and intuitive, with a dedicated "clear" button and a full keypad, so testers entered times by typing instead of scrolling. It displayed all of its timers at once, so we could check everything at a glance.
MEASUPRO Digital Timer, Clock, and Stopwatch MODEL: CCT400 PRICE: $14.99 NUMBER OF TIMERS: 4	INTUITIVENESS ★★★ EASE OF USE ★★½ DESIGN ★★ VERSATILITY ★★★ DISPLAY & ALERTS ★★½ CLEANUP & DURABILITY ★★★	This timer had clearly labeled single-purpose buttons, and its display was nice and bold. It was a little tippy, displayed only one timer at a time, and its "start/stop" button was hard to hit with one hand. Testers had to scroll to enter the time, and there was no reverse function.

RECOMMENDED WITH RESERVATIONS

	PERFORMANCE	TESTERS' COMMENTS
MAVERICK Redi-Check Four Line Timer MODEL: TM-091 PRICE: $14.99 NUMBER OF TIMERS: 4	INTUITIVENESS ★★★ EASE OF USE ★★½ DESIGN ★★½ VERSATILITY ★★★ DISPLAY & ALERTS ★★ CLEANUP & DURABILITY ★★	This compact timer was intuitive, with clear, dedicated buttons. Its audio alerts were a bit sharp, especially considering that it beeps when you press its buttons. It showed only one timer at a time, and we had to scroll to set the time and start over. Its light frame was unsteady.
MARATHON Large Display 100 Hour Dual Count Up/Down Timer MODEL: TI030017BK (black) PRICE: $14.99 NUMBER OF TIMERS: 2	INTUITIVENESS ★★½ EASE OF USE ★½ DESIGN ★★ VERSATILITY ★★★ DISPLAY & ALERTS ★★★ CLEANUP & DURABILITY ★★★	This timer was reasonably intuitive. We liked its clear digits, two volume options, and "mute" button. It was a bit tippy, but only if we knocked into it. You have to scroll to set the time, and you must hold down two of its buttons to reset, making it a fussy, two-handed endeavor.

NOT RECOMMENDED

	PERFORMANCE	TESTERS' COMMENTS
WESTBEND Triple Timer/Clock MODEL: 40053 PRICE: $11.99 NUMBER OF TIMERS: 3	INTUITIVENESS ★★★ EASE OF USE ★★½ DESIGN ½ VERSATILITY ★★★ DISPLAY & ALERTS ★★★ CLEANUP & DURABILITY ★★★	This timer was persnickety to program because its buttons were laid out in four tight rows and printed with very small type. It was also slightly tippy, required us to scroll to see the time, and couldn't reverse.
POLDER Digital Dual Timer with LED Alert MODEL: TMR-993-90 (white) PRICE: $14.99 NUMBER OF TIMERS: 2	INTUITIVENESS ★★ EASE OF USE ★½ DESIGN ★½ VERSATILITY ★★★ DISPLAY & ALERTS ★★★ CLEANUP & DURABILITY ★★★	Despite this timer's modern look, its performance didn't stack up. You have to press hour and minute buttons simultaneously to reset it; it had a supersensitive touch screen, so if we didn't press the buttons precisely, it would add time. We had to scroll to set the time without a reverse option.
TAYLOR Plan & Prep Four Event Timer with Whiteboard MODEL: 5849 PRICE: $14.22 NUMBER OF TIMERS: 4	INTUITIVENESS ★★ EASE OF USE ★★ DESIGN ★★ VERSATILITY ★★ DISPLAY & ALERTS ★★★ CLEANUP & DURABILITY ★★★	The board worked, but the timer stunk. It couldn't be set for seconds, and its tiny buttons were tightly grouped in its bottom left corner, making it easy to press the wrong one. You also have to hold down two buttons to clear it, and its buttons weren't intuitive.

FOOD PROCESSORS

Here in the test kitchen, we demand a food processor that can handle lots of chopping, slicing, and shredding while delivering high-quality results. We put 21 models through their paces, looking for a machine that could handle whatever tasks we threw at it. The space between the blades and the bottom and sides of the workbowl was pivotal: Smaller gaps promised even chopping, slicing, mixing, and emulsifying. Sharp, efficient blades also stood out, making clean cuts while dull blades created a bruised, mushy mess. The best models also had pulses that ran for only as long as we were pushing the button, giving us excellent control over our chopping. Mixing dough is a food processor's ultimate challenge, so we tasked each with a double batch of pizza dough. Some machines couldn't handle the strain, but our top performers muscled through, yielding silky, bouncy dough. Though by no means an inexpensive model, our winning food processor proves its worth in its sturdiness and performance, and it outshone fancier models costing up to three times as much. Products appear below in order of preference.

HIGHLY RECOMMENDED	PERFORMANCE		TESTERS' COMMENTS
CUISINART Custom 14 Food Processor MODEL: DFP-14BCNY PRICE: $161.99	CHOPPING SLICING SHREDDING MIXING PUREEING EASE OF USE	★★★ ★★★ ★★★ ★★★ ★★★ ★★★	With a powerful, quiet motor; responsive pulsing; sharp blades; and a pared-down design, this model aced every test. It didn't leak at its maximum stated liquid capacity. It's easy to clean and store, and it comes with a chopping blade and shredding and slicing disks. Additional blades are available à la carte.

RECOMMENDED			
THE BREVILLE Sous Chef 12-Cup Food Processor MODEL: BFP660SIL PRICE: $299.99	CHOPPING SLICING SHREDDING MIXING PUREEING EASE OF USE	★★★ ★★★ ★★★ ★★ ★★★ ★★½	Quiet and quick at most tasks, this model excelled at chopping, slicing, and shredding, but struggled to mix pizza dough. Its blades spin out of reach in the big bowl, so emulsifying and mixing were not thorough. The option to easily select thickness settings was a nice touch.
BLACK + DECKER Performance Food Processor MODEL: FP6010B PRICE: $149.99	CHOPPING SLICING SHREDDING MIXING PUREEING EASE OF USE	★★½ ★★★ ★★★ ★★★ ★★ ★½	This model performed well in many areas despite its construction's flimsy feel. Suction cup feet on its lightweight base failed to stabilize the machine, and its motor was loud. The pulse button continued running a bit long, and chopping was uneven, but its slicing and shredding were impressive, and it diced well.

RECOMMENDED WITH RESERVATIONS			
CUISINART Elite Collection 2.0 12-Cup Food Processor MODEL: FP12DC PRICE: $249.00	CHOPPING SLICING SHREDDING MIXING PUREEING EASE OF USE	★★½ ★★ ★★★ ★★ ★★½ ★★½	We liked this machine's responsive pulse button and simple control panel; shredding was exemplary, and chopping was more than acceptable. But the innovative snap-on lid didn't always latch. The motor struggled when mixing heavy pizza dough, and flour flew up into the lid and fell out messily after making pie crust.
CUISINART Elemental 11 Food Processor MODEL: FP11GM PRICE: $149.00	CHOPPING SLICING SHREDDING MIXING PUREEING EASE OF USE	★★½ ★★★ ★★ ★★½ ★★½ ★½	With a lid that went on off-kilter, this machine was tough to open and close, and its lightweight base and parts felt poorly constructed. The motor was loud, and too-long, too-weak pulses made chopping inefficient, as did narrow blades that left gaps around the edges. Pizza dough was a struggle.

NOT RECOMMENDED			
OSTER Designed for Life 14-Cup Food Processor with 5-Cup Mini Chopper MODEL: FPSTFP5273DFL PRICE: $69.00	CHOPPING SLICING SHREDDING MIXING PUREEING EASE OF USE	★★ ★ ★★½ ★★ ★★½ ★½	One of the lowest-priced products in the lineup, this machine felt flimsy, and it was incredibly loud. It wobbled on its suction cup feet, pumped a stream of air at us as it ran, and blew flour and bits of food all over the interior of the workbowl. Gaps between blade and bowl meant it failed at chopping and emulsifying.

SMALL FOOD PROCESSORS

We swear by our favorite full-size food processor, but smaller models are great for mincing garlic, dicing celery, grating Parmesan, chopping nuts, making mayonnaise, and more. To find the best on the market, we zeroed in on 3- to 6-cup models and gave them a test run. The 3.5- and 4-cup models were ideal, just large enough to handle a range of projects. Sharp, low-sitting blades were a critical feature, promising crisp cuts and thorough processing. A feeding tube was essential to slowly adding oil to homemade mayo, but only one model—our winner—had this feature. While not the right appliance for large-scale prep, a good small food processor is a worthwhile purchase. Products appear below in order of preference.

HIGHLY RECOMMENDED

	PERFORMANCE		TESTERS' COMMENTS
CUISINART Elite Collection 4-Cup Chopper/Grinder MODEL: CH4DC PRICE: $59.95 CAPACITY: 4 cups	MINCING DICING GRATING CHOPPING EMULSIFYING BLENDING DURABILITY	★★★ ★★★ ★★★ ★★★ ★★★ ★★★ ★★★	This processor had a sharp blade with great coverage. It turned out crisply cut vegetables and nuts and fluffy parsley. Its strong motor blended hummus and pesto with minimal scraping, and its small feeding tube allowed us to slowly add oil for fantastic mayonnaise.

RECOMMENDED WITH RESERVATIONS

	PERFORMANCE		TESTERS' COMMENTS
BLACK+DECKER Glass Bowl Chopper MODEL: EHC3002R PRICE: $34.95 CAPACITY: 4 cups	MINCING DICING GRATING CHOPPING EMULSIFYING BLENDING DURABILITY	★★ ★★★ ★★½ ★★★ N/A ★★ ★★★	This processor's blade was higher, but a sweeping bar to incorporate food at the bottom of the bowl helped make up for this shortcoming. Its motor was weaker than the winner (pesto and hummus were "rustic" but acceptable), and it has no feeding tube.

NOT RECOMMENDED

	PERFORMANCE		TESTERS' COMMENTS
KITCHENAID 3.5 Cup Food Chopper MODEL: KFC3511OB PRICE: $49.99 CAPACITY: 3.5 cups	MINCING DICING GRATING CHOPPING EMULSIFYING BLENDING DURABILITY	★ ★½ ★★ ★★½ ★★★ ★★ ★★★	This machine had nice blade coverage and diced mirepoix and grated Parmesan fairly well. But its motor ran fast, which made it easy to overprocess, and its blade is serrated, so it didn't chop everything cleanly.
HAMILTON BEACH Stack & Press 3 Cup Glass Bowl Chopper MODEL: 72860 PRICE: $29.99 CAPACITY: 3 cups	MINCING DICING GRATING CHOPPING EMULSIFYING BLENDING DURABILITY	★★ ★ ★★★ ★★ N/A ★★ ★★	This model's smaller bowl inhibited movement—mirepoix was a mess, and almonds were dusty. Because pressing down on the lid activates the motor, we had to unplug it every time we wanted to scrape down the sides, or it turned on with our hand inside.
NUTRI NINJA 2-in-1 MODEL: QB3000 PRICE: $99.99 CAPACITY: 5 cups	MINCING DICING GRATING CHOPPING EMULSIFYING BLENDING DURABILITY	★★ ★★ ★★ ★★ N/A ★★ ★★★	This large processor-cum-personal-smoothie-maker's powerful motor was hard to control and sprayed food up the sides of its carafe, which were lined with plastic ribs that made it tough to clean. It also doesn't have a feeding tube.
PROCTOR SILEX 6 Cup Food Processor MODEL: 70452A PRICE: $34.99 CAPACITY: 6 cups	MINCING DICING GRATING CHOPPING EMULSIFYING BLENDING DURABILITY	★ ★★★ ★★ ★★ N/A ★ ★★★	This processor had poor blade coverage: Garlic and pine nuts sat untouched in its bowl, and mayo never emulsified because half the ingredients fell below the blade. Its pulse button kept spinning far too long, and its rough serrated blade battered parsley.
BRENTWOOD 3-Cup Food Processor MODEL: FP546 (white) PRICE: $27.99 CAPACITY: 3 cups	MINCING DICING GRATING CHOPPING EMULSIFYING BLENDING DURABILITY	★ ★ ★ ★★½ N/A ★ ★★	Because of a weaker motor, a narrow canister, and poor blade coverage, this processor left Parmesan, pesto, and hummus all unacceptably chunky, even with extra processing. It also lacks a feeding tube, so it couldn't make mayonnaise.

SAUCIERS

Essentially rounded, wide-mouthed saucepans, sauciers can do everything a saucepan can do—and for certain tasks, it does them better. We gathered eight models to see if a saucier was worth bringing into the home kitchen. All eight delivered creamy risotto, satiny gravy, and smooth pastry cream, and it was a pleasure to whisk and stir in most of them. Pots with bottom surfaces measuring between 5¾ and 7 inches were best—spacious enough to keep ingredients from piling up and steaming but not so broad that they scorched. Water evaporated faster in all of the sauciers than it did in a saucepan, a boon when making reductions. Our favorite's walls slope gently down to a 5¾-inch cooking surface, encouraging broad strokes with a whisk, and the long, wide handle gave us great control. It won't replace our favorite 4-quart saucepan, but we think it deserves a place in your kitchen. Products appear below in order of preference.

RECOMMENDED

LE CREUSET 3½-Quart Stainless Steel Saucier Pan
MODEL: SSP610024P
PRICE: $250.00
CAPACITY: 3.5 quarts
WEIGHT: 2 lb 12 oz
COOKING SURFACE: 5¾ in

PERFORMANCE	★★★
EASE OF USE	★★½
CLEANUP	★★½

TESTERS' COMMENTS: With gently sloping sides and a generous opening, whisking and stirring in this saucier was a pleasure—it was also the most efficient at the evaporation test. Its lightweight frame and wide, straight-angled handle make it maneuverable and very easy to lift. One criticism: The handle became hot over time, forcing us to use a pot-holder or hold it by the back end.

ZWILLING J.A. HENCKELS Aurora 3.5-qt Stainless Steel Saucier
MODEL: 66080240
PRICE: $219.99
CAPACITY: 3.5 quarts
WEIGHT: 3 lb 13 oz
COOKING SURFACE: 7 in

PERFORMANCE	★★★
EASE OF USE	★★½
CLEANUP	★★½

TESTERS' COMMENTS: Our runner-up is heftier than our winner, with walls that slope just slightly less gently toward the cooking surface. Still, it cooks food beautifully and its wide, easy-to-grip handle extends at a comfortable angle from the pan.

RECOMMENDED WITH RESERVATIONS

ALL-CLAD Stainless Steel 3-Quart Saucier with Lid
MODEL: 4213
PRICE: $189.95
CAPACITY: 3 quarts
WEIGHT: 2 lb 10¾ oz
COOKING SURFACE: 5¼ in

PERFORMANCE	★★½
EASE OF USE	★★
CLEANUP	★★½

TESTERS' COMMENTS: This lightweight pan is easy to maneuver around the stovetop, though its cooking surface is on the small side and its walls are more sharply sloped than our top pots; that might explain why it was the slowest model to evaporate water. Some testers complained that the handle edges were sharp, but most found it easy to grip without slippage.

DEMEYERE Atlantis 3.5 qt Stainless Steel Saucier
MODEL: 5592441524
PRICE: $319.99
CAPACITY: 3.5 quarts
WEIGHT: 3 lb 11 oz
COOKING SURFACE: 6½ in

PERFORMANCE	★★★
EASE OF USE	★½
CLEANUP	★★

TESTERS' COMMENTS: The walls of this pricey saucier come close to forming saucepan-like corners. As a result, testers had to hold their utensils at a sharper angle to stir, but the food it produced was flawless. Lifting its heavier frame was made more difficult by its steeply angled handle, which felt awkward and uncomfortable.

CALPHALON Tri-Ply Stainless Steel 3-qt Covered Chef's Pan
MODEL: 1767724
PRICE: $93.49
CAPACITY: 3 quarts
WEIGHT: 2 lb 6 oz
COOKING SURFACE: 5 in

PERFORMANCE	★★
EASE OF USE	★½
CLEANUP	★★★

TESTERS' COMMENTS: The walls of this saucier slope smoothly down to the cooking surface without a hint of a corner, and testers loved the way spatulas glided around the interior, but its cooking surface is relatively skimpy. Short and slim, the handle rested uncomfortably against our palms, and cooks with large hands struggled to get a firm grip. Without rivets, cleanup was a breeze.

NOT RECOMMENDED

TRAMONTINA 3 Qt. Covered Saucier
MODEL: 80121061DS
PRICE: $69.95
CAPACITY: 3 quarts
WEIGHT: 5 lb 15⅝ oz
COOKING SURFACE: 4¾ in

PERFORMANCE	★½
EASE OF USE	½
CLEANUP	★★

TESTERS' COMMENTS: We had to lug this cast-iron heavyweight around the stovetop, and its stumpy, scorching-hot handle was no help. The small, cramped cooking surface forced us to stir vegetables frequently to ensure that they didn't steam. The abrasive side of a sponge scratched the enameled surface.

INEXPENSIVE DIGITAL THERMOMETERS

It pays to monitor the temperature of not only meat but also pies, cakes, breads, poaching water, custards, and even baked potatoes. Our go-to thermometer is the Thermapen from ThermoWorks, but at $79 for the basic model, it's an investment. In search of a cheaper alternative, we tested inexpensive digital thermometers to find out which model reigns supreme. We evaluated every model's accuracy, speed, usability, visibility, comfort, and durability with a mix of lefties, righties, small- and large-handed testers, professional chefs, and lay cooks. Most models were accurate and fast, but we found that longer probes were better—otherwise, our hands were too close to the heat. Testers also preferred large screens situated on the side of the thermometer's head, finding them easier to read at different angles. The best thermometer was lollipop-shaped and had a display that was visible at any angle for both lefties and righties. This model was also fast, accurate, and easy to use. Products appear below in order of preference.

RECOMMENDED

	PERFORMANCE		TESTERS' COMMENTS
THERMOWORKS ThermoPop MODEL: TX3100PR (purple) PRICE: $29.00 LENGTH: 7.15 in AVERAGE READ TIME: 6.33 sec	ACCURACY SPEED EASE OF USE VISIBILITY COMFORT DURABILITY	★★★ ★★★ ★★★ ★★★ ★★½ ★★★	This thermometer was fast, accurate, ambidextrous, and easy to hold. It had a few cushy extra features, including a rotating display and a backlight, which came in handy for grilling. The ThermoPop is an excellent inexpensive alternative to the Thermapen.
POLDER Stable-Read Instant Read Thermometer MODEL: THM38990 PRICE: $18.42 LENGTH: 8.75 in AVERAGE READ TIME: 6.67 sec	ACCURACY SPEED EASE OF USE VISIBILITY COMFORT DURABILITY	★★★ ★★★ ★★★ ★★★ ★★½ ★★½	Testers loved this long thermometer's audible beep when it registered the temperature. It was fast, accurate, and had a handy loop on its end and plenty of room to grip. Our only quibble: It melted when we accidentally rested it on the lip of a saucepan for a moment.
LE CREUSET Digital Instant-Read Thermometer MODEL: TR1006 PRICE: $34.95 LENGTH: 8.10 in AVERAGE READ TIME: 8.65 sec	ACCURACY SPEED EASE OF USE VISIBILITY COMFORT DURABILITY	★★★ ★★½ ★★★ ★★½ ★★½ ★★★	This bright thermometer was quick, accurate, and easy to use. We liked the small loop on the end, but its slim head was a bit small for larger-handed testers to comfortably grip over heat.

RECOMMENDED WITH RESERVATIONS

	PERFORMANCE		TESTERS' COMMENTS
ACURITE Digital Instant Read Meat Thermometer MODEL: 295 PRICE: $12.70 LENGTH: 5.75 in AVERAGE READ TIME: 9.17 sec	ACCURACY SPEED EASE OF USE VISIBILITY COMFORT DURABILITY	★★★ ★★½ ★★★ ★★½ ★½ ★★½	This quick, accurate, and straightforward thermometer had a clear, legible display, but its screen was on top of its head, meaning it was only visible from one often prohibitive angle. It was also a bit short, and it melted slightly during testing.
CDN ProAccurate Thermometer MODEL: DTQ450X PRICE: $17.90 LENGTH: 6.10 in AVERAGE READ TIME: 8.17 sec	ACCURACY SPEED EASE OF USE VISIBILITY COMFORT DURABILITY	★★★ ★★½ ★★½ ★★ ★½ ★★★	This thermometer was accurate and fast, but it was too short. Its face had lots of little buttons that were easy to accidentally press, and we never felt like we had a secure grip on its smooth, round metal head.

NOT RECOMMENDED

	PERFORMANCE		TESTERS' COMMENTS
WEBER Original Instant-Read Thermometer MODEL: 6492 PRICE: $9.99 LENGTH: 6.30 in AVERAGE READ TIME: 13.91 sec	ACCURACY SPEED EASE OF USE VISIBILITY COMFORT DURABILITY	★½ ★½ ★★½ ★★★ ★★ ★★★	Of our two copies of this thermometer, one was accurate and one was wildly erratic, reporting –7 degrees in a 32-degree ice bath and 153 degrees in a 212-degree pot of boiling water. It was also too short, and its tilting head felt a bit unstable.
FARBERWARE Protek Instant Read Thermometer MODEL: 5141007 PRICE: $13.92 LENGTH: 6.75 in AVERAGE READ TIME: 18.17 sec	ACCURACY SPEED EASE OF USE VISIBILITY COMFORT DURABILITY	★ ★½ ★½ ★★ ★★ ★	Both copies we tested of this thermometer had faulty battery chambers. The small plastic circle that's supposed to lock in place over the lithium battery was loose and would never securely screw in place—one dove right into a boiling pot of water.

GAS GRILLS

Most people choose a gas grill over charcoal because it's convenient, but whether that grill performs as it should is another matter. All too often you get one instant-burn zone and another zone so cool you could set your drink down on it. To determine which grills had the heat retention we needed, we preheated a few models for 15 minutes and mapped the heat by covering the entire grill surface with white sandwich bread. Top grills gave us evenly browned toast, and this was thanks to the grills' heat diffusers. These metal tents over a grill's burners prevent hot spots and also produce flavorful smoke when dripping fat hits them; our favorite model had extra diffusing bars between the burners for ideal heat distribution. When we tasked each model with grilling burger patties, pork butts, and 12-pound turkeys, the importance of capacity and a tight fitting lid became clear. Our winner produced smoky, tender meat thanks to the cookbox's thick cast aluminum sides and bottom and its tight-sealing lid. Products appear below in order of preference.

HIGHLY RECOMMENDED

	PERFORMANCE		TESTERS' COMMENTS
WEBER Spirit E-310 Gas Grill MODEL: 46510001 PRICE: $499 BURNERS: 3 GRATES: Enameled cast iron SIZE OF COOKING GRATE: 24 x 17 in CAPACITY: 19 burgers	GRILLING DESIGN DURABILITY CLEANUP	★★★ ★★★ ★★★ ★★★	Our winner put a crisp, brown crust on burgers and steaks. It was equally good at barbecue, rendering tender pulled pork with real smoky flavor. With a heavy-duty cookbox of thick cast aluminum and enameled steel and just one narrow vent across the back, it was easy to keep heat steady and distribute smoke. The angle of the lid when open kept smoke out of our faces. Its large, secure grease tray made cleanup easier; the sturdy, compact cart rolled without a struggle.

RECOMMENDED

	PERFORMANCE		TESTERS' COMMENTS
CHAR-BROIL Commercial Series 4-Burner Gas Grill MODEL: 463242715 PRICE: $499.99 BURNERS: 4 GRATES: Enameled Cast Iron SIZE OF COOKING GRATE: 29.5 x 17 in CAPACITY: 24 burgers	GRILLING DESIGN DURABILITY CLEANUP	★★★ ★★ ★★★ ★★	Unique, heat-spreading zigzagged steel plates beneath cast-iron grates made this grill the best at direct grilling. But its unusual interior layout left us struggling to figure out where to put water pans for indirect cooking, and there was nowhere to prop wood chip packets above the flames. Pulled pork roasted to tenderness but lacked smoke flavor. While we liked the side burner, its high, domed cover ate up space.

NOT RECOMMENDED

	PERFORMANCE		TESTERS' COMMENTS
DYNA-GLO 5-Burner Propane Gas Grill with Side Burner and Rotisserie Burner MODEL: DGA550SSP-D PRICE: $483.65 BURNERS: 5 GRATES: Stainless steel SIZE OF COOKING GRATE: 29 x 17 in CAPACITY: 28 Burgers	GRILLING DESIGN DURABILITY CLEANUP	★½ ★ ★★★ ★½	This handsome, roomy grill had five burners plus a side burner, but it ran hot and cold in different zones. Burgers got wedged under a protruding rotisserie burner in back, and a low warming rack blocked our spatula. The grease collection tray didn't channel fat, creating a mess. A big 2-inch gap at the back of the lid, open holes in the sides, and an open back panel let too much hot air and smoke escape.
NEXGRILL 4 Burner Liquid Propane Gas Grill MODEL: 720-0830H PRICE: $269 BURNERS: 4 GRATES: Stainless steel SIZE OF COOKING GRATE: 26 x 17 in CAPACITY: 15 Burgers	GRILLING DESIGN DURABILITY CLEANUP	★ ★ ★★ ★★	This was the least expensive grill we tested, so we were dubious about its value. The back of the grill surface was hotter than the front. We got visible grill marks on some burgers, while all steak came off the grill pale and soft. The open lid's shape sent smoke straight into our faces. The cookbox was thin and flimsy, and nine large vents and a 2-inch gap across the back let smoke and heat escape; no surprise that the pork butt roast was still tough after 6 hours of cooking.
KITCHENAID 3 Burner Gas Grill & Side Burner MODEL: 720-0787D PRICE: $469 BURNERS: 3 GRATES: Stainless steel SIZE OF COOKING GRATE: 24 x 19 in CAPACITY: 20 Burgers	GRILLING DESIGN DURABILITY CLEANUP	★½ ★ ★ ★	The direct heat over most of this grill's cooking surface was weak, while food on the back row scorched. Steak was "pretty sad," with a flabby, pale crust. The weak heat was a boon for barbecue, which came out tender and moist, but there was "no smoke." Abundant vents channeled heat and smoke out of the thin stainless-steel cookbox. A shallow grease tray was a hazard to move, and grease didn't channel effectively, leaving the grill interior a gummy mess.

WATER BOTTLES

Water bottles come in all shapes, sizes, and materials these days, and the options make picking one all the more challenging. We wanted to find a bottle that was easy to fill, open, close, carry, clean, and sip from. It also had to be spill-proof and exceptionally durable. Off the bat, the soft plastic pouch was too squishy and awkward for everyday use. The stainless-steel canisters were problematic, too: Testers sometimes spilled while filling them because they couldn't see inside, and they dented easily. Our favorites were made of Tritan, a clear, hard plastic that made for easy filling and supreme durability. Testers didn't like complex bottles with fussy buttons or finicky, hard-to-undo latches. As far as being spillproof and durable, nothing beat the classic screw-on lid. Our favorite had a smaller twist-on cap that opened and closed smoothly and was easy to drink from; its large opening was great for filling and made cleaning a cinch. Products appear below in order of preference.

HIGHLY RECOMMENDED	PERFORMANCE		TESTERS' COMMENTS
NATHAN LittleShot MODEL: 4313TN PRICE: $11.99 CAPACITY: 24 oz (BigShot is 32 oz) MATERIAL: Tritan DISHWASHER-SAFE: Yes	EASE OF USE DURABILITY CLEANUP	★★★ ★★★ ★★★	This bottle's clear plastic sides made it easy to fill, and its bilevel twist-on lid was secure and easy to sip from. Its tether stayed out of the way and folded into a handy carrying loop.

RECOMMENDED			
NALGENE Wide Mouth MODEL: 32 Ounce Wide Mouth PRICE: $10.50 CAPACITY: 32 oz MATERIAL: Tritan DISHWASHER-SAFE: Yes	EASE OF USE DURABILITY CLEANUP	★★½ ★★★ ★★★	This basic clear bottle was simple to fill, carry, and clean. It was easy to open and close and aced our durability testing. The only drawback: Its wide mouth was harder to drink from.
VAPUR Element Anti-Bottle MODEL: N/A PRICE: $11.99 CAPACITY: 23 oz MATERIAL: Triple-ply BPA-free plastic DISHWASHER-SAFE: Yes	EASE OF USE DURABILITY CLEANUP	★½ ★★★ ★★★	This soft pouch was durable and spill-proof and had a nice drinking spout. It was light and handy for traveling. However, its soft sides were awkward, and we felt in constant peril of squeezing too hard and sending up a geyser.

RECOMMENDED WITH RESERVATIONS			
THERMOS Hydration Bottle **with Rotating Meter on Lid** MODEL: HP4100MGTRI6 (magenta) PRICE: $12.20 CAPACITY: 24 oz MATERIAL: Tritan DISHWASHER-SAFE: Yes	EASE OF USE DURABILITY CLEANUP	★★ ★★ ★★★	This clear bottle didn't hold on to smells or stains and had a nice drinking spout, but its finicky latch and cheap plastic button were hard to open. It leaked during abuse testing and the meter for recording water intake broke.

NOT RECOMMENDED			
KLEAN KANTEEN **"The Original" Classic** MODEL: K27CPPSGF (green fatigue) PRICE: $19.95 CAPACITY: 27 oz MATERIAL: Stainless steel DISHWASHER-SAFE: Yes (except painted bottles)	EASE OF USE DURABILITY CLEANUP	★★ ★★ ★★	This bottle had an exposed drinking spout made of tacky rubber that collected dust. Its steel body meant that we couldn't see inside, and it dented during the dropping test.
STANLEY Adventure **One Hand H20** MODEL: 1001152065 PRICE: $20 CAPACITY: 24 oz MATERIAL: Stainless steel DISHWASHER-SAFE: No	EASE OF USE DURABILITY CLEANUP	★½ ★½ ★½	This steel bottle had an exposed drinking spout, and we had to hold down a button to release water. The button isn't covered, so if something nudged it, say, a shoe in a gym bag, the spout opened. It also dented when we dropped it.

CONVERSIONS & EQUIVALENTS

Some say cooking is a science and an art. We would say that geography has a hand in it, too. Flour milled in the United Kingdom and elsewhere will feel and taste different from flour milled in the United States. So, while we cannot promise that the loaf of bread you bake in Canada or England will taste the same as a loaf baked in the States, we can offer guidelines for converting weights and measures. We also recommend that you rely on your instincts when making our recipes. Refer to the visual cues provided. If the bread dough hasn't "come together in a ball," as described, you may need to add more flour—even if the recipe doesn't tell you so. You be the judge.

The recipes in this book were developed using standard U.S. measures following U.S. government guidelines. The charts below offer equivalents for U.S., metric, and imperial (U.K.) measures. All conversions are approximate and have been rounded up or down to the nearest whole number. For example:

1 teaspoon = 4.929 milliliters, rounded up to 5 milliliters
1 ounce = 28.349 grams, rounded down to 28 grams

VOLUME CONVERSIONS

U.S.	METRIC
1 teaspoon	5 milliliters
2 teaspoons	10 milliliters
1 tablespoon	15 milliliters
2 tablespoons	30 milliliters
¼ cup	59 milliliters
⅓ cup	79 milliliters
½ cup	118 milliliters
¾ cup	177 milliliters
1 cup	237 milliliters
1¼ cups	296 milliliters
1½ cups	355 milliliters
2 cups	473 milliliters
2½ cups	591 milliliters
3 cups	710 milliliters
4 cups (1 quart)	0.946 liter
1.06 quarts	1 liter
4 quarts (1 gallon)	3.8 liters

WEIGHT CONVERSIONS

OUNCES	GRAMS
½	14
¾	21
1	28
1½	43
2	57
2½	71
3	85
3½	99
4	113
4½	128
5	142
6	170
7	198
8	227
9	255
10	283
12	340
16 (1 pound)	454

CONVERSIONS FOR INGREDIENTS COMMONLY USED IN BAKING

Baking is an exacting science. Because measuring by weight is far more accurate than measuring by volume, and thus more likely to achieve reliable results, in our recipes we provide ounce measures in addition to cup measures for many ingredients. Refer to the chart below to convert these measures into grams.

INGREDIENT	OUNCES	GRAMS
Flour		
1 cup all-purpose flour*	5	142
1 cup cake flour	4	113
1 cup whole-wheat flour	5½	156
Sugar		
1 cup granulated (white) sugar	7	198
1 cup packed brown sugar (light or dark)	7	198
1 cup confectioners' sugar	4	113
Cocoa Powder		
1 cup cocoa powder	3	85
Butter†		
4 tablespoons (½ stick, or ¼ cup)	2	57
8 tablespoons (1 stick, or ½ cup)	4	113
16 tablespoons (2 sticks, or 1 cup)	8	227

* U.S. all-purpose flour, the most frequently used flour in this book, does not contain leaveners, as some European flours do. These leavened flours are called self-rising or self-raising. If you are using self-rising flour, take this into consideration before adding leavening to a recipe.

† In the United States, butter is sold both salted and unsalted. We generally recommend unsalted butter. If you are using salted butter, take this into consideration before adding salt to a recipe.

OVEN TEMPERATURES

FAHRENHEIT	CELSIUS	GAS MARK (imperial)
225	105	¼
250	120	½
275	135	1
300	150	2
325	165	3
350	180	4
375	190	5
400	200	6
425	220	7
450	230	8
475	245	9

CONVERTING TEMPERATURES FROM AN INSTANT-READ THERMOMETER

We include doneness temperatures in many of our recipes, such as those for poultry, meat, and bread. We recommend an instant-read thermometer for the job. Refer to the table above to convert Fahrenheit degrees to Celsius. Or, for temperatures not represented in the chart, use this simple formula:

Subtract 32 degrees from the Fahrenheit reading, then divide the result by 1.8 to find the Celsius reading.

EXAMPLE:

"Roast chicken until thighs register 175 degrees." To convert:

175° F − 32 = 143°
143° ÷ 1.8 = 79.44°C, rounded down to 79°C

INDEX

Note: Page references in *italics* indicate photographs.